F72:2
10601
942·01

D1356796

THE OXFORD HISTORY
OF ENGLAND

Edited by SIR GEORGE CLARK

THE OXFORD HISTORY OF ENGLAND

Edited by SIR GEORGE CLARK

ROMAN BRITAIN
AND THE
ENGLISH SETTLEMENTS

By

R. G. COLLINGWOOD, F.B.A.
Sometime Fellow of Pembroke College and
Waynflete Professor of Metaphysical Philosophy

and

J. N. L. MYRES
Student of Christ Church and
University Lecturer in Modern History

SECOND EDITION

OXFORD
AT THE CLARENDON PRESS

Oxford University Press, Amen House, London E.C.4

GLASGOW NEW YORK TORONTO MELBOURNE WELLINGTON
BOMBAY CALCUTTA MADRAS KARACHI LAHORE DACCA
CAPE TOWN SALISBURY NAIROBI IBADAN ACCRA
KUALA LUMPUR HONG KONG

FIRST EDITION 1936
SECOND EDITION 1937
REPRINTED 1941, 1945, 1949, 1956, 1961

PRINTED IN GREAT BRITAIN

PREFACE TO BOOKS I–IV

THIS volume is not a work of collaboration. It consists of two independent studies of two distinct, though inter-locking, subjects. When the general scheme of the *Oxford History of England* was being discussed, the persons who under-took to write on the Roman and Anglo-Saxon periods agreed in thinking that the abstruse and delicate problems of the English settlement ought to be handled by some third writer, specially qualified to act as an intermediary between them, and able to give such a generous allowance of time and labour to the subject as should result in advancing our knowledge of it by an appreciable amount. We thought ourselves fortunate in being thus associated with Mr. Myres; and the fruit of his researches appears as Book V of this volume. It is printed here, not in the volume which deals with the Anglo-Saxon period, because the scale of treatment makes it easier to find room for it here.

Thus each part of the present volume is a work for which its own author is individually responsible. We have, in fact, deliberately refrained from discussing the connexions between our two subjects until our manuscripts were almost complete, believing that perfect independence of treatment was, in this particular case, the best way of arriving at the truth. Each of us was already familiar enough with the other's mind, methods, and ideas to be sure that the results would be reasonably harmonious. If the reader can detect contradictions between the two works, he may be certain that they do not arise from incompatibilities of temperament or divergences of prejudice on the part of the writers, but from those differences of perspective which any period of history presents when approached from two different sides.

Histories of England traditionally begin with some account of prehistoric ages. In this work that subject has been omitted. The invasion of Julius Caesar has been taken as the starting-point, and the book begins with an attempt to describe the state of the country as it was when that invasion took place. The reason for this does not lie in any theoretical distinction between history and prehistory, for that distinction does not here arise; from the beginning of the Neolithic period at least, British chronology is determined by strictly historical methods through keying its archaeology into the chronological framework given by documents from the Mediterranean region; it lies in the fact that our knowledge of what is conventionally called British prehistory is now so large, and is growing and changing so rapidly, that it can no longer be dealt with in a mere introduction. It demands a volume to itself, and the time for writing that volume has not yet come.

In writing this study of Roman Britain, my aim has been to make a contribution to the history of Britain, regarded as a region with a personality of its own, and a part of its own to play in the history of Europe. I have tried to reconstruct the state of the country and of its people, and to determine how far these altered, and how far they remained the same, in the four centuries and a half with which I have dealt. Military and political history are discussed only so far as seemed necessary for this end. Conceived in this way, the Roman period is no longer an isolated episode in British history. However isolated it may seem when we regard it simply as an age when an alien military and political system was imposed for a time upon a distant province, it presents a very different aspect when we reflect that the people upon whom this system was imposed were people with an historical tradition of their own, who learnt from Rome not the lessons she was able to teach but the lessons their previous training enabled them to learn. I have tried to write the history of Roman Britain as if it were the chapter in a biography dealing with a man's school-days, in which he is still the same boy that he was before he left home; whereas the historian of the Roman empire is writing the history of the school.

A history of the Romano-British people has to be written with attention to the somewhat meagre literary sources, eked out by analogy from those of other provinces; but its material comes mainly from archaeology. This country has been fortunate in having a long and widespread tradition of archaeological interest, and in the last half-century it has enriched and purified this tradition by what is nothing short of a revolution in the scientific method of archaeological research. It is the great service of Haverfield to Romano-British studies that he set himself, and to a great extent accomplished, the enormous task of collecting and sifting the materials thus accumulated; but death carried him off before he could digest the results into a book. His various sketches, studies, and lectures are the *vindemia prima* from which any book such as this must start. My debt to other writers is, I hope, sufficiently acknowledged in the bibliography. But this book could never have been written without the co-operation of innumerable scholars who, for the last twenty-five years, have helped me to form my ideas by explaining to me their own. Every page, as I wrote it, has recalled the generous friendship of these colleagues and the happy relations with them which I have enjoyed.

Four special debts must be mentioned. My colleague Professor J. R. R. Tolkien has helped me untiringly with problems of Celtic philology. Several years ago I found in Mr. C. E. Stevens, now Fellow of Magdalen College, one who shared my sense of the profound importance of agrarian problems for the social and economic history of the Roman empire, and my conviction that hitherto the study of them had hardly begun. His patient researches, which he has discussed with me at every stage, have contributed more than I can hope to acknowledge to my account of agricultural life in Britain. Professor Tenney Frank honoured me by asking me to write a section on Britain for his great *Economic Survey of Rome*, and this detailed collection and discussion of economic material, which will shortly be in print, he permitted me to use as the groundwork of a great deal that appears in the present volume. And Dr. R. E. Mortimer Wheeler has allowed me to read and use in manuscript certain parts of his report on the late excavations at Verulam, shortly to be published by the Society of Antiquaries of London.

Lastly, I should like to express my gratitude to the University of Oxford, which, by creating for me the post of University Lecturer in Philosophy and Roman History, gave me for many years together encouragement and opportunity to pursue the studies whose results, having now vacated that position, I offer to it and to the public.

OXFORD, *14 January 1936* R. G. C.

The second edition embodies corrections kindly supplied by Mr. Robert Aitken, Mr. E. Birley, Dr. R. W. Chapman, Miss Mary Kitson Clark, Sir Cyril Fox, Mr. E. W. Gilbert, Sir G. Macdonald, Mr. I. C. Peate, Mr. C. E. Stevens, and Mr. R. P. Wright.

16 February 1937 R. G. C.

PREFACE TO BOOK V

BETWEEN Roman Britain and Christian England there is a great gulf fixed, a void of confusion whose obscurity remains a standing challenge to historical inquiry. And not the least of the dangers which confront those who attempt to bridge the gulf lies in the difficulty of determining the limits of firm ground upon its borders. Chronologically, indeed, it may seem possible in certain directions to narrow the chasm almost to vanishing-point. In Book IV of this volume Professor Collingwood to our great advantage has pursued the flickering torch of Roman Britain into the gathering darkness of the sixth century, far beyond the conventional limit set for earlier writers by the edict of Honorius: and when his pursuit ends, he has in fact all but reached in time the solid land on which in the next volume Professor Stenton will lay the firm foundations of Christian England. It might thus seem that there is hardly room for a special study of the period between.

Nor have I attempted in Book V to study a period of years as such, but rather a cultural phase in our history which, however much we may learn to draw together the last days of Roman Britain and the first days of Christian England, will continue to be profoundly different from either and both to demand and to repay examination for its own sake. Book V is devoted to the establishment of the English Settlements in the lowland zone of our country, and, if limiting dates must be given for the process, I would say that it started soon before the middle of the fifth century and that by 593, the traditional year of Ceawlin's death, the political evolution of territorial states had advanced so far that a new age had begun. Within that century and a half the face of lowland Britain was transformed, and it is our ignorance of the course and character of that transformation which still makes the great gulf between Roman Britain and Christian England so difficult to cross.

This being so I have deliberately devoted my space to the discussion of those problems which are directly relevant to the settlement of the English in Britain. The surviving Celtic society of the west has been left on one side in the isolation to which the coming of the English, and its own preoccupation with the memories of Rome and with the specialized problems of life in the highland regions, had forced it: it was not until after the end of our period that the conflict of religious enthusiasms over the soul of Anglo-Saxon heathendom brought Celtic society again into direct contact with English history. Nor has any attempt been made to discuss in themselves the character of Anglo-Saxon social life and organization, or the varieties of its artistic expression in the pagan period. The former subject will receive full treatment in the next volume, and, since the earliest sources on which our knowledge of its features depends belong almost wholly to Christian times, it would be not only redundant but possibly misleading to anticipate that discussion here. On the other hand, a review of the arts and crafts of pagan times would certainly be here in place: it has been reluctantly omitted mainly because it would be difficult, if not impossible, to make an exposition of the subject intelligible without the illustrations which the plan of the present series precludes. The varieties of Anglo-Saxon zoomorphic ornament must be seen to be believed, and no amount of description can convey the fantastic beauty of the Kingston brooch. But while a separate discussion was also rendered impracticable by considerations of space, I have endeavoured to introduce the main conclusions that can be drawn at present from this cultural and artistic evidence for the character of pagan society wherever it seemed relevant to the general course of the narrative.

I have tried to indicate in the Bibliography and footnotes my debt to many scholars whose work in varied fields has contributed especially in the last few years to the growing illumination of the darkness. Two recent publications—Mr. R. H. Hodgkin's *History of the Anglo-Saxons*, and the Ordnance Survey *Map of Dark Age Britain*—have rendered the paths of all students of this age immeasurably smoother than they were even two years ago, and my debt to both will be obvious. I owe it to them especially that the material on which my maps are based has been easy to verify, and that the means employed in its presentation have been easy to select: it may, however, be noticed that most of the archaeological entries on the maps had been independently collected by me before these works were published and that such differences as exist between my maps and theirs are the natural consequence of my own studies. Where in my text I have ventured to disagree with Mr. Hodgkin or to criticize his interpretation of the evidence, it has been, I

think, nearly always on topics on which he would be the first to
agree that difference of opinion is legitimate. Dr. S. W. Wooldridge's important article in *An Historical Geography of England
before 1800* (ed. H. C. Darby) was published after my chapters
were in proof: where our thought has run, as on many topics
it has, along parallel lines I can only congratulate myself on
our agreement, and regret that I was not able on some other
matters to profit earlier from his penetrating study. To Professor Stenton I owe not only the inspiration which all readers
of his works derive from them but also much special help in
matters of philology and place-names, topics which have not
been my primary field of study. Mr. E. T. Leeds has kindly
assisted me in several archaeological difficulties, and has
generously allowed me to see the manuscript of his Rhind
lectures before their publication. Messrs. C. E. Stevens, C. F. C.
Hawkes, and P. C. Gordon-Walker have all been good enough
to read my proofs and have all made suggestions which have
saved me from errors of fact and ambiguities of expression.
To them and to my wife, who by typing the whole and materially assisting with the Index has taken on herself many of the
burdensome incidents of authorship, I would record my thanks,
for I appreciate to the full how much this work owes to their
encouragement and criticism.

J. N. L. M.

OXFORD
1 September 1936

CONTENTS

Book I. BRITAIN BEFORE THE ROMAN CONQUEST

I. THE STAGE OF HISTORY

III. CAESAR'S INVASION

IV. FROM CAESAR TO CLAUDIUS

Book II. THE AGE OF CONQUEST

V. THE CLAUDIAN INVASION

VI. CARATACUS AND BOUDICCA

VII. FROM BOUDICCA TO AGRICOLA

VIII. THE MAKING OF THE FRONTIER

IX. THE FRONTIER AFTER HADRIAN

Book III. BRITAIN UNDER ROMAN RULE

X. THE MACHINERY OF GOVERNMENT

XI. THE PEOPLE

XII. THE TOWNS

XIII. THE COUNTRY-SIDE

XIV. INDUSTRY AND COMMERCE

XV. ART

XVI. RELIGION

Book IV. THE END OF ROMAN BRITAIN

XVII. FROM SEVERUS TO HONORIUS

XVIII. THE END OF ROMAN RULE

XIX. BRITAIN IN THE FIFTH CENTURY

Book V. *THE ENGLISH SETTLEMENTS*, by J. N. L. MYRES

XX. THE SOURCES FOR THE PERIOD: ANGLES, SAXONS, AND JUTES ON THE CONTINENT

XXI. THE COURSE OF THE CONQUEST IN KENT AND THE SOUTH-EAST

XXII. THE FENLANDS, EAST ANGLIA, AND THE PROBLEM OF WESSEX

XXIII. THE HUMBRENSES

XXIV. THE CHARACTER OF THE CONQUEST

LIST OF MAPS

MAP I. ROMAN BRITAIN

BOOK I

BRITAIN BEFORE THE ROMAN CONQUEST

I

THE STAGE OF HISTORY

THE country of Britain is divided by nature into two parts, each with a character of its own, a complement and contrast to that of the other. The north and west are formed by an ancient mountain-chain, worn down by ages of erosion into a plateau of hard rock, and this again has been deeply scored by water and ice, and shattered by Atlantic weather, until its seaboard has become ragged and irregular and its western parts cloven by deep valleys with mountain-masses rising steeply between them. Only in its eastern parts has it retained the character of a continuous plateau, with long stretches of uninterrupted high ground between one valley and the next.

Leaning up against the eastern edge of this highland zone, and sloping thence away to the east and south-east, lies a plain composed of newer and softer rocks. These have been deposited during successive ages in superimposed and more or less parallel strata; but in the course of time the western highlands have tended to rise a little out of the sea, carrying with them the western edge of the plain, and its eastern edge has correspondingly sunk below it, so that, if no erosion had taken place, the plain as a whole would now slope gently upwards from sea-level on the south-east to a height of two thousand feet or more on the edge of the uplands; but, since erosion always acts most powerfully on the highest ground, and so tends to reduce a slope to a level by carrying that away, its effect has been to remove the uppermost strata and expose those below them differentially, most in the west and north, least in the south and east. A traveller going from the Straits of Dover towards the Welsh mountains, therefore, finds himself alternately rising in a gentle slope, along the surface of one geological stratum, and then, where this breaks off, dropping sharply down an escarpment to the surface of the one next below it.

It is this differential erosion that determines the main lines of surface-geology, and therefore of historical geography, in the plain of secondary rocks that forms the lowland zone of Britain.

For several reasons the contrast between these two zones is a fact of primary importance for British history.

First and foremost, the two differ widely in the general character of their landscape. The softer rocks of the lowland zone yield gentle slopes and wide expanses of almost level ground; the highland zone, though in scale and wildness its mountains are nowhere comparable with those of younger mountain-ranges, is everywhere rugged and broken in the aspect of its surface, steep in its slopes, and hardly anywhere even approximately level for more than a very little space.

There is also a general difference in the character of the soil. Almost all the lowland formations, however much they differ among themselves, have this in common, that they weather into fertile soils, naturally clothing themselves with a rich growth of turf or forest trees, and capable of being used by man either for arable farming or as grass-land. In the highland zone the soils are everywhere by comparison poor, at best thin and stony, at worst so sour with peat as to be useless, and by nature chiefly given over to scrubby, stunted trees and open heath.

In climate also there is a contrast. The highland zone, with inconsiderable exceptions, has a rainfall everywhere above the average (40 inches in the year) for the entire country; the lowland zone everywhere one lower; and indeed almost all the lowland zone, except in its south-western part, has on average less than 30 inches in the year. This difference, which would in any case have a great effect on the relative habitability of the two zones, is further increased by the fact that the parts of the lowland zone which receive most rain are the chalk and oolite uplands, which most quickly absorb it; so that few parts of the lowland zone, except actual fen-land, are ever so water-logged as most of the highland zone is for most of the year. And this water-logged condition, besides being in itself an enemy to human life, lowers the temperature and decreases sunshine by evaporation and by the formation of clouds. Thus the lowland zone as a whole is warm and dry, though nowhere too dry for the free growth of vegetation; the highland zone as a whole is cold and wet. But the contrast in general or mean temperature is modified by the fact that the warm Atlantic winds which bring rain to the highland zone diminish the intensity of winter cold there, so that frosts are more intense in the lowland zone, especially towards the east coast.

These differences in respect of relief, soil, and climate between the highland and lowland zones have deeply affected the life of their respective inhabitants. In the lowland zone communications, whether by land-routes or by boat along the slow-flowing rivers, have always been easy; agriculture and stock-farming, ever since man first introduced them, have prospered on lands eminently suited to them; and neither heat nor cold, neither drought nor excessive rainfall, has ever been an obstacle to human prosperity. In the highland zone communication by land is everywhere difficult, and water-transport, except by sea, impossible; the character of the soil makes agriculture and stock-farming alike a precarious matter, with small profits and great liability to loss; and the cold, wet climate is a hindrance to every kind of activity and a handicap to every form of civilized life.

Hence, in degree, there has always been a general difference between the richer, more comfortable, and more prosperous life of the lowland zone and the harder and poorer life of the highland; and there have been differences of kind as well, arising out of the same causes. The lowland zone is not only more accessible to invasion from the Continent, it is also more attractive to invaders; because life is easier there, changes in the way of living are less hard to bring about, and consequently the history of the lowland zone shows from time to time profound changes of this kind, partly through the coming of new inhabitants, partly through the infiltration of new ideas. The highland zone is unattractive to invaders, hard to invade, and hard to conquer in detail when invaded; its landscape and climate impose peremptory laws on any one, no matter whence he comes, who settles there; all these causes, therefore, combine to make it a region tenacious of its old customs, conservative in temperament, stubborn to resist any kind of change. New peoples and new ideas, when they gain a foothold in it, do so at the price of compromise with the old; and the civilization of the highland zone, analysed at any given moment in its history, shows a curious blend of older and newer elements, the old surviving though modified by the new, the new quickly adapting themselves towards conformity with the old.

In spite of this contrast between highland and lowland zones, the relation between the two is by no means one of mere difference. The sea which rings them round and holds them together combines them into a single whole with a character of its own. From the point of view of an observer on the European mainland, Britain as a whole is deeply permeated by the characteristics especially belonging to the highland zone: conservatism of temperament, tenacity of customs, resistance to new ideas except in so far as they modify themselves under the influence of the old; and thus figures as the embodiment of a spirit of compromise, sometimes admired for its cautious and practical common sense and its loyalty to long-tried traditions, sometimes condemned for backwardness in the march of progress, blind devotion to lost causes, deficiency in logic, proneness to half-measures and hypocrisy. These characteristics of the British spirit arise from the fact that, in its relation to the Continent, Britain in general plays the same part which in particular belongs, within Britain, to the highland zone: cut off from the mainland by the sea, it is difficult enough of access to form a melting-pot in which new arrivals, whether of population or of ideas, are assimilated and absorbed, conquering only by being themselves conquered.

For this reason the rhythms of civilization in Britain have always been slower, and their pulsation less violent, than on the European mainland. The quick and brilliant flowerings of such continental movements as Celtic art, Roman imperial civilization, medieval French architecture, Renaissance art and thought, or the revolutionary spirit of the eighteenth century have seldom failed to find a reflexion in Britain; but they have been reflected there somewhat tardily and dimly, losing much of their own specific quality, and never representing that quality in its highest and intensest form, but achieving by their assimilation in the life of Britain a certain solidity and endurance, so that in compensation for their lack of a rapid blossoming they are exempt from a rapid decay, and each phase tends, far more than on the Continent, to overlap with the next and to give an impression of relative permanence.

This slowness of rhythm, which at first sight makes Britain a mere laggard in the movement of European history, a refuse-heap on the edge of the ocean into which are swept the outworn relics of ethnic migrations and spiritual fermentations, there to linger indefinitely in a confused and inert mass, has nevertheless a positive function of its own. What it lacks in brilliance and novelty, it makes up in a certain maturity or ripeness; the very habit of blending together things so diverse as the Celtic spirit and the Roman, the medieval and Renaissance, the feudal and the democratic, has constantly produced new forms of life and thought which Britain has given back to the Continent as her own peculiar contribution to the life and thought of Europe. In this way Britain has given to Europe the Irish and Anglo-Saxon scholarship and art of the dark ages, the empirical philosophy of the school of Locke, the principles of parliamentary government, and the fruits of the industrial revolution. And in many cases, within Britain itself, these new products have arisen where the spirit of conservatism is strongest, in the highland zone: the home of Irish Christianity, of Locke, Berkeley, and Hume, of Trevithick, Watt, and Stephenson.

The history of Britain in the Roman period is primarily the history of its partial conquest and occupation by Rome. From this point of view the historian's interest is focused on the question how far Britain became romanized, and in the light of what has already been said we should expect to discover a partial and tardy romanization of the lowland zone, less intense than the corresponding romanization of the continental provinces, and penetrating little if at all into the highland zone. And this in effect is what we find; but not the whole of it. There are two other facts, less interesting to the historian of the Roman empire, but more interesting to the historian of Britain.

First, the adoption of Roman civilization in the lowland zone could take a lasting and stable form only at the price of assimilation to the ways of life already established in Britain; and this is the key to the difference which we shall find to exist between two widely divergent phases of Romano-British civilization, one characteristic of the earlier part of our period, one of the later.

Secondly, the infiltration of Roman civilization into the highland zone, slow though it necessarily was, and hard to detect in the scanty evidences of its actual occurrence, might well leave behind it results more permanent and more momentous for later history than the quicker and more spectacular romanization of the lowland zone. This is the key to the part played in British history by the heritage of Roman life and thought after Britain had ceased to be a part of the empire.

So much for the larger features of British geography and their

influence on history during the Roman period; we must now
study the geographical setting of that history in somewhat closer
detail.

The lowland zone, extending as far west as the base of the
Devonshire–Cornwall peninsula and the beginning of the Welsh
hills, and as far north as the Pennines and the uplands of county
Durham and Northumberland, is a single, undivided whole.
Its landward limits, clearly marked by the outcrop of the
palaeozoic rocks, may be represented by a line beginning at
Seaton, on the Devonshire coast, and running north to the
Bristol Channel, with an outlier of highland-zone character in
the Mendips; recommencing at the head of the Bristol Channel
and skirting the Forest of Dean and the Malvern hills to the
Wrekin, and thence bending westward and northward by
Shrewsbury, Oswestry, and Wrexham to the estuary of the Dee;
beginning again near Lancaster and passing round the edge of
the Pennines by way of Manchester, Derby, and Sheffield until
it reaches the sea near the mouth of the Tees. The lowland area
thus defined stands out on the map of Roman Britain as the
region of Roman towns and villas, the region of peaceful,
civilized, romanized life.

The highland zone is discontinuous; it is broken into three
parts by two deep inlets, where the western sea has penetrated
through it to meet the lowland zone, the Bristol Channel and
the bight of the Irish Sea on the coasts of Cheshire and
Lancashire. These three parts are very different in size. The
northernmost, including the whole of Scotland, the Border
counties, and the Pennine chain, is by far the largest as well as
the farthest removed from Rome; Wales, including the Welsh
marches, is much smaller, and the Dumnonian peninsula the
smallest of all. These three regions have, from the Roman point
of view, this in common, that they are all highland regions,
impenetrable in the main to civilizing influences; but their
isolation from each other made it possible to treat them differently, and their differences of size and position made such
differences of treatment inevitable. The Dumnonian peninsula,
however uncivilized, was too small and too easy of access to be
a focus of armed opposition to Rome: it never offered serious
resistance to conquest, and never received a military garrison.
Wales was another matter; and the map shows it as studded
with a network of forts. But for the most part these had done

their work within a hundred years from the landing of the Roman armies, and were abandoned as no longer useful; conquest was here complete. The Pennine-Scottish region was never conquered in its entirety at all; such a conquest was for a time projected, but soon abandoned; and a compromise was reached by throwing a frontier-line across it and maintaining a system of forts in the conquered portion.

Thus the distinction between civil and military areas in Roman Britain, long familiar to historians, corresponds with the distinction between lowland and highland zones, but with modifications due to the division of the highland zone into three unequal parts.

The three legionary fortresses at York, Chester, and Caerleon-on-Usk served both as bases or focal points for the military region and as links connecting it with the civil. This is because all three lie on the natural frontier-line separating the highland zone from the lowland, and, more particularly, at the three points on that line where the lowland zone penetrates most deeply into the highland, the three gates of the highland zone. York, the natural capital of its own vale, stands where the northernmost tongue of lowland country is squeezed out between the Pennines and the Cleveland hills. Chester commands the gap between the Pennines and Wales, pushed as near as may be to Wales, its primary objective. Caerleon similarly commands the gap between Wales and the Dumnonian peninsula, but is thrust into the very throat of the Welsh mountains as if to emphasize the fact that Devonshire and Cornwall needed no military supervision.

The lowland zone, continuous though it is in extent, is more variegated in character than a first glance at the map would suggest. North of the Thames it is crossed over its entire extent by two ridges of hill-country: the oolite limestone ridge that begins as the Cotswolds and continues successively as the Northamptonshire uplands and Lincoln Edge, and the chalk ridge that begins in the Berkshire Downs, continues across the Thames as the Chilterns, and curves round to the south side of the Wash, reappearing in a continuation of the same curve as the Lincolnshire Wolds and, across the Humber, as the Wolds of Yorkshire. South-east of the Chiltern ridge, the chalk disappears beneath the clay of the London basin; but it rises again south of the Thames, emerging from under the tertiary

beds to form another chalk ridge, the Hampshire Downs and
the North Downs of Surrey and Kent. But for the effects of
erosion, it would rise higher still, to form a dome-like plateau
covering the Weald; but all this has gone; the North Downs
are broken off to southward by an escarpment, faced across the
sandy and clayey Wealden forest-land by the corresponding
escarpment of the South Downs, whence the chalk dips down-
ward again to the Sussex and Hampshire coast. These three
ridges of chalk are not parallel; they converge westward, and
meet in Salisbury Plain.

Salisbury Plain has thus a peculiar significance for the geology
and topography of lowland Britain. It is not only in itself a
vast plateau of chalk, it is also a ganglion from which three
chalk ridges radiate: one through the Chilterns to the Wash,
one through the North Downs to the Straits of Dover, and one
through the South Downs to Beachy Head. Yet another range
of chalk downs branches off from its south-western edge and
extends to the Dorset coast, while tangentially to it, separated
from it only by a narrow gap about Chippenham and Trow-
bridge, runs the oolite ridge of the Cotswolds.

The importance of this ridge-system radiating from Salisbury
Plain consists not so much in its elevation, which is in many
places inconsiderable, as in the character of its soil. The chalk
and the oolites are the only formations in lowland Britain
yielding large, continuous tracts of land whose soil is at once
reasonably fertile and naturally drained. Excessive moisture
is the chief enemy that human life encounters in Britain; it is
easiest for man to live, therefore, in places where fallen rain is
quickly absorbed by a porous subsoil; and subsoils of this kind
are provided by sands, gravels, chalk, and limestone. The importance of sands and gravels must be considered later on;
here it is enough to say that in the extent and continuity of their
deposits they are much inferior to the other two. An agricultural population in a somewhat primitive stage of development,
unequal as yet to the task of draining the loamy soils, and therefore taking the line of least resistance by choosing those with
a natural drainage, while at the same time civilized enough to
appreciate the value of large continuous tracts of habitable land,
where an effective political and religious organization could be
developed, would fasten upon these plateaux and ridges of chalk
and oolite as its natural home, and, as its corporate life took

shape, would tend to regard Salisbury Plain as its home-land *par excellence*, the economic, religious, and political centre of Britain.

Something of this kind did actually occur during the earliest ages of civilization in Britain. Settled agricultural life was introduced in the Neolithic age, during the third millennium before Christ; towards the end of that millennium great stone monuments were being erected in this country on a scale implying considerable wealth, a high degree of political organization, and a very definite system of religious beliefs. These megalithic monuments, there is good reason to think, were a fashion introduced by people sailing up the Atlantic coast from the Iberian peninsula and making their landfall in the south-west of Britain; many of them settled in Cornwall or worked their way by degrees northwards either to Wales and Scotland, where they settled upon the western headlands and islands, and so to the extreme north of Scotland, or else to Ireland, which is densely covered with their remains; but many others landed on the coast of Dorset, where the south-western chalk ridge reaches the sea, and established a great megalithic culture on Salisbury Plain and the Cotswolds. It is here that the megalithic civilization of Britain developed in its earliest, purest, and intensest form, as the evidence of dolmens and long barrows testifies; and it is here that, at a later date, when the cult of the stone circle came into existence, the greatest and most impressive stone circles were erected, at Avebury and Stonehenge.

The next great accession to the population of Britain was the arrival of the 'Beaker people', so called from the characteristic drinking-cup found in their graves, who came from the south-east; their remains are scattered along the eastern coast very much as those of the megalith-builders are scattered along the western. But in spite of the difference of origin there was to some extent an identity in their goal; on Salisbury Plain the two civilizations met and mingled. The same thing happened to a less degree elsewhere, notably on the Yorkshire Wolds and the limestone uplands of Derbyshire; but it is on Salisbury Plain and the chalk downs of Dorset that the evidence of fusion is greatest in quantity and most striking in quality; for at Stonehenge itself the stones appear to have been dressed with bronze tools, and bronze was unknown in Britain until the coming of the Beaker people.

In the Early Iron Age, once more, the chalk and oolite ridges maintained their importance; and once more it is on Salisbury Plain and the dry uplands adjacent to it that man has left the most impressive evidences of wealth and power in the gigantic hill-forts of the Plain itself, the downs of Dorset and Hampshire, and the Cotswolds. Thus, for two thousand years and more before the coming of the Romans, Salisbury Plain had been a centre to which every new civilization gravitated when it reached Britain, and at which it attained its highest expression of material and spiritual culture.

This ancient importance of the chalk and oolite plateaux as the regions of densest population, greatest wealth, and highest civilization comes to our minds to-day as a surprise. We are accustomed to see those regions as among the most sparsely inhabited in the country; and we are aware that this has been so for many centuries; long before the towns began to eat up the population of the country-side, we know, the medieval villages and the Anglo-Saxon villages before them tended on the whole to avoid those regions, or at most to penetrate them by creeping up their river-valleys, and to choose by preference soils of a heavier and more loamy kind. Here and there, it is true, a modern town or village, like Stow-on-the-Wold, with its Early Iron Age ramparts, inherits what may well be an unbroken tradition from prehistoric times; but these exceptions only serve to emphasize the general truth of the principle that the centres of population and wealth have shifted their ground since those times, leaving the chalk and oolite relatively bare. This is not the place to consider when and why this change came about; it is enough here to call attention to its reality, in order to insist upon the fact that when the Romans came to Britain they found a population living not like the village population of to-day, mostly on heavy soils which before they could be used for agriculture had to be both cleared of timber and also drained of superfluous moisture, but mostly on light and naturally drained soils whose timber had been cleared by a gradual process during the Bronze Age, not so much by systematic felling as by the slow encroachment of grazing animals.

In addition to the chalk and oolite, naturally drained soils are afforded by various sands and gravels. The relation of early man to this group of soils is a complex matter. Whereas it is easy to generalize about the oolite- and chalk-lands, and to accept the principle that early man settled everywhere on these except where, as in the Chilterns, they were overlaid by superficial deposits of heavy clay, no generalization will hold good of the sandy and gravelly soils. Considerable tracts of them exist in the lowland zone; for example, the New Forest, the tertiaries of the Bagshot district, the greensand which crops out under the chalk in the Weald and north of the Berkshire and Chiltern escarpments, the dry, wind-blown sand of the Breckland bordering the Fens in Suffolk and Norfolk, and the richer brick-earth that lies along the banks and terraces of the larger rivers. Both in the Bronze Age and in the Iron Age, down to the coming of the Romans, some of these tracts were densely inhabited and others practically devoid of population; and this difference cannot be correlated with differences in the quality of the soil. Of the lightest and poorest, some, like the Wealden greensand and the Bagshot and New Forest regions, were left unsettled; yet the Breckland, among the poorest of all, was densely populated in the earlier part of the Bronze Age, though in the Iron Age this population was greatly diminished. Of the riverbanks and terraces, again, some were thickly settled in the Bronze and Iron Ages. The most remarkable case is that of the Thames, where finds from the Bronze Age onwards occur in a continuous belt on both sides of the river from its mouth to the Oxford district, where they spread out fanwise over the alluvial soils from Dorchester to Eynsham. Hardly less striking is the case of the Orwell, where an almost equally dense belt of finds runs up the valley and merges into the thickly populated districts of the Breckland and the Cambridgeshire chalk. The nearest approach to a generalization would be to say that by the time the Iron Age was established the poorest sands and gravels, even where they had once been thickly inhabited, were either unoccupied or occupied only by a small population, whereas the richer alluvial soils along the chief rivers of the south-east were densely populated, and increasingly so as time went on.

Dense though it was, however, this population may have been less advanced in wealth and political organization than that of the chalk and oolite plateaux; it has nothing left comparable with Stonehenge and Avebury or with the great hill-forts of the upland regions. In part the difference may be due to lack of materials; the valley-people had no stone for making such things;

they may have erected circles of timber, and they did sometimes construct river-side forts like the Dyke Hills at Dorchester. Yet the evidence, so far as it exists, does suggest a lower degree of civilization in the valleys throughout the prehistoric periods.

As opposed to these regions of primitive settlement, there were others which early man hardly touched at all. Some of these, composed of barren sand and gravel, have already been mentioned; but the largest in extent and most important to the historian are the heavy clay-lands which hold the water on their surface and were originally covered with damp oak-forest having a dense and almost impenetrable undergrowth. The most conspicuous of these are the Weald, the London basin, the boulder-clay plateau of East Anglia, the belt of Kimmeridge and Oxford clays that separate the Berkshire–Chiltern chalk ridge from the main ridge of the oolite, the Liassic clays of the midlands, and the Trias and glacial clays of Cheshire and Lancashire. To these may be added certain extensive clay-caps overlying the chalk, especially on the Chiltern plateau. All these were in prehistoric times either uninhabited, though doubtless visited by hunters, or else inhabited only here and there, where belts or islands of less intractable soil were to be found. There were also regions of marsh-land, habitable only where islands of drier ground emerged: the Fens, the marshes of Somerset, and the country round the head of the Humber.

These inhospitable regions were not only in themselves unpopulated; they also acted in varying degrees as barriers to the movement of civilization. Thus the Weald effectively cuts the South Downs off from communication with the North Downs and the Thames valley, with the result that whereas a civilization focused in Salisbury Plain can make itself felt along the southern chalk ridge as far as Beachy Head, one centred in the Thames basin leaves that ridge as a whole unaffected. Again, a people settled on the river-banks of Norfolk would tend under primitive conditions to live in a backwater of history, untouched by influences from the south and west. The Oxford and Kimmeridge belt seems to have been a forest-wall which Bronze Age influence coming from the south-east failed to penetrate, leaving the oolite ridge singularly poor in relics of that period. And, most important of all, the vast triangle of the sparsely inhabited midland forest, together with the cold and wet clay-lands of the Cheshire gap, made it difficult for any civilization rooted in south-eastern England to affect Wales or to find an outlet on the Irish Sea.

Until the Roman road-builders set themselves deliberately to break these barriers down, the main lines of communication generally followed within the lowland zone were very different from those of Roman and all post-Roman times. They fall into two groups. First, there are the ridgeways that mark the lines of dry upland: the Icknield Way, connecting Salisbury Plain by way of the Berkshire Downs and the Chilterns with the Wash; the Harroway running similarly along the North Downs; and others along the South Downs and the Cotswolds. Secondly, there are traffic-lines following the river-valleys, partly the rivers themselves, carrying traffic in canoes, partly roads along the river-banks. The Thames was an important waterway throughout the Bronze and Iron Ages; so were the rivers that flow into the Wash, and, farther north, the tributaries of the Humber, especially the Trent and the Ouse.

For the highland zone a briefer survey will be enough. Here, as a rule, the soils are impermeable; for even the carboniferous limestone, which figures so largely in the Pennine region, is to a great extent covered either with boulder-clay or with peat; and consequently, though dry limestone soils are important wherever they occur, for example in Derbyshire, in the Yorkshire dales, and in parts of Westmorland, they are not the decisive element in the distribution of early man. The most powerful factor in that distribution was height above sea-level, or rather, above the level of more or less permanent excessive surface-water. Throughout the highland zone there are groups and belts of megalithic remains, their distribution eloquently attesting the sea-borne character of the civilization that produced them, on the lower shelves of land near the coast. In Cornwall they occur especially near Land's End; in Wales towards the headlands of Pembrokeshire and Carnarvonshire and in Anglesea; there is a sprinkling of them on the Cumberland coast with a few penetrating up the Eden valley, and they become commoner again in Galloway and round the Firth of Clyde; then, after a considerable gap, they begin again in Skye and the Outer Islands, and there are many near the northern and eastern coasts of Caithness and in the Orkneys. Inland, except for an important group on the limestone plateau of Derbyshire, they are conspicuously rare. Taken as a whole, they represent an agricultural civilization occupying somewhat low-lying, fertile, naturally drained soils, based on the sea, and derived from exploitation of the Atlantic traffic-route which connects the Iberian peninsula with the Biscayan coastlands, the peninsula of Brittany, and the western coast of Britain.

The Beaker people, coming as they did from the east and south-east, affected the highland zone very little except in the north. Here the eastern coast of Scotland from Inverness to Aberdeen, and the coastal plain of Northumberland, are densely studded with their remains, which conspicuously avoid the megalith region of Caithness, but except for that northern extremity occur freely all over the eastern coastland. But the Beaker civilization penetrated much more adventurously than the megalithic into the heart of the country, occupying the upland valleys of eastern Scotland and Northumberland, and thence working its way to the open and well-drained basin of the Eden valley. The mingling of megalithic and Beaker civilizations, which in the lowland zone we have found to be characteristic of Salisbury Plain, seldom appears, and never on a comparable scale, in the highland zone: it occurs once in Derbyshire, once in the Eden valley, and again in a region which, though geologically belonging to the lowland zone, is culturally ambiguous as between that and the highland, the Yorkshire Wolds.

Taking the Bronze Age as a whole, and setting aside northern Scotland as outside the main scope of this volume, we find a population which avoids the lowest lands and the heaviest soils as too wet and too densely timbered for occupation, and avoids the highest as too cold and exposed, but settles freely in the upland valleys and on shelves of land and foothills between the mountains and the valley-bottoms, especially where these have a permeable subsoil. Settlement is particularly dense in eastern Northumberland, with penetration up the Tweed and through the Tyne gap into the Eden basin; the dales of the central Pennines, especially Airedale, which carries a similar penetration over the watershed into the Ribble valley; the Derbyshire uplands; North Wales from Flintshire to Anglesea; western Cornwall; and the plateau of Dartmoor.

It remains to consider the natural lines for sea-borne traffic connecting Britain with the Continent, and to ask how these in their various ways affected its early history.

The first is the Atlantic route to Brittany and Spain. This impinges on Britain at its south-western extremity and there divides into two branches, one going north into the Irish Sea and so to the west coast of Scotland, the other east, up the English Channel. In prehistoric times the northern branch was the more important of the two; the eastern seems to have been of value only because it gave direct access to the Dorset coast and thus to the rich hinterland of Salisbury Plain. As long as Salisbury Plain was the heart of civilization in Britain all roads led to it; and thus, in the megalithic period, it acted as a magnet drawing sea-borne traffic from the Atlantic coastal route as far up-channel as Dorset. Apart from this deflection, the Atlantic route belonged at its British end to the highland zone; it was the pathway by which early civilization reached Cornwall, Wales, Ireland, and the west and north of Scotland.

The second route, or group of routes, crosses the Channel between Normandy and Hampshire, again with a strong tendency to be deflected towards the Dorset coast. These routes seem to have increased in importance during the Bronze Age and the earlier phases of the Iron Age; they were the main agents in developing the Late Bronze Age and La Tène I[1] civilizations of the Wessex uplands.

The third group crosses the Straits of Dover and reaches Britain at the Kentish ports, the Thames, and the rivers of Essex. This traffic-line seems first to have become important in the Early Iron Age, when it introduced a civilization of Hallstatt type into south-eastern England; from the first century before Christ it became, and remained throughout the Roman period, the most important of all.

Lastly, a fourth group crosses the North Sea from the Low Countries and Denmark. These routes were of great importance about the beginning of the second millennium before Christ as introducing the Beaker people, and again some twenty-five centuries later as the highways of Anglo-Saxon immigration; between these two dates they were of little consequence.

---

[1] The pre-Roman Iron Age on the Continent may be conveniently regarded as occupying the last millennium before Christ, of which the first half is the Hallstatt period, the second the La Tène period, both called after sites at which their characteristic civilizations were first extensively studied, and both subdivided into minor periods. English antiquaries at one time gave to the La Tène civilization the name 'Late Celtic'; this name is now little used.

II

BRITAIN IN THE TIME OF JULIUS CAESAR

ANY attempt to give an account of Britain, as it was when Julius Caesar's invasion brought it for a moment into the light of history, must begin with the question: to what race did the Britons of that age belong? or, in less ambiguous terms, since the word race is apt to carry misleading associations, what kind of men were they in bodily form and habit?

This is a question which, in the present state of knowledge, cannot be answered briefly and decisively; but something can be done towards clearing away misconceptions and indicating the direction in which an answer should be sought.

In the last century students tended to approach the question from a point of view partly archaeological and partly literary. From skeletons found in the communal burial-chambers of long barrows, they reconstructed the picture of a short, long-headed, lightly built, Neolithic race, which they connected with the similar peoples of the western Mediterranean. The beaker burials of the earliest Bronze Age gave them a strongly contrasted physical type, tall, massive, and round-headed; and they tended to think of this type as characteristic of the Bronze Age. Finally from the historical writers of the Roman age they derived an idea of the Britons in Caesar's time as a race of tall, fair warriors of Celtic speech.

All these conceptions had in them a certain degree of truth, but all must to-day be qualified; and the result of these qualifications is a picture of the ancient Britons which, if more complex in some ways, is simpler in others.

In the Neolithic period, which is as far back as we need attempt to trace the British pedigree, the whole of western Europe was inhabited by a race of long-headed men, varying somewhat in appearance, and especially in colouring, since they were probably always fairer in the north and darker in the south, but in most respects substantially alike. Into this area of long-headed population there was driven a wedge of round-headed immigrants from the east, known to anthropologists as the Alpine race. Most of the peoples that have invaded Britain, from whatever direction they have come, have belonged to the western European long-headed stock, and have therefore borne a general resemblance to the people already living there; and consequently, in spite of the diversities among these various new-comers, the tendency in Britain has been towards the establishment and maintenance of a tolerably uniform long-headed type. The chief exception to this rule is the Beaker people, who, whatever their precise origin, derived from an Alpine strain in their ancestry a strongly brachycephalous type of skull; but the total influence of this strain upon the physique of the Britons has not been great; and in estimating its importance we must bear in mind that, although the Beaker people buried their dead unburnt, so that their physical characteristics are well known to the modern archaeologist, the Bronze Age to which their coming was the prelude was in general an age of cremation: hence very little is known concerning the physical type of the population in that period as a whole. Other exceptions are the Romans themselves, using that name in a narrowly geographical sense for inhabitants of central Italy, and the Normans: these were both round-headed peoples. But apart from these exceptions (of which the Roman may be almost ignored, for hardly any skulls attributable to that type have been found in this country) practically all the skulls found in Britain, of whatever age, are of a long-headed type whose closest affinities are with the ancient peoples of north-western Europe. This applies even to the skulls found in long barrows, which are more akin to the Nordic long-headed type than to the Mediterranean.

It is not until the later Roman period, when cremation ceased to be practised and inhumation became general throughout the country, that we can assemble a sufficient mass of evidence to give us a trustworthy general idea of the physique prevalent in ancient Britain. When this happens, we find that the physical type is fairly constant. The head is moderately long, with a flattish top, giving an upright, square, and somewhat low forehead, generally marked by a transverse groove above the eyebrows: the back of the head projects strongly; the cranial capacity is about the same as that of an average modern Englishman, the stature somewhat less; the figure is as a rule sturdy and muscular.

This Romano-British type, as anthropologists call it, is so widely prevalent in the later Roman period that it may safely be regarded as having established itself before the Roman

period began. Its closest connexions on the Continent are with
Scandinavia, the Low Countries, and northern France; and it
has survived on a considerable scale in modern England. Sir
Arthur Keith, the chief living authority on this subject, raises
the question:[1] 'Do people . . . of the Romano-British type occur
in our modern population? I would answer that inquiry with
a confident Yes—in very considerable numbers, particularly
amongst the English middle classes.'

Beyond asserting the wide prevalence of this type, certainly
in the later Roman period and probably at its beginning, little
can be said here about the local and other variations which
undoubtedly existed. It is possible, for example, that the
modern prevalence of fair colouring in the east and dark in the
west is not altogether due to the Anglo-Saxon invasions, but is
connected with a much older division between north European
influences on the east of Britain and southern influences on the
west, coming by way of the Atlantic coast. It is also likely that,
in the south-east, the latest comers, whom the Roman invaders
would encounter as a military aristocracy, would be fairer than
the general bulk of the population, with whom they had not
yet been assimilated.[2]

In language, all the various British tribes with whom the
Romans came into contact, and probably all the inhabitants
of the British Isles without exception, were by the beginning of
the Roman period Celtic. Here again, views prevalent not long
ago require modification. The late Sir John Rhys called attention to a broad division of Celtic languages into two classes,
which he called Goidelic and Brythonic, most easily distinguished by the existence of a *q* sound in the Goidelic where the
Brythonic used a *p*; and he advanced the theory that there had
been two waves of Celtic immigration into Britain from the
Continent, the first of Goidels or 'Q-Celts', the second of

---

[1] *Archaeologia*, lxxi (1921), p. 161. Sir Arthur goes on to suggest that, since our
evidence is derived from 'Romano-British settlements', it does not represent 'the
real British people of the Roman period', but people 'who arrived in England
during the period of the Roman occupation'. I venture to dissent from this judgement, because I think that the inhabitants of Roman villas in Britain, about whom
Sir Arthur is here writing, were in general not immigrants but Romanized natives:
I believe, therefore, that their physical characteristics are an index of those prevailing in Britain when the Romans came.

[2] A cautious attempt to establish certain local peculiarities of physique in the
Romano-Britons has been made by Dr. L. H. Dudley Buxton in an important
paper on 'The Racial Affinities of the Romano-Britons', *J.R.S.* xxv (1935), p. 35.

Brythons or 'P-Celts'. Archaeologists then supposed it their business to discover when these two invasions took place, and what distinct types of civilization they introduced. The task was never satisfactorily accomplished; and to-day archaeologists who are also Celtic philologists no longer regard it as a legitimate problem. It is now held that the original language brought to Britain by Celtic invaders belonged to the P-variety, and that the Q-variety did not reach Ireland by way of Britain at all. In confirmation of this view it is pointed out by students of place-names that, throughout Great Britain, no trace can be found of Goidelic names, except where they can be explained as due to migration from Ireland at a time subsequent to the beginning of our era.[1]

It is not known when the Celtic language was introduced into Britain; the attempts to correlate that event with any of the various prehistoric invasions known to archaeology have been, so far, conjectural. It would be generally agreed that it cannot have been later than the beginning of the Iron Age, that is to say, roughly, the sixth century before Christ. One thing is clear: it was sufficiently early for pre-Celtic speech to have left no recognizable trace upon the British names of people or places which, from the time of Caesar onwards, Roman authors committed to writing. It is natural to expect that place-names still in use to-day might preserve such traces; but even in the case of river-names, the most conservative of all, no examples can be quoted with certainty. Professor Ekwall[2] sums up a discussion of the whole subject by saying: 'I cannot point to any definite name that strikes me as probably pre-Celtic.' At the same time it is possible, as some scholars maintain, that certain Celtic dialects in western Britain have been influenced by pre-Celtic speech; though this, if it is true, is no evidence of such speech surviving as a living language into the Roman period.

The material civilization of the Britons in the first century before Christ was by no means uniform. Archaeology, especially within the last twenty years, has told us enough about it to make possible a tentative survey of its characteristics; but this survey must be somewhat like a geological map, where one formation is shown as superimposed upon another, and the

---

[1] I. C. Peate, 'The Kelts in Britain', *Antiquity*, vi (1932), p. 156.
[2] *English River-Names* (1928), pp. liv–lv.

upper formations stop short at certain lines, beyond which the lower go forward without them. It will be enough here to attempt such a survey for that part of Britain which ultimately became Roman, omitting Ireland and most of Scotland.

The general background of British civilization at this time may be described as having a Late Bronze Age character; but over a great part of its area this background had been overlaid by newer cultural formations derived from the continental Iron Age. It will be necessary in the sequel to distinguish four of these; but first the general background must be described.

The Late Bronze Age was a period when Britain as a whole was a backward country by comparison with the Continent; primitive in its civilization, stagnant and passive in its life, and receiving most of what progress it enjoyed through invasion and importation from overseas. Its people lived either in isolated farms or in hut-villages, situated for the most part on the gravel of river-banks or the light upland soils such as the chalk downs or oolite plateaux, which by that time had been to a great extent cleared of their native scrub; each settlement was surrounded by small fields, tilled either with a foot-plough of the type still used not long ago by Hebridean crofters, or else at best with a light ox-drawn plough which scratched the soil without turning the sod; the dead were burnt and their ashes, preserved in urns, buried in regular cemeteries. Thus the land was inhabited by a stable and industrious peasant population, living by agriculture and the keeping of live stock, augmented no doubt by hunting and fishing. They made rude pottery without a wheel, and still used flint for such things as arrowheads; but they were visited by itinerant bronze-founders able to make swords, spears, socketed axes, and many other types of implement and utensil, such as sickles, carpenter's tools, metal parts of wheeled vehicles, buckets, and cauldrons. Judging by the absence of towns and the scarcity of anything like true fortification, these people were little organized for warfare, and their political life was simple and undeveloped, though there was certainly a distinction between rich and poor, since many kinds of metal objects belonging to the period imply a considerable degree of wealth and luxury.

This civilization differed a good deal in different parts of the country. In particular, towards the north and west, it was strongly tinged with Neolithic survivals, sometimes so strongly

as to give it an ambiguous character as between Neolithic and
Bronze Age types; in these parts inhumation, the Neolithic
burial rite, sometimes lingered on, and the megalithic tradition
led people to build their huts and villages with large stones,
often placed on end; the soil, too, was poorer and the whole
standard of life lower.

The chronology of this period is very vague. The Late Bronze
Age in southern Britain is regarded as beginning about 1000
B.C. and lasting until about 400 B.C.; elsewhere it is thought to
last to about 200, and in Scotland to as late as the beginning of
our era.[1] These dates, however, are not only mere approxima-
tions, but the events which they are designed to fix are only the
beginnings of slow and gradual processes. The peasant-civiliza-
tion described above may have taken shape after 1000, but it
did not cease to exist at the date when the Bronze Age is said
to have closed. What happened at that date was that it began
coming at certain points under the influence of Iron Age
fashions of life and thought, which in many respects left it
substantially unchanged. From this point of view the earlier
phase of the Iron Age may be better regarded as a period of
overlap between the Bronze and Iron Ages; a period when
some settlements, planted by new-comers from the Continent,
showed a predominant Iron Age civilization, while others went
on their way little if at all influenced by their new neighbours.
In fact, so important is this overlap between the two periods
that some archaeologists believe the characteristic implements
of the Late Bronze Age not to have been introduced until the
first appearance of iron; while it is an established fact that such
implements remained in use, even in a fairly advanced region
of southern England, until the last century before Christ. When
we speak of the Iron Age as beginning at a certain date, therefore, it must be remembered that this does not imply a general
abandonment of Bronze Age fashions, nor even the general
beginning of such abandonment; and hundreds of years after
such a date the majority of Bronze Age villages were still carrying on their old life with little change.

Of the various Iron Age cultures[2] which had by the time of

[1] These dates are those given in V. Gordon Childe, *The Bronze Age* (1930),
pp. 236-7.
[2] I am here in the main following C. F. C. Hawkes ('Hill-Forts', in *Antiquity*, v
(1931), pp. 60-97; Kendrick and Hawkes, *Archaeology in England and Wales, 1914-31*
(1932), ch. x. My first or south-eastern culture is his Iron Age A; my second

Julius Caesar established themselves upon this Late Bronze
Age foundation, the first made its appearance in the seventh
century before Christ and developed especially in the sixth.
The La Tène period had not yet begun; consequently the
civilization brought in by these new-comers was based upon,
though it did not very closely reproduce, the Hallstatt type[1]
which flourished on the Continent in the first half of the last
millennium before our era.

It is in south-eastern England that the remains of this Hallstatt immigration are chiefly found; but it impinged upon a
long coast-line, extending from Yorkshire to Dorset, and its
earliest appearance seems also to have been its most northerly.
This was the settlement on the Castle Hill of Scarborough,
where, in addition to implements of Late Bronze Age types, a
single iron object was found, and much pottery of a kind which
shows its makers to have been at least under the influence of the
Hallstatt tradition. The settlement is referred to the seventh
century. Other landings of the same general kind have been
traced on the Thames, in Kent, and in Sussex; and especially
on Hengistbury Head in Hampshire. The continental affinities
of the pottery are in part with south-western France and the
Pyrenees, in part with Holland and Champagne; but its general
distribution in Britain suggests that its main source lies in the
latter direction rather than the former, the migration from
Champagne coming at the end of the movement, about 500 B.C.

The influence of this Hallstatt immigration was not confined
to the coast. Inland sites affected or freshly settled by it are
numerous. The most important is the village at All Cannings
Cross, near Devizes, in Wiltshire, dated to the fifth and fourth
centuries, where implements of Late Bronze Age types were
found associated with a great mass of Hallstatt pottery. Another
is at Park Brow, in Sussex, where the Hallstatt invaders seem to
have destroyed a village of Bronze Age round huts and built
instead their own rectangular houses. In general, settlements

(south-western) and third (north-eastern) are his Iron Age B; and my fourth
(Belgic) is the first phase of his Iron Age C. Since all that is needed for the purposes
of this book is a broad and generalized picture, I omit much detail and ignore
complications, important for the prehistorian, which have been added to Hawkes's
scheme especially by the excavations now in progress at Maiden Castle in Dorset.

[1] Bushe-Fox, in *Antiquaries Journal*, iv. 225, calls attention to the differences which
mark off the Hallstatt material in England from that derived from the continental
sites to which the name is properly applied.

yielding the pottery characteristic of this culture occur all over the south-east, from Kent to the Cotswolds and the Wash. Many of these settlements indicate a mode of life not perceptibly differing from that of their late Bronze Age background: they are farms or villages, often undefended, lying among their little fields on river-gravels or light upland soils, mostly cremating their dead, storing their grain in underground pits and grinding it with primitive querns, not yet made with the upper stone revolving upon the lower; keeping oxen, sheep, goats, and pigs; still using bronze and even flint implements and possessing very little iron, but indicating their date by a change in the style of their pottery, which, however, is still made without the wheel.

Other settlements are of a new type, and indicate a change in the political life of the people. These are hill-forts, which now, for the first time since the Neolithic age, began to be constructed in large numbers. The hill-forts of this period, though varying a good deal in size and shape, are all alike, so far as we yet know them, in being very simply planned: they consist of a single rampart, which may be of stone, but was generally an earthwork revetted and palisaded with timber and protected by a single ditch; the size of the ramparts is not very great, and the entrances are simply planned, though excavation has in some cases revealed traces of wooden guard-rooms. These were not mere camps of refuge. They were permanently inhabited towns, containing pit-dwellings where the nature of the soil allowed it. Nor do they seem to have been the strongholds of invaders in a hostile land; rather they appear to have come into existence by degrees, as the new-comers multiplied and developed a tribal system and tribal wars, and most of them are dated to the fourth and third centuries before Christ.

This south-eastern Hallstatt culture, although apart from the construction of hill-forts it changed the face of the country and affected its civilization very little, was sufficiently powerful to resist further movements of population from without. A few objects of the La Tène period found their way into the region which it occupied, but very few; and until the Belgic invasion of the last century before Christ (and to some extent, as we shall see, even after that event) it remained somewhat stagnant and kept its original character unimpaired: presumably with a gradual fading away of the Bronze Age elements, and a parallel development of the iron industry in the Weald, whose first exploitation dates from this time.

The south-west shows an Iron Age culture of a different and later type. About the opening of the fourth century the tin trade began bringing to Cornwall influences from the Hallstatt civilization of northern Spain. The clearest evidence for this connexion is a series of late Hallstatt brooches, found at Harlyn Bay and Mount Batten, whose origin is to be sought in Galicia and northern Portugal, not far from the tin-mines of that region; but pottery found at Chun Castle, a circular stone fort in Penwith, as well as the shape of the fort itself, which re-sembles the *citanias* of Galicia, reinforces this evidence; and pottery of the same kind, from many sites in south-western England, shows that the connexion produced widespread con-sequences in opening the south-west to an Iron Age civilization.

Before long, however, Spanish influence was replaced in this part of Britain by Armorican. Presumably the Veneti of the Morbihan, whom Caesar found holding a monopoly of the coastwise trade round Cape Finisterre, were already beginning to assert themselves, and to cut off direct communication between Britain and Spain. Whatever the reason, the fact is clear that the main Iron Age culture of south-western Britain, after an initial phase in which it was dominated by that of Hallstatt Spain, settled down into a La Tène culture in close connexion with Brittany.

The main development of this culture took place in Dorset and Somerset, whence it spread along the Cotswolds into the midlands. Along the eastern edge of this area it marched with, and in many places supplanted, the earlier south-eastern culture already described, being superior to that culture both in its material equipment and in its political and military organiza-tion. Evidences of the character of its daily life have been richly provided by the lake-village at Glastonbury, which proves it by far the most advanced civilization by that time established in this country. The pottery is of good quality, skilfully made though not thrown on the wheel, and the quantities of it very large. Metal objects, both in bronze and in iron, are numerous, and metallurgy was practised in the village itself. Numerous and well-made wooden objects were found, including portions of looms and carts, as well as tubs, spoons, and other small things. And not only are all these things skilfully made, but a great many of them are beautifully decorated in that elegant, flowing, curvilinear style called by English antiquaries Late Celtic, which now for the first time makes its appearance in this country.

The political and military power of this civilization is attested by its hill-forts, which exist in great numbers and far exceed those of the south-east in the massiveness of their structure and the intricacy of their design. Their defences ordinarily consist of stone walls protected by ditches; and multiple ditches, complicated outworks, and additional defences at the gateways are common features.

Eastward the spread of the new culture was blocked by the already established Iron Age civilization of the south-east: but westward it was able to range freely, if somewhat superficially, over the highland zone, whose Late Bronze Age civilization was incapable of resisting it; and hence it is found pushing its way into Wales, establishing hill-forts at Lydney and Llanmelin in the southern marches and leaving relics of its decorated metal-work at various places in the centre and north.

Simultaneously with this south-western La Tène culture, another of the same kind was developing in the north-east. This is especially connected with the name of the Parisi, a tribe of the East Riding mentioned by Ptolemy, whose presumable origin from the Parisii of the Seine valley is confirmed by excavation of their burials, where warriors were interred with their weapons and their chariots in a manner recalling the middle La Tène chariot-burials of the Marne. Here, again, La Tène art is found in a highly developed form; and from this source it spreads widely over the north of England, penetrating into Scotland and even into Ireland. But there is nothing in this northern culture to set alongside the peaceful village-life of Glastonbury. We have, rather, an aristocracy of invading warriors, establishing their dominion over a people whose daily life is still characteristically Bronze Age. The relics of La Tène art in the north at this period are scabbards, shields, horse-trappings, and in general the implements of war; their resemblance to things found in France is so close that some of them were almost certainly brought in by the invaders, to form the basis of a native school of which more will be said hereafter.

In spite of the contrast between these two La Tène immigrations, the warrior aristocracy of the north-east ruling over a native population of alien culture and the richer and more peaceful civilization of the south-west containing in itself certain peasant elements of its own, there are also strong similarities. One is their common dependence upon continental sources of the middle La Tène period. Another is the fact that they established themselves on the outer fringe of the area already occupied by the Iron Age culture of the south-east, and by degrees joined hands, outside the limits of that area, in the midlands, so that no definite frontier can be drawn between them. A third is their common situation on the line dividing the highland and lowland zones, with the result that in both cases they pushed outward into the highland zone and there established an ascendancy over a native culture of Bronze Age type, far more tenacious and conservative than the corresponding peasant cultures of the lowland zone, ready perhaps to accept new masters but by no means ready to accept new fashions of life. In the north this feature is illustrated by the numerous hut-villages of the Brigantian region, wholly Bronze Age in general character, where excavation only very rarely yields a fragment of recognizably La Tène work. In the south-west it is illustrated by such settlements as Chysauster, in Cornwall, whose chambered houses belong to a type of architecture characteristic of the outermost fringe of the highland zone, and represented at its highest development by the brochs of north-western Scotland. At Chysauster, however, the La Tène objects found in these houses are far more numerous than those found in any hut-village of the north: a fact which, with others, goes to show that the influence of La Tène civilization over the Bronze Age peoples among whom it was established was greatest in the south-west and diminished northwards, being in Wales very slight before the beginning of our era, and in the north of England practically non-existent.

The last of these Iron Age invasions, and to historians the best known, because it led directly to the interference of Julius Caesar in British affairs, was that of the Belgae in the first century before Christ. For this event we have the testimony of Caesar himself. Within the lifetime of his informants, he says, the Gaulish king Diviciacus had governed Britain as well as a great part of north-eastern Gaul, and later Commius, whom he made king of the Atrebates in Gaul, was a man of influence in Britain; statements whose significance becomes clearer when he tells us that the parts of Britain nearest to the sea (that is, the straits of Dover) were inhabited not by people born in the island but by people who had crossed over from Belgic Gaul, at first to plunder, then to settle and till the soil; and that almost all of these still bore the names of the Gaulish tribes from which they were sprung.[1] He emphasizes the wealth and dense population of the region thus settled, and reckons its inhabitants as the most civilized of the Britons, differing little in manners and customs from the Gauls.

The evidence of archaeology supports and supplements these statements. A peculiar culture belonging to the late La Tène period was identified in the last century in a cemetery at Aylesford, in Kent, and its characteristic pottery has since then been found in Britain over an area spreading across the Thames to Hertfordshire and Essex, and reaching at its greatest extension to Northamptonshire and the Cherwell valley. In origin this culture was the product of a fusion between the middle La Tène civilization of the Marne and Aisne valleys and new settlers of German blood, arriving in that region in the second century before Christ; for the closest parallels to the material found in Britain come from the southern Belgic region, in particular the territory of the Catalauni, round Châlons-sur-Marne. The date of the migration is fixed by Caesar's evidence to within a generation before his own activity in Gaul, that is, to about 75 B.C.; and by the time of Caesar's expedition the Belgic area in Britain included the east and north of Kent, a few landing-places on the coast of Essex, and at least a considerable part of Hertfordshire.

The character of these new-comers' civilization reflects their mixed pedigree. Hitherto all inhabitants of Britain had attached themselves to what in the last chapter were called areas of primary settlement: the lighter soils, whether on the uplands or on the banks and terraces of rivers, which were naturally drained and unencumbered by heavy timber. For purposes of defence they had fortified themselves on hill-tops or promontories. The Belgae, on the Celtic side of their ancestry, inherited these same traditions; but on the German side they had the instincts of forest-dwellers, accustomed to living in woodland clearings, and an agricultural technique adapted to working heavy soils. Even at Glastonbury, the most advanced agricultural

[1] *Bell. Gall.* ii. 4; iv. 21; v. 12.

implement actually discovered is the foot-plough, and until the Belgic invasion it is fairly certain that no animal-drawn plough was used in this country except a light and primitive type which merely furrowed the surface of the soil; but the Belgae appear to have brought with them the heavy Gaulish plough armed with a coulter and designed to turn a sod. Hence, for the first time in British history, the Belgae began to clear forests, and to exploit the heavier soils on which they grew; they covered the country with isolated farm-houses[1] and stocked it with cattle; they settled in the valleys and appropriated river-crossings; they did indeed construct hill-forts, but much less systematically than the earlier Iron Age settlers, and in the course of time—though this only happened after the Julian invasion—they abandoned the hill-tops and built their towns on valley-sites which have been inhabited ever since. Even where, in the early days of their settlement, they made hill-forts, these were so far influenced by their forest-dwelling habits as to excite special remark from Caesar, who stormed two of them. 'The Britons call it a fort', he writes, 'when they have defended a tract of dense woodland with a rampart and ditch'; a description which could never have been applied to the earlier hill-forts of the open downland. They also introduced into Britain a practice which we know to have been current among the early Germans: that of delimiting their territory by means of a continuous rampart and ditch. A boundary of this kind, dated to their time, runs across the Hertfordshire plain from Verulam to Wheathampstead, with another sector north-west of Verulam; it was evidently made in the early days when they were extending their power north of the Thames, that is, just before the Julian invasion.

Their pottery, made on the wheel, was technically much superior to anything hitherto made in Britain; but both here and elsewhere they showed themselves defective in the artistic qualities with which the earlier La Tène invaders were so richly endowed. It is not until a later period, when no doubt their political predominance enabled them to attract and develop artistic talent, that we find decorative art growing up among them. At this early date they reveal themselves as good

---

[1] Caesar's *creberrima aedificia*, I take it, can only be explained in this sense. The point will become important when we have to consider the origin of the 'Roman villa'.

farmers and good organizers, capable workmen and stout fighters, men of solid utilitarian temperament: in this, too, Germanic rather than Celtic in nature.

It was the Belgae who introduced coinage into Britain. The earliest coins found in this country, apart from stray specimens of Mediterranean fabric brought by trade to the south-west, are those of the Gaulish Bellovaci, apparently struck early in the first century B.C., which are found over an area almost corresponding with that of the Belgic settlements; other types assignable to the Atrebates and perhaps to the Morini are found in the same region, sometimes spreading beyond it; these represent the coins brought with them by the invaders, with some that may have arrived by way of trade before the migration began. After the Belgic settlement coins began to be struck in Britain itself; possibly this was already happening before Caesar's invasion; but that is not certain, and in any case the main development of British coinage belongs to a later date.

In speaking of coinage in Britain, Caesar mentions that iron bars of standard weight were also used as currency. He seems here to be referring to certain objects chiefly used not by the Belgae but by the south-western tribes: objects resembling a half-finished sword with a roughly formed handle, of which large numbers have been found in Somerset, Dorset, Wiltshire, Gloucestershire, and Worcestershire. It has been contended that they are not in fact currency-bars, but merely unfinished swords; nevertheless the traditional explanation of them is probably correct, and if so they represent a form of currency used by the La Tène tribes of south-western Britain before coinage proper was introduced into the country at all.

It is time to attempt a generalized sketch of the civilization of Britain, as these various movements and developments had moulded it by the time of Julius Caesar.

In east Kent and round the mouth of the Thames a dense population of vigorous Belgic settlers were scattering their farms over the country-side, clearing forest, breaking up new land with their heavy ploughs, and reaping rich crops of wheat off the virgin soil. They were divided into small tribes often engaged in petty warfare, but their main concern was to push forward their own area of settlement towards the north and north-east. To the south they were hemmed in by the forest of the Weald, inhabited only by iron-miners belonging to an older civilization.

This civilization extended from the limits of the Belgic area to the Wash, the forests of the midlands, and the uplands of Wiltshire; it was a mixture of primitive Bronze Age elements with elements akin to those of the Hallstatt culture, to some extent affected by La Tène influences, but on the whole stagnant and backward; a peasant civilization, housed in hut-villages and scratching the lighter soils, its chiefs mostly living in hill-forts on the open downs, and even its larger tribal units— Trinovantes, Iceni, Regni—having no capital that could deserve the name of a city.

West of this lay a richer and more progressive region. The Cotswolds, Somerset, Dorset, and the lands surrounding them, supported a large population of well-organized tribesmen, primitive in their agriculture compared to the Belgae, but hardly less powerful in politics and war, and infinitely more gifted in the arts. North-eastward they were in communication with a culture like their own which dominated the midland forests from the fortress of Hunsbury, and this again linked up with the warriors of Lincolnshire and Yorkshire, who were gradually asserting their supremacy over the hut-villages of the lingering northern Bronze Age and laying the foundations of the Brigantian kingdom.

The westernmost fringe may by now have learned everywhere to talk Celtic, but its civilization was practically untouched by Iron Age influences. Cornwall had its tin trade and its ancient connexions with the civilized world; but Devonshire, Wales, and the north-west were still occupied by a backward and poverty-stricken Bronze Age population, living in hut-farms and hut-villages and owning hardly any implements except of wood and stone.

It sometimes happens that the name by which a nation or country is known to history perpetuates some error on the part of those who first used it, as when the natives of the American continent are called Indians because the European explorers who discovered it were in search of India, or when we call the Hellenes Greeks because the Romans transferred to them the name of a small Epirote tribe. The origin of the name Britain is obscure; but in all probability it enshrines a blunder of a somewhat similar kind.

Among the Belgic tribes inhabiting the continental shore of the straits of Dover in the time of Julius Caesar was one which

Pliny[1] calls Britanni. From his text, they appear to have lived immediately south of Boulogne. The Belgic invaders of Britain were drawn not from this region, but from a district a good deal farther to the south; but this was the region from which Caesar's expedition sailed, and his port of departure lay almost in the Britannic territory; it may therefore be assumed that he knew their name.

But the country which ever since he invaded it has been known as Britain—Britannia, the land of the Britanni—was not known by that name to earlier explorers. Although manuscript readings are discrepant, no doubt through a tendency to replace the earlier name by the better-known later, they contain evidence that from the fourth century before Christ, when Britain was visited and described by the Greek traveller Pytheas, the British Isles were called by many geographers, Diodorus Siculus, Strabo, Ptolemy, and others, the Pretanic Isles. Scholars agree that the name Pretani, which is thus implied as a general name for their inhabitants from at least the fourth century onwards, can hardly be identical with the name Britanni. On the other hand, there is a name with which it not only can but must be identical: it is the old Welsh Priten, the 'P'-form of which the corresponding 'Q'-form is Cruithin, the name by which Irish writers refer to the Picts. The name Picti, painted men, is a Latin translation of this word, appearing in the third century as a general term by which Latin-speaking Britons referred to the barbarian tribes beyond the frontier; later it was adopted by these tribes themselves, and became the title of the Pictish kingdom whose people were called Cruithin by the Irish.

In the light of these facts it can hardly be doubted that the true form of the name Britannic, as the name of Great Britain and Ireland, is really Pretanic or Pritenic, and that the inhabitants of these islands, perhaps already before the beginning of the Iron Age, were called Pretani or Priteni. It is a very probable conjecture that Caesar, finding himself at the outset of his expedition on the borders of a Belgic tribe called Britanni and knowing that the country he was about to invade had been lately colonized from Belgic Gaul, believed himself able to correct a widespread error by substituting the forms Britanni, Britannia, for Pretani and its Latinized correlative Pretania.

[1] *Natural History*, iv. 31.

III

CAESAR'S INVASION

WHAT motives induced Caesar to attack Britain, what he intended to bring about there by his invasion, and how long the project had been shaping itself in his mind before he set about executing it, are questions to which he has given us no answer. Yet we cannot help asking them; and unless we can find some sort of answer, at least to the first and second, the mere narrative of his campaigns must remain unintelligible.

The nearest approach in Caesar's text to a statement of his motives for the invasion is the remark that, in almost all his Gallic campaigns, contingents from Britain had been fighting on the side of his enemies.[1] In other passages also, he testifies to the close connexions between Britain and Gaul: in 57 B.C. those chiefs of the Bellovaci who had urged resistance to him took refuge in Britain when their policy broke down; he tells us that in his time there were chiefs whose power extended to both sides of the Channel; and in his general sketch of Gallic civilization he describes Britain as the cradle and school of Druidism. Every reader of his Commentaries knows that, as the years of his work in Gaul went on, he became more and more preoccupied with the problem of keeping the peace, and forestalling or repressing movements of rebellion, among the fiercely independent tribes he had conquered. It was the necessity of guarding against such risings that dictated his last acts in Gaul, before he crossed the Channel on his final British adventure; it was fear of their imminence that forced him to abandon it before he had carried it to a finish; there is little room for doubt that the same motives played a part in determining the enterprise itself.

As the event of his expedition showed, Caesar was on the horns of a dilemma. So long as Gaul was restless, Britain, a refuge and reservoir of disaffection within a few hours' sail, was an added danger: for the sake of Gaulish security, therefore, Britain must be made harmless. But so long as the restlessness of Gaul was acute a campaign across the Channel was hazardous:

---

[1] *B.G.* iv. 20. It should be noted that Caesar gives this as a reason not for invading Britain at all (for that, he gives none) but for pushing the invasion forward as rapidly as possible.

it was an incitement to revolt in Gaul while the Roman armies were overseas. Either way there was a risk. Caesar chose one risk and went to Britain: Augustus, warned by his example, chose the other and stayed in Gaul.

The question which risk to take could be decided only in the light of an estimate of possible gains; that is, in the light of an answer to the question what a British campaign might hope to achieve. It is impossible to think that Caesar had no answer of his own to this question; but he has not told us what it was. The last thing he did before sailing to Britain in 55 was to cross the Rhine and undertake a campaign in Germany; and in narrating the events of that campaign he ends with the statement that his plans had been fully carried out and his objects completely achieved. At the end of his British narrative he makes no such claim, and the contrast is significant. His reconnaissance in 55 was followed by a twenty days' thanksgiving at Rome to celebrate the happy commencement of a new adventure. Nothing of the kind followed the definitive campaign of 54. Whatever the object of the expedition may have been, neither Caesar nor the Senate thought that it had been fulfilled.

For this reason it cannot be supposed that Caesar meant only to conduct a punitive war, a large-scale raid, in order to teach the Britons that they were within the reach of Rome's arm, and to warn them against interference in the affairs of Gaul. That is what he meant to do in Germany; had he meant to do only that in Britain, he could have justly claimed that he had done it. He meant to do more.

He had taken up his command in Gaul in 58, with four legions. In that year he did little more than expel the Helvetian and Germanic hordes that threatened it from the east. In 57, with two more legions, he broke the power of the Belgae. In 56 he crushed the Veneti and carried his standards to the Pyrenees and the Bay of Biscay. He had, in fact, overrun the whole of Gaul in three years: by the beginning of 55 'Gaul was, to all appearance, conquered'.[1] The appearance was no doubt deceptive: much of the hardest work was still to come; but in estimating his intentions at the beginning of his British campaign we must be guided by the situation as it then appeared, and by his record of achievement in Gaul as it must have stood

[1] Rice Holmes, *Caesar's Conquest of Gaul*, p. 95.

in his own eyes at that time. He knew the size of Britain with a fair degree of accuracy; he knew that its inhabitants were less civilized and less highly organized both in politics and in war than the Gauls; he meant in the following year to invade the country with five legions and to keep them there for the winter; and when all these facts are considered at once, it can hardly be doubted that his plan was to conquer the whole island.

This plan was presumably formed during his Belgic campaign of 57. It was then that he visited the regions from which Britain had lately been colonized; and during that summer he had its existence and importance repeatedly impressed on his mind. It was then that he heard of Diviciacus, lately king of the Suessiones and overlord of Belgic Britain; it was then that the hostile faction of the Bellovaci took flight across the Channel; it must have been then that he made Commius ruler of the Atrebates and learnt that he too claimed to be a man of authority on the other side of the straits. And if Strabo is right in saying that the Veneti, after submitting to him in 57, rebelled at the beginning of 56 because they heard that he was about to invade Britain and feared the loss of their monopoly in the Atlantic coastwise trade, it follows that Caesar's plan was by then not only formed but already becoming a matter of common knowledge.

It was late in the summer of 55 when Caesar felt himself free to turn his attention to Britain. He had destroyed an invading force from Germany and had completed his punitive expedition across the Rhine; and he writes as if, after this interruption, he were picking up the thread of his plans where the German inroad had compelled him for a time to lay it down. It is clear too from his words that he expects a critical reader to ask, not, 'Why did Caesar go to Britain at all?' but, 'Why did he go there with a couple of legions for a hurried visit so late in this year, instead of waiting for the next summer and then invading in force?' To this question he gives two answers. First, the constant help which Britain had been in the habit of sending to his enemies in Gaul: this, evidently, was an inducement to show his hand and prove to the Britons that their own safety was in the balance. Secondly, the desirability of a reconnaissance in order to gain information about the approaches, the harbours, the country, and the inhabitants.

In view of the close connexion between Britain and the mainland, a connexion vouched for by Caesar himself, it is natural to suppose that, to many at least of his questions, answers might have been given by merchants and others in Gaul. And of the merchants he did make diligent inquiry, but failed to discover what he most wanted to know. They were only acquainted, he found, with the Channel coasts, and even there they could not tell him of a harbour able to accommodate so vast a fleet as his expeditionary force would need.

They may have known more than they were willing to tell; but Caesar himself never hints that they were concealing anything from him; and if he had believed this he had every reason to state it, as justifying an expedition which, he was well aware, needed justification. If his plan was to conquer the whole of Britain, all becomes clear. He asked the merchants, as indeed his words imply, for information not only about the Channel coast but about the entire country; they were honestly unable to give it; and he went over to get it himself. But he could not afford to explain that to his readers, because in the event he got no information whatever except about that very coast which was already well known to his informants. To state the facts explicitly would have been to confess that his reconnaissance was a failure. He did, however, see enough to convince him that what the Gaulish traders had told him was true so far as it went; and at least he did not attempt to cover his own failure by accusing them of bad faith.

His preparations were simple. He requisitioned close on a hundred Gaulish sailing craft to serve as transports, assembled them at the straits of Dover, and sent a trusted subordinate, Gaius Volusenus, to reconnoitre the opposite coast from a warship. Volusenus was away for the best part of five days, and in the light of what happened later we can infer that, making the obvious landfall at the cliffs of Dover, he explored the coast for some distance to the east and west. From the South Foreland to Folkestone he found the beach commanded by ramparts of cliff. West of that, the tidal inlet where now is Romney Marsh gave doubtful access to hilly and wooded country. But eastward he soon arrived at the open shelving beaches about Deal, with anchorage in the Downs and plain country, well cultivated, behind them. Here, he saw, a landing might be made. Had he gone farther, he would have found what Caesar wanted: a great land-locked harbour inland from Sandwich.

protected by the isle of Thanet, with the low hill of Richborough offering a perfect site for a camp. This was the port used in the following century by the armies of Claudius; and had Caesar known of it the whole course of his British campaign would have been different. Conditions in Gaul would, even so, never have permitted him to complete the conquest of Britain; but his fleet would have been secure, and the chief anxiety that crippled his operations there would not have arisen. The failure to find the port of Richborough was the blunder that marred the entire expedition. And the responsibility for it lies not altogether on the shoulders of Volusenus; Caesar himself, after the hard-learned lesson of 55, looked for another landing-place and came within a mile or two of the harbour without discovering it.

Eighty of Caesar's transports were now in the river-mouth at Boulogne; eighteen more, which he intended for his cavalry, lay a few miles farther north at Ambleteuse. Traders crossing the Channel warned the British tribes of his preparations, and several of them sent promises of submission and undertook to find hostages for their good conduct. Caesar, making use of the tribal connexions between Britain and the Continent, sent Commius back with their envoys to urge as many tribes as possible to submit; and on the return of Volusenus his armada sailed.

A force of about ten thousand men embarked at Boulogne, leaving harbour on the ebb after dark and waiting until midnight to sail. It consisted of the Seventh and Tenth legions, with archers and slingers; the cavalry were given orders to proceed to Ambleteuse, take ship there in the vessels awaiting them, and join the fleet as it passed. It was a fine night in late August; the moon was past the first quarter, and the wind fair, but light and fitful. Towards morning it died away, and the sailing-ships were almost becalmed when, about nine o'clock, Caesar halted the galleys off the little port of Dover, and waited for his transports to close.

The Kentish Britons had meanwhile changed their minds about submitting to Caesar. Perhaps further information from Gaulish traders had revealed the smallness of his force; in any case, when their envoys returned, bringing Commius with them, they found the tribes bent on resistance. Commius was seized and thrown into chains, and preparations were made for war. Charioteers, cavalry, and infantry assembled on the downs above

Dover, on the assumption that Caesar would probably land there; and consequently, when he drew near the harbour in the morning, he saw both lines of cliff, which overhung the beaches of the inlet to right and left, thronged with armed men.

These were no conditions in which to attempt a landing, even if he had originally intended it; but he knew from Volusenus' report that a better place was to be found farther eastward;[1] he therefore anchored while his transports came up on the last of the breeze, summoned his officers to the flagship, told them what he had learned about the lie of the land, and laid before them his plan, urging upon them the necessity of watching for his signals and obeying them smartly: the only way in which he could hope to throw all his force ashore at once and escape being defeated in detail.

The cavalry had ridden to Ambleteuse according to instructions, embarked with unforeseen delay, and failed to clear the harbour, having missed the evening tide. In the morning, when they did sail, they were met by a contrary wind and obliged to put back. Caesar awaited them in vain until the middle of the afternoon, when the tide turned up-channel and a breeze from the south[2] sprang up with it. As soon as he saw his ships swing to their anchors, he gave them the signal to weigh and make sail, and the whole fleet stood slowly north-eastward along the coast and rounded the South Foreland.

The Britons divined Caesar's intention, and marched across the downs, cavalry and charioteers leading, to meet him. When he reached the shelving beach selected by Volusenus as the best landing-place, and ran his transports aground on the shingle,

---

[1] I follow Rice Holmes in making Caesar land east of Dover, in spite of Commander H. D. Warburg's attractive argument (*Eng. Hist. Rev.* xxxiii (1923), p. 226), for a landing near Hythe. He shows conclusively that if Caesar's dates and times are correct the tide-stream when he weighed anchor was running south-west, and that south-west gales are overwhelmingly commoner, especially at that time of year, than north-east. But he has overlooked the facts that (*a*) the gale undoubtedly was a north-easterly one, for the cavalry transports running before it were driven westward (iv. 28); (*b*) in 54 Caesar certainly landed east of Dover, and at a place which he had chosen in 55, which therefore cannot have been far from his landing in that year (v. 8). I suspect that something has gone wrong with the numeral *quartum* in iv. 28; if the interval was more like a week, the stream would be running north-eastwards when he weighed.

[2] This was the only wind which would permit the sailing-ships both to round the South Foreland from their anchorage off Dover and to run on shore in the neighbourhood of Deal. It was only a local breeze, or it would have brought up the cavalry from Ambleteuse.

they were ready for him, the infantry a little way up the beach, the cavalry and chariots at the water's edge. His men, heavily armed as they were, hesitated to jump over the bows of the transports into several feet of water and face these strange engines under a fire of javelins, arrows, and sling-stones; and it was only when Caesar brought up his warships to reply to this fusillade, and throw into the balance the heavier fire of their catapults, that the Britons drew back a few paces and allowed the legionaries, gallantly led by the standard-bearer of the Tenth, to gain a foothold on the beach. A confused struggle followed; but by degrees the legionaries gained ground and at last formed line and charged. The Britons, however formidable in a straggling fight, were never able either now or afterwards to resist Caesar's legions in battle-formation; they broke and fled, and it was only his lack of horse that prevented Caesar from completing his victory.

This initial defeat swung the policy of the Kentish chiefs in a moment to the other extreme. They dismissed their levies, each man to his farm or village, and bringing Commius with them came penitently to wait on Caesar, who rated them soundly and ordered them to send for hostages. For the next two days the chiefs continued to come in with promises of submission.

At the end of that time the cavalry transports found the wind fair though light, and sailed for Britain. The day was far advanced, and they had nearly reached the camp, when a gale sprang up from the north-east and drove them out to sea again. Some, with the wind on the port quarter, reached Ambleteuse; the rest were blown down channel. They tried to anchor, but the waves broke over them, and they were forced to stand out to sea and feel their way back in the dark to the coast of Gaul. To the credit of their seamanship, not a vessel was lost. These Gaulish seamen knew their work; but that mystery was not possessed by Caesar. He had anchored the main body of his transports in the Downs, and beached his light warships on the shingle. That night the moon was full, and the tide almost at springs; and it is difficult to believe Caesar's statement that no one in his camp knew of the connexion between the two. The rollers, racing up the shingle before the gale, filled the hulls of his beached galleys; some of the transports dragged their anchors or carried away their cables and were dashed on shore under the eyes of the helpless Romans. In the morning the beach was strewn with shattered hulks and wreckage. There were no facilities for repairs, no spare tackle to replace what was lost, and no more ships within call. And Caesar, intending only a brief stay in Britain, had brought no supplies to maintain his men for the winter. The British chiefs in his camp saw their opportunity. In hurried whispers they exchanged an oath to raise the tribes once more, prevent the Romans from replenishing their stores from the standing wheat-fields in the neighbourhood, starve them out, annihilate them, and be rid of Rome for good and all. One by one, they slunk away from the camp.

To a less determined man than Caesar the situation might have appeared desperate. Cast away on a hostile shore with a small force of hungry men, with no hope whatever of relief by his friends, there was only one thing for him to do. The year had been dry and there was a good wheat-crop, standing ripe for harvest. He detailed fatigue parties to reap and bring into camp every day as much as they could. At the same time he turned his legionary artificers to the task of demolishing the worst damaged of his ships and using the materials to repair the rest. It was a race against time. Every day the weather was likely to worsen for a voyage, wheat would be harder to get, and the Britons might be expected to accumulate forces against him. One day their cavalry and chariots lay in ambush where they expected his men to forage, surprised the Seventh legion at work, and were pressing it hard when Caesar, thanks to the watchfulness of his sentries, was able to bring the rest of his force to the rescue. A spell of bad weather followed, after which the Britons thought the time had come for a decisive blow. They approached the camp and offered battle. But they could not face the legions; they fled, and the pursuing Romans ravaged the country far and wide before returning to camp.

Once more the Britons swung from confidence to despair. Before nightfall they were suing for peace, and Caesar was demanding twice the former toll of hostages. But he knew that he would not be there to receive them. His ships were ready; the wind was fair; the equinox was at hand, and further delay would be folly. That night he sailed back to Boulogne; and of all the tribes that had promised hostages only two sent them.

It is clear from the apologetic tone which more than once creeps into Caesar's narrative of this expedition that his conscience was not at ease. He expected to be criticized for under-taking it, on so small a scale and so late in the season, at all. He expected to be criticized for making no provision to ensure the safety of his fleet in a gale at high water of springs. He expected to be criticized for not having brought supplies, both in the way of foodstuffs and of materials for repairing his ships in the event of damage. None of these criticisms can be alto-gether rebutted. There are only two things that could be said in Caesar's defence, and neither is conclusive.

One is that he did not know how dangerous a matter it was to ship an army to Britain without having first secured a sheltered harbour for his transports. Had he understood the conditions and the perils of ocean as opposed to Mediterranean navigation, he would either never have gone to Britain in the late summer of 55, or he would have insisted on a sheltered harbour or a reserve fleet, or both. Yet it is necessary to record the fact that even his misfortunes in that year failed to teach him the required lesson, and he repeated his mistake in the year following.

The other plea in his defence is that he did after all succeed in the main object of his expedition. It was not an invasion, it was a reconnaissance; and he came away from Britain having learnt something about the country and the people. But what did he actually learn? As to how a fleet could go safely to Britain and remain there safely until it was wanted again he learnt nothing. He learnt nothing about the geography of Britain as a whole, its natural resources, or its military power. He only came into contact with a handful of East Kentish tribes, and concerning these, it is true, he gathered certain useful information, though none, surely, which the Gaulish traders had not already given him.

He learnt that the Britons, unlike the Gauls of his own time, made use of chariots in warfare, and he saw how these were handled. They served partly as a kind of cavalry, partly as a kind of mounted infantry used in conjunction with cavalry. The chariot carried a highly skilled and well-armed warrior, who might either travel independently about the battlefield dis-charging arrows and sling-stones, or else combine with the cavalry, join in their charges, and on reaching their objective dismount and fight on foot while his chariot waited near by to remove him at need elsewhere. Caesar describes these tactics with care, and pays a high tribute both to the skill with which the chariots were driven and fought and to their effectiveness in battle. At the same time, it appears from his narrative that the combined cavalry and chariot attack which he describes, though alarming to his men by its novelty and effective when used against scattered parties of infantry engaged in foraging or ravaging, was not dangerous to a legion in battle-formation. The chief tactical problem presented to him by the British charioteers was the difficulty of pursuit. On his reconnaissance in 55 Caesar was totally unprovided with cavalry except for the thirty men of Commius' bodyguard. Even in his invasion of the following year he was, like all Roman commanders of the period, inadequately furnished in that arm. Consequently charioteers could always escape him when their attack failed.

It may be added that although a few ancient writers describe the British war-chariot as having its axle armed with a scythe Caesar neither says nor implies anything of the kind; his account of their operations rather implies that they had none, and this inference is borne out by the silence of the best ancient writers and by the remains actually found in Celtic chariot-graves, whether in Britain or in Gaul.

Caesar also learnt that in at least the south-eastern part of Britain there was abundance of grain to be had at harvest-time; but his provisions for the invasion of 54 show that he did not rely on this for the support of his troops. Another lesson was that the British tribes could easily be brought to sue for peace by sustaining a defeat, and this, we shall see, was an idea which helped to control his initial strategy in the following year, with disastrous results.

Taking all this together, one cannot believe either that the information gathered in the reconnaissance came up to Caesar's expectations or that it was worth winning at the expense of so considerable an effort and at so grave a risk. Had the gale been worse, so as to destroy a majority of his ships instead of a minority; had the Britons been more energetic in preventing his troops from foraging; above all, had they collected a fleet powerful enough to hamper the movements of his returning transports, which they might well have been able to do for all he seems to have known about them, Caesar's career would have ended ingloriously on the coast of Kent. Yet, after all this is said, the judgement of history depends not on what might have happened but on what did happen; and the fact is that Caesar, like many another great commander, took risks, partly with his eyes open and partly blindfold, and that by the coolness and soundness of judgement which he invariably displayed in an emergency he extricated himself, not on this occasion only, from dangers which to a' lesser man would have proved fatal.

It was late in the autumn before Caesar left the winter-quarters where he had placed his legions in Belgic Gaul. In the meantime he had learnt from the fewness of the hostages sent across the Channel that the Britons as a whole did not mean to submit easily, and he had worked out elaborate plans for next year's campaign. He designed a new type of transport, instead of contenting himself with the standard pattern of Gaulish ship: they were lower in the freeboard and broader in the beam, and fitted with oars as well as sails. He arranged for the building of six hundred, to be done by military labour in various parts of northern Gaul: sixty of them, we know, were to be built on the banks of the Marne; rope was ordered from Spain, and the whole fleet was to be ready in the spring.

In June 54 he was back in the north, to find his shipwrights well forward with their work; but the shadow of approaching troubles in Gaul already overhung his preparations: the Treveri were planning revolt, and many of the Gaulish chiefs were lukewarm or worse. But Caesar was not to be turned from his project. He patched up the affairs of the Treveri as best he could in the time, and resolved to take with him the most discontented of the Gaulish leaders, to be hostages for the good behaviour of their tribes.

His force was now ready to sail. Eight legions were encamped at Boulogne, beside slingers and archers and four thousand Gallic horse; but of this army more than a third was to be left behind, in command of Caesar's ablest officer, Labienus, not only to protect the base of the expedition and to keep it supplied with provisions, but also to keep the peace in Gaul. His fleet consisted of 28 warships and 540 transports; 60 more were weatherbound at the mouth of the Seine, but he could do without them; and in addition there were over 200 privately owned vessels belonging to merchants and adventurers who had attached themselves to the expedition.

For over three weeks the armada lay in port, waiting for a

favourable wind. It was an anxious time for Caesar. Among the Gaulish notables in his camp were some whose disaffection only awaited opportunity or incitement to show itself; and if it was his business to see that opportunity was lacking, incitement was not. Their ringleader was Dumnorix the Aeduan, who had openly declared in his tribal council that Caesar meant to make him king, and had never forgiven him for falsifying the boast. During these weeks Dumnorix tried by every means in his power to persuade Caesar to leave him behind, pleading his terror of the sea and his religious obligation not to set foot on shipboard; finding this vain, he turned his attention to persuading his fellow chiefs of the danger they ran by putting their lives in Caesar's hand; and at last, when all else had failed and the wind was fair for crossing, he summoned the cavalry under his command and, in the confusion of a general embarcation, fled from the camp.

Not even the long-delayed fair wind could distract Caesar's mind from the peril of this new emergency. He cancelled his orders for embarcation and sent a strong body of horse in pursuit of Dumnorix, to bring him back dead or alive. But Dumnorix had gone too far to retreat; he refused to come back, and was cut down, crying out that he was a free man and member of a free tribe. His ghost had its vengeance. It was the Gaulish freedom which he invoked with his last breath that ruined Caesar's plans for the conquest of Britain.

That evening the fleet sailed. Towards midnight the light south-west breeze died away and at dawn Caesar found himself drifting up-channel on the flood tide, and saw the South Foreland receding on the port quarter. But his transports were now provided with oars, and when the tide turned he set his men to row, and work their way across the stream of the ebb to the landing-place he had chosen the year before. By midday all the ships were beached, and the army landed unopposed.[1]

The exact position of this second landing is uncertain. Caesar's words may imply either that it was identical with the landing-

[1] This time there is no difficulty about the tides. Caesar left Boulogne on the ebb, shortly before sunset, which happened about 8 p.m. The tide turned about 10, and the wind failed at midnight; between 3 and 4 a.m. it was light enough to see the coast, and by that time the current that was carrying the fleet towards the North Sea had already begun to slacken. By about 4 they had got their oars out, and soon after this the tide definitely turned. They must have been then about ten miles east of the South Foreland.

place of the previous year, which, if his own estimate of seven miles from Dover is correct, must have been close to Walmer Castle, or that it had been chosen by himself in that year for future use, in which case it cannot have been far away. It was not so far north as Sandwich, for had Caesar landed there he would have discovered the harbour of Richborough and his ships would have been safe. As it was, he allowed political and military considerations to determine his next step. Natives were brought in, who said that the tribes had at first meant to oppose his landing as before, but on seeing the vast size of his fleet had changed their minds and retreated into the interior. Caesar knew the value of a swift and unexpected stroke; he had learnt in 55 that the Britons had no stomach for a defeat, and he was confident of his power to defeat them whenever he could bring them to battle; he decided therefore that this was an opportunity not to be lost, and determined on a night march to be followed by a battle at dawn.

Leaving his fleet at anchor and a sufficient force of men to protect the camp, he marched inland with his main body soon after midnight. Early in the morning he was looking down into the Stour valley from the hills east of Canterbury, with the low sun behind him, and descried the British forces moving down from the opposite woods, cavalry and chariots leading, to dispute his passage of the river. He launched his own horse against them and they withdrew into the woods.

There is an ancient fort, now called Bigbury, on the brow of the hill two miles west of Canterbury, overlooking the river. It had been constructed as a fortified town by the Belgae not long before Caesar's time, and their weapons, agricultural implements, and household goods have been found there. Its defences were simple: a bank and ditch, doubtless a palisade, and an abattis of felled trees in the gateways. Here the Britons, demoralized by the shock of the first encounter, took refuge. Woods grew around it, and among these their skirmishers were moving in expectation of the assault. Caesar swept them aside with his cavalry and threw the Seventh legion against the fortress. The rampart and palisade together rose some twenty feet above the ditch-bottom, but under the locked shields of the front rank their comrades piled a mound of earth, swarmed over the palisade, and cleared the place with trifling casualties. No pursuit was allowed; the men had marched and fought since midnight, the country was strange, and time was needed to pitch a camp.

If Caesar was satisfied with his day's work, he was much deceived. Once more the apologetic note makes itself felt in his narrative when he describes himself leaving his fleet at anchor 'off a gentle open beach'. He had made a mistake for which he paid dearly. While he lay encamped in the Stour valley a gale got up from the east. His ships dragged their anchors, fell foul of one another, and were thrown by scores on the beach to be hammered by the full force of the rollers. The crews left on board could do nothing, and by morning very few of the vessels were undamaged.

The news reached Caesar just in time for him to stop the pursuit. Hastening back to the coast, he found that forty of his ships were a total loss, and the rest not to be repaired without much labour. He drafted gangs of skilled legionaries to the work, and sent orders to Labienus to dispatch shipwrights and begin at once building new vessels to replace those that had been wrecked. But it was not enough to repair his fleet; he now at last realized that he must protect it from like damage in the future. The only way in which he could do this, in the absence of a safe harbour, was by beaching every ship above high-water mark and then entrenching them against enemy attack. This took ten days, which could ill be spared from the short campaigning season; but it had to be done, and Caesar did it.

The negligence with which he exposed himself to a repetition of the same disaster which he had suffered in 55 is difficult to understand. Rice Holmes has argued that whereas in 55 his transports were anchored in the Downs off Walmer, in 54 his anchorage was in the Small Downs off Sandwich, where, as the *Channel Pilot* has it, 'the anchorage is much more secure than in the Downs, being more sheltered, with better holding ground and shoaler water', and where vessels driven ashore on the sand would suffer less than on the shingle beaches about Deal. This may be true; and if it were, the contrast between the two anchorages would have been some excuse for Caesar's conduct in 54; it is strange, therefore, that he has not mentioned it. All he has urged in his own defence is that he anchored off a gentle open shore, in words almost identically repeating the description of the beach where his fleet was wrecked in the previous year. The only point of contrast would seem to be that whereas in 55 his warships were beached, in 54 they were anchored with the transports. We can do no more than note the facts that, in spite of his earlier experience, he allowed his impatience to close with the Britons to prevent him from attending first to the security of his ships, and that his intelligence service failed, even after the second disaster, to reveal the existence of a safe harbour at Richborough.[1]

The earlier mishap to Caesar's shipping had encouraged the Britons to renew their resistance to him; the second had the same consequence, the more so because his armament in this year was on a much larger scale and yet proved equally vulnerable to the hostility of the stars in their courses.

The most powerful man in Britain at the moment was Cassivellaunus, king of the chief tribe among the recent Belgic settlers, the Catuvellauni. This tribe was the spear-point of the Belgic invasion. By now it had pushed its way across the Thames above London and was hard at work consolidating its position in Hertfordshire. Its capital, the stronghold of Cassivellaunus himself, was a fortress a hundred acres or more in extent, protected by earthen ramparts and a ditch still as much as forty feet in vertical depth, that can be traced on the hill-top beside Wheathampstead, a little north of St. Albans. The defences here, and the occupation within them, date from the first half of the last century before Christ; and its excavator says of the fortress: 'It is the work of men with wealth, power, arrogance; but it is the work also of men who were still, for one reason or another, uneasy in their adopted land.'[2]

When Caesar's threat to Britain became matter of common talk, it found Cassivellaunus fighting to maintain and extend his lately established lordship north of the Thames. Especially he was at war with his eastern neighbours, the non-Belgic

---

[1] Rice Holmes (*Ancient Britain*, p. 664, note 7) does not face this fact. He says, when refuting some one's suggestion that Caesar may have landed at Richborough in 55, 'it might have been dangerous to land in a harbour with a narrow entrance in the presence of an enemy'; but in 54, even granted that for this reason he might have wished to land on an open beach in the first instance, there could be no reason why immediately on landing he should not have sent his ships round there, a mere two or three miles on Rice Holmes's own theory as to the landing-place, and still less reason why he should not have moved them there after the storm instead of spending ten precious days in beaching them. Richborough was a perfectly good harbour in the time of Claudius; it cannot have been a bad one in the time of Caesar.

[2] R. E. M. Wheeler, 'Belgic Cities of Britain', in *Antiquity*, vii (1933), p. 30.

Trinovantes. Not long before Caesar's invasion the Trinovantian king had fallen in battle, and his young son Mandubracius, barely escaping with his life, had crossed the Channel and sought protection from Caesar. With Caesar he returned to Britain, hoping with his help to recover his father's kingdom. Though hard pressed by Cassivellaunus, however, the Trinovantes had not yet fallen under his rule; nor was he in any sense ruler even over the Belgic tribes of Britain, for these, as Caesar tells us, had each a king of its own and were indeed in a state of more or less constant mutual warfare. Those of Kent made common cause to resist the Roman invaders, but Cassivellaunus was not a member of that coalition.

After the fall of Bigbury, which was undoubtedly the capital of one of these Kentish tribes and, so far as we know, the most important Belgic city south of the Thames, the Kentish chiefs reviewed their situation. They saw that there was no hope of defeating Caesar unaided; and yet, after the events of 55 and his hurried retreat from the Stour valley when his fleet was smitten by the gale, they took heart to believe him not invincible. Their one hope lay in enlisting the aid of the great Cassivellaunus; and the only terms on which they could hope to do this was by offering him the supreme command.

All operations being at a standstill while the Romans were beaching and stockading their ships, there was time for the Britons to arrive at this decision and carry it out before Caesar was ready to march once more. When he did, the whole military situation had changed. Cassivellaunus had assumed control of all the British forces, augmented as they now were by the addition of his own troops; and Caesar was no sooner in touch with his enemy than he felt, as any competent general can feel on such occasions, the personality of their new commander.

He had marched only a few miles, retracing his steps in the direction of Canterbury, where ten days earlier he had never met an enemy until his triumphant dash across the Stour and through the woods of Bigbury, when he found himself engaged in a running fight with British cavalry and charioteers. He brushed them aside again and again, but they stuck to their task and, when driven into the woods, turned against their pursuers and inflicted heavy losses on them. At the end of a difficult day's march, when the Romans were fortifying their camp for the night, the Britons suddenly burst out of the woods and were upon them, hotly engaging the covering troops that had been posted to protect the fatigue-parties. Caesar rushed up the two first and strongest cohorts of two legions in support; for a moment it seemed that the Britons were cut off and surrounded; but there was a gap between the two cohorts, and the British chariots and horse streamed through while the legionaries were too much unnerved to close it, and made good their escape.

It was Caesar's first experience of what British troops could do when well led. The engagement took place just outside the half-finished camp, and every detail of it was visible. It taught him that his heavy-armed infantry, though safe enough in battle-formation, could never put up more than a passive defence against these audacious and swiftly moving barbarians, and that if he tried to pursue them with his horse the charioteers, turning upon them and dismounting to fight on foot, were more than a match for his Gaulish cavalry. They had no regular formation; they fought in isolated and mobile groups, each of which could be reinforced at need by fresh men, or dissolve at any moment into a feigned retreat, to lead pursuers on to their destruction. At the same time, he saw how these tactics could be met, and next day he put his plan into operation. He sent out nearly half his infantry, about noon, to forage: the Britons fell into the trap and attacked them recklessly. But Caesar had kept the rest of his legions and his entire cavalry force, some 1,700 men, in reserve; and the cavalry, gaining confidence from the support of the legions behind them, in a single charge swept the Britons from the field, kept them on the run so that the charioteers had no time to dismount, and routed them decisively. From that day the British levies began to melt away, and never again encountered the Romans in full strength.

By now Caesar knew that Cassivellaunus was the man against whom he was matched, and resolved to end the war by striking at his territory. This meant crossing the Thames; and from the fact that Caesar describes the kingdom of Cassivellaunus as lying eighty miles from the sea it is probable that the ford in general use—certainly not, as Caesar thought, the only practicable one on the lower reaches of the river—was somewhere in the neighbourhood of Brentford. He found it strongly held and obstructed by sharp stakes both above and below the water, but the legionaries, whose confidence was now fully restored, crossed it neck-deep while the cavalry turned the position by swimming, and the Britons fled.

This brought him into the territory of Cassivellaunus. The British king, realizing that he could not defeat the Romans in a general action, had disbanded his infantry, but had no intention of giving up the struggle. He still had 4,000 chariots, and these he used with great skill and determination, clearing the population away from before the advancing legions so that no prisoners should be taken, and incessantly harassing the Gaulish cavalry when Caesar sent them out to forage and to burn the farms. So successful was he that the cavalry could no longer venture out of touch with the main body, and the work both of foraging and of destruction was limited to what the legionaries could do in the course of their day's march.

Pressing thus grimly forward through a deserted country, whose woods were infested on every side by watchful enemies, Caesar met a body of envoys from the Trinovantes, welcoming him as their deliverer from Cassivellaunus, offering him the submission of their tribe, and promising to accept Mandubracius at his hands as their king. Their overtures came at the right moment, for Cassivellaunus had so hampered the Romans in their foraging that the provisions which Caesar had expected to find on the march had not been forthcoming. In accepting their offers and demanding hostages, therefore, he added a demand for grain, and marched into the Trinovantian territory as into a friendly land, ordering his men to respect the inhabitants and their property.

Here he received the submission of five neighbouring tribes, whose names are otherwise unknown. He also learnt the whereabouts of the Catuvellaunian capital: and nothing more plainly shows the ability of his chief enemy than the fact that he had not learnt it before. Had Cassivellaunus allowed even a handful of his subjects to be taken prisoner, the secret could hardly have been kept so long. But now Caesar's next step lay clear before him. Retracing his path westwards to the marshy valley of the Lea, he fell upon the Wheathampstead fortress from two sides at once; the resistance of its defenders was quickly overcome, and the place fell into his hands with heavy casualties and a great capture of live stock and prisoners.

But Cassivellaunus had not yet shot his last bolt. While his

charioteers were dogging Caesar's march through the Hertfordshire woodlands, he had sent instructions to the four Kentish
kings to organize an attack with every man at their disposal
upon the naval camp. It speaks well both for his own military
capacity that he conceived the plan and for the loyalty of those
who had accepted his leadership that, in so dark an hour for
himself, they carried it out. Caesar is content to tell us that it
was beaten off by a successful sortie in which the defenders
suffered little loss; but we learn from Cicero's correspondence
a fact which Caesar in his own narrative refrains from mentioning: that about this time (5 August) he was himself present at
the camp. Whether he hurried there because he heard that the
attack was imminent, or whether he went when he heard that
it had taken place, to see for himself what its effect had been
and whether his base was in any further danger, we do not
know. In either case the fact of his visit, and the added fact of
his silence about it, suggest that he may have been more anxious
about the safety of his fleet than he cared to admit; unless, indeed, as is more probable, it was the state of Gaul that caused
him anxiety, and he returned to the Channel in order more
quickly to exchange letters about it with Labienus.

Cassivellaunus knew that he was beaten. His only friends in
Britain were those of his own Belgic race, and although these
had supported him with magnificent loyalty they were now
without exception defeated. His capital was destroyed, and,
most important of all, his methods of warfare had proved decisively inferior to those of the invaders. The campaign between
Caesar and the Belgic Britons had been fought to a finish, and
the victory lay with Caesar. There was nothing to do but to
make peace. Caesar, it would appear, recognized the inevita-
bility of this step on the part of Cassivellaunus, and sent Commius to him to expedite it, perhaps by giving him a hint that
easy terms would be offered.

Historians have wondered why it was through Commius that
the British king approached Caesar, and have rightly suspected
that it could only be owing to Caesar's own initiative. Caesar
himself has told us that his reason for making peace with Cassivellaunus as and when he did was the fact that he had abandoned his original intention of wintering in Britain 'because
of sudden disturbances in Gaul'. In other words, these disturbances underlay not only his hasty visit to the coast but also his

employment of Commius as a go-between. If, as we know, he did not wish to confess that he had made that journey, he would wish even less to admit that the first overtures came not from Cassivellaunus but from himself; yet such must have been the fact. The trouble in Gaul, which was to culminate in the rising of Vercingetorix, already before the end of his British campaign determined him to winter south of the Channel. Whether he suspected that he would never cross the Straits again we cannot say, but it is clear from his own narrative that henceforth his only anxiety concerning Britain, so far as this year's campaign was concerned, was to leave it with a reasonable show of success. He received the envoys sent by Cassivellaunus and told them the terms of peace which they were to carry back to their king. He was to send hostages, pay a stated annual tribute to Rome, and refrain from molesting Mandubracius and the Trinovantes.

Caesar was still north of the Thames when these negotiations took place. On receiving the hostages, he marched back to the Channel and found his transports ready for sea. But they were not enough to carry his army and all the prisoners he had taken, whose sale as slaves was to pay the costs of the campaign, and he decided to make the crossing in two trips. In returning after the first, he hoped that the empty transports would be accompanied by sixty new ships built to his orders by Labienus, but the wind was foul and only a small part of the expected vessels reached Kent. For some time Caesar awaited the others; then, his anxiety to be gone increasing as the equinox approached, he crowded all that was left of his army and prisoners in the few ships he had, and on a calm night made his last crossing in safety.

From a military point of view Caesar was entitled to regard his invasion of Britain as a success. The chief problem of strategy had been the discovery and destruction of the fortresses belonging to the British tribes against which he was fighting; and this had been done. The chief problem of tactics had been how to deal with the British charioteers, and this had been solved not only by the discovery that they were helpless against a legion in battle-formation, but by the further discovery that a sufficient body of Gaulish horse, properly supported by infantry, could break them up and rout them by a well-timed charge. Moreover, in spite of Caesar's failure to discover a safe harbour, he had learnt how his ships could be protected against the weather; he also knew that wheat in very considerable quantities could be had in the country; he was therefore right in thinking that it would be possible for a Roman army to winter there. Britain was very far from being conquered; but the first steps towards conquering it had been taken.

From a political point of view the success, if less complete, was no less real. Over one considerable tribe a nominee of Caesar's was ruling. Several others had submitted to him without striking a blow. Of the rest with which he had come into contact, every one submitted before the end of the summer. Doubtless, as his experience in Gaul had already taught him, these submissions were precarious and were always liable to be followed by revolt; but at any rate the political consequences of his actions in Britain were as favourable as those which he had achieved in Gaul. On this side also, the omens for eventual conquest were favourable.

From a financial point of view success was more doubtful. Caesar knew nothing of the argentiferous lead-mines that were to play so important a part in the future history of Britain; indeed, not long before the final expedition sailed, the situation was well summed up by Cicero, writing to a friend: 'It is now known that there is not a pennyweight of silver in the whole island, and no hope of plunder except in the form of slaves.' The tin and iron of whose existence Caesar was aware offered no prize to a conqueror. Slaves, however, were to be had in plenty. The upshot was that Britain might pay for its own conquest in prisoners of war, but might not prove a very lucrative permanent addition to the provinces of the Empire.

None of these considerations was likely to make Caesar, at the close of his first campaign, abandon his design of conquering Britain. There is another question which might have influenced him in that direction. Throughout his Gaulish command he knew that he was working against time. It was not enough, therefore, to believe that he was able to conquer Britain; he must also believe that he could conquer it fast enough to complete his programme in the time at his disposal. Naturally, he has told us nothing about this question; we have to ask ourselves whether, as compared with his record in Gaul down to that time, the record of his first British campaign was such as to make him think his progress sufficiently rapid.

The most probable answer is in the affirmative. He believed

that the tribes which he overcame in 54 were the most civilized in the island, and must therefore have expected the rest to offer a less powerful resistance. He knew nothing of the difficulties attendant on a war of conquest in the highland zone, and nothing of the huge hill-fortresses that guarded the Wessex Downs. Nor, indeed, are we entitled to say that a soldier of Caesar's calibre would have been baulked by these obstacles. On the assumption, therefore, that Caesar's original plan was the complete conquest of Britain, there was nothing in the lessons of the first campaign to make him change his mind in the autumn of 54.

The fact that he did eventually change his mind arose from other causes. His conquest of Gaul divides itself into two main phases. In the first he was receiving the voluntary submission of some tribes and beating others into submission by pitched battles; in the second he was putting down determined and well-organized rebellions among these same tribes by means of expensive and protracted siege-operations. His British campaign falls at the line of division between the two. He went to Britain in pursuance of a plan based on the assumption that the first phase would prove permanent. It was while he was in Britain that it came to an end. That very winter his legionary camps suffered a series of attacks which were the beginning of the new phase; its ending is haunted by the tragic names of Alesia and Uxellodunum.

This change in the spirit of Gaulish affairs was the reason why Caesar's British war broke off at the end of its first campaign. Even at the beginning of the campaign there were signs in the air of its coming, and Caesar was not blind to them: he tried to guard against it by taking numbers of Gaulish chiefs with him across the Channel, and the fate of Dumnorix showed him that his precautions were not idle. Caesar was not only a great general, he was a great statesman, but a statesman's services to statecraft are to be measured partly indeed by his successes, but partly by the lessons he teaches through his failures. One of Caesar's failures was the mistake for which he paid in the senate-house on the Ides of March. Another was the mistake which he made when he set out to conquer Britain before he had pacified Gaul. And in both cases the lesson which he taught was well learnt by the subtle and patient man who took up the burden of his inheritance.

IV

FROM CAESAR TO CLAUDIUS

CAESAR's attempt to conquer Britain had failed; but its failure was due to other causes than the strength of British resistance. With a peaceful Gaul behind it, the attempt, so far as well-informed contemporaries could judge, would have been a success. This, then, was the most obvious double lesson to be learnt both by Britons and by Romans from Caesar's invasion: that whatever difficulties might arise from the dangers of ocean navigation and the power of British rulers, these difficulties were not insuperable; Rome could conquer Britain whenever she pleased, but not until Gaul was pacified and able to provide a safe starting-point for this further advance.

From Caesar's own point of view it can hardly be doubted that the conquest of Britain appeared simply as a project deferred, and that the continued freedom of the British tribes was not a reprieve but a respite. We shall find this assumption underlying Roman policy throughout the reign of his successor. The British point of view is less easy to define. A truly statesmanlike British king might have divined and shared the Roman view of the situation; but it would have been natural to take a shorter view, to insist on the fact that an attempt at conquest had been made and had ended in failure, to over-estimate the part played in this failure by the dangers of the Channel and the prowess of British warriors, and to mistake the respite for a reprieve. This at least the Britons could see: that for the immediate future they need not fear another attempt.

Cassivellaunus had sent hostages to Caesar, and this implies acceptance of his terms, namely, that tribute should be paid and the Trinovantes left unmolested. Whether he ever actually sent the tribute we are not told, but it appears that he did refrain from molesting the Trinovantes, and, that being so, the probability is that the tribute was, for a time at least, paid. For a generation and more the Catuvellauni contented themselves with the development of their own territory and its extension northward and north-westward. They no longer needed to protect their capital with defences like those surrounding the Wheathampstead fortress; if they had renounced their eastward offensive at Roman dictation, at least they feared no attack from that quarter; and it was not very long after Caesar's invasion, perhaps during the last twenty-five years of the pre-Christian era, that they abandoned their old capital and built a new unfortified one at Verulamium, in the woods overlooking the later Roman city.

The new capital reflects a new policy. The valley of the Ver gives easy access into the Chilterns and so, by way of Dunstable, to the plains beyond them. This was the line taken later by the Roman Watling Street; and along this line the Catuvellauni could penetrate without opposition into an almost uninhabited country, the upper basin of the Ouse. Here we will leave them for the present, consolidating their position and increasing their wealth, a community of prosperous and progressive farmers with little inducement to spend their time or their substance in warfare.

South of the Thames a new situation had arisen. Commius, for some years the servant of Julius Caesar, was among the Gaulish chiefs who turned against him in the rebellion of Vercingetorix, answering the last appeal of that gallant fighter and staking all that they had on the attempt to raise the siege of Alesia. When that attempt failed, Commius was in a desperate position; but now that he had declared himself he was faithful to the cause he had embraced, and became a dangerous and effective enemy to Rome. During the final phase of the Gallic war, he was at last beaten to his knees by Mark Antony, but made his peace and gave hostages for his conduct on the express condition that he should never again be compelled to look upon the face of a Roman. This condition had reference to a treacherous attempt on his life made at Labienus' command by Volusenus; but in the light of later events it was easy to read into it another interpretation; for it is recorded that at some date not specified Commius sailed with a fleet to Britain. A writer of the following century tells a story of how, pursued by the Romans, he escaped by hoisting his sails and seeming to be already under way when in fact his ships were still aground waiting for the tide; and when next we hear of him he is striking coins inscribed with his own name in the woodlands of northeastern Hampshire.

Archaeology, filling in the details of this story, has shown that some time about 50 B.C. there was a second migration of Belgae into Britain. It seems, to judge from its pottery, based upon

Normandy rather than upon the Marne valley; and it certainly reached Britain by way of the Hampshire coast. This second Belgic invasion was the movement led by Commius, who must have landed somewhere near Southampton, pushed his way up-country, and planted a city where now stand the ruined walls of Silchester.

In the course of time these western Belgae took possession of all the central part of southern England. From the Hampshire basin they pushed out in three directions. On the north their frontier is not accurately known; it probably ran along the escarpment of the Berkshire Downs and reached the Thames at Cholsey. Eastward they penetrated into western Surrey and, farther south, established themselves on the Sussex–Hampshire border. The South Downs had retained their primitive Hallstatt civilization almost untouched, and to the end they were un-influenced by the eastern Belgic culture of Kent and the Thames basin; but now the old hill-fort of the Trundle was evacuated and a new city, Noviomagus, built in the plain on the site of Chichester, defended like many Belgic cities by cross-country dikes running at some distance from the town itself; Cissbury, too, on the hill above Worthing, was evacuated, and only eastern Sussex beyond the Adur remained independent.

On the west the realm of Commius absorbed by degrees all the chalk uplands of Wessex, and along their western edge built or rebuilt a formidable series of fortresses marking its frontier. They ran in a curved line roughly from Swindon to Bourne-mouth, and comprised over a dozen strongholds, crowning the crest of Marlborough Downs from Ashdown to Devizes and the escarpment of Salisbury Plain from Upavon to Warminster, and then, after certain intermediate forts near Wilton and Shaftes-bury, ending with a number in the Stour valley, of which the chief are the imposing twin works of Hod Hill and Hambledon near Blandford; and, crowning the whole, Maiden Castle.

As we shall see, this large tract of country was not always ruled by a single king. The immediate followers of Commius, drawn from the Gaulish Atrebates, were settled in and round Silchester; another tribal name, that of the Regni, maintained itself in west Sussex. But by the time of the Claudian conquest the civilization of the whole region was fairly uniform. It was a hybrid culture in which old and new elements were mixed. The old upland agriculture went on, for the most part in peaceful, unfortified villages; here and there, especially round Silchester, there was some clearance of forest and exploitation of heavier soils; and except along the western frontier, the practice of building or living in hill-forts appears to have died out as the country became more and more peaceful under the sway of a strong central government.

There were now two distinct regions of Belgic settlement in Britain, one in Kent and Hertfordshire, the other in and about Hampshire. The history of Britain between Caesar and Claudius is to a great extent the history of these two regions, and in attempting to reconstruct it we must begin with the history of the kings who ruled them.

The fortunes of the two royal houses can be to some extent inferred from their coinage. Their founders, Cassivellaunus and Commius, both struck coins. Those of Cassivellaunus, uninscribed but identified as his with reasonable certainty, are found mainly in the Catuvellaunian territory, Hertfordshire and the lands adjoining it north-westward; a similar type is found in west Surrey and west Sussex, and is difficult to explain. Contemporary with these or on average a little later are the coins of Commius, assigned to him with certainty because at this point coins begin to be inscribed. These are mostly found near Silchester, with outliers on the Sussex coast. It would seem that in the lifetime of Commius the northern and eastern frontiers of his realm ran down the middle Thames, diagonally across Surrey and through the Weald. The Catuvellaunian house ruled north of the Thames; so far as the coins of this period go, Kent seems to have lain in neither kingdom.

Cassivellaunus was succeeded by a ruler whose name appears on the coins as Andoco, doubtless an abbreviation. He, after a short reign, was followed by Tasciovanus, who thus appears as probably Cassivellaunus' grandson. His coins are widespread and numerous; they indicate a long and prosperous reign, and, occurring as they do almost exclusively north of the Thames, chiefly in Hertfordshire, Bedfordshire, Buckinghamshire, and eastern Oxfordshire, but with scattered specimens over a wider area, they show the Catuvellauni becoming a wealthy and commercially active state about the end of the last century before Christ.

In quantity, the coins of the Commian house cut by comparison a poor figure; but they yield fairly definite historical

inferences. It seems from the evidence of this coinage that
Commius left three sons. Eppillus, at some time late in the
century, carved out for himself a short-lived kingdom in north-
eastern Kent. Tincommius at the same time ruled in Sussex and
Hampshire, no doubt from the new city of the Regni at Noviomagus. Verica succeeded to his father's more immediate possessions round Silchester, and was the most successful of the three;
for Eppillus was soon overthrown by a certain Dubnovellaunus,
of whose origin we know nothing but whom we may conjecture
to have been the last independent king of the Trinovantes,
possibly even the son of Caesar's Mandubracius; and Tincommius, not much later, was evicted from his kingdom and sent
into exile by Verica himself. Thus about the end of the century
we appear to have three kings striking coins: Tasciovanus in
Hertfordshire, the richest and most powerful of the three;
Verica at Silchester, ruling in Berkshire, Hampshire, Surrey,
and Sussex; and Dubnovellaunus at Colchester, commanding
both sides of the Thames estuary.

Soon after the turn of the century the first and third of these
kingdoms were united into one by the activity of Cunobelinus,
son of Tasciovanus, who conquered the Trinovantes and expelled Dubnovellaunus. During his long and extremely prosperous reign, which began about A.D. 10 and lasted until
between A.D. 40 and 43, his coins appear not only over the
whole area previously covered by those of Tasciovanus, but also
over Essex, Kent, and eastern Surrey. With him the capital of
the dynasty moves to Colchester, where his only mint was
situated; his father had three mints, one at Verulamium and
others at unidentified places whose names began with the letters
Ricon . . . and Sego . . . .

During the earlier part of Cunobelinus' reign Verica must
still have been ruling over the now reunited kingdom of Commius. Throughout that kingdom coins of Cunobelinus are
absent. But there are a few, scattered widely over its area,
struck by Epaticcus, another son of Tasciovanus; and it is not
unlikely that this Epaticcus was sent into the west to conquer
Verica's realm and hold it as an ally of his brother Cunobelinus.

By this time the first half of the first century A.D. was well
advanced, and three other British kingdoms were minting their
own currency. One was the kingdom of the Iceni, northward
neighbours of Cunobelinus. Their coins are derived from those

of Tasciovanus and are a good deal influenced by the mint of Cunobelinus; many of them bear the name of Addedomarus, who must have been king of the Iceni soon after the beginning of our era,[1] and evidently reigned for a considerable time.

Another was the kingdom of the Dobuni, whose coins spread from a centre near Cirencester and Malmesbury over the Cotswolds, spreading eastward down the upper tributaries of the Thames as far as Oxford, and westward across the Severn valley into the Welsh foot-hills. Southwards they come in a wedge through Somerset and Wiltshire into Dorset, with outliers in Devon and Cornwall. Their eastern limit is marked on the north by the western frontier of the Catuvellaunian kingdom, and on the south by the western edge of the realm of Commius. Six names of rulers appear on these Cotswold coins: one is known to us in full as Antedrigus, the others in abbreviated forms as Boduoc, Catti, Comux, Eisu, and Vocorio-ad. In origin, this coinage is based on imitation of western Belgic issues, especially those of Tincommius. It thus hardly begins to exist before the beginning of the first century A.D.

The third kingdom outside the Belgic area to strike its own coins was that of the Brigantes. These coins trace their pedigree back to an earlier source than either the Icenian or Dobunian; they seem to be an independent development from Continental models not much later than those which produced the uninscribed coins of Cassivellaunus, and therefore testify to independent connexions, whether by way of migration or trade, between north-eastern Britain and the Continent. They occur in Lincolnshire, Nottinghamshire, and Yorkshire.

In the generation immediately preceding the Roman conquest we thus find the more civilized part of Britain, on the evidence of coins, divided into five realms: that of Cunobelinus, extending from the Weald to the latitude of Cambridge and from the Essex coast to the Cherwell valley; that of his brother Epaticcus, south of the upper Thames and the Weald and extending westward to Salisbury Plain; that of the Iceni, consisting of East Anglia and the Fens, and ruled by Addedomarus; that of the Dobuni, stretching from the neighbourhood of

---

[1] G. C. Brooke in an important article ('The Distribution of Gaulish and British Coins in Britain', *Antiquity*, vii (1933), p. 268) has argued that the supposed Icenian ruler Antedrigus never existed, and that the coins ascribed to him really bear, under various forms, the abbreviated name of this same Addedomarus.

Oxford and Banbury along the Cotswold ridge and including the low lands of Somerset and Dorset and a considerable sphere of influence in Wales; and that of the Brigantes, centred on the Humber and spreading loosely but widely over the north.

The only case in which the coin-evidence is unsatisfactory is that of the former Commian kingdom, here ascribed to Epaticcus. Actually his coins are very rare in it, though widely scattered from northern Oxfordshire to Selsey Bill; but coins of the Commian dynasty are rare, too, when compared with those struck by the house of Cassivellaunus; and most of the pieces found in this region are imitations of early Gaulish issues, progressively repeated and degraded, which in the western part of the area passed current to the complete exclusion of any inscribed coins whatever. This is one aspect of a more general fact to be discussed later in the present chapter, namely, the relatively primitive and backward character of this region during the century before the Claudian conquest.

Before leaving the subject of coins in pre-Claudian Britain it may be well to consider two other aspects of that subject: the general pattern of their distribution on the map, and the evidence for civilization given by their style.

When all the pre-Roman coins found in Britain are plotted on a single map, it is at once evident that, with trifling exceptions, they have been discovered to south and east of a line running from Weymouth to Bristol and thence along the oolite outcrop that forms successively the Cotswolds, the Northamptonshire uplands, and Lincoln Edge. Apart from a few scattered finds in the south-west, the only exceptions of any importance are the Dobunian coins in the Severn valley and Welsh foothills and the Brigantian ones in Yorkshire. The whole of the great midland triangle bounded by the oolite-ridge, the Pennines, and the Welsh mountains is utterly barren.

Within the area thus delimited they are much commoner than anywhere else in the district which ultimately became the kingdom of Cunobelinus. This comprises an area reaching from the Thames to the Ouse and Stour and from the sea to the Cherwell; south-eastward it includes all Kent except the Weald. Outside this district are other areas where coins are fairly dense, notably round Norwich and in western Suffolk; the Nene valley; the Cotswolds and the Oxford basin; north-eastern Hampshire and the adjoining part of Surrey; the Sussex coast; and the neighbourhood of Poole and Cranborne Chase. On the positive side, it is worthy of remark that the Belgic penetration of denser forest-lands has gone far enough to appear on the map in the shape of thickly scattered coin-finds on the Chiltern ridge and round Silchester, to name the two most conspicuous cases, while on the negative side the most interesting fact is the scarcity of coins on Salisbury Plain. We shall have cause to notice, later on, the curious way in which Salisbury Plain resists new influences throughout the Roman period; it is interesting to observe that it has already taken up this attitude before the Claudian invasion.

The style of the ancient British coinage is chiefly interesting, for our present purpose, as an index of Romanization. This coinage began by imitating that of the northern Gaulish tribes, and this again originated in copying the gold staters of Philip II of Macedon which began to flood the Roman market and penetrate freely into north-western Europe towards the middle of the second century before Christ.[1] The Philippic stater has on the obverse a head of Apollo with a laurel wreath binding its tightly curled hair, and on the reverse a two-horse chariot. The copies of this coin which became the model for the British moneyers were struck by the Atrebates and other tribes of Belgic Gaul. The general characteristic of all these models is that the Gaulish craftsmen, unaccustomed as they were both to the technique of die-sinking and to the whole conception of representing human or animal forms naturalistically, reduced both designs to what, from the point of view of naturalistic art, can only be called nonsense. On the obverse the laurel-wreath has become a band of pellets somewhat resembling an ear of wheat; on either side of this are tassels, hooks, or bosses representing the locks of hair, and strange crescent-like forms derived from the outline of the face. On the reverse the two horses have been reduced to one, and that is strangely distorted and runs some risk of falling in pieces; the chariot and other accessories are becoming mere dots and streaks, *muscae volitantes*, in the field.

[1] G. C. Brooke in *Antiquity*, vii (1933), pp. 268–9, argues forcibly, in opposition to the generally received view, that it was such events as the triumph of Scipio Asiaticus in 188 B.C. and the battle of Pydna in 167, with their enormous spoils in gold staters, that brought these coins into the western market: and further, that it was the victory of Ahenobarbus over the Arverni in 121 that introduced them into central Gaul. The general chronology of the Gaulish coins is rendered more intelligible by these suggestions.

When the Britons took this coinage as a model for their own
the Apollo-head had advanced so far in disintegration that it
was past recovery and was nothing but a tangle of disjointed
elements. The British die-sinkers, whether consciously or unconsciously, set themselves the task of reducing this tangle to
order, modifying it very gradually in the direction of a decorative pattern. The element which had suffered least in the
disintegrative process was the laurel-wreath, with its tendency
to become something like an ear of wheat; the course usually
taken by the British moneyers was to duplicate this at right
angles, making a cruciform design, in whose centre they collected crescentic motives derived ultimately from Apollo's pro-
file. In the time of Tasciovanus, under whom this development
reached perhaps its highest point, this central group of motives
framed a little panel on which the king's name could be inscribed.

At the same time, the degeneration of the horse is arrested.
The Britons, like Artemus Ward, found themselves unable any
longer to conceal from the public that these things were horses,
and, simultaneously with the attempt to organize the scattered
elements of the obverse into a single decorative design, there
is visible in their work an attempt to rehabilitate the horse on
the reverse, infuse it with new life drawn from actual observation, and produce what at its best is not only a recognizable but
a vigorous and almost naturalistic animal portrait. This was
the general character of the British coinage as developed under
Cassivellaunus and taken over by Tasciovanus. A somewhat
similar character belongs to the issues of Commius and to the
Dobunian coinage derived from them, though here an independent connexion can be traced with Gaulish sources.

A new movement sets in towards the beginning of our era.
Already under Tasciovanus silver pieces, though not gold, begin
to imitate contemporary Roman work. This tendency rapidly
gathers weight. It reaches its highest pitch of intensity in the
reign of Cunobelinus, whose silver and copper is entirely dominated by it, and even his gold strongly affected. About the same
time the same change is taking place in the realm of Commius.
Of his three sons, only Tincommius uses the traditional British
designs, and he changes over to the Romanizing fashion before
the end of his reign; Verica and Eppillus invariably strike in
the new style.

This new style, then, dominates the coinage of all south-eastern Britain during the first half of the first century A.D., and towards the close of that period it even begins to affect that of the Dobuni. Broadly speaking, it may be described as a Romanizing style, and at times it may even have been practised in Britain by craftsmen imported from the Continent; but in spite of the profusion of types borrowed from Roman numismatic art, it retains a strongly Celtic colouring. Side by side with heads closely imitated from those of Augustus are others, whose savage and hirsute appearance contrasts curiously with the skill employed in their portrayal. Roman fashions are penetrating peacefully into British society; but that society itself, though welcoming these luxuries as an adornment of its life, is at heart barbarian still.

Much more interesting than the coinage, but at the same time much harder to interpret historically, owing to the difficulty of dating its products, is the artistic work of the Britons during the generations preceding the Claudian conquest. The products in question are, at their best, the work of highly accomplished artists, gifted with a sense of line that has seldom been surpassed in any school, and employed to decorate objects of luxury evidently belonging to the wealthy and warlike aristocratic class of the community: shields, helmets, scabbards, mirrors, personal ornaments, and horse-trappings. These metal goods have survived in small numbers where a vast quantity of more perishable work has evidently been lost; consequently they come to us without any context, and this is the chief reason why they are so hard to interpret. It is well, therefore, to turn first to the humble domestic craft of pottery, which may provide a background for these higher works of art.

Of the ruder pottery little need be said. All over south-eastern England it is based mainly on the Hallstatt tradition of the original Iron Age settlers; elsewhere the Bronze Age tradition still predominates, where pottery is found at all. Against this background there stand out three[1] main types of better and more civilized wares.

First, there is the decorated hand-made ware which is best known to us at the Glastonbury lake-village. The interesting feature of this ware is its decoration. Derived from Gaulish art of the middle La Tène period, it delights in boldly drawn curved

---

[1] Of the first and second something has already been said in Chapter II.

lines, spirals, and circles, S-shaped curves, wavy, zig-zag bands, and chains of lenticular or almond-shaped elements, all these, at the same time, crossed and combined with decorative motives drawn from the repertory of the Bronze Age. The predominant shape for vessels is that of a squat, wide-mouthed jar or jar-like bowl. Pottery of this kind is widely though somewhat thinly spread over the south-west, from Cornwall to Hengistbury Head and even penetrating into Sussex; inland it spreads over Dorset and Somerset and works its way along the Cotswold ridge as far as Hunsbury in Northamptonshire. It thus attests a cultural unity belonging to the same region whose central part is characterized by the Dobunian or Cotswold coinage. This culture goes back for its origins, as has been said in an earlier chapter, to the fourth century before Christ; but we are now considering its fortunes after the invasion of Julius Caesar, and here the fact of chief importance is the destruction of the Glastonbury village, apparently by raiding Belgae from the realm of Commius, at some date between that time and the Claudian conquest. During this period, then, the Dobunian civilization was being attacked by the Belgic; but the evidence of its coins proves that on the whole it maintained its independence.

Secondly, there is the wheel-made pottery of the original Belgic invaders, also derived from Gaulish La Tène models, but differing from the south-western wares in its utter lack of decoration. It is not altogether inartistic, but it produces its somewhat dry and hard effect by its elegant and decisive profiles, contrasting strongly with the squat shapes of the south-west. This, the Aylesford pottery mentioned in a previous chapter, extends between the time of Caesar and that of Claudius all over the region that has already been defined in the present chapter as the kingdom of Cunobelinus.

Thirdly, there is a type of pottery called by archaeologists bead-rim ware, which is found throughout the realm attributed to Commius and his family. This is regarded as the pottery of the second Belgic invasion, to some extent certainly influenced by fashions already existing in that area, but in the main derived from wares used in Normandy during the last century before Christ. It is sometimes hand made, sometimes wheel made; it is undecorated, except when it is rudely scratched with a comb; and it shows no evidence of artistic talent in its makers.

The only region, therefore, in which an art akin to that of the

finer metal-work has penetrated down to the level of domestic
pottery is the south-west with its prolongation into Northamptonshire. Now, the La Tène art of Britain may perhaps be seen
at its best, both in quality and in quantity, in the engraved
bronze mirrors which have always been recognized as a peculiarly British class of object. Over a score of them are known;
some are too fragmentary to give an idea of their original
appearance, but several are almost or quite perfect. Two
of them stand out as among the very best works of Celtic
art: they were both found in the region of which Glastonbury
pottery is characteristic, one at Birdlip in Gloucestershire, the
other at Desborough in Northamptonshire. The rest, so far as
their condition enables us to reconstruct them, are debased and
degenerate copies of the beautiful designs happily preserved to
perfection in these two. If we seek for parallels to the decoration
on the Birdlip and Desborough mirrors we shall find them
primarily in the Middle La Tène ornament found at sites like
Meare in Somerset, Hunsbury in Northamptonshire, and the
country of the Brigantes, and secondarily, simplified into the
relative crudity of peasant-art, on pottery in the Glastonbury
style. Thus the evidence concerning the artistic culture of the
entire belt of country that begins in Somerset, and travels along
the oolite-ridge into Lincolnshire and Yorkshire, falls into an
intelligible whole. It was into this belt of country that the best
elements of Middle La Tène art were transplanted; it was here
that they took root and, especially perhaps in the southern and
central part, blossomed into the school of British art that gave
us these mirrors.

It remains to ask when this blossoming took place.[1] The
difficulty of dating such works of art has already been confessed.
The Birdlip mirror is usually dated to the middle or second half
of the first century A.D., that is, shortly after the Roman conquest, because in the same grave with it was found a unique
and beautiful brooch which has been thought to be derived
from types of brooch worn in Germany about A.D. 40–60. In
fact, however, this brooch-type seems to have been decadent

---

[1] The reader ought to be warned that in this paragraph a view is maintained
which many archaeologists would reject. They would place the Birdlip mirror after
the conquest, on account of the associated brooch. I have long regarded the argument as weak and the conclusion as impossible, and am glad to have my doubts
shared and confirmed by E. T. Leeds, *Celtic Ornament in Britain* (1933), pp. 28–37, to
whose statement of his case I am much indebted.

during those years, and soon afterwards it passed out of use; and there is no evidence to tell us how long before this it might have influenced a British artist. We are on firmer ground in the fact that a debased and presumably late mirror was found in a grave at Colchester with pottery of the late first century B.C. The natural inference is that the school of art which gave us the Birdlip and Desborough mirrors culminated about the time of the Julian invasion.

Thus, in the early part of the century which we are now attempting to describe, the regions of Belgic settlement may have been in some ways, as Caesar thought, the most civilized parts of Britain; but just beyond their limits lay a region less prosperous perhaps in its agricultural basis, but far richer in its artistic culture, and supporting a wealthy and powerful aristocracy with a purely Celtic tradition of life and art. The northwestward movement of the Catuvellauni after Caesar's invasion brought them into contact with this Celtic region; and as the wealth and power of the Catuvellauni increased they began to develop an art of their own, based chiefly on borrowings from it. Inferior copies of its mirrors began to be used in the Belgic territory, and as time went on a new school of metal-work grew up there, which made important technical advances in the craft of enamelling.

But the taste of the Belgae for Celtic art was never very strong. At the time of their greatest prosperity under Cunobelinus their chief men were deserting Celtic fashions for Roman. Of this we have much evidence gleaned from various sites of which the richest, and also the most decisive, is the magnificent burial-mound of Lexden near Colchester. The ritual here is British; the noble or king (for the question has been raised whether this may not be the grave of 'the radiant Cymbeline' himself) was apparently buried with his war-chariot; the pottery is Belgic, but the metal-work, of which great quantities were found in the tumulus, is wholly Roman either in origin or in taste, and there is a complete absence of any trace of Celtic art. Elsewhere in the realm and age of Cunobelinus the same tendency to desert Celtic fashions for Roman, though never so overwhelming, is plainly visible: throughout the first half of the first century of our era the evidence of burials seems to show a progressively romanized court and aristocracy, soon parting with the Celtic fashions they had but lately and partially acquired.

In the realm of Commius there was indeed a less intense romanization, but there was also far less celticizing. Its capital, Silchester, was already using small quantities of earthenware from Italy before the Claudian conquest; but in many years' excavation practically nothing has been found bearing any resemblance to La Tène art. Like their more powerful neighbours and kinsmen to east and north-east, these western Belgae of the second invasion were an inartistic race, but, unlike them, they never advanced so far in wealth and power as to attract the arts of luxury; and they remained to the end a people of simple farmers and, on occasion, stout warriors.

Meanwhile the north, free from Belgic influence, was developing on lines of its own. There are here no villages with a true Iron Age culture, whether of Hallstatt or La Tène type, no hill-forts like those of the south, and no towns to compare with Verulamium or Cunobelinus's capital at Colchester. Against all these we can only set a single site,[1] the vast *oppidum* at Stanwick near Darlington: a site where a tract of plain country, a mile by a mile and a half in extent, is enclosed by a great rampart and ditch of regular Iron Age pattern, fit capital, one might conjecture, for a warrior-state embracing in its dominion all northern England. Whether or no that is the true explanation of the Stanwick earthworks, the descendants of the Middle La Tène invaders had by now grown into a Celtic warrior-caste ruling over a populace of primitive culture hardly differing from that of a poor and ill-furnished Late Bronze Age; and thus had come into existence the state of the Brigantes or hillmen. A similar process appears to have taken place in south-eastern Wales, Monmouthshire, and Herefordshire among the Silures, where, however, the influence of Dobunian culture led to a considerable development of hill-forts.

The west, where pre-Roman Celtic art in Britain reached its zenith, seems hardly to have retained its supremacy in this respect until the time of Claudius. Its northern extension on

---

[1] Yorkshire contains a number of small hill-forts, for which see Elgee, *Archaeology of Yorkshire* (1933), pp. 117–19; they are quite unlike the great forts of the south, and may have been constructed in the course of the Roman invasion. It is otherwise with Stanwick, where the rampart and ditch (100 feet across, and still some 30 in vertical height) must represent a huge permanent fortress, and cannot (*pace* Elgee, op. cit., pp. 233–4) be a medieval deer-park. The La Tène hoard in the British Museum confirms this view, whether found inside or just outside the rampart. At Almondbury, near Huddersfield, is another fortress of Early Iron Age type which ought perhaps to be mentioned together with Stanwick.

the Northamptonshire uplands was already being encroached upon by the Catuvellauni before the turn of the century. Its southern extension was threatened by the fortresses of the Belgic frontier, and almost certainly harried by Belgic raids, not very much later. Even in its centre we find, here and there, evidences of Belgic penetration into the very fortresses of the Cotswolds. Its coinage, which falls, as we have seen, almost wholly, if not altogether, after the beginning of our era, shows no evidence of artistic vitality. And when we are able to recapture the spirit of this region once more in the artistic work done there soon after the Roman conquest, we find it, with one notable exception to be considered hereafter—the sculptures of the Bath temple— strikingly inferior to what is being done elsewhere. If it is true that the Birdlip mirror was made not later than the last century before Christ, we have here a consistent picture of the art-loving aristocracy of the west as decaying, whether from internal or external causes, during the first half-century of our era. And this was the time when the leadership in the field of art passed to the north, and was taken up by the Brigantes.[1]

The economic life of the country, especially in the Belgic areas, shows a certain development during this period. Of agriculture little need be said beyond what has been said already. We have seen that in addition to the village-communities with their little fields there were already isolated farms presumably ploughing large tracts of unenclosed land, and that the latter system may possibly have been characteristic of the Belgae with their heavy sod-turning plough. We have seen that large quantities of wheat were grown, and it may be added that barley also was grown and used for brewing beer, the national drink of the Celts in every land. It need hardly be said that Caesar was misinformed when he was told that, except near the Straits of Dover, the Britons knew nothing of agriculture but lived on meat and milk and dressed in skins. Even the remoter and less civilized tribes, long before his lifetime, were cultivating the soil and wearing woollen and linen clothes.

On another point, in spite of common opinion to the contrary, Caesar appears to have had better information. He says that the Britons in his time had to import their copper.[2] As Britain

---

[1] I must once more express my debt here to Leeds, whose demonstration (*Celtic Ornament*, cit., pp. 45–8) of decadence in western art before the conquest, as exemplified by the latest pieces in the Polden Hill hoard, is most convincing.

[2] *Aere utuntur importato* (*B.G.* v. 12, 4). *Aes* may mean (1) copper, (2) bronze, the

is somewhat rich in copper, and has been a source of bronze from very early days, it has generally been thought that Caesar was wrong here. But in point of fact there is no evidence that any of the copper ores in Britain were mined before the Romans exploited them, and it is by no means impossible that the important Bronze Age foundries of this country, though deriving their tin from native sources, drew their copper from abroad, and that this state of things lasted until the Roman conquest.

Iron was being worked in large and increasing quantities, mostly, no doubt, still in the Weald, but also perhaps in the Forest of Dean, almost certainly in the Mendips, and probably in many other places also. The large hoards of currency-bars found in the south-west and the frequency with which iron objects of considerable size, like fire-dogs, were used during this period mark it as an age when iron was easy to come by and when the working of it was an art very familiar to blacksmiths in all parts of the country.

The Romans in the time of Claudius expected Britain to provide gold in payable quantities; and certainly it was being exported thence in the reign of Augustus. The Wicklow deposits, it is thought, had been worked out some centuries earlier, and therefore other sources must have been known. Possibly these were in South Wales; possibly in Cornwall; possibly in Scotland; the first alternative is the most probable, but the other districts may have produced gold also.

Of silver we hear nothing in Caesar's notes on Britain, and Cicero (as already quoted) writes to a friend that there was none. In the middle of the last century before Christ the great wealth of Britain in argentiferous lead was as yet unknown; it seems that none of the deposits had been worked except those of the Mendips, and they not on a large enough scale to attract attention. The lake-village of Glastonbury proves, however, that the Mendip lead was being regularly mined in Caesar's time and before; it has yielded several leaden objects, mostly net-sinkers, and others have been found in the earlier village, not far away, at Meare; while at the mining village of Charterhouse British coins have been found. The use of lead for such

alloy of copper and tin, (3) coinage. The context excludes this third meaning. It has also been suggested that the word here means 'bronze-ware'—saucepans and the like. It is certainly true that after Caesar's time much bronze-ware was imported into Britain; but that is not the natural meaning of the passage, which must refer to the metal, either pure or alloyed.

everyday purposes as weighting fishing-tackle proves that by
now it was cheap and common. The lead from Glastonbury
and Meare has not been desilverized; but this process must have
been introduced into Britain at an early date, if it is true, as
Strabo says, that by the time of Augustus silver was being
exported from Britain on a considerable scale.

The early British tin-trade is so controversial a subject that
some hardiness is needed in order even to mention it. Fortunately, we are here concerned only with the half-centuries
immediately before and after the birth of Christ. We need not,
therefore, discuss the difficult geographical problems—Cassite-
rides, Ictis—which surround the prehistoric tin-trade. In
Caesar's time Cornwall was still the source of most of the tin
used in western Europe and the Mediterranean, but the secret
of its origin was so well kept that Caesar himself only knew that
it came from the 'inland regions', by which he evidently meant
some region not near the Straits of Dover. Actually the carrying
trade in his own times was in the hands of the Veneti, and what
happened to it after the destruction of their shipping we can
only guess. But during the generation that followed his British
campaign the Augustan settlement of Spain opened up the
Spanish tin-mines to the Roman world, and there is little doubt
that this event was a severe blow to Cornwall. Nevertheless, the
industry continued; and soon after the conquest, as we shall see,
Roman prospectors in their systematic search for minerals found
their way to Cornwall and settled there for a time.

Whitby jet and Kimmeridge shale, out of which ornaments
were turned on the lathe and carved, were already staple products of Britain and were widely used throughout this period.
Pearls, too, were an article of commerce; Caesar himself is
recorded to have made an offering to Venus Genetrix of a
breastplate set with them.

There was, in fact, during this century, a large and growing
trade between Britain and the Continent. Caesar's campaign
against the Veneti must have crippled the Atlantic coastal
traffic; but even in his own time, he tells us, that which crossed
the Straits of Dover was more important, and this increased
steadily in bulk and value. During the reign of Augustus
Strabo enumerates the exports from Britain as comprising
wheat, cattle, gold, silver, iron, hides, slaves, and hunting dogs;
under imports he mentions bracelets, necklaces, amber, glass-

ware, and 'suchlike trifles'; and explains that the Romans have
abandoned the idea of annexing Britain because, if they did so,
they would perforce lose the large revenue collected in the form
of duties on this trade. To this argument we shall have to
return when considering Roman policy towards Britain in this
period. For the present it may be observed that, so far as can
be judged from the evidence of archaeology, the argument by
no means exaggerates the extent or value of this cross-channel
trade. Indeed, Strabo rather under-estimates it. Amphorae in
which wine must have been brought to Britain from the Roman
world are found in such large numbers that the wine-trade must
have been very considerable. Arretine pottery was coming into
general use among the wealthier classes all over the Belgic
regions, especially at Colchester itself. The Campanian metal-
work, both of bronze and silver, found in tombs at Lexden and
elsewhere in the realm of Cunobelinus has already been mentioned. Strabo is clearly right in implying that what Britain
imported from the Roman world was articles of luxury; but of
these, as the romanizing movement of the last two generations
before the conquest went forward, the variety, the bulk, and
the value steadily increased. It is not surprising to learn that
during the reigns of Augustus and Tiberius a trading-settlement
grew up on the left bank of the Thames, on the site of London,
where goods from Gaul and Italy were handled in considerable
quantities. London was already entering upon its career as the
leading commercial port of the British Isles.

It remains to consider the relations during these hundred
years between Britain and Rome.

If Caesar intended to conquer Britain, and if his intention
was at Rome an open secret, it is easy to understand an otherwise perplexing fact, namely, that Augustus is repeatedly
credited by good authorities with the same intention. Horace
states it as all but a *fait accompli*:

> Caelo tonantem credidimus Iovem
> Regnare; praesens divus habebitur
> Augustus, adiectis Britannis
> Imperio gravibusque Persis.

Dio alleges that in 34 Augustus actually set out to invade
Britain 'in order to outdo the feats of his adoptive father', but
abandoned the project because of a revolt in Dalmatia. In 27,

Dio tells us, he again started for Britain, but remained in Gaul partly because Gaulish affairs were unsettled and partly because he expected envoys from Britain, who never came. A third intended expedition is ascribed by Dio to the year 26; its cause, the refusal of the Britons to come to terms; the cause of its abandonment, the revolt of the Salassi and the outbreak of a serious war in Spain.[1]

These stories as Dio tells them are circumstantial enough; confirmed by the testimony of Horace, we cannot dismiss them as groundless fictions. Their meaning, especially in view of the words about outdoing Caesar, is plain: they refer to a project of conquering Britain and annexing it, as Horace says, to the Empire. They prove beyond a doubt that, up to the year 26 B.C., if no longer, the intention of conquering and annexing Britain was generally attributed to Augustus, and that he never disavowed it. Whether he entertained it is quite another question. Augustus had none of Caesar's adventurousness. He was the most circumspect of men. It was most unlikely that he would seriously think of committing himself to the conquest of Britain while so many urgent problems awaited solution in Gaul, in Spain, in the Illyrian provinces, and in the East. The most probable explanation of the stories that have come down to us is that Augustus, knowing, as every one knew, that his adoptive father had meant to conquer Britain and had been prevented from pursuing his plans by trouble in Gaul, allowed it to be assumed that, with the rest of his inheritance, he had taken over this project too; and it was no doubt gratifying to his rather malicious sense of humour to find that whenever people expected him to go ahead with this particular piece of work, some variant of the old excuse—trouble in Gaul—was always at hand to explain why nothing was done.

But these excuses could not be repeated indefinitely. A time came when every one must realize that Augustus had no intention of annexing Britain; and, always on the assumption that this was known to be part of Caesar's plans, a reasoned explanation was needed for the supposed change of policy. The explanation which must surely have been the official one has been recorded by Strabo in two passages.[2] In the first he argues that

---

[1] Horace, *Odes* III. v. 1–4 (cf. I. xxxv. 29). Vergil has references to Britain which, though less explicit, confirm those of Horace. Dio, xlix. 38. 2; liii, 22. 5 and 25. 2.
[2] Strabo, ii. 115–16; iv. 200.

Britain is so difficult of access that it can do Rome neither harm nor good: it is not strong enough to invade her territory, and the duties on the trade between it and Gaul bring in more than the total estimated yield of the tribute minus the cost of maintaining a garrison. In the second, the financial argument is repeated with further details, but for the argument about difficulty of access another is substituted, namely, that some of the British rulers have made their peace with Augustus, dedicated offerings in the Capitol, and 'made the whole island almost a Roman country'.

There is in all these arguments a certain strain of disingenuousness. The financial plea looks like a repetition of what Caesar had to say concerning the poverty of Britain; but by the time of Augustus it was known, and these very passages of Strabo prove it, either that Caesar was mistaken or that times had changed. A country which could afford so large a trade with the Empire could pay its way in taxes as a province of the Empire. The plea that Britain was to all intents and purposes inaccessible is equally inconsistent with the recorded fact of constant trade relations. As to the argument from the alleged friendliness of British princes, it can be checked by reference to Augustus's own autobiography. In his *Res Gestae* Augustus records with pride the names of various countries outside the Empire whose rulers had sought his friendship; and the name of Britain is not to be found there. All he can say is that he had been visited by two suppliant, and therefore doubtless exiled, princes from that country, a certain Dumnovellaunus and some one whose name begins with the letters Tim . . . or Tin . . . . These are clearly no others than the Dubnovellaunus and Tincommius of the British coins. When Augustus wrote that autobiography, Cunobelinus had been on the throne for some ten years; and Augustus can only be tactfully concealing the fact that, during all this time, he had never sent him so much as a complimentary message. The British rulers whom Strabo mentions are obviously the suppliant princes of the *Res Gestae*; and their relations with Augustus are thus evidence not of British friendship but of British hostility, a hostility quite compatible with advancing romanization in manners.

But Cunobelinus, though he never sought the friendship of Rome, never did anything to excite her enmity. He must have been well aware that, if war should break out, a single campaign would suffice to destroy him. His attitude towards Augustus was therefore one merely of reserve; and when, during the northern campaigns of Germanicus, certain Roman soldiers were shipwrecked on the coast of Britain, it was quite in accordance with his policy that the princes in whose country they landed should send them safely back to the Continent.

So far as we can divine the policy of Augustus, British conquest had no part in it. He planned and carried out a thorough pacification of Gaul, suppressing revolts and paving by all possible means the way to peace; when this was done, he embarked on his one great military failure, the attempted conquest of Germany. By the time this attempt was renounced, after the slaughter of Varus's legions, we hear no more of Britain; the arguments preserved by Strabo had done their work. Yet Augustus undoubtedly knew what the consolidation of Cunobelinus's kingdom meant to Rome. He can hardly have been blind to the fact that across the Channel a strong state was growing up, progressive in its civilization and by no means friendly to Rome in its spirit: a state whence no overtures of friendship were forthcoming, except from its exiles. He is not likely to have been deceived by the arguments which he used in explaining to others why the conquest of Britain was not being pushed forward; and in that case he must have known that, sooner or later, it was inevitable. Either Rome would find her hands free to settle an account long outstanding, or something would happen to precipitate a conflict.

Meanwhile he bequeathed to his successor the maxim that the frontiers of the Empire were best left unaltered, and in particular gave him a hint, which Tiberius treated (according to a phrase of Tacitus) as a command, against reopening the question of a British war. The new reign was a time of peace and consolidation, and saw no change in the relations between Britain and Rome. But events on either side were converging towards a crisis. The very success of Tiberius's policy paved the way for its own abandonment. The Rhine and Danube frontiers were firmly based; the east was quiet; Spain, pacified at last, was patently over-garrisoned; there were troops to spare for a forward move wherever one was needed. And in Britain Cunobelinus was growing old and his sons were quarrelling. In the light of later developments we can discern a pro-Roman and an anti-Roman party at his court, the latter led by two of his sons, Togodumnus and Caratacus, the former led by another son, Amminius.

By the time Gaius came to the throne in 37, it was a perfectly serious question of policy whether the time had not come for undertaking the long-deferred conquest. Unhappily, Gaius was a conceited and cruel tyrant upon whom his contemporaries have revenged themselves by depicting him to posterity as a lunatic; and it is impossible to discover the truth even concerning his actions, not to speak of his intentions, beneath the mass of ridicule that ancient writers have heaped upon them. In all probability Gaius had resolved to invade both Germany and Britain within a year of his accession; but the events which brought him to the Rhine in 39 arose not out of a planned campaign but out of a conspiracy against his life, which he hastened to Germany to suppress. The strange stories told of his doings there during that autumn have been explained with some plausibility[1] as a garbled version of manœuvres for the training of the troops in view of an intended invasion of Germany next year; and the fact that this invasion never took place is accounted for by the same writer as due to the arrival of Amminius, exiled by his father, bringing with him a handful of followers, and coming as a suppliant to Gaius as he lay encamped at Mainz, an event which, it is suggested, diverted his campaign of A.D. 40 from Germany to Britain.

But in attempting to plumb the motives of Gaius we are groping in the dark. All we know is that he did plan an invasion of Britain for the year 40; that in preparation for it he had a lighthouse built at Boulogne; that he assembled his expeditionary force there, made all ready for departure, and then, at the very moment of embarkation, cancelled his orders and countermanded the whole campaign. The plan had been hastily formed by an ambitious and inexperienced ruler; whatever may have been the motive for its abandonment at that critical moment, the fact that it was never taken up again is probably due less to his own instability of purpose than to the atmosphere of opposition and conspiracy with which he was surrounded at Rome, an atmosphere whose ill effect on his character is admitted even by his kindliest biographers. To the historian of Britain, however, the incident is crucial. It marks the end of the long respite from Roman invasion.

[1] J. P. V. D. Balsdon, *The Emperor Gaius* (1934), pp. 78–82.

BOOK II
THE AGE OF CONQUEST

V
THE CLAUDIAN INVASION

To the question why Claudius resolved to conquer Britain, ancient writers give no clear answer. Dio, to whom we are indebted for the only narrative we possess of the invasion, says that a certain Bericus, exiled from Britain, persuaded Claudius to attack it. But it is hardly probable that a Roman emperor undertook such an enterprise out of kindness to an exiled prince; nor does the name of Bericus reappear at any later stage in the narrative. Suetonius, the official scandal-monger of early Imperial history, alleges that the emperor was moved by the desire to celebrate a triumph; but in the same breath he observes that Britain was in a disturbed condition (*tumultuantem* is the word), which provides a motive of a quite different kind for Claudius's act: a motive based not on personal grounds but on grounds of imperial policy. Tacitus, by far the greatest historian of them all, hints that the mineral wealth of Britain had something to do with the decision; but in the brief summary of events, prefaced to his biography of Agricola, he conveys to his reader the impression that what demands explanation is not the fact that Claudius conquered Britain, but the fact that no one else had done it. For, says he, Julius Caesar had fought a successful campaign there, but in effect had only pointed Britain out, not handed it over, to his successors: pointed it out, we are to understand, not as an object of disinterested speculation or scientific study, but as a field for future conquests. Civil wars and political problems then, Tacitus continues, occupied for a while the attention of emperors; even in times of peace Augustus thought it politic, and Tiberius treated it as a command laid upon him by Augustus, to forget that Britain existed. Gaius's invasion was rendered futile by his own inconstancy and his record of ill success in Germany; it was left for Claudius to take up the task again and carry it through.[1] The question which Tacitus is here assuming, as in the mind of

[1] Tacitus, *Agricola*, xiii.

any reader, is not 'Why did Claudius invade Britain?' but 'Why was so obvious and natural a step not taken earlier?'

There is no doubt that the perspective in which Tacitus here places the Claudian invasion is the right one. The project of conquering Britain had been brought by Caesar into the agenda of Roman policy. Thereafter, the question at any given moment was not whether it should be done, but whether it should be done now, and if not, why not. Augustus, as we have seen, had more urgent things to do, and gave it out from time to time that Britain was too poor, too distant, or too friendly to make annexation expedient or necessary. By the time of Gaius none of these reasons held good. When Claudius reviewed the situation, the facts which must have weighed with him may be summed up as follows.

First, there were troops to spare. The Rhine, the Danube, and Spain were amply guarded, perhaps even excessively. The military situation is rendered a little ambiguous by doubt whether it was Gaius or Claudius who enrolled the two new legions, XV Primigenia and XXII Primigenia, which, with IV Macedonica from Spain, took the place of the three Rhenish legions sent by Claudius to Britain: II Augusta from Strasburg, XIV Gemina from Mainz, and XX Valeria Victrix from Cologne. If the new legions were recruited by Claudius,[1] the Rhine garrison was maintained at its former strength and its composition changed; if by Gaius, it was done in preparation for his own schemes of conquest, and the fact of its being done meant that unless Claudius carried out those schemes the Rhine would be heavily over-garrisoned. The fourth legion for Britain, IX Hispana, was drawn from Pannonia.

Secondly, the fiasco of Gaius's abortive invasion laid a responsibility on his successor. Whether Gaius was right or wrong in thinking the time favourable for conquering Britain, the fact that he had taken the first step towards conquering it gave Claudius an additional reason for taking up the plan again and carrying it out decisively, as a demonstration of firmness both to the Britons and to his own legions.

Thirdly, the financial arguments of Augustus were long out

---

[1] H. M. D. Parker, *The Roman Legions* (1928), pp. 93–8. *Contra*, E. Ritterling in *Pauly-Wissowa*, s.v. 'Legio', 1244–9; Syme in *Camb. Anc. Hist.* x. 788–9. It may be convenient for some readers here to be referred on to p. 138, where they will find details about the strength, &c., of legions and auxiliary units.

of date. Britain was known to be rich in raw materials, metals, wheat, cattle, slaves; there was good reason to think that, as a province, it would pay its way. Annexation would further stimulate trade, and commercial interests of every kind must have favoured it.

And lastly, the political situation was precarious. Even in the time of Gaius, the expulsion of Amminius probably indicates that the cautious and moderate anti-Roman policy of Cunobelinus was being replaced, as he grew old, by a more violent version of itself, championed by Togodumnus and Caratacus. By the year 43 Cunobelinus was dead and the anti-Roman movement had come out into the open. The exile of Bericus marks a further stage in its development: it appears that the British princes demanded of Rome that he and perhaps others should be handed back to them, and when this was refused they took up a threatening attitude. Because Gaius's expedition had never sailed they thought themselves secure from invasion, and fancied that Rome could be bullied. Threats conveyed through diplomatic channels might easily be followed by hostile action: perhaps a descent on the coast of Gaul, more probably a massacre of the Roman traders who must by now have been settled in Britain in considerable numbers. The case for invasion was complete.

It has been said that Claudius formed the nucleus of his expeditionary force by detaching three legions from the Rhine garrison and one from Pannonia; it was from Pannonia that he drew its commanding officer, Aulus Plautius. With the complement of auxiliary regiments, foot and horse, usual at that time, the total must have numbered about 40,000. As compared with Caesar's army in 54, there was one legion less but more auxiliaries; the chief effect of this would be that the Claudian force was stronger in cavalry and therefore better adapted to the tactical conditions of British warfare.

This is not the only respect in which the Claudian invasion bears traces of planning by men who had carefully and profitably studied Caesar's account of his own. The same point of departure was chosen, at Boulogne; the same method of crossing at night; the same landfall, with one significant modification, in east Kent; and the same strategy for the opening stage of the campaign.

Another resemblance, though an undesigned one, was that, as

Caesar found some of his Gaulish companions reluctant to cross the sea, so Claudius's army flatly refused to face an ocean voyage to a destination (as Dio says) 'outside the world', with the danger of being wrecked at sea or cast away on a hostile shore. But whereas in the case of Caesar's expedition the incident closed in tragedy, in that of Claudius it turned into farce. One innovation of Claudius's reign was the formation of a State secretariat within the Imperial household, staffed by freedmen; and when news reached Rome that the army of Britain was in mutiny, he sent his chief secretary, the freedman Narcissus, to deal with the mutineers. Roman soldiers were well accustomed to have an *imperator* ascend the tribunal and address them; Claudius himself, as head of the army, they would have heard with respect; but when an ex-slave mounted the platform they were indignant, until their sense of humour overcame them, and they howled the secretary down with shouts of 'Merry Christmas'—if that will serve to translate the greeting that passed from mouth to mouth at the Saturnalia, when slaves dressed up in their masters' clothes and the social order was turned upside-down. Whether because, having relieved their feelings, they thought better of their obstinacy, or because Narcissus after an inauspicious beginning handled his audience better than we are told, the mutiny died there and then, and the legions went on board.

The fleet of transports sailed in three divisions, under separate commands. It is safe to assume that there was a main body of two legions, and two smaller divisions of one each. The motive for this arrangement is recorded to have been the desire to avoid being prevented from landing. Later in the history of Britain the Romans made use of three ports on the coast of east and south Kent, Richborough, Dover, and Lympne; and three roads leading from these ports converge at Canterbury. It has therefore been suggested that Plautius sent one flotilla to each of these three ports, with orders to land and effect a concentration at Canterbury. There are two reasons for thinking this unlikely. First, the strategy of the whole invasion was modelled closely on that of Caesar's campaign; and, whereas Caesar had explored the road from the east Kent coast to Canterbury, he had left no information suggesting that good routes might be found thither from Dover and Lympne, and had once for all settled the unsuitability of Dover as a landing-place on a hostile shore. Secondly, it is a maxim of strategy that forces should not be

divided in the face of the enemy. Had the Britons prepared a
force at all equivalent to Plautius's own for the purpose of opposing him at or after landing, and had any of his three divisions
encountered it on the beach or come into touch with it shortly
after disembarkation, his campaign would have opened with at
best a rebuff and at worst a disaster which would have been
poorly requited by a successful landing on the part of the other
two divisions.

It is more likely that when Plautius divided his forces 'in order
that they might not be prevented from landing anywhere'[1] his
intention was to confuse the Britons by making feints at two
other possible landing-places, of which Dover was very likely
one, while intending actually to land at one only. Recent
excavation has proved that this one was Richborough, where
the remains of a very large camp of Claudian date have been
found. Its landward defences form a crescent-shaped line, still
700 yards long, and originally longer, with both ends resting
upon the sea; inside the area so defended were many wooden
store-houses, of which the earliest were built soon after the landing of Plautius's army. The discovery of this large land-locked
harbour, hidden away behind the Isle of Thanet, where a great
fleet could ride at anchor or lie on the beach secure from danger
in any weather, was a triumph for the intelligence service of
Claudius's army. It suggests that his staff realized where lay
the fundamental weakness of Caesar's campaign, namely, in his
failure to find a safe and commodious harbour. By good fortune,
that weakness could be mended with a very slight modification
of his strategy, for the harbour of Richborough lay only a few
miles from his own landing-place.

In point of fact, Plautius's precaution was unnecessary. The
Britons remembered the fiasco of Gaius; they had news of the
mutiny, which had lasted for several weeks; and they concluded
that there would be no invasion. Indeed, to speak of the Britons
collectively, as if they formed a single political unit, is misleading. Britain at this time, although Cunobelinus is called
rex Britanniae by Suetonius, was very far from being one realm.
Cunobelinus, to judge from his coins, ruled not only over the
kingdom of Cassivellaunus but, as has been said in the preceding
chapter, Essex and Kent as well. Within this realm local autonomies had been suppressed; but tribal identity and tribal con-

[1] Dio, lx. 19, § 4.

sciousness remained, ready to assert themselves piecemeal when occasion offered. At the moment of the invasion, Cunobelinus was lately dead, and his sons' intention was probably to divide his inheritance between them; but this appears not yet to have been done, and actually we find two of the anti-Roman sons, Togodumnus and Caratacus, exercising a kind of joint rule which must have been a provisional and temporary arrangement, favourable to the invaders.

Outside the realm of Cunobelinus were many tribal states, some of which recognized the authority of Camulodunum, while others did not. There must have been a king reigning at Silchester, whether Epaticcus or a successor of his, intimately related to the sons of Cunobelinus. Farther west, the Durotriges, a lately Belgicized tribe, doubtless had a king of their own in their stupendous fortress of Maiden Castle. The Belgicized inhabitants of west Sussex, the Regni, were ruled by Cogidubnus; the Iceni of East Anglia by Prasutagus; but alike in these cases and in those of tribes farther afield like the Dobuni, the Coritani, the Brigantes, and the Dumnonii, it is impossible to say how far the unity of tribal names and districts which has come down to us conceals a diversity of petty states, each with its own ruler, in the time of Claudius.[1]

In this state of things a unified policy for the defence of Britain was not to be expected. A Cunobelinus in his best days would no doubt have imposed such a policy, at least over the whole south-east; but Claudius rightly calculated that amid the family quarrels and party strife which marked his last years, and intensified after his death, there would be no organized resistance. Caught unprepared by Plautius's landing, the inhabitants of east Kent took to the woods, hoping to avoid a decisive battle and to wear the Romans out, as Cassivellaunus, according to what must have been their version of the story, had worn out Julius Caesar. Plautius spent the first stages of his campaign marching and countermarching in east Kent, searching for an enemy whom he never found.

In describing this phase of the campaign, Dio explains the impossibility of discovering and engaging the enemy by saying

---

[1] Tacitus, *Agr.* 12, § 1, suggests that by the time of the Roman conquest a good many tribes had abolished the kingship and had a republican constitution. But his words must not be taken as implying that all had done so; that could be refuted from other statements of his own.

that 'the Britons (of those parts) were not self-governing but were ruled by other kings'.[1] If the tribes of Kent had been independent, each would have had a king of its own, an army of its own, and a capital of its own; Plautius could therefore have attacked them in detail, stormed their fortresses one by one, and forced them one by one into submission. As it was, he might overrun the territory of any one such tribe, only to find that it contained no army to fight, no fortress to attack, and no government upon which to impose terms of peace.

Meanwhile, however, the two most active sons of Cunobelinus were mustering their forces and hastening to meet the invaders. Even now, disunion was their undoing. Instead of acting in concert, each of the two brothers independently gathered his own men around him and rushed blindly upon the Roman force. Caratacus, the abler and more vigorous of the two, reached Kent first. It is tempting to conjecture that he took up his position on Caesar's old battlefield at the crossing of the Stour; for Dio's narrative suggests that he fought on ground of his own choosing somewhere in the eastern half of the county, and no better defensive ground is to be had. But Plautius found no difficulty in driving him headlong from his position. He escaped with his life and the remnants of his force along the line of the Watling Street; and Plautius in his pursuit, somewhere along that line, met with Togodumnus and crushed him. The loss of these two engagements made it impossible to hold East Kent, and some part at least of its inhabitants submitted to Plautius. They are described as a section of the Bodunni, who were doubtless one of the four unnamed Kentish tribes mentioned by Caesar.[2]

Rome's method of dealing with conquered tribes had undergone a change in the last hundred years. Caesar would have received hostages from the Bodunni; Plautius detached a small

---

[1] Dio, lx. 20, § 1. The emendation ⟨ἄλλοι⟩ ἄλλοις, which would imply that each tribe was ruled by its own king, makes nonsense of the passage.

[2] At and before the conquest there were numerous tribes in Britain whose names are unknown to us, because the tribal names which have been preserved are mostly those of the cantons which the Romans made into units of local self-government, and when this system was created many smaller tribes were merged in larger ones and their identity lost. It is therefore an error to assume that the name of a tribe mentioned in these earlier times will reappear later. Through overlooking this, Hübner (Römische Herrschaft in Westeuropa, 1890, ch. 1) was tempted to identify the Bodunni with the Dobuni and reduce the narrative of the conquest to a strategical nightmare.

force to police their territory, planted it in a little fort there, and marched on. This way of disposing small police-forces in block-houses can be traced back to Tiberius's northern campaigns in the reign of Augustus;[1] it was part of the process by which the field-armies of the late Republic developed into the network of sedentary garrisons that guarded the frontiers of the Empire.

These first engagements were mere skirmishes. While they were going on, the general levy of fighting-men from north-west Kent and from beyond the Thames had mustered on the Med-way and encamped along the wooded hills west of the river, where they were joined by the survivors from the defeated forces of Caratacus and Togodumnus. It is probable that a bridge already spanned the river at Rochester; if so, the retreating Britons destroyed it and, imagining that this would give them sufficient respite from attack, neglected to guard the crossing. Plautius came on them unprepared. His Gallic cavalry swam the stream and charged the British charioteers, with orders to destroy their mobility by crippling their horses. Meanwhile the future emperor Vespasian led the Second legion upstream to find a ford, crossed the river, and turned the right wing of the defenders. But the position was not to be so easily won. The attack was beaten off. Next day battle was renewed on the same ground, and it was only after severe hand-to-hand fight-ing that Plautius gained the summit of the ridge, and looked down to see the Britons retreating across the plain towards Dartford.

The battle of the Medway was the decisive engagement of the campaign. It was a hard-won victory for the Romans, for a two-days' battle is a rare thing in ancient warfare; and it reflects credit both on British leadership and on the steadiness of the British troops that, though caught unawares and confronted with a simultaneous cavalry attack and flanking movement, the Britons were victors in the first day's fighting. It is clear that their whole available forces were engaged, and that their plan had been to put their main effort into the defence of the Medway.

This fact is concealed from us in Dio's narrative, and for a curious reason. From the first, the Roman plan of campaign had involved the presence of Claudius at its culminating point.

---

[1] Velleius Paterculus, ii. 120: after the defeat of Varus, Tiberius 'mittitur ad Germaniam, Gallias confirmat, disponit exercitus, praesidia munit'.

Plautius, a steady and experienced general, was to land the expeditionary force in Britain and take it through the early stages of the campaign; he was then to encounter the main forces of the enemy in a strong defensive position, and go through an elaborate comedy of professing his own incompetence to proceed farther and summoning the most unmilitary of emperors to take command and save the situation. Caesar's narrative of his own invasion, which was used throughout the campaign of 43 as a text-book by the Roman staff, would suggest to any reader that the right place for this picturesque event was the crossing of the Thames, where a great river guarded the frontier of Cunobelinus's immediate realm. Here, it was assumed, the Britons would make their chief stand and the decisive battle would be fought.

When Cassivellaunus took command against Caesar, he decided to fight him in east Kent. It was here that the battle took place after which, in Caesar's words, the Britons never again encountered him in a general action. The line of the Medway was never held against him, and consequently he never mentions its existence. Hence, when Plautius was marching across Kent in Caesar's tracks, he knew nothing of the Medway, and found himself quite unexpectedly confronted with the main army of the Britons and committed to fighting the decisive battle of the war. This explains his defeat on the first day. Plautius was fighting by the book, and on paper neither the Medway nor the Britons had any right to be there.

By comparison, the crossing of the Thames was a trifling affair. Relatively to sea-level, the land about London stood fifteen feet higher then than it does now. A trading settlement already existed at London itself, and the Thames had been bridged; but there were fords down-stream from it. The Britons in their retreat from the Medway naturally made for these fords, and crossed them with the Romans in pursuit. The Gaulish cavalry missed the fords, but some of them swam the river and others galloped for the bridge. The Britons made no attempt to hold the crossing. They continued their retreat towards Colchester. In the marshes of the Lea valley Plautius's cavalry came up with them; and now at last the Britons turned on their pursuers and checked them sharply.

There was nothing in this to cause the alarm which, according to Dio, Plautius professed to feel. A general with a free hand would have had his legions in support, and would have swept the Britons before him until he reached the unwalled city of Colchester. But Plautius was bound by the plan. If the Britons would not defend the Thames, that was their affair; his business was to make the most of his cavalry's losses, send for the emperor, and hope that by the time he arrived the enemy would have occupied the left bank in respectable force.

All went well. Claudius had reinforcements ready prepared, including a contingent of his own praetorian guards and an elephant corps; he made a rapid journey to Britain, arrived in Plautius's camp, and gave orders for a general advance. At this point our sources become contradictory. Dio says that the crossing of the Thames was opposed and a battle fought in which the emperor was victorious; Suetonius, that no engagement took place and no casualties were incurred during his whole stay in Britain; Claudius himself, in the inscription cut on the triumphal arch celebrating his conquest, that he suffered no losses.[1] If there was opposition, it must have been of the slightest; the Britons had shot their bolt at the Medway, and had no heart for another battle.

At Colchester Claudius received the submission of many tribes[2] and laid down the lines for a peaceful settlement of Britain. His biographers have noticed that alike in his administration and in his reforms he presents a curious mixture of bold innovation with an almost pedantic conservatism. The systems of government which he created, whether at home or in the provinces, never have the simple clarity of a scheme deduced from logical principles. They are patchwork affairs, composed of heterogeneous and conflicting elements. In this, his British settlement is characteristic of the man.

To begin with, there was the realm of Cunobelinus. This was the part of Britain which had directly incurred the hostility of Rome, and the occupation of its capital marked the close of the first campaign and was the occasion of the emperor's triumph. Of its royal princes Togodumnus was dead; Caratacus was a

[1] Dio, lx. 21, § 4; Suetonius, *Divus Claudius*, 17, § 2; Dessau, *Inscr. Lat. Sel.* 216. Perhaps the inscription (*sine ulla iactura*) is the source from which Suetonius gets his *sine ullo proelio aut sanguine*.

[2] Eleven kings submitted to him, according to the inscription already quoted; but that inscription was only put up in 51, and the eleven may include all who submitted down to that time. If so, however, the phrase *sine ulla iactura* is unjustified: it can truthfully refer only to the sixteen days of the emperor's own visit to Britain.

defeated and discredited exile. Here Claudius's course was obvious: this kingdom was to be a Roman province, with Colchester as its capital and Plautius as its first governor. But the straggling, half-barbaric town of Cunobelinus was no fit capital for a province. A new city was laid out on the hill-top a little way to the south-east: here in all probability was the official residence of the propraetor and the seat of Roman government; and here in the centre of the city, surrounded by the porticoes of a forum, was to stand a temple, a vast and massive building where Claudius was to be worshipped as a god.

Claudius was ready to give with one hand what he had taken away with the other. The Belgic Britons had shown themselves willing to adopt town life of a sort and able to conduct their own public affairs; these signs of grace, then, should be fostered. In his other new-conquered province of Mauretania, Claudius had converted at least one native town into a self-governing *municipium*; the same experiment should be made in Britain, and for this experiment no place could be more suitable than the Catuvellaunian capital where Tasciovanus had once reigned. Accordingly, a new city was built at Verulamium, in the valley below the old town, and endowed with municipal rights.[1]

Outside the realm of Cunobelinus there were at least two independent states which had taken no part in the war and now lost no time in submitting to the conqueror. One was the Regni of west Sussex. We have already seen that this was a region cut off from the Belgae of the lower Thames basin by the forest of the Weald, but affected to some extent by the La Tène civilization of the south-west and more decisively, later on, by the western Belgic invasion, under whose influence its people had ceased to inhabit their hill-forts and had built themselves a new capital at Noviomagus in the plain. Here, at Chichester, ruled a king named Cogidubnus. We may assume that he was no friend to Caratacus and Togodumnus; and so convincingly did he make his peace with Claudius that the emperor confirmed him in his kingdom and even enlarged its boundaries, conferring upon him a title thoroughly characteristic of his tendency to mingle innovation with conservatism: *rex (et) legatus Augusti in Britannia*. Strange though the title is, its spirit is not out of harmony with the methods of Claudius. In the following year he revived the title of *rex* for the benefit

[1] If so, it lost those rights by the early third century (cf. *C.I.L.* vii. 863).

of M. Julius Cottius, representative of the ancient native rulers of the Cottian Alps; his father had enjoyed only the title of *praefectus civitatium*, but his grandfather Donnus had been a king. Similarly in Judaea Claudius experimented from time to time in the re-establishment of client kingdoms, taking care, however, that the men whom he elevated to these petty thrones should refrain from striking out independent policies of their own.

Cogidubnus accordingly was obliged to give proofs of loyalty. He became a Roman citizen with the name of Tiberius Claudius Cogidubnus, and either he or some wealthy subject acting with his authority employed Roman artists to build a temple to Neptune and Minerva, dedicated for the welfare of the imperial house, whose dedicatory inscription, the most elegant and purely classical in Britain, still survives at Chichester to tell the story. The choice of deities is not without significance. Chichester stands at the head of the first and most easily accessible of those Hampshire harbours which, even as early as Strabo's time, were connected by regular trade with the mouth of the Seine; and the god of the sea, named together with the goddess of learning and the arts, suggests that Cogidubnus in building this temple was publicly announcing his attachment to the new civilizing influences which cross-Channel trade was bringing to his coast. How far his title of imperial governor in Britain indicated a real authority over his own people, and how far it was merely honorary, serving to cover a real subordination to Plautius, it is difficult to say, but the later history of Prasutagus suggests that his authority was genuine and not lightly to be revoked.

The second of these client kingdoms was that of the Iceni. This tribe had always held themselves aloof from their Belgic neighbours, and in all probability lived in daily fear of them. Eighteen years later they still had a king of their own, Prasutagus; either he or his father was presumably on the throne at the time of the conquest, and shared with Cogidubnus his submission to the emperor and the emperor's gift of a partial and patronized freedom. A third client kingdom ought probably to be added; that of the Brigantes.

Having conjured up this strangely devised political system for his new province, Claudius instructed his propraetor to conquer the rest of Britain, and went home to the devout enjoyment of his triumph.

VI

CARATACUS AND BOUDICCA

AFTER the battle of the Medway Caratacus vanished. He knew that it was decisive, and that all further attempts to defend his kingdom and capital must be futile. But he was a man of indomitable spirit, whose power over others rested not upon his royalty but upon his personality. He resolved to gather round him a small band of kinsmen and friends, to cut himself loose from his own country, and to rouse in the tribes as yet untouched by Rome a spirit of resistance to the invaders.

It was a bold step for the king of the Belgic Britons to take. Both he and his people were rather feared than loved by their neighbours. Their conquests were certainly resented, and their civilized manners were no doubt despised; the other tribes were likely, on the whole, to be pleased at the swiftness and completeness of their humiliation. The Regni and the Iceni, and many other neighbouring peoples, had long hated them, and had only waited to show their hand until they were no longer to be feared. Where, then, was Caratacus to go?

With the strategical instinct of a born soldier, he saw that the highland zone was the place in which the legions must be resisted, if they were to be resisted anywhere. He saw that, of its three sectors, the Dumnonian peninsula was too small and too much isolated. He saw that it was only in Wales and the north that he could hope for success. The north was already a great military power under the rule of the Brigantes; in Wales, hardly touched as it yet was by Iron Age civilization, there were the materials for another such power, lying ready to the hand of any one who could use them: a hardy and independent race, and a country designed by nature for desperate defence. He turned to Wales.

It must be asked, even though the question cannot be conclusively answered, why he did not turn first to Wessex, where the former realm of Commius offered him a people akin to his own, and where, as he travelled westward, he could find a country rich in fortresses, each one capable of stout defence. A possible answer is to be found in the defection of the partially Belgicized Regni. If Cogidubnus was not to be trusted, the same may have been true of the other chiefs in central south England.

Jealousies between them and the dynasty of Cassivellaunus may have been too strong for Caratacus to expect their sympathy. And he was no diplomat. He was a man of fiery and over-bearing temper, totally unsuited to the work of begging help from princes who thought themselves his equals and looked on him as a discredited exile. The later events of his life showed that his haughty bearing could not gain the support of a Carti-mandua, though it could win the respect of a Claudius. Such a man, driven from his own kingdom, had the best chance of success if he tried to carve out a new kingdom for himself among the masterless tribes of the west.

His temperament as a fighter helped this decision. He was not the man to conduct a dogged rearguard action, to dispute every step of an advancing enemy and to wear him out by con-stant pressure on his flanks and his communications. The course of the campaign of 43 after the battle of the Medway showed that Caratacus never had it in him to emulate Cassivellaunus's tactics against Caesar. He was a fighter of battles; his idea of warfare revolved round the conception of the decisive engage-ment. His first campaign had culminated in one such engage-ment; he had lost it; and he now set to work to prepare an army and a field of operations for a second.

Meanwhile Plautius was proceeding systematically with the conquest of the lowland zone. It is a process of which ancient writers tell us practically nothing; and archaeology has done very little to fill the gap. Beside the great camp at Richborough, there is hardly a single place where we can identify one of the marching-camps or forts which during these first years must have been scattered broadcast over the face of the country. But the few fragments of information which have reached our hands make a picture which, so far as it goes, is intelligible.

The Roman supreme command made the assumption that henceforth no great concentration of enemy forces would be encountered. Their own forces could therefore be divided into separate columns, each of which was to work in one direction and thus, by a general radial movement, overrun and pacify the lowlands. Sussex and East Anglia were friendly; therefore the area to be conquered spread fanwise from the Thames estuary westward and northward. The centre of the advance would run through Catuvellaunian territory into the forests of the midlands; the right wing would work northwards towards

Lincolnshire, the left would overrun Wessex from east to west.

Although Colchester was the capital of the new province, the centre from which these radiating lines diverged was at London. The building of roads was an essential instrument of conquest, and most of the main Roman roads in Britain must have been laid down at a very early date. When we find London the centre from which one road, Watling Street, runs north-westward to Wroxeter, another northwards to Lincoln, and a third westward to Silchester, we can hardly doubt that these were the roads built for this triple advance, and that London served as the supply-depot and base for the three columns.

Of the central column's fortunes we know nothing. It probably consisted of the Fourteenth and Twentieth legions; and it pushed its road forward along the central watershed of England, crossing the rivers close to their sources, gradually leaving the Catuvellaunian tilled lands behind and plunging into the woodland of Warwickshire. On its way it encountered the La Tène civilization of the Northamptonshire uplands, but after this its march lay through country almost uninhabited. We may wonder why so powerful a column was sent into this desolate and unpeopled land; the answer must be that its destination was already fixed on the Welsh borders and the Irish sea, and that its ultimate function was to conquer Wales before turning, if that should be necessary, against the Brigantes.

The right wing consisted of the Ninth legion. Its route lay through Cambridgeshire and round the edge of the Fens; but once more, we know nothing of its operations, unless the Roman camp lately seen from an aeroplane near Castor[1] is a relic of its progress. Unless they had already submitted to Claudius, the Brigantes must now have made peace; or rather, their queen Cartimandua did so, now if not earlier, but was unable (as we shall see) permanently to impose her will upon all her subjects.

About the left wing we know more, because it was commanded by the future emperor Vespasian, whose biography tells us that in Britain he 'fought thirty battles, conquered two powerful tribes, capturing over twenty fortresses, and annexed the Isle of Wight'.[2] He commanded the Second legion, which

---

[1] *Antiquity*, iv (1930), pp. 274-5.
[2] Suetonius, *Vespasian*, 4.

has left a trace of its presence on the south Devon coast. What the two tribes were it is idle to guess. The Atrebates of Silchester may have been one, or they may have submitted of their own free will; one must almost certainly have been the Durotriges, whose fortress of Maiden Castle was surely one of the twenty-odd that Vespasian stormed. He may have overrun the country of the Dumnonii; there are earthworks in Cornwall which may possibly be the camps of a Roman army.[1]

By the autumn of 47, when Plautius was succeeded as governor by P. Ostorius Scapula, the right wing had reached Lincoln, the left was on the borders of Devonshire and Dorset, and the centre was somewhere in the midlands. But the situation was far from satisfactory. Ostorius found the friendly tribes much harassed by constant raiding from those which were still unconquered, especially the Brigantes and Silures, the Brigantes crossing the Trent and raiding the Coritani of Leicestershire and Nottinghamshire, the Silures crossing the Severn and plundering the Dobuni. This counter-offensive was perhaps the firstfruits of Caratacus's activity in the west. Ostorius either knew or suspected that these raids were encouraged by unruly elements in the tribes that had submitted. Accordingly, after a series of sharp engagements in which the raiding forces were repulsed by his auxiliary infantry and cavalry, he drew a frontier-line across Britain, disarmed all the tribes on his own side of it, and fortified and patrolled it to keep out raids from beyond.

This frontier-line was the road which is known as the Fosse. It was meant to hold down the entire country up to the Trent and Severn; that is to say, it was planned so as to defend the Dobuni and Coritani against marauders from across those rivers. The way in which the Fosse is laid out shows that its designers regarded the Dobuni and Coritani as friendly tribes, not as enemies; it passed right through the centre of their territories and was, according to the ordinary practice of the time, studded with auxiliary units, whose duty was to patrol the neighbourhood of their various forts, and thus act as a defensive garrison for the country in which they were placed, and upon which they depended for supplies.

The Fosse begins at Seaton, by the mouth of the Axe on the Devonshire coast, where a tile of the Second legion indicates

[1] *Vict. Co. Hist. Cornwall*, i. 26, note 74.

that it once lay there in more or less permanent quarters; perhaps a tradition of this residence is preserved in the pages of Ptolemy.[1] It runs, with a directness rare even in Roman roads, to Bath and across the Cotswold plateau to Cirencester, which either was or soon became the capital of the Dobuni; here early tombstones suggest a cavalry garrison. About Moreton-in-Marsh, still following its straight line, it gradually leaves the plateau and enters the midland forest, and somewhere in this region, perhaps near High Cross, north of Rugby, where it encounters Watling Street, the Fourteenth and Twentieth legions must have had their encampments. At Leicester, a tile suggests that a detachment of the Eighth, possibly part of Claudius's reinforcements, garrisoned a fort where later, if not already, the tribal capital of the Coritani stood. The road then follows a ridge of hills on the right bank of the Trent to Newark; on this ridge a Claudian fort has been excavated at Margidunum, east of Nottingham. From Newark it runs straight across the plain to the Ninth legion's fortress at Lincoln. The two ends of this line, as well as its centre, where no river offers an impediment to the free crossing of it, were thus already well defended by legionary fortresses; it was the gaps between these points that were exposed to Silurian and Brigantian raids, respectively, and it was to protect these gaps that Ostorius planned his frontier-line.

But his disarmament of the tribes lying behind the line was unexpected, and in one quarter at least bitterly resented. The Iceni regarded themselves as free allies of the Roman people, and although they had hitherto paid their allotted tribute and provided their quota of recruits without protest, they were too proud and independent in spirit to submit to disarmament. They rose in revolt and carried with them a number of neighbouring tribes; certainly not the Brigantes, who were outside the frontier, nor the Catuvellauni or Trinovantes, who were under the direct rule of the propraetor, but small tribal units whose names have not come down to us. Realizing from the first that defence and not attack must be their part, they assembled their forces in a strong position protected by field-works

---

[1] Ptolemy, writing his *Geography* in the second century, places the Second legion near the town of Isca, and calls this a town of the Dumnonii. That should be Exeter; but Bradley (*Collected Papers*, p. 72) pointed out that he confused the Exe with the Axe. Of course, a further confusion with the Monmouthshire Usk is conceivable, but not probable.

and abattis. Scapula's legions were busy constructing and fortifying the Fosse, and he could only spare auxiliaries to deal with
the revolt; but he dismounted his cavalry, since the position was
one which only infantry could attack, and with these and his
infantry cohorts assaulted and stormed the rebels' defences. In
spite of desperate resistance, the victory was complete. The
Iceni and their allies were disarmed; but it is noteworthy that,
in spite of the revolt, they were still allowed to retain the status
of a nominally independent kingdom.

Ostorius now thought himself free to move onwards, and his
next campaign was on the northern frontiers of Wales in the
country of the Degeangli. It was now, presumably, that Watling Street was driven forward from High Cross to the upper
Severn, and a legionary fortress established at Wroxeter. Excavations have failed to discover any remains of such a fortress,
but early tombstones of men from the Fourteenth and Twentieth legions have been found there, one at least of which can
hardly have been set up later than the time of Claudius; and
the fact that the forum of the later city was designed on the
model of a *praetorium* suitable for a fortress containing two
legions[1] gives further support to the suggestion that in or about
the year 48 a double fortress was established there, in which
both those legions took up their quarters. It was from this new
base that Ostorius attacked the Degeangli, whose lands he overran without fighting a pitched battle.

He hoped in the course of this campaign to establish himself
on the Irish sea, make contact with his fleet, and effect the
separation of Wales from Brigantia. But before he had reached
his goal he learnt of trouble among the Brigantes which demanded his intervention. They were a turbulent race. Though
Cartimandua had made peace with the Romans, that did not
prevent a considerable part of her subjects from treating them
as enemies and plundering the lands of tribes whose submission
had been more complete. These were the raids which had given
trouble to Ostorius at the beginning of his term of office. His
suppression of them, no doubt accompanied by a demand that
Cartimandua should in future keep a firmer hand on her subjects, caused the more insubordinate elements among the Brigantes to turn against the queen herself, and it was this civil war

---

[1] This was pointed out by Professor D. Atkinson, excavator of the forum. His
report has not yet been published; but see Macdonald, *Roman Britain 1914–1928*.

which distracted Ostorius from his campaign in Flintshire. He marched into Brigantia so promptly that he was able to nip the revolt in the bud, punish those who had committed themselves, and pardon the rest.

If the Silures had been as tractable as the Brigantes, Ostorius would soon have been able to resume his forward movement. But conditions here were very different. The pressure on his left wing, directed against the long and lightly held Gloucester-shire sector of the Fosse, was unremitting. Punitive expeditions did not check it; negotiations were fruitless. The fact is that Ostorius was here confronted, not by the turbulent subjects of a friendly or submissive ruler, but by an organized guerrilla campaign, whose brain was Caratacus. Since his defeat on the Medway and his flight to the west Caratacus had done much to restore his reputation. Even before the arrival of Ostorius in 47 he had gained an ascendancy over the Welsh tribes and begun to lead them against the conquered west in a series of systematic raids. For the last two or three years (we are now speaking of events happening about the year 50) he had continued on the same course, achieving a substantial degree of success in spite of the garrisons in the forts of the Fosse. It was, in fact, the standing weakness of the Roman frontier system, by which small police-posts were scattered in a chain or network over the belt of country forming the frontier, that forces so minutely sub-divided were helpless against a mobile and concentrated enemy whose movements were directed by an able soldier. In such warfare the initiative lay with Caratacus, who was the right man to use it; and he was now worshipped by his followers as a national hero, the champion of their liberty, and their heaven-sent leader against the invaders.

The only way in which Ostorius could recover the initiative was by placing a strong force in the lower Severn valley, in advance of the Fosse frontier, where it could take the offensive against the Silures and break up any concentration in their country before it became a danger to the country of the Dobuni. This implied the creation of a legionary fortress on the left bank of the Severn at some point where it could be easily crossed, threatening the hostile right bank somewhat as Cologne or Mainz threatened the right bank of the Rhine. The obvious position for such a fortress was Gloucester, which is still the lowest bridge on the Severn; and here Ostorius quartered the

Second legion, bringing it up from the south where its work of pacifying the Dumnonii was now complete.[1]

But Ostorius had not forgotten the Icenian revolt, and before he undertook his final campaign against Caratacus he decided to safeguard the peace and loyalty of the south-eastern Britons by planting a *colonia* at Colchester, in order that a strong body of time-expired legionaries, living on their allotments of land and ready to take up arms again when occasion demanded, should serve as a garrison for the capital and a threat to neighbouring disaffection. This required that the Britons of the surrounding country should be dispossessed of their land after having believed that their tenure of it was secure; but Ostorius was not a conciliatory governor, and cared little for the feelings of natives when a military question was in the balance. The event showed that his judgement was at fault; the resentment caused by this expropriation created more disaffection than the presence of the colonists could quell. But it was another ten years before that harvest was ready for reaping.

In 51 all was ready for the final blow. The legion at Gloucester, planted there probably a year earlier, had already destroyed Caratacus's freedom of action among the Silures, and he had moved into central and north-western Wales, the country of the Ordovices. When he knew that Ostorius was coming in search of him, he chose his ground with care for a decisive engagement. The place which he chose resembled Caesar's battle-field at Bigbury, transposed into terms of a mountain country. A craggy hill, its summit ringed by a stone-walled fort, overlooked a river; the fort was the centre of the British position, and the rocky slopes between it and the river were to be the scene of the first encounter. Caratacus had learned that a legion in line of battle was practically invincible to the British warriors, with their fluid and shifting formations; but he calculated that no troops, however well drilled, could keep shoulder to shoulder while advancing over such steep and broken ground, and that his skirmishers stood a good chance of repulsing every Roman charge before

---

[1] There is no proof that the Second or any other legion ever had a fortress at Gloucester. But Tacitus's statement that Ostorius placed a legionary fortress in the country of the Silures, or at least on its borders, cannot refer to Caerleon-on-Usk, which was not founded until about 75; and not only is Gloucester the natural place for it, but the shape and size of the Roman town there are exactly those of a legionary fortress, and suggest that this may have been its character in the first phase of its history.

it reached the walls of the fort where his last stand was to be made.

To Ostorius, though his total force, legions and auxiliaries together, far outnumbered that of Caratacus, the British position seemed wellnigh impregnable; and the skill and ardour with which Caratacus was preparing his defences, placing his men, and encouraging every unit to do its best, made the Roman general, as he watched him, realize the mettle and quality of his antagonist. But his men were in high spirits, and their officers keen to lead them; and Ostorius, knowing that it would be a soldiers' battle where everything must depend on the spirit of the troops, resolved to fight. He divided his forces into several columns and launched them simultaneously against different points where the river seemed fordable and the hill easy of access. Their first rush carried them across the stream and far up the slope. At the walls of the fort they were brought to a standstill, galled by a constant fire of missiles from above; but they locked their shields overhead, tore down the stonework, and broke in on every side. The Britons retreated, fighting stubbornly, to the very summit of the hill; here, surrounded and hopelessly outnumbered, the remnant of the defenders at last yielded. Among the prisoners were the wife and daughter of Caratacus, and his brothers, but Caratacus himself had, for the third time, fled from the scene of his defeat and escaped to renew the war elsewhere.

This time his hope was vain. In Wales he had shot his bolt; there remained Brigantia. His only chance was to persuade Cartimandua to abandon her position of a client ruler and raise the standard of rebellion. But Cartimandua was deeply committed to Rome. Not only had she made submission, she had called upon Roman aid against her own rebellious subjects, and knew that if she made Rome her enemy her own throne was forfeit. She threw Caratacus in chains and sent him to Ostorius as a pledge of her loyalty; and the last son of Cunobelinus, after facing with dignity the emperor and populace assembled to triumph over him, ended his days in honourable captivity at Rome.

In Britain, now that the assembled levies of Wales were routed and the fidelity of Brigantia proved, it seemed that the war was over. No more operations in the field were undertaken. Ostorius began to build forts in the country of the Silures, treating them as a conquered tribe that only needed now to be kept quiet. But the Silures were only awaiting an opportunity to avenge their hero; and the dispersal of the Second legion in working-parties over the country-side gave them their chance. At a concerted moment the whole tribe rose. The half-built forts were attacked and destroyed; the legion's *praefectus castrorum* and eight centurions, with many rank and file, fell in bringing support to the hard-pressed working-gangs; and although in spite of these losses the legion beat off the Silurian attack, the assailants did not give in. They hung about the fortress, and watched for an occasion to strike a blow. Once they overwhelmed a foraging-party and cut up the cavalry sent out to rescue them; routed the auxiliary infantry sent in support of the cavalry; and were only put to flight when Ostorius, now present in person, led out his legions, when they escaped into the gathering dusk. This was only one of many engagements in which the Silures, by swift and well-timed strokes, inflicted heavy loss on the Romans and suffered little in return, sometimes carrying off prisoners and plunder, sometimes merely destroying, but always making good their escape before the counter-blow could be delivered. Their spirit was only heightened by learning that the Roman governor had sworn to exterminate the entire tribe; and their example, backed by gifts of plunder and prisoners, had already begun to have its effect upon other tribes hitherto submissive, when Ostorius, worn out with fruitless work and disappointments, died.

Before his successor, Aulus Didius Gallus, could arrive matters had gone from bad to worse. The Second legion had been beaten in the field, and the Silures were carrying destruction far and wide into Roman territory. The first task of Didius was to recover lost ground, clear his subjects' land of Silurian raiding-parties, and re-establish a state of defence in the Severn valley. No sooner had he done this than the Brigantes began to be troublesome. They were the most important of the tribes that had been worked upon by the recent Silurian successes. Cartimandua stood obstinately faithful to Rome; but Venutius, hitherto the partner both of her throne and of her policy, now put himself at the head of a faction to dethrone the queen and turn the whole power of Brigantia against the Romans. Didius hurriedly dispatched a force of auxiliaries, by whose help she succeeded, not without difficulty, in maintaining her position against the rebels; a legion followed, which eventually put down the rising. Thus for the second time Cartimandua was confirmed in her rule by the armed intervention of a Roman propraetor.

Didius governed Britain from about 52 until 58. An elderly and unenterprising man, he was content to protect his province against dangers threatening it from Silurian aggression and Brigantian turbulence without advancing its frontiers; his only forward step consisted in the establishment of a few auxiliary forts, no doubt in the country of the Silures.[1]

The next governor, D. Veranius Nepos, was ambitious and energetic. He came out to Britain resolved to make his mark. He inherited a long tradition of ill success against the Silures, who were quiet but far from cowed; and he determined to settle accounts with them promptly. His premature death, before he had held office for a year, put an end to the insane hope, revealed when his will was read, of completing the conquest of Britain within two years. In 59 he was succeeded by C. Suetonius Paulinus, one of the most distinguished soldiers of the day.

Paulinus's first two years are said to have been marked by conquests and by the establishment of new auxiliary forts. It is possible to infer the direction which this forward movement took. The Brigantes were quiet again under the submissive Cartimandua. The Silures were not finally conquered until half a generation later. It is clear, therefore, that Paulinus, satisfied with the position established on these two flanks by Didius, took up the project of an advance to the Irish sea where some ten years earlier Ostorius had been compelled to lay it down. He had at his disposal the Fourteenth and Twentieth legions, lying at Wroxeter; with these he repeated Ostorius's march through the country of the Degeangli, building forts as he went, and penetrated steadily and deeply into North Wales.

By 61 he had reached the Menai Straits, and in that year he proposed to conquer Anglesey. He built transports for his infantry; his cavalry were to swim or ford the shallows. His crossing was opposed by a strange and awe-inspiring assembly.

---

[1] Tacitus, *Agric.* xiv, § 3. We do not know how far the territory of the Silures extended eastward; I assume that the Severn was the boundary between them and the Dobuni. In any case, the plain on the left bank of the river was almost uninhabited.

Among the groups of warriors women in ceremonial dress, bearing lighted torches, ran hither and thither; behind them were druids, standing by the fires of human sacrifice, their hands raised in prayer for help against the invaders. The Romans at first shrank from so weird a sight; then, recollecting themselves, leapt ashore, fell upon warriors, priests, and women indiscriminately, cut them down, and flung them into their own fires. It was not a battle but a massacre. Beyond lay the fertile plain of Anglesey; but before Paulinus had overrun the whole of it he had news which turned him headlong back.

Prasutagus, king of the Iceni, had submitted to Claudius in the year of the conquest without striking a blow, and had been allowed to retain his throne as a client king. As we have seen, even the resistance of the Iceni to the disarmament ordered by Ostorius did not lose them this status. But in 61 Prasutagus died; and, whatever may have been the intention of Claudius, the policy of Nero was unfavourable to the continuance of client kingdoms; in Pontus and in the Alps, on the death or abdication of their rulers, he abolished them and established in their place the standard type of provincial government. Prasutagus left a widow, Boudicca, and two daughters, and by the old trick of making the emperor a coheir he had attempted to secure his children in their inheritance. But no sooner was he dead than a tempest of calamities burst upon his country. The royal line was treated as extinct and its property confiscated. The emperor's procurator, Decianus Catus, extended the confiscation to the property of all the Icenian nobles. The procurator's servants fell upon the palace, and in the sack Boudicca was flogged and the princesses raped. Nobles and kinsmen of the dead king were seized as slaves. The debts which had been incurred in the process of romanizing the upper classes of Icenian society—a process involving vast purchases from the traders who swarmed over the country in the wake of the legions—were hurriedly called in by panic-stricken financiers, chief among whom was the apostle of mercy and the simple life, the philosopher-statesman Seneca. And in the midst of all this ruin and outrage, the officers of the Roman government appeared, reiterating their twin demands for recruits and tribute-money.

Furious at this breach of faith, terrified at the prospect of endless future oppression, and burning to avenge the insult to their royal house and nobility, the Iceni rose at Boudicca's call. The

rising spread to the Trinovantes, who had neither forgotten nor
forgiven the confiscation of their land by Ostorius when he
founded the colony of Colchester. The rebels resented not only
the ordinary levies and taxes of the empire but, still more, the
special demands upon them made for the upkeep and service
of Claudius's temple, the symbol of Rome's dominance among
them.

And now the price had to be paid for Ostorius's neglect of
administrative detail in his thirst for military success. The disarmament which he had ordered had been a farce: weapons
were in every man's hand. The colony which he had founded
had neglected the most elementary precautions of defence: it
was an open town, where unarmed men retired from the legions
lived at their ease. Too late they heard the mutterings of the
coming storm. Stories were passed from mouth to mouth, how
the buildings of the colony had been seen upside down in a
mirage at sea; how the tide had flowed red with blood and had
left on the beach things like heaps of human bodies; how strange
cries had been heard in council-house and theatre. The statue
of Victory fell from its base. Women screamed suddenly in the
streets.

Paulinus was 250 miles away. There was no legion within
120. The procurator sent 200 half-armed men; the citizens
could muster a handful more. When Boudicca's warriors appeared, on every side at once, there was no thought of defence.
The few who had weapons fled to the temple, whose massive
stone base was the only thing that could resist sword and torch.
The rest of the town went up in flames. When the fire died down
nothing was left except the blackened temple and its few score
defenders, and in two days that was empty.

At Lincoln the Ninth legion was commanded by a gallant
soldier, Quintus Petillius Cerialis. As soon as he heard that the
Iceni had risen, he marched to the rescue of Colchester with a
vexillation of two thousand men. Before he reached it all was
over, and Boudicca had turned to meet him. Swamped by
sheer numbers, the legionaries went down fighting. Only the
cavalry, with Petillius himself, made good their escape, and fled
closely pursued to the very gates of their fortress, where they
shut themselves in and beat off their pursuers.

One other Roman escaped whom Rome could well have
spared. Decianus Catus, the procurator whose rapacity and

violence had been the chief cause of the disaster, did not stay
to share the consequences of his own action. He found a ship,
and crossed over to Gaul.

This was the news that reached Suetonius as he lay encamped
in Anglesey. He had with him, beside auxiliaries, the Fourteenth legion and a part of the Twentieth; the rest was guarding
the fortress at Wroxeter or building roads and forts in North
Wales. His first thought was for his depot and base of supplies
at London; but that was 230 miles away, hardly to be reached
even by the best infantry in a week of forced marches, and in a
week anything might happen. He made a bold decision. Leaving his infantry to follow, and sending a galloper to summon the
Second legion from Gloucester, he rode for London at full speed
with his cavalry. The country was ablaze; at any moment he
might encounter Boudicca's host and be engulfed; but he rode
on, and reached London in safety.

London was a large straggling town, unwalled, full of peaceful traders and military stores. It was utterly incapable of defending itself. But the supply depot was no doubt, according to
custom, entrenched and palisaded, and held by a handful of
troops. If the Second legion arrived in time (and three or four
days' marching should bring it) the non-combatants could be
herded within the ramparts, and Suetonius, with one legion, his
own cavalry, the depot troops, and such citizens as he could arm,
had at least a chance of beating off the Britons until his main
body should come up. There were unknown factors as well.
After chasing Petillius to Lincoln, Boudicca might waste time in
storming auxiliary forts on the line of the Fosse and elsewhere;[1]
in that case his main body would reach London before her.

He had not been more than a day or two in London before
he knew that his hope of defending it was vain. The Britons
were hastening southwards. London was clearly their objective.
And, worst of all, the Second legion failed him. At the moment,
no legate was in command; and the officer in charge, the prefect
of the camp, lost his nerve and refused to face the risk of another
disaster like that which had overtaken the Ninth. For Suetonius
to remain in London, with the force at his disposal, would be
suicide. His duty was clear. He must rejoin his main body, and

---

[1] When he wrote the *Agricola* (xvi, § 1) Tacitus was under the impression that
Boudicca had actually done this; later, in the *Annals* (xiv. 33, *omissis castellis*), he
corrects his earlier statement.

choose time and place for a defensive battle in which, despite the enormous odds against him, there should be a bare possibility of success. He hardened his heart to the prayers of those whom he was leaving to certain death, and taking with him all who could march, set off again up Watling Street.

At Verulam, still less defensible than London, the same ordeal awaited him. He pressed on, and somewhere in the midland forests he met his troops and made his preparations for a last stand. Meanwhile Boudicca reached London. There was no resistance, and no prisoners were taken. To this day, men digging in the city find everywhere the layer of ashes which is all that was left when her men had done their work.[1] Then they turned to Verulam, and that went too. In those three towns it was said that 70,000 perished, by sword or gibbet, on the cross or in the fire.

Suetonius had only 10,000 men to meet a triumphant and confident enemy that far outnumbered him. But he knew that their success would make them reckless, and that if he could avoid being surrounded and keep his men steady all might be well. He chose a battle-field where flank and rear were protected by dense woods, so that the attack must be delivered square on his front; and placing his cavalry where they could strike at the flanks of his assailants, he awaited the event. The Britons, an unwieldy host accompanied by their wives and children in wagons, only cared to trap him on his own ground; they drew up their wagons so as to close the only outlet, and came on to offer battle in front of them. Suetonius did not wait until they were ready to rush him. He charged, foot and horse together, and swept them in confusion against their own wagon-barrier. The surprise was complete, and escape impossible. Men and women, even the wagon-horses, were cut down until the narrow front was choked with the dead. The British host was wiped out as completely as the towns it had destroyed. Boudicca took poison; when the news reached Gloucester, the prefect of the Second fell on his sword.

The revolt was over, but there was much still to do. Reinforcements were sent from Germany and the Ninth legion brought

[1] There is a place in Spitalfields where the bones have been found of people who appear to have been buried by cartloads. Archaeological evidence of date is lacking; but their skulls are like those of Italians of the same time, and it is possible that they were some of the Roman settlers who perished in Boudicca's massacre (Morant, *Biometrika*, xxiii (1931); Buxton, *J.R.S.* xxv (1935), p. 40).

up to strength; and now Suetonius took the field for vengeance. New police-posts were scattered over the country, and the land of the guilty and suspect tribes was ravaged with terrible thoroughness. As the year wore on, famine helped. The rebellion had begun in the spring, and fields had remained unsown, partly because every man had joined the rebels, partly because they had counted on using the vast supplies stored in London for the use of the Roman troops.

While Suetonius thought only of pushing his vengeance to the uttermost, the new procurator, Julius Classicianus, thought of a province ruined and sources of revenue dried up. He begged Nero to recall Suetonius and send out a more humane governor, to practise a policy of conciliation and repair, instead of aggravating the effects of what now could not be undone. The emperor sent a commission of inquiry under his freedman secretary Polyclitus, with orders to settle the differences between Classicianus and Suetonius and to see to the pacification of the rebels; for in spite of the governor's ruthlessness, the tribes had even now made no formal submission, and it was said that they were holding out on the procurator's advice, in hopes of better terms from another governor.

The commission decided that enough punishment had been inflicted. Suetonius, to whose soldierly mind it seemed that clemency towards natives was only a name for weakness, refused to accept the decision; and Nero had to recall him, to his bitter resentment, on the pretext of a mishap to his fleet. The campaign against the rebels was stopped, and in the autumn there arrived a new governor, C. Petronius Turpilianus, fresh from his consulship in the first half of the year, with instructions to conciliate his subjects and keep the peace. These instructions he faithfully obeyed.

In the pages of Tacitus, whose incomparable prose has given us the story of these years, Suetonius is a hero despised and rejected by a wicked emperor, and Classicianus and Turpilianus are abject and self-seeking cowards. But the verdict of Tacitus cannot stand. In the time of Nero, Britain certainly still needed soldiers like Suetonius, but she also needed statesmen to guide and foster the peaceful life of her Romanized tribes: *parcere subiectis* as well as *debellare superbos*. The story of Caratacus is the story of a gallant losing fight, honourable alike to victors and vanquished. The story of Boudicca from first to last is a story of horror and shame, a story of things that ought never to have happened. For the people of Britain, Caratacus has always and justly been a national hero. It may seem harsh to refuse the same title to Boudicca. But the real hero of her story is Classicianus, who stood up to Suetonius in his hour of victory as the champion of the British people. Classicianus died before he laid down his office, and his ashes were laid to rest in London. His tomb[1] is among the possessions of the English nation; and in honouring its stones we are honouring the man by whose work that story, opening in violence and wrong, was made to end in the establishment of a lasting peace.

[1] One part of it, found on Tower Hill in 1852, has long been in the British Museum, where it has now been joined by another piece of the inscription, found in 1935, which makes its identification certain. Cf. *Antiquaries Journal*, xvi (1936), pp. 1, 208.

VII

FROM BOUDICCA TO AGRICOLA

FOR ten years after Boudicca's rebellion history tells us little of British affairs. But its very silence is informative. Tacitus, who dismisses these years in a few scornful sentences,[1] neglects them because they were a time of peace, when Roman arms were gaining no glory in frontier-wars, and when Roman governors were disgracing their office by conciliating their subjects and allowing their sword to rust unused. If warfare is but an instrument of policy, and if the end of policy is the establishment of peace and prosperity, the achievements of Petronius Turpilianus and of Trebellius Maximus, who succeeded him in 63, were more important than those of the soldier-governors whom Tacitus praised. But of these achievements in detail we know nothing. Hints, hardly amounting to proofs, are offered by archaeology of peaceful development and growing civilization in the British country-side at this time. The towns destroyed by Boudicca were rebuilt and others enlarged. It was during this decade that a cautious administration and financial economy allowed the conquered Britons to settle down into contentment and prosperity, to recover from the wounds that had both excited and accompanied the Boudiccan rebellion, and to lay a foundation for the more spectacular advance in romanization which is associated with the name of Agricola.

The military situation had reached a point of equilibrium. In the west the flames of the fire lit by Caratacus had died down. Wales, still unconquered, was quiet, no longer threatening the security of the lands east of the Severn. Brigantia was a client kingdom. The Second legion at Gloucester, the Fourteenth and Twentieth at Wroxeter, and the Ninth at Lincoln (the evidence for placing them at these sites has already been considered) remained stationary, and afforded with their attached auxiliaries an ample garrison for the frontier-line.

If anything, the garrison was excessive. In 67, when Nero was planning a great expedition to the East, he was so well satisfied with the results of his peaceful policy in Britain that he judged

---

[1] *Agric.* xvi, §§ 3–6. In the *Histories* he mentions Britain, with one exception (iii. 45), only so far as concerns the intervention or non-intervention of its troops in the civil wars.

three legions enough for its needs, and withdrew the Fourteenth, which had won great fame by bearing the brunt of the campaign against Boudicca, to be part of his expeditionary force.

But Nero's days were numbered. In the following spring Julius Vindex, a romanized Gaul, set in motion the forces that were to destroy him. Governor of one of the Gaulish provinces, he raised a revolt against Nero and approached the army commanders of the west for support. One of them, Sergius Sulpicius Galba, legate of Hispania Tarraconensis, was to be the new emperor. It is hardly possible but that Vindex should have appealed to the governor of Britain as well; and, if so, this appeal may have been the occasion of the trouble, briefly recorded by Tacitus, that arose between Trebellius Maximus and his legions. Trebellius was a man of no military experience, who in his pursuit of peaceful administration had allowed his troops to become idle and undisciplined. A mutiny broke out, in which Trebellius at first barely escaped the swords of the legionaries, and finally, giving way to their demands, resumed for a time a nominal and ineffective control.[1] Such an event might have been caused by an intention on Trebellius's part of throwing in his lot with Vindex, and a refusal by his legions to follow him. In any case, during the later course of the civil wars it was often said that the army of Britain would never appear on the Continent, as if its decision on that point had been once for all expressed.

When Galba's short reign had begun and ended, and when Otho was being attacked by Vitellius, the British legions could no longer ignore the very existence of the civil war. The Fourteenth, by now in Pannonia or Dalmatia, declared for Otho; but the troops in Britain joined the party of Vitellius; and now once more trouble broke out between the governor and his legions. The ringleader against him was one Roscius Coelius, legate of the Twentieth. Trebellius accused Roscius of insubordination and lax discipline; Roscius accused the governor, whose financial policy made him unpopular with the men, of impoverishing the troops. From the legions, disaffection spread to the auxiliaries, and the governor was compelled to leave his province and take refuge with Vitellius. Once more, it is a

---

[1] Tacitus has two different stories: the above in *Agric.* xvi, § 5, another in *Hist.* i. 60. In combining them I follow Anderson, *Agric.*, loc. cit.; but perhaps the *Hist.* version corrects the *Agric.*; cf. p. 101 note.

reasonable conjecture that Trebellius had wished to bring his legions across the Channel to the support of the Vitellian armies, and that their refusal was the cause of his flight. Though nominally on the side of Vitellius, not a man from the army of Britain took part in the campaign which set him on the throne.

That campaign culminated in the battle of Bedriacum, near Cremona, in April 69. The victory of the Vitellian armies was complete. A mere vexillation of the Fourteenth had been present to share the defeat of the Othonians, and the legion as a whole, arriving in Italy soon afterwards, claimed to be still unbeaten. Rather to get rid of it than because it was needed there, Vitellius sent it back to Britain, sending out at the same time a new governor, Vettius Bolanus. Since Trebellius's flight the province had been governed by the three legates of legions, Roscius Coelius putting himself at their head. The legion went, not without recalcitrance. Presumably it returned to its old quarters. A later tombstone at Lincoln naming one of its veterans is not evidence that in this, its second, residence in Britain it shared that fortress with the Ninth.

Bolanus governed Britain in the same peaceful manner as his two predecessors. But conditions there were beginning to change. Cartimandua had divorced her husband Venutius and married his armour-bearer Vellocatus, and, presuming on the high favour she enjoyed with Rome since her betrayal of Caratacus, had attempted to impose her new consort upon the tribe as partner of her throne. But Venutius was a popular figure; now Caratacus was gone he was regarded as the first warrior in Britain; and the Brigantes were indignant at the queen's treatment of him and her preference for a squire. The tribal leaders joined him in revolt against Cartimandua and repudiation of the Roman alliance. For the third time Cartimandua appealed to a Roman governor for help. Bolanus sent to her aid a mixed force of auxiliaries, who after severe fighting rescued the queen but left her realm in the hands of Venutius. Brigantia, after being a precarious ally of Rome for twenty years and more, was now an open enemy, and the military equilibrium of the British frontier was at an end.

At the same moment storm-clouds in the east were threatening Vitellius. In the summer of 69 Titus Flavius Vespasianus, governor of Judaea, who had commanded a legion in Britain under Claudius, was declared emperor, and his partisans began to march upon Italy, gathering legions as they went. Vitellius, collecting forces to resist them, took what he could from Britain. From the Fourteenth he had nothing to hope; it was actually in communication with Vespasian's friends; but he had already some British troops with him, for when he marched into Italy after Bedriacum he was accompanied by 8,000 men from the Second, Ninth, and Twentieth. He pressed Bolanus for auxiliaries as well, but the situation on the Brigantian marches was now such that none could be spared, and Bolanus answered evasively.

While the first of the Flavian armies was threatening Italy from the north-east, its commander, Antonius Primus, sent a message to the Batavian chief, Julius Civilis, requesting him to prevent the legions of the lower Rhine from coming to the help of Vitellius. Civilis promptly organized a rebellion which, beginning among his own tribesmen, soon had the whole Rhineland aflame. Meanwhile Antonius entered Italy, met the Vitellians before Cremona, routed them, stormed their camp, and sacked the city. By December Antonius was in Rome and Vitellius dead. One of the new emperor's first tasks was to put down the rising of Civilis; in this work a leading part was taken by Q. Petillius Cerialis, a man both formerly and afterwards celebrated in British history, and by the Fourteenth legion, recalled from Britain for that express purpose and never again sent back there.

Vespasian's rule was accepted in Britain without serious demur. His old corps, the Second legion, was eagerly in his favour and carried the others with it. For the moment, Bolanus was left in command. Though a Vitellian, he had shown himself a lukewarm one, more intent on governing his province than on fighting the private battles of the emperor who had appointed him. But Vespasian had no intention of leaving him there permanently. The fall of Cartimandua had radically changed the British situation. The largest tribe in Britain, separated only by the Humber and Trent from Roman territory, had become hostile, and was being ruled by a tried and honoured warrior. In such conditions it was useless attempting to maintain the peace that had lasted for nearly ten years. The wisest course would be to reinforce the army of Britain, to replace Bolanus by a first-rate soldier, and to take the offensive against Brigantia at the earliest possible moment, namely, the moment when the revolt of Civilis should be at an end.

That event furnished both the troops and the man. Vespasian himself had, during the civil war, raised a new legion, II Adiutrix, from the marines of the fleet at Ravenna, when it came over to his side; in the Batavian rising this legion fought under Cerialis against Civilis, and after the final battle lay for a time in camp at Neumagen. It was not needed for the permanent defence of the Rhine, and by the spring of 71 it was ready to be used elsewhere. As for a new governor, especially appointed for a war against the Brigantes, nobody could be more fit than Cerialis himself. As a former commandant of the legion at Lincoln he knew Britain, and especially the north; he had fought there with conspicuous gallantry in the Boudiccan war; lately he had shown initiative and courage in his work for Vespasian during the last weeks of Vitellius's reign; and finally he had crushed Civilis and brought a dangerous and expensive revolt to an end. As soon as he was at liberty, therefore, Vespasian sent both him and the Second Adiutrix to Britain.

For three years Petillius Cerialis governed Britain. During that time he pressed the war against the Brigantes with ruthless energy, and ended, says Tacitus, by either annexing or overrunning a great part of their country. The words are vague; and other sources can add little. Excavations have shown that the earliest Roman occupation at York goes back to about this time, and make it very probable that, at the beginning of his governorship, Cerialis either moved the Ninth legion bodily to York, lodging it there in a new permanent fortress, or else established there a camp of the kind that antiquaries call semi-permanent, which a large force might use as its advanced base during a campaign. Perhaps a semi-permanent camp for the Ninth legion was constructed at York in 71, followed by a permanent fortress a year or two later. In any case, we may ascribe to Cerialis the beginning of what was to be, until the close of the Roman age, the principal military centre of northern Britain.

The choice of York for this centre was a good one. Up to that point the Ouse is navigable to vessels of considerable size; and there the vale of York is crossed by a ridge of relatively high ground, safely above flood-level, dividing the low-lying forest and swamp to southward from other marshy ground to northward. This ridge is the true centre for all offensive strategy in north-eastern England. It is not a defensive position; it is not a position at which to block the movements of invading enemies;

it is a position from which to strike. Two natural lines of communication run north and south along the vale of York, both
used by Roman roads: one on the west, from Doncaster by
Wetherby to Catterick, one on the east, from Brough-on-Humber
by Stamford Bridge to Northallerton. York lies midway between them, and is the only point from which both are easily
accessible. Road traffic between York and Lincoln, or between
York and the north, can use either indifferently. Eastward all
the Wolds and Cleveland hills are within two days' march; westward the Aire gap, the easiest of all the Pennine passes, gives
direct access to the Lancashire plain.

Another large camp of the same period has been identified
and partly dug seventeen miles farther to the north-east, at Malton. This lies in the very centre of those eastern uplands which
in prehistoric times were the richest part of Yorkshire;[1] and a
general intending to cripple the Brigantes by ravaging their best
agricultural land might very well have established himself here
even before he seized the strategic position on the Ouse.

Elsewhere no certain traces of Petillius's campaigns have been
found. The Brigantian power was of such a kind that an effective blow at its heart would paralyse its whole body. Its warriors
once decisively beaten, its richest lands in central and eastern
Yorkshire occupied, and its fortress at Stanwick destroyed, further resistance was impossible. To a skilled and experienced
soldier, with forces enough at his disposal, this was no impossible
task in three years' fighting; and in this sense, even if he left
much of their outlying territory untouched, the conquest of
Brigantia was complete by the time Cerialis laid down office.

Thus triumphantly begun, the forward movement went on.
Ever since the time of Ostorius Scapula, whose frontier on its
northern wing had now been left far behind, the Brigantes and
Silures had been the two chief dangers to the security of Roman
Britain. The Brigantes conquered, it was the turn of the Silures.
In 74 Cerialis was succeeded by another able and energetic
governor, Sextus Julius Frontinus, a man greatly respected by
his contemporaries, and still represented by his writings on warfare, on surveying, and, in particular, on the water-supply of
Rome, a service which owed much to the vigorous reorganization
and reforms carried out when he was at its head. Petillius, so
far as we can envisage him, was a pure soldier; Frontinus was

[1] On this district, see Richmond, *Arch. Aeliana*, ser. 4, xiii (1936), pp. 325-7.

a man of high distinction as lawyer, engineer, and administrator;
and we may be sure that during his governorship there was
progress in the political and economic life of Britain as well as
in the military affairs of which alone information has reached us.

Even that information is scanty enough: a single sentence, in
which Tacitus writes that Frontinus 'conquered the powerful
and warlike Silures, overcoming both the valour of his enemies
and the difficulty of the ground'; and a later passage in which
he tells us that the Ordovices of central and north-western
Wales had, before Agricola's arrival, almost annihilated a cavalry
regiment stationed in their territory, and that a single short
campaign by Agricola sufficed to reduce them. This implies
that Frontinus, in addition to overpowering the Silures, undertook considerable operations farther afield, planted garrisons
among the Ordovices, and by the end of his governorship left
Wales as a whole conquered, though still able to rebel.

Archaeology adds confirmation and a few details. Excavation
in the legionary fortress at Caerleon-on-Usk has given ample
proof that in its original form, with clay ramparts and wooden
buildings, it was built about 75. As Cerialis pushed his right-
wing legion forward from Lincoln to York, planting it in the
centre of the tribal territory he was attacking, so, it is clear,
Frontinus moved up his left-wing legion from Gloucester to
Caerleon in the heart of the Silurian country. Here again the
choice of a site was well made, and the new fortress became a
permanent feature of Roman Britain. The tidal Usk, like the
Ouse, gave an easy approach for shipping. Alternative roads,
either by the coast or inland through Monmouth, led in two
days' march to Gloucester. Wroxeter lay not more than twice
that distance by easy ways to northward. As an offensive centre,
Caerleon lies on a coastal road leading into Pembrokeshire and
commanding all the valleys of the southern Welsh hills, and in
the vale of Usk, the best of all lines for penetrating the Silurian
hinterland. 'No other site in south-eastern Wales is comparable in
respect of general accessibility from every point of the compass.'[1]

A few miles to the east, a hill-fort in Llanmelin Wood marks
the probable site of the chief Silurian stronghold. The settlement here, founded by Celtic colonists from across the Severn,
apparently in the second century before Christ, was subsequently
enlarged, and towards the middle of the first century A.D. its

---

[1] R. E. M. Wheeler, *Prehistoric and Roman Wales* (1925), p. 223.

defences were improved. About the year 75 occupation ceases abruptly, and never begins again except for the building of a few medieval huts in and about the site. At about the same time the first traces of occupation appear in the town of Caerwent on the plain below. Frontinus, when he conquered the Silures, did not destroy the tribe as a political entity, but built them a new capital where, under the eyes of the legion, they could learn to live like Romans and manage their own affairs in their own city, henceforth called Venta[1] of the Silures.

Westward and northward Frontinus built roads and studded them with forts. The best known of these, dated with fair certainty by excavation to his rule, is the Gaer near Brecon in the vale of Usk: 'A pleasant, sheltered place where a permanent garrison might live with tolerable safety and in ample comfort.'[2] Another of his posts has been identified as far afield as Pembrokeshire. Other forts to south and north of Brecon, Coelbren in Brecknock and Castell Collen in Radnorshire, are probably of the same time; and it is likely that further digging would give similar results at many other forts in South Wales.

To Frontinus, in view of what Tacitus tells us, we may also ascribe the early Flavian forts in the upper Severn valley, marking a line of penetration from Wroxeter into the country of the Ordovices: the Forden Gaer near Montgomery, and Caersws, the strategic key to central Wales, where to-day the roads divide that lead left and right of Plynlimmon to Aberystwyth and Machynlleth. Even in the extreme north, Caerhun and Segontium by Carnarvon are archaeologically dated either to Frontinus or very soon afterwards: but here the evidence points, on the whole, rather to Agricola than to his predecessor.

There is a curious contrast between the abundance of archaeological evidence for the work of Frontinus in Wales and its paucity for that of Cerialis in Brigantia. To Cerialis we can ascribe only the fortress at York and the great camp at Malton; not a single *castellum* dating from his campaigns has been identified; whereas Frontinus can claim not only the Caerleon fortress but, with tolerable certainty, half a dozen *castella* as well. Comparisons of this kind are dangerous; the difference may very well

---

[1] Venta is a common Celtic town-name, but its meaning is unknown. It cannot be connected with the plausibly identical Spanish *venta*, an inn.

[2] R. E. M. Wheeler, *The Roman Fort near Brecon* (Cymmrodorion Society, 1926), p. 69.

be due to the excellence of the work done by Welsh archaeologists at Roman military sites in the last ten years; but it is at least an interesting fact that, until the present time, only a single auxiliary fort (Margidunum) earlier than Frontinus has been discovered in Britain, although scores must have existed; and a possible reason might be that Frontinus, trained engineer that he was, introduced into Britain a better and more solidly constructed type of *castellum*, the type, in fact, of which Agricolan examples are well known and widely distributed. Of Agricola's *castella*, says Tacitus, not one was ever taken either by storm or by siege, so skilfully were they placed and so well provisioned; and it is conceivable that some part of his success in this matter may have been due to his adoption of improvements originally made by Frontinus.

It was late in the summer of 78, when Frontinus was succeeded by Gnaeus Julius Agricola, the third of Vespasian's fighting governors. His fame as a figure in British history rests in great part, doubtless, on his own merits; but in great part on the life which his son-in-law Tacitus wrote of him; so that it is difficult for the historian of to-day to keep a just proportion between his achievements and those of his predecessors, *carent quia vate sacro*. Nevertheless it must be attempted.

Agricola, born in the highly romanized Provence, had already spent much of his life in Britain. He had served there as a young man under Suetonius Paulinus, had fought through the Boudiccan rebellion, and had won a good name as a zealous officer, keen to learn all he could of the province and its army. He gained experience of administration in Asia Minor and Rome, and at the beginning of Vespasian's reign went back to Britain to command the Twentieth legion, suspected of disaffection. Under Bolanus, we are told, he learned to repress his thirst for military fame, but later commanded his legion in the Brigantian wars of Cerialis, after which he was sent to govern Aquitania and then, after a brief consulship, became governor of Britain. For all Tacitus's praise, he remains a somewhat unattractive character: an able man, evidently, both in the field and in administration; a man of sound judgement, and incorruptible; but cold, calculating, obsequious to authority, yet grudging in his submission; incapable of inspiring enthusiasm like Cerialis or reverence like Frontinus; in his last years, after a longer term of office in Britain than most, a man with a grievance, resenting his recall, living in gloomy retirement for safety's sake, and nursing his spleen.

His achievements in Britain were genuine and important; but the rhetoric of Tacitus has tended to exaggerate them, and to an incautious reader appears to give him credit for what in reality was the work of his predecessors. It is only with an effort that we recognize how completely Cerialis had already paralysed Brigantia and how nearly complete was Frontinus's conquest of Wales by the time Agricola reached Britain. His first campaign, late in the summer of 78, finished the work of Frontinus by conquering Anglesey and massacring the Ordovices; his second, in 79, overran Brigantia and sprinkled it with a network of forts. That is the year of the inscription on the leaden waterpipes of the legionary fortress at Chester; and the construction of the fortress itself should most probably be dated to the beginning of Agricola's governorship, the Twentieth legion and the Second Adiutrix being now placed there in preparation for his northward advance. His real forward movement began in 80;[1] in the next year he completed the conquest of the Lowlands as far as the Forth and Clyde, studding the country as he went with *castella*, built in timber and earthwork, some meant for permanent police-forts, others designed to be held only until the tide of conquest should have flowed on.

At the Forth–Clyde line he halted for a summer, partly for some operation overseas which the text of Tacitus does not sufficiently describe, partly to create a naval base (perhaps at Ravenglass on the Cumberland coast) for a projected invasion of Ireland which was never accomplished. In 83 he moved forward again, marching into central Scotland by way of Stirling and encamping here and there upon navigable rivers in order to have his army supported and supplied by his fleet. Tacitus ascribes this movement to fear of attack from the Caledonian tribes, now mustering in league to oppose him; but it is not to be thought that Agricola would otherwise have been content to make the Forth–Clyde line a permanent frontier. His ambition was certainly to conquer all Britain. What Tacitus means is that this threatened hostile concentration induced him to cancel his plans for an Irish campaign and proceed at once to take the offensive in the north.

---

[1] *Novas gentes*, Tacitus, *Agric.* xxii, § 1, implies that until then he had been going over old ground.

Agricola's plan for this summer was to carry a chain of posts a certain distance along Strathmore, the great valley that separates the Perthshire mountains from the Ochil and Sidlaw hills: then, resting this line on the sea (doubtless on the Tay near Perth) to strike from it north-eastward up Strathmore itself and north-westward up the valleys of the Earn and upper Tay. He meant to establish himself in this offensive position before the summer of 83 was at an end; and, hoping in this way to anticipate the enemy's concentration, he divided his forces into three parts in order to push forward the work of occupying and fortifying the entire position. In this he was successful, despite a dangerous attack upon the Ninth legion, whose failure did nothing to discourage the Caledonians. Next year their concentration was complete. The Mons Graupius, where it took place, has never been successfully identified. If the above account of Agricola's doings in 83 is correct, the effect of that year's campaign had been to force upon the Caledonians a place for their concentration outside the area now occupied by the Roman armies, that is, outside the region limited on the north by Inchtuthill, the Roman fortress at the confluence of the Tay and Isla. Since the words of Tacitus[1] suggest that it took place not very far from the sea, it would therefore be natural to place the Mons Graupius in or near the north-eastern part of Strathmore, near Forfar or Brechin; and the importance of this region in early Caledonian history is well enough attested by the existence, close to Brechin, of two great hill-forts, the White Caterthun and the Brown Caterthun, 'among the largest in Scotland, placed on rival summits of an isolated ridge . . . with the Highlands of Forfar at their back and the Lowlands of the same county at their feet'.[2]

It was late in the summer when Agricola fought his famous battle and destroyed the assembled armies of Caledonia. No time was left to establish police-posts in the country of the defeated tribes: all he could do was to march, ostentatiously at leisure, through as much of it as possible, while making his way back to winter quarters, receiving hostages from some, and upon others content to leave an impression of his might. Meanwhile his fleet cruised northwards and ravaged the coast to its farthest extremity before it, too, returned to port for the winter.

[1] *Praemissa classe*, *Agric.* xxix, § 2.
[2] Christison, *Early Fortifications in Scotland* (1898), p. 256.

In the following year Agricola was recalled. Tacitus alleges that Domitian cut his term of office short from jealousy, fearing a comparison between Agricola's genuine success in Britain and his own derisory claims to success in Germany, and thinking it dangerous that a private citizen should thus outstrip an emperor in military renown. Modern writers, estimating more justly the importance of Domitian's German campaigns and recognizing that Agricola had already enjoyed more than the customary length of office in Britain, have preferred to think that the emperor, having obtained independent advice about the prospects of further conquest, judged it impossible for Agricola to carry out his programme, and recalled him in order to prevent further waste of the empire's resources. This would explain Agricola's resentment, but it demands a very unnatural rendering of the famous phrase in the *Histories* of Tacitus, *perdomita Britannia et statim omissa*. When Tacitus writes that Britain was completely conquered and then let go, he must on this view mean that it was not conquered, but could have been conquered had Agricola not been recalled.

Taken literally, the words of Tacitus imply that the battle of Mons Graupius was a decisive victory, a final destruction of the enemy's armed forces, and the end of the war. There is plain evidence that both he and Agricola so regarded it. Not only in the *Histories*, but in the *Agricola* itself, the statement is explicitly made that Agricola completed the conquest of Britain; and in the governor's own speech before the battle he is made to say that this conquest would be finished by that day's victory.[1] Moreover, the opinion cannot have been peculiar to Agricola and his friends. It is clear from precedents that, according to the generally received theory of the time, a general who had invaded an enemy's country, found and destroyed his armed forces, and planted permanent garrisons at strategic points there, was regarded as having conquered it even without overrunning and pacifying it in detail. To recognize this we need go back no farther than Cerialis and Frontinus. Cerialis was recalled after breaking the resistance of the Brigantes and establishing a legion at York. There is no suggestion that he had a grievance because he was not left in Britain until all Brigantia was overrun.

---

[1] Tacitus, *Agric.* x, § 1: 'tum primum perdomita est'; ibid. xxxiii, § 3: 'finem Britanniae non fama nec rumore, sed castris et armis tenemus: inventa Britannia et subacta.'

His position with regard to Brigantia in 74 was, in the eyes of contemporaries, exactly analogous to that of Agricola ten years later. Similarly, Frontinus at his recall had done all the decisive work towards the conquest of Wales; it is not suggested that Vespasian injured him by leaving the final settlement to Agricola. In short, Domitian treated Agricola strictly according to precedent in recalling him after his decisive victory, and not ungenerously in giving him seven years in which to achieve it. There is no reason to doubt the sincerity of the welcome which, according to Tacitus himself, he had ready for his returned servant.

But if Agricola, Domitian, Tacitus, and all other contemporaries thought it a decisive victory, it is even more difficult for modern historians to agree with their opinion than to realize that they sincerely held it. This is, no doubt, because Scotland has so often and so successfully resisted conquest that we find it hard to believe in the possibility of what, to these Romans, seemed easy. But the theatre of Scottish national resistance has always been the Lowlands. When they have been penetrated, when southern and central Scotland have been conquered, history does not teach us that the Highlands can resist by themselves. The nearest military parallel to the situation of Agricola after Mons Graupius is that of Cumberland after Culloden; and if Cumberland's pacification of the Highlands was a grim business, that was because the political situation was complicated by partisanships and loyalties which had no existence in the time of Calgacus. If, as seems probable, the Caledonia of those days was ruled by a Celtic warrior-aristocracy like that of the Brigantes, whose peasantry had little kinship in culture and tradition with themselves, a single decisive battle entailing the destruction of that aristocracy would be the end of resistance.

Perdomita Britannia is, therefore, no rhetorical exaggeration. It expresses accurately the opinion of Romans at the time; and, so far as we can judge, that opinion was correct. Whether Agricola's other opinion was correct, that Ireland could have been conquered with a single legion and a modest force of auxiliaries, is another question altogether. Agricola had never been to Ireland. But his success as a soldier entitles his opinion to be heard with more respect than it has commonly received.

Agricola's real grievances against Domitian were two: that he

was never employed again, and that Caledonia, which he had
conquered, was allowed to slip out of Rome's grasp. On the
first head we can say nothing. As to the second, the main facts
are clear. They are, that Agricola's military dispositions in
Scotland were designed by him as a base for further advance;
that this advance, if made forthwith, should, according to the
best judges, have been a simple matter, entailing no more pitched
battles; and that it was not made. It is equally clear that Domitian's reason for not making it was the concentration of his
military efforts elsewhere, on the Rhine and the Danube, efforts
which, about the year 86, entailed the removal of the Second
Adiutrix to Moesia and the permanent reduction of the British
army to three legions. By this change of policy Agricola's wave
of Caledonian conquest was frozen into immobility the very
moment it had broken; and he ended his days feeling, truly
enough, that his crowning victory had been made fruitless.

The details are far less clear. Historians once believed that
immediately upon Agricola's recall much of Scotland, if not the
whole of it, was evacuated. Early in the present century, excavation at Newstead in the Tweed valley proved that here at
least there had been a garrison for some years after that date.
Following up this clue, Sir George Macdonald[1] showed that the
same thing had happened farther north, at Camelon, Ardoch,
and Inchtuthill. He also showed that this continued occupation
had not been undisputed, but that these forts had from time to
time been roughly handled by native risings. How long this
state of things continued is not yet settled beyond dispute. In
his latest work he regards it as having probably outlasted the
reign of Domitian by at least eight or ten years, that is, until at
least 104–6; others, arguing from the absence of characteristic
Trajanic pottery, date its close before the end of the first century.[2] It would be more important than settling the exact date
when Agricola's dispositions finally broke down if we could
know what exactly they were. The analogy of earlier conquests
compels us to believe that a legionary fortress, planted somewhere in Caledonian territory, was an integral part of his plan.
As long as there were four legions in Britain, this was possible;

---

[1] 'The Agricolan Occupation of North Britain', in *J.R.S.* ix (1919). Cf.
Macdonald on the Newstead evidence in Curle, *A Roman Frontier Post* (1911),
pp. 401, 415.
[2] Macdonald, *The Roman Wall in Scotland*, ed. 2 (1934), p. 2; Pryce and Birley,
'The First Roman Occupation of Scotland', in *J.R.S.* xxv (1935).

but we do not know whether a legion was ever placed there, either by Agricola or by his successor. If it was, it must have been withdrawn at latest in 86 when the British legions were reduced to three. At Inchtuthill, however, the 'great camp' of fifty acres, with its twenty-foot ditch, its massive rampart, its built roads, and its wooden hutments, forcibly recalls the permanent legionary *hiberna* of the Flavian period; and although further excavation is needed to assess its meaning more accurately, the most probable explanation of the discoveries made there is that it was the fortress of a legion, built in the year 83 or 84 and evacuated either on Agricola's recall or, at latest, in 86.[1] Even then the place was not deserted, for there are traces of an auxiliary garrison living on the same site after the abandonment of the great camp. But if this reading of the evidence is correct, the withdrawal of a legion from Strathmore, with its inevitable result in the fatal weakening of the whole position there, was the virtual evacuation of Caledonia.[2]

[1] The excavations (1901) are reported in *Proc. Soc. Ant. Scot.* xxxvi. Sir George Macdonald, reconsidering their significance in his paper of 1919 already quoted, concludes that the great camp was 'the winter quarters of a small army . . . in all probability Agricola's' (*J.R.S.* xix. 115), and kindly informs the writer that his meaning was, and is, to explain Inchtuthill as a permanent fortress.

[2] In this chapter I have opted for the later of the two datings (77 or 78) for the beginning of Agricola's term of office in Britain and consequently (since its internal chronology is fixed) for all its incidents. I have been induced to do so by Mr. Eric Birley's pointing out to me that by *Agric.* xxxix the battle of Mons Graupius was fought after Domitian's triumph over the Chatti, which must be dated late in 83 (*Camb. Anc. Hist.* xi (1936), p. 164, note 2).

VIII

THE MAKING OF THE FRONTIER

OF British affairs for a generation after Agricola's recall ancient writers tell us little or nothing. During the latter part of Domitian's reign a governor of Britain, Sallustius Lucullus, was put to death for daring to call a new type of lance by his own name; apart from that scrap of scandal preserved by Suetonius, we are left to read the story as best we can from archaeological evidence until the accession of Hadrian.

Inscriptions give us the names of several governors. In 98, the second year of Trajan's reign, a certain Nepos, successor perhaps of the ill-fated Lucullus, had just laid down that office and had been followed by T. Avidius Quietus, whom we know as a friend of the younger Pliny. By January 103 the governor of Britain was L. Neratius Marcellus, brother of the distinguished jurist Neratius Priscus whom Trajan, according to Roman gossip, intended for his own successor on the Imperial throne. Marcellus's term of office was then probably nearing its end. The next name is that of Q. Pompeius Falco, who was presumably the first governor appointed by Hadrian, and was immediately followed by A. Platorius Nepos, who supervised the building of the Wall.

Another officer of some importance, about the same time, is a commander of the legion at Chester, T. Pomponius Mammilianus Rufus Antistianus Funisulanus Vettonianus. The inscription mentioning him used to be dated to the late second century, but this is an error;[1] and the officer named by it was perhaps a brother or relative of Pliny's friend Mamilianus, who was consul in 100, if not the same man.

Nothing can be said as to the doings of any one of Trajan's governors. But excavation has told us something about military developments during that reign, though it is not easy to put the details together into a coherent picture. The focus of interest falls partly on Trajan's Dacian and eastern wars, partly on his internal administration; and nothing happened in Britain,

---

[1] As Haverfield saw: *Ephemeris Epigraphica*, ix. 535. The inscription (*C.I.L.* vii. 164) closely resembles in style others from northern Britain which date from Hadrian's reign: e.g. *C.I.L.* vii. 371, 373, set up by the Hadrianic garrison of Maryport.

whether in peace or war, comparable with Trajan's great undertakings elsewhere. Conqueror though he was, he did not regard the resumption of Agricola's northern conquests as an object worthy of his attention; on that adventure he accepted Domitian's verdict, and his military policy in Britain is best understood as an anticipation of Hadrian's: the policy of establishing a permanent frontier and renouncing all conquest beyond it.

The final result of this policy, as consummated by Hadrian, was to cut Great Britain in two by means of a continuous rampart and ditch, garrisoned by troops housed in forts along its line and provided also with fortlets at regular intervals, the so-called milecastles, and signal-towers between them. But before considering the steps by which this final result came about, it is necessary to understand the Roman conception of a frontier and to know something about the history of the Imperial frontiers in general.

To the Romans the continuous lines of fortification which are so much the most conspicuous feature of the British frontier were no necessary part of a frontier as such. Their word for a frontier, *limes*, originally meant a pathway; in military usage it means the strip of cleared and open land in which runs the *via*, the made and metalled road: and hence it comes to mean that strip with everything which it contains, road, forts, and signal-towers. Thus *limes* becomes the regular word for a military road complete with all these appurtenances, irrespectively of the direction in which it runs, whether forwards to the front of one's position, or transversely across it. This is the stage which the development of the word's meaning has reached by the earliest years of the empire, when military writers freely use it to signify a strategic road driven forwards into the enemy's country, like Agricola's road through Northumberland into central Scotland. But in the Flavian age, when frontiers began to be more thought of than conquests, it comes to bear a special sense, the sense of a frontier, conceived as a road of this same type running transversely and marking the limit of Roman occupation.

Throughout the history of the Roman empire, the Imperial frontiers for the most part retained this character. In Africa and in the east there are none of any other type. But often, where it was convenient, such frontier-roads were placed on the bank of a great river, which gave at once a convenient line of demarcation and a certain obstacle to unauthorized crossing of the line. Augustus, who first took in hand the organization of a frontier system for the Roman world, used the Rhine and the Danube in this way; his attempted conquests in Germany were designed to replace the Rhine by the Elbe.

During the German wars of the early first century, the Romans encountered a different type of frontier. Some of the German tribes surrounded their territory with continuous earthworks. One of these, found in recent excavations, proves to have been an earthen bank thirty feet wide and faced in front with a massive upright revetment of timber. Similar tribal boundaries, as we have seen in an earlier chapter, were introduced into Britain by the Belgae in the first century before Christ. These works appear to have given the Romans the idea of adding upon occasion to their own standard type of frontier, the fortified road, a new feature, namely, a continuous rampart. Such an addition never became general. We have certain knowledge of its existence only in three cases: from the Rhine to the Danube in upper Germany and Raetia; across the Dobruja from the Danube to the Black Sea; and in Britain.

Compound frontiers of this type, combining the idea of a road with its forts and signal-towers and the idea of a continuous obstacle, began to be constructed in the reign of Domitian. To this reign, and probably to the years 87–9, belongs the great earth rampart of the Dobruja, a work about 50 feet thick and still standing in places as much as twelve feet high. It is furnished with an extraordinary number of forts, surrounded by turf ramparts, which have been occupied only for a short time and then superseded by others smaller in size and fewer in number; and alike in the massiveness of its construction and the strength of its garrison it suggests an emergency measure following on a military disaster, which has been identified with the defeat of Cornelius Fuscus in 87. The earthwork itself is reasonably explained as an enlarged imitation of an earlier one, following almost the same line, which is probably a tribal boundary. The whole line must have been abandoned when, at the beginning of the second century, Trajan planted a legion sixty miles north of it, at Troesmis on the bank of the Danube.

It was Domitian also who first erected a continuous frontier-barrier in Germany; but this was of a much simpler type. His

war against the Chatti in 83 resulted in the building of several
forts in the Main plain, at and around Frankfurt, and the enclosing of this whole area with a frontier carried along the watershed of the Taunus and driven in a straight line across the
lower ground. This frontier was composed of a string of earth
fortlets connected by wooden signal-towers, and in front of these
a wattle fence. Later, all this was reconstructed after the rising
of Saturninus in 89, and at the same time the area enclosed was
extended both to north and to south.

Thus, by the end of the first century, the standard pattern
of Roman frontier was well established: a road, with forts and
signal-towers along it, which might run either across country or
along a river-bank; and precedents were already established for
adding in front of this, as occasion seemed to demand, some
continuous obstacle, whether fence or earthwork. But with
regard to this addition there was no settled rule, either as to its
existence or as to its nature; it would not be added at all unless
local conditions required it, and if so its character would be
what seemed to suit the place and the time. Each provincial
governor, if called upon to construct a frontier, would use his
own judgement as to how it should be done, unhampered by
precedent except in the one essential, that it should be a road
with forts and signal-towers at intervals, though each governor
would doubtless know what had been done in other provinces.

At the end of the last chapter it was pointed out that the
removal of the Second Adiutrix from Britain to Moesia about 86
made it impossible for the British army to hold all Agricola's
conquests for long, unless the frontier tribes should remain
quiet. Evidence of destruction and rebuilding at sites in central
Scotland shows that they did not. Until about the close of the
century, however, it is certain that these conquests were maintained: at some time after that they were abandoned. There
is no reason to connect this abandonment with any further movement of troops out of Britain, whether to Dacia or elsewhere;
the situation in northern Britain by itself is enough to explain it.

This abandonment of the Agricolan position in Scotland
could hardly be carried out at a time when so much thought
had already been given to the subject of frontier-lines without
the creation of a definite frontier somewhere farther to the
south: and this would presumably be a transverse road, with
forts and signal-towers, to which a continuous obstacle might or

might not be added. For such a frontier either of two positions would be especially suitable: the Forth–Clyde isthmus, where Agricola himself had set up a temporary frontier-line in his campaign of the year 80, or the Tyne–Solway line, which was similarly used by him, it would seem, two years earlier, and where finally the Hadrianic frontier was placed. The Forth–Clyde line was rejected: if Strathmore could not be held, the Forth–Clyde isthmus was little better. Geographical conditions therefore led almost inevitably to the Tyne and Solway.[1]

On the Tyne–Solway line there are three things, each of which might be regarded as in some sense a *limes*. There is Hadrian's Wall, with its forts, milecastles, and turrets, and the military way running close behind it. There is the earthwork which English antiquaries call the Vallum, following the same line a little way south of the Wall. And there is the Stanegate, a fortified road a little way farther south again. The construction of the Wall, whatever problems of detail it may still present, is dated beyond dispute to the earlier part of Hadrian's reign. If, then, we are looking for traces of a Trajanic frontier on or near the same line, the Vallum and the Stanegate must be examined.

The Vallum is a broad and deep, flat-bottomed ditch, whose upcast earth has been neatly arranged in two parallel mounds set back some twenty feet from its north and south sides. This symmetrical section makes it tactically neutral: no force of troops on one side of it has any advantage over one on the other. In spite of repeated and careful search, no trace of palisades belonging to it, on the mounds or elsewhere, has ever been found. Although, with its steep sides, it was in its original shape a formidable obstacle, it cannot be regarded as in any sense a work of defence or fortification. That it is of Roman date, and belongs, like the Wall, to the early second century, is established beyond doubt. It runs from the north bank of the Tyne, close to Newcastle (the exact termination is not known, but it seems to have been less than a mile upstream from the Roman bridge and fort there) to the south bank of the Solway at Bowness, a distance of about seventy English miles.

[1] A suggestion was at one time made by Haverfield (*Edinburgh Review*, April 1911) that the frontier, after central Scotland was abandoned, was placed on the Tweed. It is, of course, possible that Newstead was held for a time after sites farther north were evacuated; but there is no evidence that anything like a *limes* was ever constructed in the Tweed valley.

Antiquaries of the last century tried to explain the Vallum as a southward defence for a strip of frontier-territory, varying in width but nowhere more than half a mile across, whose northern edge was the Wall. When a closer study of its original shape made this view impossible, Haverfield in the last years of the century proposed to regard it as a civil or legal boundary somehow corresponding to the Wall as a military obstacle. The difficulty of understanding why two continuous works were needed for these two purposes led later archaeologists to suggest that Hadrian's original frontier had been a line of forts and signal-towers connected by the Vallum, which they explained as a mere line of demarcation without any military purpose; and that to this original Hadrianic frontier-system the Wall had then been added as a military obstacle, in order to ease the work of the garrison.

Apart from various other difficulties, this suggestion was based on the assumption that the Vallum was older than the Wall; and of this no definite evidence had ever been found. The prima-facie evidence was, in fact, against it; for on several occasions, when the Vallum approaches a fort belonging to the Wall, it swerves from its usual straight line and makes a deviation southwards so as to avoid the fort. This looks as if the Vallum were either contemporary with the Wall, or later than the Wall; if it is to be regarded as earlier, the prima-facie evidence must be explained away, either by supposing that the forts standing in these deviations are earlier than the Wall and belong to the presumed Vallum stage of the frontier, or by supposing that they belong to the presumed Wall stage but occupy the sites of earlier and perhaps smaller forts contemporary with the Vallum.

Expedients like these made it theoretically possible to regard the Vallum as earlier than the Wall; and the question arises whether in that case the interval between the two might be sufficient for the Vallum to be the required Trajanic frontier.[1] But the balance of evidence is against this alternative. The forts that stand in the Vallum deviations are now known to date, in some cases and therefore probably in all, from Hadrian's reign, and no evidence exists that any of them superseded a Trajanic fort occupying the deviation before it.[2] The Vallum itself has

---

[1] This identification was proposed by Birley, 'A note on the date of the Vallum', in *Arch. Aeliana*, ser. 4, xi (1934), p. 146.

[2] A fragment of what might be a small Vallum fort has been found under the

in many places been purposely filled up to facilitate operations connected with the Wall; and botanists who have examined the material from the ditch at these places say that it has lain open only for a very short time, certainly not long enough for the interval between a Trajanic frontier and one dating from about 122. Lastly, recent work in Cumberland has excluded the possibility that the Vallum can be at all, however little, earlier than the Wall: for it is now known to make a deviation in order to avoid, not a fort, but a milecastle belonging to the Hadrianic series, built on ground where no earlier structure ever stood. It is therefore necessary to look for the Trajanic *limes* elsewhere than in the Vallum; and this means asking whether it can be more plausibly identified with the Stanegate.

The Stanegate is a road which runs from Carlisle along the north bank of the Eden by Low and High Crosby to Irthington, where it crosses the Irthing and passes close by a fort at Brampton Old Church; passing another fort at Easby, it travels up the left bank of the Irthing to another at Nether Denton and another at Throp, close to Gilsland, whence it climbs to the heights north of the Tyne valley to forts at Carvoran, Haltwhistle Burn, Chesterholm, and Newbrough. After this its course is uncertain. It may cross the North Tyne near Chesters; it may continue down the valley to Corbridge.

On this line decorated 'Samian' pottery of Trajan's reign is common. Considerable quantities of it have been found at Carlisle, Nether Denton, Birdoswald (whose oldest structural remains, earlier than the Vallum, would seem to indicate an outpost of the same system north of the Irthing gorge), Chesterholm, Chesters, and Corbridge. Rougher pottery, dated to the same period, has been found at Throp and Haltwhistle Burn. Thus all along the Stanegate evidence of occupation in Trajan's reign is definite and voluminous. That road itself, in some form or other, apparently goes back as far as Agricola; some of the sites on its line, notably Carlisle, Chesterholm, and Corbridge (if Corbridge may be regarded as belonging to it), undoubtedly

---

stone fort at Birdoswald (*Cumb. and West. Trans.*, N.S., xxxiii (1933), pp. 253–4), but no evidence was forthcoming for dating it to Trajan; pottery of that reign was found close by (ibid. xxxii (1932), p. 141), but this might equally well have come from the buildings that stood on the same site before the Vallum was made (ibid. xxxiv (1934), pp. 120–4). Nor is there any reason for ascribing a Trajanic date to the scrap of turf rampart at Castlesteads (ibid. xxxiv, pp. 163–4). The evidence for Trajanic Vallum forts, at the time of writing this, is nil.

do so; but the systematic fortification of it belongs without a doubt to the time of Trajan. The Stanegate, then, would appear to be the *limes* constructed in that reign after the evacuation of Scotland. In the absence of literary records and inscriptions no closer date can be given; and we do not yet know how this *limes* ran east of the North Tyne. It may possibly have followed the road known as the Devil's Causeway to near Berwick-on-Tweed; but until the course of that road has been explored with the spade this must remain mere guesswork.

Elsewhere in Britain there are traces of a widespread reorganization in Trajan's reign. To some extent this was a matter of routine. Hitherto, so far as we know, all Roman military buildings in Britain had been of timber, with earth or turf ramparts; stonework seems hardly to have been used except in bath-houses, where the hypocaust system of heating required it. But at least by Domitian's reign earthen forts were being replaced in Germany by stone; and in Trajan's time this fashion spread to Britain. It was now that the legionary fortresses at Caerleon and York, and probably at Chester, too, received stone-revetted ramparts and stone internal buildings. At York, an inscription enables us to date the change, or at least some important phase of it, to 108–9; at Caerleon, another tells us that it was in progress about the turn of the century. Many auxiliary forts were treated in the same manner. The best examples are in Wales, where Segontium, near Carnarvon, received stone internal buildings, Caerhun in the Conway valley both these and stone ramparts, and Brecon stone ramparts and a beginning of stone internal buildings, never completed.

More important is evidence suggesting that garrisons were being moved about. At Castleshaw, in the hills east of Manchester, a large fort was abandoned at about the beginning of the century, and a very small blockhouse built on its site. Certain reductions in the size of forts, made by cutting off one end, have been tentatively ascribed to this reign, but without definite proof: examples are Castell Collen and Tomen-y-Mur in Wales. This need not mean that Trajan was withdrawing auxiliary units from Britain for his wars in the east, for at the same time we find certain new forts being erected, such as Hardknot Castle in Cumberland and Gellygaer in Glamorgan, the latter dated by an inscription to between 105 and 112. Such as it is, all this suggests that, over and above a tendency to reconstruct old forts partially or wholly in stone (perhaps in some cases after enemy destruction, but more probably after natural decay of the wooden buildings), the reign of Trajan witnessed two shufflings of auxiliary regiments, which may or may not have been simultaneous: a movement of certain units from their Agricolan quarters in the far north to the new Stanegate *limes*, and, farther south, a shifting of others from forts which it was now decided to evacuate into others now built for the first time.

On the whole it is probable that these movements and changes were due rather to a spirit of reorganization, characteristic of Trajan, than to necessity imposed by military disasters on a large scale. Had there been a great rising in Britain during this reign it is probable that we should have heard of it from some ancient writer. Small local disturbances there may well have been. Now and then, an auxiliary fort may have been destroyed. But the only reason for imagining a disaster of any magnitude is the unexplained disappearance of the Ninth legion. The last dated record of its existence is the inscription of 108–9, already mentioned, at York. By about 122, when Hadrian's Wall was being built, it was replaced at York by another legion, the Sixth Victrix from Vetera on the lower Rhine, and had ceased to exist as an effective corps. But its disappearance cannot be dated earlier than the beginning of Hadrian's reign, when the Stanegate frontier had been for some time in existence; its annihilation cannot therefore have been any part of the events leading up to the evacuation of Scotland and the establishment of that frontier.

When Trajan died in the summer of 117 on his way back to Rome from the east, he was succeeded by P. Aelius Hadrianus, a native like himself of Italica, near Seville, his cousin by birth, his kinsman by marriage, his ward in boyhood, and his life-long friend. As a young officer in the legions of the Rhine and Danube, fighting with Trajan through the Dacian and Parthian wars, first on his staff and later in command of a legion, and then governing lower Pannonia, Hadrian had served long in a sound military school and had seen almost every part of the European and eastern frontiers. Promoted somewhat rapidly by the emperor's favour, he was at Trajan's death governor of Syria, the most important military command in the empire. He was not, like his predecessor, a soldier of genius; but a good soldier he was, and much more besides: to the solid traditions of soldier-

ship and statesmanship which he inherited from men like Trajan
and Vespasian he added something comparable with the scholarship of a Claudius and the artistic interests of a Nero, but mixed
these elements in such a way as never to incur the charge of a
pedantic learning or a frivolous aestheticism. He not only
created a stable and efficient system of imperial frontiers, he
also inaugurated a new age in the history of Roman taste; he
was both a patron of original ideas in architecture and himself
an architect of originality; he was a painter and a lover of
painting; a lover of literature and a writer who, after a lifetime
of idle versification, wrote on his deathbed five lines of poetry.

Except for one brief visit to the Danube, Hadrian spent the
early years of his reign in the capital. Then, in 120 or 121, he
set out on the first of the voyages that were to occupy the next
ten years of his life. The account of these voyages that has come
down to us is fragmentary and confused, but it gives us a clear
enough picture of a man tirelessly energetic, bewilderingly ver-
satile, throwing himself with equal energy into the adornment
of towns, the redressing of peasants' grievances, the reviewing of
troops, or the inspection, afoot and bare-headed in all weathers,
of league upon league of frontier. Wherever he went Hadrian
left his mark. New laws were enacted, new buildings rose from
the ground. But nowhere has he left a more impressive monument than in Britain.

During the first few years of his reign matters there had not
gone too well. At the time of his accession, says one ancient
writer, the Britons were in successful rebellion against Roman
rule; and another says that under Hadrian the Romans suffered
heavy casualties in Britain.[1] The two statements must refer to
one and the same event, namely, a rising in Britain, accompanied by a grave disaster to the Roman arms, in the first two
or three years of the reign. With that disaster must be connected
the disappearance of the Ninth legion.[2] Consequently the

---

[1] *Scriptores Hist. Augustae*, Spartian, *Hadr.* § 5; Fronto, p. 218 N.

[2] Ritterling, in Pauly-Wissowa, *Realencyclopädie*, s.v. 'Legio', cols. 1668–9, has
pointed out that this connexion, although he does not reject it, gives rise to a
difficulty: for certain persons are known to us who served as tribunes in the Ninth
and thereafter passed through other stages in the senatorial career at a rate which,
if that legion really ceased to exist in 117–19, was extraordinarily slow. He asks,
therefore, whether the annihilation of the legion might not have happened in a
revolt at some later date in Hadrian's reign. To my mind, its absence from the
inscriptions of the Wall, plus the fact that Hadrian brought the Sixth to Britain
(surely to replace it), makes that impossible. In any case, the existence of these

situation with which Hadrian had to deal in Britain was not
unlike that which had confronted Domitian in 87 in the Dobruja:
a badly defeated frontier-army to be reinforced, its morale
restored, and its positions secured against further attack. This
serves to explain why Hadrian's British frontier works are in
point of strength so much like Domitian's in the Dobruja, and
so unlike Hadrian's own works in Germany.

It was from Germany that Hadrian's British journey began;
and it is instructive to see how he reorganized the Domitianic
limes there before ever he visited Britain. The whole frontier-
line was surveyed afresh and in some places moved to a better
position. The auxiliary regiments acting as its garrison, instead
of lying in forts at some distance behind the line, were brought
up to fresh ones built upon the line itself. Finally, the entire
line was defended by means of an oaken palisade, a massive
work, still to be traced by the stumps of its uprights below
ground-level, but rather an obstacle to unauthorized traffic than
a fortification proper designed to stop the inroads of hostile
armies. The aims governing these alterations are greater uniformity, greater efficiency, greater ease of working: and the chief
means by which these results were achieved were the erection
of the palisade and the placing of its garrisons as close to it as
possible.

In certain ways Hadrian's reorganization of the British frontier resembled these changes in the German. Obviously he
surveyed the whole line afresh, and, if a friend's reference[1] to
his 'British walking-tour' is to be taken in its natural sense, he
did it not only in person but on foot. As we do not know how
Trajan's frontier ran on the east, we cannot tell how he altered
it there, except that the bridge and fort on the Tyne at Newcastle, being called Pons Aelius after him, are certainly his work;
but in the centre he moved it up from the north slope of the

---

survivors is proof that the disappearance of the legion was not due to literal
annihilation in the field. But a legion that had only suffered severe losses in action
was normally brought up to strength by drafts from elsewhere; the suspicion arises,
therefore, that the Ninth had not only been cut up, but had disgraced itself, which
would account for its survivors' slow promotion.

[1] The friend was a certain Florus, who wrote in mock commiseration of the
emperor's hard life a doggerel running:

> Ego nolo Caesar esse,
> Ambulare per Britannos,
> Scythicas pati pruinas.

Tyne valley to the heights of the Whin Sill, which even in Trajan's time the troops must have actually patrolled; and on the Irthing he transferred it bodily from the south side of the valley to the north, where one or two outposts were already being held. In both these cases he was following the principle which he had observed in Germany when he moved the garrisons up from such low-lying forts as Wiesbaden and Frankfurt to the ridge of the Taunus, increasing their efficiency even to the detriment of their comfort. On the west he carried the line down the south shore of the Solway to Bowness, where the firth ceases to be fordable.

As in Germany, again, he built along this line a continuous barrier. The country through which it was to run was not rich in heavy timber, and therefore the barrier could not be a palisade; but throughout its eastern and central part there was abundance of good building-stone and of limestone for burning, and in the western part, where stone became scarcer and no lime was to be had, it was easy to build, as local conditions prompted, either in cut sods or in clay. This was the original plan for Hadrian's Wall in Britain. Beginning at the new bridge and fort at Newcastle, the Wall, 10 Roman feet thick and 20 feet high, including its parapet, built of stone with a rubble and mortar core, and protected in front by a 30-foot ditch, was to run westward in this shape as far as the Irthing, 40 English miles; then, with the change in geological conditions, the build of the Wall was to change, and it was to go forward as a turf-work, or made of clay where turf was not ready to hand, for another 30 miles to Bowness-on-Solway. At regular intervals of a Roman mile there were to be fortlets, walled in stone or turf as the case might be; between each of these and the next, two stone towers for signalling. These milecastles and turrets (to give them their current names) were to be solid with the Wall and of one build with it. At irregular intervals were sixteen forts, almost all of them built actually in contact with the Wall, and each housing an auxiliary regiment.

The chief difference between this Wall and the German palisade is one of material. But there is also a very considerable difference of strength. The British work is much the more powerful, and, especially with its great ditch in front and its rampart-walk on the top, has the air of a genuine fortification intended to be used in warfare. Closer study shows that this appearance is deceptive. A wall-top 7 or 8 feet broad, to which access was provided only by ladders every 500 yards and narrow stairways a mile apart, lacking artillery, lacking bastions, and, above all, garrisoned only with an average of 150 men to the running mile, was never intended by Roman engineers for use as a fighting-platform. Like the German palisade, it was meant as an obstacle to raiding and plundering, and doubtless also to smuggling; and since, if it were properly patrolled, no one could cross it without attracting attention, especially when laden with loot or merchandise, its efficiency must have been perfect. The fact that it was so much stronger than the German palisade no doubt reflects the fact, already noted, that the British frontier was restless. The border tribes were in a dangerous mood; the Roman armies had lately suffered a grave defeat; and in this respect conditions here resembled those which led to the construction of Domitian's earth wall in the Dobruja, thirty-five years earlier. Even granted that the Wall was incapable of resisting siege-tactics, it would be an obstacle to the movements of armed bands, and would thus protect the Roman posts against being surrounded, cut off, and crushed in detail, while giving their garrisons a better chance of reinforcing threatened points and marching out through the northern gates of their forts to engage the enemy in the open.

As often happened with Roman buildings of great size, the original plan of the Wall underwent modification before the work was finished. In the east and centre it was decided to reduce the thickness from 10 to 8 Roman feet, and at the same time to extend the length for $3\frac{1}{2}$ miles down the Tyne to a new terminal fort, still called Wallsend, where a clear view can be had down the last reach of the tidal river. When this change was made, the stone Wall had been built westward from Newcastle for half its intended distance, as far as the north Tyne; on the remainder of its line the foundations had been laid and the milecastles and turrets built. Between the north Tyne and the Irthing, therefore, the curtain of the Wall was completed to the new 8-foot gauge. The decision was also made to replace the turf Wall by stone; this replacement, at the eastern end of the turf Wall line, was put in hand at once, but it was not completed for many years.

The Hadrianic frontier presents one other feature, the ditch known as the Vallum, of which some account has already been given.[1] The purpose of this work has always been a perplexing question; but close study of its actual features, partly as visible on the surface of the ground and partly as revealed by the spade, has gradually eliminated one hypothesis after another, narrowing down the field of possibilities, until to-day the very stringency of the conditions which a theory of its purpose must satisfy should make it easier to see in what direction the truth is to be sought.

The chief facts to be considered are, that the Vallum in its original shape was a formidable obstacle to traffic, but incapable of military defence, and so designed, indeed, as to look ostentatiously unmilitary; that this obstacle is carried with remarkable thoroughness, admitting no interruption whether from hard rock subsoil, morass, or ravine, right across the country from Tyne to Solway, close behind the Wall; that, according to the latest results of excavation, it was made at the same time as the Wall itself; and that the only original ways across it are solid causeways opposite the Wall forts and perhaps also opposite the milecastles, each surmounted by a stone gateway. In sum, the Vallum is a second obstacle parallel to the Wall and provided with a corresponding series of controlled openings for traffic, differing from it in its deliberately unmilitary design.

Now, a Roman frontier had two functions, one military or defensive, the other financial, as a line where traffic passing between the province and the unconquered country outside it passed through supervised openings and paid duty. And it is a peculiar feature of Roman administration that the financial service under the procurators was entirely separated from the military service under the provincial governors. The sentry on guard at the gate of a fort was responsible to the commandant; he, whether or not through the mediation of a legionary commander, to the governor of the province; and he to the emperor. A customs officer was responsible to the procurator, and he to the emperor directly, without any intervention of the governor. And not only were these two services separate, but relations between them were delicate: friction and jealousy were not unknown.

Before the building of Hadrian's Wall, continuous frontier-works, where they existed at all, had been structurally separate

---

[1] Above, p. 124. The name Vallum, as a piece of Latinity, is incorrect: Romans would have called it *fossa*. But the current name has been applied to it ever since the time of the Venerable Bede, and has earned a prescriptive right to stand.

from the forts of their garrisons. It may be conjectured (we have no proof) that the openings in the barrier were controlled by customs officers, while obviously the sentries of the garrisons looked after their own fort gateways. But on Hadrian's Wall the forts, with one or two exceptions, formed part of the barrier itself, so that a man passing through the fort was passing the line of the barrier; and (again with one or two exceptions) there was no way of crossing the barrier except by thus going through a fort, unless, indeed, non-military traffic was allowed to pass through milecastles; if it was, the same problem would arise there.

From a military point of view, this new method of planning the forts in relation to the barrier was no doubt an improvement. If traffic crossing the line of the barrier was compelled to pass through a fort, the military control over such traffic was tightened. But the question must now have arisen, how to provide for the customs officers? Hadrian, a stickler for military discipline, may very well have thought it unwise to give the procurator's men an official position at fort gateways, where the authority of the commandant should be undisputed. The simplest solution on paper, though a cumbrous and expensive one, would be to have a second barrier behind the Wall; to make this barrier look as unmilitary as possible, consistent with efficiency; and to provide it with a crossing opposite each fort, where the customs officers could do their work. The Wall as a whole would be controlled by the governor, the Vallum by the procurator; the distinction between the two reflecting and symbolizing the separation between the military and financial services.

There is no proof that this explanation of the Vallum is correct. All that can be claimed for it is that it fits the facts. The one thing which is certain is that, whatever may have been the original purpose of the Vallum, it was soon disused. Everywhere in the neighbourhood of forts the whole work was destroyed and its ditch filled in very soon after it was made; elsewhere, earthen causeways were thrown across it at short and regular intervals, which in some places were cleaned out again and in others left where they were. To the garrison, the whole thing was a nuisance; and it was no doubt discovered before long that the customs officers could, after all, be accommodated at the fort gateways without disastrous consequences; or, perhaps, in some cases, that even when the Vallum ditch had been filled in the old gateway could still be used as a customs-house.[1]

Hadrian's visit to Britain fell in 121 or 122. He left the province in charge of A. Platorius Nepos, an intimate friend of his own, who, since his consulship in 119, had been governing Lower Germany; and it was this governor who carried out the construction of the new frontier-works. The task was a heavy one. To dig the ditch of the Wall alone, it was necessary to move nearly two million cubic yards of soil and subsoil, much of it solid rock; and in some places, where the rock is basalt, it can still be seen how fiercely the ditch-diggers grappled with their task, splitting the stone and lifting the blocks with cranes, until they gave it up not as impossible but as an addition not, at such cost, indispensable to the barrier of the Wall. The Wall itself, with its core of rough stone and mortar—essentially a concrete structure—faced on either side with ashlar, contained over two million cubic yards of material, of which the stone had to be quarried and cut, and the lime burnt. In Northumberland these materials were to be had close at hand, and on certain stretches of the Wall the Roman quarries are still visible not far behind its line; in Cumberland, when the change was made from turf to stone, a change which was probably begun under Platorius himself, they had in many cases to be brought up from quarries several miles to southward, where beds of suitable stone were found exposed in steep river-banks. In addition, there were rivers to be bridged, and about sixteen new forts to be built, all in the most elaborate manner, of stone throughout. The highest quality in construction was everywhere demanded; no trouble or expense was spared to make details like fort-gateways and bridge-abutments monumental alike in strength and magnificence; and beside all this, the Vallum has been calculated to entail a million man-days of labour in mere earthwork. Even to-day, when these vast works remain only in shattered fragments, they are a monument of Roman purposiveness than which none more impressive exists in any country, and a fitting memorial to an emperor distinguished above others for his ambition as an architect and his remorseless demands on the labour of his troops.

---

[1] The gateway long survived at Benwell (*Arch. Aeliana*, ser. 4, xi (1934), p. 182); perhaps at Housesteads (ibid., p. 188) and certainly at Birdoswald (*Cumb. and West. Trans.*, N.S., xxxiii (1933), p. 252) it was very soon disused. Practice was not rigidly uniform.

For it was the legions that built the Wall. According to Roman tradition, every legion contained within itself technical specialists of every kind, and was competent to do every sort of constructional work that an army could need, whether temporary or permanent. Its efficiency as an engineering unit, for earthwork, woodwork, or masonry, was no less important than its efficiency in battle, and Hadrian himself, in his addresses to his troops in Africa, which have been preserved on stone where they were delivered, laid equal stress upon each. The sculptures on Trajan's Column, which may almost be regarded as contemporary pictures of the building of the Wall, show half-armed legionaries digging ditches and erecting fortifications, while auxiliaries act as covering troops. The Wall itself has yielded evidence of how this work was organized. Along its line over 150 small inscriptions have been found, generally cut on the ordinary stones of the facing, which simply give the name sometimes of a legion, sometimes of a cohort, but most often of a century, the smallest unit into which the legion was divided. They show that the work of building the Wall was partitioned out in lengths to individual centuries, just as, according to inscriptions from elsewhere, the ramparts of forts were divided. These lengths were quite small; now and then the inscriptions give measurements, which vary from 19 to 30½ *passus* (31 to 50 yards) but are most often between 35 and 40 yards; and the way in which the same centuries and legions reappear in different parts of the Wall proves that the whole, or at any rate the main, strength of the three legions was concentrated on building one short sector at a time, and then moved on to another.

Here and there, in the western part of the Wall, there are records of a different kind: once, near Birdoswald, a sector was built by men from the fleet; and in four places the work is recorded to have been done by British tribes: Durotriges, Dumnonii, Catuvellauni, and perhaps Brigantes, acting not as mere labour-gangs under legionary supervision, but as independent units signing their own work. But whereas the naval inscriptions are Hadrianic in style and must refer to the original building of the Wall (or rather, to the replacement of the turf Wall by that of stone), these tribal inscriptions seem all to be of later date, and refer to the rebuilding of the Wall in the time of Severus.

The completed work employed a large garrison. Each fort

housed an auxiliary regiment, either of foot or of horse; the total strength of these must have been, on paper, about 10,000 men, of whom probably one-fifth were cavalry. If we add the forts on the Cumberland coast, which were certainly an integral element in the Wall scheme, the depot at South Shields, and the outposts north of the line, we get a total of about 14,000 men for the fighting garrison of the frontier. But the existence of the milecastles and turrets, forming a system quite distinct from the series of forts, suggests that there was, independently of this fighting garrison, a patrolling garrison, one small unit of which occupied each milecastle and served the two turrets immediately adjacent to it. For the entire Wall, and the system of signal-stations which prolonged its line down the Cumberland coast, this patrolling garrison can hardly have numbered much less than 5,000 men.

In order to understand the military situation thus created, it is necessary to consider what troops a governor of Britain in the early second century had at his disposal. We have no statistics; but it is possible to draw up an army-list for Britain in Hadrian's reign whose margin of error is probably not very large. This is partly because inscriptions of the early second century are common; but it is even more because we happen to possess half a dozen military diplomas dating from that half-century. These were documents, engraved on bronze, issued to auxiliary soldiers on their discharge, and certifying their good conduct while with the colours and the conferment upon them of the rights of Roman citizenship, which during their service auxiliaries, unlike legionaries, did not enjoy. In particular, the right of legal marriage was always specified, though in such terms as to make it clear that previous marriages, though not hitherto legally binding, had already been recognized, and were now further dignified with a legal sanction. These diplomas were issued in batches to men of certain regiments; any one diploma, therefore, gives a list of all the regiments to whose time-expired men copies of it were issued; and when we put together seven lists of this kind, all belonging to Britain, and dated respectively to 98, 103, 105, 122, 124, 135, and 146, we have a working basis for a catalogue of auxiliary units in Britain for that time; to which, in point of fact, only very small additions can be made from other sources.

The results are as follows. Three legions, each numbering

5,600 men, of whom 120 were cavalry, give 16,800 troops of the first class. Of the 68 auxiliary units which we can identify, 16 are *alae* or cavalry regiments; one of these a milliary unit, 1,000 strong, the rest quingenary (nominally 500, actually on paper 480): total 8,500. Of the auxiliary cohorts (infantry regiments, but sometimes having a cavalry contingent) 7 are milliary, 45 quingenary: total, 29,500. The auxiliaries thus number 38,000 in all, and the grand total for the army in Britain comes to 54,800. This, of course, is merely paper strength; we do not know what percentage of it could be reckoned upon as effectives. On the other hand, there may have been a few auxiliary units of which we have not heard.

Of these 68 auxiliary regiments, the forts of the Wall itself took up 16 or 17; and if we add the forts of the Cumberland coast, the outposts in front, and the supporting posts within two or three days' march of the frontier—a doubtful quantity, for we do not exactly know how many were held—the number of regiments required by Hadrian's scheme north of the latitude of York amounts to about 50. This leaves only about 20 regiments for the rest of the province, in which we actually know of some 40 *castella*. The presumption, therefore, is that the network of auxiliary forts which had been thrown, in varying patterns, over northern and western Britain was now to a very considerable extent drained of its garrisons, which were moved up to the Wall and its neighbourhood. And this presumption is borne out by archaeological findings. In Wales, most of the existing forts seem now to have been evacuated except for a military caretaker or a skeleton garrison. The same thing certainly happened at some forts in the southern Pennine region; but our knowledge is not detailed enough to describe the process in full.

It would be an exaggeration to say that the auxiliary troops, which did the ordinary work of policing the country-side, were withdrawn from every other part of Britain in order to provide for the needs of the frontier. But the frontier absorbed two-thirds of them; and this policy must have been based on the assumption that the whole country behind the frontier was, if not completely pacified, very nearly pacified, and that in future any considerable concentration of force would be needed only to protect the province against invasion from the unconquered north. Danger of invasion from elsewhere, later so pressing, did not yet exist.

This movement of troops towards the frontier affected even the legions. The Sixth, now stationed at York, and the Twentieth at Chester, still maintained the two northern fortresses; but it was no longer thought necessary to keep the Second at Caerleon up to full strength. About the time when the Wall was built, excavation in that fortress shows traces of a decline in occupation. The head-quarters of the legion were not moved, but it seems that large drafts were more or less permanently absent. It may not be an accident that, of inscriptions connected with the building of the Wall which name a legion, by far the largest number record work done by the Second Augusta;[1] nor that the only case known to us of legionaries serving in the garrison of a Wall fort is that of a draft from the same legion at Housesteads;[2] and although one would expect the patrolling garrison to be composed of irregular troops, presumably consisting of the units called *numeri* which certainly existed on the Wall in the third century,[3] there is a possibility that in the original organization of the Wall some part of this work was done with the help of men from that legion.

One curious result of this northward movement appears in Wales, where some period not earlier than the second century saw the construction of numerous massively fortified hilltop towns. These fortresses cannot have been built without the knowledge and consent of the Roman government, and it is a bold but not improbable idea that they were built at its instigation. If the government was by now sufficiently convinced of the Welsh tribes' loyalty, it might have enrolled their militia as an irregular native force for the defence of their own country, and encouraged them to fortify their dwellings. The date of this Welsh development is not very satisfactorily fixed, but it may have begun in Hadrian's reign and intensified later, when raids from Ireland became dangerous.[4]

[1] Of inscriptions probably recording original (Hadrianic) work on the Wall, 25 belong to the Second legion, 14 to the Sixth, and 11 to the Twentieth.

[2] *Ephemeris Epigraphica*, ix. 1177; by the style, later than Hadrian.

[3] Birley, 'A note on the garrisoning of the Wall', *Arch. Aeliana*, ser. 4, ix (1932), p. 210.

[4] Wheeler, 'Roman and Native in Wales', *Y Cymmrodor*, 1920–1, p. 40.

IX

THE FRONTIER AFTER HADRIAN

BEGUN probably in 122, Hadrian's Wall can hardly have been finished until 127 at earliest; if in its finishing we include the replacement of turfwork by masonry as far as the Solway, a good deal later. The main part of the work was done before Platorius left Britain, which may have been about 126. After his recall we know nothing of military affairs there for some time. The province was governed, about the years 130–4, by Julius Severus, who was transferred to the east in order to suppress a Jewish revolt; the fact is good evidence for his success in Britain. It is therefore all the more puzzling to find that by 140, two years after Hadrian was succeeded by Antoninus Pius, drastic changes were being made in the British frontier-system. The general nature of these changes is clear; what is difficult to understand is their motive.

From 140 to 142 Q. Lollius Urbicus, governor of Britain, conducted a war of conquest in the Border country and the Lowlands. Reopening Agricola's road over the Cheviots, and establishing a supply-depot at Corbridge where it crossed the Tyne, he fought his way to the Forth–Clyde isthmus, and there, at the end of the war, built a second barrier on the model of Hadrian's Wall. Like that, the new work, known to antiquaries as the Antonine Wall, was a continuous rampart stretching from sea to sea, with a ditch in front and a series of forts, connected by a road, attached to its southern side. But it differed from Hadrian's Wall chiefly in its simpler design and less elaborate structure.

In design it lacked two prominent features. First, there was no Vallum. Even if the explanation of the Vallum's purpose suggested above is correct, it does not follow that there were no customs officers on the Antonine Wall, but rather that, by this time, a *modus vivendi* had been reached by which they could be accommodated in the forts.

Secondly, there were no milecastles and turrets, and the forts, which, apart from a few platforms apparently serving as bases for beacon-fires, were the only regular structures connected with the Wall, were on average much smaller than those of Hadrian's system and much closer together. The Wall was only 37 miles long instead of 73; and along its line, which is everywhere chosen with the greatest skill so as to command a view of the valley to northwards, there seem to have been no less than 19 forts, placed therefore on average only 2 miles apart instead of $4\frac{1}{2}$ as on Hadrian's barrier. In size they fall, so far as their dimensions are known, into four groups: first comes Mumrills, in a class by itself, at $6\frac{1}{2}$ acres, with a large commandant's house suggesting that it may have been the residence of the senior officer on the Wall; then Balmuildy and Old Kilpatrick, both in positions of importance and measuring 4 acres each; then a group of 5 at about 3 acres; and lastly 4 that measure between 1 acre and 2.

This double feature, the absence of milecastles and turrets, together with the smallness and close spacing of the forts, indicates a departure from the Hadrianic model in the matter of organization. Instead of two separate garrisons, one consisting of whole regiments kept intact for use in the field, the other of small units patrolling the line, there was on the Antonine Wall only one garrison, whose units were split up so as to discharge both functions: no doubt with consequent loss of efficiency as fighting forces. That a system of this kind was adopted is clear from the small size of the forts. A milliary cohort required a fort of at least 4 acres, preferably 5; a quingenary cohort, one of at least $2\frac{1}{2}$. Castlecary on the Antonine Wall has yielded inscriptions of two different milliary cohorts, one of which is known to have had a cavalry contingent. Such a cohort can hardly have settled down in quarters covering less than 4 acres; Castlecary measures little over 3. Similarly, the quingenary cohort which has recorded its presence at Rough Castle can never have lodged in the bare acre of ground which the ramparts there enclose.

Evidently, then, the forts of the Antonine Wall were not meant to be occupied each by a complete regiment. The units must have been subdivided, except for a few inhabiting the largest forts; elsewhere it must have been a frequent practice to detach a century or two from a regiment occupying a fort of moderate size, and thus form a garrison for one of the smallest forts. So distributed, the total garrison of the Wall, according to careful estimates, did not exceed six or seven thousand men.

Even this small force, however, seems not to have been wholly composed of auxiliaries. Evidence for identifying the garrison has been found at no more than eight forts, and in five of these it suggests that, whether permanently or only for a time, the place was held by a draft from a legion or legions: in two cases the Second alone, in one the Sixth alone, in one the Second and Sixth, and in one the Second and Twentieth. If these cases are a fair sample, perhaps a third of the total garrison consisted of legionaries. This fact, taken together with the way in which auxiliary regiments were subdivided between various forts, shows convincingly enough that the garrisoning of the Antonine Wall was planned with a view to economy in men.

Economy in labour was considered no less carefully. Here again the contrast with Hadrian's Wall is striking. The ditch that lies in front of the rampart is even larger than Hadrian's, but the rampart itself, instead of stone, is made of turf in the western and central part, of clay in the eastern. Hadrian himself had laid it down that turfwork was very much easier to construct than masonry. And the measurements increase the contrast. The turf part of Hadrian's Wall is twenty feet wide at the base; the Antonine Wall is only fourteen, which implies that, if the height of the turfwork was the same in the two cases,[1] the Antonine rampart required, for any given length, only two-thirds of the turf that would be required by Hadrian's. The forts, again, instead of being massively walled in stone, with monumental gateways, were surrounded for the most part with turf or earthen ramparts whose timber gateways were commonly of the simplest design; where stone was used, the construction was simple and inexpensive. Even the official central buildings in the forts were not uniformly of stone, and the barracks were of the cheapest, wooden hutments which in some cases had thatched roofs.

Both in construction and in organization, then, the Antonine Wall bears the marks of a deliberate effort after cheapness, at the cost of a serious decrease in efficiency. The same thing is to be seen if we consider its strategic position. Both its flanks, especially the left, lie unprotected upon narrow estuaries, easily crossed by the smallest craft in almost any weather. If we recollect the care with which Hadrian (in addition to maintaining ships in the Solway, as he presumably did) fortified the whole of the north-west Cumberland coast for thirty or forty miles beyond the terminus of the Wall, the complete absence of Roman posts on the Clyde below Old Kilpatrick becomes so striking that we cannot put it down to negligence. These various features of

[1] See Richmond in *J.R.S.* xxvi (1936), p. 191.

the Antonine Wall, when considered together, seem less like a series of oversights than parts of a deliberate policy, based on the assumption that a powerful frontier-work on that line was not needed.

This impression can fortunately be verified by comparing the Antonine Wall with the new frontier-line constructed by the same emperor, only some five years later, in Germany. The contrast is striking. On the 'outer *limes*' there is no subdivision of fighting units, and no confusion between the fighting and patrolling garrisons. Exactly as on Hadrian's Wall, the distinction is carefully made between major forts accommodating cohorts or *alae* and fortlets and signal-towers for the patrolling garrison. And all these structures alike are solidly walled in stone, the major forts amply large enough for their garrisons. From every point of view the standard of strength and efficiency displayed by the new Antonine *limes* in Germany is fully equal to anything in Germany of Hadrianic date, and far superior to that of the Antonine Wall. It is evident, then, that the new features of the Antonine Wall are not due to any general cause, such as a cheeseparing policy on the part of Antoninus Pius, or a decline in the efficiency of Roman military engineering, or a less exacting conception of what was demanded in frontier-works. Their explanation must be sought in conditions peculiar to Britain.

Any attempt to find such an explanation must begin from the fact that we have to do not with a shifting of the frontier, but with a doubling of it. Hadrian's Wall was not evacuated. Some of its garrisons were moved to the new line, but others were not; and the places of those that were moved did not lie vacant. The First Cohort of Tungrians, for example, was moved from Housesteads on the old Wall to Castlecary on the new, and an inscription seems to show that its place was taken by a draft from the Second legion.

In Germany, too, the new frontier created by Pius was a double one, that is, he added a new line to run in front of one already existing. And this was not because the tribes beyond it were peculiarly dangerous; on the contrary, the district beyond it seems to have been to all intents and purposes uninhabited. It has been suggested by the highest authority on the German frontier that the motive of this double line was not to keep enemies out, but to keep subjects in: to prevent certain barbarians, lately conquered and deported to this region, from leaving their new homes and escaping into the wilds of Germany.[1]

If the Antonine Wall, like the 'outer *limes*', was designed rather because of what lay behind it than because of what lay in front, its unprotected flanks are no longer a fault. And if we can find reason for thinking that the potential enemies against whom it was built were, through some special cause, unusually weak, the unusual weakness of the Wall itself becomes only reasonable. In order to pursue this line of inquiry we must go back to the time of Hadrian and consider the relation between his Wall and the natives tribes through whose territory it ran.

Hadrian's frontier, as we saw, was established after a military disaster to consolidate what had become a dangerous position. The conception underlying it, although the Wall was not in the strict sense a fortification, was defensive: not a tactical defence, but a strategical defence. There is nowhere any suggestion that Hadrian launched a counter-attack against the northern tribes whose activities were compelling him to build his lines; on the contrary, all his available military force was thrown into building and digging. And, if he did not visit his wrath on the tribes outside the Wall, neither does he seem to have taken any severe measures against those who lived behind it. What we know of the history of native villages in Brigantia suggests that they were little, if at all, affected by Hadrian's visit. They may have been more closely supervised by an increased force of police-troops, but there was no depopulation, no devastation. The history of native arts and crafts tells the same story.

When the north of England and the south of Scotland were conquered in the Flavian period, they had been as yet very little affected by the fashion, so richly developed in the south, of building hill-forts.[2] This is sufficiently attested by the extreme rarity of such forts, to this day, in northern England south of the Wall. When we turn to the Lowlands, the contrast is startling. The highest levels, whether of the Cheviots or of the central lowland plateau, are bare of them; but all round the upper basins of the Tweed, Annan, and Clyde they come in crowds. The counties of Dumfries, Roxburgh, Selkirk, and Peebles number them by hundreds, and a dense sprinkling

---

[1] Fabricius, in *Der obergermanisch-rätische Limes*, Lieferung xlviii, 53.
[2] See above, ch. II, p. 23.

of them stretches over the Lammermuirs to the Forth and the sea.

As yet little is known in detail about these forts; but the little that is known shows that in some cases at least they were inhabited in the second century,[1] and in the circumstances this must imply a date between the Roman evacuation of Scotland and its reoccupation under Pius, for we can hardly imagine them to have been built under the very eyes of the Roman cohorts. It is likely, then, that the reigns of Trajan and Hadrian saw a rapid growth of little forts all over the most fertile regions of the central and eastern Lowlands; and it is even possible that this growth was in some way conditioned by a desire to control the lines, by now already existing, of the Roman roads. This movement had probably begun before Hadrian's Wall was built, and may have been one factor in the military situation which led to its building. If so, that building certainly did not stop it.

A development of this kind may well have caused serious questionings. Hadrian, in the conditions in which he found himself, was doubtless right to be content with a strategic defence and refrain from anything like a counter-attack; but was it possible to maintain that policy for ever? Were not the lowland tribes taking advantage of their impunity to gather a force, and establish a position, which would one day menace the safety of the Wall itself? Was it not wiser to anticipate that day and strike first?

Any stroke based on reasoning like this must aim at placing in Roman hands the entire control of the lowland area. The distribution of native forts is proof that the movement had gone too far to be dealt with by any mere raid. Further, it is clear that in its nature the stroke must be designed, not so much to defeat the lowland tribes in a decisive pitched battle, as to crush their strongholds one by one and forestall any renewal of the movement that had created them.

At this point good fortune offers us a verification of the hypothesis. One possible method of achieving this end would have been to sprinkle the country with auxiliary garrisons as dense as those of northern England. This Lollius did not do, and for an excellent reason. We know already that he did not possess the troops. Even if he completely denuded Britain of auxiliaries as far north as the latitude of York, he would only have twenty or

[1] Cf. Childe in *Antiquaries Journal*, xiii (1933), p. 1.

twenty-five regiments at his disposal, and these, when the necessary
new frontier had been provided for, were not nearly enough.
A second possible method was to depopulate the country, not
completely, but sufficiently to secure the end. The brief account
which we possess of the Antonine conquest in Scotland[1] mentions that it involved a 'removal' of those barbarians whom Lollius conquered. The phrase, taken in itself, might be thought
ambiguous; it might conceivably[2] refer, not to the transplantation of a barbarian tribe, but to the rout and flight of a barbarian
army. Yet this is not its most natural meaning; it rather suggests a dislodgement of the tribes from their strongholds, involving not their destruction, as Agricola had destroyed the
Ordovices, but their removal to other homes.

Here, once more, the history of the German frontier throws
light on the British.[3] When the 'outer *limes*' was built and the
inner line parallel to it reorganized, about 148, a division was
made, as we have already seen, between the fighting garrison
in the major forts and the patrolling garrison in the fortlets.
This patrolling garrison, as constituted by the Antonine reorganization, seems to have consisted entirely of *numeri* or small
irregular units of Britons, first apparently placed on the old
inner line, later moved forward to the outer. The number of
these units shows that there must have been, at this time or
just before it, a very large transplantation of Britons to the
Württemberg forests, not only, if Professor Fabricius has interpreted the evidence aright, of able-bodied men drafted into new
formations, but of entire tribes, placed in new homes where
their menfolk could be made useful and kept under supervision. This at once confirms and explains the statement of
Capitolinus.

The motives which led to the building of the Antonine Wall
are now clear. Hadrian's was to remain the chief bulwark of
the province; but there was need to relieve it of a threat,
gradually becoming more and more serious, from the tribes of
the central and eastern Lowlands, which may have been in-

---

[1] *Scriptores Hist. Aug.*, Capitolinus, *Antoninus Pius*, ch. 5, § 4: 'Britannos per Lol-
lium Urbicum legatum vicit, alio muro caespiticio submotis barbaris ducto.'

[2] If taken as an echo of *summotis velut in aliam insulam hostibus*, Tacitus's words
describing Agricola's fortification of the same isthmus (*Agric.* xxiii), as Sir George
Macdonald (*Wall*, ed. 2, p. 49) suggests.

[3] Fabricius, 'Ein Limesproblem', in *Festschrift der Universität Freiburg*, 1902; and
more recently in *Der obergerm.-rätische Limes*, Lieferung xlviii (1932), pp. 49–55.

creasing in numbers and were certainly, by building their forts
everywhere, increasing in strength. The Wall was finished, and
force was available for a counter-attack. The strategy for such
an attack had been settled once for all by Agricola; all that was
needed was to repair his roads and reoccupy the sites of his forts.
He had even driven a *limes* of the earlier Flavian type, a mere
chain of military posts, across the Forth–Clyde isthmus, choosing their sites, as usual, so skilfully that his choice could be
accepted as final; and, in fact, almost every fort on the Antonine
Wall where any digging has been done has yielded traces of an
Agricolan work beneath it. The plan of Urbicus, then, was first
to destroy the lowland native forts and deport the tribes to
which they belonged; the forts are almost all in the central and
eastern districts, so that a campaign in Galloway and Ayrshire
was not called for; and then to reoccupy the isthmus with a
limes of the new type, following Agricola once more in throwing
out advanced posts beyond it as far as Inchtuthill. It was assumed that the lowland tribes were the chief enemy to be dealt
with, and that central Scotland would give comparatively little
trouble. And because the Lowlands had been to a great extent
cleared of their inhabitants, it was possible to build the new
limes cheaply, hold it lightly, and support it with an unusually
thin network of forts in the rear.

On these assumptions the scheme was in itself reasonable; but
the cost must be counted. The new barrier, with its lines of
communication and outposts, however lightly held and supported, could not be manned with less than about twenty auxiliary regiments; it would consume almost all the balance which
Hadrian's scheme had left over for the southern Pennines and
Wales. These districts could not even now be altogether emp-
tied of troops, but their garrisons were drastically overhauled
and redistributed. One hint of such redistribution reaches us
from the Forden Gaer near Welshpool, where, by an exception
to the general rule for Wales, a more intense occupation begins
just at this time. The policy adopted was to cut down auxiliary
garrisons to the barest margin of safety, and to get the rest of
the men whom the scheme demanded by drafts from the legions,
which until then, except for possible inroads by Hadrian on the
strength of the Second, had been kept intact as mobile forces
for use in the field. In two ways the new move was a gamble:
it assumed that the central Scottish tribes would not be

dangerous, and it assumed that, behind the frontier, Britain was pacified.

Urbicus cannot have been unaware of these risks; and we may wonder whether, in taking them, he meant to take them as a temporary measure or in perpetuity. Granted the insecurity of the Antonine Wall's strategic position, the slightness of its works, the makeshift character of its organization, and the strain which, even so, it imposed on the resources of the province, it may be thought to resemble a temporary measure, to last until the pacification of the Lowlands had stood the test of time, rather than a revision of the frontier system designed for permanence. In the end, as we shall see, the northern Wall was peacefully and deliberately evacuated. If this was from the first intended to be its end, its lack of resemblance to other frontier-works of the same period is easier to understand. Recent excavation has shown, for example, that at Mumrills, the largest of all its forts, the commanding officer's quarters were at first of timber, a thing hardly to be expected at that time in a structure of such importance designed to be permanent. But this is a question which we have no means of answering.

The scheme went through without a hitch. By 142 or early in 143 the new Wall was finished. Its lighter structures were easier and quicker to build than those of Hadrian, and more efficient methods of working were adopted. Instead of dividing up the work wastefully among centuries engaged on short sectors at a time, six powerful working-parties were made up, two from each legion; and it seems that the entire length of the Wall was divided into nine sectors, of which the first six, beginning on the east, were simultaneously made, Wall and ditch together, by these six gangs, which then joined forces to complete the last three. The building of the forts was entrusted to their future garrisons. Each gang signed its work by erecting, at each end of every sector which it made, a stone slab recording the name of the gang and the length of the sector; and it is the text of these 'distance-slabs' that informs us how the work was done.[1]

It was soon to be proved that, of the risks involved in the new

---

[1] We owe the interpretation of their evidence to Sir George Macdonald (*The Roman Wall in Scotland*, ed. 2, 1934, ch. x), who has also put forward an hypothesis as to how this original scheme was thrown out of gear by the unexpected difficulty of cutting the ditch through the basalt of Croy Hill.

frontier system, one at least was greater than had been realized. We are told by Pausanias that Antoninus Pius annexed the territory of the Brigantes because they had invaded some un-identified district which he calls the Genunian region. The statement reads as if Pausanias conceived the Brigantes as living outside the Roman frontier, whereas by now they had long been subject to Rome (it is probable that their territory did not extend far north of Hadrian's Wall, which as a military line was, of course, under no obligation punctiliously to respect tribal boundaries), and had, indeed, a capital in the Roman style at Aldborough. But sense can be made of it by supposing that what Pausanias was referring to was not a frontier war, but a revolt, and in that case it was no doubt a revolt directly due to the weakening of the garrisons in Brigantia entailed by the building of the Antonine Wall.

The revolt can be dated[1] by the help of inscriptions and coins. Inscriptions show that a certain C. Julius Verus brought re-inforcements from Germany for all three British legions in the time of Pius, built or rebuilt forts at Brough in Derbyshire and Birrens in Dumfriesshire, the first certainly and the second perhaps in Brigantian territory, and that his work at Birrens fell in the year 158. In that same year, another inscription tells us, repairs were carried out on the masonry of Hadrian's Wall; and excavators have noted that in various buildings of the same Wall new floors have been laid at a time which cannot be very remote from this, sometimes over layers of dark matter which might be caused by the burning of their woodwork. Coins of Pius tell us that in 155 his troops gained a consider-able victory in Britain.

Many of these facts, if not all of them, must be connected with the event recorded by Pausanias. The Brigantes evidently rose about 154; the auxiliary garrisons in their territory were too few and far between to control the rising in its early stages, and the legions were too much weakened by the absence of drafts on the frontier to put it down. Verus, bringing reinforcements, suppressed the revolt in 155, and the victory was thought great enough to justify a special issue of coins. If so, the revolt may well have been serious enough to involve a certain amount of

---

[1] As Haverfield pointed out: 'Julius Verus, a Roman governor of Britain', in *Proc. Soc. Ant. Scot.* xxxviii (1902–3), p. 454; for the coins, Macdonald, *Wall* (cit.), p. 10.

damage to Hadrian's Wall, taken unexpectedly in the rear, and the destruction of some forts immediately to the north of it.

The trouble may even have spread as far as the Antonine Wall. Buildings in the forts there show signs of having been twice destroyed before being finally abandoned. Neither destruction can be accurately dated by archaeological or indeed any other evidence; but it is a reasonable conjecture that the first of them may have happened at or about the time of the Brigantian revolt. If this conjecture is correct, the inference follows that not one only, but both of the risks entailed by Lollius's distribution of his forces had been under-estimated. Nevertheless, no radical change was made. Apart from details here and there, too scanty to serve as the basis for a theory, we do not know on what principles the rebuilding of the Antonine Wall forts was planned. At Mumrills the wooden house for the commanding officer seems to have been handsomely rebuilt in stone; at Cadder, on the contrary, a stone house was replaced by a timber one. At Rough Castle the rampart was strengthened by adding a new rampart-walk, and it is thought that the size of the garrison was reduced. No generalization can be based on details like these. Nor can we even be sure how far Julius Verus strengthened the auxiliary garrisons of Brigantia, and how far he merely rebuilt their forts and restored the *status quo*. In either case, he was only patching a system whose weaknesses were fundamental.

It is therefore not surprising to learn that within a very few years trouble again broke out in Britain. Verus was succeeded as governor by M. Statius Priscus, who was there when Pius died in 161 and was succeeded by Marcus Aurelius. The new reign opened darkly. The *Historia Augusta* enumerates a severe flooding of the Tiber, a war in Parthia and the rout of the Roman governor of Syria, an invasion of unconquered Germans into the provinces of Germany and Raetia, and a British war. This last was dealt with by sending out a new governor, Sextus Calpurnius Agricola, doubtless to succeed Priscus, under whom the trouble must have arisen. Of its nature we know nothing. There are traces of his rule on Hadrian's Wall: a building dedicated to the 'Invincible Sun-God' at Corbridge, an altar to the 'Syrian Goddess' near Carvoran, a building at Ribchester, were set up while he was governor, or even at his express command; but whatever temporary success he may have enjoyed, war broke out again, unless the *Historia Augusta* is hopelessly confused, in 169. Another and more trustworthy writer tells us that in 175 Marcus sent to Britain 5,500 auxiliary cavalry. He was evidently aware that so long as the present frontier system there was in being the army of Britain urgently needed reinforcement; but his wars on the Danube forbade more effective action.[1]

Matters came to a head in the reign of Commodus, who succeeded his father as sole emperor in March 180. The last war of which we know anything definite began within the frontier; this time it came from outside. The tribes of central Scotland, encouraged no doubt by the feeble defensive power of the Antonine Wall, attacked it in force and swept across it into the Lowlands. It was a critical moment in the history of the British frontier, not only as the gravest blow it had ever yet suffered since its first definite organization by Hadrian, but as the death-knell of an age. Hitherto the initiative had lain with Rome. Henceforth it lay with her enemies. The barbarians were never again to forget the triumphs and the plunder that awaited them beyond those barriers. Rome, however successfully she maintained her defences in the future, was never again to win a decisive victory. With this invasion began the long process which, checked again and again, was never reversed until the helpless Britons of two centuries and a half later wrote their lamentation to Aetius: 'The barbarians drive us into the sea, the sea drives us back to the barbarians.'

The exact date of the war is not known. Cassius Dio gives an account of it under the year 184; that, however, was the year of its ending, the year when Commodus took the title Britannicus and issued coins commemorating a British victory. Dio's account has reached us only in an abridgement, but it is, as usual, far superior to the vague generalities of the *Historia Augusta*:'[Of the wars waged by Commodus] the greatest was in Britain. The tribes in that island crossed the wall which

---

[1] *Scriptores Hist. Aug.*, Capitolinus, *M. Antoninus*, ch. 8, § 7, ch. 22, § 1. Cassius Dio, lxxi. 16. If we could be sure that the archaeologists are right in now dating the first destruction of the Antonine Wall to *c.* 154 and the second to 180–3, an interesting result would follow in connexion with these British disturbances under Marcus: since on that view the Antonine Wall was unaffected by them, they must have been internal revolts, and thus testify to incomplete pacification of the province. I have not drawn this inference in the text because the details of the chronological scheme for the Antonine Wall periods are not, in my opinion, sufficiently certain to warrant it: there is really nothing to prove that the first destruction did not happen in 161–2.

divides them from the Roman fortresses, and did great harm. They slew a (Roman) general and the men under his command. Commodus, greatly alarmed, sent Ulpius Marcellus against them.'[1] A description of Ulpius follows: a hard man, sparing and austere in his own life, relentless in his demands upon others; fanatical in his refusal of food and sleep, and strangely ingenious to invent new disciplines for his army. 'Such then was this Marcellus; who inflicted a terrible defeat on the barbarians of Britain.'

From this passage it is evident that the war began not as a revolt, but as an invasion. The tribes beyond the Wall broke in and destroyed a considerable force, apparently commanded by the governor in person. A new governor was sent out, who repulsed the invaders. Ulpius Marcellus, as an inscription from Hadrian's Wall tells us, was already governor of Britain in the joint reign of Marcus and Commodus (177–80); Dio's words imply that the war broke out under his successor, and that Ulpius was sent back to retrieve the disaster.

Only one Wall is mentioned, and that in terms which might apply to either; for 'the Roman fortresses' here are the permanent quarters of the legions. But Hadrian's Wall, according to the findings of archaeology, suffered no disaster at this time;[2] and it is easiest to identify Dio's Wall with the Antonine barrier, and to see traces of the invasion in the second of the two destructions which, as we already know, overtook the buildings of that Wall in the course of their history. On this assumption, the story of the war is that the tribes of central Scotland overwhelmed the Antonine Wall, ravaged the Lowlands, met and destroyed a considerable force sent to stop them, but failed to break the much more solid barrier of Hadrian. The field army, beaten and demoralized, was brought up to fighting-pitch again by the stern vigour of Marcellus, and attacked the invaders once more, this time successfully. An inscription at Carlisle records the dedication of a shrine 'to the divine companions of the god

---

[1] Cassius Dio (Xiphiline's abridgement), lxxii. 8. *Hist. Aug.*, Lampridius, *Commodus*, ch. 13, § 5, speaks vaguely of a revolt in Britain, and ibid., ch. 8, § 4, seems to confuse this war with the soldiers' rebellion to be mentioned below.

[2] Until lately it was assumed that a great destruction everywhere traceable on that Wall could be brought into connexion with this passage of Dio. The consequences of this assumption were, however, difficult to accept; and within recent years new discoveries have shown that the destruction actually took place later, on the occasion of Albinus's removing his troops to Gaul.

Hercules', with whom Commodus was pleased to identify himself, 'on the rout of a vast horde of barbarians'; Professor Rostovtzeff, who has restored the inscription, sees in it a commemoration of Marcellus's victory.[1]

If that is the story of the campaign, its lessons were not difficult to read. The Antonine Wall had proved powerless against an attack from the north, and it had now become evident that the possibility of such attacks was a thing to be reckoned with. The position in Scotland was untenable. Hadrian's Wall, on the contrary, had signally justified itself. It had not only checked the barbarians, it had given the shattered legions time to recover their morale behind its shelter and prepare their counter-stroke at leisure.

If the latest reading of the evidence is right,[2] this lesson was understood and its practical consequences drawn by Marcellus himself. The third and last period of construction on the Antonine Wall is now regarded as his work; but the buildings thus reconstructed seem not to have been long occupied; and there is much to show that when they were finally abandoned, which in any case happened before the end of the century, they were methodically dismantled not by triumphant enemies, but by the Romans themselves, for altars and inscribed slabs, which enemies would take special pleasure in destroying, were hidden out of harm's way in the ground. All this suggests that when Marcellus had defeated the invaders his first act was to repair the Antonine Wall, as a demonstration of strength, and that then, when order was restored and the frontier quiet, he

---

[1] *C.I.L.* vii. 924; *J.R.S.* xiii (1923), p. 91.

[2] Sir George Macdonald's, in *Wall* (cit.), ed. 2. After the first scientifically conducted excavations on the Antonine Wall, the evidence of the coins found there was interpreted as indicating that the Wall was finally abandoned when the invaders of 180–4 destroyed it: the first intermediate destruction being assumed to date *c.* 155, the second was associated 'with the operations of Calpurnius Agricola or with a later rising in the reign of Marcus' (op. cit., ed. 1, 1911, p. 401). Sir George now thinks the interval of time thus allowed for, between the first and second destructions, insufficient to account for the state in which remains of the second period have been found (ed. 2, p. 479), and therefore dates the second destruction to 180–4 and ascribes the third period to Ulpius Marcellus himself. This reopens the question, when was the Antonine Wall finally evacuated? Sir George, on an exhaustive review of the evidence, comes to the conclusion that this event took place early in the reign of Commodus and was in fact carried out by Marcellus in an orderly and deliberate way. The evidence does not amount, in my opinion, to proof, though this is not the place to go into details; none the less, I am disposed to think that on the balance of probabilities this view is the right one, and adopt it in the text.

deliberately razed the fortifications and evacuated the position, withdrew to Hadrian's line, and made that for the future the single frontier of Roman Britain.

It must have been soon after this event that Marcellus was recalled. We are told that Commodus had it in mind to make away with him on account of his virtues, but finally spared him. Perhaps the emperor was angry with the man who had sufficient strength of mind to abandon the Antonine Wall; perhaps, on the other hand, he accused Marcellus of driving his troops to mutiny by the unreasonable severity of his discipline. For it is certain that, when Marcellus was succeeded by Helvius Pertinax, the future emperor, the army of Britain was in a dangerous mood, airing grievances and ready for violence. The story of these mutinous moods is a confused one, as such stories generally are. At one time the men attempted to set up an emperor of their own, one Priscus; at another, they took it into their heads to send a deputation, 1,500 strong, to wait upon Commodus and denounce his trusted minister, Tigidius Perennis, as a traitor. The idea was not an invention of their own. Perennis had a son who was in command of the Illyrian army; and certain Illyrian soldiers in Rome went to the emperor and informed him that Perennis meant to put this son on the throne in his stead. Apparently the deputation from Britain went to back up the statement of these Illyrians. In any case they gained their point; Perennis lost at once his power and his head. His fall took place in 185, and it was after this event that Pertinax was sent to restore order in Britain. He put down the mutiny, not without danger to his own life, when once more the mood of the troops abruptly changed, and they declared themselves willing to serve whatever emperor he liked, preferably himself.

The real importance of these outbreaks lies in the fact that they foretold a new civil war. The assassination of Commodus in 193 brought about a situation much like that following the death of Nero in 69. In both cases the army took upon itself the nomination of a successor. In both cases the praetorian guards were the first in the field; in both cases their choice was a failure, and the matter was left to the arbitrament of the sword, each army fighting the rest in support of its own man. The praetorians chose Pertinax, but he alienated his supporters by incautious reforms, and the soldiers who had crowned him butchered him, and proceeded to hold an auction, offering the empire to the highest bidder. So contemptible a farce could only end contemptibly. Didius Julianus, to whom the majesty and godhead of an emperor were knocked down for cash, paid his money but never received his goods: he remained a futile and incompetent old man, waiting in fussy inactivity while Septimius Severus, the grim African who commanded the legions of upper Pannonia, made all ready for his destruction.

By July Julianus was dead and Severus was in Rome. His first act was to disband the praetorian guards and substitute a bodyguard of his own choosing. He knew that Pescennius Niger in Syria and Clodius Albinus, the successor of Pertinax in Britain, were possible rivals, and he preferred to deal with them singly. He conciliated Albinus by giving him the title of Caesar, virtually appointing him as his own successor, and marched to the east, where he crushed Niger and fought various frontier wars. The story of his breach with Albinus is not altogether clear; but evidently neither believed that a breach could be avoided, and each was manœuvring for position when it should come. Correspondence treasonable to Severus passed between Albinus and the senate: it came to the emperor's hands, and he declared Albinus a public enemy. In reply, Albinus had himself proclaimed emperor, crossed with all the troops he could muster into Gaul, and set up his court at Lyons. Septimius was already in Pannonia, and by February 196 his army confronted that of Albinus outside Lyons. Albinus, decisively beaten, committed suicide.

Albinus's bid for the throne was a disaster to Britain, not because it was made in vain, but because it was made at all. There can be no doubt that, the Antonine Wall once given up, Hadrian's frontier was equal to its work. Nothing that the tribes beyond it could do at this time need have caused its defenders a moment's uneasiness. In fact, so far as our knowledge goes, down to the very end of its history Hadrian's Wall never fell before a frontal attack. It was captured by the enemies of Rome only when its garrison was either withdrawn or else in league with those same enemies. But now, not many years after one successful invasion, the door was deliberately thrown open to another by Albinus's removal of the garrisons to fight for him in Gaul.

The consequence has long been known to archaeologists. All along Hadrian's Wall forts, milecastles, turrets, and the very fabric of the rampart itself, have been towards the end of the second century wrecked with astonishing thoroughness. It was no mere question of burning whatever would burn. At a fort like Housesteads visitors can still see how the great squared stones of the gateways have been forcibly levered sideways out of place, down to the lowest course. At the neighbouring mile-castle the piers of the north gate have been forced bodily away from the walls with such violence that large stones bonding them into the walls had been snapped in two, and the flags of the floor, when the milecastle was first dug, were found to have been tilted up on edge with the impact of masonry falling on them. Elsewhere, the same tale is repeated over and over again, how the debris of this destruction is full of stones from the ruined masonry of the buildings in which it lies. In many places the Wall itself has been dismantled to the very foundations. Nor is all this peculiar to the Wall. It happens all over the north. Even at the legionary fortress of York the foundations of the stone rampart put up in Trajan's time have been deliberately undercut and the wall thrown down, length by length. At Chester Severus's men had to rebuild the walls of the fortress from ground-level.

This flood of destruction which swept over northern Britain as far south as the latitude of York and Chester cannot be accur-ately dated by archaeology alone. All that can tell us is that its effects were repaired by Severus, beginning at least as early as 198; and we may be sure that no government with the smallest degree of self-respect (a quality lacking neither in Ulpius Marcellus, Pertinax, nor Albinus) would have allowed its fortifications to lie thus ruined for a day longer than was necessary. Archaeology further tells us three things about the damage itself. First, it was plainly the work of men at leisure. It was not done in the heat of a siege; it was done in a cold fury of destruction by men unopposed and uninterrupted at their work. Secondly, it did not spread to the walled towns of civil-ized Britain. Thirdly, unlike the destruction of the Antonine Wall, it was not done by the garrisons themselves, intending a final abandonment of their fortifications, for it is not associated with deliberate concealment of altars and other things that in such a case would have been piously preserved from outrage.[1]

---

[1] There is one interesting exception to this rule: the great hoard, so to call it, of altars buried at Maryport and discovered accidentally in 1870. But against this

One of the first acts of Severus, when his victory was complete, was to send to Britain a new governor, Virius Lupus. It is recorded that when Lupus reached Britain he found it overrun by the Maeatae, a tribe or confederacy of Scotland; and so firm was their hold on some considerable part at least of the province that, unable to drive them out by force, and learning that the Caledonians, who lived farther to the north, were likely before long to join them, he bribed them to be gone.[1] The inference can hardly be doubtful. These Maeatae were descended from the remnant of some of the tribes whom Urbicus had deported. A dozen years before they had watched Marcellus's men destroying the forts of the Antonine Wall; and when Albinus withdrew the garrisons from northern England they realized that the time had come to avenge the wrongs of their forefathers. They swept in, no one resisting them, and deliberately treated every Roman building they could find in the same manner, arguing that without their fortifications the Romans could do nothing. If they did not destroy the walls of towns, it was because their inhabitants could beat them off. They were not prepared for siege-work, and could destroy only where no opposition was offered.

Once the country was clear of them, Lupus made it his first business to rebuild the forts they had wrecked. It was he, no doubt, who robbed the cemetery at Chester for stone to reconstruct the north wall of the legionary fortress, whose demolition in the eighties gave us the finest collection of Roman tombstones in the country: he, too, that reconstructed the walls of York. But at these sites there is no inscription to identify him as the rebuilder. For that we must go first to Ilkley, where he restored a building in 197 or early in 198; Bowes, also in Yorkshire, where he rebuilt the regimental bath-house before the middle of 198; and perhaps Brough-under-Stainmore, the next fort west of Bowes, where a scarcely legible stone records work done

must be set the numerous cases of the opposite kind: second-century monuments thrown down and smashed and now existing only in fragments. And it is curious how few building inscriptions of Hadrian's own time from Hadrian's Wall have survived even in this fragmentary state.

[1] The Maeatae are described as living 'near the Wall that bisects the island' (Dio, lxxvi. 12). In view of the fact that elsewhere Dio, mentioning one Wall only, means the Antonine Wall (above, p. 151), the Antonine Wall is probably meant, which places the tribe on or near the Forth-Clyde isthmus. For Lupus and the Maeatae, Dio, lxxv. 5. The Caledonians, according to Ptolemy, lived in the central highlands of Perthshire and Inverness-shire, south-east of Glen More.

apparently about the same time. Evidently Lupus was hard at work in Brigantia. He must also, surely, have begun the enormous task of repairing Hadrian's Wall.

Later historians have handed down to us a persistent tradition that made Severus the actual builder of the Wall. Until it was known how thoroughly that masterpiece of Hadrian's had been ruined by the Maeatae, the existence of such a tradition was hard to understand; and in fact it misled generations of scholars, and for long divided opinion into two camps according as Hadrian or Severus was supposed to be the builder. But if the Wall itself was razed to ground-level by the mile together, and its attendant works shattered often to their foundations, the work of Severus was so extensive that the tradition is not ill founded and the credit which it gives him not undeserved. Unfortunately we know hardly anything of how this great work of restoration was carried out, or at what speed. By 205–8 it was far enough advanced to have reached the internal buildings of the forts, and even to have extended north of the line to an outpost such as Risingham; and inscriptions tell us that the tribal communities of romanized Britain built certain sectors of the great rampart, no doubt at their own expense.[1] All this indicates a vast effort of reconstruction, extending from 197 to 208, in which every nerve was strained and every source of labour tapped in order to make the frontier system, as it had been at the end of Hadrian's reign, a going concern once more.

To do this, it was not necessary for Severus to visit Britain in person. The system had been designed once for all by Hadrian; to reconstitute it was work that any intelligent subordinate could do; and it was done successively by Virius Lupus, Alfenus Senecio, and one or two other governors coming between them. But Hadrian's work had been incomplete without the offensive against Scotland that followed it under Antoninus Pius. Severus, therefore, in forming his plans for the treatment of the British frontier, was not content merely to restore the Hadrianic fortifications; he meant also to emulate Antoninus Pius in overrunning and depopulating as much as should prove necessary of Scotland, though without repeating his mistake of creating a second, and indefensible, frontier-line. It is clear that his policy was, structurally and topographically, a return to Hadrian, but

---

[1] Not necessarily of their own free will; perhaps rather by imperial orders. For burdens imposed by Severus on towns, cf. p. 203.

politically, a partial return to Pius. First the fortifications were
to be built, then, when the troops had finished that task and
could be spared for a different one, the country north of them
was to be ravaged.

In 208 the first part of the programme was finished, and
Severus came over to conduct the second part himself. From
208 to 211 the emperor, now ageing and losing strength year
by year, pressed home a series of campaigns into the heart of
Scotland. Like Agricola and Lollius before him, he used the
road that crosses the Cheviot at Makendon and the Tweed at
Newstead; he created afresh a base at Corbridge, and a naval
station at Cramond on the Forth; and by immense labours of
road-building and forest-clearing he is said to have advanced
almost to the northern extremity of Britain. And, in fact, there
are Roman camps, which may well be his, as far north as Aberdeen and beyond.

The impression which the narrative of these campaigns, as
given by Dio and Herodian, leaves on a reader's mind is one
of great efforts and heavy casualties fruitlessly borne, in blindly
striking at an enemy who could always strike back but never
stood still to be hit: guerrilla warfare skilfully waged by light-
armed warriors and charioteers, who had learnt the lesson of
avoiding a pitched battle and confined themselves to hampering
the movements of Severus in every possible way and wearing
him out by ceaseless attrition of men and material. And these
at any rate are facts: that Severus died, worn out by his labours,
at York in 211, and that his sons forthwith broke off the Caledonian war and returned to Rome.

It looks like the story of a misguided and wholly unsuccessful
war. Yet after its conclusion the British frontier enjoyed unbroken peace for nearly a hundred years. If the war ended in
complete failure for Rome, why did the Scottish tribes do
nothing to follow up their victory? In part, that was due, no
doubt, to the excellence of the Hadrianic frontier and to the
efficient way in which Severus's lieutenants had restored it. But
it is difficult to say that the second phase of his frontier policy
was a failure unless we are first sure what it was meant to
achieve. Certainly not the complete conquest of Caledonia; if
that had been its aim the elaborate reconstruction of Hadrian's
Wall would have been sheer waste. Certainly not the restoration
of the Antonine Wall, or he would have got to work on that,

as he did on restoring Hadrian's, as soon as he had possession of the ground on which it stood. In fact he never even temporarily reoccupied the sites of its forts, although many of them lay on his lines of communication.[1] It seems that he did not intend a permanent occupation of any part of Scotland; the forts which, according to Dio, Caracalla evacuated at the end of the war need not be more than a few places like Cramond, meant to be held only for its duration. The evidence, such as it is, suggests that his campaigns were meant as wars of devastation, designed to inflict the heaviest possible losses on the tribes that had risen during the absence of Albinus: punitive expeditions, visiting the wrath of Rome on enemies outside her grasp but not outside her reach. In the course of them he seems to have followed the example of Lollius Urbicus in deporting captives to the German frontier: at Walldürn there was a corps of *Brittones gentiles* which first appears in the third century and is thought to owe its origin to the campaigns of Severus.[2] If this was his aim, to prove that Rome could strike deeply beyond her own frontier, punish those who had attacked it, and carry them off into captivity, his success may have fallen short of his desire, but it was not negligible; and the lesson may have contributed much to the security which Britain enjoyed in the generations that followed.

[1] Sir G. Macdonald, *Wall* (cit.), p. 480, note, observes 'there is no scarcity of coins of Severus and his family in Scotland, but none has ever been found on the Forth and Clyde line, or indeed in any *castellum* save Cramond', where no less than nine have turned up.

[2] *O.R.L.* Lieferung xxi, p. 13; Lieferung xlviii, p. 52.

Postscript. Fellow students (e.g. Richmond, *J.R.S.* xxvi (1936), pp. 190–4; and some others by letter) have not much liked what I say about the Antonine Wall. It may be of use to repeat here the logical framework underlying it, so as to clarify the issue. (1) The A. W. fell disastrously, once at least in fair fight, twice in forty years (this is common ground). (2) It was therefore much too weak for the work it was called upon to do (this is the same thing in other words). (3) But this weakness was not typical of Roman *limites* (cf. Hadrian's). (4) It is therefore exceptional, and must be treated as such. (5) The questions thus arise: (*a*) Wherein did this weakness consist? (*b*) Why was it tolerated? (*c*) Why, in spite of it, was the A. W. created at all?—These are the questions I have tried to answer; I hope it will now be clear why I felt obliged to ask them.

BOOK III

BRITAIN UNDER ROMAN RULE

X

THE MACHINERY OF GOVERNMENT

ONE feature of the settlement by which Augustus established himself in the new office of *princeps* was a division of the provinces into two classes, one to be controlled by himself, the other by the senate. Senatorial provinces were to be governed as they had been during the Republican age, by men of consular or praetorian rank, chosen by lot from the senior members of their class; imperial provinces were in theory all alike governed by the emperor himself as holder of the *proconsulare imperium*, but actually by legates of his appointing, each of whom ruled in his own province unless the emperor happened to be there. The full title of such a legate was *legatus Augusti pro praetore*, that is, in his capacity of governor he ranked as a praetor, in order that the emperor's proconsular power should be superior to his own; but in provinces garrisoned by more than one legion the governor was always a man of consular rank. This was the case in Britain, which, as possessing either four or three legions, was reckoned one of the most important of the imperial provinces. The emperor's representative in charge of a province like this, with his miltary command, his *ius gladii*, and his five fasces, was a man invested with less dignity than the governor of a senatorial province ruled by a proconsul, but with more power; it was important that he should be carefully chosen both for ability and for loyalty, and in order that he should learn to know his province well but should not become too powerful it was the usual practice of emperors to retain him in office for a term of not less than three years and not more than five.

Among the subordinates of the propraetor the chief were, on the military side, the officers commanding legions. These, like himself, were *legati Augusti*, delegates and nominees of the emperor, responsible therefore to the emperor, but subordinate to the governor as commander-in-chief of the military forces of the

province. Normally a *legatus legionis* accepted without question
the authority of the propraetor; but occasions were not unknown
on which a weak governor failed to command his obedience, and
we have already seen, in the case of Trebellius Maximus, how
such failure might arise, and that it might put the governor in
an untenable position.

On the judicial side a governor might have a *legatus iuridicus*
as his assistant. Such an office does not seem to have been common; elsewhere we know of it only in Spain and Upper
Pannonia; but in Britain the names of no less than five *legati
iuridici* are known, of whom the first occupied that position in
the governorship of Agricola, and the last in the early years
of the third century. It is not known whether the office came
into being under the Flavians, as some historians conjecture;
but it seems that such an official was a regular part of the
British governor's staff from at least the Flavian period to
at least that of Severus.[1] Like the legates of legions, the juridical
legate was directly nominated by the emperor, but it does not
follow that he relieved the propraetor of responsibility for jurisdiction; he seems rather to have been a subordinate, appointed
to assist the hard-worked governor of a large and exacting province in the performance of one part of his duties.

A subordinate of either kind was capable of governing a
province in the absence of the propraetor. We have seen how,
during the civil wars following Nero's death, the three legionary
legates governed Britain in the interval between Trebellius
Maximus and Vettius Bolanus. Similarly, we learn from an
inscription that about the beginning of the third century M.
Antius Crescens Calpurnianus, juridical legate, governed in the
absence of the then propraetor.

The same could be done, it would seem, though here the
evidence is less decisive, by an official of a very different type,
namely, the procurator. In theory the procurator was simply
the emperor's steward; in practice, he was the head of the
financial service in an imperial province. He was not a man of
senatorial rank, and his relation to the governor was somewhat
ambiguous. He was not under the governor's orders, but the

---

[1] Gsell, *Essai sur le principat de Domitien*, pp. 140–1, conjectures that C. Salvius
Liberalis Nonius Bassus, who was *legatus iuridicus* in Britain *c.* A.D. 79, was the first
and that the office was, for Britain, created by Vespasian. Domaszewski, *Rhein.
Mus.* xlvi (1891), pp. 599 sqq., would place his appointment later, under Domitian.

head of an independent department and responsible directly to the emperor; consequently, in spite of his inferior dignity and powers, he was capable of acting independently, and the actual relations between him and the governor depended partly on their respective characters and partly on the orders each received from their master. The emperor might, and often did, use his procurator as a check, or even as a spy, on the activities of his governor, for the procurator's humbler position and entire dependence on the emperor's favour would tend to make him a faithful servant; and conversely, a governor might sometimes use his influence, though he could not use the method of direct command, to check a procurator whose rapacity was in his opinion oppressive to the inhabitants of his province. The events preceding and following Boudicca's rebellion are typical of what might happen when relations were strained; and in the crisis of the rebellion itself the colonists of Colchester, it will be remembered, appealed to the procurator, the governor being out of reach, for armed protection, though the personnel at his command was inadequate to provide what was needed.

The business of this financial department may be grouped under various heads. The chief source of revenue was the land-tax, based on a survey dividing land into private property, communal property, and state property, and classifying it according to its productivity. In addition to this and the poll-tax paid by a conquered population, there were levies in kind, the *annona*, paid in grain and devoted to the maintenance of the military establishment. A good governor might do much for the welfare of his provincials by checking abuses here; Agricola, for example, we are told, found that the Britons were being compelled to buy grain from the Roman stores to meet their obligations, and to carry their produce long distances for delivery when there were fortresses near at hand. There is in existence a *modius* or corn-measure of Domitian's reign, found close to Hadrian's Wall, certified as measuring $17\frac{1}{2}$ *sextarii* but actually holding about 20; it has been thought that this may have been dishonestly used to obtain 15 per cent. more *annona* corn than was justly due.[1]

The procurator was also in charge of imperial property, whether public or personal to the emperor; such property in-

---

[1] Tacitus, *Agric.* xix; Haverfield on the 'Modius Claytonensis', in *Arch. Aeliana*, ser. 3, xiii. 85.

cluded domain lands and also mines, quarries, and certain industrial establishments. Indirect taxes too came under his department; of these the most important were the customs duties, *portoria*, levied on all goods passing the imperial frontier. There were many other taxes, not all of which need be here mentioned: the five per cent. legacy duty was not at first applied in the provinces, being levied only on Roman citizens, until Caracalla extended the citizenship to all provincials, but they were liable to imposts on trade, on purchase of slaves, and so forth, and in especial to the *aurum coronarium*, an extraordinary levy, theoretically payable on the accession of a new emperor, but sometimes demanded on other occasions.

As to the details of this financial system in its application to Britain, we know little or nothing. Tacitus records, doubtless on Agricola's word, that the Britons were good tax-payers unless exasperated by official insolence. Inscriptions add over a dozen to the two names of procurators that Tacitus has preserved. A writing-tablet has lately been found in London, branded on the back with the legend 'issued by the procurators of the province of Britain', and a number of stamped tiles, also found in London, testify to the existence there of an official building belonging certainly to some body of financial officers, though their exact identification is in dispute. Taken in conjunction with the tablet, however, they can be most reasonably attributed to the procurators, and used as evidence that London (the chief centre of trade, and as we have seen originally the military arsenal) was the seat of financial administration. The totals of income and expenditure for the province are impossible to conjecture; but with its enormous military establishment we can believe Appian when he says that as a whole it did not pay its way.

Within the general framework of a Roman province there was plenty of room for local self-government. In the first place, there were institutions of strictly Roman character. Of these the most important was the *colonia*, which was a settlement of time-expired legionaries on the land. Its members were therefore Roman citizens. They lived in a town and held allotments outside it, so that culturally they enjoyed an urban life and all its institutions, while economically they had the status of independent farmers. It is true that the title of colony could be conferred in an honorary sense on communities very different from this in origin, but so far as we know it never was so conferred in Britain; Tacitus goes out of his way to remark that it had not been given to London, in spite of its size, wealth, and importance as a commercial centre and military depot. A colony received a charter conferring upon it, among other rights, that of electing four annual magistrates, *duoviri iuri dicundo* for jurisdiction and *duoviri aediles* for building and finance; and it was to some extent free from interference by the provincial governor in its affairs. In Britain we know of four colonies: Colchester, founded A.D. 50, Lincoln, founded under the Flavians, Gloucester, under Nerva (96–7), and York, perhaps under Antoninus Pius (see p. 171).

The *municipium*, like the colony, was a community of Roman citizens, or if not of full citizens at least of persons enjoying the so-called Latin franchise. The essential difference between it and a colony was that whereas a colony was an offshoot of the Roman state from within, a *municipium* was a community taken into the state from without. Like a colony, it received a definite constitution; its magistrates, called *quattuorviri*, corresponded to the two pairs of *duoviri* in a colony; but in the case of a *municipium* this constitution was conferred by grant upon a community already existing. In Britain we have only one known example, that of Verulam (cf. p. 86).

Towns of either type had a constitution modelled on that of Rome herself. There was a quasi-senate, called *ordo*, whose members were called decurions, and were ex-magistrates. It was a permanent executive body which dealt with the ordinary business of the town by decree, and was consulted on all matters of importance by the magistrates. The magistrates were elected by the general citizen body; but apart from this the citizens as such had no voice in public affairs, which in practice were controlled by the *ordo*. Every such town had a college of *Augustales*, existing for the purpose of maintaining the emperor-worship which was everywhere carefully fostered as an institution promoting the spiritual unity of the empire; the *Seviri Augustales* appear to have been the annual magistrates of this college, and thus the chief religious officials of the community. A greater or less extent of land round a colony or *municipium* was 'attributed' to it; the inhabitants paid taxes to the town and could plead in its courts and serve in its militia, though they were not citizens.

M

Self-government of a simpler and less highly organized kind extended far beyond the limits of these peculiarly privileged cities. Even the smallest communities which could in any sense be called towns reproduced to some extent the same constitutional pattern. Where a group of houses grew up outside a military fort, as soon as it attained sufficient importance (and the evidence shows that no very high standard was imposed) it was recognized as a *res publica* classified under the title of *vicus*, which means either a subdivision of a town or a separate village; given a body of councillors, called *vicani*; and allowed to elect its own magistrates, two *magistri* or *vicomagistri*, and two aediles. In this way, whenever we find in a province such as Britain anything in the least resembling a town, even so humble an affair as the cluster of houses beside a fort often is, we can be sure that it enjoyed, possibly within very narrow limits, the right of managing its own affairs, settling its own disputes, raising and spending money, and so forth.

All this applies to urban communities either Roman in origin or (in theory at least) completely romanized. But the same flexibility which caused self-governing institutions to spring up on a scale adapted to their environment, wherever anything existed to which the name of Roman or romanized urban community could be applied, caused the same principles to be extended, so far as that was found practicable, to the native population itself. The method of bringing about this extension was to take over the political system of the natives as it stood, and modify it in the direction of conformity with the same universal model. Britain, before the Romans came, was a country whose political life was the life of a number of independent tribes, mostly ruled by kings, and so related among themselves that smaller tribal units could be absorbed into larger ones without altogether losing their individuality. There is no quite certain trace in Britain of the *pagi* into which the tribes of Gaul were subdivided;[1] and the process of replacing monarchical by republican government, which had already gone a long way in the Gaul of Caesar's time, does not seem to have gone far in Britain by the time of the Roman conquest. In Gaul, outside the ancient Province of the south, the Romans retained this tribal system as a weapon of local government.

[1] There is a possible trace: the *curia Textoverdorum* of *C.I.L.* vii. 712: cf. Stevens, *Arch. Aeliana*, ser. 4, xi (1934), p. 138.

The tribal aristocracies easily became romanized in manners and thought; they were induced to build towns, a capital city for each tribe, in the Roman style; and in each of these towns the native republican institutions were readily modified, with little more than verbal alteration, into an executive *ordo* and annual magistrates. By the time Britain was conquered a precedent was thus well established for retaining the tribal units and making them into units for a local self-government rooted in native tradition and at the same time conformable to Roman usage. We have already seen how far Roman conservatism went in this respect, by using even the kings of these tribes, when they were willing to be so used, as imperial legates. In a town like Noviomagus of the Regni (Chichester) there must have been, for a generation after the conquest, a complete microcosm of the Roman constitution: the king Cogidubnus in the position of vice-emperor, an *ordo* of local notables representing the senate, and annually elected officers corresponding to the magistrates of the imperial city. But we have also seen that this was a temporary expedient, adopted only to ease the transition from barbarian freedom to the full membership of the Roman commonwealth which Tacitus called servitude. Ultimately, all these tribal units settled down into the standard constitutional pattern of a municipality, differing mainly in the legal status of their members; for these *civitates* (in a British context the word practically means tribes) did not enjoy Roman or even Latin citizen-rights.

This system was applied to the greater part of Britain, at least in the lowland zone. But its application involved a certain degree of artificiality in the units. A great many small tribes which had existed in Caesar's time now ceased to exist, being absorbed into larger ones or grouped into new units. It is possible to give what seems to be a fairly complete survey of the resulting units.

In the south-east, the tribes of Kent were united into a single unit with a capital at Canterbury, Durovernum Cantiacorum. Separated from these by the forest of the Weald was the *civitas* of the Regni, with its capital at Noviomagus. The district south of the middle Thames became the canton of the Atrebates, with its capital, Calleva, at Silchester. North of the Thames, instead of a tribal unit of Catuvellauni, there was the *municipium* of Verulam with its territory; and farther east, instead of a *civitas* of Trinovantes, the colony of Camulodunum. East Anglia became the canton of the Iceni, with capital Venta Icenorum, the now-deserted site of Caistor-next-Norwich. The Cotswolds, ancient kingdom of the Dobuni, became the *civitas Dobunorum*, with Corinium (Cirencester) as its capital; beyond this, in the Severn valley, the territory of the colony at Gloucester. South of this, and west of the Atrebates and Regni, was a belt of country which had formed the western fringe of Commius's kingdom; it extended from south-eastern Hampshire obliquely to the Bristol Channel, and was made into an artificial unit under the name of *civitas Belgarum*, with its capital, Venta Belgarum, at Winchester. Beyond this again lay Dorset, the country of the Durotriges; their capital, Durnovaria, was at Dorchester, close to their prehistoric fortress of Maiden Castle. And the whole western peninsula, probably beginning at the river Axe, was the territory of the Dumnonii, whose capital Isca was on the site of Exeter. West of the Severn were the Silures, whose capital was yet another Venta, now Caerwent. In the midlands, Ratae (Leicester) was the capital of the Coritani; Viroconium (Wroxeter) that of the Cornovii. Lincolnshire must have been attributed to the *colonia* of Lincoln. In Wales we have no trace of *civitates* except for that of the Silures; the other tribes of which we know—Demetae in the south-west, Ordovices in the centre and north-west, Degeangli in the north-east—do not seem to have had self-governing institutions and certainly had no romanized capitals. Their land may have been altogether under military government; the Degeangli, for example, were probably administered directly by the legionary commandant at Chester, whose mines and tile-works were in their territory. Finally, the Brigantes formed a *civitas* with capital (Isurium) at Aldborough. But much of Yorkshire must have been attributed to the colony at York; and the northern Pennines and frontier district as a whole, though historically Brigantian, were doubtless under military administration.

As to the boundaries of these districts we can only guess; and therefore it is difficult to be sure that the list is complete. There is one obvious omission. Whatever may have been the exact status of London, it was so large and so important a town that it must have possessed, not only *ordo* and magistrates of the standard kind, but sufficient public resources to make it in effect a power in the land. But it was not a tribal capital; it was not originally, and probably never became, a *colonia*; and there is

no evidence that it ever became even a *municipium*. Its wealth
was derived from commerce and industry, and in the absence
of municipal rank it cannot have possessed the *territorium* which
was peculiar to that rank. The omission of London from the
above list, therefore, is more apparent than real; for nothing
that we know of London entitles us to regard it as the centre or
capital of any district, belonging in a special sense to itself.

It was the policy of the empire to foster self-government on
the part of provincials not only in their various tribal units,
but to a certain extent even in the province as a whole. The
machinery by which this was done depended on the institution
of emperor-worship. In each province there was a centre where
this worship was carried on by officials specially appointed on
behalf of the province as a whole. Representatives from every
part of the province (in the case of Britain, no doubt from the
tribal *civitates*) met annually in the *concilium provinciae*, the provincial council, whose chief business was to elect a provincial
high priest for the due performance of the rites of worship, and
to raise the money which that performance required. But this
council had other duties and powers as well as its primary
religious function. It had direct access to the emperor as representing the corporate voice of his subjects in the province, and
in that capacity could express its opinion of the merits or defects
of a governor. Normally it exercised this right only by passing
a vote of thanks to a retiring governor, but on occasion it might
pass a vote of censure. No doubt this was rarely done, but cases
of it are on record.

In Britain, the meeting-place of the provincial council was
the temple of Claudius at Colchester, which was obviously
marked out by its history under Cunobelinus to serve as the
centre of provincial life and opinion. But the system made a
bad beginning. Britain was not a unity, and the attempt to
make it into one by setting up a provincial council was premature. This is shown by the revolt of Boudicca, in which the
hatred of the rebels was especially directed against the temple
of Claudius and all that it implied, that is to say, against the
very institution which the Romans had intended to serve as an
expression of their subjects' wishes. After this we hear no more
of it. That the provincial council continued to exist we cannot
doubt. But we cannot even be sure that it continued to meet
in Colchester. A fragmentary inscription from London suggests

the possibility that, by the early part of the second century, the seat of emperor-worship may have been transferred to a place less dangerously associated with ancient tribal enmities.[1] There is also in London a tombstone to the wife of a *servus provincialis*, a slave belonging to the provincial council, which is additional evidence of the same transference.[2]

If the question is asked: where was the capital of Roman Britain? no answer can be given unless we distinguish between four possible senses of the word capital: religious, civil, financial, and military. We have seen that the religious capital was first Colchester, and later London; the move having been accomplished early in the second century, perhaps immediately after the Boudiccan revolt. The civil capital would be the seat of the governor's residence and offices. We do not know where this was at any time; but what Tacitus says about London suggests that it was not there in the days of Boudicca. Perhaps that, too, was first at Colchester and later moved to London, which would certainly be the most convenient place for it when London had grown to the largest town in Britain, and the most accessible. The financial headquarters, as we have seen (p. 164), were in London. Reference has been made in an earlier chapter to the tombstone of Julius Classicianus, who became procurator during the course of Boudicca's rebellion. This tombstone was found in London, and if, as is probable, it indicates that Classicianus died before he laid down his office, the natural inference is that he lived and worked in London, and that the procuratorial offices were already there just after the rebellion, perhaps before it also.

Perhaps the likeliest suggestion would be that, before the Boudiccan revolt, Colchester was the civil and political capital, London the financial; and that in consequence of the revolt London became capital in all three senses.

Certainly London was marked out by nature to serve such a purpose. But it does not follow that the most convenient centre for the military administration would be found there. London is between 150 and 200 miles away from each of the three legionary fortresses, and 300 from the Wall, where from Hadrian's time onwards the military organization of the province had its

---

[1] *C.I.L.* vii. 22; the sense of the inscription seems to have been 'to the divinity of the Emperor and to the Province of Britain'; that rendering, and the date given in the text, are Haverfield's (*J.R.S.* i. 151). [2] *C.I.L.* vii. 28.

centre of gravity. By the time of Severus there was at York something called a *domus palatina*, an imperial residence, and although this does not imply that York was in every sense the capital of Britain, it may not inconceivably point to the existence there, perhaps from an earlier date than this, of a general head-quarters for the army. More probably, however, this *domus* was merely the residence of the governor of Severus's new province, Lower Britain.

Such was the general plan of governmental machinery by the time Roman Britain had crystallized into definitive shape under Hadrian. The drastic revision of the entire scheme by Diocletian will be described in a later chapter; here a few minor alterations, falling between Hadrian's time and the end of the third century, must be mentioned.

Something has already been said of the Brigantian revolt in the reign of Antoninus Pius. Pausanias, our authority for it, says that it was followed by Roman annexation of a great part of the Brigantian territory. This seems at first sight strange, since the whole of Brigantia was already well within the Roman frontier. But it has already been pointed out that one large part of that region must have belonged, partly as colonists' allotments and partly as attributed land, to the *colonia* of York, and that another large part was probably administered not from the tribal centre at Aldborough, but by the military authorities of the frontier district. It is therefore easy to understand the words of Pausanias as meaning that the reduced portion of Brigantia which in 154 was still governed by the tribal authorities was now still further reduced by transferring a large part of it to one or other category of land under direct Roman rule.

Another alternative is even likelier. The documents attesting the colonial status of York, unlike those for the three other colonies in Britain, are all of a late date, and are consistent with the possibility that the *colonia* there, as distinct from the legionary fortress and the usual *canabae* forming a settlement outside its walls, did not begin to exist until the Antonine period. Knowing as we do that the Brigantes were punished for their revolt by 'cutting off', as Pausanias puts it, a great part of their land, it is very probable that what Julius Verus actually did was to create the colony at York, to give the colonists allotments in the fertile vale of the Ouse, and to annex to their community in the form of *ager attributus* a considerable proportion of the rest. This is all the more likely because Aldborough, whose walls are thought to be of Hadrianic date, lies so close to York that if the *colonia* there existed in Hadrian's time it is hard to see how the allotments and attributed land of the colony could avoid jostling the Brigantian capital, in which case one might have expected Hadrian to move the native town to another and more distant site.

The only other innovation that need be considered here is the division of Britain by Severus into two provinces. The fact is baldly stated by Herodian[1] as having happened immediately after his victory over Albinus at Lyons. No hint is given of his motive in making the division, nor of how it was made; but a passage of Dio,[2] whose evidence is borne out by various inscriptions, tells us that the Second and Twentieth legions were in upper Britain, the Sixth in lower. An inscription found some years ago at Bordeaux adds the information that Lincoln, like York, was in lower Britain.[3] From a couple of inscriptions once existing at Greta Bridge, on the Stainmore road from York to Carlisle, which mention officials belonging to the upper province, no inference can be drawn, except that persons officially attached to the upper might on occasion be seconded for duty in the lower.

The general purport of the division, from a military point of view, is clear, especially when it is recollected that Severus restored the Second legion to its full strength, recalling its drafts from the north, and reoccupied in force at least one *castellum* in Wales, namely, Segontium at Carnarvon. Whether because he did not trust the Welsh tribes, or because there was already reason to fear raids from Ireland (both are possible, but there is no positive evidence for either), Severus used the retrenchment of forces in the north, due to the reorganization of the frontier on Hadrian's line, for strengthening his position in the west; and this new arrangement was accompanied by a new distinction between a western command, including Wales with the legionary fortresses naturally belonging to it, and a northern command comprising Brigantia and the Wall.

The natural result of this arrangement would be that upper Britain, having two legions, would be governed by a legate

---

[1] iii. 8. 2.   [2] Dio, lv. 23.
[3] *J.R.S.* xi. 102: an altar set up in 237 by a '*sevir Augustalis* of the colonies of Eboracum and Lindum in the province of Britannia Inferior'.

of consular rank, lower Britain, since it had only one, by a praetorian. When a general concentration of troops was needed the consular would take command. A system of this kind, however, would naturally tend to leave traces in the inscriptions, of which it happens that we possess a fair number for the thirty years following the change; not only is nothing of the kind traceable there, but the texts make it improbable that such a system was actually in force. We find, in the early years of the third century, a governor of consular rank recording his presence in Northumberland without any mention of his belonging strictly to the upper province. Possibly, in view of the exceptional importance of the York command, with its enormous number of auxiliary troops, it was allotted to a consular governor in spite of possessing only one legion. In that case, the two commanding officers being of equal rank, it is possible to accept an explanation of Severus's motive for the change which would not hold good if one were under the other's orders. The adventure of Albinus, he may have thought, proved that the entire army of Britain was too large a force to be left safely in the hands of a single governor. It could be divided in two without seriously weakening the frontier, and for political reasons this was accordingly done. It thus falls into line with the general policy of Severus, according to which frontier armies are so divided up that no one governor commands more than two legions.

From a civil point of view, the division probably implied that London and the greater part of the civilized region fell in upper Britain, whose governor would accordingly use London as his capital, while that of the lower province had his residence at York, this being doubtless the *domus palatina* to which Severus retired after the conclusion of a campaign in Scotland. How the division between the provinces ran we do not know; most probably from the neighbourhood of the Wash or Fens to that of the Mersey; for East Anglia in Roman times, as to-day, was more closely connected with the Thames basin than with Lincolnshire.

XI

THE PEOPLE

HOWEVER difficult it may be to give a generalized account of the population of Roman Britain, its character, its distribution, its density, and the changes which it underwent during our period, the attempt is worth making, if only as a framework into which the details to be considered in later chapters may be fitted. The difficulty is due to the fact that here, as usual in ancient history, we have no statistics, and without statistics any sketch of the general state of a country is at best shadowy and vague, and all too probably wrong in essential points. The possibility of attempting it at all depends on the accumulated labour of many generations of archaeologists, studying and describing the remains of the period found in various parts of the country. By compiling these results and assembling them into descriptive lists such as Haverfield contributed to many volumes of the *Victoria County Histories*, and by plotting the fruits of many such compilations on a map, which has been admirably done in the map of Roman Britain published by the Ordnance Survey, it is possible to obtain a general picture of the population in its relation to the land, a picture which, so long as its limitations, due to the character of the materials on which it depends, are never forgotten, can claim a certain approximation to the truth.

The Ordnance map depicts the distribution of the Romano-British population exactly as it depicts, for example, the Roman road system. Here and there it shows a stretch of road a few miles long, ending in the air, not because the compilers thought that the Romans built roads leading from nowhere to nowhere, but because the farther course of these roads has never been exactly discovered. Similarly, it shows the entire highland zone as, apart from the Roman forts which it contains, almost empty of inhabitants. This is not because we believe it to have been uninhabited, but because sites there, other than these forts, which have been proved by objects found in them to have been inhabited during the Roman period are very rare. Again, it shows large areas within the lowland zone, such as Lincolnshire and the Fens, as sparsely inhabited, because when it was compiled the exploration of these areas had been very incomplete;

in both cases much progress has been made in the last few years. Hence, in using the map for the purpose of the present chapter, two limitations must be borne in mind.

First: in proportion as any section of the people was un-romanized, the chances of its being adequately represented on the map diminish. This is a consideration of the utmost importance for any attempt to estimate from the map the total numbers of the population. If we believed that practically the whole of the people was appreciably romanized we could rely on the map to give us at least a fair sample not only of its distribution, but of its numbers; whereas, if we suppose any given fraction—say one-half—to have been untouched by Roman civilization, we should be obliged to infer that concerning this half the map tells us nothing whatever.

Secondly, a special density or rarity of entries on one part of the map may be due, either to special density or rarity of the population (that portion of it, of course, with which the map is concerned) in the corresponding part of the country, or else to special intensity or backwardness of archaeological exploration in that district. For this reason the map cannot be used for our present purpose apart from some acquaintance with the history of research in different parts of the country.

With these qualifications, the map gives us a scheme of distribution somewhat as follows.

In the lowland zone, the areas of primary settlement contain the vast majority of the inhabitants. They are dense in its central ganglion, the chalk plateau of Salisbury Plain; dense on the plateaux of Berkshire and Hampshire and on the chalk ridges that run from these centres into Kent, Sussex, and Dorset; dense again, though less so, on the ridge that runs by way of the Chilterns and Cambridgeshire to the Wash. The same is conspicuously true of the oolite Cotswold–Northamptonshire–Lincolnshire ridge. But the chief river-valleys, and some low-lying lands, too, have a large population, especially the middle and upper Thames from Staines to Oxford and above, the Cam near Cambridge, the drier parts of the Fens, and the coastal strip on the Sussex–Hampshire borders from Brighton to Southampton. The forest of the Weald is conspicuously empty; so, to a less extent, are the heavy lands of Norfolk and Suffolk; so, too, the clay belt between the oolite ridge and the chalk.

Beyond the oolite ridge we enter a region almost devoid of

inhabitants. The Severn valley above Gloucester, the whole midland belt stretching thence to Leicester and Derby, and the marshes of the Ouse basin to the north, all these show hardly anything except a few settlements on the Avon, a few posting-stations on the main roads, a town and a group of villas at Leicester. The triangle whose corners lie at Gloucester, Lincoln, and Chester is the most sparsely inhabited region in Britain.

So far, in dealing with the lowland zone, we need make comparatively little allowance for the first source of error. All over that area sites even of the humblest villages so constantly yield traces of Roman influence to the excavator's spade, even if only a few potsherds, that we shall probably not be far out if we assume a certain degree of romanization in every section of the people, down to the humblest: not enough to justify us in calling them romanized in manners and life, but enough to justify us in thinking that their settlements have not been omitted from the map in very large numbers for lack of evidence to date them.

In the highland zone all is changed. Here the degree of romanization is so low that when settlements are dug whose general character would suggest ascribing them to this period, it is not always that they contain even a potsherd to make the dating certain. Although, therefore, the highland zone contained no lack of inhabitants, their unromanized condition has banished them from the map, and their distribution must be gathered from other evidences.

Beyond the belt of sparse population there are, on the fringe of the highland zone, three outposts, as it were, of romanized life. The first is in Monmouthshire and Herefordshire, with a few towns and a sprinkling of villas. The second is in Shropshire, with a large town at Wroxeter and a few villas. The third is in central Yorkshire, the richest of the three.

There is evidence for a dense average population of the highland zone in the character of the Roman towns bordering upon it. The upper Severn basin, the country of the Cornovii, contains very few villas and not many other inhabited sites dated to the Roman period. If we knew nothing of its capital, Wroxeter, we should think of it as a somewhat sparsely inhabited region. But Wroxeter, with 170 acres within its walls, is the fourth town of Britain in point of size. Its public buildings were among the largest and most magnificent in the country. Such a town cannot have existed in a thinly populated district. Though other evidence for a dense population hereabouts is wanting, Wroxeter by itself is evidence enough. Caerwent, again, though a small town in size, is remarkable for the closeness with which houses are packed into its walls; as we shall see, it must have contained at least as many people as Silchester, though its area is smaller by more than half. This points, by the same reasoning, to a dense population in the canton of the Silures. If the Silures and Cornovii were so numerous, we may fairly suspect that the tribes of the highland zone in general were hardly less so, as, indeed, their hill-top towns prove.

As to the distribution of these inhabitants, the highest and wildest parts of the highland zone were hardly inhabited at all: nobody lived in the heart of the Lake District, for example, or on the main plateau of the Pennines. Again, the valley-bottoms, where the heavy mountain rains caused frequent floods, and where woods and swamps made cultivation difficult, were seldom occupied. But on the lower hills, on the knees of the mountains, and on the shelves of drier ground between the hill and the valley, especially when the soil was permeable and not too much soured and sodden with peat, there was a large population, often larger than the same kind of land carries to-day; probably not less in average density than the population of the lowland zone.

In all parts of the country the distribution of the inhabitants during the Roman period has a character which separates it from that of the modern population and assimilates it to the prehistoric. Everywhere it is the areas of primary settlement which were occupied: in the highland zone, the naturally drained slopes above valley-level; in the lowland, the chalks, oolites, gravel, and brick-earth. To-day these areas have everywhere been, if not deserted, at any rate robbed of their primacy by a gradual process through which areas of secondary settlement, heavier lands impossible to cultivate without a great expense of labour in forest-clearance and drainage, have been brought under cultivation. In Wiltshire, the river-valleys that dissect the plateau of Salisbury Plain are to-day cultivated from end to end, and studded with chains of villages; in Roman times they were empty, and the people lived on the plateau itself. The same contrast can be seen in the Berkshire Downs and the vale of the White Horse below them, or the South Downs near

Brighton and the strip of low country along the coast, or the Cotswold plateau and the Worcestershire plain.

The shift of population from the primary areas to the secondary has been, perhaps, the greatest change that Britain has undergone since first it began to be inhabited. It has been described as a 'valleyward' shift, and to some extent the epithet is just; but strictly it was a 'forestward' shift. Its essence was a change of habits by which, instead of choosing land to cultivate where cultivation was easiest, because the land was unencumbered either by dense timber or by excess of moisture, men began to cultivate, undeterred by these obstacles, wherever the land was good. Before the shift took place, wooded and waterlogged land was regarded as uninhabitable. After it had begun, such land was reckoned as in no way disqualified for occupation. The result, at lowest, was a great increase in potentially cultivable land and consequently in the total population and wealth of the country; at best it might be an even greater improvement, if the new land brought into cultivation was intrinsically, once it had been cleared and drained, better and more fertile than the old; and in such cases there would be a tendency for the new land not only to rival the old in population, but actually to drain it of inhabitants.

This shift did not take place all at once. But, broadly speaking, in the time of Julius Caesar it had hardly begun; by the time of Domesday it was, if not complete, at any rate far advanced. We think of the Romans as a great civilizing power, and it seems natural to assume that a movement of this kind, resulting in so great a development of the country's unexplored wealth, might have been due to them. But that assumption only seems natural because we unconsciously liken the Roman settlement of Britain to, for example, the English exploration and development of central Africa, which was from the first deliberately planned as a means of increasing the production of wealth by applying European methods of cultivation to soils hitherto, by European standards, neglected.[1] How false the analogy is may be seen from a study of the actual distribution of inhabitants in the Roman period, which reveals the fact that,

[1] The motive, combined with that of introducing the blessings of the Christian religion, appears, for example, on almost every page of Livingstone's books: *Expedition to the Zambesi, 1858–1864*, p. 588: 'the favourable soil and climate render it probable that with skill in cultivation this country might be made to exceed many others' [in production of cotton].

whenever the great forestward shift of population took place, it did not take place then. Throughout that period the vast mass of the people, in highland and lowland zones alike, continued to live as it had lived in prehistoric times on the areas of primary settlement, nibbling here and there at the forests and planting a few farms in clearings, but for the most part preserving its prehistoric habits with regard to choice of cultivable land unchanged.[1]

The distribution of inhabitants in the Romano-British country-side, then, is qualitatively prehistoric, being based for the overwhelmingly greater part on the areas of primary settlement: and with regard to the exceptions, with their evidence for a slight and hesitating valleyward and forestward tendency, it must be remembered that this tendency had set in before the Roman conquest, owing to the settlement of the Belgae. Apart from these exceptions, of which the most remarkable is the Roman drainage and colonization in the Fenland, the chief characteristic of the Romano-British distribution is quantitative. 'In Romano-British times practically the whole of Salisbury Plain, Cranborne Chase, and the Dorset uplands were under plough'; and a recent survey has shown that the same is, broadly speaking, true of the South Downs.[2] Without changing their habits, Roman influence apparently stimulated the inhabitants of Britain to exploit more completely those soils which they already knew how to till, a fact which probably indicates a rise of population, as well as the existence of an incentive to increase production in order to meet the demands of the tax-collector.

When the attempt is made to estimate not merely the relative density of this population in various parts of the country, but its absolute density, the difficulties thicken. We probably know all the towns of any size that Roman Britain contained, and the areas of nearly all; excavation has shown us roughly how far these areas were ever full of houses; consequently we can make

---

[1] The general facts have been laid down once for all by Sir Cyril Fox, whose intensive study of the Cambridge region proved that a widespread, though sparse, occupation of forest-land set in during the Roman period (*Archaeology of the Cambridge Region*, pp. 224–5). But the total results were small, and the Domesday distribution pattern was the product of a decisive change 'wrought between 650 and 1050 A.D.' (*Personality of Britain*, ed. 2 (1933), p. 71).

[2] O. G. S. Crawford and A. Keiller, *Wessex from the Air*, p. 9; *Antiquity*, ix (1935), p. 443.

a fair guess at the total number of town-dwellers. Of villas there were certainly a great number which are still undiscovered; but it is most improbable that the unknown ones were more numerous than the known; and here again the size of a great many has been ascertained, and a guess can be made as to the number of persons they would probably contain. The villages of peasants enjoying a low degree of romanization are known to the number of some 700, and here again we know the size of a good many; but the number of unknown ones is far harder to guess. And finally, when we come to the population of the highland zone, data fail us altogether. The result is, roughly speaking, that we can estimate the more or less romanized inhabitants of Britain, including the army and its dependents, at about half a million souls; but this leaves it an open question what fraction of the whole was sufficiently unromanized to slip through the meshes of our estimate. Perhaps, if we allow another half-million for that, and estimate the total at a round million, we shall not be very far wrong.

It still remains to ask whether during the Roman period this population, taken either as a whole or in its various sections, rose or fell. Much has been written of decline in the population of the Roman empire, but the best modern opinion holds that this decline was probably limited to Greece and Italy, and that in some other regions there was actually an increase.[1] We must therefore approach the question, as it affects Britain, with an open mind.

In the case of town-dwellers it is certain that, after rising to a peak in the second century, numbers must have greatly diminished. The evidence for this decline will be discussed in the next chapter. The inhabitants of villas, on the contrary, increased, though the increase here can hardly be thought to balance the decrease in the towns. With regard to the village-dwellers, who in any case made up the large majority of the population, it is hard to say anything definite. The abolition of tribal warfare no doubt at first brought about a rise; but in villages, as in villas, there is evidence that the Roman peace brought with it the practice of infanticide, which would tend to stabilize numbers. Here and there villages seem to have grown larger as time went on; but on the other side of the account we must place some which were deserted. On the whole, it is probable that the rural

[1] Rostovtzeff, *Social and Economic History of the Roman Empire* (1926), p. 328.

population tended to rise, rather than fall, under Roman government; but the evidence does not allow certainty.

The tendency to take up land in forest-clearings certainly points to a rise; but we do not know at what time this tendency was chiefly operative. If we could generalize from the case of a villa in a forest-clearing in Wychwood, near Oxford, which is known to have begun its existence in or even before the Flavian age, we might be disposed to think the tendency characteristic of an early period, when the newly established *pax Romana* was causing population to rise, and when equilibrium had not yet been reimposed.[1]

The population of the highland zone probably rose a good deal during the Roman period. That is the natural inference from the numerous hill-forts that were built both in Wales and in the lowlands. Probably the relative or absolute cessation of tribal war caused an increase which was not checked, as it was in the lowland zone, by various by-products of civilization.

In an earlier chapter some account has been given of the physical characteristics of the Britons before the Roman invasion. The question must now be asked how far these characteristics were affected by the invasion and the events to which it led. There are two classes of evidence to be considered: historical evidence for immigration, and anthropological evidence for change in physical type.

There was certainly a great deal of immigration, especially but not exclusively at the beginning of our period. The Roman conquest itself brought into Britain some 40,000 soldiers of non-British origin; when to this number we add traders and camp-followers of every kind we cannot put the number of immigrants at less than 100,000, and the probability is that it was even larger. And during the generation that followed the landing of Claudius's army the influx of foreigners must have continued, though it probably declined and, by the end of the first century, was no longer very considerable. The great majority of these early settlers either made up the army, and therefore went where the legions went, or else were engaged in trade and may be supposed to have taken up their abode for the most part in

---

[1] *Antiquity*, iii (1929), pp. 261–76. In reconsidering the views there stated, I have thought it desirable to allow a much larger figure for unromanized village-dwellers, and to attach more weight to the possibility of a rise in rural population during the Roman period. I have to thank Mr. H. J. Randall and Dr. R. E. M. Wheeler for observations on the former point, ibid. iv (1930), pp. 80–95.

London, and to a lesser extent in Colchester, Verulam, Chichester, Silchester, and the other Roman or romanized towns of the south-east.

If we ask where they came from, the answer, so far as we can give it, is derived from a study of early tombstones. We have about fifty tombstones of the first or very early second century which give some account of the origin and occupation of such settlers. Of these, forty-five commemorate legionaries; the rest were either civil officials or traders. From Italy proper there are only four, two of them soldiers; from Cisalpine Gaul nine, all soldiers; from the Province in southern Gaul four, all soldiers; from the rest of Gaul eleven, seven of them soldiers; from Spain six soldiers; from Germany a single soldier; from the Danubian provinces fourteen soldiers; from Greece, Asia, and Syria five, two of them soldiers. On the evidence of these tombstones, the legions of the invasion would seem to have been recruited chiefly in Gaul, whether Cisalpine, Provincial, or Lugdunese, in the Danubian provinces, and in Spain, whereas the traders and officials apparently came from Italy, northern Gaul, and Greece.

Inscriptions of later date, as we should expect, add comparatively little. The main fact which they reveal is that, after the original invasion, reinforcements for the army, when needed on a large scale, came almost exclusively from Germany and to a less extent from the upper Danubian provinces. The influx of German soldiers, whether individually or (still more) in blocks, is shown to have been very considerable in the late second century and early third, after which inscriptions fail us. In general, units of the Roman army, from whatever source they were originally derived, tended to settle down and take root in the country where they were quartered. Among the auxiliary regiments in the army of Britain, over half came from northern Gaul and the Rhineland, a quarter from the Danubian provinces, and almost all the rest from Spain. The great majority were thus derived from regions where the people differed little either in physical character or in civilization from the Britons; and when once they had settled in Britain they would recruit themselves, according to Roman custom, on the spot, and consequently would assimilate themselves somewhat rapidly to the country of their adoption. The evidence of inscriptions certainly tends to show that this local recruitment proved inadequate for the maintenance of their strength; but it also shows that when new drafts were needed from elsewhere they were drawn mostly from the Rhineland.

Thus, apart from the initial influx of legionaries, mostly from Gaul, the Danube, and Spain, the physical influence of the Roman army on the population of Britain, as judged by inscriptions, cannot have been very great. We should expect it to show, if at all, in a tendency towards the establishment of German physical characteristics, and we should expect this tendency to appear only in the north.

There is another source of racial mixture which must be considered. Especially during the later period of the empire, it was not unusual to transplant considerable masses of inhabitants from one district to another. Burgundians and Vandals from northern Germany were planted in Britain in this way by Probus in the third century, Alamanni from the upper Rhine by Valentinian I in the fourth.[1]

Apart from these transplantations, the historical evidence applies almost exclusively to the earliest period of the occupation. That of physical anthropology applies only to its later phases; for it depends on the measurements of bones, especially skulls, and this becomes available only in the third century, when cremation went out of fashion and was replaced by inhumation. Thus the historical and anthropological evidence are mutually complementary: the first gives an account of the immigration and settlement which occurred chiefly in the first generation of our period; the second gives us a view of the population some two to three centuries later, when, in spite of easy communications both within Britain and between it and the rest of the empire, it is reasonable to assume that a stable condition had been reached.

The results of anthropological study are curiously uniform and definite.[2] The Romano-British physical type, whose general features have already been described in an earlier chapter (*supra*, ch. ii, pp. 16–18), occurs all over Britain in skeletons of the third and fourth centuries. It is not confined to the native villages; skeletons found in villas and in the cemeteries of towns show exactly the same type. The importance of this fact appears when it is recollected that the native Romans or central Italians

---

[1] Zosimus, i. 66; Ammianus Marcellinus, xxix. 4.
[2] Buxton, 'Racial Affinities of the Romano-Britons', in *J.R.S.* xxv (1933), pp. 35–54.

of the time belonged to an altogether different type, being as definitely round-headed as the Britons were long-headed; while other inhabitants of the Mediterranean region such as Maltese, Sicilians, and ancient inhabitants of Egypt and Spain, though they resembled the Britons in being long-headed, differed sharply from them in the very much smaller size of their skulls. Thus the absolute measurements of the average British skull in length and breadth differentiate it clearly from one belonging to the so-called Mediterranean race, while the proportion between these measurements distinguishes it no less clearly from one of the Alpine race, to which the Romans belonged.

When allowance is made for normal variation from the average, skulls of the Roman period found in Britain belong with surprising uniformity to the standard Romano-British type. Even in the legionary cemetery at York, from which we possess a large number of bones, there is no trace of the Alpine type to which a large number of the Claudian legionaries must have belonged, and which is admirably represented by the portrait-tombstone of the centurion Favonius Facilis at Colchester. In other words, by the time cremation gave place to inhumation, the effect of that Alpine immigration on the physique even of the legions themselves had disappeared, and even the army was no less British in physical type than the ordinary townsfolk or villa-dwellers or peasants. Or rather, no less Nordic, if the word is understood in its proper technical sense, as a label for the tall and long-headed race which in prehistoric times inhabited the whole of north-western Europe, though on the Continent that race is now confined to the lands bordering on the Baltic and North Seas. For within that race it is possible to recognize varieties differing slightly from one another; and there is a difference of this kind between the standard types of Romano-Britons and Anglo-Saxons. The legionary cemetery at York has yielded a large number of male skulls which, though not very different from Romano-British, are in size and shape identical with Anglo-Saxon. They are, no doubt, to be explained by reference to the reinforcements sent at various times, as we have already seen, to the British frontier armies from the Rhineland.

Groups of skulls have turned up here and there in England which closely resemble the Italian type. Unfortunately, not one of these groups can be dated by archaeological evidence to the Roman period; but as one was found at Richborough there is a possibility that it may represent a population which was either descended with little native admixture from original Italian settlers, or, more likely, one which was reinforced from time to time by new-comers from the same source. Another was found at Dunstable in a barrow of the fifth or sixth century; here, too, therefore, there is a suggestion of a settlement whose blood was in the main Italian. A third and very interesting case is that of a large collection of skulls found at Spitalfields in London, belonging to people who appear to have perished in some pestilence or other catastrophe, and to have been buried in cart-loads. Their physical character so closely resembles that of skulls from Pompeii that the evidence for a population of Italian blood is here very strong; and, as we already know, London is the place where such a population is most likely to have existed. It is tempting to see here the victims of Boudicca's massacre; for though at that date cremation was in general use it may have been dispensed with in clearing up the ruins of a destroyed city, where all the timber that could be had was needed for reconstruction.

The inference from this anthropological material is definite. In some places, notably Richborough and London, there may have been populations whose debt to an Italian ancestry was visible in their bodily appearance; in the north, a Germanic physical type may have had its influence on the army; but elsewhere, in town and country alike, the later part of the Roman period saw Britain inhabited by a race highly uniform in physique, and in that respect definitely and characteristically British, owing nothing physically to the Italian influence to which, culturally, they owed so much.

XII

THE TOWNS

THE Mediterranean world is a world of town-dwellers. By her early tradition, Rome, like the cities of Greece, rested upon an economic foundation of landed property, and in the last resort implied the conception of the citizen as farmer; but politically and socially the civilization of the Mediterranean depended on the life of the town, and implied the conception of the farmer as citizen. And citizenship was no metaphorical expression or legal fiction; it meant bodily presence in the city, personal attendance at assembly and law-court, participation in a kind of life which could not be lived except in towns. Deep in the mind of every Roman, as in the mind of every Greek, was the unquestioned conviction which Aristotle put into words: that what raised man above the level of barbarism, in which he was a merely economic being, and enabled him to develop the higher faculties which in the barbarian are only latent, to live well instead of merely living, was his membership of an actual, physical city. Man's bodily and animal existence might be satisfied by the country; his spiritual needs could only be satisfied by the town; hence the town was at once the symptom and the symbol of all that was highest and most precious in human life, all that raises man above the beasts of the field.

It is necessary to dwell on this conception, because to us it is a little strange. We inherit the words that once expressed it: words like politics from the Greek and words like civility and civilization and citizenship from the Roman; but for us these words are sublimated into metaphor, and we have forgotten, what the Greek and Roman never forgot, that originally they had no meaning in abstraction from the bricks and stones of the city itself. This is because we are heirs of another tradition. Historians of art have shown us that the northern European peoples have never wholly accepted the principles of Mediterranean art, according to which the artist's highest aim is faithfully to depict the human body; and that, with them, the artist is most himself when he is designing formal patterns. There is a like difference between their conceptions of civilization. For the northern peoples, public life needs no town. Its elements already exist in every man's household; and its higher forms crystallize into shape round a tree or a stone where men meet together, and culminate in the court of a king who lives nomadically from manor to manor.

The Greek expressed his yearning after that good life, without which mere life is worthless, by speaking of his city as divine, and of himself, in the words of Pericles, as in love with her. For men of the north, these same yearnings find expression rather in the words of Gunnar, when he turned back from exile and safety to the meadows and homestead of his farm and the death foretold him. 'Fair is the Lithe; so fair that it has never seemed to me so fair; the corn fields are white to harvest, and the home mead is mown; and now I will ride back home, and not fare abroad at all.'[1] And northern men, in spite of all the south has taught them, still tend to think rather in Gunnar's way than in that of Pericles: conceiving the town as a merely economic fact, a place where man only makes a livelihood, and finding room for the development of his higher faculties only in the country.

In northern countries to-day these two heritages are so intertwined that neither by itself can satisfy all man's desires. But when the Romans conquered Britain the two were still separate, and that conquest, in one of its most significant aspects, is the story of their first encounter. Julius Caesar grasped and stated once for all the essential character of contemporary British life, as it appeared by contrast with that of his own country, when he said that Britain was rich in people and cattle, and covered with farms, but that all they had for towns were tracts of woodland fenced against assault.[2] Nor is the contrast invalidated by pointing to the great hill-top towns of the west like Maiden Castle, which Caesar did not know, or to the growth of native towns in the south-east after his time. These hut-clusters were in no sense the nuclei and symbols of British civilization; they were not so much cities as slums.

To convert Britain into a province of the Roman empire, then, was to civilize it in the most literal sense of the word: to furnish it with towns. The same problem had already confronted the Romans in northern Gaul, and the solution adopted there was applicable here too. The hill-top fortresses of the Gallic tribes, places like Alesia and Gergovia and Bibracte, stood not only for tribal warfare and for a freedom that was inconsistent with

---

[1] Njáls saga, *The Story of Burnt Njal*, tr. G. W. Dasent, ch. lxxiv.
[2] Putting together *Bell. Gall.* v. 12, § 3 and 21, § 3.

imperial unity, but also for a barbarism inconsistent with romanization in manners and in the whole spirit of public life. Where they had not been already destroyed in the wars that ended Gallic independence, the policy of Rome was, in general, to decree their abandonment, and to build in the plains below them new cities after the Roman style, properly planned with straight streets at right angles, dignified with public buildings, and surrounded by walls that were at once a defence and an ornament. In such a city the ancient tribe was still to recognize its political centre, but its institutions underwent a change parallel to, and symbolized by, the change from hill-fort to city.

By the time Britain was conquered, this change in Gaul was half a century old, and had proved its soundness. Naturally, therefore, it provided a formula for Britain. If the Gaulish tribes could be converted into self-governing units of the empire by giving each a romanized capital, the same could be done here. In some cases we can even trace a process, identical with that which had created Augustodunum in the plains below the hill of Bibracte, by which a hill-top town was deserted and a new city built close by: thus the settlement in Prae Wood was replaced by Verulam, Maiden Castle by Dorchester, Llanmelin by Caerwent. In others, the appropriate valley site was apparently already occupied, as at Silchester or Winchester or Chichester or Canterbury, and all that was necessary was to convert the hut-cluster into a romanized city.

But there was a difference between the two cases. Northern Gaul before Augustus had developed its towns a good deal further than Britain before Claudius, and to that extent was a good deal better prepared for the change. The story of the Roman wars in Britain contains no sieges comparable with those which Caesar describes in Gaul; the towns of pre-Roman Britain were for the most part either less populous or less powerfully fortified than those of pre-Roman Gaul, and most of them must have fallen at the first assault. Caesar carried Bigbury and Wheathampstead by a *coup de main*; Claudius walked into Camulodunum; Maiden Castle itself shows no trace of Roman siege-works thrown up across its ditches or against its ramparts. And inside British towns, the spade has brought to light no such houses, squarely built and alined on streets, as those of Gaulish Bibracte. If it is true, as historians have said it is, that the towns of Roman Gaul survived the barbarian invasions when those of Britain went under (and although the contrast has been exaggerated there is a grain of truth in it), some part of the explanation may lie in the fact that in Britain the idea of living in towns was a newer thing than it was in Gaul, and that the Roman town-building movement was in consequence more artificial.

It also proceeded far more slowly. Excavations at Silchester, Caerwent, and elsewhere have given us a very complete picture of what a Romano-British town was like when it arrived at its full development; but for an accurate view of the stages by which this development was reached we have to rely almost wholly on work done since 1912, when the Society of Antiquaries began their work at Wroxeter; and especially on the same Society's excavations of 1930 and later in Verulam. The importance of this last piece of work is twofold. Partly it is due to the modern methods available for the exploration itself, which have yielded historical data that were lacking in, for example, the excavation reports on Silchester; partly to the intrinsic importance of the site, than which no town in Britain could have given us fuller and more precise evidence for the character of Romano-British urban life at its best.

So far as excavation has recovered the buildings of the earliest Verulam, the town which Tacitus calls a *municipium* and which Boudicca's men destroyed, they were of a very simple kind: mere huts, clustered beside Watling Street and spreading southward in ribbon-development along it, with mud floors and walls of wattle and daub, not very different from the huts of pre-Roman days. It is plain that the Roman government in the time of Claudius made no attempt to create a town on the Roman model; and this is all the more interesting in view of their readiness to make it a *municipium*. Backwardness in material civilization was evidently, to the Romans of those days, no barrier to the enjoyment of the highest legal privileges.

This earliest town developed rapidly. Industries on a small scale grew up in it. The equipment of daily life was hardly more romanized than the architecture; of all the pottery found in its huts, three-quarters is of the Belgic kind used before the conquest, which implies that its inhabitants were for the most part not foreign traders, flocking in to exploit the new province (for these would have built houses of a far more Roman kind, and brought household goods such as to furnish a civilized life), but

Catuvellaunian tribesmen, not of the upper classes alone, ready
to adapt themselves to the new régime and make a profit out of
the new fashions it had introduced. We catch here a glimpse
of the process by which the Celtic style in arts and crafts so
rapidly died out and gave place to the general reign of Roman
fashion. The Belgic tribes had never been deeply imbued with
Celtic taste, and the same romanizing movement that had
flourished under Cunobelinus was now being carried a stage
farther in the workshops of Claudian Verulam.

A similar process was going on elsewhere. It must have been
at this time that Cogidubnus began royally to adorn his capital
of Noviomagus with a classical temple and doubtless other buildings in the Roman style; the *colonia* of Colchester was building
the great temple of Claudius, a structure more than twice the
size, measured in floor-space, of the famous Maison Carrée at
Nîmes; London was a vast and swiftly growing collection of
military storehouses and the dwellings and warehouses of traders.
Other tribal capitals too must have been growing quickly, if
somewhat chaotically and squalidly, with sharp contrast between a few handsome public buildings, where the authorities
were anxious to show themselves in the van of progress, and a
mushroom-growth of hovels where artisans hammered and
chiselled and modelled, blew at forges, or handled crucibles and
hot metal with the tongs.

So quick and so complete had been the success of the Roman
armies, so ready the conquered British to accept the *fait accompli*,
that no one thought of danger. These straggling, kaleidoscopic
townships went unwalled, without even a palisade against possible enemies. The tempest of Boudicca's men fell upon them
unawares, and wiped them clean away.

For a progressive and thriving town, fire is not an unmixed
evil. Verulam rose from its ashes not indeed transfigured, like
Wren's London as it ought to have been, but better built with
rectangular wooden houses, and fenced foursquare with a ditch
and palisaded bank. The men who made these defences had
confidence in their city: they enclosed 140 acres of ground, an
area only exceeded by three other towns in Britain even at the
height of their prosperity, and nearly half the size of London
itself. The houses which now begin to appear are the standard
smaller town-house of all the north-western provinces. They are
detached buildings, long and narrow, one gable-end facing the

street. At first they were generally built in timber, with this front end open to serve as a shop; the whole house is like a large cart-shed or garage, where people lived and plied their industry and sold the produce. These open-fronted wooden houses are typical of the late first century in Britain; in construction a link between the ruder huts of an earlier stage and the similar stone houses of a later; characteristic of a time when towns were growing fast and buildings had to be put up cheaply and quickly, but when romanization had already reached the point of dictating the architecture of even the humblest town-dwellings.

Such were the houses of the poorer townsfolk all over Britain in the Flavian age, when Agricola, and doubtless other governors as well, began officially to encourage town life. By this time the towns were already serving at least three purposes. Legally and politically they were seats of local government, where the magistrates of the tribe did justice and its *ordo* met to transact its public business; commercially they were markets for the country round; and industrially they were the homes of artisans working busily to supply the ever-growing demand for goods made in the Roman style. But in architecture and in the character of their household furnishings they were still very primitive, far behind the towns of northern Gaul; at Verulam, for example, a quarter of the pottery used in the Flavian period was still purely native in fashion. Their social life was British rather than Roman, and even their magistrates and decurions were not always at ease in the Latin tongue. This lag of equipment behind function was what Agricola set out to correct. He urged the tribal senates to adopt town-planning schemes and to sink money in handsome buildings, temples, markets, halls of justice, public baths; he encouraged their members to learn Latin, adopt the Roman style in manners and dress, and build themselves houses such as Roman gentlemen should live in. If money was lacking for these public works, he advanced it from government funds; if advice was needed, he furnished technical experts.

Thus, by the end of the first century, the Roman towns in Britain had laid down the main lines of their development. Everywhere they had chessboard street-plans, enclosing blocks whose size and shape varied from town to town, but whose regularity bears the hall-mark of the Roman surveyor. In or near the centre of each town was a forum, a market-square surrounded on three sides by shops and flanked on the fourth by a basilica, an aisled and colonnaded hall such as any modern town of like size might envy. In a little tribal capital like Silchester, a bare hundred acres in extent, the basilica measured 240 feet by nearly 60, and is estimated to have stood 60 feet high. To compare this with a modern town hall, one may reflect that, if provided with chairs in the modern style, it would easily have seated 4,000 people: twice as many as, according to the current estimate, the city contained. Public baths were built where hundreds could bathe at once; the Flavian bath-house at Wroxeter had hot and cold rooms each measuring 80 by 35 feet, and the rest to match. Amphitheatres, with banks of earth carrying wooden seats capable of holding some thousands of spectators, were erected outside the chief towns.

The first thing that strikes the spectator of this development is its scale. Even down to the present day, no English town has ever been so lavishly supplied with public buildings, relatively to the size of its population, as was the average tribal capital by the end of the first century. A town hall that would hold every man, woman, and child in the city, and more; a second building where they might all watch shows at once; another, where every one of them might bathe daily; such things are hard to believe in these times, when all the public halls and theatres and picture-palaces of an English town will together hold only perhaps a tenth of its population. These public buildings were, no doubt, planned and executed by a small autocratic body; but they were not intended for the use of that body; they were patently designed for the use of the entire city populace. The successive enlargements of the public bath-house at Silchester, for example, show how its accommodation must have been increased for every increase in the population of the town. Just as emperors provided amusement and sanitation for the population of Rome, so, according to their scale, these local governments of provincial districts, each trying to make its own city a miniature Rome, provided the same gifts for all the people within their city boundaries. Free corn they may not have had; the humbler householders worked for their living; but in other respects the formula *panem et circenses* held good no less in the little towns of Britain than in the capital of the empire. As for the upkeep of these huge public services, that was met out of

the tribal exchequer, fed by taxes on its members and by voluntary contributions from its rich men.

We can glean a hint or two even as to the technical staff that
helped the tribal authorities to plan these buildings. The forum
of the average Romano-British town is not designed on the
model of the typical forum as it existed in Roman towns of the
south. It seems rather to have been planned after the pattern
of the head-quarters building in a legionary fortress. The
resemblance even extends to measurements: the forum of an
ordinary small town is laid out like the central building of a
fortress for one legion; that of Wroxeter, where once two legions
lay encamped, is like the head-quarters of a double fortress.
Again, the private houses in these towns have little resemblance
to the ordinary town-house of Italy; they have no *atrium* and
peristyle, like the houses at Pompeii, nor are they tenement-
houses like those of Ostia and Rome. The larger ones are
courtyard-houses like the commandant's house at a military
site; the smaller resemble the *canabae* commonly found in the
civil settlement outside such a fort. In these ways the planning
of the Romano-British town betrays the hand of the military
architect; the experts whom Agricola lent to the tribal senates
must have been his own army engineers.

Assuming that during the Flavian period tribal capitals thus
planned were built at a dozen places in Britain, mostly in the
south-east, but extending westwards to Exeter, Caerwent, and
Wroxeter, and northwards to the Brigantian Aldborough, it is
easy to see what one result must have been. Each town was a
focus of intense romanizing influence; but this influence operated primarily on its own inhabitants, and only to a very small
extent on any one else. Farmers and villagers living at some
distance from the town, even in the most favourable cases, must
have been very much less affected by it than even the humblest
residents in the town itself. These country-dwellers, or at any
rate the more substantial of them, could vote in the city as
citizens of the tribe at the annual election of magistrates. They
would visit the town when they were involved in cases at law.
Many of them would go there now and then to market, and see
something of town life. But in no case, unless they were rich
landowners who were members of the *ordo* and therefore probably had town-houses of their own, could the romanizing
power of the town work upon them as it would work upon its

permanent inhabitants. The Flavian movement for the development of towns, therefore, would inevitably divide the population of Britain into two classes, distinct not in social standing or in legal status or in blood, but in habits and education and culture: one somewhat intensely romanized, the other romanized in a much lower degree or hardly at all. And there is good evidence that this was what actually happened. The townsfolk, even the poorest and lowest in the social scale, learnt Latin; learnt in many cases to read and write; learnt to live in a Roman way. The country-folk, and in particular the villagers, acquired hardly anything of all this. The larger landowners, as we shall see in the next chapter, became to some extent romanized, roughly in proportion to their wealth; the peasants remained Celtic.

How far this vast plan of town-building was actually carried out during the last quarter of the first century is a question that cannot be answered in detail. But there is evidence that the sudden change in their habits was not accepted, even by the tribal aristocracies, without some reluctance. Tacitus, describing the work done by Agricola in promoting it, tells us not only that he gave 'private advice and public assistance', but that he praised those who were forward to accept his policy and rebuked those who were backward, 'so that competition for his favour acquired the force of compulsion'.[1] This passage shows not only that the responsibility for building romanized cities rests on the Roman government, as their official policy imposed upon the British tribes by what in practice amounted to coercion, but also that a certain degree of backwardness to obey that command was perceptible even to the governor who most skilfully and energetically pursued the policy. The tribal aristocracies must have found that the habits of a people are not changed without difficulty; they probably found, too, that even with the help of government grants the money needed for these vast buildings was not easy to come by. They evidently felt that, in view of these obstacles, the policy was one into which they could not throw themselves with much enthusiasm.

This reluctance was no doubt least in the regions nearest to the Continent, where romanization had already taken root, and increased towards the north and the west. It is the less surprising to find material evidence of it at Wroxeter, on the

[1] *Agric.* xxi, § 1.

north Welsh borders, in a striking shape. The great public
baths of that town, as laid out in the Flavian period, were never
finished. Whether because interest declined or because money
ran short, the building, which would have been among the
finest in Britain, remained a mere shell of brickwork, its roof
never put on, its walls never plastered, and its furnaces never lit.

There is some reason to think the Wroxeter baths no isolated
case. They seem to be symptomatic of a failure to carry the
Flavian town-building policy to its logical conclusion. Such a
policy would be complete, as recent excavation at various sites
has shown, only when every town was surrounded by walls
comparable in massiveness and in architectural character with
its public buildings. It used to be thought that the towns of
so peaceful a province, sheltered behind its entanglement of
frontier-garrisons, were originally designed to be unfortified,
and that they provided themselves with walls only when the
troublous times of the later imperial age made them necessary.
This is now known to be a mistake. The *colonia* of Colchester,
undefended at first, was furnished with magnificent walls and
monumental gates soon after the Boudiccan rebellion. Verulam, as we saw, was simultaneously given an earthwork and
palisade defence. At Caerwent and probably at Silchester
earthen defences of the same kind were thrown up at an early
date. The walls of London were certainly built not later than
the first half of the second century; it is now thought that they
date from the reign of Hadrian. And it was not until the reign
of Hadrian that the earthworks of Verulam were replaced by
stone walls.

Hadrian, according to his biography in the *Historia Augusta*,
'set many things right in Britain', besides building the Wall.
The excavations of Wroxeter and Verulam have given the words
a new meaning. They reveal Hadrian as the emperor who revived the town-building policy of the Flavian age, rescued it
from stagnation, and carried it through to within sight of the
end. At Wroxeter, where the ruin of the half-finished baths
stood as a monument of failure and bankruptcy in the very
centre of the town, he encouraged the authorities of the Cornovii
to demolish it, to build a splendid forum in its place, and to
erect a bath-house on a new site. The story is revealed by the
inscription that stood over the gateway of the forum, happily
preserved where it fell, dating its erection to Hadrian's reign

and its completion to A.D. 130, some eight years after his visit to Britain. At Verulam, where houses had begun to straggle southward along Watling Street outside the Flavian earthwork, a new effort made in his reign swept away the earlier defences and laid out a fresh line, enclosing 200 acres of ground and carrying a massive wall of flint and brick, whose gates were not unworthy to be compared with those of the great Gaulish cities.

These facts show that when the town-building policy was no longer being constantly urged upon the British tribal senates by a governor like Agricola, it failed to preserve its momentum. The reasons were probably economic. The capital expense involved must always have been disproportionate to the tribal revenue, and could be met only by constant help from the central government or by remorseless taxation. But whatever the reasons may have been, the fact is that the central government which had initiated the policy found itself obliged to keep up a constant pressure if it was to be fully carried out.

Even with Hadrian, the development of the Romano-British towns was not complete. The stone walls of Caerwent seem not to have been built until the second half of the second century; the theatre at Verulam about the middle of the century. It was the age of the Antonines that saw the towns of Britain reach their apogee. This was the time when their population was largest, their public buildings most splendid, and their private houses most luxurious. At this point, therefore, we may pause for a moment to survey their achievement and estimate the return they gave for all the effort that had gone to their creation.

We find tribal capitals to the number of a dozen: Canterbury, Chichester, Winchester, Silchester, Cirencester, Dorchester, and Exeter south of the Thames; north of it Leicester, Wroxeter, Caerwent; and Aldborough beyond the Humber. Verulam, too, was in fact a tribal capital, differing from the rest in promotion to municipal rank. These represent the romanized urban life of the Britons. London, the largest of all, and by now almost certainly the seat of government, was perhaps rather cosmopolitan than British, though doubtless its inhabitants were for the most part natives of the province. Bath, too, a luxurious and fashionable health-resort, was a cosmopolitan town that stood outside the tribal system. The colonies of Colchester, Gloucester, Lincoln, and York, in spite of their military origin, were becoming increasingly British as the British element came to preponderate in the army, and were growing less and less different in character from the ordinary run of the larger towns. Smaller towns were numerous. We know about fifty, varying from busy industrial centres to mere posting-stations along the main roads.

In spite of the scale and magnificence of their public buildings, so far in excess of our ordinary modern standards, all these towns, compared with our own, were very small. London contained within its walls 330 acres; Cirencester 240; Verulam 200; Wroxeter 170; Colchester 108; Silchester only 100. Some of the towns which in the preceding paragraph have been classified as large covered no more than 30 or 40 acres. Nor were the inhabitants as a rule at all closely packed within the defences. There were no blocks of flats. The houses were detached and stood with plenty of elbow-room. At Silchester, where the entire town-plan has been recovered, at Caerwent, where the plan is hardly less complete, and at Verulam, where trenching has been done with the express purpose of settling the question, it is proved that there were considerable areas towards the outskirts of the town where no houses were ever built. The walls were evidently laid out on a generous scale to make room for large increases of population, and more land was included than was ever required. When we ask ourselves, therefore, what population a town of a given size probably contained, we must be guided by the analogy not of a densely packed modern city with houses touching one another all along its streets, but of a residential town where they stand free.

In Silchester, with 100 acres of land, there were only 80 houses. Half of these are of the humblest kind, inhabited doubtless by a single family with few slaves or none. Even the largest could hardly contain a very large body of slaves in addition to the family. It has been estimated[1] that Silchester might have contained as many as 2,000 inhabitants; as this implies an average of 25 to a house, it ought to be considered extremely generous, and any one who proposed to reduce it by half would be difficult to answer. The evidence of Verulam shows that Silchester was not peculiar in the smallness of even its maximum population relatively to its size.

[1] Oman, *England before the Norman Conquest*, p. 181. In view of the acknowledgement in the preface, we may assume this estimate to carry the authority of Haverfield's approval.

But there was no constant ratio of population to area. Caerwent was less than half the size of Silchester, but it seems to have contained quite as many houses, if not more: judging by the way they stand in the excavated *insulae* there may well have been a hundred in the 44 acres enclosed by the walls. In this Caerwent was perhaps exceptional. It seems to have been laid out as a city almost simultaneously with the neighbouring legionary fortress at Caerleon; in its rectangular plan and in its area it owes something to the model of such a fortress; unlike many Romano-British towns, it had defences from the first, owing, no doubt, to the wildness of the hardly conquered frontier district in which it was planted; and the later growth of population had to accommodate itself as best it could to this pre-existing plan. At Silchester, on the contrary, the defences, even in their earlier form as earthworks, seem designed so as to accommodate themselves to a pre-existing town with streets laid down and houses already spreading along them. Caistor-next-Norwich in this respect resembles Caerwent; Cirencester and Wroxeter and London are like Verulam or Silchester.

We may therefore assume an average population of one or two thousand in the smaller tribal capitals, rising to two or three times that number in a place like Wroxeter and even more at Cirencester or Verulam. But even Verulam in the Antonine age is likely to have held, perhaps, nearer 5,000 inhabitants than 10,000; London itself possibly not more than 15,000.[1]

The smallness of these town populations makes it easier to conceive their relation to the life of the country as a whole. Economically, the towns were parasitic on the country-side. They had to be fed by it, and the goods they produced, together with the services they rendered as markets and trading-centres, were no adequate return for the food they consumed and the expenditure which they demanded for the upkeep of their public services. They had their industries; but these consisted only to a small extent in the production of goods needed in the country; most of them were luxury-trades whose produce was mostly used in the towns themselves. They did a large business in retail trade, selling pottery made in Gaul and other imports,

---

[1] The discrepancy between these conjectural figures and the statement of Tacitus that Boudicca massacred 70,000 persons at Colchester, London, and Verulam is not necessarily fatal to the conjecture. The estimate for Boudicca's victims is likely to be much exaggerated; it must also include refugees.

but, here again, the total quantity of these goods which found its way into the country districts was the barest fraction of what the towns consumed. From the strictly economic point of view the towns were a luxury. Their function was cultural and political. They stood for the decencies and elegances of civilized life, and they provided a link between the Roman government and the mass of the people, to whom those decencies and elegances were things out of reach. Their populations, rich and poor alike, thus formed a privileged section of the people, privileged to enjoy the blessings of romanization at the expense of the country-folk.

The strictly economic point of view was not, of course, that which the central government had in mind when it forced this policy on the Britons. Its motives, so far as they were conscious at all, were partly political, the desire to find means of governing a conquered people, and partly cultural, the desire to create wherever possible that urban life which to the Roman mind was identical with the best life. These motives so completely dominated Roman policy that it is hardly relevant to judge its results by economic standards, to insist that town life in Britain was a luxury, and to ask whether it was a luxury that Britain could afford. But if we do insist upon raising this question, the answer to it will depend on the ability of Britain to pay for the luxury, and this again will depend on the outlay which it required. It is the very smallness of the towns that justifies in a strictly economic sense, if anything can, the policy of creating them.

The general aspect of such a town in the Antonine period is familiar from excavations. In the open centre of the forum markets were held, while in the shops opening inwards upon the market-place, and sometimes outwards too upon the surrounding streets, retail trade was carried on. The excavations at Wroxeter have shown how one of these shops might be full of Samian pottery from Gaul; another might specialize in coarser pottery; in another, a packing-case full of whetstones awaited the customer. In the basilica the public business of the tribe was being done, and behind it was a row of offices where the magistrates worked in private with their clerical and technical staff. In the streets, which were well paved and well drained, and provided with side-walks for pedestrians, the older wooden shacks had been replaced by well-built houses, half-timbered above and roofed with tiles and slates, but standing on stone

foundations. In the smaller ones, artisans were at work, and the
things they made were offered for sale in elegant shop-fronts
forming the street-face of the house. Different towns to some
extent specialized in different industries; Silchester had its
dyers, Wroxeter its iron-workers; but in all of them there were
blacksmiths, bronze-workers, joiners, stone-masons, and all the
trades required by the daily life of the town.

These smaller houses were more for use than for luxury; but
the larger were not only roomy, but handsome. Their living-
rooms were large and adorned with tessellated pavements and
frescoed walls, and some of them were heated with hypocausts.
Even if they had no upper stories, about which there is no conclusive evidence one way or the other, the best had from a dozen
to twenty rooms, of which a good many would be about twenty
feet square. Here is ample space for a rich man's family, with
reception-rooms and bedrooms all on a good scale, and a large
retinue of slaves. In plan these large houses are curiously shape-
less, and their appearance can hardly have been impressive to
the eye of an architect; but they were comfortable, convenient,
spacious; and, surrounded as they were by gardens and opening
on the street through private gates, they were pleasant places
for an easy life.

One general characteristic of these town houses, large and
small alike, is the absence of baths. For the daily bath which
the Roman took before dinner, their inhabitants went to the
public bath-house. Here they met their friends, took their exercise, and went through all the sociable and leisurely ritual of the
Roman bath: the undressing, the cold room, the warm room,
the hot room, and back; the massage and the cold douche, and
so to the dressing-room and home to dine. Sometimes, as in the
later bath-house at Wroxeter, there were two suites of rooms,
doubtless for men and women; as a rule there was only one, and
sometimes an emperor would discover laxities, and issue an edict
that men and women were to bathe at different times. This
happened often enough to show that, in a general way, public
opinion saw no harm in mixed bathing.

Even visitors were provided for. At Silchester there was a
large building which has been identified as an hotel. As strangers
would not be entitled to use the city bath-house, it had a private
one of its own. Doubtless other towns had the same.

Most towns, if not all, had a public water-supply brought by an aqueduct, not a stone or brick one, striding across country like those of the drier south, but a covered channel cut in the ground, tapping a neighbouring stream. When enough had been provided for the public services, the surplus was available for private use, though for the most part private houses relied on their own wells.

For amusements, there was the amphitheatre. Gladiatorial shows were perhaps too expensive to be common, but beast-baiting was cheap, and the fondness of Britons for cock-fighting was already notorious. Verulam was not unique in possessing a theatre; Tacitus mentions another at Colchester; but Verulam's is the only one revealed as yet by the spade. The Verulam theatre was built about 150. Both from its plan and from what we know of the drama in Roman times, we can be sure that it was not used for the production of classical plays; but singers and dancers may have performed there, and, as no amphitheatre has been found, it probably served as a bull-ring and cock-pit.

The religious needs of the people were supplied by temples, of which every town contained a certain number, where gods of mixed origin were worshipped: partly Celtic, partly Roman, partly from the east. The temples were small buildings, not designed for congregations; the ritual was kept going by priests, and individual worshippers could attend as they pleased, bringing their petitions and their offerings. In every town, too, there were *collegia* of the ordinary Roman type: guilds or clubs partly religious, partly social, partly based on business interests; subject to legal control and authorization, and thus part of the public life of the community. One of their functions was to provide the burial expenses of their members in the cemeteries which lay along the roads outside the city gates.

Finally, as a body capable of defending itself, the town had its walls, and could man them at need by calling up its own militia.

Throughout the Antonine period this urban life continued to flourish. When the forum at Wroxeter was burnt down about A.D. 160, it was rebuilt. At Verulam private houses were tending to increase in size and numbers down to the beginning of the third century. But at some time before the middle of that century a change began to make itself felt. Evidence has long been known pointing to a great decline in the prosperity and population of the towns before the end of the Roman period. At Silchester, the excavators found that in the best houses people

had, at some late date, lived squalidly, lighting their fires and
doing their cooking upon tessellated pavements. At the time,
this date was assumed to fall in the dark years after the departure
of the Romans; but now there is no need for such an hypothesis.
At Caerwent, a rudely constructed amphitheatre has been built
over the deserted ruins of houses inside the town, clear proof
that, at a time within the Roman period, the population was
much diminished and land within the walls no longer in demand
for building.

Further light came with the discovery that at Wroxeter the
forum had been again burnt down about A.D. 300 and never
rebuilt. The life of the town had not come to an end; the overthrown columns of the portico, lying half-buried in the street,
had been worn on their upper surface by the traffic of long years;
but the unrepaired destruction of the forum showed that the
trade of the town was ruined, its finances exhausted, and its
public life paralysed. For at least a hundred years at the end of
its history, Wroxeter was a town economically and politically
decayed.

But it was only the Verulam excavations that drew all this
together into a coherent and detailed picture. There it was
found that by about A.D. 275 the walls were partly ruinous,
the theatre was long disused and demolished by service as a
common quarry for the town, and the houses were everywhere
falling into decay. Verulam 'must at this time have borne some
resemblance to a bombarded city'.[1] The vigour of its life was at
so low an ebb that no reconstruction was being done. All this
indicates a decline of the most far-reaching kind, which had
probably made some progress by the middle of the century.
The catastrophic manner in which this decline smote a great
and central town like Verulam, far away from the frontiers,
shows that it was not due to barbarian invasion: its causes,
whatever they may have been, were not peripheral, but central.

What, then, were these causes? That is a question which
carries us far beyond the confines of British history, and here
its obscurities and intricacies can only be dealt with in the
briefest outline. First of all, it must be recognized that if we
divide the life of Roman Britain into the three heads of urban,
rural, and military, the disaster that overwhelmed Verulam
affected the first of these alone. Rural life, as we shall see in

---

[1] R. E. M. and T. V. Wheeler, *Report on Excavations at Verulam* (1936), p. 28.

the next chapter, continued to prosper: indeed, it prospered increasingly. The defence of the frontier was not impaired. What happened was that the cities, which until now had stood for romanization and had enjoyed a privilege of civilized life, suffered a blow of the most devastating kind: a blow which left them unable to recover from it.

This did not happen only in Britain. A decay of city life is to be traced in the middle of the third century all over the empire. So general is it, that as lately as 1926, before Verulam had told its story to the excavators, the historian of the economic life of the empire, commenting on the 'rapid and disastrous decay' of cities at that time, observed: 'The only exception seems to have been Britain, where the third century appears to have been a time of peace and prosperity.'[1] Something was happening all over the Roman world which was cutting away the foundations of urban civilization: so widespread that it can only have been due to some universal cause, so cumulative that no recovery from it was possible.

Professor Rostovtzeff, who has painted a picture of this decay, using the entire map of the Roman empire as his canvas, traces its origins back to the reign of Septimius Severus. Where earlier emperors had fostered town life as the principal object of their care, Severus openly recognized the army as the basis of his power, and set on foot a movement by which the centre of gravity of the empire's life was transferred from the town to the camp. The urban aristocracies, instead of being helped and protected, were plundered by a system of taxation and levies that bore upon them with especial severity. The voluntary contributions by which wealthy decurions had always from time to time borne a share in the expenses of the city's public services were converted into forced levies on capital, and these were developed to such an extent that the position of decurion, instead of being sought as an honour, was one to be avoided as a grievous burden. Everywhere men of substance tried to escape it, and the government found it necessary to make such escape illegal. Caracalla, when in 212 he issued his famous *constitutio* extending Roman citizenship to a far wider circle, was in effect enlarging the number of persons liable to these burdens; for, while the exact purport of the measure is doubtful, it may

[1] Rostovtzeff, *Social and Economic History of the Roman Empire*, p. 422. His chapters ix–xi are fundamental for any discussion of the problems involved.

have affected the cities only, and in them only the wealthier classes.[1] As the century drew on, the evils of a system by which emperors raised money and resources in kind through arbitrary requisition and compulsory levies became more and more intense. While certain classes, notably imperial officials and tenants of imperial estates, were exempt from municipal burdens, these burdens gradually dissipated the wealth and undermined the spirit of the propertied classes, and in particular those of the towns. By the middle of the century the currency had collapsed owing to reckless inflation, and one ephemeral emperor after another had made matters worse by equipping himself as best he could through pitiless use of the weapon of compulsory requisition. Depopulation set in; people left the cities and took refuge in the woods; and a semblance of prosperity remained only where the individual household, living on the land, could produce all it needed for its own subsistence.

That a process of this kind was going on in the third century, there is no doubt. Its cause, however, is very obscure. Professor Rostovtzeff has explained it as the effect of a social revolution. The third-century army, he points out, was in the main an army of peasants. The Antonine emperors, by raising the status of the peasantry, had set them on the road towards the development of class-consciousness; and by the third century, he thinks, the army had become aware of itself as representing that class, and had begun to conceive a fixed hatred and envy of the town-dwellers as a class of persons privileged at their expense, entrenched in the enjoyment of a civilized life denied to themselves. These motives, Rostovtzeff contends, used the emperors as their tools, and turned the central organization of the empire to the destruction of that very urban life whose development had hitherto been its chief function.

Three points may be distinguished in this interpretation of third-century history. First, that the towns were victimized by a predatory financial policy which found in their accumulated wealth an easily tapped source of revenue. There is no doubt that this was the case, in Britain as elsewhere. Proof of it is to be found in the tribal inscriptions of Hadrian's Wall, referring, as we have already seen, to its Severan reconstruction rather than to its original erection, and indicating that the local authorities, the urbanized aristocracies of the tribes, had been

[1] Rostovtzeff, *Social and Economic History of the Roman Empire*, p. 369.

called upon to rebuild parts of the Wall at their own expense. Secondly, that this policy indicates a new attitude towards urban civilization, an attitude, if not hostile, at least not decisively favourable. It was no longer a central point in the provincial policy of Rome that city life should be fostered and encouraged. For whatever reason, the towns were no longer an end in themselves. This, too, was evidently the case in Britain. Town life is allowed to decay when the military establishment was being most carefully maintained and when country life was on the up-grade. Obviously, this implies a new scale of values in which less importance is attached to the towns. Thirdly, this change is explained as due to a definite sense of hostility towards the towns on the part of the peasants. On this head the British evidence does not allow us to return a definite verdict. We have no reason to think that either the forces which, about the time of Severus, checked the development of town life in this country, or the forces which by degrees converted this check into a disaster, originated in hostility between the British peasants and the British aristocracy. The actual state of the province, so far as we can detect it, seems to have been peaceful, and the wrecking of town life must have been due to administrative action of a kind universal at that time throughout the empire. This accounts for its violence at Verulam, and its relative slightness in the more outlying parts of the country. In one way Britain suffered less than most parts of the empire: with the exception of Spain it was the only region which never, during the period of anarchy, set up a single pretender to the imperial throne. The Gallic emperors, Postumus, Victorinus, and Tetricus, were unable to arrest the process of decay, and during its temporary independence under Carausius Britain fared no better; but perhaps the Gallic empire and the Carausian period withdrew Britain to some extent from the agonies of the rest, and left it battered and bankrupt, but quiet.

As to its bankruptcy there is no doubt. One of the most remarkable features of the late third century is the numerous and vast hoards of coin that were buried not because the country was unsafe, but because Britain was feeling the effects of the same inflation which multiplied the price of grain in Egypt by 6,000 between the early third century and the time of Diocletian. At Verulam an attempt was made to establish a local currency: a hoard found in the ruins of the theatre contains thousands of tiny coins, certainly of local minting, which must for a time have passed current while the inflation was at its worst.

It was in the last years of the century that the revived strength of the central government, due to the work of Diocletian, brought Britain once more under the direct control of Rome. The visit of Constantius Chlorus in 297 led to a great reorganization of many things in Britain; most of them will be dealt with hereafter, but here one aspect of Constantius's work concerns us. At Verulam, the end of the third century is marked by a determined attempt to revive the life of the town. The defences were repaired. The theatre was rebuilt, and even enlarged. Old dwelling-houses were restored, and new ones built, some on a large scale.

Whether Verulam represents the rule or the exception we do not know. At any rate, no similar restoration took place at Wroxeter. In the case of Verulam, Constantius was reversing the policy of the last hundred years, and instead of bleeding town life was transfusing blood into it. Probably the new policy was only half-hearted, and applied only to a few of the most important towns. In any case it failed. The decay of civic spirit and of faith in the value of urban life had gone too far to be revived by administrative means. By the middle of the fourth century the effects had worn off. The greater part of Verulam was uninhabited, a waste of empty land and ruined houses. Here and there squatters lived among the ruins. The theatre had become a rubbish-tip, and its orchestra and auditorium were silted up beneath foot upon foot of domestic refuse. Close round it, a shrunken and impoverished population lived in slum conditions.

There is no reason to think that in this degraded condition fourth-century Verulam was worse off than other towns. The evidence of squatters' occupation at Silchester and of the deserted and ruined forum at Wroxeter, on the contrary, suggests that it was typical. But the significance of these facts must not be misunderstood. They do not imply a break-down or abandonment of the system of local administration. Shrunken and impoverished though they were, these towns were still the capitals of self-governing tribes. They still had their permanent decurions and their annual magistrates. Politically, they were in theory at least, and to some extent in practice, unchanged. The change was a cultural one. The towns of the first and second century had been the privileged vehicles of Roman civilization. The third century saw that privilege destroyed. Whether it was destroyed by the envy of the unprivileged peasantry, as Rostov-tzeff thinks; or because of the helpless rapacity of ephemeral rulers who had no way of supporting themselves except by plundering those whom it was easiest to plunder, the simple and superficial explanation of the historical materialist; or because the deep-rooted Celtic tradition of life, which had in it no place for the town, was not to be overborne by the most earnest efforts of Roman governors; this, at any rate, is certain, that the Britons of the fourth century had given up their earlier belief in, and desire for, the kind of civilization which they had inherited from the Graeco-Roman city-state. The first attempt to romanize British life, by imposing upon it the civilization of the town, had failed. It was when its failure was most complete that the second attempt, based on the spontaneous development of the country house, began to display its most brilliant successes.

XIII

THE COUNTRY-SIDE

EVEN when the towns were at the height of their prosperity, by far the largest part of the inhabitants of Roman Britain were country-folk, living either in villages or in the isolated farm-houses, large or small, which are called villas; and of these again, though some worked at industries like mining, pottery, and so forth, the great majority were occupied in agriculture. We should probably not be far wrong if we reckoned that at no time during the Roman period did agriculture occupy less than two-thirds of the inhabitants of Britain.

Something has already been said about agriculture in pre-Roman Britain, and of the development it received at the hands of the Belgae, leading to production on a scale which made it possible to export wheat and other produce. This surplus of production over and above what was needed for the subsistence of the agricultural population was diverted by the Roman con-quest into two channels: the imperial taxes, especially the *annona* or wheat-tax for the maintenance of the army and the govern-ment officials, and the local taxes which went to support urban life. The Roman Peace, coupled with these two demands for surplus produce, must have stimulated agriculture from the first, although neither archaeological evidence nor literary sources afford any hint that the Romans taught the Britons to use any new agricultural methods. The agricultural life of the British country-side is in substance and character British in almost every detail known to us; what is Roman about it is the political framework into which it is fitted, and to a certain extent the manners and customs of the people who pursued it.

In the four *coloniae*, people lived according to Roman custom in towns who were engaged in cultivating their plots of land in the neighbouring country-side. This combination of agriculture with town life may possibly have become general. Many towns were surrounded by regions in which villas and villages are rare. Round Canterbury, for instance, the country seems to have been almost deserted by comparison with the dense villa-population of north-western Kent. This and similar cases elsewhere may indicate that people lived in the towns and worked on the land

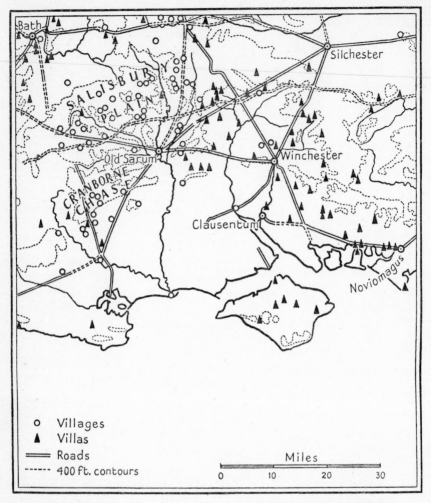

MAP II. VILLAS AND VILLAGES IN HAMPSHIRE AND WILTSHIRE

outside them; but the evidence is not conclusive, and is not borne out by finding agricultural implements in town-houses, except where (as in one case at Silchester) the house was that of a blacksmith or ironmonger. Certainly, too, agriculture was practised by the people dwelling in the civil settlements at military forts, and increasingly so as time went on and the garrisons of the frontier army became more and more like bodies of peasantry. For the most part, however, the agricultural population lived scattered on the land itself, either in villages or in villas.

The distinction between these two types of settlement is of fundamental importance. The villa is a house, large or small, with or without outbuildings, but marked by two characteristics. Economically, it is an isolated farm-house standing in its own land, not clustered with others into a village. Culturally, it is more or less thoroughly romanized in architecture and furniture: it has rectangular rooms, nearly always hypocausts in some of them, generally a suite of baths, and perhaps always painted plaster for decoration on the walls; the things used in it, pottery and so forth, betray a romanized habit of life.

The village is a group of huts, not houses: one-roomed, nearly always circular in shape; sometimes pit-dwellings sunk into the ground, sometimes stone-built structures standing wholly above it; they are never neatly alined on streets or laid out in a regular plan, but clustered shapelessly, generally within some kind of a ditch or fence; and although the people who lived in them used Roman pottery and coins to a certain extent, their daily life was affected by Roman ways very little, and in some cases, especially in the highland zone, not at all.

Seen from the point of view of medieval and modern England, where the distinction between the manor or castle of a land-owner and the cottages of his tenants and labourers is so familiar a fact, this distinction between villa and village naturally suggests a similar relation. But the analogy is misleading. If we look at the relation of villas to villages on the map, instead of finding one villa normally associated with one village or, in the case of a large villa, a group of villages, what we actually find is that cases of such association are very rare, if, indeed, they genuinely exist at all; and that certain regions, so far as we can tell, were exclusively occupied by villas, others exclusively by villages. Thus, Salisbury Plain and Cranborne Chase are

especially rich in villages, and have been so thoroughly explored
that we may be certain few, if any, villas could have escaped
discovery. Yet, though villas are common on their outskirts,
hardly a single one is known in either district. Other regions,
again, of which the Cotswolds are the most conspicuous instance,
are densely covered with villas but contain no villages. There
are, no doubt, districts containing both; but the possibility of
either existing without the other shows that the relation between
them is something quite different from the relation between
two social grades within one and the same economic system.

We have, in fact, to do with two economic systems existing
side by side. The villa is self-contained. It is the residence of
a Roman or romanized person whom, if we like, we may describe as a landlord or gentleman; but it does not segregate him
from his social inferiors. Whatever the scale of a villa in size and
in romanization, it always contains enough room for the entire
staff of an estate; and in many cases we can detect certain parts
of its buildings which must have provided quarters for the
labouring population. The village, too, is self-contained in the
sense that whole tracts of agricultural country could be inhabited by villagers and no one else.

There seems to have been a further distinction in agricultural
methods. Romano-British villages are constantly found to co-
exist with arable land divided up into small fields, irregular in
shape, but as a rule tending towards a square or rectangle. A
vast amount of information on this subject has been collected in
recent years, partly by field-work on the ground, but far more
by air-photography, to which the discovery of these so-called
'Celtic fields' is really due. The result of this very extensive
work has been to establish two generalizations: that Romano-
British villages, broadly speaking, always have fields of this kind,
and that villas never have them. The difference between village-
economy and villa-economy thus extended to the lay-out of their
arable land. The villas cultivated large open fields, the villages
small enclosed ones.

This suggests a difference in tenure. The undivided arable
land of the villa points to undivided ownership or tenancy; the
small fields of a village suggest that its arable land was divided
into parcels held, on whatever tenure, by individual villagers.
The two systems might conceivably rest on an original distinction between land owned by individuals and land owned in

common by villages and parcelled out from time to time among their members.

It also suggests a difference in agricultural technique. All over the Roman world, people used various types of the light wheelless plough which the Romans called *aratrum*; but here and there they found the Celtic peoples using the heavy wheeled plough, invented, as Pliny says, in Raetia, which the Gauls called *caruca*. The essence of the invention was that by supporting it on wheels the cultivator could use a much heavier implement with a much higher penetrating power. Even on light soils this gave the *caruca* an advantage, for it could do at one operation as much work as the *aratrum*, by cross-ploughing, could do in two; but also the *caruca* could be used on heavier soils where the *aratrum* could not be used at all. To utilize its penetrating power to the full, the wheeled plough was fitted with a coulter or vertical knife in front of the share, to cut the soil in preparation for turning a sod, and a share designed to lift the sod sideways so that the mould-board could turn it clean over, whereas the *aratrum* in its simplest form did little but grub the soil like a pig's snout and heap it into a ridge on either side of the furrow.

Of these two types of plough, the *aratrum* would be the more suitable for the small fields of village-arable, which are seldom more than an acre or two in extent, and whose peasant cultivators must have used plant of a cheap and simple kind. The open fields of a villa, on the contrary, would suit the more powerful and expensive *caruca*, especially in view of the fact that villas are sometimes situated on heavy soils where the *aratrum* would be useless. In fact, it has lately been pointed out that in France both kinds of plough have survived into modern times, together with two types of field-system: the *araire* being co-extensive with systems of plots resembling the 'Celtic fields' of Britain, the *charrue* with open fields divided into strips.[1]

Both *aratrum* and *caruca* were used in Roman Britain. The *aratrum* is represented in the little bronze statuette of a cloaked and hooded British ploughman found at Piercebridge, in the county of Durham, and now in the British Museum; it shows an implement (no doubt the ordinary Romano-British plough) whose action was of the grubbing kind described above. Large coulters clearly belonging to a *caruca* have been found not

[1] Marc Bloch, *Les Caractères originaux de l'histoire rurale française* (Oslo, 1931).

only at pre-Roman Belgic sites in Britain, but also at Roman sites: Silchester, Great Chesterford in Essex, Witcombe in Gloucestershire; so that the heavy coulter-plough, which was introduced into the country, as it seems, by the Belgae, certainly played its part in Romano-British agriculture.[1]

Can we go a step farther, and argue that the *aratrum* was used by the villagers, the *caruca* by the villa-dwellers? The evidence is in favour of such an hypothesis but is not sufficient to prove it. The Piercebridge model was found far away from the nearest villa: the building at Great Chesterford where coulters were found is a typical villa, and so is the house at Witcombe. The Silchester coulters, being found not on the land but in a town, tell us nothing definite. The Belgae, according to Caesar, lived in isolated farms; but they did not introduce the isolated farm into Britain; it existed there before they came. Perhaps what they did was, by introducing the *caruca*, which was adapted for use in open fields and not in little enclosed plots, to give a new impetus to open-field cultivation, which for them was associated with the existence of isolated farms, and thus enable the agriculture of the isolated farm to outdistance its rival, the agriculture of the villages, tied as that was to the system of cultivation by small plots. And at the same time the association of the *caruca* with the isolated farm made it possible for isolated farms to encroach on forest-land and begin cultivating heavy soils with which the *aratrum* could not cope.

At the Claudian conquest, therefore, it seems likely (one can say no more, the evidence being so slender as it is) that two systems of land-tenure and of cultivation existed side by side, corresponding with two types of settlement. There was the village, with its communal land divided up into little fields parcelled out among the members of the commune and cultivated with the light plough, and there was the isolated family farm, with its open fields, cultivated, where Belgic influence had made itself felt, with the coulter-plough, and tending here and there to encroach on the heavier soils of the forest-land. It was thus already becoming clear that, of the two systems, one had in it germs of progress, the other was relatively stagnant. The village-economy was rigid and unprogressive because the minute subdivision of land and the smallness of the capital commanded by any individual made reforms all but impossible. The more

[1] Karslake in *Antiquaries Journal*, xiii. 455; Hawkes in *Antiquity*, ix (1935), p. 339.

substantial and independent farmers, the class qualified by wealth and circumstances to embrace new movements, were the dwellers in the isolated farms. These independent farmers, after the conquest, by degrees acquired Roman ways of living, and their farms became Roman villas; the villages were too poor and too unprogressive to undergo any such change, and they retained their primitive character.

If it is true, as the above account implies, that what we may call the villa-system in Roman Britain was the romanized version of a system of land-tenure and cultivation already existing before the conquest, and in especial stimulated and developed by the Belgic settlement, there ought to be some positive evidence that such a system existed before the Romans came. There is such evidence; but it is scanty, and still needs to be confirmed and supplemented by scientific excavation at villa-sites in the south-eastern counties of England.

In the first place, what we know of Celtic economic life suggests that isolated farms must have been quite common in pre-Roman Britain. And this is borne out both by Caesar's statement that he saw them in Kent,[1] and by the fact that isolated farms exist to this day in Ireland, Wales, Cornwall, and Scotland, the parts of the British Isles that were never either romanized or saxonized, at least as commonly as elsewhere, and traceable back to a remote antiquity. It does not follow, of course, that they were all associated with open-field cultivation.

Further, there is archaeological evidence for the existence of pre-Roman isolated farms in the lowland zone; one dating from the Bronze Age has recently been dug on Harrow Hill near Worthing in Sussex: evidence, too, that such farms existed in the Roman period in an un-romanized shape; an example has been dug on Rockbourne Down in Wiltshire. In the highland zone, un-romanized isolated farms of the Roman and pre-Roman periods are common. And lastly, there are several villas in the south-eastern counties where excavation has revealed traces of pre-Roman occupation on the site, either certainly or presumably belonging to a pre-Roman farmstead: examples are at Otford (Kent), Newport (Isle of Wight), Knowl Hill (Berkshire), and perhaps Ashtead (Surrey) and Folkestone (Kent). The classical example is at Mayen in the Eifel, where

---

[1] See above, p. 28.

a complete farm of the La Tène period has been studied in all the phases of its conversion into an ordinary Roman villa. Nothing so conclusive has been found as yet in Britain, but the British evidence, slight though it is, suffices to justify the assumption that the principle proved for Germany holds good for Britain also.

It does not, of course, follow that all Roman villas occupy the sites of pre-Roman farms. On the contrary, if the farm-economy was more efficient and progressive than village-economy, and in particular better adapted to the tillage of cleared forest-land, extensions of cultivation during the Roman period would largely come about through the planting of new villas on virgin sites, in forest-clearings and elsewhere. There is evidence that something of this kind actually happened. In the Cambridge district a few villas were placed in forest-clearings where no earlier finds occur; the same thing happens on the edge of the forest in southern Berkshire. That this development took place, or at any rate began, at an early date is proved by the villa lately dug at Ditchley, near Oxford. It stood in a clearing of Wychwood forest, and excavation has shown that in its first form, as a timber house of Roman type, it dates from at least the Flavian age, if not from the reign of Nero. The Roman period also saw some extension of village-economy, but this will be considered later.

The history of the villa-system in Britain is still very obscure, owing to the fewness of the sites on which really scientific digging has been done. We know a great deal about the architecture and furnishings of these villas at the time of their greatest prosperity, but it is very seldom either that this time can be accurately dated or that search has been made, underneath its remains, for those of earlier buildings on the same site. From the evidence of coins picked up on villa-sites it is abundantly certain that most of them were flourishing in the fourth century; excavation has proved that some were first built at this time, others in the third century, others in the second. Broadly speaking, the villa-system appears to have been growing, slowly but without a check, from the first century to the fourth. In Kent, on the Hampshire coast, and in the Isle of Wight there was already in the late first century a considerable development of villa life, which spread, before the century was over, as far north as the Thames valley and as far west as Somerset. Evidently the richer

land-owners began rebuilding their country houses after a
romanized pattern quite soon after the conquest.

The building of villas may be regarded as a second movement
of romanization, distinct from that of the towns, and having
certain special features of its own. Its most remarkable feature
is its spontaneity. It was not due to an influx of settlers from
abroad taking up land in Britain. Partly that is shown by the
continuity between villas and pre-Roman buildings existing on
the same sites, which attests the reconstruction of old farmsteads
in a new style; partly by the entirely British type of skulls found
at villa-sites; partly by general historical considerations, such as
the improbability of foreign settlers at so early a date going anywhere except to the towns. For these and similar reasons no
student of the subject is disposed to reject the statement of Haverfield that 'the inhabitants of the villas were, so far as we can tell,
romanized natives of Britain. Here and there a settler from
Gaul, or even from Italy, may have found his way to the island
and acquired landed estate. There is, however, a singular absence of proof or indication of any such thing. We seem clearly
to be dealing with an indigenous native population.'[1]

This movement may have been encouraged by government
policy, offering easy terms to settlers on uninhabited land; but
in great part it must have been spontaneous. It was no doubt
connected with the movement of urban romanization, and in
one sense a reflection of it; for the people who first converted
their farms into villas were very likely just those wealthy Britons
who had a seat in the *ordo* of their tribe and a house in the
tribal capital, and learnt there to live in the Roman style; but
it indicates a genuine spontaneity, because it shows how these
persons wished to live, when they were no longer performing
their official functions under the eye of the governor and under
the pressure of his known policy.

At the same time, it was confined to one class. It was a privilege of the well-to-do, and the peasants of the villages did not
share in it. In this way also it differed from the romanization
of the towns, which affected rich and poor alike.

Another difference is revealed by its history. Partly because
of its spontaneity, partly because of its diffusion, it possessed a
staying power which the urban romanization lacked. Nothing
can be more striking than the contrast between the collapse of

[1] *Roman Occupation of Britain*, p. 232.

the towns in the third century, with the complete failure of every effort to redeem it, and the continued and increasing prosperity of the villas. When Haverfield described the late third and fourth centuries as the golden age of Roman Britain, he had in mind the evidences of this widespread rural prosperity and civilization. The evidence of decay in the towns had not yet come to hand; when it did, the prosperity of the villas only appeared more striking by contrast.

Haverfield went so far as to suggest that it was the reign of Septimius Severus which, in particular, marked a forward movement in the civilization of the villas. The evidence on which that suggestion is based, though never amounting to proof, is still valid to-day. We have seen that it was precisely the Severan age that saw the first check to the rising tide of urban prosperity. The two things can hardly be unrelated. If it is true that the early third century was the time when systematic pillage of the cities 'dealt a mortal blow at the civic spirit of the higher classes, and induced them to conceal their wealth and appear as poor as possible',[1] these same causes would lead the wealthier land-owners to spend more time and money on their estates, and to improve their country houses rather than keep up their town houses.

Once this movement of land-owners back to their estates had begun, other causes contributed to accentuate it. Before long, the currency began to depreciate. The consequent rise and uncertainty of prices made town life unpleasantly precarious. Not only was trade ruined, but people living in towns must have had difficulty in procuring food and necessaries of every kind. In the country, where most things that a household required were produced on the estate, people could live on their own granaries and store-rooms, unaffected by fluctuations in the value of money. Before the end of the third century the wealthier classes had learned to think of their villas as places where they could live in a degree of comfort and security not possible in the towns. The habit of country life, once reaffirmed and strengthened by such inducements, was not to be broken. The attempt of Constantius to re-establish the town as the centre of civilized life beat against it in vain. The Roman civilization of Britain had left the towns and transplanted itself to the villas.

[1] Rostovtzeff, *Social and Economic History of the Roman Empire*, p. 400.

The extent and distribution of this rural civilization can be studied on the map with a considerable degree of accuracy, for Roman villas have so long been an object of interest to people of all kinds in England that records of their discovery are voluminous and, on the whole, trustworthy. We know about 500 of them. Of these 90 per cent. lie not only in the lowland zone but south-east of a line joining the Severn and Trent. Even within this restricted area there are certain districts where they hardly occur. They are densest in north-west Kent round Maidstone; west Sussex; the Hampshire basin east of Salisbury and south of Silchester; the Somerset–Dorset borders round Ilchester; the Avon basin round Bath; and the Cotswold plateau round Cirencester, with a belt of them extending thence along the oolite-ridge through Northamptonshire into Lincolnshire. Their absence from the Weald, the New Forest, and the clay belt joining Oxford to the Fens, is due to a total scarcity of population in those districts. On the other hand, their rarity in Cranborne Chase, Salisbury Plain, and the middle Thames valley is connected with the fact that here the village-population is extremely dense. Their relative scarcity in East Anglia seems to be connected with the first cause rather than the second.

Outside this area there are one or two in Cornwall, a fair number in the extreme east and south of Wales, a very few in the midlands, especially near Leicester, and over a dozen in Yorkshire.

It has already been remarked that in some cases they have been placed on heavier soils than were commonly tilled before the Roman period. But these cases are very exceptional. Most villas were built upon the lighter soils, chalk and oolite and gravel, which needed little clearing and no drainage. As compared with villages, however, they tend to select a rather special type of site: a valley-slope facing south or east, not too high up, with shelter from wind, exposure to the sun, and water close at hand. The villages of Salisbury Plain lie out on the wind-swept summit of the plateau; the villas of the Cotswolds nestle warmly on the sides of the valleys, basking in the sunshine.

In ground-plan, the great majority belong to one pattern: a row of rooms all entered from a corridor or veranda running along the front, with a wing jutting forward at each end. Often there is a corridor along the back as well; sometimes it runs all round. The front door is in the centre of the corridor, and leads through it into a central room which might be described in house-agents' language as the 'lounge hall'. In a house of average size there will be two or three other rooms on each side of this, and the best living-rooms will be in the wings. Such a plan would give seven or nine rooms as a normal number; but some villas of the same pattern are smaller, many are larger, and some have begun on this scale but have had additions made to them. Whether they ever had upper stories is not known; probably as a rule they did not. They were generally built in timber and plaster on a stone foundation, with tiled or slated roofs.

Houses of this kind are as common in Gaul and Germany as they are in Britain, and scholars have differed as to whether the type is a Celtic invention or an importation from the Mediterranean world. Neither alternative seems quite to fit the facts. The partisans of a Celtic origin cannot point to such houses existing in Celtic lands before the Roman conquest; those who think that it came from the Mediterranean cannot produce satisfying parallels from the architecture of the south. It seems most probable that the type was invented in the Celtic regions under Roman rule and influence, and should be regarded as a testimony (not the only one) to the existence of a specifically Romano-Celtic civilization.

A villa of this kind has certain accessories which, except perhaps in the very poorest, were regarded as indispensable. A rectangular, walled farm-yard lay in front of it, and generally surrounded it on all sides. This farm-yard contained other buildings: barns, stables, and quarters for the farm labourers. The house proper was thus reserved for the master and his family, no doubt including domestic slaves. There was always, except in the poorest villas, a suite of baths, either in the house itself or forming a separate building. A well in the yard supplied water, unless, as was sometimes the case, it was laid on by means of an aqueduct; and sometimes it is possible to recognize a threshing-floor, a dovecote, or the circular track of a horse-mill.

Among the humbler villas, a certain number belong to a quite different type of house. This is the so-called basilican house, or, more simply, the barn-dwelling. It is an oblong building with two rows of posts running along its length and dividing it into a nave and two aisles, exactly like the barns which are still to be seen in many parts of the country. Partitions, inserted as required, cut off rooms at the end or the sides for privacy; some of these could be fitted with hypocausts and tessellated floors, and the whole could be, and generally was, fitted up and finished in the conventional Roman style with painted wall-plaster and glass windows. Sometimes a barn-dwelling serves as labourers' quarters to a corridor villa. The Celtic origin of this type is reasonably certain, though Britain has shown as yet no pre-Roman examples.

Corridor houses might be built on a considerable scale—some of them have twenty rooms or more—though none in Britain attain the size or elaboration of the best continental examples. But the finest British villas are planned on a different principle. They are built round a large courtyard, quite distinct from the farm-yard, and entered through it. This inner courtyard is surrounded by a veranda off which the rooms open, and of these rooms, which may go up in number to thirty or forty, some are designed and decorated on a scale, and with a magnificence, worthy of Roman domestic architecture at its best. A villa like Bignor in Sussex or Woodchester in the Cotswolds gives an impressive picture of the wealth, comfort, and elegance of the life lived by the wealthiest Romano-British landed gentry. It is unfortunate that we know so little about the dates at which these splendid country houses were built; but where we can trace in the walls themselves the evidences of alterations, these are generally enlargements, and suggest that throughout their life, until about the middle of the fourth century or even later, their history was one of increasing prosperity. Nowhere do they give any hint of a general decline in the standard of living or of civilization parallel to that which took place in the towns.

Of these various types of country-house, most were farms; such industries as existed in them were confined to the workshops of the estate carpenter, the estate blacksmith, and so on. Here and there, industries were carried on in another spirit: the villa became a factory. But this, which is common in Belgium, is rare in Britain. A few villas were given over to iron-working; some, in the Mendip region, seem to have been employed in smelting lead; one in Surrey had tile-works on a commercial scale. In three cases, to be discussed in the next chapter, large-scale fulling establishments for the preparation of woollen cloth were inserted at some late date into pre-existing villas, and seem to have ousted all other occupations. Again, houses of the same pattern might be used as the residence of a mining manager, the bailiff or lessee of an imperial estate, or even the officer in charge of a legionary tile-works.

Apart from such rare cases, the general run of villas were the country houses of land-owners farming their own estates, presumably by means of slave labour. The existence of great and wealthy land-owners is a commonplace of imperial history, and even the evidence for their increasing prosperity in Britain as time went on is in harmony with what we know of the empire at large; for the richest were able to weather the difficulties of the later period, and gather into their own hands an ever-increasing proportion of the wealth of the country.

Whether every such villa represents an independent holding is a question we cannot answer with certainty. The largest must, no doubt, have been the centres of genuine estates. But in some places there are groups of small villas, lying close together in such a way as to suggest that there may have been some closer relation between them. One such group, in Oxfordshire, has been studied by Crawford.[1] It has, at some date, been surrounded by a defensive rampart and ditch enclosing about twenty-two square miles of country and containing at least five or six villas, besides half a dozen other Roman sites. One of the villas is the well-known large one at North Leigh; another the small one already mentioned at Ditchley (Watts Wells). This defence reinforces the impression already given by the close grouping of the villas, that they may in some sense form a single unit. Now there was in Gaul a unit, technically called *fundus* or estate, represented by the Romano-Gaulish place-names ending in -*acum* which are so common in the French country-side. Such a *fundus* might consist of a group of small villas; and on this Gaulish analogy it may perhaps be conjectured that in Britain, too, a villa-group might form a single estate, where the owner of the whole group lived in a large house like North Leigh while the rest were farmed by his tenants.

The staple crop of all British agriculture, both before and after the Roman conquest, was wheat. The Romano-Britons continued the prehistoric custom of harvesting before the ears were

---

[1] *Antiquity*, iv (1930), p. 303. The assumption there made, however, that Grim's Ditch dates from the late Roman period, is no longer permissible since the recent excavation of it by Mr. D. B. Harden (*Oxoniensia*, ii, forthcoming).

ripe; but what may have been a new practice was introduced, that of drying the grain in a kiln. The underground furnaces of such kilns exist both at villas and at villages. The ancient practice of marling the land still went on. There is no evidence that even the wealthiest villas drained their land. Here and there vines were grown and wine made: during the earlier imperial age attempts were made to prevent this being done in the north-western provinces, in order to give Italian wine-growers an advantage in the market; but Probus in the third century gave permission to the Gauls, Spaniards, and Britons to plant vines and make their own wine; and a quantity of vine-stems have actually been found near a villa in Hertfordshire, on a sheltered south-western slope.

The ordinary live stock of a villa included horses, cattle, sheep, and pigs; geese were often kept, and dogs and cats were, of course, indispensable. A villa thus provided could keep itself in bread, meat, milk, and cheese; wine or beer; wool for spinning and weaving by its own women; raw leather; timber for burning and for joinery; tallow for candles: in short, almost everything it needed for its own subsistence. If it learned to do without such foreign luxuries as oil and imported wine, its chief demands on the outside world would be for iron and other metals, pottery, linen, window-glass, and other things for repairs about the house, and certain industrial processes like tanning and fulling which it could not carry out for itself.

Important though it was, the villa-population was not nearly as large as the un-romanized peasantry of the villages, which in fact must have comprised the great majority of the inhabitants of Britain. Many settlements which must be classified as villages were industrial, but most were agricultural, and to these we shall here confine our attention.

It is possible to describe at least certain features of this peasantry's life; but many features are hopelessly obscure; and when we try to describe their history, we find ourselves in a darkness lit only by the faintest gleams. Their chief employment was the growing of wheat in their small fields; outside its patch of subdivided arable, a village would have pasture-land, for they kept oxen, sheep, pigs, and even a few horses. Their implements reveal a profoundly peaceful existence. Weapons, even hunting-weapons, are hardly ever found in them. The defences with which they are commonly surrounded were evidently not against human enemies, but against wolves. Their little round huts, whether wattled and thatched or built beehive-fashion in stone, show no trace of Roman influence in plan or construction, except that in a few cases an exceptionally prosperous and civilized village plastered and painted its huts as if they were Roman houses; and Roman influence on the furniture of their daily life is correspondingly slender, chiefly visible in the most prosperous, and there mostly confined to importations of coin, superior pottery, and metal goods.

The excavations of Pitt-Rivers on Cranborne Chase have given us an admirably complete picture of this architecture and furniture, as it existed on the chalk downs of Wiltshire. Of that picture it is true, as Haverfield wrote, that 'to these men the Roman objects which they used were the ordinary environment of life', and that 'round them too clung the heavy inevitable atmosphere of the Roman material civilization'.[1] But the Cranborne Chase villages, as later exploration has shown, were exceptional in the degree of their romanization. This is the only region in which drying-kilns for corn have been found in village sites; and elsewhere there is never such profusion of Roman goods. It seems, in fact, that whereas a fairly high degree of romanization existed in villages of southern England, this declines rapidly towards the north and west; and in the highland zone only a few odd potsherds of recognizably Roman type attest the date of villages which might otherwise be prehistoric.

Apart from its influence on their manner of daily life, which may easily be exaggerated if we forget that a native village may obtain its pottery and implements from the civilized world without using them in a particularly civilized way, the Roman conquest no doubt had many other effects upon these villages. By stopping tribal warfare it tended to increase their population; but to some extent this result was compensated by the introduction of infanticide. Not, perhaps, altogether. Here and there new village settlements seem to have arisen in Roman times. In Sussex, a tiny village has been excavated which is unique in consisting of rectangular huts instead of round ones; this was a foundation of Roman date. The suggestion has been made, too, that where village-fields are laid out with exceptional regularity this may be a sign of Roman influence in land-

---

[1] *Romanization of Roman Britain*, ed. 4, p. 46; *Roman Occupation of Britain*, p. 218.

surveying.[1] In Anglesey there are several villages which began
to exist in Roman times, but as these are industrial they do not
affect the present question. On the whole, evidence of a general
rise in the lowland-zone peasant population under Roman rule
is wanting.

Where such evidence is decisive, it points not so much to a
general rise as to special local conditions. This is the case in
the Fens, where recent study has revealed a large village-
population, with settlements and fields of the ordinary kind,
whose existence depends on large-scale drainage-works dated to
the Roman period. It is not to be supposed that the peasants
undertook this reclamation of fenland at their own expense. It
points rather to capitalistic enterprise. Such land would presumably be leased from the State on condition of its being cultivated; and the same lessee who did the draining must have
found peasants to do the cultivation. The possibility of such
development must be connected with the increasing power both
of the large land-owners and of the State, the largest of all.

Against an increase in this direction, however, must be set off
certain evidences of decline in others. Some villages were undoubtedly deserted during the latter part of the Roman period.
The clearest case is Rotherley in Wiltshire, where Roman coins
are quite common, but only go down to the latter part of the
third century. At the neighbouring village of Woodcuts they
die out in the Constantinian age. Other villages in Wiltshire
yield evidence of a similar kind. When we remember how
widely fourth-century coins circulated, and in what numbers
they are found on the sites of villas, we can hardly doubt that
a great depopulation of the Wiltshire downs was going on during
that time. It cannot have been due to warfare or raiding. The
villas show that it cannot have been due to a falling-off in
agricultural prosperity as a whole. It is far more likely to be
connected with the very prosperity of the villas and to indicate
a deliberate transplantation of village-dwellers to serve the
policy of capitalistic landlords or a socialistic State.

We can even hazard a guess as to what this policy might have
been. In the next chapter some account will be given of the way
in which the woollen industry developed in the third and fourth
centuries. A similar development, many years later, made Sir
Thomas More utter his famous remark about sheep eating men.

[1] Park Brow, Sussex: Wolseley in *Archaeologia*, lxxvi; Curwen in *Antiquity*, i. 278.

If the chalk-lands of southern England, after having been so intensively cultivated as we know they were, became sheep-walks during the later Roman period on a scale such as to support a great woollen trade, depopulation was inevitable. Whether the peasants moved from the chalk downs were settled on the newly drained fenlands is a question which must wait for answering until we know more about the history of that settlement.

This raises the question: what was the economic and legal status of the British peasant? Was he a free part-owner of communal land, or was he a *colonus*, a tenant on the soil of a master? And was this master public or private? Were the areas of village-economy imperial estates or were they owned by British landlords?

These questions are impossible to answer with certainty. There were, of course, imperial estates in Britain as elsewhere; we have proof of it in an inscription from a villa close to Bath, which was the residence of a bailiff in charge of one. And there were *coloni*; there is a reference in the Theodosian Code to *coloni* and *tributarii* of decurions in Britain. In general, it is unlikely that most of the villagers under Roman rule would retain the status of free property-owners. Many of them would almost certainly become *coloni*, although their status may not precisely have resembled the Roman colonate elsewhere, since Roman law was always flexible in its adjustment to the traditional institutions of subject races.[1] And it is on the whole most probable that, where we find large tracts of country exclusively inhabited by peasants, like Cranborne Chase and Salisbury Plain, we have to do with imperial estates, either administered directly for the emperor by procurators, or leased to *conductores*. Where villas and villages are mixed in the same region, as in Sussex, we may suspect that the villagers were *coloni* on the estates of the villa-owners. As in northern Gaul and Germany, the economic development of Britain may have tended towards converting free peasants into *coloni* of great land-owners,[2] if, indeed, they were not already in a somewhat similar position of dependence even before the conquest.

If we ask how far the empire or the individual land-owner

[1] Cf. Mitteis, *Reichsrecht und Volksrecht*, p. 8.
[2] Cf. Rostovtzeff, *Social and Economic History*, pp. 209, 212. I concur in the author's view (p. 213) that Britain was not a land 'of peasants and small proprietors'.

cared for the welfare of these humble masses of its population, the answer is not reassuring. In the higher products of Roman civilization they had no share. That many of them spoke Latin is not certain; evidence that, even in the most prosperous villages, any one could read and write is singularly scanty. Certainly there was no systematic attempt to educate them or to improve the conditions, whether material or spiritual, of their life. Unlike their social equals in the towns, nothing was ever done for them; unlike their social superiors in the country, they were never able to do much for themselves. As the years went by, there was no general increase in their prosperity. On the contrary, as time went on, they became more and more liable to arbitrary exactions and oppression of every kind. As the power of the great landlords and of the central government increased in the fourth century, they became increasingly servile in their position. Nor were they unconscious of it. The contrast between power and wealth on the one hand, and poverty exploited and oppressed on the other, was so glaring that in Gaul peasant revolts became a regular feature of late imperial history. For Britain we have no evidence of them, but that may be only because our literary sources are so defective. A survey of the state of the people in fourth-century Britain shows at least that, of the material conditions which might lead to such revolts, none was lacking.

XIV

INDUSTRY AND COMMERCE

THE effect of the Roman conquest on British industry and commerce was rapid and decisive. Hitherto, those who could afford it indulged their taste for Roman metal-work, wine, and so forth by purchasing these things from enterprising Gaulish merchants. The steady trickle of Roman goods into Britain to meet this demand was purely a luxury traffic and did very little to disturb the economic life of the country. After the conquest, living in the Roman style was, for the British aristocracy who wished to be abreast of the new régime, no longer a luxury but a necessity. There was a sharp rise in the demand for such goods as were needed by any one who was to live in that style. The importation of luxury articles into Britain during the latter half of the first century, as witnessed even to-day by the contents of our museums, was enormous. Britain possessed or produced nothing whose exportation could be so developed as to balance this influx of costly goods. The only valuable exports whose production was stimulated by the conquest were metals, and these, being state property and not articles of commerce, could not be reckoned in the trade balance. If agriculture showed an increased productivity, as may well have been the case, the increase was fully accounted for by what the army and officials absorbed in the form of *annona*.

The consequence was twofold. First, there was a heavy and rapid drainage of money into the pockets of traders, especially foreign traders; debt, principally incurred by the highest classes of society, whose need of imported goods was greatest; recourse to the money-lenders, foreigners once more; and heavier debt. We have already seen how this vicious circle underlay Boudicca's revolt. Secondly, there was an attempt to balance the trade account by developing industries within Britain capable of satisfying the demand for goods of Roman patterns. The British craftsman was a skilful and experienced workman; in pottery he was good, in metal-work he was first class. He set himself to make for home consumption articles of the kind which at first his countrymen had been obliged to purchase from abroad.

The extent to which the British manufacturer was capable of doing this was limited. He could not produce foodstuffs capable of competing with Italian wine, Spanish sauce, or Spanish olive-oil. Apart from one isolated attempt, he never set out to compete with Gaulish red-glaze pottery. He could not make saucepans and colanders to rival those of Campanian metal-workers. But he could turn out excellent ironmongery; he could make little things, both useful and ornamental, in bronze; he soon learnt how to make glass, at least in the shape of window-glass; he began making pots, not, indeed, able to compete with Gaulish ware, but adequate to the humbler needs of households where such wares were used. In short, though he could nowhere oust the foreign trader in respect of the best and most expensive things, he could and did supply, in large and increasing bulk, what might be called the second-class furniture of a romanized everyday life.

By the reign of Hadrian the importation of foreign goods had notably declined. A great deal was still coming into the country, but far less than a generation earlier. This is a measure of the British artisan's success in solving his problem: adjusting himself to the requirements, both in utility and in taste, of a romanized society, and developing an output whose quality and quantity were abreast of them. Industrially, Britain was now in great part self-sufficing; and the prosperity of both town and country life in the Antonine period is testimony to the fact.

The third century saw a further change. With the decay of romanized town life, the need of imports declined. The Gaulish pottery manufacture was dying out, and its place was only partially taken by the pottery and glassware of the Rhineland; Britain was beginning to rely more and more on its own potters for the satisfaction of all its demands. A pewter industry grew up, replacing the importation of foreign table-silver. Oil was largely replaced, it would seem, by tallow, and foreign wine by home-grown wine under Probus's edict or by the old Celtic drink, beer. The villa-life of the later empire depended very little, even for its luxuries, on foreign trade. The consumer was asking less, the home producer was offering more: and in the third and fourth centuries the two met. Once more, as in the time of Cunobelinus, the imports that Britain required to maintain the standard of life which she set herself were only a marginal fraction of all that she consumed.

This equilibrium might seem to promise stability; but it was not stable. A stable equilibrium is one which can reassert itself after being disturbed; it is therefore relative to the nature and violence of the shocks which it is liable to sustain. The economic equilibrium of the fourth century was no longer being undermined by the administrative anarchy of the third; the government had by now been re-established on a firm basis; but it was exposed to barbarian attack from without and to peasant revolt from within. How these worked on fourth-century Britain we shall see in the sequel.

From this rough preliminary sketch we must turn to details. By far the most important source of wealth in Britain, after agriculture, was her mineral deposits. They were already known in Caesar's time, and Tacitus was no doubt well informed when he said that they were among the considerations which prompted the Claudian invasion. Within a few years from the landing of Claudius's armies, Roman miners were working the argentiferous lead of the Mendips, whose silver had been an article of export as early as the time of Augustus. They found and worked the same minerals in Shropshire, Derbyshire, Flintshire, Yorkshire, and Northumberland; gold in South Wales; copper in North Wales and Anglesey; iron in the Weald, the Forest of Dean, and a great many other places; and coal in all the chief coalfields of England, South Wales, and southern Scotland. In the third century they took over and revived the Cornish tin-mines.

It was a general principle of Roman provincial government that mines and quarries were state property.[1] So far as we know, this principle was always observed in Britain. But this property might be administered in several ways. It might be managed by procurators directly in the emperor's interest; it might be under military control; or it might be leased to private companies. All three methods have left their traces in this country. Labour was supplied by slaves, prisoners, and condemned criminals, and by provincials under forced labour; free labourers working under contracts are known in some parts of the empire, and may conceivably have been employed in Britain. The labourers were lodged in some cases underground, and there is evidence of their living and working in fetters; but

---

[1] Actually the legal situation was somewhat complicated (cf. Davies, *Roman Mines in Europe*, pp. 3-4) and does not entitle us to lay down *a priori* that all mines in Britain were state property, though most of them certainly were: details are considered below.

conditions varied, and the Mendip miners seem to have lived in a tolerably civilized town, while the gold-miners of South Wales may even have had pit-head baths. Mining was a job which the Romans understood well and carried out efficiently; their workings were well designed, ventilated, and drained; and it may be safely assumed that in a country such as Britain the output of the industry increased enormously under their rule.

So far as we know, the only regular gold-mining operations were carried out at Dolaucothy in Carmarthenshire. The workings still visible are Roman in character, with their drainage adits and aqueduct to supply water for washing the ore; the settlement beside them includes a Roman bath-house which, unless it was for the private use of the manager, for which it seems too large, must have been for the miners; and a considerable quantity of jewellery proves that goldsmiths worked on the spot. The mine must have been state property, and may conceivably have been under military control, though of this there is no evidence. How far gold was being produced elsewhere in Britain we do not know. There may have been other places in Wales, and possibly in Cornwall and Scotland, where gold-washing was done on a small scale by natives working on their own account; perhaps even some mining.

The most important mines of Britain were lead-mines. Lead itself was much in demand among the Romans, especially for water-pipes, but their chief object in working it was to obtain silver, which they extracted from it by cupellation. In this process the lead is melted in a strong current of air on a bed of bone-ash; the bone-ash absorbs the lead, and the silver is left in a pure state in the form of pellets. The saturated bone-ash, which is known as cupel, may then be re-smelted to recover the lead, and this was cast into pigs marked *ex arg(entariis)* to indicate that it had been through the silver-works. The Romans practised cupellation with great efficiency; the lead so marked contains only 0·01 per cent., or even less, of silver. Incidentally, these pigs, bearing the names of emperors, lessees, or military authorities, give us much information about the history and organization of the industry.

The lead-ores of the Mendips, as we know from a pig dated A.D. 49, were already in full work within six years of the Claudian invasion. A considerable town grew up there at Charterhouse, and there is evidence that work went on right through the

Roman period. All the pigs bear imperial inscriptions showing that they were state property, and one, of Nero's time, has the name of the Second legion, proving that for some time they were under military control; this may have ceased when the legion moved into the valley of the Usk. The lead was exported, as pigs traceable to the same region indicate, by way of Southampton to Gaul; much of it must also have been used nearer home, for instance, at Bath.

A less important lead-field in Shropshire and on the borders of Wales, whose chief workings lie about ten miles south-west of Shrewsbury, was being worked in the first and second centuries under military control from Chester: pigs bear the names of Hadrian and the Twentieth legion, and coins of Antoninus Pius have been found in the workings. Some distance to the north there were considerable lead-mines in Flintshire, also worked by the Twentieth legion. Finds in the workings show that they were exploited in the first, second, and third centuries.

The Derbyshire lead-mines were among the chief in Britain. They were chiefly in the valleys near and north of Matlock. Pigs of Hadrian are found, and others, later in date to judge by their style, are inscribed with the names of private persons who must be lessees. This is the only case in Britain where the practice of leasing state mines to *conductores* is known to have existed. The capital of the mining district seems to have been called Lutudarum, and all pigs belonging to it bear an inscription giving some abbreviation of that name; they are numerous, and have been found as far afield as Sussex, the Humber, and the river Carron in Scotland. The workings yield finds which show that the industry was still flourishing as late as the fourth century.

The Yorkshire lead was already being mined as early as Agricola's time near Pateley Bridge and Grassington; and there is some small evidence that the deposits of Alston Moor, which were to become so important in later years, were worked as well; but these northern mines never, so far as we know, throve like those farther south, especially those of Mendip and Derbyshire, whose output must have been very large and a considerable source of revenue to the state.

The Cornish stannaries, by the time of the Roman conquest, had been eclipsed in importance by those of north-western Spain. Nevertheless, an attempt was made by the Romans to work them in the Flavian period. A small mining settlement of the late first and early second centuries, altogether Roman in type, has been found near Bodmin. It did not last very long, and no others like it are known. The inference is that the industry was left in native hands, as it generally was to some extent elsewhere,[1] and that a private Roman speculator who put money into tin-mining found that it did not pay. But about the middle of the third century, when the Roman world began to fear the exhaustion of its mineral resources, we find a change of conditions in Cornwall. Roman coin becomes common; milestones indicate road-making under imperial direction; and it is evident that the state had in some way undertaken control of the industry. The result was an increase of output. It is now that tin and pewter vessels begin to play a conspicuous part in domestic life. This state of things lasted down to the end of the Roman occupation, to judge from pewter ingots found in the Thames at London, which bear Christian symbols and stamps hardly earlier than the late fourth century.

Copper was mined by the Romans in Shropshire, at Llany-mynech, where the workings have yielded finds of the second and fourth centuries and refuse showing that the miners lived in a cave that formed part of them; and on the Great Orme's Head and in Anglesey, where the ore was smelted in hut-villages. The little round furnaces, after firing, smelting, and removing the slag, contained at the bottom a round cake of copper; and cakes of this kind, known as bun-ingots, are found in Anglesey and the north-west of Wales, stamped with names which show that the industry was leased to private companies. The villages give us a hint of how natives lived under capitalistic control. They are ordinary native settlements, peculiar only in being laid out with an attention to straight lines that is very un-Celtic; evidently the mining company had some say in the planning of its workmen's villages; and in their furnaces they burnt coal, which the company must have brought for a considerable distance, the nearest coal-field being seventy or eighty miles away.

Coal, in fact, was much valued by the Romans. They mined it wherever they could get it, generally at outcrops, but sometimes by shafts and galleries; they used it extensively for metallurgy and domestic heating; and the Anglesey mining villages

[1] 'Tin seems nearly always to have been worked by free miners.' Davies, op. cit., p. 6.

are not the only case in which they carried it long distances. Tyne-
side and Cumberland coal was regularly worked, and bunkers
of it have been found in forts on Hadrian's Wall and near
it; the same thing happens in the lowland coal-field and the
forts of the Antonine frontier. The southern Yorkshire and
Lancashire coal-fields were similarly worked, and the discovery
of coal at industrial sites in that part of Britain, including North
Wales, is as common as it is in the military sites of the north.
Similar finds in Monmouthshire and the surrounding counties
show that the south Welsh and Dean coal-fields were exploited
no less regularly, and the same is true of the Somerset deposits,
which deserve special mention, not only for the remarkable fact,
recorded by a third-century writer, that the sacred fire in the
temple of Sulis at Bath was stoked with coal instead of wood,
but also for the way in which coal, doubtless from the Somerset
mines, found its way to villas and villages scattered over Wiltshire and even as far afield as Buckinghamshire. The use of coal
even in peasant villages indicates that it must have sold quite
cheap, and that transport for it presented no difficulty. As to
the ownership, management, and control of this large coal output we know nothing. In the north it must all have been in
military hands, but in Somerset, bearing in mind the character of
the deposits, one might rather suspect individual outcrop-work-
ing by free native miners, who might have hawked their own
winnings in panniers on donkey-back or in some such inexpensive way.

Iron, as we know from Strabo, was already by the time of
Augustus reckoned an important British product. At that time
it was no doubt the Wealden ores that were chiefly worked.
The Romans turned their attention to these ores quite soon
after the conquest, and worked them on a large scale. The slag-
heaps of Roman date are numerous and very large; they yield
coins as early as Nero, and those of Vespasian are especially
common and indicate a great development of the industry in the
Flavian period. The Forest of Dean, too, was extensively mined
for iron-ore as early as the first century, and numerous Roman
slag-heaps occur there; the actual methods of working have
been studied in a third-century mine at Lydney on the southern
edge of the Forest. These two regions were the chief sources
for iron in Britain; but it was mined in a great many other
places as well, notably in Warwickshire, Northamptonshire,

Rutland, Norfolk, Lincolnshire, Nottinghamshire, Cheshire, Lancashire, and Northumberland. In fact, there is no considerable area of Roman Britain in which iron-ore of some kind was not won and worked.

Iron-ore was smelted either in a primitive bowl-furnace, a hole in the ground lined with clay, the blast being introduced over the edge of the bowl, which, with various modifications, is found all over the country, or in a free-standing shaft-furnace, generally contracted to a chimney at the top and having a hole for tapping the slag near the bottom; but it does not seem certain that the shaft-furnace was used in Britain until after the Roman period, though it was freely used in less backward provinces. The purpose of smelting was not to bring the ore to the melting-point of iron and liquefy the metal; when this happened accidentally, the resulting cast iron was thrown away as useless; it was to produce blooms of impure iron which were then purified of slag by heating and hammering. Consequently iron could be produced only in small quantities; for since the Romans had not invented a water-driven trip-hammer (as, for that matter, they had not invented water-driven bellows for furnaces) the size of a bloom was limited by the weight of a hammer that could be wielded in the hand. If too large a bloom were made, the hammer would not be heavy enough to force the slag out of it. Accordingly, when large quantities of iron were needed, it was necessary to re-heat a number of blooms and weld them together. Iron-work of excellent quality was already being done by the Celts of the La Tène period, and though the Romans undoubtedly increased production and developed a large and thriving industry, turning out iron goods in great quantity and enormous variety, they do not seem to have introduced British iron-smelters and blacksmiths to any new technical processes.

About the ownership and management of iron-mines nothing is known. In the empire at large 'iron was normally produced by independent labourers in the forests',[1] and this may have been so in many parts of Britain; but here and there such facts as the great size of the Wealden slag-heaps, the advanced mining-methods of the Forest of Dean, or the concentration of smelting-works at a town like Ariconium, suggest a higher degree of organization, whether depending on private companies and capitalists or on state ownership or control. It is

[1] Davies, op. cit., p. 6.

possible that the state never asserted its ownership of the lesser
British iron-mines, and left it to develop in the hands of British
owners; it may have confiscated the most valuable of them.
The rapid development of output in the late first century does
not suggest that the industry was left entirely to the enterprise
of individual labourers.

The making of iron goods was done in all parts of the country:
every town had its blacksmiths, every fort its regimental smithy,
every villa its forge. But there are slight traces of special local
developments in the direction of wholesale manufacture. In
London we seem to trace master-cutlers called Basilius, Olon-
dus, and Aprilis; and it is hard to see why so many caltrops
have been found in a peaceful town like Wroxeter unless there
was a specialized iron-working industry there, forerunner of
Birmingham Small Arms.

The bronze-working industry, too, was widely diffused. To
some extent it probably existed in most towns of any size. But
definite evidence of its existence on a large scale comes mostly
from the north and west. Certain types of brooch, for example,
are peculiar to the Severn valley and its neighbourhood. Others
were made in the north, at places like Brough-under-Stainmore
and Stanwix near Carlisle, where in both cases the finding of
flawed castings demonstrates the presence of the industry; and
made in such quantities that they achieved the commercial success of a wider market, and were sold all over Britain and even
in some cases beyond the Channel. Probably there was much
more bronze-working going on all over Britain than we know
about; otherwise it is difficult to account for the tenacity with
which the tradition of Celtic art survived among the metal-
workers of the lowland zone. But this is a subject that must be
considered in a later chapter, when we attempt to trace the
history of art in Roman Britain.

Of goldsmiths and silversmiths there is little to say, except
that they existed: we have, for example, an inscription from
Malton in Yorkshire mentioning a goldsmith's workshop run by
a slave; and, in addition to much jewellery that is either certainly or probably of native make, there are some rather handsome silver plaques in the British Museum, native offerings put
up at shrines, which must have been made by a silversmith on
the spot. Mention has already been made of the pewter ware,
certainly of British workmanship, which in the fourth century

was turned out in large quantities to meet the demand among villa-dwellers for a cheap substitute for silver dinner-services. In style and taste this was entirely Roman, with nothing Celtic about it.

Glass was made in various places, but nothing better than window-glass seems to have been produced; for table glassware Britain always depended on the Continent.

No industry has left such abundant and instructive traces of itself as pottery. Wherever potters work they leave broken sherds and 'wasters' that have warped in the firing; where the industry attains any considerable size, or remains in one place for any considerable length of time, the quantity of this refuse is enormous. It is not unusual to find deposits from a foot to three feet thick, extending over large areas; or to find several hundredweight of it in merely exploring a site by means of trial trenches. In consequence, pottery-sites are easy to detect, and the evidence for the kind of wares they produced is always abundant; comparison of these with wares found on excavated sites makes it possible to date their activity; and the size of the deposits, together with the duration of the time they cover and the relation between their contents and the pottery found at other places, gives information about the scale and organization of the industry and about its market.

Potteries existed in every part of the country, and show enormous variety in size, in the length of their history, in the kind of wares they made, in their organization, and in the diffusion of their produce. Districts in which they were especially common were the Kentish bank of the Thames, the New Forest, the Nene valley round Castor, and the upper Thames near Oxford. Early in the Roman period, as in the preceding period, the industry was mainly in the hands of small local establishments supplying in the main a purely local demand; the result is a considerable variation in fabric and in shape from one district to another. But the Roman conquest of itself tended to produce a certain uniformity; the uniform civilization which grew up in the towns and to some extent filtered through into the country-side, and the army, moving about from place to place and carrying everywhere its standardized requirements, began by degrees to accustom Britons in widely scattered districts to use wares of uniform kinds and to transport them for considerable distances. By the middle of the second century we find British potters adapting themselves to the needs of a romanized public by producing vessels more or less modelled on Roman patterns: a fusion is taking place between Roman and Celtic pottery-shapes, and a system of distribution is growing up by which wares of special kinds, produced in special districts, find their way to consumers all over the country.

In the central and later parts of the Romano-British period this process has developed to a high degree of complexity and efficiency. The general standard of potter's work is by now remarkably uniform and, from a merely technical point of view, remarkably high. The rude hand-made wares which prevailed in the pre-Roman age have not, indeed, wholly disappeared, but for the most part they have been superseded all over the country by well-made and well-baked pottery, thrown on the wheel and produced in mass, each district making its own special kind or kinds. The vast majority of this huge output is wholly inartistic in design; the hybrid Romano-Celtic taste which it represents has lost all interest in delicacies of shape, and cares for nothing except cheapness and utility; but from a strictly utilitarian point of view the entire population of Britain, rich and poor, peasant and citizen, has profited by a great improvement in its domestic crockery, both in quality and in quantity.

Even at this period the organization of the industry was far from uniform. At one end of the scale we have the potteries of the Castor district, a large group of establishments fixed permanently in one place, where well-to-do manufacturers lived in houses resembling the villas of prosperous farmers, surrounded by the smaller but still romanized houses of their work-people and by kilns of an unusually elaborate and efficient type. Here the industry was evidently worked on a capitalist basis, with highly organized methods of manufacture and distribution. The characteristic ware of the Castor kilns is found all over Britain, and there are indications of the way in which it was shipped in barge-loads by river from the pottery wharves. At the other end of the scale are the New Forest potteries, where small independent workmen lived in temporary wigwams and fired their pots in little primitive kilns, moving on to another site when the fuel close at hand was exhausted. Here the distribution must have been as individualistic as the manufacture; Mr. Heywood Sumner,[1] to whose labours our knowledge of the New Forest industry

[1] *Excavations in New Forest Pottery Sites* (1927), pp. 82–5.

is chiefly due, has worked out the distribution of its produce, and
has pictured the potters carrying their goods on donkey-back
from house to house and from village to village within a radius
of thirty miles, though the best of their wares went farther, and
are found all over the south of England.

This difference between concentrated capitalistic production
and free individualistic industry on a small scale does not imply
a corresponding difference between Roman and Celtic traditions in design, or between more advanced and more primitive
technique. The shapes of New Forest vessels are quite as romanized, and their technical qualities quite as good, as those of
Castor. In fact, Castor ware has often been held up as the outstanding example of Celtic taste in design surviving in Romano-
British industrial products. This is a question to which we must
return. For the moment, it is enough to say that the nomad
potters of the New Forest show a spontaneity in their design and
a taste in their decoration which make their work far more
pleasing than the stereotyped patterns of Castor ware.

This lack of uniformity in organization, so clearly to be discerned in the pottery trade of Roman Britain, does not tend to
disappear as time goes on. Both the Castor and the New Forest
potteries were already flourishing in the third century; there is
no evidence that the large producer was tending to oust the
small in the fourth. And what can be proved for the pottery
trade may be supposed true for others. The economic system
of the Roman world contained plenty of room for large and
small producers to work side by side.

In one sense, however, a sense in which even the New Forest
potters may be called large producers, large-scale production
definitely triumphed over small. The prehistoric form of industry, where, generally speaking, every village made its own
pots and the total amount of transport required between producer and consumer was very small, disappeared. Pottery became a thing made by highly skilled specialists, and distributed
to consumers who could no more make it for themselves than
a modern English village, which not long ago made its own
tallow candles and horse-shoes, could supply itself with electric
light bulbs or spare parts for a tractor. The concentration of
skill and the diffusion of trade combined to create a situation
in which every one could obtain far better crockery than before;
but if the centres of production should for some reason cease

working, or the system of communications become disorganized, the failure of supply would leave people not only unprovided with good crockery, but no longer able to replace it with poorer stuff of their own making. As we shall see, this is what happened in Britain towards the end of the Roman period.

A similar tendency towards concentrating production and enlarging distribution is seen in the non-commercial industry of the army. At first, not only legionary fortresses, but even individual *castella* very often had their own pottery-kilns. The only proof which we possess that the Ninth legion was for a time encamped at or near Carlisle is the fact that it had potteries and tileries five miles away at Scalesceugh; the short-lived Trajanic fort at Hardknot supplied itself with most of the crockery it needed from its own kilns in Eskdale. By degrees, this small-scale local production died away, until in the late fourth century we find practically every military site in the north of England depending for the greater part of its supplies on certain establishments in Yorkshire, where almost incredible quantities of pottery were produced, miserably tasteless and worse than barbarous in design (since barbarians have generally the time and the interest to adorn what they make) but cheap and efficient to the last degree. In this case a further change is involved, namely, in the personnel of the labourers. At first these were soldiers, legionary or auxiliary as the case might be; but the late Yorkshire potteries, though evidently under military control, were run with native labour, and native traditions of craftsmanship are unmistakably at work in shaping the quality of the output.

The making of bricks and tiles was hardly less widespread than potting, and in many ways followed a similar development; but there was no native industry on which to graft it, and it consequently remained far more Roman in character. In addition to legionary and auxiliary tileworks, of which examples are numerous, some towns had their own, as municipal property; and there is even one case of an imperial tilery, near Silchester, whose products are stamped with the name of Nero. We can also identify native firms. Tile-workers as a class were more romanized than potters. The British potter, for all we can learn, was generally illiterate; he hardly ever signed his wares or wrote inscriptions on them, as potters in other provinces often did; but tile-makers were apt to scribble phrases in Latin on their wet clay: a date, a name, a remark about a girl, or an observation on the habits of a fellow workman.

The only other industry which need be mentioned here is that connected with textiles. Unlike pottery, this was an industry which for the most part always retained its primitive domestic form: spindle-whorls and loom-weights are found everywhere, and every household, rich and poor alike, did for itself most of the spinning and weaving that it needed. But in the later part of our period a tendency made itself felt towards developing a textile trade in Britain, like those which had long existed in more advanced regions of the ancient world. By the end of the third century cloaks made of British cloth were a sufficiently important article of commerce to appear in the list of goods whose prices were fixed by Diocletian's edict; and in the fourth century there was an imperial weaving-mill, doubtless for the production of this same cloth, at Winchester.[1]

The evidence of these official documents is seconded by that of archaeology. No less than three villas are known which at some date subsequent to their original building have been wholly or partially converted into factories devoted to fulling cloth. At Darenth in Kent a large villa and its separate bath-house were almost entirely turned into a large *fullonica*, and a new building was added for drying-rooms. A less spectacular, but still remarkable, case is at Chedworth, where a bed of fuller's earth lies near the villa, and where the whole northern wing of a very large house was converted to the same uses. An example on a smaller scale has been discovered at Titsey in Surrey, where one wing of a villa has been turned into a *fullonica*, the other into a drying-room. These developments, although they are not dated, probably belong to the third or even the fourth century, and their scale makes it obvious that they were designed for commercial purposes.

The conversion into factories of villas, which hitherto had presumably been homes of mixed farming, shows that the development of the woollen industry on a commercial scale was accompanied by a reduction in the number of independent farms, as well as a reduction in the area of arable. Plough-land was being laid down to grass, large sheep-farmers were buying

---

[1] Diocletian's Edict, xix. 36. *Notitia Dignitatum*, Occ. xi. 60: *procurator gynaecii in Britannis Ventensis.* As Haverfield pointed out, Venta in this connexion is most unlikely to be Caistor-next-Norwich or Caerwent, and must be Winchester.

out the smaller land-owners, and, as was said in the last chapter, downland villages were being deserted, doubtless in order to enlarge the area available for sheep-walks. The relation of these private fulling establishments (as we may suppose they were) to the state mills at Winchester implies that the state mills dealt only with wool grown on imperial domain lands. Cranborne Chase, where we find the deserted villages, was in the administrative district whose capital was Winchester, and the absence of villas in it suggests that it may have been an imperial domain. Elsewhere, private growers might weave their own cloth and bring it for fulling to a private *fullonica* in the neighbourhood.

Before attempting a general sketch of Romano-British commerce, it is necessary to say something of the lanes along which it travelled, the lines of communication.

The 5,000 miles of Roman road which are known to us in Britain form a system intelligible enough in its main lines, but obviously planned to serve the needs of conquest and government rather than those of civil traffic. The whole system radiates from London, and gives the impression of having been designed so as to provide the most direct communication from point to point of a network whose nodal points are the *coloniae*, the legionary fortresses, and the tribal capitals. If London was the seat of the provincial government, nothing could have been better arranged to suit the needs of a legate who wished to keep in touch with the score or so centres of administration. But, useful as it was for such official traffic, and consequently also for through traffic of a private kind, whether in passengers or in goods, the system was of little service to local traffic. Instead of running along belts of relatively dense population like the North and South Downs or the Cotswolds, its main lines cut them crosswise, in order to penetrate as quickly as possible the belts of sparsely inhabited forest that lay between them.

Local traffic, therefore, must have preferred roads other than these imperial highways: old ridgeways like the Icknield Way of the Berkshire and Chiltern escarpment, or the Harroway of the North Downs; roads built by local authorities for their own convenience, like the White Way of the Cotswolds; and many others that must have existed of the same kinds, now unknown. Even officials may have found the original road-system inconvenient, in its neglect of everything except the shortest distance.

The *Antonine Itinerary*, a road-book generally ascribed to the early third century and claiming an official origin, gives directions for travelling between London and Chichester not by the direct road, the Stane Street through the uninhabited Weald, but by a road twice as long, that passes through the tribal capitals of Silchester and Winchester and the port of Bitterne. From London to Lincoln it neglects the straight road through Castor, and takes the traveller round either by Verulam and Leicester or by Colchester. From Chester to Carlisle it specifies the long way round by York, instead of the short way through the forests of Lancashire. These deviations may possibly represent the actual routes followed at the time of compilation by the imperial postal service, which existed not for the convenience of the subjects, but for that of the central government.

All main roads were wide (20 or 24 feet is a normal breadth), metalled with gravel for summer or winter use, and well provided with bridges or paved fords. Local roads were of lighter construction, but we may think of them as passable for ordinary traffic all the year round. The four-wheeled wagon of the Celtic provinces, as we see it represented in so many Gaulish sculptures, was the chief means of transport, whether commandeered by officials and soldiers, or used by the country-folk coming and going on their lawful occasions.

There was also a good deal of water-borne traffic. Beside the cross-Channel trade, which for commercial purposes came increasingly to depend on the tidal harbours of London, Southampton Water, and the Humber, inland waterways were much used, especially in the east, where rivers are largest, by dug-out canoes sometimes running up to forty and fifty feet in length. Vessels varied in size from large oak-built sailing-ships to the leather and wicker coracles which the Britons used even in the open sea.

Like other provincials, the Britons soon became accustomed to Roman coinage and regarded it as necessary for commerce. At first the official coins were much imitated; in the second century they were so abundant that imitation was no longer needed, and at the same time the last lingering remnants of the pre-Roman native coinage, which was still being used in the south-west in the Antonine period, died out. In the early third century official coins become scarce again, and local copies are common; with the depreciation of the later third century these become enormously commoner, and the monetary chaos of that time is reflected in the vast hoards of coins, sometimes very barbarous, that had become worthless. It was now that Carausius for the first time opened an official mint in London, with another at Colchester or Bitterne, and possibly a third at Wroxeter. London issued copper until about 325; but by now the reforms of Diocletian had put the coinage on a new and firm basis, and throughout the Constantinian period the Britons had as much as they needed. The decline and disappearance of money after this must be discussed in a later chapter.

The history of Romano-British commerce is very obscure. Literary and epigraphic sources are almost non-existent; and archaeology, while it tells us much about imports, gives us practically no information about exports, which mostly took the form of raw materials. Of the imports which it reveals, so many were sent as supplies for the army that we cannot use its evidence without great caution for an estimate of commercial activity.

Pottery, especially the red-glazed 'Samian' ware of the Gaulish factories, was imported in very large quantities, first from southern and then from central and eastern Gaul, from the early days of the occupation until the decay of the industry in the early third century. Probably the bulk of it was shipped to London and thence distributed over the country, where it was sold in the markets of the towns. The quantity which found its way to the villas was relatively small. When this ware ceased to be imported, its place was to some extent, though a much smaller extent, taken by pottery of other kinds and glass from the Rhineland. Judging from Rhenish inscriptions, this trade was partly in the hands of British merchants.

Metal goods of all the more expensive kinds, especially saucepans, jugs, and lamps, were at first imported from Italy in large quantities; but this did not last long; by the second century little metal-work was coming in except the Belgian enamels of the Namur district. By this time the British home industries had become capable of supplying most of what the home market demanded.

Italy and Spain sent wine, oil, and the inevitable fish-sauce; but here, too, the importation diminished as time went on, and most of what came over in the second century seems to have been destined for military consumption. In short, by the third century, and even more by the fourth, the archaeological evidence for imports on a large scale has practically vanished.

Exports must have continued on the general lines already laid down, according to Strabo, in the time of Augustus: wheat, cattle, iron, hides, slaves, and hunting-dogs. British dogs remained famous throughout the history of the empire; we can distinguish at least three breeds, the Irish wolf-hound, of which a statuette has been found at Lydney, a light, fast animal valued for its scent, and some kind of bull-dog. Oysters were not only eaten in large numbers all over Britain itself, but were valued by gourmets as far away as Rome. Pearls, too, were exported, though not of the best quality. There are traces of manufactured goods being exported: brooches made in northern Britain were for a short time traded up the Rhine,[1] and the fourth-century export of cloth has already been mentioned.

Whether the export of wheat survived the Roman conquest, with its resultant demand on British agriculture for levies in kind, we do not know. More than one author speaks of wheat shipped from Britain to the Rhineland in the time of the emperor Julian, and it is often assumed that this refers to a continuance of the same export trade.[2] But the writers in question make it clear that there was no question of a commercial transaction; the shipment was an *annona*, a forced levy in wheat, which one author describes as an enlargement of one regularly levied; and it was needed to support communities which, having been just re-established in rebuilt towns, could not at the moment support themselves. It was in fact an emergency measure, like so many levies in the fourth century, whose existence throws little light on the question whether those who were forced to pay it were able to pay it without distress out of their surplus produce, and none at all on the question whether they were in the habit of exporting such produce commercially. In the same way, when Constantius Chlorus at the beginning of the same century drafted British masons and carpenters off to Gaul, to rebuild

---

[1] In *Archaeologia*, lxxx. 50, 56, I associated these with the transplantation of lowland tribes under Antoninus Pius (see above, p. 146). Professor Fabricius has pointed out to me that this view is not tenable; the brooches are too early in type, and they do not occur in the right district, which is farther south than the Cologne-Mainz region in which they have been found.

[2] Zosimus (iii. 5) describes Julian as building 800 sailing barges to carry wheat 'to those whom he had restored to their own cities'. Ammianus Marcellinus (xviii. 2) explicitly calls this wheat *annona*. Eunapius (15) mentions the same event.

the city of Autun, the fact did not imply that British craftsmanship was in demand on the Continent, like Italian craftsmanship at the court of Francis I: all it implies is that Britain had
suffered less than Gaul in recent troubles and could be called
upon to assist her, in this case by *corvée*.

Internal trade was at first carried on chiefly through the
medium of the *fora* in towns. The excavations at Wroxeter,
already referred to, have shown us how one shop in such a
forum might specialize in Samian pottery, and so forth. But
there must also have been local markets in the country, not
only at small towns, but also at places where nothing to call
a town can be recognized; one such place has been identified
at Woodeaton, close to Oxford, in a region remote from towns
but full of villages and small villas.[1] Unlike the forum at Wroxeter, Woodeaton continued to thrive down to the end of the
Roman period, and especially in the third and fourth centuries.
The fact is of interest because it shows what happened to retail
trade when the towns were no longer capable of handling it.
Woodeaton drives a larger and larger trade precisely when the
Wroxeter forum falls into ruin; that is to say, the decay of the
towns as commercial centres is compensated by the rise of small
country markets, part and parcel of the change, already described, by which the economic centre of gravity shifts in the
third century from the town to the country-side. At the same
time, much retail trade must have been carried on by hawkers
and pedlars. We have already found reason to conjecture such
a thing in the cases of coal and of New Forest pottery. Another
obvious example is that of charcoal; there must have been
numerous charcoal-burners, independent labourers working
nomadically in the forests, and peddling would be the best way
of bringing their produce to their customers. Perhaps the salt
produced on the coasts of Essex, Lincolnshire, and elsewhere,
and at the brine-pits of Cheshire and Worcestershire, was in the
same case.

Thus in the fourth century, when the country-side enjoyed
the highest degree of romanization, the collapse of town life
did not imply the collapse of trade. People who lived in the
villas could get what they needed, when it could not be produced on the estate, by attending rustic markets and receiving
visits from itinerant hawkers. The villa-dweller could sell his

[1] J. G. Milne in *J.R.S.* xxi. 101–9.

surplus produce—cattle, wheat, cloth, and so on—at periodical fairs in the neighbourhood, and buy what he needed either there or, with money received there, from pedlars offering their own produce for sale at his door. This kind of trade had, of course, existed ever since prehistoric times, when it is attested by the hoards of itinerant bronze-workers; it certainly existed throughout the Roman period, for how else did Samian ware and other imported goods reach native villages many miles from the nearest town? In the third century, and still more in the fourth, it became the standard type of commerce, the country-dwelling Briton, here as elsewhere, reverting to type after the Roman's attempt to urbanize him had failed.

In conclusion, a word may be added about trade across the frontiers. The volume of trade with Scotland was very consider-able. It went by three routes: overland across the Wall, up the west coast, and up the east coast. Most of it probably went over-land, and crossed the Wall either at Portgate, where the great road to Scotland went through, or at Housesteads, where a special gateway existed to serve it, and where the civil settle-ment outside the fort, developing rapidly in the early third century, seems to have served the purpose of a market. A Ger-man scholar[1] has pointed out that the old-established fairs of the present day are often, in his own country, held on sites which have been used in the same way ever since Roman times; and it is tempting to conjecture that Stagshaw Bank Fair, held on Dere Street just south of the Wall, is the lineal successor of the market where traders from the unconquered north sold the goods that they had brought past the customs-house at Portgate. The western sea-route, which has left us a trader's inscription at Bowness-on-Solway, ceased to exist by the fourth century, doubt-less owing to Irish raids; but the eastern route went on well into the middle of that century, carrying Rhenish pottery and glass, brooches, and coins along the coasts of Fife, Angus, and Moray, and as far afield as Caithness and the Orkney brochs. Pottery, wine, bronze goods, and ironmongery were the chief exports; in return, Britain received cattle, leather, furs, and probably slaves and wild animals; possibly, too, gold, oysters, and pearls.

With Ireland, conditions were very different. Until loot began to enter that country at the end of the Roman period, practi-cally nothing of Roman origin reached it except coin, and this

[1] Drexel in *Germania Romana*, ed. 2 (1924), ii. 12.

occurs almost exclusively on the east coast, chiefly in Ulster and
near Dublin. The dates of these coins show that they cannot
all have been brought home by raiders, for many of them are
too early; it seems rather that the Irish carried over to Britain
small quantities of their own produce, possibly cattle and slaves,
and especially hides, for which Ireland was afterwards so famous, and sold them for good Roman silver. One closer contact
is recorded. Cormac mac Airt, high king of Ireland in the
middle of the third century, raided Britain and carried home
a Pictish princess. His queen became jealous, and with reason.
She stipulated that the princess should grind a certain quantity
of meal every day; but the captive was by now unequal to the
labour. So the king sent to Britain 'for an artificer who could
construct a mill', which was evidently a water-mill after the
Roman pattern. The meal was ground, and the terms of the
compact fulfilled.[1]

[1] Keating's *History of Ireland* (c. 1633), tr. Dinneen (1908), ii. 337. I owe the
reference to Mr. C. E. Stevens.

XV

ART

THERE is a certain artificiality in applying to the ancient world, which knew nothing of any distinction between art and manufacture, that separation between the two which is demanded by modern ways of thinking. The historian is often conscious of a certain embarrassment in the presence of his subject; aware of his own thought as perplexingly alien to that which he is thinking about, and of himself as a thing that would seem very strange to the people whose deeds and ideas he studies; and this is never more so than when he applies the modern conception of art to the ancient world, where that conception is so brilliantly exemplified, and whose men were so utterly unconscious of the conception itself. But we have to think as best we can, and unless we thought in the conceptual vocabulary of our own times we should not be able to think at all. In distinguishing, therefore, between two things, the technical quality of Romano-British artisans' work and its artistic quality, we are helping ourselves to understand their world: if we feel a scruple for doing it by making distinctions which they would repudiate, let this apology to their shades suffice.

At its lowest terms, the history of Romano-British art can be told in a couple of sentences. Before the Roman conquest the Britons were a race of gifted and brilliant artists: the conquest, forcing them into the mould of Roman life with its vulgar efficiency and lack of taste, destroyed that gift and reduced their arts to the level of mere manufactures.

That statement is not so much untrue—it is as true as any statement so concise can be—as inadequate; simplified to the point where simplification of itself becomes falsehood. We shall have to supplement it, and in supplementing to modify it; but first we must expand it, to get out of it all the truth it contains.

The art of pre-Roman Britain, offshoot though it was of the continental La Tène style, had developed in a way of its own. The finest works of continental La Tène art have in their repertory of motives a large remnant of naturalistic material: the lotus and the palmette are still everywhere recognizable, even though in a shadowy form, as if remembered in a dream; human masks, often strange and terrifying, are common; birds and

beasts not rare. In their style, they have a certain fullness or
roundness. The artist has not altogether lost his sense for the
solidity of things. His world may be a dream-world, but the
dream has three dimensions. And in their tradition they stand
sometimes within sight of Graeco-Etruscan work, sometimes
even more clearly in sight of eastern models, Scythian or Ira-
nian.[1] These, however, are not the dominant characteristics
even of continental La Tène art; they are recessive; they appear
most strongly in its early days, and as time goes on they tend
to be overcome by their own opposites: naturalistic motives
gradually turn into abstract patterns, the plump forms become
more and more wire-drawn, and the reminiscence of southern
and eastern originals fades away into an art that is more and
more turned inward upon itself.

It was in the La Tène II period, the third and second centuries before Christ, that the migrations took place which
planted this art on British soil. By that time the process above
described had already gone some distance. The founders of
British Celtic art took with them to their new home a vocabulary of decorative motives consisting almost exclusively of S-
shaped and spiral curves that had once been tendrils, and by
now had forgotten their origin, and a tradition of weaving these
and certain other motives into subtle and delicate linear patterns. The effect of transplanting the La Tène tradition to
British soil at this particular point in its history was to make its
British development continue as it were in a straight line, along
the tangent to the curve of its development on the Continent,
a thing which often happens in the history of ideas. Cut off from
its original source, British art lost almost all vestige of naturalism, and much of its plastic feeling; and although it could still
do fine work in the round, it became chiefly an affair of
abstract design in two dimensions.

British La Tène art at its best was thus an intensely specialized
thing. It is hardly an exaggeration to say that the artist had
nothing to do except think out abstract patterns of curving lines.
As craftsman he had to execute them in this or that material,
adapt them to this or that object, shield or helmet, tankard-

---

[1] The characteristics which I am trying to describe may be found with the eye
of faith (for the illustrations are not very good) in the objects figured in Déchelette's
Manuel d'archéologie préhistorique, vol. iv (ed. 2), pp. 742, 744, 754 (top), 841-4. I
confine myself to quoting what is most easily accessible.

handle or mirror; but as artist the only thing that occupied his mind, apart from his central care for curved line, were such minor considerations as colour and background. This concentration on abstract design, practically all of it made out of a single type of line, is a most unusual thing in the history of art: to a person brought up in the nineteenth-century belief that the artist must always be returning to nature for his material and his inspiration, a monstrous and unnatural thing: a thing out of which no good could come. Yet, in fact, the artists of pre-Roman Britain produced work, and a considerable quantity of work, which grows more impressive as one becomes more familiar with it, and more able to place oneself at the point of view from which they themselves looked at it. No school of art maintains a constant level; but among the works of this British school there are individual pieces so perfect, so entirely rich and harmonious in design, that within the narrow limits of the problem he has set himself we cannot deny to their maker the name of a great artist.[1]

If there was some great art in the Britain of that time, there was much that was good. Even the second-rate artists were trained in a school which gave them a firm grasp of abstract curvilinear design, and even their trifling works in metal or in the pottery of peasant-settlements show a wonderful purity of taste and sureness of hand. With the Roman conquest a rapid and disastrous change comes over the whole spirit of British craftsmanship. In taste, the standards of classical art in its degraded imperial form, and the commercialized provincial variety of that degradation, begin to dominate the minds of those who set the fashion. In manufacture, mass-production takes the place of individual design and execution. Within a generation, every trace of La Tène art has disappeared except in the north, where it lingers for another half-century; at last it dies out there also, and by the late second century everything that meets the archaeologist's eye is infected with the uniform and sordid ugliness of drab Romano-British daylight.

In that daylight, it is true, we can see works of art. Rome taught the Britons to carve stone, to paint wall-plaster, to decorate floors in mosaic. But, of all the results, there is hardly anything that rises above the level of dull, mechanical imitation

[1] Examples are the Birdlip mirror at Gloucester (Leeds, *Celtic Ornament*, fig. 9) and one of the Polden Hill enamels in the British Museum (ibid., plate i, no. 4).

to that of even third-rate artistic achievement. The Roman models themselves were poor enough; the empire was not an age of good taste; but there is perhaps no province where local attempts to reproduce them failed so dismally as they failed in Britain. Elsewhere the provincials threw themselves with a certain degree of confidence or even enthusiasm into the production of romanized works of art, and if they produced nothing great, at least they produced something competent: something that was no disgrace either to the Roman tradition or to their own skill. But on any Romano-British site the impression that constantly haunts the archaeologist, like a bad smell or a stickiness on the fingers, is that of an ugliness which pervades the place like a London fog: not merely the common vulgar ugliness of the Roman empire, but a blundering, stupid ugliness that cannot even rise to the level of that vulgarity.

Had we known nothing of pre-Roman art in Britain we might have accepted this fact with resignation, shrugged our shoulders, and dismissed the British provincial as a person of no artistic talent. Knowing as we do what brilliant artistic work he was producing before the Romans came, we cannot say that. The thing demands explanation; and all the more urgently when we find the same Celtic art which disappeared at the beginning of the Roman period rising mysteriously from its grave, enfeebled and uncertain of itself, but unmistakable, when that period is over. Where have its seeds been preserved? And why have they been hidden so completely for three centuries and a half?

There are two questions here which must be dealt with separately. First, why did anything so well established and well developed as British La Tène art fail to survive the Roman conquest? Why did it not continue to live and flourish under the new régime? And secondly, granted that it did die out, surely the artistic talent that had produced it was not extinguished: why did it not turn its powers to the production of works in the Roman style and produce a provincial school of art comparable, for instance, with that of the Moselle valley?

The complete answer to the first question will only become evident when we have answered the second. But in the meantime it is useful to remember that however impressive the quality of pre-Roman art in Britain may be, the total bulk of it is not large. Even in the west and north, where it is most at home, the number of its known works is curiously small. Not only are the finest works rare (that is in any case to be expected), but even its humbler manifestations in decorated pottery, well known in the Somerset lake-dwellings, are not at all common at other inhabited sites. No part of Britain was ever saturated with works in this style.

Outside its home districts, moreover, it is either rare or alto-gether absent. None of it has been found at Silchester; little at Colchester, and that little not of the best; comparatively little anywhere in the Belgic area, apart from finds which are earlier than the Belgic settlement. The Belgic tribes, which politically and culturally were the dominant force in Britain just before the Roman conquest, were not and never had been the heirs of this artistic tradition. They inherited a good La Tène style in the elegant though somewhat obvious shapes of their pottery; and after achieving their ascendancy they attracted to them-selves a certain number of craftsmen representing the best British school; but the general effect of their domination was to under-mine the taste of that school and substitute the Roman fashions to which their own eclectic taste on the whole inclined.

Thus the social basis of the best pre-Roman art in Britain was somewhat narrow, and was already becoming insecure before the Roman conquest; and this fact certainly had something to do with its rapid submergence. But an even more important cause lay in its own artistic quality. To make great art, or even good art, by the purely abstract manipulation of curved lines is a feat of extreme difficulty, demanding the rarest combination of favourable circumstances: above all, a certain isolation from disturbing influences, permitting the artist and his patron to develop their canons of taste in unconsciousness that any other kind of art is possible. The dream-like quality which to some extent pervades all Celtic art here reaches its culmination. So delicate is the meditative poise of the best early British art, that a touch will destroy it. Granted the peculiar character of that art, it could never survive contact with the cruder, grosser art-work of the Roman empire, whose very crudity is in such a contact its strength.

We have, then, an art of extreme delicacy rather than robust-ness, and one whose appeal is aristocratic rather than popular; an art whose existence depends on isolation, concentration, and unspoilt sensitiveness of eye. The high demands which it makes both on the artist and on his patron are not reinforced by any adventitious appeal, whether sensuous or patriotic or religious. There is nothing here that could enable it to outlive the shock of conquest and absorption in a society whose standards were different. Even if left to itself, such an art, after achieving the perfection which we know it did achieve, would decay of itself, merely through having exhausted its own somewhat narrow possibilities of development.

It was natural, therefore, that the art of the pre-Roman Britons should perish at the Roman conquest. It was equally natural that it should survive for a time on the outskirts of romanization, among the village bronze-workers of Brigantia, and then die out there too, while continuing to exist in Ireland and unconquered Scotland. But in the meantime the people who had shown themselves capable of producing and enjoying it had passed under Roman rule. Why (this was our second question) did they not continue to show their talent by producing good works in the Roman style which they had adopted?

In order that this question may become answerable, we must first of all understand that there is no such thing as an abstract and general artistic talent, biologically transmissible like the shape of a skull. Art is a phenomenon not of biology but of history; and the historical possessions of a people, their traditions and culture, are inherited in a way quite different from that in which biological characteristics are inherited. Biological conceptions like that of race throw no light, but only darkness, upon historical problems, breeding error and superstition where what we want is fact. If we wish to answer our question, we must beware of all talk about racial talent. The artistic power of a people is not an innate power to produce good art: it is a tradition, handed down from generation to generation, telling the members of that people what kinds of artistic problem they must set themselves and how problems of that kind can be solved.

But the continuity of a cultural tradition is not the same thing as the continuity of a school. The continuity of a school is a conscious continuity: it depends on one person's teaching another, explicitly, what to do and how to do it. The continuity of a cultural tradition is unconscious: those who live in it need not be explicitly aware of its existence. The continuity of tradition is the continuity of the force by which past experiences affect the future; and this force does not depend on the conscious memory of those experiences. In the life of a people, a great experience in the past affects the way in which the generation that has had it teaches its children to look at the future, even though they never knew what that experience was.

The British people had achieved its first great artistic experience through the intensely abstract curvilinear design of the middle La Tène school. It was bound, therefore, to respond to contact with a new art in one of two ways. If that new art provided opportunity for the perpetuation and development of this particular experience, it would welcome it, converting the traditional motives of the new art into means for continuing that line of artistic growth to which it had already committed itself. If no such opportunities were offered, it would accept the new motives, if forced to accept them, in a dull and uncomprehending manner, like a pupil uninterested in his lesson, and do stupidly and blunderingly what it was told to do, not from stupidity, but because it was preoccupied with its own thoughts: betraying this preoccupation from time to time by doing work, crude and childish, no doubt, quite unlike what it was wanted to do, but expressive of its own desires, and therefore bearing the stamp of conviction. The one thing it could never do is to behave as if its own great experience had not happened to it, and learn its new lesson with an open mind. A people, like a single human being, is what its past has made it.

Of these two reactions, the first would make for healthy artistic development. From such a contact both Roman art and the British people would gain something of value. There would arise a school of Romano-British art having the same kind of double parentage as the Anglo-Italian madrigal of the Jacobean age, or the Flemish-Italian painting of the early Renaissance. The British people would have incorporated the Roman tradition in its own artistic experience, and would be able to go on to the next stage in its development. The second would be in the main a waste of time, unproductive for both sides; Roman art teaching the Briton nothing but what he was glad to forget, Britain contributing to Roman art nothing of which it could be proud. After the end of the contact, Britain would be left to take up her own artistic problem where she had been forced to lay it down.

The tradition which Rome brought into her provinces was completely unsuited to the needs of a mind trained as the artists of Britain had been trained. This had nothing to do with its artistic merits: it depended on the traditional problems which Roman artists set themselves, not on their success in solving those problems. Primarily, Roman art was concerned with the representation of living forms, and in particular the human form. Its sculpture, its modelling, its painting, were based on a naturalistic tradition as old as Greek art and older. Secondarily, it was concerned with the manipulation of masses, the creation of dignified and expressive architectural shapes. Here again it was rooted in the age-old tradition of the Mediterranean world.

It was a strange fatality. Representative art, the idea of making a picture that should be a picture of something, was all but incomprehensible to the British artist. A master in formal design, he was a child in the portrayal of nature.[1] What Roman art might have taught him in that direction, and might have taught him quite well, for in spite of its artistic poverty it had behind it a formidable amount of knowledge and technical skill, was a lesson he did not in that stage of his development wish or need to learn. And the one direction in which it might have aroused his interest, the non-representative art of architectural design, was closed to him because of his specialized concern with design in the flat, patterns in two dimensions. Conversely, the one point in which the Briton excelled was a point in which the Roman artist was uninterested. Had the Briton encountered classical Greek art, or Byzantine art, or Moorish art, his mind would have lighted up with new ideas about linear patterns; but Roman art had nothing of the kind to offer him. Again, had he been trained, like the Gaul and the German, in the work of the early La Tène period, with its naturalistic elements and its feeling for solid shape, the contact with Roman art might have appealed to that training and produced something in Britain like the sculpture of northern Gaul and the giant columns of Germany; but the training was not there, and the response never came.

The artistic romanization of Britain is therefore a melancholy story, not because Rome failed to impose her standards—she succeeded all too well—nor because Britain lacked artistic apti-

---

[1] I do not forget the exceptions. But I think no one will quarrel with Leeds's valuation of them (op. cit., pp. 86–7): 'It is not that they failed entirely, but that their efforts were bound in the very nature of things to result in what must be admitted is very poor success.'

tude, for she had it in plenty, but because teacher and pupil were at cross-purposes. If the abundant evidence for this fact is to be appreciated, the history of Romano-British art must be distinguished from the history of Roman art in Britain. It goes without saying that works of art in the standard Roman taste were imported into Britain, and that others, legionary tomb-stones and the like, were made in Britain by hands that were not British. When we try to set these on one side, and look solely at things made in Britain by Britons themselves, after they had become romanized, the story of failure is clearly legible.

There is one work which stands out so far above all rivals that any discussion of Romano-British artistic achievement must begin with it. The Gorgon's head on the shield of Sulis-Minerva, in the pediment of her temple at Bath, shows what might have happened if a genuine school of Romano-British sculpture had come into existence. As it is, we cannot even be sure that it is the work of a British hand; for a Gaulish sculptor from Chartres has recorded his presence at Bath, and the pediment may be his. In any case, it is the work of an artist brought up in the La Tène tradition, using Roman motives, and therefore it is to our purpose.

From the Roman point of view, the Gorgon head is merely one feature of the shield, and the shield is merely an accessory of the divine figure that holds it. On the Bath pediment the Gorgon is the centre of interest, glaring, ferocious, apotropaic, like the human or demonic masks of early La Tène art. Like them, it is male, not female as a Gorgon should be; its beard and moustaches are tangled with the snakes of its own hair; and the rendering of its features, which is wholly unlike anything Ro-man, recalls in unmistakable detail the same Celtic originals. Romano-British religious syncretism had asked for a Gorgon: the Celtic sculptor responded by supplying a mask whose an-cestry is sought for in vain among the Gorgons of Hellenistic and Roman tradition, but can be found at once when we turn to the history of Celtic art. The shield is merely its frame, and all else is crowded away into corners. The goddess has dis-appeared.[1]

[1] Apotropaic masks are a commonplace of La Tène I art. For examples, with the moustache of the Celts to indicate sex, cf. Déchelette, op. cit., pp. 744, 754, 841; with beard as well, developing strongly in the direction of the Bath head, p. 938 (the Klein-Aspergle flagon). The frowning forehead recalls the stone head from Heidelberg in the Carlsruhe museum, not figured in Déchelette. I cannot but think

The success of the Bath sculptor depended on his finding, at one point in the repertory of Roman art, opportunity for doing the kind of work that he understood. A Gorgon head is in fact simply an apotropaic mask, a hideous face to scare away demons and the evil eye; and the artists of the La Tène I period had spent much of their time making such things. Its full face and floating hair make a design in the flat, where subtleties of modelling are not required; what is required is a training of the same kind that went to the making of the British mirror-backs. The Bath sculptor knew all about apotropaic masks, and he knew all about decorating a roundel with a pattern of snaky lines. For once Roman art had asked him to do the things that he could do well.

This work stands alone; there is nothing in Britain to set beside it. That, together with its obvious derivation from the La Tène masks, which hardly occur in this country,[1] increases the possibility that its sculptor may not have been a Briton at all, but Priscus of Chartres or one of his Gaulish colleagues. If, yielding to these doubts, we no longer claim it as native work, the evidences of Romano-British sculpture fall entirely under the second of the two alternatives set forth above: cases where the British artist, finding the demands of Roman style too un-congenial to arouse his interest, fulfilled them only in a per-functory and incompetent manner. Here and there he has seized upon a complex of drapery-folds and worked it out into a pattern of flowing lines, or given to a human or animal face one of the two standard expressions, grotesquely ferocious or dreamy and half-asleep, that mark the faces of early La Tène art. When this happens, which is not often, he breaks through the placid con-ventionality of the Roman style, and shows that the Celtic tradi-tion is still alive in him. It is working uneasily behind the façade of romanization, unable to express itself by remodelling that façade, and unable to rest until it has found expression.

In metal-work we find a variation on the same theme. All over the lowland zone Celtic art withers at the coming of Rome. In the highland fringe it not only survives for a time, it even

that Haverfield and Stuart Jones had overlooked these sources when they put forward the attempted derivation of the Bath Gorgon from Hellenistic and Roman originals in *J.R.S.* ii (1912), pp. 134–5.

[1] The set of three from Welwyn (*Archaeologia*, lxiii, pl. 2) are the only ones I know of. They are, however, not of the ferocious kind, of which we have no examples in Britain.

develops into new forms, not unworthy of its best tradition. Partly this is because romanization is here less rapid and overwhelming; partly, one may suspect, because northern Britain had already produced a style of its own, less delicate and finedrawn than that of the south, a style in which feeling for mass had not been entirely sacrificed to subtlety of line. In Brigantia and in Scotland Celtic art is more like modelling and less like draughtsmanship; forms are plump and solid, recalling those of early La Tène work on the Continent; and it is thanks to the heritage of what Leeds has called the northern 'boss' style that the bronze-workers of those parts made, in the early second century, so many brooches distinguished at once for solidity and elegance, and the greatest genius of them all, applying La Tène patterns to a Roman type of brooch, produced at some time not later than the end of the first century what Sir Arthur Evans once called 'the most fantastically beautiful creation that has come down to us from antiquity', the gold fibula found at the Roman fort of Aesica.[1]

In Ireland and unconquered Scotland the La Tène tradition lasted on. But in the Roman north it died out in the course of the second century as completely as it did in the lowland zone. Yet, somewhat as the Celtic spirit here and there reveals itself in sculpture by some un-Roman treatment of a conventional Roman motive, so in metal-work we find, thinly scattered in place and time, little pieces of design showing that Romano-British bronze-workers, though no longer able to produce things comparable with the art of their pre-Roman forebears, never entirely lost their hold on the same tradition. Embossed or enamelled brooches and the like, found not only in Northumberland and Westmorland but in Berkshire and at Silchester and Verulam, and dated to the third or fourth century, bear triple spirals whose treatment, elementary though it is, places them in the descent of Celtic art and proves that, all over Britain, that art remained alive behind the façade of romanization.

Pottery teaches the same lesson. In the designs on Castor ware, despite the mass-production and the romanized organization of the industry, slender threads of Celtic tradition are visible. The running animals, the leaf-scrolls, and the rare and

---

[1] *Archaeologia*, lv. 186. The brooch has often been figured, e.g. in my *Roman Britain* (1934), fig. 37. Leeds, op. cit., p. 109, adds the weight of his authority to the earlier of the possible dates proposed for it in *Archaeologia*, lxxx. 40–2.

bad human figures, are all Roman; but the way in which these motives are used preserves a distinct, though far-away, reminiscence of the flowing decoration that surrounds the shoulders of Gaulish and even western British vessels of the La Tène period. Both here and in the stamped or painted ware of the New Forest there is a suggestion that the surviving Celtic spirit in British design is drawing new nourishment from contact with similar survivals in northern Gaul and the Rhineland. But these Celtic traces in late Romano-British pottery, though in quantity they far exceed those visible in metal-work, are in quality far more elusive. Often we seem vaguely to feel that a design, taken as a whole, is tinged with a Celtic flavour, when on looking more closely we see that everything in it is Roman.

The revival of Celtic art at the end of the Roman period is by now a commonplace, though it remains a debated question how much of what goes by the name of Anglo-Saxon art is due to that revival. Into that debate we need not enter. Fortunately, there is one class of works, intensively studied in late years, which gives us an admirable sample of the products of British craftsmanship at about the time of the Roman evacuation. These are the metal hanging-bowls whose suspension-rings are attached to the vessel by means of little plates bearing different kinds of ornament.[1] The type of vessel is late Roman; the ornament is sometimes late Roman, sometimes Celtic; but Celtic of a style in general more akin to the Christian Celtic art of the following centuries, with its spiral and trumpet motives, than to the earlier La Tène art with its S-shaped figures derived from the classical palmette. In these patterns we see, as in the pottery, but far more clearly, motives of Roman origin, especially the curvilinear triangle known as the pelta, undergoing absorption into a style that is not only recognizably Celtic in its general tone and feeling, but explicitly obeys the two great principles of pre-Roman British art: the positive principle that the artist's work is to create a harmonious design made up entirely of curves, and the negative principle that this design must be wholly abstract, a picture that is not a picture of anything.

No less significant than the quality of the hanging-bowls'

---

[1] Romilly Allen in *Archaeologia*, lvi. 39; R. A. Smith in *Proc. Soc. Ant.* xxii. 66; Cowen in *Arch. Aeliana*, ser. 4, viii (1931), p. 329; Kendrick in *Antiquity*, vi (1932), p. 161; Wheeler, ibid., p. 292; Clapham, ibid. viii (1934), p. 43; Leeds, *Celtic Ornament*, ch. vi.

ornament is their distribution. It is emphatically and almost exclusively (when allowance has been made for examples carried off as loot by raiders) a lowland zone distribution. A quarter of them come from Kent and the neighbourhood of London; three-quarters from the part of England that lies southeast of the Fosse. The inference is clear: they are an indigenous product of Romano-British art, in its latest phase and in the most romanized part of the country. The analysis of their ornament and the map of their distribution conspire to prove that the revival of Celtic art to which they testify was not due to a refertilization of the old stock by new influences washed back from the outer Celtic world where Rome had never ruled, but was thrown up by that old stock itself, out of its own continuing vitality.

Revival implies survival. But what exactly survived? Not a school, handing down a conscious heritage of motives and treatment; to postulate that would be not only going beyond our evidence, it would be going against what evidence we have. Not a racial temperament, if there is such a thing; to assert that would be to confuse history by an admixture of pseudo-biology. The facts reviewed in the last few pages show that, throughout the Roman period, British artists were working under what may perhaps be described as a permanent strain, pulling them away from the spirit of Roman art in the direction of one totally different. The spirit of Roman art was naturalistic. It sprang from an interest in observing and recording the appearance of things. The mind of its artists was turned outwards, to play upon the external world; it stored itself with memories of men and women, beasts and birds and plants, and out of these memories it built up its repertory of motives. The art of the La Tène world was symbolic. Where it used naturalistic motives, as in the early animal forms and apotropaic masks, it used them not because of an interest in the appearance of things, but because it could by their means express the artist's emotions. The inward-turned mind which began by using natural things for this purpose found before long that the purpose could be served even better by ceasing to think about natural things, and expressing the same emotions in abstract patterns. Just when the British artist had triumphantly made this discovery, he was brought within the orbit of Roman naturalism. He tried to accept it with docility, but his mind was still preoccupied with the ideal of a symbolic art.

Thus the symbolism of La Tène art acted like a vortex into which were thrown the fragments of the Roman artistic tradition. Wherever possible, these fragments, throughout the centuries of our period, were sucked down into that vortex and there transmuted into materials for a symbolic art. Whenever the student of Roman Britain finds anything of native workmanship which he feels to have any artistic merit, the Bath Gorgon, the Corbridge lion, the Aesica brooch, Castor or New Forest pottery, or the like, he has found something that has undergone this transmutation. Wherever the fragments resisted absorption into the vortex, and floated unchanged on its surface, we find dull and clumsy imitation of Roman work by men who seem utterly devoid of artistic gifts. Finally, when the naturalistic Roman art itself is dying back, and has no longer the energy to impress its ideals on a distant frontier-land, the British artist is set free. He has learnt little, and has forgotten much; but he has preserved intact the ideal of a symbolic art, and is able at last to begin again the task of realizing it: a task which, this time, will not be interrupted, but only assisted by borrowings from the south and east, until it has achieved the triumphs of Lindisfarne and Bewcastle.

XVI

RELIGION

THE story of Romano-British religion offers a curious contrast to that of Romano-British art. Whereas in art the Roman tradition and the British were so deeply antagonistic that no compromise between them was possible, and the only result of their contact was to drive the British tradition underground, in religion there was on both sides an easy polytheism, tolerant and hospitable, which permitted mutual borrowings and encouraged compromise from both sides. So long as Celtic religion wore an intolerant nationalistic shape, in the form of Druidism, Rome saw in it a danger to her own imperial policy; but Druidism in Gaul had already been abolished by Claudius before Britain was conquered, and on this side of the Channel the conquest of the people and the destruction of their Druidical organization went hand in hand. Negatively, after the suppression of Druidism, there was nothing that Rome need demand of British religion; she could leave it alone. Positively, all she asked was participation in the imperial cult through the provincial assembly; and this had no effect whatever on the general religious views and practices of the people.

Hence, whereas British art all but perished under romanization, British religion throve on it. Or rather, it hardly underwent romanization at all. It survived unchanged, within a political framework admirably fitted to foster just such local autonomies and idiosyncrasies. At first, enthusiastic Britons like Cogidubnus embraced the worship of the Roman gods; but this lead was not long followed; by degrees the tide of romanization ebbed away; everywhere Celtic forms of worship raised their heads, and even won the adherence of the conquerors. The Romans were always willing to come to terms with the *genius loci*; they could not do it in art, but they could in religion; and consequently the history of Romano-British religion is the history of a blend of cultures in which, by degrees, the Celtic prevails. We shall consider in turn the two components of this blend, the Roman element first.

The gods of official Roman religion have left their records so lavishly in the inscriptions that we can form a detailed idea of their worship as it affected people who used that form of

3720.1   S

dedication. To judge the significance of these records, we must remember that Britain is extraordinarily rich in military inscriptions, and correspondingly poor in others; that inscriptions only tell us about the habits of the most romanized parts of the population; that, of those parts, they tell us more concerning official and public acts than about personal and private ones; and that the vast majority of those we possess date from the second century: by the middle of the third they have become very rare, in the fourth they have practically vanished.

The supreme god of the official imperial cult, Iuppiter Optimus Maximus, claims a much larger number of dedications than any other. With these may be reckoned the dedications to the deity of the emperor. Almost without exception, these record acts of official worship by military units or their commanders, and to a less extent by other public bodies. The evidence is quite clear that the worship of Iuppiter was an official military cult which never sank deep into the private lives even of men in the army, and *a fortiori* had no effect on the general body of the people. It is significant, too, that Iuppiter kept himself proudly aloof from all contamination with Celtic religion. Once he shares an altar with the native Cocidius; once he condescends to take a Celtic epithet, Tanarus, the 'roarer', possibly in reminiscence of his own thunder. Otherwise he stands for the cleavage between Rome as ruler and Britain as subject: he is the symbol of the *raj*.

After Iuppiter, by far the commonest of the Roman deities is Mars. But he is in a quite different position. Often, in the second[1] and early third centuries, he is the object of an official military cult not very different from that of Iuppiter. But in two ways he shows a closer contact with the life of the people. The little rude altars on which private soldiers, generally anonymous, recorded their personal devotion never bear the name of Iuppiter, but often that of Mars; he was therefore a living reality to the rank and file of the army. But also, he was very freely identified with Celtic deities, Belatucadrus, Camulus, Cocidius, Corotiacus; or adorned with Celtic epithets like Rigisamus, 'most royal': in short, he went native without compunction, and thus formed an important link between the Roman and Celtic elements of British religion. And in that process he ceased to be in any special sense a soldier's god; many

[1] In spite of von Domaszewski, *Religion des röm. Heeres* (1895), p. 34.

of his Celticized avatars belong to an entirely unmilitary sphere of provincial life; thus he formed a point of contact between the religion of the army and that of civil life.

Mercury, like Mars, made a place for himself in the heart of the common soldier; always a genial and condescending god, he was worshipped for good luck in a variety of ways, especially by means of rude carvings or scratchings on stone, hardly recognizable except by the wings on his head and sometimes the rod and purse in his hands. To some extent, the same popularity belonged to Hercules, to Neptune, and to Silvanus, god of the wild, worshipped by hunters. But none of these three has left any trace of absorption into the religion of the natives. There is nothing in Britain comparable with the influence which Mercury, through his popularity with the mass of the Gaulish people, has exercised on the place-names of modern France. Vulcan, god of the smithy, became the patron of many *vici* where industries were carried on outside the gates of military forts; but he, too, failed to win favour with the Briton. Apollo and Diana come rarely, and almost wholly for official purposes; Apollo sometimes identified with a youthful Celtic god, but easily beaten in that endeavour by Mars. Minerva appears only in an official or semi-official capacity; as a rule worshipped by the scientific branches of the army, architects, and the like.

Minor hangers-on of the Roman pantheon are found mostly in the form of miscellaneous genii, the spirit of a place or a community or even a person: the genius of a fort or an official building, of a legion or auxiliary regiment or *collegium*; these are mostly official dedications. More interesting, because they might convey a suggestion of local cults not yet discriminated by their own proper names, are the common dedications to the 'genius of the place'; but when we look at them in detail, the suggestion is hardly confirmed: they come from places like Bath, Lincoln, Chester, York, Carlisle, and are consequently documents of Roman religion pure and simple, not Roman recognition of native deities. Even the officer who set up an altar by the Antonine Wall to the 'genius of the British land' was worshipping a spirit Romanly conceived.

Eastern religions came, as a matter of course. The army, in the third century, contained many devotees of Mithras, and his temples existed on Hadrian's Wall. The Iuppiters of Doliche and of Heliopolis in Egypt have left traces. From Egypt, too, came Serapis and Isis; and worship was paid to the Syrian goddess and the Asiatic Cybele. But these eastern influences worked only on the army and, to a far smaller extent, on the most romanized and cosmopolitan of the towns. On the general mass of the people they had no effect at all.

When we turn to the Celtic religious element, the material is far richer and more varied. We have some forty names of deities or groups of deities. Of these, a dozen represent local cults concerning which something definite can be said; eight or ten are deities more or less widely known in the Celtic world, and probably imported into Britain by worshippers from other Celtic lands; and of the rest we know nothing, and can only guess that some of them were native to the soil, and others brought from overseas.

It will be worth our while to review the cases in which we can identify local gods, worshipped at one place or in one quite small region. These cults, rooted in the soil and purely Celtic in origin, have an interesting history. A few of them were sufficiently important to attract the attention of Romans, or at least of persons worshipping in the Roman way, at an early date; but these are the exception. As a rule, the evidence suggests that the little local gods emerged slowly and timidly, one by one, into the light of romanized or half-romanized cults, and that this emergence, generally speaking, was confined to the highland zone. Except at Bath, which is a somewhat special case, we do not know the name of a single local god in the lowland zone; for isolated dedications, like that to Ancasta at Bitterne or Andescocis at Colchester, are not proof.

Let us look at the evidence. Sulis,[1] the goddess of the hot springs at Bath, came into her own at a very early date; her temple, with its classical architecture and very unclassical sculpture, was probably built in the Flavian period. But less than thirty miles away across the Severn, Nodens, the hunter-god of the Forest of Dean, who survived in later mythology as Nuada of the Silver Hand, king of the Tuatha dé Danann, and later still as King Lear, had to wait for his splendid temple, with its hostelry and baths and precinct, until the pagan revival initiated

---

[1] She is traditionally called Sul; but Professor Tolkien points out to me that the Celtic nominative can only be Sulis, and our authority for believing that even the Romans made a nominative Sul on the analogy of their own word *sol*—perhaps meaning the same—is not good. The Celtic *sulis* may mean 'the eye', and this again may mean the sun.

by Julian the Apostate, though, no doubt, his hill-top above Lydney had always been sacred ground. The dwelling-place of Nodens owed its fortune to the fact of its being close enough to the lowland zone to be drawn within the orbit of romanization; the remoter Welsh fastnesses must have been full of gods concerning whom we know nothing.

In the north things were different. Here the highland soil was no less tenacious of its deities, and by degrees the frontier army found them out and gave them their due. There must have been many shrines to the goddess Brigantia. She was worshipped at Birrens in Dumfriesshire as early as the second century, but most of the dedications to her, scattered from the southern Pennines to Corbridge and to Castlesteads on Hadrian's Wall, are in the style of the third. A few other local gods of the north were already worshipped in the second century. One was Maponus, 'the youth' or 'hero'—perhaps a descriptive term for one whose real name might not be uttered—whose shrine seems to be recorded by the entry Maponi in the Ravenna Cosmography, and whose dedications come thickest at Corbridge in that century, though in the following century we find his worship spreading here and there over the north. Romanizing religion identified him with Apollo; but when some third-century Germans put up an altar to him in north-eastern Cumberland they called him simply Maponus.[1]

Another local god early recognized was Cocidius. His temple, Fanum Cocidi, appears in the Ravenna Cosmography, and, to judge by the distribution of his altars, must have been in the Irthing valley. Thereabouts several altars were dedicated to him in the middle of the second century; in the third he was much worshipped along the Wall between Carlisle and Hexham, and in the forts to the north of it, and we have one altar as far away as Lancaster. Coventina, the lady of the sacred spring by Carrawburgh on the Wall, whose little temple has been excavated, was recognized as early; and the coins thrown into her spring show that her cult lasted to the end of the Roman occupation, when the Wall was finally abandoned in Gratian's reign. At Benwell, also on the Wall, a temple was built to a pair of local gods, Anociticus and Antenociticus, also in the second century.

[1] It is noteworthy that individual dedicators describing themselves as Germans repeatedly address themselves to gods with pure Celtic names; often, no doubt, local.

Many others make their appearance in the third. In the reign of Caracalla a temple was built to Matunus, the 'kindly one', near Elsdon in mid-Northumberland. In the same district, though the cult is also found in Cumberland, Mogons, the 'doughty one', was worshipped: sometimes he appears in the plural, as other Celtic deities do. Belatucadrus, the 'fair shining one', often identified by Roman worshippers with Mars, was greatly honoured in the district south and west of Carlisle and also eastward along the Wall. Condatis, the god of a river-mouth or watersmeet, was worshipped on the lower Wear; he, too, identified with Mars. In the Lune valley there was Contrebis or Ialonus Contrebis, the 'god of a fair open place dwelling among us'. On the western part of the Wall we find Latis, goddess of some pool or stream.

All this shows the extent to which Celtic religion, in the shape of small localized cults, survived the Roman conquest and imposed itself on the minds of the conquerors. As time went on, to judge from the coins in Coventina's well and from the temple of Nodens, the process must have intensified; but inscriptions fail us. We have enough, however, to show that in the region of the Wall the local cults of Celtic religion, so far from being neglected or persecuted or swamped beneath the weight of imported worships, steadily reasserted themselves, not here and there only, but everywhere. We can even trace the way in which natives living close by the Wall took the lead in this reassertion. There is an altar from the Tyne valley, set up as early as the second century by a body calling itself the 'curia of the Textoverdi', that is, the pagus or canton of that name, doubt-less a subdivision of the Brigantes, to a goddess whose name, not wholly legible, may be Saitada, the 'lady of grief'.

These local cults, of which we have knowledge only because they are commemorated by inscriptions in Latin, testify to the easy relations that existed between Celt and Roman in the matter of worship. Both officially and unofficially, the Roman was ready not only to tolerate Celtic religion, even in its hum-blest local manifestations, but to join in it; the Celt was ready to welcome that co-operation and not anxious to keep the Roman at arm's length. Thus understood, the religious dedica-tions which we have been analysing are documents telling of the relation between the garrison and the natives, un-romanized as these were, in the frontier district. They do not attest

romanization of the local cults. Not a single one of these dedications, except that of the Textoverdi, was put up by members of
the frontier tribes; these continued to worship in their own way,
leaving no epigraphic record. In that religious fellowship, the
Celt was the dominant partner. The Roman garrison, as it
gradually took root in the soil, did not impose its own culture
on its neighbours; on the contrary, it went to school with the
inhabitants, in order to learn the religions of the soil and to
take its part in them.

In the lowland zone also Celtic religion survived. Here, too,
its survival was a revival as well: its part in the life of the country
became more and more predominant as time went on. But it
shows itself in a different way. In the south-eastern counties,
from Norfolk to Dorsetshire, we find temples of a peculiar kind:
little buildings, often standing on hill-tops, whose ground-plan
is a square within a square, showing that such a temple consisted of a single room surrounded by a portico. Temples of this
kind occur widespread over Gaul and Germany, especially in
the Seine and Moselle valleys. Like the commonest kind of
villa, they are neither a Roman type of building nor a Celtic;
the type is one that came into existence in Celtic lands under
Roman rule, and has been appropriately called the Romano-
Celtic temple. We have seen that the local cults of the highland
zone were for the most part completely un-romanized in themselves, though admitting Romans to their worship. In these
temples, on the contrary, the cult itself is half-romanized, yet
remains half-Celtic: a state of things recalling the mixture of
Celtic and Roman elements in the Castor or New Forest pottery,
described in the last chapter.

We do not yet know at what date Romano-Celtic temples
began to be built; but we know that most of them belong to a
late period and that they were being put up in the third and
fourth centuries. No British example has told us the name of
the god worshipped there; but from examples on the Continent
we may suspect that their patron deities had been at least as
much romanized as their architecture, and had generally Roman and Celtic names coupled together, like Apollo Moritasgus
at the similar temple on Mont-Auxois. This official acceptance
of an *interpretatio Romana* at the head-quarters of the cult was a
very different thing from the casual and unofficial way in which
a Roman worshipper of such a god as Cocidius might identify

him now with Mars, now with Silvanus, or alternatively give him no name but his own. We know enough about the history of Romano-Celtic temples to be sure that the blended religion for which they stood was making headway in southern Britain during the latter part of the Roman period, and up to its very end.

Of the imported Celtic deities, by far the most popular were the three Mothers. Their cult seems to have originated in Cisalpine Gaul and the lands bordering on it across the Alps; it spread early to the Rhineland and thence to Britain, where it is commonest in the army, but is well attested elsewhere. Other deities from the Rhine and Moselle are the Suleviae; Grannus, identified with Apollo; Lenus, identified with Mars; Nemetona, from the neighbourhood of Trier. These are local in origin; but Epona, the horse-goddess, and Camulus, another of the many Celtic gods who became Mars by *interpretatio Romana*, seem to have been more generally worshipped. Finally, we are left with a host of Celtically named deities of whom we can hardly say whether they were native or imported: Ancasta, Andescocis, Harimella, Setlocenia, Vanauns, Viradecthis, and many others.[1]

There remains one curious cult of which a word may here be said. About forty little altars are known, mostly from the central part of Hadrian's Wall, but reaching out to Netherby on one side and with single outliers as far as Catterick and York on the other, dedicated to a god apparently called Vitiris. The dedicators were humble persons, and barely literate; often they write *deo veteri*, 'to the old god', instead of *deo Vitiri*, and may even have thought that was what they meant; sometimes they wrote *hvitri* or *hveteri* or *vheteri*, as if the word began with an aspirated or voiceless consonant. Sometimes the dedication is to one god, sometimes to a group; sometimes the group is of goddesses. Interpretation of so confused a mass of material is hard. It has been thought that the dedicators were pagan die-hards, worshipping 'the old gods' in a time of prevailing Christianity; but that fits neither the facts nor the probabilities. It has been thought, on the strength of the aspirate, that the word

---

[1] I omit, as of very slender historical interest, the more Germanic of these imported deities: Mars Thincsus and the Alaisiagae of Housesteads, the Suebian Garmangabis of Lanchester, the Unseni Fersomari of Old Penrith. They are linguistic curiosities; but as religious phenomena they are related to the Germanic elements in the army precisely as imported Celtic gods are to the continental Celtic.

is a Germanic divine name; but philologists will have nothing of the idea.

The distribution of these altars strongly recalls that of the local cults already described. In style the altars are exactly like those of, for example, Belatucadrus. The names of the dedicators are either non-committally Roman or Celtic. In one case the god is identified with Mogons. In the light of these facts, the most probable explanation of this mysterious worship is that it belongs to the class of cults which it so strongly resembles at every point: in other words, that a local god with some name like Vitiris had his sanctuary, like Belatucadrus and Cocidius, not far from the Wall, probably near Carvoran, at which fort a quarter of all the known dedications have been found; that he resembled his neighbour Mogons not only in being ambiguously one or many, but in other ways sufficient to make identification possible; that, like Belatucadrus, but even more so, he became popular in the third century among the rank and file of the army, and that his cult differed from its chief rivals only in having its centre farther to the east, thus spreading into County Durham and down into Yorkshire instead of into Cumberland and Lancashire.

What emerges most clearly from this survey of Celtic religion in Roman Britain is its variety. There is no trace whatever of any god or gods dominant over all the Celtic world. Travellers, it is clear, may take their gods with them; and in exceptional cases they may become naturalized in their new country; but in its broad general character this religion is a localized religion: its gods have homes, and it is at these homes, or near them, that they are normally worshipped.

This kaleidoscopic, fissiparous character was at once its strength and its weakness. Later, Britain was called a land fertile in tyrants or petty local rulers; it could be described with equal truth as a land fertile in petty local godlings. The reign of these godlings was not disturbed by romanization; but Roman rule by degrees created a consciousness of unity, the unity of a single peace and a single culture, which needed some kind of religious expression. That need Roman religion could not satisfy. It had long ceased to be taken seriously as a living faith by the Romans themselves; it lacked the confidence which it required if it was to impose itself on the minds of the British provincials. A universal civilization demanded, as its complement and completion, a universal religion. Without understanding this demand it is impossible to understand the success of Christianity.

How Christianity first came into Britain we do not know. It was not long before the Britons themselves asked the question and offered answers. A story grew up, based on a confusion between the name of Britain and that of Britium in Mesopotamia, that in the year 167 king Lucius sent to the pope for missionaries, and was baptized together with his people; later, it was said that the first seeds of the faith had been brought by St. Peter, or by an emissary of St. Paul, or by Joseph of Arimathea, planting the sacred thorn at Glastonbury; or that the father of Caratacus, Bran the Blessed, was the first to preach Christ among the Britons. Taken literally, these stories are pious inventions. But they were invented in order to explain a fact: the fact that Christianity did reach Britain at an early date and did make very considerable progress there. By the beginning of the third century Tertullian could claim that parts of Britain inaccessible to the Romans had been conquered by Christ, which seems to imply that the new religion had not only worked its way into the more romanized parts of the country, but had already spread beyond them into the highland zone. A little later, still in the first half of the century, references to British Christianity occur in Origen; vague and rhetorical, but enough to confirm us in thinking it a solid reality. It appears, then, that Christianity established itself in Britain at least as early as the second century, and that in the third it was gathering momentum. The terms in which it is mentioned make it clear that such leading men as Tertullian and Origen thought it a reproach to themselves and their church that the movement had not gone farther. When Origen says that of the Britons most have not yet heard the Gospel, he is not merely stating a fact, he is making a demand: he is seeing Christianity as something essentially expansive, dynamic, having just that confidence in itself and in its power to conquer the world which Roman religion lacked.

In the fourth century this movement emerges into daylight. The Diocletianic persecution in the early years of that century has given us the names of three martyrs: Alban of Verulam, Aaron[1]

---

[1] There is no need to be sceptical about his name; we have the actual stamp of a silversmith called Isaac, who worked in Britain later in the century.

and Julius of Caerleon. We know nothing in detail about them. The later story that Alban was a soldier belongs to a time when Britons vaguely imagined that all Romans in Britain had been soldiers; but the tradition that he was executed not in the town but on the neighbouring hill where now his abbey church stands is very likely true. In the same persecution it appears that many churches were destroyed. Gildas, who probably knew more of ecclesiastical history than of military and political, says that when it was over there was a great restoration of them and a building of many new ones.

By now Britain possessed a church sufficiently organized to have its voice in the general affairs of Christendom. The Council of Arles, in 314, was attended by three bishops representing British communities: Eborius, bishop of York; Restitutus, bishop of London, and Adelphius, 'bishop of the *civitas colonia Londinensium*', where an unhappy slip of the scribe's pen has cheated us of knowing in which of the *coloniae* the third bishopric was. A priest and a deacon went with them. The entry '*Eborius episcopus de civitate Eboracensi*' suggests that the scribe did not know the name of the bishop of York, and invented one out of his head; but that is no reason for doubting the existence either of the see or of the mission. The Council of Nicaea in 325 does not seem to have included British representatives; but its condemnation of Arianism was accepted, we are told, by all the British churches. In spite of the insinuations of Gildas to the contrary, it is evident that the Christian communities of Britain had a firm hold on the essentials of doctrine as laid down by Athanasius, and were well enough instructed to resist the plausible and attractive Arian attempt to convert Christianity into a superior kind of paganism.

It is not quite clear whether Britain sent representatives to the Council of Sardica, convened by Constantius II and Constans in 343; but in any case her churches accepted the decisions of that council, vindicating Athanasius once more. In 360 they sent three bishops to the Council of Ariminum; possibly more; all we know is that there were three who were too poor to travel at their own expense, like their brethren from Gaul, and therefore accepted Constantius's offer to have their expenses paid by the *fiscus*, rather than by raising a subscription among their congregations.

These facts show that, when the last persecution was over,

Christianity emerged in Britain as something widespread in all
parts, and in the more civilized regions organized in local communities of the approved type, each presided over by its bishop.
They show that British Christianity was a recognized part of the
general body of such communities, welcome at its councils, and
its opinion valued. They show, too, that it was poorer than
most of the provincial churches, which implies that as yet it had
few adherents among the great men who lived in the villas and
in whose hands the wealth of the country was now concentrated.
We may picture it as already deeply rooted in the populations
of the shrunken and impoverished towns, and making its way
by degrees among the peasantry. And (combining Tertullian's
much earlier statement with inferences from the history of much
later times) we may conjecture that it had already taken root
over much of the highland zone. Of one thing we may be certain: that the poorer classes among whom it was especially
acceptable included, especially outside the towns, considerable numbers whose degree of romanization was very small;
people whose names and speech and manners, in spite of
three centuries of Roman government, were still prevailingly
Celtic.

When the general character of this movement is realized, the
paucity of archaeological evidence for it is no longer surprising;
for archaeological evidence of all kinds is scanty in fourth-
century Britain, and always scantiest in the case of the poorer
and less romanized sections of the people. The tale of that
evidence is soon told. A little undated church at Silchester
testifies to a small community of Christians in that town at
some late period in its history. Three tombstones suggest by
the turn of their phrasing Christian ways of thought: all come
from the north, two of them from military sites, and they show
that Christian influences not only spread beyond the civilized
south and its towns, but even affected the army. In the south,
the sacred monogram for the name of Christ appears cut into
the floors of villas, or worked into their mosaics, at Chedworth
in Gloucestershire and near Frampton in Dorset, and scratched
on pewter dinner-services at Appleshaw near Andover in Hampshire and elsewhere. The same symbol is found, never very
commonly, on other movable objects. These things belong to
the fourth century, mostly to a late period in it. They show
that as time went on Christianity worked its way up the social

a

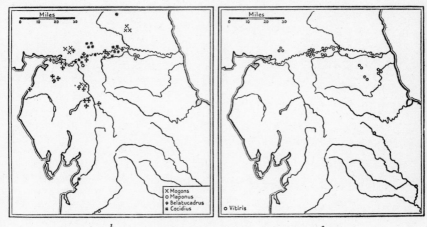

b   *c*

MAP IV. *a:* LOCAL CULTS OF CELTIC RELIGION
b AND *c:* DEDICATIONS TO CERTAIN CELTIC GODS OF THE
FRONTIER REGION

scale and, before the end of that century, had made considerable progress even in the wealthiest classes.

Even at the end of the century, however, we have no reason to think that Christianity was more than a minority religion. New pagan temples, that of Nodens among others, were still being built and maintained on a considerable scale. Perhaps during the reign of Julian a governor of Britannia Prima restored a pagan 'giant-column', the only one of which we know in Britain, at Cirencester.[1] It seems that paganism was meeting the challenge of Christianity by special efforts; we get the impression of a state of things in which the old faith and the new were competing freely for the mastery, each relying on its own intrinsic merits: the same state of things which we find elsewhere in the empire, in the biography of such men as St. Augustine. The outcome of this struggle, so far as we can now reconstruct it, will be discussed in a later chapter.

[1] Fragments of what may be the base of a second have lately been turned up at Chichester; *J.R.S.* xxvi (1936), pp. 263–4 and plate xxviii; *Antiqs. Journ.* (1935), pp. 461–4.

BOOK IV
THE END OF ROMAN BRITAIN

XVII
FROM SEVERUS TO HONORIUS

At the end of Book II the narrative of military and political affairs was carried down to the death of Severus. For the next half-century there is nothing of moment to record. Down to about 225 the finishing touches are being put to the frontier-works—a new drill-hall here, a battery for heavy catapults there; then inscriptions become rare, literary sources shrink in quality and quantity, and doings on the frontier fade from our view. We have, however, enough archaeological evidence to show that the Severan reorganization was a success. If there were frontier wars, they were easily settled, and have left no trace on our records. As late as the reign of Gordian III (238–44) we find large-scale reconstruction still going on in auxiliary forts; after that, inscriptions of the middle and late third century are practically confined to milestones recording the repair of roads, and showing that in this at least the work of the central government was energetically carried on, however emperors might rise and fall. Arguing from the efficiency of the road-surveyor's department, we may infer that the architects in charge of the frontier-works, though there was now nothing spectacular for them to do, were equally efficient.

When Postumus set up his independent Gallic empire in 258 there is nothing to show that Britain was in any way affected, whether for good or ill, by being governed from Gaul instead of from Rome. His successors, Victorinus and Tetricus, were accepted with equal indifference; and so, when Tetricus had submitted to Aurelian, was the restored connexion with the centre of the empire. And the subsequent adventure of Bonosus, who tried to set up a seat of empire at Cologne and revive the independence of the Celtic provinces, forms part of British history only to the extent that Bonosus was the son of a British schoolmaster; his mother was a Gaul and his home was in Spain. He was crushed by Probus, but the governor whom Probus sent to Britain revolted against him and was assassinated by his orders, after which he is said to have settled a number of Vandals and Burgundians in the island. The story is most intelligible if we suppose a considerable part of the British army to have been involved in the enterprise of Bonosus, so that Probus found it necessary to stamp out the embers of rebellion there and to reinforce the garrison with new troops.

The central government of the third century, increasingly embarrassed by military and economic problems, was not equal to the task of administering the whole empire; and even after the suppression of the Gallic empire the centrifugal tendency remained alive. It only needed an external shock to bring it into action. The disturbances on the continental frontier which had proved so formidable to Gaul and the Danubian provinces produced no immediate effect in Britain; she was in fact able to provide skilled labour, at the beginning of the fourth century, to repair their effects in Gaul; but about the beginning of Diocletian's reign the Channel seas began to be infested with Frankish and Saxon pirates, whose movements were a kind of secondary tremor due ultimately to the same shocks.

The Romans had maintained a fleet in the Channel, the *Classis Britannica*,[1] from the first century onwards. Its existence by that name is first attested by Tacitus in connexion with the rising of Civilis in A.D. 70; but it seems to have existed, with head-quarters at Boulogne, as early as the reign of Claudius. This was the fleet used by Agricola in his northern campaigns, and a detachment of its men, as we saw, was employed in the building of Hadrian's Wall. Tiles stamped with its mark show that it had a permanent station on the British side of the Channel at Dover, and another at Lympne. Some of the same tiles found their way into the fabric of a villa on the cliff-edge at Folkestone; but the conjecture that the villa was a residence for its commander is more attractive than convincing.[2]

In 285, the year after he became emperor, Diocletian appointed Maximian as junior colleague to himself with the title of Caesar. This use of the collegiate principle, the division of the supreme power among a board of co-regents, was Diocletian's method of solving the problem which had led to the splitting off of the Gallic empire. Maximian was sent to Gaul, where he had to deal with a revolt of Gallic peasants, a frontier

[1] Atkinson, 'Classis Britannica', in *Historical Essays in Honour of James Tait*, 1933.
[2] Winbolt, *Roman Folkestone*, 1925.

war on the Rhine, and piracy in the Channel. For the last purpose he strengthened the *Classis Britannica*, and put in command of it a native of the Low Countries, a Menapian called M. Aurelius Mausaeus Carausius, whose massive head, short, straight nose, bearded jowl, and bull neck expressed a resolute and unscrupulous character. His command did not include the province of Britain, or rather of either British province, for the Severan division was still in force; it was a purely naval appointment. Carausius was at once successful. He caught pirate ships by scores and seized great quantities of plunder from them; but instead of restoring it to its rightful owners or sending it to the imperial treasury he kept almost the whole for himself. Maximian, believing that he was using his position to allow the pirates a free hand at first and then descend upon them when laden with spoil, thus indirectly enriching himself at the expense of the provincials, ordered his arrest and execution.

Carausius once more acted promptly. He crossed over to Britain and declared himself emperor. He won the legions to his cause, defeated some auxiliary regiments that resisted him, and strengthened his position by pressing Gallic merchants into his ranks, raising mercenaries from among the tribes he had been fighting, and enlarging his fleet. Thus, either in 286 or 287— the year is not certain—Britain set herself up as an independent empire, on the model of Postumus's Gaul.

As soon as Maximian had his hands free, and could build himself ships, he attacked the usurper. But his fleet, after being severely handled by bad weather, was defeated; and the two Augusti (Maximian had been raised to that rank in 286) decided to acknowledge Carausius as one of themselves. They conferred on him the title of Augustus, confirmed him in his possession of Britain, and added to his command the south shore of the Channel, apparently as far inland as Rouen, where he seems to have set up one of his mints. On their side, the arrangement was accepted without enthusiasm; they never recorded it on their coins, and they meant it to stand only until such time as they could conveniently revoke it. But for Carausius it was all-important: it meant that he could now appear, at any rate in the eyes of his own subjects, as an emperor *de jure* instead of a usurper. His government was good: we know of it only from the statements of his enemies' flatterers, and they find nothing to dispraise. He certainly defended Britain against her new enemies with vigour and success; and it has even been thought, not without support from archaeological evidence, that he may have built the Saxon Shore forts of which something must be said later. On the whole, however, that is improbable.

In 293 Diocletian's mask of friendship was thrown off. Two new Caesars were appointed; one of them, Constantius Chlorus, was placed in command of transalpine Gaul, and at once began to encroach on the realm of Carausius. He captured Boulogne after a long siege, and thus deprived Carausius of his continental possessions. Soon afterwards Carausius was murdered by Allectus, his own financial minister, who took his master's life in order to escape punishment for his own misdeeds, and succeeded to his power. But his reign was short. In 296 Constantius had a fleet ready. He sailed in two divisions, from Havre and Boulogne. The weather was bad, and in mid-channel a fog came on. But it served his purpose, and allowed his prefect Asclepiodotus to slip unobserved past Allectus's fleet, waiting for him off the Isle of Wight, and enter the Solent. On landing, Constantius burnt his ships, a sign of the grim struggle which he believed to await him, and marched towards London.

Allectus had made his own preparations. It is evident that he had stripped the whole country of troops. For the first time since Clodius Albinus crossed to Gaul, the frontier was left undefended. The northern tribes took their opportunity; they broke in, and along the Wall we can trace the destruction they left behind them. But all was in vain. His motley barbarian army was routed; the rout became a massacre; Allectus, fleeing, fell into the hands of Constantius's men and almost had his wish, that in death he should be unrecognized.

Carausius may have been honoured in Britain; none regretted Allectus. It may have expressed the general feeling when a medal was struck showing Constantius arriving at the gates of London greeted by a kneeling figure and surrounded by the legend *Redditor Lucis Aeternae*. He had restored to Britain the light of Roman civilization.

It was no empty boast. There was much to do, and Constantius set himself to do it. All along the Wall defences lay in ruins, partly through neglect, partly through barbarian havoc. Everywhere, like Severus before him, Constantius rebuilt them, and put the frontier in order once more. Farther south he rebuilt the fortress of York; the multangular tower that

still stands there is his work. In the heart of the civilized province he restored the walls and public buildings of Verulam,
and doubtless other towns too; it may have been he that added
the bastions to London Wall.

Most important of all, he dealt drastically with the menace
of Frankish and Saxon piracy. Along the Saxon Shore, as it
came to be called, the south-eastern coast from the Wash to the
Isle of Wight, inlets and harbours are guarded by massive forts
of the late Roman period. In lonely places their walls stand
to-day between twenty and thirty feet high, thicker and higher
than the fort-walls of the early empire, and guarded by bastions
in whose tops can still be seen the sockets for heavy artillery.
Excavation has dated them to the late third century, and there
can be little doubt that so sweeping a scheme of fortification
was the work of a master builder such as we now know Constantius to have been, acting in co-operation with the new re-
organizer of the Roman world.[1]

On the west coast also defences had to be provided. By the
middle of the third century Ireland was becoming restless. The
movement which was to produce settlements along the Welsh
coast, and later, in Argyll, was to set on foot the process by
which the names of Caledonia and Pictland were succeeded by
that of Scotland, had already begun. It was hope, not fear, said
Tacitus, that moved Agricola to fortify the coast facing Ireland;
in his day the initiative still lay with Rome. It was fear, not
hope, that induced Constantius (for the work is almost certainly
his) to abandon the legionary fortress at Caerleon-on-Usk and
create a new one, in the Diocletianic style of military architecture and resembling the forts of the Saxon Shore, at Cardiff.
Segontium, the fort on the hill above Carnarvon, was abandoned at the same time, and a new one built on the same principle down by the river; and a new fort, small in size, but in
design (as the visitor can still see for himself) like others of
the period, was constructed to command the harbour at Holyhead.[2]

These new coastal fortifications have, almost without exception, one tactical feature in common. They lie close to the shore,
not on headlands or points of vantage, but on harbours. They

[1] Society of Antiquaries, *Reports on Excavations at Richborough.*
[2] Wheeler, 'The Roman Amphitheatre at Caerleon', *Archaeologia*, lxxviii. 154;
'Segontium and the Roman Occupation of Wales', *Y Cymmrodor*, xxxiii. 70, 95.

have evidently been designed to work in the closest co-operation with naval units. Each was a fortified base for a squadron engaged in patrolling the coast. A description of the new coastal patrols has perhaps been preserved by a fourth-century military writer, who tells us that in Britain (that is, in the Roman fleet there) the warships had attached to them a special kind of light craft with twenty rowers a side, used for scouting and called in navy slang 'Picts', because they were camouflaged by being painted sea-green, hulls and sails and men's clothes and faces and all, to make them invisible.[1] The *Classis Britannica* must have been reorganized into a dozen or more of these patrols, each stationed at a naval base which was no mere port and dockyard but a strongly fortified point with a military garrison. The significance of this double system can only be guessed at. Either it implied that raiding bands, whether of Franks and Saxons or of Scots, might be expected to land in strength and destroy the naval bases while the patrols were away at sea; or it was designed to protect these bases against the brigandage of revolted peasants, like those which had already begun to give so much trouble in Gaul. Between these alternatives the evidence does not permit us to choose.

The work of Constantius involved some redistribution of military units. How this was carried out in detail we cannot say; for inscriptions are by now almost entirely lacking, and it is not clear how far the dispositions given in the much later *Notitia Dignitatum* apply to this period. If we are justified in supposing that the garrisons of the Saxon Shore as there described still preserve the arrangements made by Constantius, the inference will be that he moved the Second legion from Caerleon to Richborough and garrisoned the other forts with units of which most were probably new creations; only one of them was derived from the early imperial army of Britain.

Reorganization of a far more sweeping kind, involving the entire political and military system of the empire, had already been set on foot by Diocletian and was to be carried farther by Constantine; and of this, since Britain was now drawn into it, some account must be given.[2] The new system, inaugurated in

---

[1] Vegetius, *De Re Militari*, iv. 37.
[2] What follows is only a crude outline of a complicated subject. For details, cf. E. Stein, *Geschichte des spätrömischen Reiches*, vol. i (1928); more briefly, H. M. D. Parker, *History of the Roman World* (1935).

293, involved three main features: a reform of civil administration, a reform of the army, and a reform of the imperial power; the whole being designed with the utmost care so as to create a strongly centralized despotism. Instead of one emperor there were now to be four: two senior, Augusti, and two junior, Caesars. Each Augustus was to retire from office twenty years after his original appointment as Caesar, and to be succeeded by his junior, who would then appoint a Caesar of his own. The empire was divided into four parts, each member of the tetrarchy being responsible for one; but an Augustus might on occasion enter the territory assigned to either of the Caesars.

This fourfold division of the supreme executive power broke down before many years were over; but in the meantime it had done good work. The two new Caesars, Constantius, who was placed in command of the north-west, and Galerius, who ruled the Balkan provinces, were able soldiers, and Constantius was evidently, as we can judge from his work in Britain, a statesman as well. The steadily increasing prosperity of the British country-side in the early fourth century must be put down, in part at least, to his credit.

The principle governing the new civil and military system was that these two sides of imperial administration should be completely separated. For purposes of civil government the empire was divided into twelve new units called dioceses; of these Britain formed one, and was governed by an official called *vicarius*. The *vicarius* was, however, not directly responsible to the emperor; he was subordinate to the praetorian prefect of Gaul, who was in effect the viceroy of the north-western emperor, resided at Trier, and governed what had once been the Gallic empire—the whole of transalpine Gaul, Britain, and Spain. But the hierarchical principle went a step farther. Within the diocese were a number of provinces. These were now quite small units. In Britain there were four: Britannia Prima, Britannia Secunda, and two called after the two Caesars,[1] Maxima Caesariensis after Galerius Maximianus, and Flavia Caesariensis after Flavius Constantius. Maxima Caesariensis was governed by a man of consular rank; the others by *praesides*.

The military service, though now entirely detached from the

---

[1] Bury's suggestion that they were called after a town in Britain called Caesarea, which he conjectured to be Verulam, is unconvincing ('A lost Caesarea', in *Cambridge Hist. Journ.* i, 1923).

governors of provinces and the *vicarius*, was at first, until Constantine abolished this arrangement, under the control of the praetorian prefect. The reforms now put into operation, at first by Diocletian and later developed by Constantine, were designed to serve various purposes: to create large, mobile field-armies in addition to the garrisons of the frontiers; to increase the total strength of cavalry; and to increase the efficiency of the higher command by recruiting it from professional soldiers. The garrison-army, instead of being liable for general service in the field, became a purely local militia, the so-called *limitanei*, operating for defensive purposes within the limits of its own province. The field-army, commanded (under the supreme control of the emperors) by officers called *magistri*, consisted of two classes of troops, *palatini* and *comitatenses*, in each of which there were both cavalry, now become the senior arm, and infantry.

How these reforms affected Britain in detail is far from clear. We do not even know in what parts of the country the four new provinces lay. The 'giant-column' at Cirencester, already referred to, suggests that this town fell in Britannia Prima, and may even have been its capital; in which case Prima must have included the whole south-west of England. York must have been another provincial capital, and the head-quarters of the *vicarius* were doubtless at London. As for the military organization, the *Notitia* enumerates three commands: the *Dux Britanniarum*, with head-quarters at York, in charge of the frontier district; the *Comes Litoris Saxonici*, in command of the coastal forts from the Wash to the Solent; and the *Comes Britanniarum*, in charge of a field-army. The duke of Britain and the count of the Saxon Shore may possibly have been created by Constantius or his son Constantine the Great. But the count of Britain does not seem to have existed so early. Even as late as 368 there seems to have been no such officer, and the units placed by the *Notitia* under his command include some at least that were not raised until the fifth century.[1]

There is no need here to repeat the story of how Diocletian's tetrarchy collapsed, leaving Constantine master of the world.

---

[1] Bury ('The *Notitia Dignitatum*', *J.R.S.* x (1920), a paper of fundamental importance for understanding of the *Notitia*) has pointed out that the counts of Italy, Strasburg, and Britain represent 'a new class of *comites*', commanding not groups of *limitanei* but local mobile forces, and argues that this class was not introduced until the early fifth century. See below, p. 297 *seqq.*

He was the natural son of Constantius by Helena, no British
princess as later legend would have it, but a woman of humble
birth. He was a little over thirty when his father died while they
were both in Britain. Constantius had, it seems, repeated in
certain ways the story of Severus. Like him, he first rebuilt the
fortifications of the frontier and then undertook a punitive war
against the tribes to the north of it; for we know that in 306,
after the restoration of the Wall, he revisited Britain to fight the
Picts, and we are expressly told that this campaign was not
undertaken with any view to the annexation of territory, and
the writer implies that it was not a defensive war waged for the
purpose of driving out invaders.[1] After a brilliant victory, in
which his son took part, he died at York, and Constantine assumed the title of Caesar. This was a claim for which he would
have to fight; but his own affairs did not distract his mind from
those of Britain. We have no less than five milestones, coming
from all parts of the country, dated to the seven short months
of his Caesarship, which proved that his first act must have
been to embark on a sweeping scheme of repairs to all the main
roads.

Constans, who succeeded Constantine on his death in 337,
had some trouble with Picts and Scots, who now begin to appear
as partners in the work of raiding British territory. The Scots,
as we already know, were the inhabitants of Ireland; the name
Pict begins to be used about the end of the third century as a
new collective name for those of central and northern Scotland.
It seems to be simply the Latin equivalent or translation of the
Celtic name Priteni, which means 'painted' or 'tattooed'. That
old custom, like the custom of using chariots in warfare,
lingered on outside the Roman province. Later, the name of
Picts was adopted by the Caledonians themselves, and became
their national name. In the winter of 342–3 some emergency
arose which induced Constans to visit Britain in person, and
make a treaty with the barbarians, giving them concessions in
return for their promise to keep quiet. To judge by the ordinary
procedure of the later empire, we must infer that Constans
allowed certain colonies of Picts and Scots to settle within his
territory. One such colony seems to have been established in
the late third century, in which case we may suppose that the
new treaty gave it formal recognition; viz. that of the Deisi, a

---

[1] *Anonymus Valesii*; Eumenius, *Paneg. Constantino Aug.*, 7.

tribe from County Meath, who are found in the fifth century occupying the Gower peninsula and adjacent parts of South Wales; one may think, too, of those Irish settlers who, if the *Historia Brittonum* tells truth, were expelled from North Wales by Cunedda at the beginning of the same century. What seems to have happened in the reign of Constans, then, was not a frontal attack on the Wall, where archaeology gives us no evidence of any disaster, but a movement of mixed immigrants by sea into the western coastlands, where Roman patrols and garrisons were thinnest. The policy of Constans was to give these settlers the position of *foederati* and hope that they would accept that position loyally; the Roman garrisons of Wales were quite inadequate to keep them in order if they should be inclined to give trouble.

In 350 Constans was murdered, and the *comes* Magnus Magnentius, a Gaul from Amiens, placed on the throne. He was gladly welcomed not only in Gaul but in Britain, Spain, and Italy; for Constans had made himself unpopular everywhere. Three years later Constantius II overthrew the usurper and proceeded to destroy those who had followed him. Among these was Martinus, *vicarius* of Britain, a man universally beloved and devoted to the interests of his people. The emperor sent one of his civil servants, Paulus by name, to arrest the partisans of Magnentius. He acted in so arbitrary and oppressive a manner that Martinus, driven beyond endurance, attacked him sword in hand, and failing to kill him turned the sword upon himself. The death of so good a public servant, and the savage vengeance which Paulus wreaked upon his victims, was described as an eternal stain upon the rule of Constantius.

Soon afterwards Constantius appointed as Caesar for the Gallic provinces his cousin Julian, a young man of brilliant promise and high character. Julian never visited Britain; but we have already had occasion to consider the significance of his shipment of British corn to the Rhine in 359, and early in 360, on hearing at Paris that the Picts and Scots had broken their treaty with Constans and were ravaging the frontier districts, he sent his *magister militum* Lupicinus to Britain with a field-army to drive them out. The occasion is memorable as the first on which a genuine invasion of barbarians, on a scale so large as to require the services of a mobile force to check it, is recorded. In other frontier provinces it had often happened before; in Britain never; and this immunity must have contributed much to the peace and prosperity which down to at least the middle of the fourth century reigned everywhere in the British country-side.

Lupicinus does not seem to have been particularly successful. He is described as an able soldier, but conceited, pompous, greedy, and cruel. His stay in Britain was cut short by the troubles arising out of Julian's elevation to the rank of Augustus, and four years later we are told that Picts, Scots, Saxons, and Attacotti[1] were plundering Britain without pause. Julian had fallen in the east in 363; in 368 Valentinian I, while fighting invaders in north-eastern Gaul, heard that these raids had brought matters to a desperate crisis. A concerted plan had been formed by the Picts, Scots, and Attacotti with the Saxons and Franks: one host was to invade Britain, the other simultaneously to overrun the northern coast of Gaul. Britain was attacked on three sides at once. The Picts assailed Hadrian's Wall, helped by the treachery of its garrison, the so-called Arcani. The Scots, already established in force on the west coast, swept over the fertile lowlands from that side; the Franks and Saxons landed in force on the south-east. The disaster to the Roman arms was complete. Nectaridus, count of the Saxon Shore, and Fullofaudes, duke of Britain, both fell in the general rout of their troops.

Valentinian was too much perturbed to act with decision; but after various false starts he sent Count Theodosius, a distinguished soldier, across the Channel with a large force. Theodosius, landing at Richborough, found the country swarming with barbarian bands, laden with captives and booty, and London in a state of siege. His first step was to throw himself into the capital, reorganize the government, and begin collecting the information without which it would be rash to engage so vast an enemy. In the following spring he set to work to clear the country of invaders. This task was barely finished when he found himself confronted with a new danger. A certain Valentinus, a Pannonian by birth, who had been living in Britain, was tampering with the troops and plotting a rebellion. He was unmasked and executed; but Theodosius realized how deep was the demoralization on which he had been reckoning, and forebore to probe farther into the conspiracy.

This incident, together with the treachery of the Arcani, suggests that the *limitanei* of Britain were at this time hardly to be

---

[1] This seems to be a collective name for certain groups of Irish, with a social rather than ethnic meaning.

trusted as watch-dogs of a peaceful and wealthy diocese. All but barbarians themselves, and a peasant militia rather than a well-disciplined army, it is hard to resist the impression that their sympathies were more on the side of the barbarian without and the peasant within, the potential invader and the potential rebel, than the rich landowner whose property they were ordered to protect. If the garrison of the frontier had not only betrayed it to the Picts, as we are expressly told they did, but had made common cause with them to the extent of joining them in their plundering expeditions to the south, it is easy to see both why Valentinus found it so easy to enlist them on his side, and why Theodosius was obliged to disband the Arcani. The phrase 'barbarian conspiracy', applied by Ammianus to the whole invasion, assumes a new and sinister meaning.

Theodosius restored the Wall and reconstructed its shattered buildings; we can still recognize the handiwork of his masons. He did not, however, rebuild the milecastles and turrets; those were henceforth left unoccupied; it has been suggested that the Arcani whom he abolished were the patrolling garrison of the Wall, who used these buildings as their quarters.[1] And, like Severus and Constantius before him, he launched a fierce counter-attack at the invaders, pursuing them to their homes by land and sea and ravaging their countries.

Archaeology permits us to add a further fact about the reorganization of Theodosius. Along the Yorkshire coast, from Huntcliff near Saltburn to Filey, there are stone signal-towers, surrounded by curtain-walls whose corner bastions could have mounted a small catapult, crowning the headlands and commanding the sea. Excavation has proved that they were occupied about the years 370–95, which implies that they were part of a coastguard system inaugurated by Theodosius in order to prolong the defensive works of the Saxon Shore and thus give protection to the north-east coast against raiders who had now become venturesome enough to sail direct across the North Sea for a landfall at Flamborough Head and the cliffs of Cleveland. They worked, we may imagine, in connexion with a fleet based on the Humber, and could send signals either to it or to the duke of Britain's head-quarters at York.

One other detail is recorded. We are told that when, after suppressing Valentinus, he resumed the course of his labours,

[1] Birley in *Arch. Aeliana*, ser. 4, ix (1932), p. 213.

rebuilding towns, forts, and frontier-works, 'he so completely restored to its former state the province which he had ceded to the
enemy's rule that on his restoration it had a regular governor
and the emperor, as if to celebrate a triumph, ordered it to be
henceforth called Valentia'.[1] And in confirmation of this we
find in the *Notitia Dignitatum* the number of British provinces
increased to five, Valentia having, like Maxima Caesariensis, a
governor of consular rank.

Where was Valentia? Charles Bertram of Copenhagen, who
has deservedly been called the cleverest and most successful literary impostor of modern times, placed it, in his bogus account of
Britain by 'Richard of Cirencester', in the region between the
two Walls;[2] and so hard is it to disentangle Bertram's inventions
from the body of credible knowledge that while this chapter was
being written a new book reached the writer's hands in which
a very distinguished scholar describes Galloway as situated in
the Roman province of Valentia. But this identification was
wrong. It is quite certain that for Theodosius the frontier of the
empire lay where it had lain for nearly two centuries before him,
on Hadrian's Wall. What Ammianus tells us makes it clear that
Valentia was a region which at first he had meant to leave in
the enemy's hands (it therefore cannot have been the district
immediately south of the Wall), but recovered from them when,
in the course of organizing his reconquests, he found himself
more successful than he had expected. There is only one part of
Britain which will fit these requirements. Valentia must have consisted in great part at least of those Welsh districts which for some
time past had been in the hands of Scotic settlers.[3] These were
deprived of the status of *foederati*, incorporated in a new province, and governed directly by a Roman consular. Significantly,
the old fort at Carnarvon seems now to have been rebuilt.

Another new name now appears in Britain. Perhaps to celebrate this same victory, the name of London was changed to
Augusta. The new name was used officially by the moneyers of
Magnus Maximus and the imperial clerks who compiled the
Notitia; but it never displaced the old in the daily life of the
citizens, and the Saxon settlers never heard the ancient capital
mentioned by any other name but that of Londinium.

---

[1] Ammianus Marcellinus, xxviii. 3.
[2] The suggestion was first made by Camden; but Bertram gave it seeming
authority.   [3] This was first pointed out to me by Mr. C. E. Stevens.

The only other incident of British history belonging to the reign of Valentinian I is the settlement of a tribe of Alamanni from the neighbourhood of Mainz, with their king Fraomar, they to become a regiment of *limitanei*, he to command them with the rank of tribune. They have left no trace in the British sections of the *Notitia*, and we cannot tell where they were settled; but it was probably where frontier troops were most needed, on or near the Wall.

Valentinian was succeeded as emperor of the west by his son Gratian. Before the young emperor had been on the throne three years, his eastern colleague Valens perished at the hands of the Goths in one of the greatest disasters of Roman history, the battle of Adrianople. Gratian, realizing the need of seeking out the best military talent in such an emergency, called to his court the younger Theodosius, son of the saviour of Britain. His father had been treacherously murdered by Valens, and the son, now 33 years old, had since then been living quietly on his Spanish estate. He was given the rank of *magister equitum*, and began the career which in a few months brought him to the position of Augustus, as emperor of the east.

Theodosius had served under his father in the British war; with him had served another Spaniard, Magnus Maximus, who stayed in Britain and rose there to high command. He had a successful career, and had victories to his credit (the Picts and Scots, in spite of their defeat in 369, were still giving trouble), when in 383 he decided to claim the throne of the western empire. Gratian's position was weak; he had lost the confidence of the army, and Maximus shared the general feeling against him. Our authorities differ as to whether or not he was moved by jealousy of his old comrade's rapid promotion, but they agree as to his ability and courage. He denuded Britain of its best troops and crossed the Channel. Near Paris he encountered Gratian's army, which deserted to him. Gratian fled and was murdered at Lyons by one of his own men, and Maximus became master of Gaul and Spain, the old union of the north-western provinces. But he was unable to protect them. The defence of the Rhine frontier kept him busy, and Hadrian's Wall was once more swamped, in its under-garrisoned condition, by the northern barbarians.

This was the end of the Wall. It has long been known that the coins found on it go down to the reign of Gratian and there stop. That by itself does not prove that its history ends with Gratian. But of late, since the events leading to the Roman evacuation of Britain have become a matter of controversial interest, excavators working there year by year have paid special attention to the last phase of its history, and conditions have entirely changed since, in 1915, Haverfield declared it an open question whether the Wall might not have been held after 395. We are now familiar with the actual work of the Theodosian restoration; we know that the occupation which followed it was a short one; and we know that after the disaster which closed that occupation there was no rebuilding.[1]

Even after the fall of Maximus in 388 the central government was not at once in a position to re-establish its hold on Britain. It was not until 395 that Theodosius, leaving his eleven-year-old son Honorius to occupy the throne of the west, left also his general Stilicho as regent. By 399, and again in 400, we find the court poet Claudian triumphantly celebrating the liberation of Britain from Saxon, Pictish, and Scotic invaders. In 399 he writes that the sea is peaceful now the Saxon is conquered, and Britain secure since the Pict is broken; in 400, celebrating the first consulship of Stilicho, he makes Britain express her gratitude for the fact that she no longer fears either Pict or Scot, and no longer from all along her coast sees the Saxon bearing down with every shift of the wind. Between 395 and 399, that is to say, Stilicho had taken measures for the defence of Britain.

It would be pleasant if we could identify one part of Stilicho's work with the erection of the Yorkshire coastal signal-towers to which reference has already been made. Unfortunately the evidence from their excavations makes this impossible. It shows, rather, that they were occupied until about 395, having evidently been left in working order by Maximus, and were then destroyed by enemy action. We must look for traces of Stilicho elsewhere.

Archaeologically, if we except the very probable case of the

---

[1] As a sample of the type of evidence, cf. Richmond in *Cumb. & West. Trans.* xxx (1930), p. 171: 'not very long after 375 the enemy looted and burnt an unevacuated barrack, still in working order. There is no evidence for later occupation' (Birdoswald). If certain late traditions current in Wales are at all to be trusted (his court at Carlisle; his horsemen on the Wall; his shadowy connexion with the office of *Dux Britanniarum*; cf. Rhys, *Celtic Britain* (1884), p. 119), Cunedda and his tribesmen were employed as frontiersmen on the Wall between its evacuation by the regular *limitanei* and his transference to North Wales by Stilicho, for which see p. 289.

tiles stamped with the name of Honorius from the Saxon Shore
fort at Pevensey, they have not been found. But they seem to
exist in the pages of the *Notitia*. This contains a survey of the
forces under the command of the duke of Britain, divided into
two parts. First comes a list of fourteen units stationed, so far
as we can identify their stations, in Yorkshire, county Durham,
and Westmorland. Then comes a second list, headed *item per
lineam valli*, and enumerating the forts of Hadrian's Wall with
some others. Now the *Notitia* as we have it was, so Bury has
proved, a working copy for office use which was compiled in or
about the year 428. The presence in it of the section on
Hadrian's Wall, which had been finally abandoned for forty-five
years at that date, shows that we cannot trust it to contain no
anachronisms; but if we recognize the *per lineam valli* section as
an anachronism, and cut it out of the text, we are left with a dis-
position of troops which is quite intelligible on the assumption
that the Wall and the Cumberland coastlands were irrecoverable,
and that the purpose of the supreme command was to protect the
vale of York, the only part of the north where Roman civilization had ever taken root. If this was the plan executed by
Stilicho, together with a restoration of the Saxon Shore, the
words of Claudian become intelligible, and as accurate as a
court poet's words need be.

It remains to ask whether Stilicho's reorganization involved
any special measures against the Scots. We are told by the
author of the *Historia Brittonum* that one Cunedag or Cunedda,
at a date very soon before the end of the fourth century, came
from Manau Guotodin with his eight sons to Guenedota or
Gwynedd, which is north-western Wales and Anglesey, expelled
the Scots from that region, and founded a local dynasty. Manau
Guotodin was identified by Rhys with the country of the
Otadini; and even if this is wrong Cunedda seems to have lived
in the north before going to Wales. The spontaneous migration of a tribe from that district across Brigantia to Wales, while
Britain was under Roman government, is improbable in the
extreme; but the transplantation of a tribe from one frontier
district to another is a commonplace of late Roman history. The
story of Cunedda must indicate that, just before the close of the
century, the Roman government applied this well-worn device
to the Scotic problem: enlisting a tribe from the north and
planting it with the status of *foederati* in the west, there to act

as a local militia under its own king, and replace the unruly Irish, who had hitherto been allowed to possess the land. If the date given is correct, and it is at least circumstantial—146 years before the reign of Mailcun—the transplantation of Cunedda was part of Stilicho's work.

XVIII

THE END OF ROMAN RULE

IF Britain was as grateful for the Stilichonian reorganization as Claudian would have us believe, her gratitude did not last long. Rome herself was in danger, and in 401 or 402 Stilicho found it necessary to withdraw troops for his own Gothic war. Claudian, who is once more our authority, describes these troops as 'the legion that protects the remotest Britons, curbs the fierce Scot, and scans the forms tattooed upon the bloodless skin of the dying Pict'. It would be rash to insist on the words of such a description. They need not even refer to a legion; the term may be used by poetic licence for troops in general; and the reference to Picts and Scots is conventional padding, offering no clue to identification of the legion, if legion it was. Claudian, in fact, tells us nothing except that the garrison of British *limitanei* was sensibly weakened, and we can add nothing to what he tells us.

When Alaric was defeated at Verona in 403 it is unlikely that the British troops were sent back. The danger was checked, but not ended; and in 405 the fresh invasion of Radagaisus had to be met. In the autumn of 406 the army of Britain, in despair at the peril in which it found itself, set up a usurper named Marcus, in the hope of providing more efficiently for the defence of the country. Marcus was very soon murdered, and was followed by another usurper called Gratian, who only survived his elevation by four months. The army, however, was determined to have an emperor of its own, and its third choice fell on a certain Constantine. He began his career by sending to Honorius and explaining that he had acted under compulsion; Honorius replied by acknowledging him, and Constantine crossed over to Gaul. He made what arrangements he could for the defence of Britain in his absence, but in effect his action must have further weakened the already inadequate garrison there, while he devoted his attention to securing the Rhine frontier and consolidating his own position by adding Spain to his realm.

The Britons had less reason than ever to be satisfied. The emperor whom they had created was neglecting their interests and leaving them to shift for themselves; accordingly they revolted against him, expelled his governors, and sent protestations of loyalty to Honorius while arming themselves for their own defence. But in 410 Honorius was in no position to do anything for them. The attempts of Constantine to protect the eastern frontier of Gaul had broken down; Alaric was marching on Rome; Stilicho, the main defence of the western empire, had lost both his place and his life; and all the emperor could do was to reply instructing the British *civitates* to arrange for their own safety as best they could.

Up to this point the story is clear. It leaves us with a well-defined situation in Britain. There were still troops in the island, left behind by Constantine; but now that his representatives had been expelled there was nobody to command them and nobody to carry on the work of civil administration in the diocese. The Britons, who had no intention of parting company with the empire, had asked Honorius to make good these defects; unable to do so through force of circumstances, he instructed the tribal authorities to carry on with both sides, civil and military, of the work of government, until such time as he could send them nominees of his own; and his instructions were obeyed.

Beyond this point all certainties vanish. Until lately it was believed that Honorius was never able to do what he could not do in 410, and that in this year Britain ceased to be a part of the Roman empire. Within the last few years this view has been challenged; indeed, it has been confidently denied; and it has been held for an established fact that, shortly afterwards, the broken connexion was made good in its entirety, and remained good for another generation. It is therefore necessary to consider what reasons there are for holding one view rather than the other, or whether the truth may not be found somewhere between them.[1]

It need hardly be said (the existence of the controversy is enough to show it) that ancient writers have nothing decisive to say, one way or the other. We have accounts of Constantine's usurpation from Olympiodorus, Zosimus, Sozomen, and Orosius. Zosimus tells us how the Britons set up a government of their own and how Honorius confirmed it; but none of these writers either says or definitely implies that direct government from Rome was or was not renewed at a later date. Attempts have been made to extract something definite out of casual references in other writers. One chronicler writes that in the

---

[1] The reader who wishes to go into the documents and literature for the discussion which follows will find references in the Bibliography.

reign of Honorius 'Britain was for ever lost to the Roman name'. This seems conclusive for the traditional view; but a partisan of the other view points out that the writer in question is inaccurate in his facts and prone to exaggeration, and counters with a quotation from Prosper Tiro showing that in 422-32 Britain could still be called a 'Roman island', in contradistinction to a 'barbarian island' like Ireland. It is hardly worth while to retort that no one doubts the continued Romanity, in some sense, of Britain at that time; the only question is whether it implied the regular reception of administrative officers from Rome.

Nor can any argument be safely drawn from this very lack of conclusive statements. The condition of historical literature in the fifth century is not such as to justify the assumption that, had Britain been recovered as an integral part of the empire, we should have heard of it. None the less, that silence imposes the onus of proof on those who maintain that an event took place of which contemporary writers and subsequent historians give not so much as a hint.

From continental writers we turn to British. Gildas, who lived in the sixth century in Britain, Ireland, and Brittany, is not an historian but the writer of a tract for the times. In the course of it, however, he makes historical statements which bear on our problem.[1] The Britons, he tells us, rebelled against Rome and sent the tyrant Maximus to Gaul; whereupon the country was set upon and ravaged by the Picts and Scots. The Britons dispatched envoys to Rome bearing letters of submission and begging for help; and the Romans sent a legion which cleared the country of invaders and returned, instructing the Britons to build a wall in order to keep them out for the future; which they did, but not being shown how to do it they built it of turf, and so it was useless. The legion went home in triumph, and the barbarians broke in again. Again a petition for aid was sent to Rome; again it was granted; and this time the victorious army itself built a stone wall from sea to sea. But even this failed to keep the barbarians out; and a third time the Britons sent their appeal, to 'Agitius in his third consulship', but this time it was rejected, and the Britons had to fend for themselves.

In literary form, this story is a 'triad' in the traditional Welsh style: it might be called the 'Three Groans of Britain', but that the triad has been expanded into a homily. In matter, it

---

[1] *De Excidio et Conquestu Britanniae*, chapters 13-20.

obviously mixes fact and fiction. Gildas knows a good deal about Maximus, who became an important figure in Welsh folk-lore; but the 'first vengeance' looks very much like a reminiscence of the campaign of Theodosius (the fortifying of the frontier and the triumphant return are both conspicuous features of that campaign as narrated by Ammianus) complicated by an attempt on the part of a Briton to explain the existence of the Antonine Wall, in complete ignorance of its true history; but if that is so Gildas has inverted the order of Theodosius and Maximus. The second devastation and second vengeance, unlike the first, are described with no historical detail whatever; their only point is that they lead up to the construction of a stone wall; and they might very well be nothing but a myth invented to explain the Wall of Hadrian. The third petition evidently contains a reference to the third consulship of Aetius in 446; here, therefore, we are back in the region of history, and we can use the authority of Gildas, for what it is worth, to assert that a fruitless appeal was made at that time.

Any attempt to base a theory of Roman reoccupation upon the story of Gildas must fail. Apart from the suspiciously poetic form of the narrative, his ignorance even of early fifth-century history is shown by two crucial facts: first, that from the days of Maximus onwards he believed that there was no Roman government in Britain; secondly, that after Maximus he knows of no other British usurpers. With his passion for symmetry and rhetorical effect he could never have refrained from mentioning Constantine, had he heard of him. It is therefore going beyond the limits of reasonable interpretation to say that Gildas in describing the first vengeance is giving an account of Stilicho's reorganization, and, in describing the second, an account of one which followed the rescript of Honorius in 410. All his narrative proves is that he knew a good deal about 'Maxen Wledig', something about Theodosius, and something of great interest, not elsewhere preserved, about Aetius; not that he knew anything of events between 388 and 446.

We turn to archaeology. Inscriptions are lacking. We have only one which falls anywhere near this time. It is a rudely cut slab from one of the Yorkshire signal-stations, recording its erection by a certain Justinian. If this was the Justinian or Justin who served, as we are told, under Constantine III, and if the claim of erection really means re-erection, the slab is evidence for a restoration of these signal-stations at that usurper's command; but those which have been dug show no signs of rebuilding, and it is possible that the reference is to some other Justinian, a generation earlier, in charge of the original work.

Pottery and architectural remains tell us nothing; Britain has yielded no parallels to the fifth-century sites that have been explored on the German frontier.

There remain coins. Nothing could be more striking than the contrast between the abundance of fourth-century coins found in Britain, and minted down to the year 395, and the extreme rarity of any belonging to a later date. Except for a very few of Constantine III, the fifth-century coins that are known from British sites are no more than might have found their way into a land outside the borders of the empire. This might seem decisive against any reoccupation; but the case is not so clear as that. In 395 the western mints almost ceased to issue copper, and coin of every kind became much rarer, except so far as old issues were still used, with a sprinkling of gold and silver which were more carefully handled and rarely lost. Sites on the middle Danube, certainly occupied in the middle of the fifth century, have produced coin-series remarkably like that from Richborough; and a comparison between coin-finds in Britain and those of northern Gaul, so far as it has gone in recent years, seems to show that their difference on the two sides of the Channel is not so very great. We have in Britain, it is true, nothing quite parallel with the Furfooz gold hoard of Constantine III, John, and Valentinian III;[1] but even in Gaul that is exceptional; and our present knowledge does not justify us in asserting that the prima facie case against reoccupation, based on the cessation of coins in Britain about the time of Constantine III, is valid. Here, too, the evidence is inconclusive.

One source of information is left. The *Notitia Dignitatum* contains a detailed account of the civil and military establishment maintained in the diocese of Britain. The brilliant article by Bury, to which reference has already been made, argues that the copy of the western *Notitia* from which our text is derived was a manuscript written in or about 428, which was subsequently

---

[1] Blanchet, *Les Trésors de monnaies romaines* (1900), p. 270.

used in the office of the *primicerius notariorum* and there corrected
and added to from time to time. Whatever occurs in it, therefore, describes either a state of things existing in 428 or one that
came into existence later; for when the copy was first made up
in that year any considerable section which was out of date
would have been omitted. It follows 'that Britain as a whole
was still held by the empire in 428'.

This view of the *Notitia*, together with the inference drawn
from it, has been accepted and developed with great learning
and acuteness by the accomplished German historian, Dr. Ernst
Stein. In France it has been less successful: Monsieur Ferdinand
Lot, a distinguished specialist on the later empire, has discussed
it only to reject it, and maintains that the text owes its present
form to 'unintelligent or over-cautious functionaries who did
not venture to suppress what had long ceased to correspond with
the facts'. In this country no historian has altogether accepted
it, chiefly, no doubt, owing to the impossibility of reconciling it
with the known details of Romano-British history.

The crux is Hadrian's Wall. It figures in the *Notitia*; but the
evidence for its evacuation some forty-five years before Bury's
date for the original manuscript is not now doubted by any
scholar acquainted with it.[1] This section of the *Notitia*, therefore, was long out of date when it was included in the copy;
and with this the general principle, that nothing out of date
can exist there, falls to the ground. Nor is this surprising. No
great knowledge of official documents is needed to convince a
student that they often contain entries which, in Monsieur Lot's
words, have long ceased to correspond with the facts. And this
need be no reproach to the officials. Any government which
had lost a frontier district, and had the smallest expectation of
reclaiming it, would keep a record of its organization as a
matter of course. How else would the details of that organization be available when it was possible once more to make them
effective? And where would the *primicerius* keep them, if not in
the *Notitia*?

What is certainly true of the Wall may be true of Britain as
a whole. The independence granted by Honorius was not, on
either side, intended to be permanent. Whether or no the

---

[1] Not British scholars alone. The only German writer who has studied this
evidence in detail and at first hand, Professor Ernst Fabricius, accepts it: Pauly-
Wissowa, xiii, col. 634 (1925).

official régime in Britain actually was restored, its restoration was contemplated. If Britain was lost in 410 and if a fresh copy of the western *Notitia* had been needed about the year 415, the civil and military services of the diocese would certainly have been copied into the new manuscript—not out of anti-quarian interest, and not in order to deceive, but for the con-venience of the government. Whether the same would be true of a copy made in 428 is a question we have no means of answering: nothing entitles us to answer it in the negative.

The purely general argument for reoccupation, based on the mere presence of Britain in the document, is therefore insuffi-cient. But there remains a special argument of an altogether different kind. This was already stated by Bury, and it has been admirably worked out by Dr. Stein. Among the officers ascribed to Britain is one called *comes Britanniarum*. Unlike his two col-leagues, the count of the Saxon Shore and the duke of Britain, he commands a force consisting not of *limitanei* or fixed garrison-troops but of *comitatenses*: a mobile field-army of six cavalry and three infantry units. No such officer and no such force are men-tioned anywhere in our literary sources; and as late as 360 and again in 368 it is reasonably certain, from the narratives we possess, that nothing of the kind existed.

Moreover, this silence concerning a count of Britain in the fourth century extends to the case of four others, who together form a well-defined class of officer. Like him, the counts of Italy, Strasburg, Illyricum, and Spain command small armies of *comitatenses* which are confined to certain localities; whereas, in general, *comitatenses* have no such territorial restriction, but are part of the general field-army of the empire, eastern or western as the case may be. They are peculiar, too, in their rank. Whereas other commanders of field-armies have the title of *vir illustris*, these five, like the commanders of frontier-armies, have the lower rank of *vir spectabilis*.

None of these five counts can be shown to have existed before the fifth century. The first occurrence of what looks like such a command occurs in 409, when Generidus was appointed in Illyricum; but he appears to have borne the title *magister militum*, which places the fully developed form of such commands, with the title *comes*, after that year. It has been conjectured that it originated with the reorganization carried out by the Patrician Constantius in the second decade of the century. The count of

Britain, therefore, cannot have existed until after the rescript of Honorius.

Bury presses this argument one stage farther. The *Notitia* contains two lists of field-units: one, in the fifth and sixth chapters, showing their division as between the master of foot and the master of horse; the other, in the seventh, showing their distribution as between the various western provinces. Theoretically, every unit should appear in both lists. Actually, there are about twenty in the second list which do not occur in the first, as well as a dozen which we can identify only on the hypothesis that their names are given somewhat differently in the two cases. This discrepancy is explained by suggesting that the second list was drawn up later than the first, and that the additional units found there were enrolled after the first list had been compiled. If the first list was up to date in 428, as on Bury's view it must have been, the additional units came into existence after that year. Five of them occur in the army of the count of Britain, as well as three doubtful ones. That officer's command, therefore, either first came into existence or (what for our purpose comes to the same thing) was completely re-organized after 428.

There is a second alternative, which is adopted by Dr. Stein: the first list may have been an earlier one, copied out un-corrected into the 428 manuscript, and the second may represent the actual state of things in that year. It would not matter, argues Dr. Stein, that one list was incorrect if the other was correct; and as we already know that out-of-date material was sometimes allowed to stand in the fair copy, we may accept this as possible. In either case the conclusion stands, that the count of Britain's command must have come into existence after the supposed severance of Britain from the empire.

At this point our minds may return to Gildas. May there not, after all, have been a 'second vengeance' as he describes it— a purely temporary expedition sent from Rome, or rather from army head-quarters in Gaul, in answer to a petition from the neglected cities of Britain, without any re-establishment of per-manent civil government? Bury has forestalled any such hypo-thesis by showing that, of the five counts we are discussing, three fall into line with the general run of officials in having assigned to them the insignia proper to their office, and are given each a chapter to himself in the book; two have no insignia and are only mentioned in the general provincial list. These two, the counts of Illyricum and Spain, had therefore no definite and settled standing in the imperial hierarchy; which he explains by suggesting that they were only appointed *ad hoc*, and 'it was not intended to make them part of the permanent military establishment'. But on this showing the count of Britain, with his insignia and large staff, cannot have been appointed only for the purpose of a single campaign; he must have been a permanent official.

Even granted, then, that the general argument based on the date of the *Notitia*, and the impossibility of its including out-of-date material, is worthless, there remains a powerful argument for the conclusion that, after the rescript of Honorius, the British establishment was augmented by the addition of a permanent officer in command of a permanent field-army. This conclusion depends on the assumption that a count of this kind cannot have existed at an earlier date. This assumption, however, is certainly probable; and until it can be discredited we must accept as probable the reoccupation of Britain, perhaps after a considerable interval, by the field-army of the count.

We have next to consider what this implies. It might entail the existence of a *vicarius* and his staff, residing in London. It might entail the existence of provincial governors: not necessarily of all, but possibly of some. It might entail the existence of a certain number of *limitanei*: certainly not all those mentioned in the *Notitia*, but possibly those of the Saxon Shore. A civil and military reoccupation of this kind might very well have been restricted to a comparatively small area in the south-east. To be effective, it is not likely to have extended far into the west and north.

For checking these guesses we have a possible clue in the distribution of late coins. Broadly speaking, the coins on any given Romano-British site, except the forts of the Wall, where they end with Gratian, and the villas, where they die out as a rule somewhat earlier, go down to Arcadius and the early years of Honorius, and there stop; these last being usually present in fair numbers, but a good deal less common than those of the Constantinian dynasty. At Richborough, on the contrary, the latest coins are by far the commonest. The contrast between Richborough and a site like, say, Wroxeter lies not in the coin-series ending at a different place—it ends everywhere, apart from rare isolated outliers, at 395—but in its ending there in a different way: at Richborough with a vast increase at the end, at the average town-site with diminution at the end.

The Richborough type of coin-series points to an intense occupation not only up to 395, but for some time afterwards; new coins not being minted, old ones are being used instead, and are being shipped there for some purpose in large numbers. The excavators of Richborough held that the coin-finds showed 'an intensive occupation lasting well into the fifth century'.[1] Moreover, they suggest regular communication with the Continent, from which alone these repeated consignments of money can have been brought. The fact that so few, relatively speaking, found their way into the interior, suggests that they were either hoarded there by the authorities who imported them, or spent at Richborough itself—for example, in payment to troops quartered there. It is possible, then, that the count of Britain had Richborough as his head-quarters.

But these coins, which came so abundantly to Richborough itself, must, if there was an effective occupation of the country, have spread pretty freely wherever that occupation extended. We have, therefore, to ask whether there are any other parts of the country where a coin-series of the Richborough type is found. There are: at several sites in East Anglia we find the same thing happening on a much smaller scale; and again in Wiltshire and at Weymouth. If a diagonal line is drawn across the map from the middle of Dorset to Cambridge and the Wash, the segment of England lying south-east of it, including (it may be noted) nine of the major towns, and over half the known villas, comprises all the sites in which coin-series of this characteristic type have been found.

It would seem possible, then, that the area which the count of Britain was meant to protect was this south-eastern region, which was probably governed by a *vicarius* at London. Excavations in Saxon Shore forts have entirely failed to find elsewhere any coin-series comparable with that of Richborough, and we must therefore infer that the other Saxon Shore forts were not re-garrisoned. But the walled towns of the romanized communities, defended by their own militia, served as fortresses; and outside the south-eastern area there may have been other unromanized *foederati*, as well as Cunedda's tribe in the hills of Snowdonia.

[1] Soc. of Antiquaries, *Reports on Excavations at Richborough*, ii. 8.

It remains to ask how long this reoccupation[1] lasted. Its beginning must certainly be associated with the work of the Patrician Constantius, who re-established Roman control in Brittany about 417. Its close has been associated with the Gallic chronicler's entry under 442: 'Britain, distressed by various defeats and other happenings, becomes subject to the Saxons.' But, even if that entry could be regarded as a sober statement of fact, we already know that the British tribal authorities were capable of managing their own affairs. The beginning of Saxon government is therefore not the same thing as the end of Roman; there was most likely an interval between the two, when the government was neither Roman nor Saxon but British. Of this phase we have, in fact, dated evidence. When St. Germanus of Auxerre visited Britain to combat Pelagianism in 429, he put himself at the head of the local militia and led them to victory over a host of barbarian invaders. It follows that there was no Roman field-army in the country at that time, nor do the narratives of his visit contain any hint of imperial officials either civil or military.

The last phase of Roman government, therefore, began in or about 417 and ended some years before 429. It may be some comfort to think that this much of historical reality, shadowy though it be, underlies the 'second vengeance' in the story of Gildas. However it may have ended, both sides still no doubt believed that it was to begin again; and it was only in 446, after the vain appeal to Aetius, that hope was abandoned.

[1] It ought to be added that, by asserting that there was such a reoccupation, the writer is abandoning Procopius's statement (*de bello Vand.* i. 2) that after Constantine III Britain was never recovered by the Romans but was ruled by 'tyrants'; and assuming that Procopius was misinformed on the subject.

XIX

BRITAIN IN THE FIFTH CENTURY

B Y the end of the fourth century Britain had sustained repeated
inroads of barbarian enemies from three sides. The story of
the great invasion in the reign of Valentinian I, as told by Ammianus, proves that then at least raiding bands had penetrated
into Kent and the immediate neighbourhood of London, and
makes it probable that they had overrun the greater part of the
country. Any attempt to estimate the condition of the diocese by
the year 400 must begin with the question: how did this experience,
and others which followed it, affect the life of the people?

The towns, though they may have suffered by the ravaging
of the country round them and the consequent shortage of food-
supplies, suffered nothing worse. Raids of this kind can have
had no effect on their walls, however lightly these were manned
by the shrunken population within. Even the Vikings failed to
storm Paris; and much smaller towns than Paris must have been
able easily to beat off the much less formidable assaults which
were all that the mixed raiders of the fourth century could have
made. Excavation on town-sites has verified this: so far as the
archaeologist knows, cities were not sacked during those years.[1]

In the open country the danger was far more serious. The
wealth of the villas would make them the first object of attack
by invaders chiefly in search of spoil; and a villa was not designed as a stronghold. A few have been found up and down
the country which seem to have been regularly fortified with
earthworks and presumably palisades, but this is exceptional.
The farm-yard wall of the ordinary villa was a very poor protection for its inhabitants and household goods against a band
of greedy plunderers. It was no doubt from the rich villas of
Kent that the robber gangs whom Theodosius saw roaming the
country-side, on his way from Richborough to London in 368,
had raided the stuff with which he found them laden.

Undoubtedly, then, grievous harm had been done to the villas
all over Britain by the end of the fourth century. But we must
try to determine what kind of harm this was, and how far fatal
to their prosperity.

---

[1] At Caistor-next-Norwich, human remains in a house burnt about this time
may prove one case to the contrary: *J.R.S.* xxi. 232.

To get an answer to this question that shall be at once generalized and accurate will never be possible, until scores of villas
have been dug by the most scientific methods; but we have
certain indications which point, when taken together, towards
a possible answer. It has long been known that the coins picked
up on villa-sites have a tendency to die out before the close of
the fourth century. This decline is far from uniform. In some
villas the coins leave off about the middle of the century; in
others they last until near its end. Moreover, these coin-series
seem rather to fade away than to break off abruptly. A case can
certainly be made out for arguing that a great many villas, if
we could assume that the end of their coin-series must coincide
with the end of their history, were finally destroyed during these
invasions; but the assumption is not justified. There is another
way in which the cessation of coins at villa-sites can be explained.

As opposed to the town, where daily life without money is
hard to conceive, the villa was all but self-supporting. The few
things which it wanted, and could not provide for itself, must
be bought; but in case of need most of them could probably be
had by barter, and there is a good deal of evidence that, all over
the west, barter was reappearing in the economic life of the late
fourth century. If we imagine that this was happening in the
British country-side too, we can envisage a state of things in
which the ordinary villa could live without any money at all.
It is still easier to imagine this moneyless existence if we suppose
that, owing to barbarian raids, the ordinary traffic of the country places by means of markets and pedlars had declined and
that the standard of living in the villas themselves had declined
too: both of them almost inevitable consequences of these inroads.

Another factor must be taken into account. Reference has
already been made to the peasant revolts which gave Maximian
so much trouble in Gaul towards the end of the third century.
This is not the only time at which we hear of them. Bacaudae
(to give these peasant rebels their Gaulish name) are a commonplace of fifth-century history; and it is to be observed that a
rising of Bacaudae is a regular consequence of barbarian inroads
into Gaul. Britain, at this late period, is exceedingly poor in
literary records of its social condition; but by the evidence of
archaeology the likeness between the two countries was so close
that Gaulish documents can be used to throw light on British

affairs; and towards the middle of the fifth century Salvian drew a vivid picture of the Bacaudae and of the conditions which created them.

The underlying cause of these recurring peasant revolts, as expounded by Salvian, was the contrast, not in wealth alone but in security, between rich and poor. The great landowners were favoured by the incidence of taxation, and could pass on their burdens to the poor. The legal and administrative system of the late empire favoured economic tyranny. It was in the power of a rich man to deprive a poor man of all he possessed; and Salvian gives examples where the power was exercised without pity and without appeal. Hence, to the poor, 'the enemy is kinder than the tax-collector'; it needed only the occasion of a barbarian inroad to convert exasperated peasants into Bacaudae and bring into existence wandering bands of broken men, escaped slaves, and despairing debtors.

One other thing in Salvian's picture is to our purpose. However frequent these risings may have been, and however difficult it was to suppress them owing to the general sympathy felt for those who took part in them, they did not actually destroy the prosperity of the country. Barbarians and Bacaudae did their worst, and to the outward eye the fair land of Gaul still seemed a paradise.[1]

The same legal and administrative system, the same distinction between rich men in great villas and poor men in village huts, and the same barbarian invasions, were present towards the end of the fourth century in Britain. Causes being identical, it is hardly to be doubted that effects were identical too; and that the wandering bands which Theodosius saw in Britain included large numbers of Bacaudae. But every man who became a Bacauda ceased to be a productive labourer. Consequently the rich estates, in addition to suffering actual plunder and the deprivation of trade, suffered a diminution in their own productive powers.

These three causes, taken together, sufficiently account for the dying away of coinage in villas, without assuming that, wherever coins die out, a villa was destroyed and left desolate. In some cases that may have happened. But if Salvian's further point can be applied to Britain, it did not happen normally.

[1] Salvian, *De Gubernatione Dei*. Cf. an article on him by Thouvenot, *Antiquity*, viii (1934), p. 315.

The villas continued to exist, but they existed in a condition where impoverishment and public disorder had thrown them back on their own resources and reduced them to the primitive economy of the independent household.

It happens that we can check this inference by one explicit record. It was about the beginning of the fifth century that St. Patrick, a lad of fifteen, was carried off by Irish raiders from his father's villa. We do not know where it was. 'Bannavem Tabernae', as the manuscripts give the name, suggests Bannaventa, which we know as a British place-name, but we cannot locate it. It is not the Bannaventa on Watling Street near Daventry, for it was near the western sea—perhaps somewhere not far from the Bristol Channel. Certainly it was not, as some have thought, by the Clyde; for Patrick's father was a decurion, member of the governing class in a romanized society, and there can have been no decurions north of the Wall. He belonged to that class which suffered most at the hands of raiders and rebels; his own son and his two daughters were taken prisoners in a raid; yet when Patrick revisited his home many years later his family were still there. Troubles came and went; life and property suffered, but life went on, the old homes were inhabited, and the land yielded its fruits.

The mention of Patrick leads to another and a very important fact about British society at the end of the fourth century. His father Calpurnius was not only a decurion and landowner, he was also a deacon of the Christian church. Here too he is typical. Despite the traces of a pagan revival which we have noted as appearing towards the end of the century, it is certain that by this time Christianity had made a good deal of progress in almost every class of British society. It began, as we have seen, among the poorer inhabitants of the towns. Although the number of recorded bishops is small, we cannot doubt that every town of any size in Britain had by now its bishop, for the bishop of the early church was not the head of a large territorial diocese, he was simply the head of a Christian community such as every considerable town must have possessed. By the end of the fourth century the upper classes of society were partly Christianized too; and it is only among the *pagani* of the country districts that we can suppose paganism to have been still general. Even there, however, Christianity may have been taking root; for Gildas, writing about the middle of the sixth century, seems to imply that in the west, at least, it had supplanted paganism among the country people. His book is in the main a denunciation of the sins of the Britons, in particular those of Wales; and among the many reproaches which he has to bring against them, there is not a word of heathenism. All he says is that it had once existed: that 'before the coming of Christ . . . divine honours had been heaped by a populace, blind as it then was, upon mountains and hills and rivers, then fatal to salvation, now useful for the ends of man'. The rural cults of Celtic religion, in other words, had disappeared. But a great deal of paganism still existed, both in the towns and in the country, early in the fifth century; and, even at the end of the sixth, the sub-Roman communities in surviving towns like London were not decisively Christian. Had that been the case, their bishops would have played an important part in the negotiations between the British church and Augustine.

During the first half of the fifth century Roman Britain was trying to stand on her own feet. The tribal authorities had their first lesson in complete self-government when Honorius instructed them in 410 to look after themselves. The violence of the break was diminished by the reoccupation of a few years later. Even after the second break there was still hope of reunion with the empire when times should mend, and the Britons carried on with the business of government in the belief that they were trustees of Roman civilization and Roman order. Thus, when in 429 St. Germanus paid his first visit to the island he found it suffering still from barbarian inroads, but ruled by its own men. At Verulam he visited a man described by the strange-sounding title of *vir tribuniciae potestatis*; but the phrase has no reference to the *tribunicia potestas* of the emperors, or even to the position of tribune commanding a regiment; for *tribunus* is a recognized title of certain administrative officers in the later empire, and Germanus's host was no doubt simply the chief magistrate of the municipality.

The state of a British city after the final departure of the Romans is admirably illustrated by the sequel. An invasion by Picts and Saxons was going on; and Germanus not only helped to organize the militia, but led them out to battle himself, and, so says the story, taught them to use the new and terrifying war-cry 'Alleluia', which cheered them to victory. One might think that the Britons had sunk low indeed to need the services of a visiting bishop as their general; but Germanus in his youth had been a soldier of high distinction, and it was in his capacity as military expert that he lent such effective aid to his hosts. The Britons had the will to fight; what they lacked was experienced leadership, both in politics and in war.

This was inevitable; it was everywhere the result of late imperial government, where all executive power had been transferred to the officials of the centralized and bureaucratic state, to the suppression of local initiative and civic spirit. Early Roman history has been described as the history of ordinary people doing extraordinary things. In the late empire it took an extraordinary man to do anything at all, except carry on a routine; and as the empire had for centuries devoted itself to the breeding and training of ordinary men, the extraordinary men of its last ages, Stilicho, Aetius, and their like, were increasingly drawn from the barbarian world. The paralysis of will which affected the British civic governments, and expressed itself again and again throughout their latest history, was only one example of this universal phenomenon. The Romano-Britons, trained for generations to obedience, were a ready prey for any upstart of coarser fibre and more brutal energy who should learn the easy trick of turning their docility to the service of his ends. We shall see how this fate befell them about the middle of the century.

In spite of this decay of initiative and these constant disturbances, there was no catastrophic decline in comfort and material welfare. As in Salvian's Gaul at the same time, the daily life of the country went on, to all appearance outwardly prosperous. In certain ways, no doubt, economic life was much damaged by unsettled conditions. It was especially industry that suffered. What cripples the archaeologist, when he attempts to cope with fifth-century problems, is his inability to identify the pottery of the period. The almost entire absence of recognizable Romano-British pottery belonging to the fifth century not only makes him unable to date its dwellings, or to assert positively that such and such a town or villa was inhabited at that time; it has also led him, too often, to say that if there was no pottery there was no habitation, and so to deny that there was any fifth-century Romano-British life at all. It is more probable that raiding and sabotage destroyed the relatively few centres of production at which the industry was carried on, or rendered unsafe the country roads along which its products were hawked for sale, and that pottery was a thing which to a great extent the fifth century learnt to do without, using leather bottles and wooden platters and the like instead.

Archaeological material of certain other kinds is now beginning to be distinguished; possibly, in time, we shall become able even to distinguish some sorts of pottery.[1] It is now agreed, for example, that for an unknown but considerable period of time in the fifth century Britain was striking her own coins, modelled on the still current issues of the Constantinian dynasty and the Gallic empire—barbarous certainly in style, and often very small in module, but no smaller and no more barbarous than those which were being struck in the same country during the financial chaos of the late third century.

This diminished and precarious outward prosperity was accompanied by the ever-increasing inner wealth of a Christian faith which in Britain, as elsewhere, came more and more to fill and satisfy the minds of a people whose hold on the externals of life was weakening and whose hope of a well-ordered society was dying. It was during this half-century that Christianity put forth its fairest flowers in the garden of decaying Romano-British civilization, and at the same time addressed itself consciously and deliberately to the task of evangelizing the Celtic world where it had never been romanized.

British Christianity has by now ceased to be anonymous. Its leaders are no longer mere figure-heads of shadowy congregations: they stand out in all their individuality as living men. The first, and not the least interesting, is Pelagius, a cultivated and sensitive layman who must have come from the most romanized social stratum in the most romanized part of the country. He left Britain about 380 and never returned; we come across him from time to time, an elusive and gracious figure, beloved and respected wherever he goes, travelling in Italy and Africa and the east with his friend the Irishman Caelestius: a strangely assorted couple—the Briton silent, smiling, reserved; the Irishman voluble, controversial, pugnacious, and upholding in season and out of season the doctrines which Pelagius had devised but would never be so uncivil as

---

[1] For example, the Rev. Angelo Raine has shown me pottery from what is described as a post-Roman stratum at York, quite good in quality, which looks like an unfamiliar kind of Romano-British ware.

to defend. Their travels could be worthily described only by a Cervantes or a Fielding, had either been able to understand theology.

The theological issue was at once simple and profound. Augustine was teaching his doctrine of grace: how the power to do great things that flows outward from the human will is a power not originating in that will itself, but flowing through it, using it as vehicle and means of expression, its source being God, and man's power being then greatest when he is most aware of himself as the open channel through which God's power flows into the world. Once in Rome, soon after Augustine's *Confessions* were published, Pelagius was hearing them read aloud by a friend. He came to the words: 'Give what Thou commandest, and command what Thou wilt.' Pelagius, stirred out of his usual calm, broke out, 'I cannot bear it.' To him, such mysticism was the negation of human freedom, and a belief in it must sap the will to self-discipline and self-improvement upon which alone man could base a vigorous practical life. Yet Augustine, the fiery man of action, knew more about the human will than Pelagius the reserved and dreaming wanderer. It was the ineffective, unpractical man who insisted on the freedom of the will; the strong man knew that such insistence was the unconscious betrayal of inner weakness. Augustine was right: a determinism of the kind which he preached is indispensable to sound ethical doctrine. Pelagius in opposing it was expressing in terms of philosophical thought the same paralysis of will that his countrymen were revealing in action: Augustine's thought, still to-day dominating civilization like a colossus, expressed the demonic energy of the early Christian mind, conscious of itself as drawing on stores of energy that were not finite, like the human personality, but infinite. In the controversy that raged from 411 to 418, though Pelagius's sanctity of character was everywhere acclaimed and though some of his writings were hailed as 'indispensable', his condemnation was a foregone conclusion, and he vanishes from history, his face set eastward, elusive to the last.

Beside him we may place the figure of Fastidius, a man of the same generation or somewhat younger, whose book, *On the Christian Life*, was composed in Britain between 420 and 430, and addressed to a British lady. Like Pelagius, he was an educated man, typical of the best upper class of his time. His Latin is simple and elegant, his thought delicate and just. His book has been compared, not unfairly, with the less mystical chapters of Thomas à Kempis. If it lacks the intellectual force of Pelagius, and if the morality it teaches is no more than the morality of a peaceful, leisured, retired life devoted to piety and charity, where faith moves no mountains, it expresses none the worse, and not unattractively, the ideal of a Christian life as it was taught by a bishop to his flock in fifth-century Britain.

Outside the circle of romanized society, however, mountains were being moved. At the heart of the empire, the church had its men of action, though the state lacked them. When Ambrose was bishop in Milan and the soldier-saint Martin was doing his pioneer work for monasticism in Gaul, a Romano-Briton called Ninian was being educated in Rome. Shortly before the end of the century he resolved to spend his life in advancing the frontiers of Christendom, and chose as his field Galloway, the district inhabited by the Picts of the Nith. On his way back to Britain to take up this work he visited Tours and studied the monastic system of St. Martin, for whom he conceived the warmest enthusiasm. At Whithorn Ninian built in 397 his Great Monastery, the first of its kind in Britain, and dedicated it to his patron. Its whitewashed stone walls—strange fashion, to the Picts, of building a house—gave it the name of Candida Casa, under which it became famous. His work was not confined to Galloway: St. Ninian's well at Brampton in Cumberland, and St. Martin's church within the walls of the Roman fort there (for many early Christians, like St. Cybi at Holyhead, chose Roman forts for the sites of their churches, whether because they found British communities living there, or in order to emphasize the truth that Christianity was the spiritual heir of the Roman empire) show that he evangelized the Irthing valley, once sacred to Cocidius.[1] It may have been Ninian who destroyed the local cults of the Wall region; he certainly blazed the trail along which, in the seventh century, Irish missionaries travelled from Iona to the Tyne and Yorkshire. A tombstone, perhaps of the late fifth century, to a Christian called Brigomaglos (the name is given with its Celtic termination), found at Chesterholm close to Hadrian's Wall, shows how this evan-

---

[1] Dedications to early saints often indicate only a revival of interest in them at a later date; but for this example cf. W. G. Collingwood in *Cumb. & West. Trans.* xxv (1925), p. 9.

gelization of the Border country made its mark in the villages
that still existed on the sites of Roman forts.

Not long after this we can trace similar events in Ireland.
Christianity had already found its way there; but it had made
little progress at the time of Patrick's captivity early in the fifth
century. Like Ninian, Patrick was conscious of a personal call
to his work; and like him he got the training for it in the south.
He spent some years at Lerins, the island near Marseilles where
St. Victor was introducing Egyptian monasticism into Gaul.
He also studied at Auxerre under St. Germanus, and elsewhere.
In 432 he was consecrated bishop for the purpose of working in
Ireland, and worked there for thirty years. He was not alone:
another Briton, Palladius, had been sent there in the previous
year by pope Caelestinus, and established a connexion between
Irish Christianity and Ninian's realm in Galloway.

These cases testify to the intimate connexion between the
British church and those of Gaul and Italy. When the empire
was splitting up, the unity of the church was asserting itself
with increasing vigour. The temporal isolation of Britain by no
means implied a spiritual isolation. At the beginning of the
seventh century Augustine of Canterbury found such isolation;
but, even so, he found no backsliding. The Celtic Easter which
he commanded the British church to abandon was the Easter
of the Council of Arles as modified by Leo I in 455, when temporal contact between Britain and Rome had ceased for a
generation, but ecclesiastical contact was still unimpaired. Between 450 and 600 this and other matters at issue had been
altered at Rome. The only reason why Britain had not received
the alterations was that she was cut off from Rome, not by the
'Departure of the Romans', but by the coming of the Saxons,
which thrust a barrier of paganism between the churches of
Britain and of the Mediterranean world.

The closeness of this spiritual contact is shown by the history
of Pelagianism in Britain. Pelagius himself never taught there.
We are explicitly told that the number of Pelagians there was
never large. The general body of the British church was as
loyal to the anti-Pelagian Council of Carthage in 418 as it had
been to anti-Arian Nicaea in 325. In spite of opinions to the
contrary, there is no Pelagianism in Fastidius. The only reason
why it appeared in Britain was that certain Pelagians, exiled
from Rome by the decrees against them in 421, made their way

there and began to spread their doctrine. Characteristically, the Britons appealed to the pope for help against this invasion; and this was the cause of St. Germanus's missions, first in 429 and again about 447. It is curious that the appeal for temporal aid in 446 was accompanied by another for spiritual aid within a year; and significant of the relation between church and state, that one succeeded where the other failed.

This did not exhaust the services of St. Germanus to Britain. What Ninian was to Galloway and Patrick to Ireland, St. Illtud was to Wales: the first outstanding figure in her Christian history, the founder of a great monastery, and the teacher of a constellation of great men; and Illtud was a disciple of St. Germanus, who thus becomes at one remove the founder of Welsh Christianity. Patrick, too, learnt from Germanus and was at Auxerre a fellow student with Illtud. Another was Paulinus, whose tombstone we have; both he and Illtud are described as teachers of St. David.

With this consolidation of Christian teaching round the outer fringe of Britain the barbarian pressure on her from the west died away. At the beginning of the fifth century we are in what may be called the classical period of Irish piracy. Niall of the Nine Hostages, high king of Ireland from 389 to 405, is its greatest figure; much of his life was spent in plundering Britain and Gaul, and he met his death in a raid, at sea off the Isle of Wight, doubtless at the hands of a Romano-British coastal patrol. A hoard of Roman coins and silver found near Coleraine, and an even greater one found on Traprain Law in Haddingtonshire, represent the fruit of such raids in the second decade of the century. By 429 we hear of Saxons and Picts encountered by St. Germanus, but no longer of Scots.[1]

About this time a new movement sets in, whose cause is as obscure as the causes of such movements generally are. Britons from the west are beginning to pour into Armorica and laying the foundations of the future Brittany. The movement went strongly forward between 450 and 550, but it began earlier. It was certainly not due to Saxon pressure in Britain, nor to Scotic; all one can say is that it reaffirmed in a new way a certain solidarity of culture and population which always unites the

---

[1] The familiar combination of Picts and Scots does, it is true, reappear in the *Historia Brittonum* in connexion with the landing of Hengist; but the *ipsissima verba* of the passage cannot be pressed; there is a *Romanica invasio* in the same sentence.

sea-divided fragments of the British highland zone and tends, whenever opportunity offers, to embrace Brittany as an outlying part of the same zone.

When we try to form some idea of the state of Britain about the year 450 we find ourselves in a region where the light is dim. But the landscape is not featureless; and when our eyes become used to the twilight its larger features are clearly enough discernible.

For about a quarter of a century Britain had ceased to receive aid or control of any kind from the central government of the empire. With the final disappearance of *comes* and *vicarius* a number of persons whose presence helped to swell the romanized element in society had gone. But this number was not large. The *comes* took away his staff and some 5,000 rank and file who were much more barbarian than the upper classes, at least, in the country they had been protecting. The *vicarius* also took away his staff, and so did the *praesides* of provinces, if indeed any were left. The officials who departed were a mere handful. Some traders may have suffered a panic and gone too; but there was no general exodus of romanized people. It is unthinkable, for instance, that any bishop deserted his flock merely because the government of the country had been entrusted to his own friends and relations instead of imperial bureaucrats. The 'Departure of the Romans' contributed very little to the cessation of Roman life in Britain.

Nor was it ruinous either to the political fabric or to the well-being of the country. At first, for a space of time which we may roughly equate with the second quarter of the century, it left Britain more exposed than ever to Saxon and Pictish raids. The *civitates* were unable to cope with them, and there was much distress and destruction. But the destruction was very far from complete. By 446 the *civitates* were still able to issue a corporate appeal to Aetius; their government, that is, was still in existence, though feeble and discredited. All the country needed was strong leadership, and it might still recover; economically, as we shall see, it did recover.

This leadership came; but from an unexpected source. We find, now beginning to appear, the names of a new class of persons whom Gildas sometimes calls tyrants: not those tyrants in which according to Jerome Britain was so fertile, usurping emperors like Maximus and Constantine III, but tyrants of a quite different kind, of whom Vortigern is typical. Vortigern was the king of a district in Wales, like Cunedda before him; from the point of view of the late empire, he would be described as the king of a tribe of *foederati*, half-romanized, living on the frontier and providing for its defence. In the fifth century such a king might have either a Roman or a barbarian name; that made no difference to his nature. We learn from the *Historia Brittonum* that it was Vortigern who invited Hengist and Horsa to settle in Kent, and fought with them there after he had quarrelled with his guests. We have no reason to doubt the substantial truth of the story. Vortigern is also described as acting in part from fear of one Ambrosius, who seems to have been his younger contemporary, no doubt identical with the Ambrosius Aurelianus mentioned by Gildas.

We thus know three things about Vortigern. He was a local king in Wales; he had authority in Kent; and he was afraid of Ambrosius. We must infer that by about 450 a tribal king of this kind was able to extend his sway over great parts of Roman Britain which under the terms of Honorius's rescript should have been ruled by their own tribal authorities, and that in doing so he was likely to come into conflict with men whose power, like his, was more than merely local, whether they came from the highland zone or, as Ambrosius must have done, from the lowland. Thus by 450 the system of government by which Roman Britain ruled itself as a loose federation of *civitates* with elected magistrates of the Roman municipal type was breaking down. The lack of initiative which we have already noted as the fatal flaw in that system had left it, in times of trouble, a victim to men trained to command, very much as the same thing was happening about the same time in Gaul.

About the middle of the fifth century, Roman Britain is thus turning into a congeries of warring states, each dependent for its existence on the prowess of the man at its head. These men are drawn not altogether from the most romanized class of its population, but largely from the Celtic peoples of the less romanized fringe, in which case their political traditions are not those of the city but those of the tribe. In their frequent warfare with each other, and their constant warfare with wholly unromanized invaders, the latter drawing the most powerful of them towards the east, where invasion was now most serious and where the conscious helplessness of the municipal govern-

ments no doubt made them welcome, they were led naturally
to the expedient (in Britain as old as Carausius) of enlisting
these invaders themselves in their service. In fifth-century language, this meant not enrolling mercenaries but creating new
settlements of *foederati*. Vortigern has come down to us as the
first of them to employ this device. From the Roman point of
view it was neither strange nor culpable. If Vortigern appears
in history as the Frankenstein of Roman Britain, it is not because
what he did was in principle wrong. It is because his invitation
unwittingly opened the flood-gates to one of those mass migrations of which the British movement to Armorica was already
giving an example.

The new political order was efficient. Gildas, who must have
spoken with men who remembered it, explicitly tells us that the
time which followed the vain appeal to Aetius was one of un-
exampled prosperity, and he says that this was due to a new
vigour in the military and administrative life of the country. It
is curious, but it is a fact, that this age of prosperity coincides
with the age whose beginning is marked by the *adventus Saxonum*
in 449. The vain appeal of 446 evidently marked the bankruptcy of the romanized *civitates*. Failing to get help from
Rome, unable to help themselves, they called in Vortigern;
he, to their horror, encouraged their worst enemies to come
and settle in their land; but (whether in spite of that policy or
because of it) he did what they had asked him to do. His
strong and unscrupulous rule gave them peace and plenty, and
freedom from the constant raids which they had tried in vain
to check.

But, as Gildas also tells us, this period of prosperity was a
period of moral degeneration. The higher civilization of the
lowland zone was undermined by truckling to the lower civilization of its new masters. Men like Vortigern imposed their standards on Britain. From 455, when the new Easter was accepted
by the British church, we hear of no more cultural and spiritual
contacts between Britain and the Mediterranean world. We
meet with no more men like Pelagius and Fastidius. The culture
of the romanized upper classes has sunk into discredit and fades
away, now that its owners have confessed their inability to control the political situation, and abdicated in favour of what to-
day would be called a dictatorship. Roman Britain is now
rapidly dying, and we are reaching the 'sub-Roman' period,

when men lived on the relics of Romanity diluted in a pervading medium of Celticism.

Thus, from the middle of the century onwards, the general tone of Romano-British society became more and more barbarized. As the Saxon settlements grew in strength, the Roman civilization of the lowland zone was declining into a Celto-Roman civilization where Celtic elements were more and more prevailing over Roman. Latin must have been less and less used. Rome was becoming a memory.

This backwash of Celticism over the romanized regions, both attested and dated by the story of Vortigern, is traceable by archaeological evidence. At Silchester a tombstone was found, with an inscription in Ogams containing the name of a certain Ebicatos and written in the Irish, as distinct from the British, form of Celtic. An Irishman who died in Silchester and left friends able to make him an epitaph in his own language must have been a member of an Irish colony in the town. The Scotic raids, as we saw, had died away; the Silchester inscription shows a state of things in which parties of Scots are settling down peacefully in the lowland zone, and retaining their own language and customs.

A second piece of evidence is the refortification of the old hill-fort at Cissbury on the South Downs, dated to what is vaguely called by archaeologists the end of the Roman period.[1] Iron Age hill-forts are not likely to have been refortified by the romanized *civitates*, and it is hard to imagine the generation of Fastidius and St. Germanus doing such things; it accords rather with the age of the war-lords, when Vortigern came out of his Welsh fastnesses and overran the south.

Accordingly, when it is asked what ultimately became of Roman civilization in Britain, the terms of the question must not be misunderstood. We must not imagine a town like Silchester or a villa like Bignor, at the height of its romanization and prosperity, confronted by Saxon settlers or war-bands. When the Saxons were settling in the lowland zone, the civilization of that zone was not so much Roman as sub-Roman. Its material and spiritual possessions were so deeply and increasingly tinged with Celticism, and what Romanity they had was so typical of the latest imperial age, that they would hardly be recognized as Roman at all by persons whose idea of Roman culture is derived from the early empire.

---

[1] *Antiquaries Journal*, xi (1931), p. 14.

Such as it was, what became of it? Some have thought that it came to an end by the destruction of cities, the burning of villas, the massacre of villagers, and in a word the extermination of the people, except so far as their remnant fled into the west or were enslaved by the English; or, if they are men of less blood-thirsty imaginings, by wholesale emigration to kindlier lands. Others have believed that it stood firm, conquered its con-querors, and brought England within the circle of the countries whose historical tradition is based on Rome. Neither view is wholly right. The truth is too complex for such crude generali-zations; if they are posited as the horns of a dilemma, the facts of history slip between them.

How are we to set about answering the question? Physical anthropology, valuable though it is, does not help us here, be-cause we are concerned not with the inheritance of physical characteristics but with the survival of a tradition, and either of these two things may happen in the absence of the other. The study of language does not help either. The replacement of Latin and Celtic by English, though it certainly attests the dominance of Germanic culture over Romano-British, does not tell us what happened to the submerged element. The study of institutions, which promises in the future to tell us a great deal, must go farther before its results can be handled by any one but a specialist in Early English antiquities.

There is one incontrovertible fact. Great numbers of places, inhabited in the Romano-British period, were deserted at some time, and this desertion was in the main peaceful. Let us con-sider the evidence.

Of the major towns of Roman Britain, four (Verulam, Sil-chester, Wroxeter, and Caistor-next-Norwich) became unin-habited and remained so until modern times. It is an open question whether others, perhaps many others, lay waste for a while and were later reoccupied by the English themselves. This, however, was by no means universal. London and others, in all perhaps a majority of the chief towns, always remained inhabited, though with the shrunken populations characteristic of the late Roman age, and de-romanized as well as shrunken.

In the case of the smaller towns, evidence of complete deser-tion is the rule rather than the exception. In the case of the villas, it is a rule to which exceptions are unknown. Not a single villa in the country has been found underlying a Saxon dwelling or has yielded evidence of permanent occupation in the Saxon period. Strangely enough, the same thing is to a great extent true even of village-sites, where we should most expect continuity of occupation. Here and there places exist which have been villages both in Romano-British and in Anglo-Saxon times. But there are large tracts of country (Salisbury Plain is the classical instance) where population-maps of the two periods have been compiled with great thoroughness, and where the two are mutually exclusive at almost every point.

Apart from certain large towns, then, the detailed maps of archaeological finds look exactly as if the English invaders had exterminated the Britons all over the lowland zone and had left their dwellings desolate. And Gildas's story of ruin and massacre has seemed to lend colour to the idea that something as sweeping as this did actually happen. But let us keep our hold on the archaeological facts. All four of the deserted major towns, and several minor ones, have been excavated; and the excavators have in every case looked for evidence that the towns finally perished in some such way. The results are decisive. These towns came to an end, not by fire and sword, but by decay and evacuation.[1] They were abandoned and left to fall down.

Villas tell the same story. Here and there excavators report one which seems to have been violently destroyed; but in the few cases where sufficient care has been taken to read the evidence they have mostly ended like the towns, in simple decay. Excavations in villages have produced only one example of what seems a massacre. At Woodcuts Pitt-Rivers found the skull of a child who had been killed by a sword-cut delivered from behind. But Woodcuts, as we know, was deserted in the middle of the fourth century; and if there was ever a massacre there it was the work of Roman soldiers, perhaps employed to dislodge the unhappy peasants from their home.

When did this widespread and peaceful evacuation take place? So far as archaeology goes, it might have happened almost everywhere by about 400. But although some of it may have happened during the second quarter of the century, we cannot think that it was anything like complete until long after 450, unless we are prepared to reject Gildas's statement about general prosperity at and after that date. All that archaeology entitles us

---

[1] The Caistor-next-Norwich evidence (p. 302) does not refer to the town as a whole.

to say, therefore, is that it happened early enough to prevent
Anglo-Saxon objects from reaching these places in appreciable
quantities before they were evacuated. A century or more may
well have elapsed during which the two races lived side by
side, with very little intercourse or contact of a kind that
would have led to an exchange of goods.

Where did all these people go? That most of them went to
Wales, already densely inhabited, is inconceivable. Some of
them may have swelled the emigration to Brittany, but according to tradition the colonists of Brittany came from the highland
zone. On the whole it is probable that the greater part of them
were absorbed by degrees into the population of the English
settlements, and that in this way a stream of Romano-Celtic
history and tradition mingled with the life of England.

In the highland zone this general dislodgement of the people
did not happen. When early English history emerges into the
light of day, that zone is still everywhere inhabited by British
peoples, preserving their sub-Roman heritage at least to this
extent, that they are everywhere Christian and everywhere keep
some faint tincture of Latinity, setting up tombstones after the
Roman model to their dead. But the story of these peoples must
not be here pursued.

It does not follow that there were not wars, and fierce ones,
between the sub-Roman Britons and the gradually encroaching
Saxons. One such period of warfare, very destructive to the
Britons, appears to have begun not long after the Saxon settlements began. Gildas refers to this period a widespread destruction of towns, partly due to the Saxons and partly to internecine
warfare between British states, and says that it was brought to
an end by the victories of Ambrosius, who seems to have made
himself a great power in the land at some date which we might
roughly guess to be about 470–80. But the peace thus realized
did not last long; before the end of the century the Saxons were
pressing forward again.

We have some archaeological evidence for wars of this kind,
but it should probably be referred to a later period of conflict,
beginning towards the end of the sixth century. The Wansdyke,
a huge earthwork running from the Bristol Channel near Cleve-
don to the Marlborough Downs and the neighbourhood of New-
bury, has been proved late Roman or post-Roman in date, and
can be nothing but the work of some British chief organizing

the defence of the south-west against invaders, probably West
Saxons. In the north, there is a strange building called The
Castles, near Hamsterley in county Durham, where Britons have
built themselves something as like a Roman fort as they could
make it, lurking concealed among deep woodlands and valleys.
Scattered lengths of earthwork along the eastern slope of the Pennines play a part for the northern sector of the highland zone
parallel to that of Wansdyke in the southern. Such forts and
limites stand to those of the Roman Empire as the rude Welsh
tombstones, sometimes with Ogam as well as Latin inscriptions,
stand to imperial monuments.

For the wars at the end of the fifth century we have evidence,
definite in its statements but hard to interpret, from Celtic
sources. The *Historia Brittonum*, in its oldest stratum, which was
used by Bede early in the eighth century and therefore must
have been written down within 200 years of the events it professes to describe, tells us that 'in those days (after the death of
Hengist) Arthur fought against them (the Saxons) with the
kings of the Britons, but he himself was *dux bellorum*'. Then follow the names, and a few scanty details, of his twelve battles,
ending with 'the battle at Mons Badonis, in which there fell in
one day 960 men under the sole onslaught of Arthur; and no
one overthrew them except him alone, and in all his wars he
was victorious'. Gildas, who mentions what must be the same
battle under the name of 'the siege of Mons Badonicus', seems
to place its date about 500–3; Bede in 493; the ninth-century
Annales Cambriae in 516. That there was such a battle, and that
it resulted in a British victory of so crushing a nature that for
at least forty-four years afterwards the Saxons never took up
arms again, is beyond question: Gildas, a contemporary witness, is our evidence. We may, then, take the fact of some such
series of engagements as those ascribed by the *Historia* to Arthur,
closing in decisive victory and long peace, as established by the
testimony of these two independent sources.

Of these sources, the later ascribes all the victories to Arthur;
the earlier, Gildas, does not mention him, except possibly in an
oblique allusion. There was, among the British leaders whom
he took it upon himself to rebuke, some one named or nick-
named The Bear, Ursus; and if he is not identical with the
Cuneglasus named in the same passage (an obscure one) his
name may represent Arthur's, twisted through the Celtic *artos*,

bear. Yet this is unlikely, because forty-four years, Gildas says, had elapsed between the siege of Mons Badonicus and the date of writing: too long, probably, for the victor to be still alive; certainly too long if we accept the statement of the *Annales Cambriae* that only twenty-one years after that engagement the battle of Camlann was fought, and the later tradition that this was the battle in which Arthur fell. But, for what this is worth, the Cambridge thirteenth-century manuscript of Nennius glosses the passage of the *Historia* by observing that 'Artur, translated into Latin, means *ursus horribilis*'. It must be left an open question whether Gildas refers to Arthur or not.

In either case, the historicity of the man can hardly be called in question. The fact that his name in later ages was a magnet drawing to itself all manner of folk-lore and fable, and that an Arthurian cycle grew up composed partly of events transferred from other contexts, no more proves him a fictitious character than similar fables prove it of Alexander or Aristotle, Vergil or Roland. It tends rather to prove the opposite. The place which the name of Arthur occupies in Celtic legend is easiest to explain on the hypothesis that he really lived, and was a great champion of the British people.

His name, Artorius, is a recognized though not very common Roman family name. In the second half of the fifth century, when he was born, a person bearing such a *nomen* is likeliest to have come from a region, and a class in that region, where romanization was still relatively high. He was therefore probably the son of a good family in one of the *civitates* of the lowland zone, and we may write off the later legends of his noble parentage and birthplace as fictions designed to give him a more honourable pedigree.

His place in the military organization of his age is clearly stated in the *Historia Brittonum*. Whatever later stories said, he was not a king, still less king over all the kings of Britain. To call him *dux bellorum* implies that the governments of his day entrusted him with a special military command: in the same way Bede describes St. Germanus as *dux belli*. To say that he fought 'with the kings of the Britons' implies that this commission was valid all over the country, and that he fought not in any one kingdom or region, but wherever he was wanted, co-operating with the local levies. His was, in fact, a mobile field-army of the kind which, early in the fifth century, had been commanded by the *comes Britanniarum*. When the Britons appealed to Aetius, complaining that they were being harried over the length and breadth of the land and asking for help, the purport of their petition is obvious: they were asking him for a new count of Britain. Now, half a century later, they created one for themselves; and this, though they or their historian had forgotten his correct title, is what in effect Arthur was.

So far, we are relying only on the earliest stratum of Arthurian legend, the passage in the *Historia Brittonum*. In its main lines, that passage becomes intelligible as soon as we interpret it in the light of fifth-century Roman military practice and envisage Arthur as the commander of a mobile field-army. One corollary is that the sites of his twelve battles must not be sought in any one part of Britain. That the names are genuine is obvious. Not only are they part of the oldest tradition, but there is hardly one whose site is established beyond controversy, whereas a forger would have offered corroborative detail by putting them at well-known places, as Geoffrey of Monmouth takes Arthur to Winchester, York, Lincoln, and so forth. The story of the twelfth, at first sight so improbable, only needs interpretation to set the seal of truth on the whole. When it is said that 960 Saxons fell under the attack of Arthur alone, the implication is that, on this one occasion, he was co-operating with no local king but was using his own force by itself.

It may be permissible to carry the argument a step farther. If a romanized Briton late in the fifth century thus revived the office of *comes Britanniarum*, he would model his mobile army, so far as possible, on similar armies of the period. The chief feature of Roman warfare in that century was the lately established supremacy of the cavalry arm. In 378 the battle of Adrianople had proved that a charge of heavy cavalry could roll up and destroy a vastly superior force of the best Roman infantry, and ever since then the Roman practice had been to rely more and more on mounted troops. The late empire was in fact the age which established the ascendancy of heavy cavalry, clothed in chain-mail, over infantry. Already in the first twenty years of the century the count of Britain commanded six regiments of cavalry to three of infantry, and any one thereafter, reviving his office with some knowledge of what it implied, would know that a count of Britain should be a cavalry general.

Even without that historical knowledge, any Romano-Briton

of the late fifth century, educated enough to know something about warfare as practised on the Continent in his own time, would understand the use and value of heavy cavalry. Such a man, looking around him, would be struck by the fact that in Britain cavalry was now extinct. The local militias of the low-land zone, whose main work was to defend their own city walls, can hardly have included any mounted men. The Celtic tribes of the highland zone had no horses that could carry a man in battle; if they no longer used chariots, which lingered long after this in Ireland, they fought on foot. The Saxon invaders were infantry, fighting with spears, and having little or no body-armour; it was not until later that they learnt from the Britons to wear mail shirts, and they never became cavalrymen. Their tactical disci-pline, too, was elementary, though their individual valour and strength were considerable. Against such an enemy, a small force of ordinary Roman cavalry, resolutely led, must prove invincible.

If, as we have argued, Arthur came of a good romanized family in the lowland zone, these ideas would be commonplaces to him. If he was also a man of sufficient acuteness to grasp their implications, and sufficient practical ability to carry them out, the story of his successes is explained. Any one who could enrol on his own initiative a band of mail-clad cavalry, using as mounts the ordinary horses of the lowland zone and relying for armament on the standard work of contemporary smiths, and could persuade the British kings of their value, might have done what Arthur is said to have done, ending with the single-handed destruction of a host which, raised in a last desperate effort to crush him, had succeeded in penning his force within the ram-parts of some British hill-fort reconditioned, as we have seen that Cissbury was, for defence against the invaders.

These are conjectures. But they are based on the facts of fifth-century warfare; and the probability that they may be correct is at least slightly increased by the fact that the traditions which first appear at a much later date, and are embodied so far as we are concerned in the twelfth-century romance of Geoffrey of Monmouth, revolve round the conception of Arthur as the creator of a band of knights. The word 'knight' has for us a medieval colouring; and certainly, as used by a twelfth-century writer, it describes a familiar type of contemporary armament and tactics, the heavy mail-clad cavalry whose charge was the dominant feature of medieval warfare until Boroughbridge and

Crécy proved that the English longbow had found the answer to it. But the knight of the middle ages was in fact only a survival or revival of the late Roman *eques cataphractarius*,[1] clad as he was in a shirt of mail, with arm-pieces and leg-pieces attached to it, 'an armament which, as Ammianus and Vegetius tell us, made horsemen invulnerable'.[2]

Through the mist of legend that has surrounded the name of Arthur, it is thus possible to descry something which at least may have happened: a country sinking into barbarism, whence Roman ideas had almost vanished; and the emergence of a single man intelligent enough to understand them, and vigorous enough to put them into practice by gathering round him a group of friends and followers, armed according to the tradition of civilized warfare and proving their invincibility in a dozen campaigns. There are other elements in the tradition which may have a foundation of truth. After the final victory, Arthur's occupation as champion of the Britons was gone. Twenty-one years later was fought the battle of Camlann—the battle, it may be, of Camboglanna or Birdoswald,[3] 'in which Arthur and Medraut fought', and Arthur is said to have fallen. Medraut, according to the story, was one of Arthur's own knights; which suggests that during those years of peace dissension had broken out in the band itself, and finally it was destroyed in a battle of one party against the other.

Whatever may be the truth about the details of his career, Arthur left behind him an imperishable name, and the people he had saved could not believe that he had died. They attached to him the belief, found in many countries, that a lost leader has only gone into hiding and will one day come back at need; and it is not long since a party of antiquaries, visiting an ancient hill-fort, were accosted by a frightened old man asking if they had come 'to take away the king'. In such hopes and fears, if our conjecture is right, the mind of the British people has embalmed its memory of Roman Britain. For Arthur, I have suggested, was the last of the Romans: the last to understand Roman ideas and use them for the good of the British people. The heritage of Rome lived on in many shapes; but of the men who created that heritage Arthur was the last, and the story of Roman Britain ends with him.

---

[1] As Couissin has shown: *Les Armes romains* (Paris, 1926), pp. 516–17. [2] Ibid.
[3] As Crawford convincingly suggests in an article on 'Arthur and his Battles', in *Antiquity*, ix (1935), p. 289.

BOOK V

THE ENGLISH SETTLEMENTS
XX

THE SOURCES FOR THE PERIOD: ANGLES, SAXONS, AND JUTES ON THE CONTINENT

THE period of some two centuries which lies between the collapse of Roman government in Britain and the arrival of St. Augustine has long been recognized as the most difficult and obscure in the history of our country. Yet within it changes more profound and far-reaching than in any other corresponding period took place: and these changes modified the physical character of our people, determined the fundamental structure of our language, laid the basis of many of our institutions, and made possible an economic exploitation of our natural resources on a scale never attempted in prehistoric or even in Roman times. And as the result of this domestic exploitation came first the possibility and finally the problem of a population expanding towards the limits of subsistence, and becoming in its turn the centre of expansion overseas. Many other and later factors have determined the direction, the character, and the extent of that expansion, but it is not too fantastic to believe that its beginning lay in this period, in the silent and strenuous conversion of the primeval forests of central and southern England into the arable fields and profitable swine-pasture of countless Anglo-Saxon communities. Until the Anglo-Saxon invasions, the pattern of human habitation in this country had been largely determined by the forces of nature, the presence and absence of downland, forest, and fen: five centuries later the distribution of Domesday *vills* shows that man for the first time has mastered his environment: henceforth he can live, within limits imposed by his own prudence, almost where he will.

In the period under review nothing, of course, could have been farther from men's minds than such a conception of the meaning of events. To the Roman world the forces of civilization were giving way to barbarism, and in so far as the civilized attempted consciously to appreciate the causes of their troubles, they not unnaturally attributed them to divine vengeance on one another's sins. Nor were the barbarians themselves, so far as we can penetrate to the thoughts which they were themselves unable to express, conscious in any way of their destiny. Long after this period was over they still regarded the forests and their contents with superstitious terror, and peopled the fens with all the army of the Evil One. That, notwithstanding this, they contined to fell the forests and to drain the fens, is a fact whose significance only the later historian can appreciate. All that was visible at the end of our period was the destruction of the fabric of Roman imperialism in Britain, the disappearance of its civil and military machinery, and of many of the arts of life. Instead had been built up a group of precariously founded barbarian kingdoms, whose rulers were still living largely on the spoil of their neighbours, even if many of their dependents were already slowly settling down to the ceaseless routine of subsistence agriculture.

The purpose of these chapters is to inquire by what stages this change took place, and how deep it penetrated into the structure of society. In the past the most diverse answers have been given to these questions, and we are confronted at the outset by the fundamental obscurity and uncertainty of the whole subject. It is necessary, therefore, first to consider the reasons for this obscurity. How does it come about that a period in which such important changes are known to have occurred should be so difficult to understand?

The best way to answer this question is to look for a moment at the sort of evidence upon which our knowledge of the period depends, and to contrast it with that on which we rely for the times before and after these dark centuries. It will be at once clear from the earlier chapters of this book, or from a glance at the bibliography, that our knowledge of Roman Britain is based on an unequal blend of two main groups of evidence. Since Britain was part of the Roman empire, the most important facts of its history are known from the historians who described at different periods the story of that empire, but since the province was remote from the Mediterranean lands which were the centres of Roman political life, and since in any case there were comparatively few Roman historians of importance whose works have survived, and not one of them after Julius Caesar had visited Britain, we have from these sources only the barest skeleton of a story. It is, however, fortunately possible to supplement that story from the results of archaeological excavation, and the character of Roman remains is such that a maximum of historical information can be derived from them. The principal reasons for this are three. Firstly, Roman occupation-sites are extremely abundant and easily classifiable, so that the evidence of individual forts, towns, villas, or villages can be constantly checked by that of other examples of their own and other classes. Secondly, Roman provincial culture was very well supplied with material goods, in such durable materials as bone, metal, and pottery; and many categories of these goods, being more or less mass-produced, are closely datable. Thirdly, the occurrence of coins and inscriptions provides the means by which such close dating is readily made possible. From these sources a very clear idea of the political, social, and economic history of the province under Roman rule has been slowly built up. If we compare this evidence with that upon which our knowledge of later Saxon history depends we shall see that a great change has occurred. There has been an enormous improvement in the quality of the literary sources, many of which give detailed and often contemporary accounts of the political history; while on the social and institutional side the evidence of the chroniclers and biographers is supplemented by, for example, the laws of the kings, and by the land-charters which they granted to churches and laymen. Thus each of these periods provides material which is of first-rate importance for elucidating its history. In the one that evidence is to a large extent archaeological, in the other it is mainly literary: but in both it is there to be used.

But for the two intervening centuries we have no contemporary sources of any sort approaching in value those available for the periods before and after. Such material as we have of a literary kind is moreover rendered more difficult of interpretation by its division into two groups representing the traditions of invaders and invaded. On the Anglo-Saxon side there is indeed no contemporary evidence at all, for the very good reason that the invaders were illiterate. It is true that in the *Anglo-Saxon Chronicle*, compiled in the reign of King Alfred, we have a series of annals attached to dates in the fifth and sixth centuries which offer an outline of the traditional story of the settlement of Kent, Sussex, and Wessex,[1] but while we may agree

[1] See Appendixes I and II.

with such claims as have been made on philological grounds for the high antiquity of certain of these annals, not even the boldest of their defenders would claim for them the authority of a contemporary annalist. It is clear that they consist in the main of stories preserved for several generations by the uncertain channel of oral tradition, groups of incidents culled from the sagas of the royal families, forced into an annalistic framework and attached to dates which at best are traditional and at worst arbitrary. And even where, as in the works of Bede, the Northumbrian monk whose *Ecclesiastical History of the English Nation* was finished in 731, we find these stories treated in the sober spirit of a scientific historian, it is none the less necessary to remember that Bede lived in more settled and simplified circumstances two centuries after the age of conquest, that he was inevitably influenced by the political geography of his own day, and that his own interest, in any case, lay not in the age of settlement but in the age of the conversion to Christianity. When Bede really set himself to tabulate in the chronological summary at the end of the *Ecclesiastical History* the most memorable certain events of the period with which we are concerned he found exactly nine;[1] and these nine included two eclipses of the sun, three events of ecclesiastical interest in Ireland, Scotland, and Rome, one which associates the sack of Rome by Alaric with the end of Roman rule in Britain, and two which give vague and inconsistent time-signals for the arrival of the Angles in this country. He notes only one specific event, and that not without ambiguity, which is directly relevant to the problems before us.[2] For the crucial period of the early settlement from 449 to 538 there were apparently in Bede's considered judgement no datable events to be recorded at all. In estimating the place which the precisely dated annals in the Chronicle should take in our story, it is wise to bear in mind the salutary scepticism of Bede.

Nor are the literary sources on the British side very much more helpful. There is indeed one contemporary source in Gildas, an ecclesiastic of strong traditionalist views, who wrote in the second quarter of the sixth century either in Brittany or

---

[1] *Hist. Eccles.* v. 24.

[2] 'In 547 Ida began to reign, from whom the royal stock of the Northumbrians is derived, and remained King for twelve years.' Bede does not tell us whether this event represented the first Anglian incursion into Bernicia.

in western Britain. He preserves information of vital importance
on the condition of things in the region that he knew and for
the years of his own life. For the rest his book is interesting
mainly as showing the distance which separated the most cultivated element among the surviving Britons from the Roman
civilization and mentality to which they still felt that they belonged: it illustrates, too, the shortness of Celtic folk-memory,
and the limitations of geographical vision which a century of
political chaos had produced. And Gildas was no more concerned than was Bede to record the progress of Anglo-Saxon
settlement. Considering the avowed purpose of his work, which
is rather hortatory than historical, we are fortunate indeed to
be given so much first-hand information by this embittered
preacher.

It is hardly necessary to devote more than a word or two to
the rest of the literary evidence from the British side. The Irish
and Welsh annalists supply an occasional and too often dubious
date: the Lives of the Saints are almost without exception viti-
ated as historical sources by the picturesque but repetitive
imagination characteristic of medieval hagiology. Their value
lies mainly in the echoes they retain of the social conditions of
the sixth and seventh centuries in the Celtic lands. Both the
annals and the biographies, in the form in which they have
reached us, are far too late to be used with confidence as original
authorities for the period.

There remains the *Historia Brittonum*, a compilation composed
or edited early in the ninth century by a Welshman Nennius or
Nemnius, whose notion of historical method is best described in
his own words. *Coacervavi*, he says, *omne quod inveni*—'I have
made a heap of all that I have found.' It is customary to treat
this uncritical attitude of Nennius as a fatal objection to the
Historia Brittonum as a source for the period. In fact, of course, it
is the one thing which saves it from the contempt into which
later writers such as Geoffrey of Monmouth and Henry of
Huntingdon have fallen. Had Nennius used his sources with
the same literary skill which they employed, he would have lost
the interest of historians as completely as they have done. It is
precisely his ignorance and his stupidity which caused him to
jumble together good and bad materials without amalgamating
them into a single whole, and each successive commentary on
the evolution of his curious book makes it more possible to sort

out the different elements of which it is composed. But while it may be agreed that some scraps in the heap are more valuable than others, that some indeed provide information unobtainable elsewhere, it is not from such material as this that a satisfactory history of the time can be made.

Then there is the archaeological evidence. Here at any rate is tangible material from the years under review, and while its quantity in no way compares with that from the Roman period, it is, at any rate on the Anglo-Saxon side, quite impressive enough. On the British side, however, it is curiously lacking. Apart from the notable but somewhat uninforming mass of Christian tombstones from Wales and the other Celtic districts, and a range of numismatic evidence whose precise extent and significance is only beginning to receive the consideration which it may turn out to deserve, there is a singular dearth of archaeological evidence which might help us to understand the ultimate fate of Roman Britain. The material on the Anglo-Saxon side is also, though fairly abundant, far less satisfactory than could be desired as a basis for historical reasoning. In the first place nearly all of it is derived from cemeteries rather than from habitation-sites, and it is obvious that groups of objects from graves, however carefully they may be excavated—and many Anglo-Saxon cemeteries were unfortunately dug at a time when the importance of isolating and recording separately the contents of each grave was imperfectly understood—cannot provide historical evidence of the same value as that derived from the successive rebuildings of a town or the superimposed strata of a single house. A simple comparison may help to impress this point. If nothing but the cemeteries of Roman Britain had been available for study more than half this book could not have been written. And if the student of Roman Britain had also been deprived of the coins and inscriptions which in the last resort form the basis of his dating-evidence, it is no exaggeration to say that it could not have been written at all.

Yet this is the unhappy position of the Anglo-Saxon archaeologist, and in the absence of coins and inscriptions he is compelled to do what he can to interpret the story of the graves with the more treacherous weapons of typology and analogy. He is forced, that is to say, to date his material either according to its place in an evolutionary series of designs or by comparing it with more closely datable objects elsewhere; and it is easy to see that while both the evolutionary series and the comparison may be correctly made, there is no necessary correlation between either and the historian's time-scale expressed in the passage of years. And since, as we have seen, most of the objects concerned come from graves, and a man may have buried with him objects of value made at every stage of his working life (apart altogether from the disputed question of heirlooms), it is clear that the hope of obtaining, within a total range of no more than two hundred years, dates close enough to be of real use to the historian who seeks precision to a decade is fore-doomed to disappointment.

With these limitations it is not perhaps surprising that the archaeological evidence for the Anglo-Saxon period is unable to supply by itself the numerous chronological deficiencies of the literary sources. In the effort to do so its professors have on occasion been led to extravagances of dogmatic assertion unjustified by the nature of their material. But when this material is properly understood, and its limitations respected, there remain wide aspects of the period which can be strongly illuminated by its use. It must further be remembered that the whole subject is still in its infancy, and that attention has hitherto been mainly concentrated on the study of objects such as brooches and other metal-work whose durability and intrinsic worth deprive them of much of the evidential value for close dating inherent in more breakable artefacts such as pottery. It is safe to say that the contribution which may one day be made by archaeology to an understanding of this period has hardly yet been realized even by its most ardent students. By plotting the distribution not only of the cemeteries, but of every type of object which they contain, it should be possible to determine not only the extent of the conquest by the end of the pagan period, but also the routes taken by the settlers, with far greater accuracy than can be done at present. It should be possible to learn more of the continental provenance of the different groups of invaders, of the kinds of country in which they preferred to make their settlements, and of their culture, religion, and daily life. We may even hope to illuminate, if not very powerfully, the relations of the new-comers to the native population. Archaeology can already say in general which were the areas of the earliest settlement, but it cannot in the nature of things give us a chronological narrative, or indeed any dates which are close enough to tell the historian much that he does not know already of the detailed course of the invasions.

Other classes of evidence may be brought into use in the search for material relevant to these dark centuries. Physical anthropologists may one day be able to speak with more authority than seems possible at present on the vexed question of Romano-British survival. The study of place-names is essential to an understanding of the social conditions under which the settlement took place and of the institutional ties which first bound the settlers together. It should be possible to use certain classes of names, those in particular which contain either the primitive group-termination -*ingas*,[1] or the names of heathen gods or holy places, as a body of direct evidence for the distribution of the new-comers second in importance only to that of the pagan cemeteries. Historians have sometimes been reluctant to use the evidence of these primitive names as positive indications of occupation in the earliest period owing to the difficulty of determining how long they continued to be formed. But a detailed comparison of the areas in which they occur with those which have produced material evidence for settlement in the pagan period provides ample proof that the great majority of them are without doubt contemporary with the use of the pagan graveyards, though a few may have been formed here and there as late as the second half of the seventh century. Good reasons can in fact be given for believing that these names provide an invaluable means of supplementing and checking the pattern of early Anglo-Saxon settlement which the cemeteries display,[2] and they will be so used in the survey of the course of the conquest attempted in Chapters XXI–XXIII.

Enough has now been said to show what form the answer to the question with which we started must take. The period is difficult to understand, not only because of its inherent confusion, but because of the inadequacy of the historical evidence. In fact it is not too much to say that for most of the events of this time the elements which contribute to historical proof are lacking. Even when we can be certain that an event of importance did occur—say the siege of Mons Badonicus, which seems

---

[1] On these names see F. M. Stenton in *Introduction to the Survey of English Place-names* (1924), 50, and E. Ekwall, *English Place-names in* -ing (1923).

[2] See, for a fuller discussion of this question, J. N. L. Myres in *Antiquity*, ix (1935), 455–64.

to have ended one stage in the progress of Saxon settlement—
it is often impossible, as in that instance, to say exactly when or
where it happened, or, for that matter, exactly what took place.
For the most part the evidence of the different classes which we
have discussed is insufficient to cohere into a single story at all,
and this is true even of different elements within one general class.
There is no point of contact, for example, between the West
Saxon annals in the *Anglo-Saxon Chronicle* and the British story
of Ambrosius Aurelianus and Mons Badonicus as preserved
by Gildas, though the two series of events are represented as
contemporary and apparently belong to the same quarter of
England. In the same way the current disagreement among
archaeologists over the dating of Kentish jewellery makes it
virtually impossible for the historian to use the evidence which
the most beautiful objects produced in England, or indeed in
western Europe, in this period should be capable of contributing
to his story.

This being so, it is hardly surprising that the conclusions
which historians have reached in the past on many of the most
fundamental questions of these years have differed widely from
one another. Different minds differently trained have inevitably
attached greater importance to different parts of the evidence.
Where finality is impossible, the subjective element inherent in
all historical writing finds full play, and no one who ventures
to write on this period can expect to win general agreement
among those best qualified to judge his work. It is none the less
necessary to attempt constantly fresh syntheses of the material
in the light of the fresh evidence which so rapidly accumulates,
and it will be the aim of these chapters not merely to summarize
what appear to be the more significant contributions which the
different branches of the subject have to offer to the common
stock of knowledge, but to set them against the only background
which is common to them all, the background of the English
country-side. If there is any period of our history which demands more than another a geographical treatment it is this.
For the facts of geography determined the course of Anglo-
Saxon settlement, and the surest—indeed the only—way to an
understanding of its difficulties will be a knowledge of the landscape of England as it was in the fifth century of our era. And
as that landscape was broken up into certain broad natural
divisions, so will the survey of the conquest be divided into

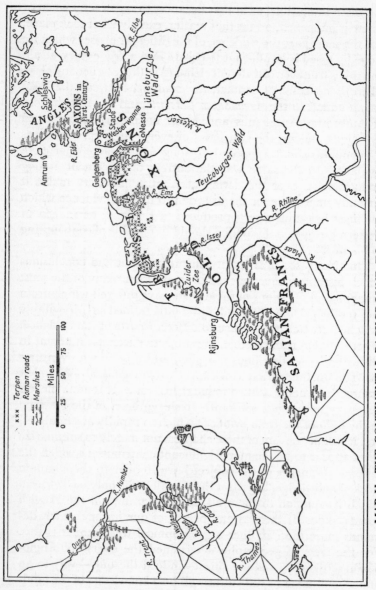

MAP V. THE CONTINENTAL BACKGROUND TO THE ENGLISH SETTLEMENTS

regional studies, in each of which the relevant evidence of every
kind will be considered in detail. Such a treatment will inevitably involve some repetitions, and the disjointing of topics
which are more usually treated as unities. It may perhaps be
said that it will lead to confusion of purpose, and a missing of
the wood for the trees. To that criticism there is one very simple
reply. The Anglo-Saxons too were confused of purpose, they
also found the trees too thick to make much sense of the wood.
And if we attempt to follow them in their detailed and individual solutions of what were always local problems, we are the
less likely to lose sight of them ourselves. To treat the conquest
as a mass of minor difficulties in an essential environment of
rivers, forests, and downland is to treat it as they did themselves.

And the light that is to be thrown upon these difficulties must
come impartially from every source that seems capable of
generating it. Neither the literary nor the archaeological evidence can be used as a touchstone of historical truth, for it has
been shown that neither is worthy of this distinction. And much
of the evidence must necessarily come from documents such as
the land charters which belong in themselves to succeeding
centuries. They can none the less be used discreetly but without
apology to illustrate the conditions of the settlement, in the same
way as it is possible on occasion to read between the lines of
the later literary evidence to the fuller understanding of earlier
times. When Bede, for example, discusses the motives which led
to the foundation of Lastingham,[1] when the anonymous biographer of St. Cuthbert portrays the Saint sight-seeing in the
ruins of Roman Carlisle,[2] or Felix of Crowland describes the
eighth-century attitude to the Fens,[3] they are unconsciously
illuminating our period as clearly as their own.

Enough has been said in Chapter XIX to describe the geographical and social conditions of Britain on the eve of the Saxon
settlement. But before we pass to a discussion of the settlement
itself, it will be as well to say something about the antecedents
of the settlers. It is not possible here to discuss fully the complex
and obscure history of the Teutonic peoples of north Germany
in the Roman period, nor would it be relevant to the present
purpose. None the less an attempt must be made to appreciate

---

[1] *Hist. Eccles.* iii. 23; see p. 454.   [2] *Anon. Vita S. Cuthberti*, § 37; see p. 440.
[3] W. de G. Birch, *Memorials of S. Guthlac* (1881), § 19; see p. 385.

the situation in the north German coastlands which made the invasions possible, and to indicate such tribal strains and cultural affinities as seem to have been dominant among the different groups of the new-comers.

It will be as well to indicate at the outset that the question, 'Where did the invaders come from?' is one which must be kept distinct from the question 'In what parts of England did they settle?' The two problems are no doubt intimately related, but any attempt to answer both at once is bound to raise more difficulties than it solves. In the one passage in which he allows himself to discuss the matter, a passage as celebrated as it is confusing, Bede tried to give clear-cut replies to both questions in this way.[1] The reinforcements who joined the *foederati* whom the British king settled in Kent came, he says,

'from three powerful German peoples, the Saxons, Angles, and Jutes. From the Jutes are descended the Cantuarii and the Victuarii, that is, the people which holds the Isle of Wight and that which to this day is called the *Jutarum natio* in the province of the West Saxons set opposite the Isle of Wight. From the Saxons, that is from that region which is now called that of the Old Saxons, came the East Saxons, South Saxons, and West Saxons. Moreover from the Angles, that is from that country which is called Angulus, and from that time to this is believed to remain uninhabited between the provinces of the Jutes and the Saxons, are sprung the East Angles, Middle Angles, Mercians, the whole stock of the Northumbrians . . . and the other Anglian peoples. Their first leaders are believed to have been two brothers Hengist and Horsa . . .'

Reduced to its lowest terms Bede thus answers the question of origin by saying that the invaders were Saxons, Angles, and Jutes; that the Saxons came from what was called Old Saxony in his day; and that the Angles came from a country which bore their name, and lay between the land of the Saxons and that of the Jutes. His answer to the question of settlement in Britain is to suggest that three tribal movements from these three regions resulted in the occupation of Kent, the Isle of Wight, and southern Hampshire by one; of Essex, Sussex, and Wessex by the second; and of the rest of the midlands and the north and eastern coastline by the third. In the last case the emigration was so complete that the old homeland remained, he believed, still uninhabited in his day. Nothing more need be said at the moment

[1] *Hist. Eccles.* i. 15.

about this second problem which will be discussed more fully later on, except to observe that Bede's clear-cut tribal migrations are difficult to reconcile with the archaeological remains or with other literary evidence not inferior in authority to his own. Indeed Bede himself makes no attempt elsewhere in his book or even in this chapter to conform to his own tripartite division. It looks as if he may have put in this passage as an afterthought, a desperate attempt based on the political geography of his own day to introduce a semblance of order into the confused conditions of two hundred years before.[1]

With the continental origin of the invaders we are more immediately concerned. It seems clear, in spite of attempts which have been made to explain his words differently, that Bede meant to imply that the Jutes came from Jutland, the Angles from the area in eastern Schleswig of which a part is still called Angeln, and the Saxons from the north German coastlands somewhere between the Elbe and the Rhine.[2] It may be noted that an earlier authority than Bede, the sixth-century writer Procopius, divides the invaders of Britain between the Angles and the Frisians;[3] and while he lived far away in the eastern empire and was prepared to believe some very queer things about Britain, he probably derived his information from Angles who are known to have accompanied a Frankish embassy to Constantinople in his day, and there are, as we shall see, other reasons for believing that the mention of Frisians among the inhabitants of Britain was not the most imaginative of the tales with which the Angles on that mission entertained the Byzantine court. Literary tradition thus settled Britain with immigrants drawn from the whole continental coast-line between Jutland on the north and Holland on the south; and before considering what other evidence can be brought to bear on the question it will be as well to examine the condition of the population in this area at the relevant date.

[1] A careful study of the text of this chapter suggests strongly that the passage quoted above was an insertion by Bede himself at a late stage in the revision of his work. For as it now stands the leadership of Hengist and Horsa is most naturally read as applying to the Angles who are discussed in the previous sentence rather than to the Saxons or Jutes. If, however, the three ethnological sentences are removed Hengist and Horsa become again the leaders of the Kentish *foederati* which Bede clearly took them to have been. His later insertion has thus broken the thread of his narrative, and confused its sense.

[2] As early as the tenth century Bede's words were thus interpreted by Æthelweard.   [3] *Gothic War*, iv. 20.

For this purpose it will be necessary to go back some distance into German history. At the end of the first century Tacitus in his description of the Ingaevones, the group of peoples who occupied the north-western seaboard of Germany, mentions among many others less relevant to the present purpose the Frisians, the Angles, and the Eudoses.[1] The Frisians already occupied the coastland which still bears their name in northern Holland, and the Angles and Eudoses, whose precise position at that time was probably no clearer to Tacitus than he makes it to us, could at least be described as 'defended by rivers and forests' in an area which made natural their common participation with other tribes in the rites of Nerthus on an island of the Ocean. And whether the Ocean in this instance means the Baltic or the North Sea there is nothing improbable in the idea that they occupied approximately the regions which Bede seems to have thought appropriate many centuries later for the Angles and the Jutes.

Tacitus, however, makes no mention in this passage or anywhere else of the Saxons. The first mention of them is to be found in the *Geography* of Ptolemy, a writer who lived in the middle of the second century, though it is often supposed that he derived much of his information from a source which was about a hundred and fifty years earlier. Ptolemy places the Saxons 'on the neck of the Cimbric peninsula',[2] by which he probably meant us to understand the modern Holstein. On the coast between them and the Frisians—from the Elbe, that is, as far as the Ems—both he and Tacitus agree in locating the Chauci, a tribe which in Tacitus' time at any rate could be described as 'the noblest of the German race'. They played in fact much the same part, as the centre of a loose tribal confederacy, as the Saxons themselves played two centuries later in precisely the same area. The exact relationship between the two has indeed become one of the most controversial points among continental scholars who interest themselves in the archaeology and ethnology of this part of Germany. The fact that the Saxons first appear settled in this region in the middle of the third century not long after the last mention of the Chauci hereabouts in Roman sources, coupled with their apparent similarity of character and habits, has caused some to regard the two peoples as essentially the same. Others, noting Ptolemy's distinction between them, as

---

[1] *Germania*, 40.   [2] *Geography*, ii. 11. 7.

well as the appearance of the Chauci in later disturbances near the Roman frontier on the middle Rhine, have concluded that an emigration of the latter from the coastlands between the Elbe and the Weser and their movement south-westwards left their former districts open for Saxon settlement. Others again have seen archaeological reasons for believing that the Chauci quickly lost the pre-eminence which they enjoyed in the days of Tacitus, and that the Saxons' westward expansion completed their disintegration by driving some south-westwards towards the Rhine, and reducing the remainder to subjection in the least attractive part of their old country, the salt-marshes along the coast between the Ems and the Elbe.

It is fortunately unnecessary for our present purpose to pursue these different solutions of the *Chaukenfrage* to a decision. There is at any rate good reason to believe that by the middle of the third century at latest the Saxons were in full possession of the whole region between the lower Elbe and the Weser, and their growing power was being felt still farther afield. But before passing on to those later manifestations of Saxon energy which are our primary concern, it will be as well to examine more closely some of the causes which prompted this expansion. There is in the first place archaeological evidence to suggest that far back in the days when the Saxons were the near neighbours of the Angles in Schleswig and Holstein they were already a populous and prolific folk. The numerous and well-furnished cemeteries of the so-called Bordesholm-Nottfeld culture, which German archaeologists have recognized as representing this phase of Anglo-Saxon history, indicate a population already willing and able to take advantage of any opportunities for expansion. With the southward movement of the Lombards who had until the middle of the second century occupied lands on the lower Elbe such an opportunity occurred and was seized: about 200 the Saxons seem also to have spread into eastern Holstein, and in the next fifty years, as we have seen, they replaced or absorbed the Chauci in the lands between the Elbe and the Weser.

Now it is clear that this important westward movement and still more the extensive raiding which succeeded it and first made 'Saxon' a name of terror to all civilized men, which it was to remain for many hundred years, was in part at least a reaction to the disturbed conditions of the Roman world during the third

century. It is at least possible, as we have seen, that the movement of the Chauci, which preceded if it did not directly pro-
mote the Saxon advance, had been inspired by a desire to fish
in the troubled waters of the frontier river, the Rhine; the Saxon
raids on the Salian Franks and their direct assaults on the province of Britain were alike the outcome of their knowledge of
Roman military weakness; and the continuing uncertainties
of political control in the empire, implying as they did an
irresponsibility and local independence among the generals on
whom the burden of frontier defence lay, were quite sufficient
temptations to the more active of the Teutonic tribes, keenly
alive as they had always been to the pleasures of plunder and
piracy.

But this agreeable prospect was soon cut short by the military
revival of the empire and the drastic reconstructions of Diocletian and Constantine. The forts of the Saxon Shore in Britain
may stand as types of the new realism which the barbarian
emergency had forced upon the government of Rome. And for
a while, as has been indicated above,[1] the patch upon the old
garment held; and if Saxon raids continued on a large scale, it
would seem from the silence of our records, and the apparent
prosperity of the British country-side at this time, that they
returned very often empty-handed. Westward expansion by land
beyond the Rhine was checked in the same way and for the
same reason, and the Saxon people soon found themselves popu-
lating the coastland between the Elbe and the Ems to the limit
of its capacity.

Such at least is the impression created by the archaeological
evidence. Few parts of the German world can have been so
thickly settled as the Saxon coastland in the fourth century. In
the comparatively small district surrounding Stade on the western edge of the Elbe flood-plain, for example, no less than forty-
five cemeteries of this period have been identified,[2] while farther
west the great graveyard of Wester Wanna, itself apparently in
no way exceptional in size, contained in all probability as many
as four thousand cremation-urns. The country inland from the
marshy coast was fertile and comparatively free from pine-forest,
while even in the marshes the thickly scattered mounds or *Terpen*,
many of them still covered by villages bearing names strongly

---

[1] See Ch. XVII.
[2] A. Plettke, *Ursprung und Ausbreitung der Angeln und Sachsen* (1921), 61.

reminiscent of eastern England,[1] suggest that the Saxons soon found themselves adopting the curious life half-way between the land and the sea, which was described by the elder Pliny as that of their predecessors the Chauci two centuries before.[2] Westward beyond the Weser the same coastal conditions prevailed, and here too the artificial mound-settlements are thickly spread; and although there would seem to be less evidence of over-population in the more unattractive hinterland, the comparative absence of scientific excavation in this area has probably combined with a deeper sinkage of the coastland to limit unduly the evidence for intensive Saxon occupation.

Beyond the Ems, however, the Frisians like the Chauci farther east had been living on the artificial *Terpen* raised above the surrounding marshes for centuries before the coming of the Saxons, and the careful excavations of Dutch scholars on many of these mounds have shown that everywhere from the fourth century onwards the native population had been reinforced and perhaps dominated by immigrant Anglo-Saxons working their way down the half-drowned coast-line in search of fresh outlets for the settlement of their people. Here too the distribution of the remains shows that it was not only the coastlands that attracted the settlers. Numerous inland sites north and east of the Zuider Zee have produced material so closely parallel to that of the Anglian invaders of England as to suggest one easy explanation for Procopius' idea that these invaders were themselves in part Frisians.[3]

As the fourth century wore on it would seem that even the forces of nature took a hand in increasing the pressure of the Saxon population on the means of subsistence. It is probable that the whole north German coast-line had been slowly sinking for some centuries, and that the widespread practice of living on artificial mounds had arisen as man's natural reaction to the slow advance of the sea. It would certainly appear that the ever-increasing size and height of the mounds which all the excavations have revealed is to be explained not merely by the

---

[1] e.g. Middlum (Middleham), Marsum (Marsham), or Stadum (Stadham).

[2] Orosius (vii. 32) describes the Saxons as 'a people of the Ocean, settled in pathless swamps and on the sea shore'; he almost echoes Pliny's fuller description of the Chauci (*Nat. Hist.* xvi (1), 1): the latter is quoted in translation by R. H. Hodgkin, *History of the Anglo-Saxons* (1935), i. 14.

[3] Some, but by no means all, of the sites are marked on J. H. Holwerda's map (Kaart III) in his *Nederlands vroegste Geschiedenis* (1925).

increase of the population but also by the rising level of high-water mark. There are reasons for believing that this sinkage, which eventually culminated in the Carolingian age with the formation of the Zuider Zee, the Dollart, and the Jade Bay, was proceeding at an accelerated pace from the fourth century onwards; and while it would be going too far to say that the Anglo-Saxons were driven to migration to escape the flooding of their homes, it is easy to see that the gaining of the sea upon the land would press more severely upon a people whose increasing population caused in any case a land-hunger which became stronger with the passage of years. While all the Teutonic tribes bordering on the Roman frontiers were watching with increased restlessness the weakening of its defences, and were themselves feeling far away in Asia the westward pressure of Huns and Avars, the Anglo-Saxons crowded on the German coast were thus faced in addition with troubles of their own.

Meanwhile the Roman frontiers and the Roman morale were slowly returning to something of their condition in the third century. Julian and Valentinian I might succeed for a time in defending the west and might even carry their arms beyond the frontiers of the empire, but in 378 came the battle of Adrianople, the death of Valens, and the pouring of the Gothic hordes into the heart of the Eastern Empire. Already by 367 the Saxons, as has been seen above,[1] were renewing with increasing success their old assaults on Britain: already they could show themselves capable of overwhelming the defensive system of the Saxon Shore, and of destroying at one blow the personnel of its higher command; and though such successes were no doubt remembered because they were exceptional they none the less showed the seriousness of the situation. It only needed the permanent weakening of the Roman garrisons in Britain to make the Saxons the arbiters of its destiny, and we have seen above how the withdrawal of troops by Maximus and Constantine III provided precisely the stimulus which the raiders needed. Whether or not the first decade of the fifth century saw the removal of the last substantial Roman forces in the province, it was in any case from thenceforward only a matter of time before the Saxons began to look on Britain no longer as a source merely of plunder and booty, a happy hunting-ground for piracy and slave-raiding, but as offering a more permanent way of escape from the in-

[1] p. 284.

creasing discomfort of their lives at home.[1] At least it was a land with room and to spare, one in which the marshes could be left on one side as a dwelling not for men but for demons and goblins.

Thus far we have traced in outline the Saxon's progress to the threshold of his settlement in Britain, but his traditional partners the Angle and the Jute have been left far back in the days of Tacitus. But of some of the Angles certainly, and possibly of the Jutes too, we have already said something in following the story of the Saxons, for it must be remembered that the latter term came to embrace in the common parlance of those within the empire the whole group of north German peoples whose homes lay along the coast-line beyond the Franks, and whose behaviour was associated in the popular mind with desperate valour and barbarity, and their appearance with a trail of burning farmsteads, wrecked villages, and a panic-stricken countryside. To the frightened provincial the precise ethnology of those who looted his villa was a matter of indifference—Angles or Jutes, they were all Saxons to him. And it is to this fact that much of our confused information on the subject must be ascribed. For the Celtic peoples, following in this respect the usage of their Latin-speaking ancestors, continued for centuries to label all the Teutonic inhabitants of Britain as Saxons: even Penda of Mercia, sprung, as it appears, from the purest Angle stock in England, from the old royal family of the Anglii of Angeln, appears in the Welsh annalists as 'Panta the Saxon'. To this day it is the Sassenach rather than the Angle or the Jute who is sometimes contrasted unfavourably in Celtic circles with the Brython and the Gael. And the matter is not made easier by the later practice of the Angles themselves. For they too, when they learnt in the seventh century to write Latin, adopted at times the convention customary in that idiom, to the denial of their own tribal origins. Wilfrid, bishop of York, an Angle of noble birth, can describe himself to the pope as *Episcopus Saxoniae*,[2] and the Abbot Hwætberht can address a letter from Wearmouth in Northumbria *de Saxonia*.[3] It is thus not

---

[1] It will be seen in the next chapter that this transition from raiding to settlement seems not to have taken place on a memorable scale before the middle of the fifth century: a fact more readily consonant with the suggestion advanced in Chapter XIX for the presence of military forces in Britain during at least part of the period 410–46 than with the older view that the final 'withdrawal of the legions' occurred in or before 410.

[2] Eddius, *Vita Wilfridi*, c. 30.   [3] Bede, *Hist. Abb.*, § 19.

surprising that Bede himself, in spite of the precision with which, as we have seen, he places the Jutes in Kent, can speak of the invaders of that region in the very same chapter as *Anglorum sive Saxonum gens.* In these circumstances the attempt to base clear-cut tribal distinctions on the literary evidence soon loses contact with reality.

It is, however, more than probable that this unscientific confusion in the employment of names does reflect more by accident than by design a very real confusion in the ethnology of the invaders. All over the German world the smaller tribes of earlier days had been hammered out in the stress of the migrations into large confederacies bearing sometimes, as with the Saxons and the Goths, the name of their most powerful constituents, sometimes, as apparently with the Franks and the Alemanni, a group-name which had not in the early days been that of a single tribe at all. We know that the Angles in early times were the close neighbours of the Saxons in Schleswig-Holstein: and we know from *Widsith* as well as from the archaeological evidence that some part at least of the tribe was still there in the fourth century. Yet, as we have seen already, there are reasons for connecting the settlers of certain of the Anglian districts of England rather with invaders whose immediate cultural antecedents were in Frisia[1] than with direct immigrants from Schleswig; and we shall shortly have to observe similar parallels between other so-called Anglian areas and the Elbe–Weser region of Germany which has been shown to be predominantly Saxon. On the other hand a strong case has been made out for believing that the royal families, not only of the Anglian districts of England but even of Kent and Wessex, were of Anglian rather than of Saxon origin in their continental homes; and the impression that some part at least of the Angles had moved southwards from Schleswig in concert with the Saxons is strengthened by the existence of the later continental code known as the *Lex Anglorum et Werinorum,* for, whatever the precise location of the Angles and Varni for whom it was composed, it can at least be said that they did not live in Schleswig.[2] If Bede was right in his belief that the continental home of the Angles was left empty by their emigration he was certainly

---

[1] For the Frisian connexions of the later Northumbrians see J. N. L. Myres in *History,* xx (1935), 258–62.

[2] See H. M. Chadwick, *Origin of the English Nation* (ed. 1924), 102 ff.

wrong in conveying the impression that all the emigrants had found fresh homes in Britain.

Now if there are good reasons for thinking that part at any rate of the Anglian invaders of Britain were already so mingled with their Saxon neighbours before leaving the Continent as to constitute for all practical purposes an Anglo-Saxon rather than a pure Anglian group, it may be said at once that the problem of the Jutes can only be solved if some such notion of racial or cultural dilution is taken for granted. It will not be possible to say our final word on the Jutish question until we come to examine in detail the evidence for the settlement of Kent, but it may be desirable at this stage to mention some aspects of the matter which are relevant to the present discussion. We have been bold enough above to assume that the Eudoses of Tacitus may be related both by name and by geographical position to the Jutes of whom Bede was thinking in the famous passage which has been quoted, and though this may be no more than an assumption, it provides at any rate a starting-point for the argument. But if there was at one time a tribe of this name in Jutland there are strong reasons for believing that the greater part of it had ceased to be there at the time of the migrations to Britain. In the first place, apart from the one passage in Bede there is no other mention of the Jutes in this area; and the only later notice of them which gives any sort of geographical information[1]—a letter of about 540 from Theudebert, king of the Franks, to Justinian in which he mentions their voluntary submission[2]—associates their name so closely with that of the continental Saxons as to raise the probability of their settlement, perhaps, as place-name evidence has been held to indicate, in the Ems–Weser area,[3] somewhere within the extensive region which by that time was associated with the Saxon name. There is furthermore archaeological evidence for a fairly complete cessation of burials in the early cemeteries of western Jutland

[1] The passage in Venantius Fortunatus (*Carmina*, ix. 1. 73) in which a string of tribes is mentioned as subject to Chilperic, king of the Franks (about 580), including the Danes, Jutes, Saxons, and Britons in that order, cannot be used, as by R. H. Hodgkin, *History of the Anglo-Saxons* (1935), i. 83, to suggest that the Jutes in question are to be placed in Jutland. For the order is determined solely by the necessity of fitting the names into a hexameter, and has no geographical significance whatever.

[2] Bouquet, *Rerum Gallicarum Scriptores*, iv. 59; quoted by Chadwick, op. cit., 92.

[3] So Siebs, quoted by R. H. Hodgkin, *History of the Anglo-Saxons* (1935), i. 370.

about the end of the second century, which may not improperly be connected with a Jutish emigration more or less simultaneous with the Saxon expansion into the old coastlands of the Chauci.[1] It may further be noted that the various scraps of evidence which throw light on the antecedents of the Kentish royal family seem to connect the career of its founder Hengist with almost every part of the Anglo-Saxon homeland except Jutland itself. The scraps of evidence, it is true, are not all of them of the highest authority, but they possess a certain general persuasiveness from their mutual independence and from their common silence on the subject of Jutland. By the Ravenna Geographer Hengist is associated once more with Old Saxony: by the *Historia Brittonum* with Oghgul or Angel, the home of the Angles. And if we may accept the tempting and by no means impossible identification of the Kentish Hengist with the warrior of that name who appears in *Beowulf*, and whose activities in Frisia are dimly discernible in the fragmentary poem of *Finnsburh*,[2] we are offered at once a possible explanation of his appearance in Kent and of the local legends which have long associated his name with several parts of Holland. Such an identification will further assist in the understanding of the dialectal and social similarities which seem to link Kent more closely to Frisia than to any other part of the Continent. And while the archaeological evidence is here, as will be seen, unusually difficult to interpret, it does at any rate combine with all the other testimony to preclude a direct influx of settlers on a large scale from Jutland. Indeed if the crucial passage of Bede is discounted, as Bede almost seems to discount it himself, it is easiest on all grounds to regard Hengist as an adventurer who had accumulated his *comitatus* all down the German coast and with greater success perhaps in Holland and the Rhineland than elsewhere. Whether he himself came from Jutland or from a more southerly settlement of its one-time inhabitants, his followers had little but the name to connect them with the former area. Indeed there is nothing but Bede's statements to suggest that they were ever called Jutes at all. There appears to be no echo of the word among the place-names of Kent, nor is there any reason to believe that they referred to themselves by this name: conscious

[1] A. Plettke, *Ursprung und Ausbreitung der Angeln und Sachsen* (1921), 60.

[2] Chadwick, op. cit., 49–50; M. G. Clarke, *Sidelights on Teutonic History* (1911), 186–7.

perhaps of their own mongrel ancestry they spoke of themselves simply as the Cantware, the Men of Kent.[1] It is curious to remember that the evidence for a *Jutarum natio*, whatever meaning we may attach to the phrase, in southern Hampshire is actually stronger than that for the Jutes of Kent, for here it rests upon the significant evidence of place-names as well as on the testimony of Bede.[2]

This preliminary discussion of the Jutish question has taken us beyond the limits of our inquiry into the origin of the invaders, and has formed a bridge to our second problem: What parts of Britain were occupied by the different peoples we have been describing? Bede's answer to the question has been before us, and may serve as the basis of our own; but it is already clear that Bede has unduly and perhaps consciously simplified the confused issues of the age of settlement. Apart from the Jutish difficulties there is no cause to quarrel with his general identification of the invaders with the people of north Germany from Angeln to the mouths of the Rhine, and on certain of his specific derivations there will likewise be widespread agreement. It is clear that in Mercia, for example, which Bede mentions among the Anglian areas, the royal family of Penda and his successors claimed descent from the old royal house of Angeln itself, and there is no reason to throw doubts upon this claim: so too the pedigree of the kings of Essex was unique among the genealogies in leading back to Seaxneat, the traditional and peculiar deity of the Saxon peoples, to whom Bede attributes the settlement of this area. Elsewhere, however, the case is not so clear: the kings of Wessex traced their ancestry to an apparently Anglian stock, connected in some way with that of the royal house of Bernicia; and the fact that the West Saxons seem habitually to have used the terms Angle and English in describing themselves and their language is less easy to explain as a mere literary convention than the parallel practice of the Angles in calling their own part of England Saxony.

These phenomena are, however, only specimens of a growing body of evidence which is tending to demonstrate with increasing emphasis the artificiality of these tribal distinctions in the migration period. The word Saxon, which had once been the name of a small folk on the neck of the Cimbric peninsula, had

---

[1] There is evidence for this as early as the Laws of Hlothere and Eadric (before 686).   [2] See p. 364.

widened its scope to include all the peoples between the Elbe and the Rhine and eventually became, like our use of 'Vandal' and 'Hun', little more than a term of abuse. And such detribalizing of the old names was not merely a manner of speaking: it corresponded to a very real disintegration of the old tribal unities themselves. In earlier days the *princeps–comes* relationship so fundamental in German society had always lain at the basis of the tribe's coherence; but now it came to expand outside the tribe, and in expanding broke up the coherence it had once secured. In a period of confusion a man's power depended on the size of his following, and a successful leader would win followers from many directions; nor would the enrolment of new recruits be obstructed by too strict inquiries into their tribal antecedents. It is thus no longer possible to conceive of the settlement of Britain as a well-ordered immigration of tribal unities, each springing from a circumscribed continental area, depending for its discipline on the claims of kinship, and retaining its individuality unimpaired in its new home. Kinship no doubt was an important matter, as the evidence of the earliest place-names may serve to remind us, but it was overshadowed at this time, as in all times of crisis, by gifts of leadership and the force of personality.

The tribal confusion which thus prevailed in the settlement of England may be illustrated in a convincing way by considering for a moment the archaeological evidence. If we were to examine the characteristic artefacts in bronze or pottery from the three continental areas from which as we have seen the bulk of the invaders must have come—the Angle homeland in Schleswig, the Elbe–Weser area, and the Frisian coast—we might expect to find regions in the traditional Anglian or Saxon parts of England where parallels to each can be found. Not many classes of objects have hitherto received sufficiently detailed study to be used with confidence in this connexion, but such evidence as we have does not suggest a division of the country along quite the lines suggested by Bede. It is at least interesting to observe that the characteristic saucer-brooches of the Saxon homeland in the Elbe–Weser region are familiar in this country not only, as we should expect, in Saxon districts but in a rather striking manner in parts of Middle Anglia.[1] Of the equal-armed brooches, which are even more markedly Saxon on the

[1] E. T. Leeds in *Archaeologia*, lxiii (1912), 159–202.

Continent, three out of the five known English examples come also curiously enough from Middle Anglia. And while it is in general true that the cruciform brooches, as their more northerly distribution on the Continent would lead one to expect, are typical of Bede's Anglian districts of England, yet early examples have been found in some numbers in Kent,[1] and also on at least two sites in the West Saxon area in Berkshire.[2] For the Kentish examples an explanation may most readily be found in the fact that Frisia is as much a home of the cruciform brooch in the migration period as is Schleswig. But this, while it may be important in forming our estimate of Kentish culture, rather serves to emphasize the confusion elsewhere than to explain it, for it opens the way to the probability that some of our more northerly users of early cruciform brooches in the admittedly Anglian districts are as likely to have come from Frisia as from Angeln.

There is the same impression of tribal mixture to be gathered from the ceramic evidence. Apart from certain unusual forms such as the window urns—vessels in whose side or base a fragment of glass has been intentionally inserted and whose continental distribution is mainly Saxon, while the English examples are found in Middle Anglia and in Kent[3]—the cremation-pottery in this country has never been subjected to a detailed analysis. A Saxon or Angle element in certain cemeteries in Kent has indeed been recognized. It has further been observed that while cremation as a burial rite is far commoner in England in the Anglian than the Saxon districts, the urns themselves as often as not exemplify forms and styles of decoration which are characteristic of Saxon rather than of Anglian areas on the Continent. In particular the very widespread use of stamped ornamentation on the English pottery is a feature which can only have been developed out of the parallel practice in the Saxon homeland: it cannot at any rate have come from Schleswig, where its employment is throughout most unusual. The ceramic evidence will moreover as a result of detailed analysis certainly support the notion of a strong Saxon influence in Middle Anglia, which has already been observed on other grounds: it will probably

---

[1] Eleven are listed by Åberg, *Anglo-Saxons in England* (1926), 29.

[2] East Shefford and Frilford: E. T. Leeds, *Archaeology of the Anglo-Saxon Settlements* (1913), 64.

[3] F. Roeder in *XVIII. Bericht der röm.-german. Kommission* (1928), 149.

also suggest that East Anglia received more direct immigration from Schleswig than Northumbria, where there are some striking parallels with the pottery of the Frisian *Terpen*.

It is now possible to sum up the foregoing discussion on the antecedents of the Teutonic settlers who poured into Britain during the fifth and sixth centuries. We have seen that Bede's view of the dominant part played by men of Angle and Saxon stock in the movement is fully borne out by every other line of inquiry. It has been possible to amplify his conception by assigning to the Angles not merely their homeland in Schleswig but a part in that wider complex of kindred peoples for which the word Anglo-Saxon is as appropriate before as after the conquest of Britain. And behind Bede's words that the Saxons came from Old Saxony it has been possible to envisage this same amalgam of restless and marauding folk extending their domination till they reached the Rhine, and capable of forming separate settlements far away on the Seine and the Loire. And amongst them, cheek by jowl with native Chauci and Frisians, were fragments of many northern tribes besides the Angles, including perhaps even those *Saxones Eucii* who may have been Bede's Jutes. The break-down of the Roman defences in the west during the fifth century was but the final factor in creating conditions on the north German seaboard which the old tribal bonds were no longer adequate to control. And so the Saxons, lacking, it appears, the common loyalties which a centralized military monarchy was imposing at this time on their neighbours the Franks, feeling only here and there, as individuals rather than in the mass, the discipline of personal service in the Roman auxiliary forces, and far less affected as yet than the Franks by the softening contacts of Roman civilization, began to pour over the sea with a common purpose but little unity of command. Their purpose was the settlement of the island province which had for centuries past been the goal of their plundering expeditions: their leaders, if we are not mistaken, were drawn from the ablest of their noble families, men who guarded more carefully than their humbler followers the traditions of their tribal origin and of their descent from gods and heroes.

But the very complexity of the continental situation as well as the specialized evidence has made it impossible to follow Bede too closely in that distinction of the three areas of tribal settlement in Britain which seems to have been little more than an attempt, in part abandoned as soon as made, to read back from the dominant elements in the kingdoms and *provinciae* of his own day to the conditions of the age of conquest. And as we come to consider in the next chapters the course and character of that conquest we shall find other distinctions among the invaders as significant as the traditional division into Saxons, Angles, and Jutes. There will be men who bury their dead like Roman provincials, and others who cremate them as their Teutonic forefathers had always done. There will be kings who boast their descent from Caesar, when others are content with Woden and Seaxneat. There will be men who find it natural to live huddled together in villages, and others who prefer isolated farms. Some will inherit or develop a taste for elaborate gold jewels set with garnets and enamel, while others will cling to their ancestral ornaments of bronze. All these contrasts and many others among the makers of England are as relevant to the story as the matter of tribal origins. It is time to turn from the preliminary inquiry to the course of the conquest itself.

XXI

THE COURSE OF THE CONQUEST IN KENT
AND THE SOUTH-EAST

THE first problem which confronts us in examining the course of the Anglo-Saxon conquest is that of the date at which it can be said to have begun: the date, that is, not of the first barbarian raids, for it was to meet these that the defensive system of the Saxon Shore had been planned right back in the third century, but the date at which raiding gave place to the first successful attempts at widespread and permanent settlement: the event which seems to have remained in the memory of the dark ages as that of the beginning of an epoch, the moment of the 'Adventus Saxonum'.

It is hardly surprising that the literary sources should give us a bewildering variety of answers to this question, for strictly speaking it is a question which cannot be answered at all. It is as useless to expect the consistent assignment to a single year of the date at which raiding gave place to settlement as it would be to demand a single date for the beginning of the British empire. In both cases there is no one event to be chronicled but a continuous process extending over a considerable period, and the most that can be expected is a rough approximation. The search even for that is complicated by the attempts of our sources to achieve the impossible as well as by the blunders of their chronological calculations.

There is no need to waste time over the more obvious of these blunders. No one now believes, as Nennius sometimes did, that the 'Adventus Saxonum' was in 375, and the mistake which led to his belief has probably been traced to its origin: it is fairly safe, too, to regard his other suggestion, 428, as the result of a misunderstanding of Constantius' *Life* of St. Germanus.[1] Other proposals deserve more careful consideration. Bede's opinion wavered between 446–7 and a date a few years later in the joint reign of Marcian and Valentinian III (between 450 and 455); and in the second view he was followed by the compilers of the *Anglo-Saxon Chronicle*, who, with a bungled reference to the same emperors, placed the landing of Hengist and Horsa in 449. On

[1] These points are discussed fully by H. M. Chadwick, *Origin of the English Nation* (ed. 1924), 45 ff.

MAP VI. THE SOUTH-EAST OF BRITAIN

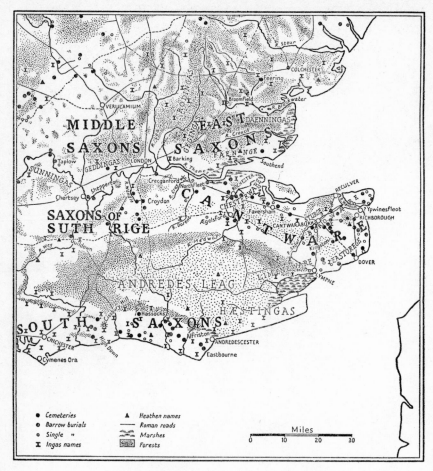

MAP VI. THE SOUTH-EAST OF BRITAIN

the other hand two related south Gaulish chronicles, for both of
which some claims to contemporaneity can be made, dated, not
apparently the beginning, but the completion of the Saxon
conquest of Britain in 438-9 and 441-2 respectively.[1]

The problem seems thus to resolve itself into the question
whether the process of settlement took place during the course
of the first half of the fifth century and reached some advanced
and decisive stage in or before 442, or whether it only began on
an impressive enough scale to be described as the 'Adventus
Saxonum' somewhere in the decade following this date. Here
is a straightforward issue, and one of importance for a true
understanding of the period.

At first sight it must seem that the weight of authority behind
the two views is very unequal, that the probable contemporaneity of the Gaulish chronicles renders their statement im-
mensely more impressive than the theorizings of Bede, who,
careful and conscientious as he was, lived nearly three centuries
later and claimed no definite authority for his never very precise
dating of this point. But there are reasons which lead one to
question this first impression. In the first place a closer inspection of the entries in the chronicles raises doubts of their precise
meaning. If the authors meant by 'Britanniae', as they must
have meant, the Roman provinces of Britain as a whole, their
statements are demonstrably false: for Cornwall was not conquered by the Saxons until the ninth century, and most of
Wales retained its independence until the wars of Edward I.
A contemporary authority capable of making blunders of this
kind has little claim on our confidence: whether or not some
decisive stage in the conquest took place in 438 or in 442, the
chroniclers have expressed themselves in a way which deprives
their statements of any evidential value: what they say is, as it
stands, untrue, and it is a waste of time to conjecture what they
ought to have said. But even if we assume that they meant, not
what they said, but that, for example, the south-east of Britain
as far as the Fosse Way had passed by 442 under Saxon dominion, there is other fifth-century evidence which is hard to
reconcile with such an idea. In Chapter XIX the information

---

[1] *Mon. Germ. Hist.*, *Auct. Ant.* ix. 661, *sub anno* 438-9: 'Britanniae a Romanis
amissae in dicionem Saxonum cedunt'; this chronicle ends in 511; ibid., 660,
sub anno 441-2: 'Brittanniae usque ad hoc tempus variis cladibus eventibusque latae
in dicionem Saxonum rediguntur'; this chronicle ends in 452.

on this point which can be legitimately extracted from the *Notitia Dignitatum* has already been examined. The story of St. Germanus's visits to Britain in 429 and again shortly before his death in 449 has also been discussed. We need only remind ourselves that the defeat of the Saxon and Pict raid in the course of the first visit, and the reception of the saint by a Romano-British nobleman on the second, are sufficient to show that, to put the matter at its lowest, the Saxons were not at that time the only or even the dominant political force in the south-east of England. And it is fair to note also that Gildas, writing here of events only half a century before his birth, speaks of a last and unsuccessful effort of the Britons to secure help from the Roman authorities, an effort dated to the years closely following 446 by a reference to the third consulship of Aetius. Such unusual chronological precision on the part of Gildas must surely cover a genuine tradition and one which rules out the suggestion that the conquest had been in any significant sense completed four years earlier. That it was still far from complete when Gildas was writing in the second quarter of the sixth century, we in fact know from his own contemporary words.

If the views of the south Gaulish chroniclers thus turn out to provide no sure guide to the period at which Saxon settlement on a wide scale began in Britain, is the tradition preserved by Bede of any greater value? Bede, as has been mentioned, uses two different reckonings, neither of which professes to give an exact year for the 'Adventus Saxonum', and he makes no attempt to discuss their respective merits. One places it 'about 446–7',[1] and the other between 450 and 455.[2] It is highly probable that the first of these traditions is based merely on Gildas, for in his narrative the deliberate settlement of federate Saxons in the eastern part of Britain follows, after two chapters only, the appeal to Aetius of 446.[3] For this date, therefore, the authority may be no more than a conjecture, and one with little justification, for while Gildas assigns no duration to the period of British success and consequent decadence which he places between 446 and the Saxon settlement, it is hard to visualize it as no more than twelve months. For the other date, in which, as we have

---

[1] *Hist. Eccles.* i. 23; ii. 14; v. 23.
[2] Ibid. i. 15; v. 24; *De Temp. Rat.*, § 489.
[3] The even closer sequence of the two events in Bede's own account, based on Gildas, in *De Temp. Rat.*, § 483, strongly suggests this inference.

seen, Bede is followed by the compilers of the *Anglo-Saxon Chronicle*, there must, however, have been a source independent of Gildas, for the latter neither mentions nor implies the joint reigns of Marcian and Valentinian which Bede uses to provide the date: it is none the less perfectly consistent with the general course of Gildas's narrative, and with the evidence for the visits of St. Germanus, both of which will fall before the period of settlement began. The literary evidence will take us no farther than this.

It might be supposed that archaeology would be an assistance at this point, for it should surely be possible to say whether the earliest Saxon material which occurs in quantity in Britain belongs to the first or to the second half of the fifth century. Nothing illustrates the limitations of the archaeological evidence for this period better than the fact that this cannot be done with any degree of certainty. The archaeologist can indeed arrange his material in a typological sequence and he can say at what point in that sequence the material from England becomes common enough to justify the assumption of considerable Anglo-Saxon settlement. But unfortunately he cannot directly relate this point to the passage of the years; he is in fact as anxious to learn from the historian the date of the 'Adventus Saxonum' as the historian is to learn it from him, for if the date was once established with certainty it would enable him to argue as from a fixed point both backwards and forwards to the dates of earlier and later material in his evolutionary series.[1]

But if the historian cannot expect much help from archaeology in making up his mind on this question, he has at least, as has been seen, two independent strands of literary evidence pointing to the years round about the middle of the fifth century: Gildas's dating of the arrival of Hengist and Horsa *after* and perhaps fairly soon after the third consulship of Aetius in 446, and Bede's date of unknown origin in the joint reigns of Marcian and Valentinian III (450–5). Two other scraps of evidence may be held to point in the same direction. It has already been

---

[1] The chronology of the archaeological material adopted, for example, by A. Plettke (*Ursprung und Ausbreitung der Angeln und Sachsen*, 65 ff.) is based very largely upon the assumption, here rejected, that the 'Adventus Saxonum' is to be dated to the first decade of the fifth century. F. Roeder's detailed studies of the equal-armed brooches, window urns, &c. (see Bibliography), envisage a dating for the invasion more consistent with that here adopted.

observed (Ch. XIX) that while the British church was still
sufficiently cognizant of continental affairs to adopt the alteration in the mode of calculating Easter which was made in 455,
it was thirty years later so out of touch with Gaul as to be un-
responsive to the further change which took place at that time.
The inference is clear: at some point in those thirty years the
pressure of immigrant Saxons had either established an im-
pervious barrier of heathenism across the natural lines of communication between Britain and Gaul, or had so disorganized
the native church as to render it unconscious of ecclesiastical
changes on the other side of the Channel. Such a state of affairs
might naturally result from the chaos and devastation which in
Gildas's account followed after a brief interval upon the 'Adventus Saxonum'. It may further be argued that the pedigrees
of such of the Anglo-Saxon royal families as provide any evidence for the date of their first establishment in Britain all point
to a period in or after the third quarter of the fifth century for
their arrival. Thus in Kent Hengist and Oisc (from whom
the family were later known as the Oiscingas) occur in the
pedigree in a position quite appropriate to the traditional chronology: Icel, after whom the Mercian kings were called Iclingas, appears five generations above Penda and is thus likely to have
flourished between 450 and 500: and in East Anglia it was traditionally the father of Wuffa (the eponymous hero of the Wuffingas)
who established the kingdom, not earlier probably than 500 since
Wuffa's grandson, Raedwald, was still king after 616. There is
no reason to believe that any of the known dynasties had
British connexions before the middle of the fifth century. Constantius' *Life* of St. Germanus precludes the possibility that
Saxon domination, in south-eastern Britain at any rate, began
much earlier than this, and there is no direct suggestion from
any source of a date for the first settlements later than say 460.
If the 'Adventus Saxonum' is placed within ten years of the
middle of the fifth century, it can hardly be far wrong;[1] and a
useful lead may be given to the archaeologist, which will be
accepted in the following pages in estimating the material evidence for the spread of Saxon settlement.

It has been a matter of some importance to determine this

[1] This must not, of course, be taken as excluding isolated earlier settlements:
the Dorchester (Oxon.) burials (see p. 394) must in any case be earlier than 450.

preliminary inquiry, for, as will soon be clear, the archaeological evidence must play an increasingly large part in forming our picture of the pattern of Teutonic settlement in its early stages in Britain. It is indeed only for Kent and Sussex that we have any information from literary sources attached rightly or wrongly to precise dates within the first forty years after the 'Adventus Saxonum' at all. And although this information is confined to six entries of the *Anglo-Saxon Chronicle* relating to Kent and three relating to Sussex, paralleled as the Kentish entries seem to be by the story in Gildas and Bede and the much fuller if more dubious account in Nennius, it has not unnaturally been regarded in default of evidence for other districts as describing the earliest establishment of the Saxon invaders in Britain. But if, bearing in mind the chronological scheme adopted above, we bring the archaeological evidence to our aid, it will be seen that besides the south-eastern area of Kent and Sussex there were at least two other centres of settlement which are likely to be as early as that of the south-east. Of one of these, which radiates from the Fens and the river valleys which flow into the Wash, there are no literary accounts at all: of the other, focused on the river system of the Humber estuary, it is barely possible to catch a distant echo by reading between the lines of Bede and other seventh- and eighth-century writers.[1] For the rest the story, such as it is, must be built up from the archaeological evidence, checked and supplemented here and there by the information derived from the distribution of the earliest types of place-names. In fact it is clear that contemporaneously with the recorded events in Kent and Sussex, the whole eastern seaboard of Britain was increasingly affected by the penetration of the newcomers.

The next three chapters will be spent upon a survey of this penetration, and the evidence for its course in the three main areas from which it appears to have radiated. And first following the tradition of the earliest settlements let us look at the story in Kent and in the south-east.

The familiar tale of Hengist, Horsa, and Vortigern need hardly be retold at length. It is, however, of some interest to appreciate the stages in the growth of this the most famous of all English historical myths. In its earliest form, that of Gildas, written down within a century of the events described, a possibly

---

[1] See J. N. L. Myres in *History*, xx (1935), 250–62.

deliberate obscurity on the author's part deprives us of such detail of personal names and local topography as he may have known himself: 'a proud tyrant' seeking to repel the repeated devastations of the Picts and Scots planted a colony of Saxons in 'the eastern part of the island', and this colony, repeatedly reinforced from its homeland, eventually turned upon the Britons and perpetrated what seemed to the author a more disastrous raid than any of its predecessors, for it spread from sea to sea and involved a widespread destruction of the surviving Romano-British towns, accompanied by an unparalleled massacre and upheaval of the population. Bede, writing two centuries later than Gildas, gives as a tradition the names of the tyrant Vortigern, the Teutonic leaders Hengist and Horsa with their pedigree, and the facts that Horsa had been killed in battle and that his monument was still to be seen in the eastern parts of Kent:[1] all this Bede learnt no doubt from the ecclesiastical friends at Canterbury whom he mentions as his sources, and so direct from the eighth-century traditions of the Kentish court. The laconic entries of the *Anglo-Saxon Chronicle*, put together in their present form at the end of the ninth century, are derived in part from Bede, but they add topographical details of battles between the invaders and the Britons, some of which from their poetic phraseology are certainly derived from early sagas, no doubt also of Kentish origin: it may be noted that the dating is at least partly artificial, four out of the six entries being suspiciously separated by eight years from one another.[2]

How this straightforward tradition was developed in the Celtic lands before the eighth century was over, and how the story of Vortigern was interwoven with a mass of legend dealing with the miracles of St. Germanus, is amply illustrated in the pages of Nennius and for the most part may be safely ignored by the historian. Some of the more significant elaborations of the story

---

[1] *Hist. Eccles.* i. 15. If there was really a monument to Horsa in Bede's day in eastern Kent, the fact is of considerable interest, for it may imply that the first generation of invaders was here sufficiently in touch with Roman ways to understand the practice of setting up inscribed memorial stones; if so, either some at least among them were literate, or they made use in inscribing the monument of literate sub-Roman masons. But it may be that the monument was a Roman one, and that all parts of the original inscription had disappeared but the letters HORS (from some such word as *cohors*): perhaps the hero himself, whose name is apparently unparalleled, owes his existence solely to what was thought to be his tombstone. For other views see E. Wadstein, *On the Origin of the English* (1927), 28–9.

[2] See Appendix I.

will be noticed later; for the moment it will be enough to observe that its essence probably contains a genuine folk-tradition
going back to the actual period of the settlement. The calling
in as federates of one set of barbarians to defend a frontier
region against another, and the granting of lands and *stipendia*
for their support, ring true to the practice of the fifth century;
while the difficulties caused by the ever-increasing numbers and
ambitions of such *foederati* can be paralleled over and over again
on the Rhine and Danube frontiers of the Roman empire. The
events which led up to the battle of Adrianople in 378, and the
subsequent inrush of Goths into the eastern empire, bear a
striking similarity, though on a much larger scale, to the story of
Hengist and Vortigern in Kent. There is no reason to doubt
that its conquest followed in the first instance a course familiar
enough in the days when the direct enforcement of Roman
authority was steadily shrinking back from the frontier provinces of the empire.

Such an origin for the Teutonic occupation of Kent raises
questions of the greatest interest, some of which will be more
appropriately discussed at a later stage. It will be necessary,
for example, to inquire what bearing such a view may have upon
the peculiar character of later Kentish institutions, the problem
of Romano-British survival,[1] and more immediately upon the
general course of the conquest of southern England. Before
considering this latter question it will be advisable to examine
such other evidence as there may be for the settlement of Kent
itself.

There are two ways in which archaeology may help us to
understand the settlement: the distribution of the pagan cemeteries may reveal the areas which were first or most thickly
populated, and the grave-goods which they contain may
throw light on the cultural affinities of those who used them;
and in the first of these inquiries we may hope to derive some
assistance from the distribution of the earliest types of place-
names.

Following these clues it becomes clear that the pattern of
Teutonic settlement in Kent was determined by physical geography—the principal areas of woodland and marsh—and the
natural and artificial lines of communication represented by the
rivers and the Roman roads. The kingdom of the Cantware

[1] See Ch. XXIV.

grew in fact out of the ruins of Roman Kent; and that had been a region whose social structure, with its numerous towns and still more numerous villas, was one of the most highly developed in the provinces of Britain. That structure was still, it is true, based primarily on those dry and easily cultivable soils beloved of prehistoric man, but it was already extending beyond them into the richer and heavier lands of natural forest. To this pattern in general that of the Teutonic settlement conforms, although here and there it may be possible to catch glimpses of a temporary return to natural conditions in some of the forested areas which had yielded in part to the intensive cultivation of Roman agricultural estates. Thus the marked abundance of villas and other settlements which lined the Medway valley from Rochester as far south as Maidstone in Roman times is only faintly echoed in the early Teutonic distribution. There are no large Jutish cemeteries here far south of the Downs, and only a trickle of early place-names in -*ingas* remains to suggest that some advantage was still taken of the wide clearings of agricultural land which presumably remained from Roman days.

On the other hand, there is, as we should expect with an immigrant culture, a more striking concentration of Teutonic than of Roman remains in the open country of east Kent: both in Thanet, the traditional home of the first *foederati*, and thence thickly up the valleys of the two Stours towards Canterbury and Watling Street, where the village of Sturry still preserves in its name the memory of the primitive 'province of the Stour men', and in its remarkable early cemetery the relics of the men themselves. Between Watling Street and Richborough a group of cemeteries and a scatter of early place-names centre similarly on Eastrey, the *villa regalis* of the early 'eastern district' of the Cantware. The Watling Street and its immediate neighbourhood, forming as it did the great highway of Roman communication from the Channel ports to London and beyond, is likewise marked by cemeteries and early place-names all the way from Dover to the borders of Surrey, and it is especially interesting in the light of barbarian behaviour elsewhere to find that the proximity of each important Roman centre on this route—Dover, Canterbury, Faversham, and Rochester—is marked by considerable Teutonic settlement, and that three of the four became the centres of early administrative districts under the kings of Kent.[1] And if we look southwards across to that other early provincial unit which took its name Lyminge from the Roman coastal fortress of Lemanis (Lympne), we see here too, as everywhere in Kent, that the pattern of Teutonic settlement was based, confusedly perhaps, but still unmistakably, on that of Roman times. More must be said on this point later: its relevance at this stage to the tradition of a first settlement of barbarians in this part of Britain alone within the old order of society needs no further emphasis.

But if in this matter the literary, archaeological, and institutional lines of inquiry seem to lead to a happy convergence, the same can hardly at present be said of our second question: what light do the contents of the Kentish cemeteries throw on the cultural connexions of those who used them? It is possible at least to recognize in these cemeteries the tribal complexity which, as has been shown in the last chapter, was concealed by Bede beneath the enigmatic word Jute. We can distinguish at least two principal cultures and several minor groups.[2] One, represented mainly but not exclusively by settlements on the north coast along the Thames estuary, is that of a people who still on occasion cremated their dead, and whose material equipment relates them most closely to the settlers of the Saxon districts in the upper Thames valley: it is more than probable that their immediate provenance, like that of the less distinctive group who for a time used early cruciform brooches in Kent, was on the *Terpen* of the Frisian sea-board, though the idea that that was

---

[1] It is difficult to understand or to accept Baldwin Brown's statement (*Arts in Early England*, iv (1915), 740–1) that 'Saxon cemeteries have not been found in any obvious connexion with the important Roman urban centres of Kent'. It is avowedly based on a dictum of C. Roach Smith (*Coll. Ant.* vi. 139), and even if true in the mid-nineteenth century can hardly be defended now. Dover has produced at least two Saxon brooches and other remains; Faversham is the site of one of the most famous of all cemeteries of this period; at Rochester Baldwin Brown himself admitted the existence of two cemeteries; and even at Canterbury, which Kendrick has rashly asserted to be surrounded by an area totally immune from Jutish settlement (*Antiquity*, vii (1933), 451), there are certainly one and probably two Saxon vessels in the Museum from the city itself, quite apart from the important neighbouring cemetery at Sturry. For the early administrative divisions of Kent see J. E. A. Jolliffe, *Pre-Feudal England: The Jutes* (1933), ch. i.

[2] Two minor groups may be seen in (*a*) the users of the early cruciform brooches listed from seven sites by N. Åberg, *Anglo-Saxons in England* (1926), 29; and (*b*) the users of saucer-brooches listed from at least six sites by E. T. Leeds, *Archaeologia*, lxiii (1912), 198. Neither seems quite to equate with the first of the two main Kentish cultures, though the three are closely related and largely overlap.

only a stepping-stone from more northerly homes is rendered plausible by their partial retention of the habit of cremation. The other culture, which is more especially characteristic of Kent, is at once thoroughly distinct from that of any other part of Anglo-Saxon England, except for a pale reflection in the Isle of Wight and the neighbouring coast of Hampshire, and is more closely related on the Continent to the Frankish districts of the middle Rhine than to any of the lands bordering on the North Sea. It is marked by a universal practice of inhumation, by wheel-made pottery of sub-Roman character and strongly Frankish technique, by the use of precious metals, garnets, glass, crystal, shells, amethyst beads, and other luxuries in personal adornment, and by a skilful employment of enamel, niello, and filigree techniques unparalleled in any other part of Britain. Within this culture it is possible to distinguish between a more barbaric school of craftsmanship prevalent on the whole in Thanet and the valley cemeteries north and south of Watling Street, and a more delicate and luxurious tradition, whose finest products occur mainly near the line of Watling Street itself, and in the development of which both classical and British factors have sometimes been discerned.[1]

It is unfortunately impossible at present to make much use of the beautiful products of the Kentish jewellers' craft in these centuries in a strictly historical context, for both the absolute dating of the series as a whole and the relative position of different groups of objects and of individual pieces within it are still subject to acute and learned controversy. Some believe that the bulk of this lovely jewellery was already in use about A.D. 500, others that its *floruit* should be put a hundred years later and treated as an artistic counterpart to the political expansion of Kent under the rule of Æthelberht.[2] The historian impressed alternately by the arguments of either school, but convinced by neither, can only use the divergence as an illustration of the archaeological commonplace that the more intrinsically precious and artistically attractive objects are always the

[1] The distinction of these two schools has been worked out by T. D. Kendrick in *Antiquity*, vii (1933), 429–52. Its historical significance, if any, is not generally agreed.

[2] The later dating, still more generally accepted, is best exemplified by Åberg, *Anglo-Saxons in England* (1926); the earlier dating, suggested by S. Lindqvist, *Vendelkulturens Ålder och Ursprung* (1926), is best studied in English in a modified form in Kendrick's article in *Antiquity*, vii (1933), 429–52.

most difficult to date. For on the one hand their beauty and value may lead to exceptionally long use and thus vitiate altogether the evidence derived from humbler associated finds; and on the other it is too often impossible to distinguish, in comparing objects of different degrees of technical perfection and artistic merit, between the effects produced by varying skill in contemporary craftsmen and those due to imitation or mere decadence arising from the passage of time.

What little can be safely deduced by the historian we may now briefly summarize. We see the cultural equipment of the inhabitants of Kent as profoundly different not merely from that of Jutland but from that of the rest of Teutonic England: these differences may in some sense be taken as symbolic of the historical paradox which has simultaneously made Kent the natural channel whereby continental modes and fashions have at all times flowed into the country and yet left it isolated from the rest of England: it has served so often as a cultural bridge, and yet remained culturally unique. And within that unique cultural equipment we can distinguish elements which spring from different sources, and some of these can legitimately be used to tell us more than others. We can safely argue from the differences between the Saxon-Frisian cremation culture of Sturry and Northfleet and the main run of Kentish inhumation cemeteries with their markedly Rhenish affinities to differences of blood and provenance, and the earlier date of the former seems assured; but it may be quite unsafe to see in the distinction between the two main groups of garnet-set jewellery, or even between the barrow burials of Kingston and the flat cemeteries of the Stour valley, anything more than two contemporary fashions. And remembering the tradition of an original treaty settlement, the initial and continuing prosperity of the land, the obvious, if divergent, continental associations, the possibility of British survival, and the proximity of Frankish Gaul, we may well conclude with a recent authority that the Jutish nation 'was made after the conquest. It was to all intents made in Kent.'[1]

If we are to agree with this as a provisional solution of the Jutish question in Kent, we must, it appears, agree also with an important corollary which may be found to affect our whole conception of the settlement of England south of the Thames. Bede, as we have seen, places a *Jutarum natio* not only in Kent

---

[1] R. H. Hodgkin, *History of the Anglo-Saxons* (1935), i. 102.

but also in the Isle of Wight and in a province still in his day called by their name on the mainland opposite the island.[1] Elsewhere he speaks of the river Hamble as flowing through the lands of the Jutes, and describes the efforts made in 685-6 by Caedwalla, king of Wessex, to extirpate the island Jutes and replace them by West Saxons.[2]

Now for the settlement in the Isle of Wight and on the Hampshire coast of a people who were called Jutes and were culturally akin to the inhabitants of Kent there is the strongest possible evidence independent altogether of Bede. The cemeteries of the island, notably that of Chessel Down, have produced almost every object characteristic of Kentish culture except the most elaborate forms of gold and garnet jewellery.[3] On the mainland the memory of Jutish settlement was still preserved after the Norman Conquest in the New Forest, 'which in the tongue of the English is called Ytene',[4] and the name may also be preserved in the tenth-century form *Æt Yting Stoce* applied to what is now Bishop's Stoke in the Itchen valley.[5] That the Meonware in eastern Hampshire were also Jutish has been strongly urged on institutional grounds, and it is a suggestive fact that Droxford in the Meon valley is the site not only of a cemetery with Jutish affinities, but also of a manor whose medieval custom 'strikingly recalls the gavelkind of Kent'.[6] Place-name evidence of a more general kind has also been held to link together Kent and southern Hampshire.[7]

It may be taken as certain that Bede was right in connecting closely the people of these three areas. He can, however, hardly have been right in visualizing that unity as a proof simply of common origin in Jutland, for we have already seen reasons for minimizing the tribal homogeneity of the Cantware, and for believing that their peculiar culture was largely formed in Kent itself. From this it must surely follow that the Hampshire settlements which preserve this association of the name Jute and a Kentish culture are themselves offshoots from Kent at a period

---

[1] See p. 336.   [2] *Hist. Eccles.* iv. 16.
[3] The evidence is well summarized by Baldwin Brown, *Arts in Early England*, iv (1915), 746-51.
[4] Florence of Worcester (ed. Thorpe, ii. 45), *sub anno* 1100.
[5] Grundy in *Arch. Journ.* lxxviii. 112; Karlström, *O.E. Compound Place-names in -ing* (1927), 32.
[6] On the Droxford cemetery see Baldwin Brown, *Arts in Early England*, iv (1915), 745; on its manorial customs J. E. A. Jolliffe, *Pre-Feudal England: the Jutes* (1933), 88, n. 5.   [7] E. Ekwall, *English Place-names in -ing* (1923), 20.

when the latter region had already developed something of its distinctive character.[1]

After all allowance has been made for the uncertainty which surrounds the dating of Kentish antiquities, there is, it would seem, no insuperable objection to this idea. The people of the Isle of Wight seem certainly to have been fond of using discarded Roman trinkets, but that is a habit which they shared with the Cantware and with the South Saxons, and it can hardly be pressed as an infallible sign of very early date. But if, allowing rather over fifty years for the formative period of Kentish culture, we place the settlement of the western offshoots early in the sixth century there are, as it happens, two fragments of literary evidence which, for what they are worth, may be held to corroborate the suggestion. In the first place it is natural to ask what led the Hampshire Jutes to make so long a journey from Kent. Why did they not merely push westwards along the coast and take up the splendid open lands beyond the Pevensey marshes, the Sussex coast plain between the downs and the sea? There can be only one answer: it was already occupied by the South Saxons; only beyond their western limit at Selsey was it possible for the colonists to settle where they are later found on both sides of the channel separating the Isle of Wight from the mainland. Now according to the traditional chronology, which in default of other evidence may be provisionally accepted, the South Saxons first landed in 477 near Selsey Bill, and by 491 they are represented as controlling the coast as far east as Pevensey.[2] Not before the turn of the fifth and sixth centuries, therefore, would circumstances have arisen to make intelligible a Kentish settlement of southern Hampshire and the Isle of Wight. Then secondly it is possible that in a garbled form the compilers of the *Anglo-Saxon Chronicle* have allowed a memory of this very settlement to survive. Under the year 514 the mysterious figures of Stuf and Wihtgar make the first of their brief appearances in the West Saxon annals. Later on it will be necessary to discuss the value of these annals as a whole,[3] but without unduly anticipating that discussion it may here be noticed firstly that the absence in the *Chronicle* of all mention of the Jutes as participating in the settlement of Hampshire and the Isle of Wight is certainly due to the deliberate policy of its compilers; and

---

[1] As is suggested by R. H. Hodgkin, *History of the Anglo-Saxons* (1935), i. 101.
[2] See Appendix I.   [3] See pp. 397–9 and Appendix II.

secondly that while Stuf and Wihtgar are described under the year 534 as closely related to Cerdic and Cynric the founders of the West Saxon royal family, who are represented as conquering the Isle of Wight for their benefit, yet there is excellent testimony of the same date as the *Chronicle* that these heroes were in fact Jutes.[1] This evidence is the more impressive in that it is derived from the family traditions of King Alfred's own mother, who was descended from them, and that it occurs in the work of Bishop Asser, who was himself in all probability closely associated with the king in the compilation of that final version of the *Chronicle* which has come down to us. And whether or not the enigmatic Wihtgar was a fiction evolved perhaps as early as the seventh century out of the Wihtware,[2] the people of the Isle of Wight, his or their association with Stuf, against whose existence no destructive doubts of this kind need be raised, connects the latter inevitably, as does the annal for 534, with the settlement of the island, which we know in any case to have been Jutish. Impossible as it is wholly to disengage the scraps of genuine tradition from the tangle of West Saxon propaganda in which the compilers of the *Chronicle* have embedded them, and unreliable as the precise dating of the whole story may be, we can hardly help regarding as highly significant these hints of Jutish settlement in the Isle of Wight and southern Hampshire at exactly the period to which the other evidence which we have noticed seems to point. Not only, therefore, are we justified in accepting the derivation of these settlements from Kent, but we can also date them with some confidence to the early years of the sixth century.

Between these two related peoples lay, as we have seen, the South Saxons, whose settlement must next claim our attention. There is fortunately no great difficulty connected with them. The story in the *Chronicle* brings their leader Ælle to land at

---

[1] Asser, *Life of King Alfred* (ed. W. H. Stevenson), c. 2. It may be noted that the reading of MS. E of the *Chronicle* s.a. 514 definitely dissociates the victory of Stuf and Wihtgar from the arrival of West Saxons recorded in the same year, while that of MS. A telescopes the two events, thereby creating the impression that the heroes were themselves West Saxons. This is a direct contradiction of Asser's statement; and if it is the correct reading constitutes the clearest evidence for the deliberate elimination of Jutish tradition by the *Chronicle*'s compilers.

[2] The philological objection to the connexion of Wihtgar and the Wihtware has been forcibly stated by W. H. Stevenson, *Eng. Hist. Rev.* xiv (1894), 27. It is to some extent discounted by the appearance of the islanders as Wihtgara instead of Wihtware in the Tribal Hidage.

Cymenes ora with his three sons, Cymen, Wlencing, and Cissa, in 477, and the last that we hear of him is in 491, when a bloody and successful siege of the Saxon Shore fort of Anderida (Pevensey), which had apparently been used as a shelter by Romano-British refugees, ended with a spectacular massacre of its defenders.[1] If it is legitimate to argue from the three brief entries in the *Chronicle*, there is here a suggestion of an eastward movement along the coast from west Sussex, for Cymenes ora may be reasonably identified with the Cumeneshora in the bounds of a Sussex charter, a spot now represented, owing to extensive coastal erosion, only by the Owers Banks off the western shore of the Selsey peninsula.[2]

Ælle and his sons are figures in whom the more critical historians of the past have not felt much confidence. Yet Ælle himself appears again in a famous passage of Bede,[3] as the first of the Saxon Bretwaldas, and this claim, which must be discussed later, is more than enough to confirm his existence: of his sons it need only be said that if Chichester was not called after Cissa it was called after another early hero of this name; that the same may be said, though with rather less confidence, of the relation of Cymen to the traditional landing-place; and that the curious patronymic Wlencing may have something to do with Linchmere and perhaps also with the village of Lancing.[4] If the great stronghold of Cissbury owes its nominal association with the family only to later antiquarian imagination, the guess was for once appropriate enough, for its extensive refortification at this time, after a long disuse in the Roman period, is eloquent of the terror which Saxon raiders and settlers inspired, and shows that early Iron Age camps, as well as deserted Roman forts, could be brought into commission again in times of need.

The main lines of Saxon settlement in Sussex were clearly laid down by the topography of the country and are amply illustrated by the distribution alike of the pagan cemeteries and the earliest types of place-names. It was essentially a coastal settlement separated on the east by the Pevensey marshes from the territory of the Haestingas, who were themselves cut off from

[1] See Appendix I.   [2] Birch, *Cart. Sax.* 64; *Eng. Place-name Soc. Sussex*, i (1929), 83–4; G. M. White in *Antiquaries Journal*, xiv (1934), 399–400.   [3] *Hist. Eccles.* ii. 5.   [4] *Eng. Place-name Soc. Sussex*, i (1929), xiii–xiv, denies the connexion with Lancing; Ekwall, *Oxford Dict. of English Place-names* (1936), s.v., accepts it.

the Limeneware of Kent by the treacherous swamps and varying shingle banks of Romney and Dungeness.[1] On the west
again the low and shifting coast beyond Selsey and Bosham
provided good harbourage but set a natural limit to coastal
settlement, while on the north behind the escarpment of the
Downs the Andredesweald stretched unbroken from the borders
of Kent to the chalk plateau of Hampshire. On the plain between the Downs and the sea, and in the river valleys which
provided ready access for the more adventurous into the wooded
hinterland, the South Saxons established the arable lands of their
'seven thousand families',[2] with increasingly extensive pastures
in the distant Weald. It may not be too fantastic to see in the
distribution of three types of place-names in Sussex the slow
expansion of the original folk: in the -ingas names of the coast-
plain, the river valleys, and the fertile strip of dry land along the
northern base of the chalk escarpment the earliest settlements;
in the -hams which follow so strikingly the course of the river
valleys into the Weald a symbol of the next stage; and finally
in the -tons with their fine disregard of the facts of geography an
unconscious record of final domination over the forces of nature.

The cemeteries may help to elaborate the picture of Sussex
in heathen times. Their distribution, strictly limited to the chalk
downs and their immediate surroundings, is even narrower than
that of the -ingas place-names. In at least two cases, Hassocks
and Ringmer, a burial-place with a long pre-Saxon history was
re-used by the invaders; and these instances may serve as a cor-
rective to the impression of unusual ruthlessness which has
sometimes been drawn from the massacre of Anderida and the
striking absence of Celtic place-names even in the Weald—an
absence, however, which rightly considered means little more
than that permanent settlements in the forest were as rare in prehistoric as in early Saxon times. Although cremation is by no
means so uncommon as is sometimes asserted,[3] the South Saxons
were on the whole an inhuming people, and the fact has some-

---

[1] Archaeological evidence for the Haestingas in the pagan period is at present
lacking; but their early settlement is attested by a group of archaic place-names.
Those familiar with the navigation of this part of the English Channel assure me
that to bring a fleet of open boats to land safely in the Hastings neighbourhood
would be in most states of the weather a more difficult task than on the chalk
beaches west of Beachy Head.   [2] Bede, Hist. Eccles. iv. 13.

[3] It has been recorded on at least five sites: Eastbourne, Hassocks, High Down,
Moulscombe, and Saddlescombe.

times been used to suggest a connexion rather with the Saxon
settlements round Boulogne and in the Seine valley than with
the German homeland. Little comparative evidence is, however, available from these settlements: their place-names usually
quoted in this connexion are indeed certainly Saxon, but they
do not give the impression of such antiquity as the earliest names
in Sussex, and no archaeological material of any kind seems to
be associated with them. While the general culture of the Sussex
cemeteries is markedly Saxon, as may be shown by, for example,
the frequency of saucer-brooches, yet there are certain features
like the button-brooches, garnet-set jewellery, and the prevalence of elaborate glassware, which link it both to Kent and to
the Isle of Wight; and a rather high proportion of objects with
romanizing ornamentation reminds us that the Sussex coast had
been thickly spread with Roman villas, and of the possibility
that the custom of inhumation may have been learnt as well
from the natives of Britain as from those of Gaul. We may think,
if we will, of the 'Saxons who followed Aella to Sussex' as 'campaigning . . . long in France or Britain',[1] but we should bear in
mind that adequate grounds for the suggestion are still to seek.

While a writer of the early eighth century could appropriately
describe Sussex as a 'province which has impregnably resisted
the attacks of other districts owing to the difficulty of the terrain
and the density of the forests',[2] it would be a mistake to over-
emphasize its cultural isolation. That easy contacts by sea with
Kent and the Isle of Wight were responsible for many common
elements in the material equipment of the whole south-eastern
littoral is not difficult to understand: it is more surprising to find
striking similarities between the Sussex cemeteries and those of
Surrey, separated from them by the whole breadth of the Weald.
Here, as in Sussex, there is little or no evidence for pagan Saxon
settlement in the Weald; the cemeteries are to be found either on
the chalk of the Downs or on the well-drained slopes to the north
and south of the plateau, which, like the terraces of the river
valleys that flow through the Downs into the Thames, were to a
large extent spread with gravel and provided those light soils
which the earliest invaders found easiest to work.

Here settled a people closely allied, as their cultural equipment indicates, with the more Saxon elements of the Cantware.

[1] R. H. Hodgkin, *History of the Anglo-Saxons* (1935), i. 106.
[2] Eddius, *Vita Wilfridi*, c. 41.

The Thames must in any case have been the route by which Surrey was settled, and it is in the Wandle valley, the nearest tributary to London, that the earliest remains, including cremation-cemeteries, have been found. Here, too, in close proximity to the Stane Street, which formed the main line of communication across the Weald, are to be noticed at Mitcham and Croydon some of the closest parallels in glass and metalwork to the cemeteries at High Down and Alfriston in Sussex.[1] Other early remains from Guildown, where the river Wey intersects the chalk hills, again include cremations, and illustrate parallel fashions in brooches and pottery with those of Hassocks, Alfriston, and other sites on the south coast. The distribution of the earliest types of place-names here again supplements and confirms the archaeological evidence, hinting, however, at a thicker concentration of early settlements in the Wey valley south of the Downs than the distribution of the cemeteries by itself would suggest. In this south-western part of Surrey, west and south-west of Godalming, there is, moreover, a striking group of places whose names contain those of heathen gods and thus show that the area was populated, however thinly, before the conversion to Christianity.[2] In accepting this interesting result of place-name study at its face value we must, however, notice that this may well have been a corner of England to which the new religion came late. Surrey lay midway between the early centres of missionary activity in Kent and Wessex, and there is in fact no evidence of any Christian enterprise in the county until the establishment of Erconwald's monastery at Chertsey between 664 and 673; nor is even this foundation known to have been a centre of widespread preaching. The survival of pre-Christian religious elements in the place-names between Guildford and Farnham may thus point to the unusually late survival in this area of a living tradition behind the old religion. And bearing this possibility in mind, we may note with interest the fact, in itself perhaps no more than a coincidence, that it is only here and in Sussex, where a late survival of paganism is better docu-

---

[1] R. H. Hodgkin (*History of the Anglo-Saxons* (1935), i. 107) believes that the cultural contacts between Surrey and Sussex were entirely by sea. The distribution of the objects points, however, clearly to the use of Stane Street, and the absence of pagan settlement in the Weald should not be interpreted as implying that the forest constituted an impassable obstacle to passage along the Roman roads through it: in Roman times, too, it was very thinly inhabited, but the roads were built to be used.   [2] *Eng. Place-name Soc. Surrey* (1934), xi–xii.

mented, that place-names are known which combine a word signifying a pagan temple or holy place with the name of its proprietor or priest. Though they may, of course, be much earlier in origin, there was nothing in these two areas to prevent the formation of such names as late as the third quarter of the seventh century.

So far we have considered the factors which link the settlement of Surrey to that of its southern and eastern neighbours in Sussex and Kent. But the name Surrey, Suthrige, the southern district, is there to remind us that at one time its political connexions were with the regions to the north of the Thames. Now there is no period after the end of the sixth century in which the political balance of the southern kingdoms made the evolution of such a name possible. As far back as there is any record Surrey was dependent upon either Kent or Wessex, and it may well be that the entry of 568 in the *Anglo-Saxon Chronicle* shows it passing for good from the orbit of the former to that of the latter kingdom.[1] The name Surrey takes us back, therefore, to a very primitive phase of our political geography, to a time in the early days of the settlement when it 'may have formed the southern province of an early people settled to the north as well as to the south of the Thames'. It has been plausibly suggested that 'a territory comprising both Middlesex and Surrey would be large enough to support one of the smaller peoples of the sixth century'.[2] It may thus be appropriate to consider at this point the somewhat meagre evidence for the early history of the districts on the north side of the Thames estuary.

Of the origin of Middlesex practically nothing is known. While its name belongs to a series of which the other members, Essex, Sussex, and Wessex, were all in historical times independent political units with well-established dynasties of their own, Middlesex was already dependent on Essex before the earliest time to which our records refer, and no traces are preserved of a separate royal family. A cemetery at Shepperton, marked by cremation-urns as well as inhumation-burials, belonged clearly to the same early group of river-side settlers as the Mitcham-Croydon folk in Surrey, or the Northfleet Saxons in Kent; and an ill-explored settlement at Hanwell, which was probably of the same people, practically completes the total of

---

[1] 'in this year Ceawlin and Cutha fought with Æthelberht and drove him into Kent . . .'   [2] *Eng. Place-name Soc. Surrey* (1934), xiv, xv.

our archaeological knowledge. That Middlesex itself contained in early times one or more of those *regiones* which we have seen to characterize the primitive Teutonic settlement of much of south-eastern England can be seen from an eighth-century charter in which Æthelbald of Mercia speaks of the *regio* called Geddinges (Yeading) in the *provincia* of the Middle Saxons.[1] From the seventh century onwards, at any rate, the history of Middlesex was dominated by that of a reviving London, and it is a matter of some difficulty which will be considered in the final chapter to assess the part played in the period of settlement by this same factor; it is interesting to guess, but not easy to determine, the significance in this connexion of the fact that in very early times the Saxon settlers round the metropolis were given a name which places them in the same political company as the distinct and powerful units of Wessex, Essex, and Sussex. After the end of the sixth century at least the implied comparison could hardly have been less appropriate.[2]

East and north from the Middle Saxons lay the kingdom of Essex, embracing in historic times not only the county of that name and, as we have seen, Middlesex and London, but also the greater part of Hertfordshire. The evidence for the settlement of this area presents us with difficulties of interpretation of a kind which have not confronted us elsewhere. In Sussex and Kent, in spite of minor problems, there is a general consensus between the archaeological and place-name evidence; even in Surrey and Middlesex there is no real conflict, and it is possible to attribute the apparent scantiness of the cemeteries in the latter county in part at least to the density of later population in the vicinity of London and to the consequent widespread disturbance of the natural ground-levels by centuries of unrecorded building and commercial exploitation. But the almost complete absence of pagan Saxon remains in rural Essex and Hertfordshire is a phenomenon which demands different treatment. Apart from two or three sites near Shoeburyness and Southend where remains of markedly Kentish character have been found, an isolated and luxurious burial also of Kentish

[1] Birch, *Cart. Sax.* 182. The charter is itself a late copy.
[2] The distinct nomenclature of Middlesex and of its southern appendage Surrey, and the traces of primitive provincial divisions which each contains, are among the hints which suggest that in the formative period of Saxon settlement London was a completely negligible factor in the political geography of the Thames basin: it did not lend its name to a Saxon *provincia*, as, for example, Lindum did to Lindsey.

type at Broomfield, some ill-explored but apparently extensive cemeteries near Feering and Kelvedon, and a few remains in the area round Colchester, the archaeological map of Essex in this period is practically blank, and it would be difficult on these grounds to argue for any considerable occupation in pagan times except on the less marshy parts of the coast-line. Yet it is difficult to agree with such an interpretation. For not only is it certain from the literary evidence that the kingdom of Essex was by the beginning of the seventh century a political unit of sufficient vigour to control the development of the port of London, but the extensive distribution of primitive place-names, both of those in -*ingas* and of those containing the names of pagan deities, strongly suggests a widespread pre-Christian occupation not only on the coast-line but far into the forested interior.

Many reasons have been put forward to account for the absence of archaeological remains in Essex, but it can hardly be said that any wholly satisfactory solution of the problem has been given. It can be plausibly argued, for example, that a treacherous shore well protected by quicksands, and backed by a tangle of forest extending for miles over a desolate expanse of London clay, constituted as unattractive a prospect for the early settler as was offered by any part of the English coast; but the distribution of the early place-names, mainly, it is true, on the drift gravel of the river valleys, is there to warn us against overestimating the deterrent effect of such surroundings on the East Saxon folk. And if, on the other hand, we are tempted to think that the settlers may quickly have abandoned both cremation, which is not known in Essex at all, and the deposition of relics with the inhumed bodies, which is here only less uncommon, under the influence of a country-side which, like that of Kent, had been 'Romanized to an extent unparalleled elsewhere',[1] a glance at the map of Roman Britain will remind us that south and central Essex at least is in fact almost as devoid of Roman as it is of Saxon archaeological remains. No single villa-estate is known between the Thames, the Blackwater, and the road from London to Chelmsford; and the only traces of Roman occupation in this whole area apart from a couple of potteries and a longshore village or two on Thames-side, and the coastal fort at Bradwell on the Blackwater, consist

[1] R. E. M. Wheeler, *London and the Saxons* (1935), 58.

B b

of a few poverty-stricken hamlets on the marshland by the Crouch and three or four indeterminate and closely related sites huddled together in the central forest. Hardly any area in southern Britain outside the Weald gives archaeologically such an impression of poverty and backwardness as the centre and south of Roman Essex.[1]

It may well be, however, that this poverty of the Roman background is itself the clue to the scarcity of Anglo-Saxon remains. An area such as this was hardly one to invite the attention of raiders outside the immediate environs of the Roman towns. The more vigorous and enterprising bands of settlers in the age of conquest turned naturally to the exploitation of those parts of Britain whose natural advantages of soil and situation had already brought about the most extensive agricultural development under Romano-British enterprise. These regions were doubly attractive: not only were they blessed by nature, but the hand of man had already accomplished much of the preliminary work of turning virgin scrub into arable and pasture, and had at the same time rendered access and communication easy for the new-comers. But the greater part of Essex had not apparently been developed in this way: it lay still under the immemorial domination of oak, ash, and thorn. We should therefore expect here to find Anglo-Saxon penetration occurring comparatively late in time after the more attractive areas had been occupied already, and to be the work of a weaker and less ostentatious body of invaders, a people whose failure to compete successfully with their more vigorous neighbours in the struggle for the best land might be reflected archaeologically in the poverty of their material equipment. And it would not be surprising if traces remained to suggest that the settlers, when they came, took advantage of such areas of previous habitation as they might find in the forest, and made them the centres of their own pioneering activities.

These conditions seem all to be fulfilled by the known data for Essex. The scarcity of recorded pagan cemeteries and the meagreness of their grave-goods are best explained by a combi-

---

[1] See *Map of Roman Britain* (Ordnance Survey, 1928). In the whole of Rochford Hundred, for example, no Roman building is known, 'nor have the foundations of one been located': W. Pollitt, *Archaeology of Rochford Hundred and south-east Essex* (1935), 26. Farther north round Colchester the country-side had been more extensively cleared for the lands of the Roman colony, and here, significantly enough, the Saxon remains approach a more normal frequency.

nation of late date and material poverty. No traditions either of the antiquity or the prowess of the early kings of Essex were strong enough to find their way into the *Anglo-Saxon Chronicle* or the pages of Bede, and the only point of interest in their genealogy, their descent from Seaxneat rather than from Woden, wargod ancestor of all the other noble dynasties of England whose pedigrees are extant, is itself an echo of a different, and perhaps inferior, social status. Taking all the evidence into consideration we find no reason to believe that the settlement of Essex had progressed far before the middle of the sixth century.

Some further light on its character may be thrown by a study of early place-names. Here, as in Sussex and Kent, the groupnames in *-ingas* are the most useful, and the Essex examples are of peculiar interest from several points of view. In the first place they show a remarkable contrast to those of Sussex, whose distribution in the regions of earliest settlement suggests a number of small but distinct communities jostling one another for a share of the available land. But whereas in Sussex two or three different *-ingas* names may occur within the limits of the same modern parish, it is more usual to find in Essex one such name covering a group of contiguous parishes, like the eight Rodings which spread over a district of more than twenty square miles.[1] In contrast with the Sussex examples it is only possible to regard this phenomenon as the result of the gradual expansion of a scanty population based on a few scattered centres over the untouched lands which surrounded their original clearings. Thus something of the same provincial groupings may have grown up in Essex as in Kent, with the difference that here the provinces or *regiones* were often the result of the expansion and subdivision of a single folk, and thus sometimes retained the original group-name in *-ingas*. On the other hand, in more densely populated Kent they were the product of co-operative fusion between contiguous but not necessarily related groups, and their names in consequence are never group-names in *-ingas* but are normally those of their administrative centres.[2] We have thus further proof of the sparseness of the original settlement in Essex, and it is interesting to note further that such names of early

---

[1] See J. H. Round, *Commune of London* (1899), 12.

[2] See J. E. A. Jolliffe, *Pre-Feudal England: the Jutes* (1933), 39 ff. and map p. 94, for the early *provinciae* of Kent. The Limeneware, Boroware, and Chesterware were all named from administrative centres which had been Roman walled sites: the others, except Eastrey, bear the names of Teutonic *villae regales*.

regiones as are not, like the Rodings or Bede's *in Berecingum* (Barking), simple patronymics, seem often to have been drawn from
the ever-present environment of forest or marsh in which the
settlers lived. Such are, for example, the 'Fen folk' of Vange,
who may once have covered a wide area among the creeks and
marshes of Thames-side, and the Daenningas or 'forest-dwellers'
of Dengie Hundred, whose *regio* (the word used of them in an
eighth-century charter) probably included in early times the
whole country between the Blackwater and the Crouch.[1] These
names are altogether consistent with our tentative picture of
Essex in the sixth century: they carry us back to an atmosphere
of wild and undrained country in the greatest possible contrast
to the sub-Roman, almost suburban, environment in which the
culture of contemporary Kent was flourishing.

None the less it may be possible to see in the distribution of
these early folk-names in Essex a hint that the invaders took
advantage of the few clearings which their predecessors had
made in the forest in Roman times. Thus the Rodings land
had been traversed by a secondary Roman road, and two minor
occupation-sites are known to have existed near the north and
south ends of it; while the Gegingas, whose territory lay in the
valley of the Wid along the main road from London to Chelmsford, may also have included on their eastern border the only
three small Roman sites that are known in this part of the forest.
On the Thames estuary and the marshy coast there is a similar
and unmistakable correlation between the Roman river-side
settlements and the line of early names from Barking to Vange;
and the same is true of the waterways and islands on the south
of the Crouch. But one can hardly argue from such parallelism
to continuity of occupation, still less to strong cultural influence
of the earlier on the later people. If these areas were still populated by Britons in the sixth century they were hardly of a kind
whose culture was worth borrowing. The East Saxons, faced
with a task which had daunted all previous inhabitants of Essex,
were not unnaturally content, in the choice of these spots among
their earliest centres, to follow the lines of least resistance.

Thus far we have surveyed the separate and widely different
conditions under which the earliest Teutonic settlements in the
south-eastern parts of Britain took place. It has been necessary
in so doing to emphasize the differences rather than the like-

[1] *Eng. Place-name Soc. Essex* (1935), xxiii.

nesses between the component kingdoms and provinces of this area. It is hard at first to see much common ground between the prosperous and well-organized Cantware, with their sumptuous practice of inhumation, and the backward pioneers of Essex, who had little or nothing to spare for their dead; and it is easier to contrast than to compare the habits of either with those of the cremation-folk of Surrey or with the mixed traditions of the Sussex Downs. But it may be as well to remind ourselves of the other side of the picture. Many of the differences which strike us so strongly may have arisen like the Jutish culture of Kent itself in the course of the sixth century after the main lines of the settlement had been laid down: they may be the product of secondary and subsequent causes, differing in different localities. Are there reasons for believing that behind these contrasts lurks anything approaching a common story for the age of settlement itself?

To some extent we have already offered an affirmative answer to this question. We have seen grounds for believing that the settlers of Kent were closely related in blood to those of Hampshire and the Isle of Wight; that elements of their culture were shared by the Saxons of Sussex, who had much in common with those of Surrey; and that the latter in their turn were certainly derived from a branch of the same folk as the Northfleet Saxons of Kent. What little we know of the archaeology of Essex can be paralleled more closely in Kent and Sussex than in the culture of its nearer neighbours in East Anglia or the Cambridge region.[1]

It would be easy to supplement these similarities by the evidence of institutions and place-names. The primitive institutional community of the whole area south of the Thames between the Kentish coast and the Hampshire plateau has so impressed a recent investigator that he has claimed the complete region as a 'Jutish South-east'; and even if this explanation of the phenomena does not win general acceptance, the similarities are none the less there.[2] And there are striking parallelisms, too, between the earliest strata of the place-names in all the districts we have been considering. The evidence is detailed and not all the de-

---

[1] The political isolation of Essex from East Anglia in this period can be further illustrated from the disuse of the roads which in Roman times connected them. See C. Fox, *Archaeology of the Cambridge Region* (1923), 285 and map.

[2] J. E. A. Jolliffe, *Pre-Feudal England: the Jutes* (1933), 73 ff.

tails are necessarily relevant, but as a whole they possess a cumulative force. Thus the same personal name underlies Barling (Essex) and the two Birlings of Sussex and Kent; there is Cocking in Kent and another in Sussex; the Feering, Patching, and Tillingham of Essex are paralleled by the Ferring, Patching, and Tillingham of Sussex; while the Bobbing, Halling, and Terlingham of Kent are matched by the Bobbingworth, Hallingbury, and Terling of Essex. It may be no accident that Eashing in Surrey contains a name early confused with that of the Oiscingas, the royal family of Kent. And quite apart from the personal names we have the opinion of those best qualified to judge that the nomenclature of Surrey, for example, 'presents many features in common with that of . . . Kent, Sussex, and Hampshire'.[1] Not all these features, of course, belong to the earliest age, but when all allowance is made for later developments as well as for the different strains of Saxon and Jute there remains enough to suggest far back in the past a basic community of settlement and interest among the peoples of south-eastern Britain.

At this point it is legitimate to inquire what light the literary sources can throw upon the question. It is useless to expect from Gildas, whose narrow western vision was limited by racial prejudice and by dearth of accurate information, any detailed account of the activities of Saxon and Jutish settlers far away in Kent or Sussex. His general picture of the course of events in the second half of the fifth century is none the less valuable, and must be treated with respect, not only because we have no other guide, but for the better reason that in the latter part of his story at any rate he was commenting on events within his own and his readers' memory. It will be remembered that his narrative is the earliest to suggest that a treaty settlement of some kind underlay the first occupation of the Saxons, and all subsequent writers from Bede and Nennius onwards have placed the scene of these events in Kent. And while it would be foolish to regard the detailed elaborations of the *Historia Brittonum* as sober history, it is interesting in this connexion to observe that in the eighth or ninth century it was already thought that the lands won by this treaty settlement before the general outburst which put an end to all peaceful relations between Briton and Saxon were by no means limited to the eastern parts of Kent. Vortigern's authority was thought of as extensive: after the first settle-

[1] *Eng. Place-name Soc. Surrey* (1934), xx.

ment of the invaders in Thanet, he proceeded in return for Hengist's daughter to hand over the rest of Kent without consulting its local king, and finally, after the murder of the British chieftains and his own capture, he recovered his freedom by the more interesting surrender of Essex, Sussex, and Middlesex.[1] The details of the story are worthless, but after what has been said above we can hardly ignore this further underlying hint of a common framework beneath the Teutonic settlement of the whole south-eastern area.

Returning to the firmer ground of Gildas's account[2] we find that the break-down of relations between the federate Saxons and their British employers was followed by a period of chaos during which barbarian raiding spread rapidly in every direction even to the western sea, the towns were destroyed, and the native population was subjected to the alternatives of massacre, flight, slavery, and emigration. This period of disaster, whose duration is not indicated, was ended by a restoration of British confidence under the leadership of a *vir modestus*, Ambrosius Aurelianus, whose personal qualities coupled with his Roman name and distinguished ancestry were adequate to stem the tide of conquest. Finally, after a period of alternating victory and defeat, an end was put to further Saxon advance by a great slaughter of the invaders at the *obsessio montis Badonici*; and the interval of peace and quiet following this event, which Gildas places in the year of his own birth, was still continuing at the time when he was writing, perhaps over forty years later, and in any case in the second quarter of the sixth century.

We shall never know where Mons Badonicus was, nor who besieged whom at the famous siege: nor is it possible to extract from the contradictory chronology of our various sources the exact year in which this outstanding event took place. But it does seem possible to narrow it down to the period between 490 and 516, and though the limits are all too wide, they do at least give us the vital information that for some years before this time the Saxon penetration of southern England had been hotly contested, and that, for the greater part of the first half of the sixth century, it had altogether stopped.[3]

It will be necessary to come back later to the bearing which this established chronology may have on the traditional story

---

[1] *Hist. Britt.*, chs. 37 and 46.
[2] Gildas, chs. 24–6.   [3] See Appendix III.

of the foundation of Wessex.[1] It is more interesting, as well as more important, to relate it, if possible, to such information as can help us to understand the course of the Saxon conquest of south-eastern England. We may remind ourselves of the two groups of traditions in the *Anglo-Saxon Chronicle* dealing with the establishment of Hengist's dynasty in Kent between 449 and 488, and that of Ælle in Sussex between 477 and 491;[2] and we may remember also Bede's notice of the latter hero as the first of the kings of the Anglo-Saxons who established an *imperium* of some sort over all his Teutonic neighbours.

Of the dates in the Kentish annals the first and the last are alone likely to be significant, for the intervening episodes from some saga of Hengist and Æsc are fitted artificially into the annalistic scheme,[3] and are not important for the present purpose. Since the initial date 449 comes probably from the influence of Bede and is quite consistent with Gildas's story, the only additions to our chronology here are thus the accession of Æsc, following presumably the death of Hengist in 488, and his reign of twenty-four years, culled probably from some regnal list, taking the story down to 512; after which complete darkness descends on Kent until after the middle of the sixth century.

Bede's reference to the Bretwaldaship of Ælle has always been a matter for bewilderment to the historians of this period, for in later times the isolated and backward Sussex was perhaps the least likely of all the Teutonic kingdoms to have established a supremacy of this sort. Such reasoning, however, ignores the distinction between the mobile commands of the age of settlement and the territorial monarchies which later grew out of them: and in fact the very improbability of the story in the conditions prevailing after the middle of the sixth century is the strongest guarantee of its essential truth. Even the most fervent South Saxon patriot would hardly think of inventing such an unlikely tale; nor, if there was any suspicion of its authenticity, should we expect to find it reported without comment by Bede. Now the last that is known of Ælle is his conduct of the siege of Anderida in 491. There is no means of knowing when he died, but he is hardly likely, if the date 477 given for his landing is

---

[1] See pp. 399, 402.   [2] See Appendix I.

[3] Note the regular spacing of the events at intervals of eight years after 449: 457, 465, 473. To avoid confusion I follow the *Chronicle* in calling Hengist's successor Æsc, though there is little doubt that his name was Oisc, as in Bede and the genealogies.

approximately accurate, to have outlived his contemporary Æsc in Kent. He must have died at the end of the fifth or early in the sixth century, and it is clear that his Bretwaldaship died with him. Into such obscurity in fact did the house of Sussex fall that not even the names of Ælle's successors as her kings are known for more than two hundred years.

The relevance of these Saxon traditions to the British tale of Gildas can scarcely be mistaken. The chronology of the two stories dovetails together in the most convincing way. It can hardly be a coincidence that the career of the kings of Kent and Sussex, hitherto marked by triumphant victories, plunges into obscurity in the very period in which we know that the British rally under Ambrosius Aurelianus was bearing fruit, and loses itself altogether with the death of Æsc six years before the last possible date for Mons Badonicus. It is hardly surprising to find Æsc himself figuring in later Celtic story as the Saxon leader at that obscure but decisive encounter. Nor need we be troubled by the absence of all mention of it among the traditions of the invaders: it is easy to see that the break-up of the hegemony of Ælle and the political impotence which followed Mons Badonicus in Kent and Sussex were topics over which Teutonic folk-memory preferred to draw a veil.

We are now in a position to bring together the scattered threads of the evidence and to weave them, without any undue dogmatism, into a coherent fabric. We may begin with the treaty settlement of federates in Thanet in the middle of the fifth century and the inroads of cremating Saxons in the Thames valley and Surrey. We can see them, if we think fit to use for a moment the spectacles of Nennius, extorting, under the able leadership of Hengist, extensions of their original territories to include first the rest of Kent itself and then perhaps a wider concession in Essex and Middlesex, of which little use seems to have been made; the arrival of Ælle and his Saxons on the Sussex coast may perhaps have been encouraged or accompanied by similar arrangements. In the second generation at any rate this adventurer won his way to a general *imperium* over the whole Teutonic complex, and with the final rupture of relations with the British encouraged his followers to the widespread raiding and destruction of which Gildas so bitterly complains, and of which the settlement of Kentish offshoots in southern

Hampshire and the Isle of Wight may remain as one permanent memorial. Roused at length from their demoralized confusion by the ability of Ambrosius the Britons recovered confidence, and after a period of unstable equilibrium the struggle reached its turning-point at Mons Badonicus. The Teutonic supremacy represented by the Bretwaldaship of Ælle collapsed, and in place of irresponsible raiding and indiscriminate and scattered settling all over the south and southern midlands of Britain, the invaders fell back upon an intensive occupation of their more easily exploitable bases on the coasts and rivers of Kent, Essex, Surrey, Sussex, and Hampshire. Here they drove their roots firmly into the soil, and in so doing began to lose the memory of common military action in the localized problems of forest-clearing and land-reclamation, while the leading families of the earlier age not unnaturally found themselves playing a fresh role as the established dynasties of new territorial states. And while geographical position and local environment led in Kent to a growing prosperity based on trade and commercial inter-course with the Continent, and the same factors brought a cer-tain stagnation to isolated Sussex, the East Saxons only half emerged from complete obscurity by an ill-matched union of primitive pioneering in the forests and a dubious control over a London whose revival depended more upon the activities of the Cantware than on their own. Such a reconstruction of the course of the Saxon conquest in south-eastern Britain seems at least to harmonize as well as can be expected the sometimes discordant notes of all our evidential instruments.

XXII

THE FENLANDS, EAST ANGLIA, AND THE PROBLEM OF WESSEX

IT is necessary to consider next the even more obscure circumstances which made the Fenland, between what were later known as East and Middle Anglia, a focus for the early Teutonic settlement of the midlands. In this inquiry we have no literary sources of any kind to help us, and the main reason for their absence is easy to understand. The forces of nature which made this region one of the greatest highways for the penetration of settlers from the east have simultaneously deprived it of those natural frontiers and easy lateral communications which were essential for the formation of a territorial state.[1] Such states grew up in the sixth century and later round the fringes of our area, and some were better placed and better led than others, and so cut a finer figure in historic times. Even so there were few that preserved echoes of early tradition to the days of Bede and Alfred. But in no part of England can the essential contrast between the age of settlement and that of consolidation be more strikingly illustrated than round the margin of the Fens, for it was there, on ground afterwards the borderland between the conflicting territorial interests of East Anglia, Mercia, and Northumbria, that the earliest Anglo-Saxon communities of the midlands had their unremembered homes. The sagas of their noble families were lost in the welter of later political discord: the settlers themselves lacked in the critical period the conservative and centralizing forces of a royal court or an episcopal *familia* which helped elsewhere to turn the local traditions into annals, and to perpetuate the memory of kings and the years of their reigns; and in default of these factors they became a people who have no memorial. The very names of their more prominent groups, such as the Gyrwe, are preserved only accidentally in later writers, and others more obscure can be read in the mysterious catalogue of the Tribal Hidage;[2] and from this barely intelligible relic of the alien administration of seventh-century

[1] The geographical aspects of the Fenland at this period are discussed by H. C. Darby in *Antiquity*, viii (1934), 185–201.

[2] A facsimile and transcription of the Tribal Hidage can be found in R. H. Hodgkin, *History of the Anglo-Saxons* (1935), ii. 389. It contains a list of tribal units together with the number of hides attributed to each.

Mercia the most painstaking research has succeeded only partially in restoring the local nomenclature of some of the earliest folks on the margin of the Fens. But these scanty records give us little but names. It is rather the graves of the dead, their distribution and their contents, which remain to convince us that here in the earliest days lay some of the crucial and most populous centres of the Anglo-Saxon people.

At all periods in our prehistory, it would seem, the estuary of the Wash, and the winding waterways which led west and south-west from its shallow and variable shore, have acted as a magnet to successive hosts of invaders, and the ships of the Saxons pressing on their silent way through the Fens were but following the course of many earlier craft bearing peoples only less civilized. It is, however, by no means certain that the earliest of the Saxon parties who entered England by this easy route found the Fenland through which they passed such a forbidding and desolate waste of waterlogged country as is often supposed. For while it has until recently been commonly thought that the whole area except for occasional patches of rising ground such as the Isle of Ely, Crowland, or March remained through prehistoric, Roman, and Saxon times an uninhabitable morass, our knowledge has been revolutionized of late by the use of air photography, and by the excavation of a few of the numerous habitation-sites whose existence has been revealed by this means.[1] From this important work has emerged, in addition to remarkable evidence for occupation in the Bronze Age and even earlier times, the fact that in the Roman period large areas of the Fenland which are now only rendered habitable by elaborate systems of drainage were populous and highly cultivated, for they display many sites of native villages and groups of associated Celtic fields. It is not certain at present how far this intensive exploitation was made possible by natural and how far by human agencies. It may be that both a higher elevation of the land in relation to the sea, and also an extensive system of dykes and causeways constructed by Roman engineers —of which traces still remain[2]—played their part. Nor do we

---

[1] The activities of the Fenland Research Committee are the main source of this new understanding of the Fens. For a summary of its important work on the Roman village site of Welney see *Antiquity*, x (1936), 94.

[2] The Car Dyke is the best known of these artificial waterways. Its importance in determining the character of Saxon settlement in the Cambridge region is discussed by T. C. Lethbridge, *Camb. Antiq. Soc. Comm.* xxxv (1935), 90–6.

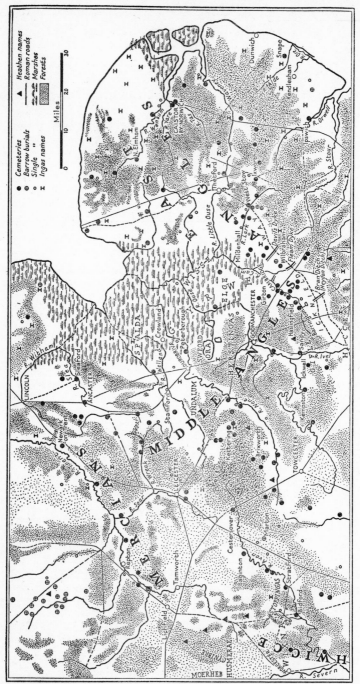

MAP VII. THE FENLAND SETTLEMENT AREA

know how long the exploitation continued: if the evidence of
the sites hitherto excavated can be taken as typical, it would
appear that the southern fenland at least was tilled and occupied down to the end of the Roman period. Whether in the
first half of the fifth century the general sinkage of land-levels
on both sides of the North Sea produced here some of the same
disastrous effects which, as we have seen, may have contributed
to the emigration of the Anglo-Saxon peoples from Frisia and
north Germany, or whether, as is highly probable, this area was
early the scene of Saxon devastation and the artificial drainage
system was soon wrecked by the break-down of the old society
and by the ignorance and carelessness of the new-comers, is not
clear. But it is legitimate to guess that by the second half of the
century, when the invaders were themselves settling down to
systematic agriculture, the Fenland had not only gone out of
cultivation but had become largely uncultivable, for the Saxons
in the pagan period and for centuries afterwards made little
serious attempt to settle in it. Even the islands were regarded
in the seventh and eighth centuries as places so surrounded and
infested with material and spiritual horrors as to be unfit for
normal human habitation, and suitable only for the occupation
of the most holy ascetics. Nothing illustrates better the horrid
fascination which the Fens held for the Anglo-Saxon mind than
the vivid description given by his early biographer of St. Guthlac's life at Crowland 'among the murky thickets of the more inaccessible solitude', of his wretched hovel constructed apparently
in the remains of a chambered tumulus, and of his incessant
struggles with demons whose antics seem inextricably mingled
in the saint's disordered mind with the more mundane if no
less disturbing activities of Celtic-speaking Britons, 'those bitter
enemies of the Saxon people', who still survived in this haunt of
lost souls and masterless mortals.[1] The contrast between this
picture and that of the prosperous agricultural landscape which
the air photographs show us in this area in the fourth century
demonstrates as nothing else can the return to primitive conditions of life which the coming of the English here at any rate
involved.

In the Fenland proper then the early settlers did not make
their homes, and there is no reason to believe that they ever
attempted the construction of artificial habitation-mounds upon

[1] Felix, *Vita Guthlaci* (Birch, *Memorials of S. Guthlac* (1889), § 19).

its borders similar to those with which many of them must have been familiar on the flooded Frisian coast. Here such expedients were unnecessary, for it was possible and more pleasant to follow the river valleys till they passed out of the swamps, and to settle on the gravel terraces and more easily drained soils beyond. The distribution of the cemeteries shows that this process began early and soon brought a mass of settlers into permanent homes. They poured into west Suffolk by the valley of the Lark; they settled thickly on the upper Cam, especially in and around the little Roman town which occupied the site of Cambridge, and farther on about Barrington and Haslingfield; they penetrated up the Ouse into central Bedfordshire, and its tributary the Ivel took the ancestors of the Gifle and the Hicce of the Tribal Hidage to their later homes; farther north other bands, separated from the last by the wooded tract which afterwards gave its name to the Herstingas, pressed up the Nene and its tributaries and settled over much of Northamptonshire; beyond what is now Rockingham Forest were still others following the Welland into Rutland and Leicestershire, and perhaps farther afield across the watershed and down the Wreak and the Soar towards the Trent. And finally along the northern limits of the Fenland it was easy to work up the Witham and the Slea towards Ancaster or to find a way to the drier ground of the south Lincolnshire wolds.

Such were the main areas of settlement opened up by the invaders who found their way into the Wash. In no other region of England is there such a significant concentration of grave-goods for which a really early date can be taken as reasonably certain. To mention only those objects whose manufacture before the end of the fifth century is generally agreed, we may note the occurrence of cruciform brooches at Mildenhall, West Stow Heath, and Ixworth in north-west Suffolk; at Trumpington, Girton, Soham, Malton in Cambridgeshire as well as four from Cambridge (St. John's) itself; and finally from Brixworth in Northamptonshire.[1] Primitive brooches of a kind represented nowhere else in England have been found at Luton and Kempston in Bedfordshire[2] and equal-armed brooches at Haslingfield and Little Wilbraham (Cambs.) and again at Kempston (Beds.). If we turn to the early ceramic evidence there

---

[1] Listed by N. Åberg, *Anglo-Saxons in England* (1926), 184.

[2] Both illustrated by R. H. Hodgkin, *History of the Anglo-Saxons* (1935), i. 113.

is the unique English example of a spout-handled urn from Great
Addington (Northants.) and primitive window urns from Haslingfield and Girton (Cambs.), Kempston (Beds.), and from
Stamford on the borders of Lincoln and Rutland.[1] Some of the
earliest types of ordinary cremation-urns known in England
have come from Little Wilbraham, Girton, and Cambridge
(St. John's); Ickwell and Sandy (Beds.); and Kettering (Northants.). In the uncertainty of the archaeological chronology it
would be unwise to argue from any one of these instances to a
settlement before A.D. 500, but the cumulative effect of such a
catalogue is irresistible, and there need be little reason to doubt
that the Teutonic settlement of the lands radiating from the
Fens had already made much progress before the end of the
fifth century. The point is well brought out on Map X.

Here as everywhere it is interesting to observe the relation
of these sites to the areas most thickly populated in Roman
times. The contrast between the condition of the Fens themselves in the two periods has already been noticed. But this very
exceptional area apart, it can easily be seen that the general
distributions of Roman and Saxon population are markedly
similar. In both there are concentrations in the Lark and Cam
valleys notably round Cambridge; and in Bedfordshire, Northants., and south Lincolnshire a tendency for the two distributions to converge upon the same areas is clear enough. A closer
examination will, however, reveal significant minor differences.
In Roman times it seems that more than a beginning had here
been made with the clearing and exploitation of the forest.
Both in the upland clay belt that separates this area from Essex
and again west of Cambridge there are signs of Roman penetration of the woodland, and it has been pointed out that in its
decided preference for the lighter and more easily worked soils
the early Anglo-Saxon population shows a closer parallelism
with that of the Bronze Age than with that of Roman times.[2]
So, too, the break-down of trade and industry could hardly be
better illustrated than by the abandonment of the Roman pottery centres round Castor and Durobrivae with their halo of
prosperous villas in the surrounding country-side and the re-

[1] For the dating of the window urns and equal-armed brooches see F. Roeder
in *XVIII. Bericht der röm. german. Kommission* (1928), 149; *Jahrb. der Prov. Museums
Hannover*, v (1930).
[2] See C. Fox, *Archaeology of the Cambridge Region* (1923), 224, 274-5, 296, and
his distribution-maps.

appearance in early Saxon times of Peterborough, an important prehistoric site, as the natural focus of the Nene valley where it enters the Fens. On the other hand the concentration of Saxon settlements in and around Cambridge in the earliest period serves to remind us that the building of the Roman roads and the canalizing of traffic which they implied had permanently modified the lines of natural communication and made it both necessary and possible for the new-comers to extend here and there from the start beyond the limits of primary prehistoric settlement.

We must next inquire into the influence which this early distributing-centre of Teutonic invaders may have had upon the original establishment and subsequent growth of those political units which, as already mentioned, grew up round its borders rather than within its direct orbit. The more important of these are the later kingdoms of Lindsey, Mercia, Wessex, and East Anglia. The settlement of Lindsey may be dismissed at once, for there can be no doubt that its origin is to be traced to the more northerly settlement-area of the Humber estuary, and it can thus be discussed more appropriately at a later stage. The only reason for mentioning it in this connexion is to emphasize the distinction between north and south Lincolnshire which is marked as well by the distribution of its pagan cemeteries as in its subsequent administrative divisions.[1] For while the northern part of the county, the modern Parts of Lindsey, alone appears to have constituted the early kingdom of that name,[2] the two southern divisions, the Parts of Holland and Kesteven, do belong naturally to the Fenland area. But the settlers who made their way up the Slea and those who found homes round Spalding and Boston, while they may be represented by the Spalda, and perhaps by other unidentified folk of the Tribal Hidage,[3] were never strong enough to attain independent political existence. Like the rest of the Middle Angles, they fell rapidly under the control of more powerful neighbours.

The problem of Mercia, too, may be better deferred to a later stage. For while, as we have seen, it is more than likely that many of the early settlers on the middle Trent, which is evi-

[1] See C. W. Phillips's map of Anglo-Saxon remains in Lincolnshire in *Archaeological Journal*, xci (1934), 138.

[2] F. M. Stenton in *Essays in History presented to R. Lane Poole* (1927), 145-7.

[3] The East Wixna of the Tribal Hidage are probably to be located somewhere in this area: see p. 409.

dently the region out of which Mercia first grew, may have arrived there from the Fenland by way of the Welland, the Wreak, and the Soar, yet the Trent valley itself is part of the Humber basin, and there are reasons for believing that the early Mercians had more in common with the other Humbrian peoples than with the Middle Angles of the Fens.[1]

This is, however, the most appropriate point to consider the scanty material for the origin of East Anglia. Here, too, there are only scraps of literary evidence to help us. We have, for example, the information that the royal family were known as the Wuffingas. They were so called after the Wuffa who was the grandfather of Raedwald, and Raedwald we know as the king who temporarily extended the rule of East Anglia over the other kingdoms soon before the death of Æthelberht of Kent in 616.[2] Wuffa therefore can hardly have been reigning much earlier than the second quarter of the sixth century, And even if the *Historia Brittonum* is right in stating that it was Wuffa's father who 'first reigned in Britain over the East Angles'[3] the literary traditions will scarcely allow the establishment of the dynasty before 500 at the earliest. It is, however, fairly clear from the archaeological evidence that there were Anglian communities in Norfolk and Suffolk some years before this date.[4] The evidence of early finds from the valley of the Lark has already shown one group of these people pressing eastwards into Suffolk from the Fens, and both these and another group on the little Ouse east of Thetford had easy contacts with, if they were not themselves the source of, the folk who used some early cemeteries beyond the watershed round the upper waters of the Waveney. A number of graveyards and a corresponding group of early place-names on the eastern border of the Wash and along the north Norfolk coast-line imply direct settlement from the sea, extending perhaps as far inland as North Elmham, where the site of the later bishopric is appropriately marked by a pagan cemetery.

---

[1] See pp. 416–17. [2] Bede, *Hist. Eccles.* ii. 15.

[3] *Hist. Britt.*, § 57. In Kent, too, the dynasty acquired their patronymic of Oiscingas not from the first king Hengist but from his son and successor Oisc.

[4] Cruciform brooches of fifth-century types have been recovered from cremation-urns at Castle Acre and Caistor by Norwich. The cremation-pottery from East Anglia includes some of the earliest-looking examples in the whole country, e.g. from Caistor by Norwich, Markshall, Shropham, and Fakenham (Norfolk) and Culford (Suffolk). One of the Caistor pots has an almost exact double, probably by the same potter, from Hammoor in North Holstein (Kiel Museum).

Much of the east coast both of Norfolk and Suffolk is unattractive to invaders from the sea, owing in part to its exposed
and stormy beaches of windswept shingle, in part to the undrained swamps and lagoons formed by the blockage and diver-
sion of many of the river-mouths. But two areas at least seem
certainly to have been occupied in this way. The valleys of the
Yare, the Wensum, and the Tas, which include the interesting
and important group of cremation-cemeteries south of Norwich
and close by Venta Icenorum, the Roman capital of the Iceni,
whose land the East Angles were to usurp, constitute one; and
the low-lying stretch of Suffolk coast between the Orwell and
the Alde is another. Here lay several early cemeteries, as, for
example, at Ipswich[1] and Snape, while Rendlesham between
them was the only *vicus regius* of the East Anglian kings in the
seventh century whose site is known.[2] Both these areas, it is
interesting to note, have their examples of early place-names.

From this brief survey it can be guessed that originally the
East Angles consisted of a number of independent folks whose
individual activities may have led them far into the country
before the Wuffingas established a political control over all. At
least three separate movements, from west, north, and east, can
probably be detected in Norfolk; and at least two more, one
from the Fens and the other from the sea, are discernible in
Suffolk. And something of its early federate character remained
in East Anglia down to historic times with the administrative
duality of the North Folk and the South Folk, and the diocesan
division between Elmham and Dunwich. If we add to this
amalgam the suggestion of a not inconsiderable British survival,
at any rate in the Brandon area of west Suffolk,[3] it is perhaps
easier to understand how the Wuffingas found it advisable to
trace their descent from Caesar as well as from Woden[4] and to
follow the reasoning which led the greatest of their number,
Raedwald, when the tidings of Christianity reached him, merely
to add a Christian altar to the pagan temple where already,
perhaps, he attempted to syncretize the religious diversity of his
people.[5]

---

[1] Certain features of the Ipswich burials have suggested a late date for the
cemetery, but *some* early settlement seems likely from the occurrence of cremation.
[2] Bede, *Hist. Eccles*. iii. 22.
[3] H. J. Fleure, *Races of England and Wales* (1923), 20.
[4] *Hist. Britt.*, § 57.
[5] Bede, *Hist. Eccles*. ii. 15.

But if the East Angles were a federation of several smaller peoples, they were fortunate in possessing, for all practical purposes, but a single line of contact by land with the rest of Anglo-Saxon England. To the west the Fenland cut them off from the more northerly parts of Middle Anglia, and to the south the forested claylands towards Essex seem to have proved only less impassable, as the significant disappearance of both the Roman roads that led northwards from Colchester to Venta Icenorum and to Cambridge respectively seems to indicate.[1] It was only along the narrow corridor of open country between the Fens and the forest that it was easy to pass south-westwards by Newmarket towards Royston and Hitchin. Along this route ran the Icknield Way, the prehistoric line of communication between south-western England and the east coast, a road already worn both by peaceful traffic and by warlike invaders far back in the Bronze Age, two thousand years before the coming of the Angles. By this route there can be little doubt that in the days of Raedwald East Anglian hosts went out to conquer their neighbours beyond the Fens, to win for their king the brief Bretwaldaship which Bede records, and perhaps to begin that clearing and settlement of the upland forest which continued steadily through the later Saxon centuries, until its full effect, a conquest of nature more significant than the political triumphs of Alfred and Athelstan, can be read in the unconscious record of Domesday Book.[2] By this route, too, came the revenge of the rising Mercia, and it may one day be possible to read in the Fleam Dyke and the Devil's Dyke and other members of that great series of dramatic earthworks which span the gap between fen and forest the successive attempts to demarcate a permanent frontier between these rival states. At each of them at least have been found the weapons and bodies of men who must have fallen fighting in their defence.[3] His-

---

[1] See p. 377, n. 1.

[2] Compare the map of pagan Saxon remains with that of Doomsday vills in C. Fox, *Archaeology of the Cambridge Region* (1923). There is a remarkable group of villages in the clay uplands of Cambridgeshire towards Essex whose names include the element 'west'—Weston Colville, West Wickham, Westley Waterless. There are no corresponding 'east' villages near by, and, as Professor Chadwick has suggested, they imply a movement of colonization from East Anglia, for which the Bretwaldaship of Raedwald provides the likeliest context.

[3] C. Fox, op. cit., 292–3. Since Fox wrote the Devil's Dyke, Fleam Dyke, and Bran Ditch have all been proved post-Roman: see *Camb. Antiq. Soc. Comm.* xxxi, xxxii, and xxxv (1935), 91; *Antiquity*, iii (1929), 148 ff.

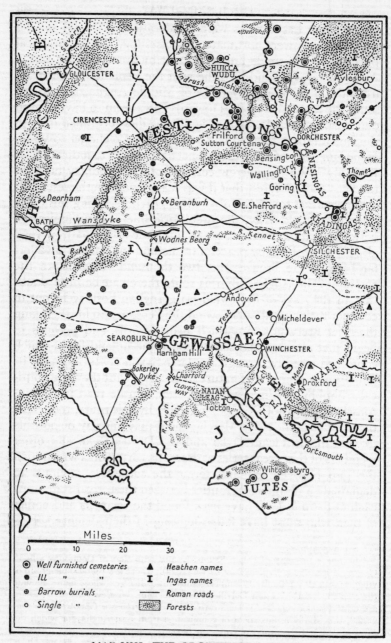

MAP VIII. THE GROWTH OF WESSEX

torians have seen in the twin nuclei, and long continued administrative duality, of the town of Cambridge a further indication of a remote time when this part of the Cam was a frontier, and East Angle and Mercian glared at one another across Magdalene Bridge.[1] However this may be, there are at least reasons for believing that the early settlements on the site, so strongly evidenced on archaeological grounds, had been temporarily destroyed before the end of the seventh century; for when in 695 the monks of Ely set out in their boat in search of a stone coffin for the body of St. Etheldreda, they found Cambridge deserted, a *civitatula quondam desolata* in which poking about among the ruins of Roman buildings they soon discovered and removed what they were seeking.[2] And it may well be that behind this scene lies the clue to one of the most puzzling phenomena of this region, the almost complete absence of the most primitive types of place-name in an area where archaeology points without hesitation to early and widespread occupation. The fate of the Cambridge settlements is not likely to have been unique. A district which had been repeatedly devastated and resettled in the seventh century can hardly be expected to retain many traces of an archaic type of nomenclature which was never given time to take root.[3]

But the Icknield Way was more than a corridor along which Mercian and East Angle could wrestle for the control of Middle Anglia: it was also, as we have mentioned, the natural route from the Fens to the Thames valley, and beyond that to the chalk uplands of the later Wessex. Before leaving this part of the subject it is therefore necessary to consider whether in the fifth and sixth centuries this route was used as it had been repeatedly used in prehistoric times; whether, in fact, the people of the upper Thames valley entered England in whole or in part by the Wash and the Bedfordshire Ouse. We are face to face with the thorniest of all political problems in this period, the question of the origin of Wessex.

So far as topographical considerations are concerned it must be admitted that the upper valley of the Thames and its tributaries between Goring and the neighbourhood of Fairford were likely to attract an early and populous group of Saxon settlers.

[1] A. Gray, *Dual Origin of the Town of Cambridge* (1908), pp. 14 ff.
[2] Bede, *Hist. Eccles.* iv. 19.
[3] For further illustration of this relationship between the pagan cemeteries and the early place-names see J. N. L. Myres in *Antiquity*, ix (1935), 455-64.

The gravel terraces which line the rivers, and spread out here and there, as to the north of the confluence of the Thames and Thame at Dorchester, to form wide areas of well-drained soil, constitute an ideal *milieu* for the valley settlement of pre-historic man, and air photography has demonstrated that this whole region maintained an unusually dense population at least as early as the Bronze Age, and continued to support it right down into the Roman period, in which it is noteworthy as an area in which native villages are exceedingly numerous, though villas, for some social reason which awaits investigation, are less frequent. Its focus lay, not as in later times at Oxford, but some ten miles farther south in the triangle of country which contains, in close proximity, the prehistoric hill-fort of Witten-ham Clumps; the Roman market-town of Dorchester which became also the seat of the first West Saxon bishopric; the great manor of Bensington, a *villa regalis* of the early Saxon kings; and the later stronghold of Wallingford, the site of a tenth-century *burh* at a vital crossing of the Thames and the head-quarters of an important medieval honour. This district, which has been described as the strategic centre of southern England, dominates the intersection of two of its natural lines of traffic, for it is here, between Wallingford and Goring, that the Icknield Way crosses the river route of the Thames where the latter passes between the Chiltern Hills and the Berkshire Downs.

In all this region evidence of Saxon occupation in the pagan period is widespread, and its early date has been generally agreed in view first of the prevalence of cremation, which in so romanized a district can hardly be otherwise explained; secondly of the close and obvious relationship borne by several of the cemeteries to their Roman predecessors, from which it is legiti-mate to argue for some cultural contact between the settlers and surviving natives; and finally of the presence in them of a num-ber of brooches and other objects of the earliest types. Two burials of a man and a woman in the artificial earthwork known as the Dyke Hills at Dorchester have produced indeed the earliest Teutonic objects ever found in this country—so early, however, that it is doubtful whether they can belong to the period of Saxon settlement at all. If they are not indicative of casualties to a raiding-party in the last phase of the Roman occupation, they may suggest the presence on the upper Thames of one of those nests of river-pirates who were able to maintain themselves in parallel circumstances in Gaul in the midst of an otherwise peaceful and romanized country-side.[1] These burials apart, however, the evidence as a whole hardly warrants, perhaps, the assumption of so early a date as that suggested for the occupation of the Cambridge region, but there can be little doubt that the upper Thames valley was full of Teutonic immigrants by the beginning of the sixth century. That these immigrants were the nucleus of the folk soon to be known as the West Saxons is strongly suggested by the essentially Saxon character of their remains, by the geographical relationship borne by this area to those whose occupants were called the Middle and East Saxons respectively, by the fact that Dorchester-on-Thames in the heart of this area was the site of the first West-Saxon bishopric, and by the absence of evidence for extensive settlement bearing the signs of so early a date in any other part of the later kingdom of Wessex.

But if these seem to be convincing reasons for thinking that the settlers of the upper Thames valley constituted the nucleus of the West Saxon people, the question of the route by which they reached their homes is not at all so easily determined. Three possible sources for the immigration have been put forward: the Fenland region to the north-east, the lower Thames valley to the east, and the Hampshire and Berkshire uplands to the south. Where such remarkable divergences of opinion are possible it is necessary to examine somewhat closely the evidence upon which each view depends.

The positive reasons which have led Mr. E. T. Leeds to claim for the Thames valley settlements a cultural parentage in the Cambridge region are almost entirely archaeological. He has drawn attention to the fact that in the cemeteries of south-western Cambridgeshire and in Bedfordshire occur many if not all of the grave-goods characteristic of the upper Thames and other Saxon districts, and that the country between the head-waters of the Ouse and Oxfordshire is also marked by culturally similar remains. The distribution of the saucer-brooches is the most important element in this evidence, but Mr. Leeds is also able to point to the suggestive fact that the only examples of early equal-armed brooches from English sites other than the three which we have already mentioned in discussing the evi-

[1] As suggested by T. D. Kendrick and C. F. C. Hawkes, *Archaeology in England and Wales* (1932), 305.

dence for early settlement in Cambridge and Bedfordshire have come from Abingdon and Sutton Courtenay in Berkshire, in the heart of the West Saxon area on the upper Thames.[1] It would also be possible to draw attention to certain schemes of decoration characteristic of the early cremation-urns of this region, which seem to owe their popularity to the fashions which evolved in Cambridgeshire, Bedfordshire, and Northants., rather than to inspiration from the south or south-eastern littoral.

The historical conclusions which Mr. Leeds has drawn from this survey of the archaeological evidence have been the occasion for considerable controversy, not only because they touch the origin of the kingdom of Wessex out of which eventually the political unification of England took shape, but also because they seemed to involve a direct attack upon the established literary tradition, according to which the West Saxons fought their way slowly northwards from the neighbourhood of Southampton Water and were not securely established in the Oxford district until the third quarter of the sixth century.[2] Mr. Leeds's argument appeared to contradict both the date and the direction of this movement, and thus raised in a somewhat acute form the question of the relative value of the two main sources for our knowledge of the early Saxon period. For his view contained the implications, which he has since made more explicit, not only that the evidence of grave-goods can be properly used to demonstrate the course and character of an invasion entirely unrecorded in the literary sources, but also that if, as in this instance, archaeology seemed to tell a story contradictory of the literary tradition, then archaeology must be right and the literary tradition wrong. In this way a notion of conflict between the two types of evidence was set up, which has served to obscure the issue, and to render more difficult than perhaps need be the solution of an admittedly complex problem. But it may help to simplify the matter if we remember that where the archaeological and literary evidence for these years appear to tell different stories, it is more likely that those stories are complementary than contradictory, for it is hardly possible to allow a direct contradiction between two lines of inquiry whose raw material has no point of mutual contact.

But before attempting to apply this doctrine to the present

---

[1] *History*, x (1925), 97; *Antiquaries Journal*, xiii (1933), 229; Leeds and Harden, *Anglo-Saxon Cemetery at Abingdon, Berks.* (1936), 26 and Pl. iv.   [2] See Appendix II.

instance it is necessary to examine the credentials of the literary tradition. The *Anglo-Saxon Chronicle*, compiled in the form in which we have it in the last decade of the ninth century, at the court and under the inspiration of King Alfred of Wessex, has a series of annals dealing with the traditional foundation of that kingdom by Cerdic and Cynric, heroic figures from whom it is clear that the West Saxon royal family had for centuries before that claimed descent. These annals give a far fuller account of the origin of Wessex than is provided in the same *Chronicle* for any other of the heptarchic kingdoms, and their character is illustrated by the interesting survival in the Preface to the *Chronicle* of what appears to be another and shorter version of the same tradition in which, within the same general framework, are to be found somewhat striking divergences both in the general chronology and in the relative importance assigned to different personages in the story. It is thus clear that we are not dealing with a series of annals preserved as such from a very remote period, and therefore likely to be trustworthy in their detailed ascription of certain events to certain years, but rather with a general body of tradition recording in the main the exploits of one family, which for the purposes of an annalistic form has been re-written or condensed as a series of decisive events each assigned to a definite year. The contradictions between the Preface and the Annals may thus be sufficient to destroy the value of either as a secure foundation for a detailed political narrative, but they undoubtedly strengthen the impression that the story as a whole rests on a broad basis of folk-memory.

Without attempting, therefore, to attach to the detailed notices an importance which is out of proportion to their intrinsic value, and avoiding equally the temptation to discredit the whole account by reference to the evident contradictions between its different versions, we may agree that a tradition of some antiquity lies behind the landing of Cerdic and Cynric at Cerdicesora, a site which has been plausibly placed in the neighbourhood of Totton at the head of Southampton Water, somewhere about the turn of the fifth and sixth centuries. This tradition seems further to have preserved in at least an intelligible order a record of battles at places connected with Cerdic's name suggesting a movement along the line of an ancient route to Charford-on-Avon, and thence to Old Sarum in Wiltshire.[1] After this, in a series of annals associated with the name of Ceawlin, we are presented with what purport to be the decisive events in the creation of an empire based apparently upon the upper Thames valley, events whose source in a separate saga of this king is easily to be seen from the poetic phraseology of the annals, and the obviously artificial chronology.[2] Of the exploits of Ceawlin more must be said later,[3] but here it should be noted that mixed up with the preceding part of the story are entries purporting to record the deeds of other heroes besides Cerdic and Cynric. Behind some of these annals, such as those mentioning Stuf and Wihtgar, may lie in reality an independent tradition of the Jutish occupation of the Isle of Wight and southern Hampshire early in the sixth century,[4] while others, such as the notice of Port's appropriate arrival at Portsmouth, can only be saved from condemnation as antiquarian inventions by invoking a coincidence which is stranger than fiction.[5]

It must, however, be admitted that not only the tale of Port but the whole group of these annals will scarcely resist detailed criticism. Certain of them may bear philological traces of an origin in documents two centuries or more before the time of Alfred: the obvious interest shown by their compiler in linking known place-names with the deeds of traditional heroes may be susceptible in some cases of a less damaging interpretation than it demands in others,[6] but it is hardly possible to leave the study of the story as a whole without the realization that it is built

---

[1] The relevance of this route to the story in the West Saxon annals has been suggested by O. G. S. Crawford in *Antiquity*, v (1931), 441–58.

[2] Except for the battle of Deorham in 577, and the note of his death in 593, both dates that might well be known independently, the Ceawlin annals are all spaced in multiples of four years at 556, 560, 568, 584, 592. These are the only instances in the West Saxon annals of such rhythmic dating except for three possibly accidental pairs 519, 527: 530, 534: 552, 556—of which the last has probably been drawn into the Ceawlin sequence. See Appendix II.

[3] See p. 424.   [4] See pp. 365–6.

[5] As is done by W. H. Stevenson in *Eng. Hist. Rev.* xiv (1899), 35, 37. The force of the argument, powerful enough if applied either to the case of Port and Portsmouth, or to that of Wihtgar and Wight, is fatally weakened by the necessity of applying it to both.

[6] The case of the entries associating Cerdic with place-names containing his name is, of course, on a totally different footing from those of Port and Wihtgar, for there is no certainty or likelihood that any of the Cerdic place-names existed before the traditional date of his arrival. They are in fact, as Hodgkin has urged (*History of the Anglo-Saxons* (1935), i. 129–30), a source of strength rather than of weakness to the champions of Cerdic as an historical figure.

up out of a handful of incidents selected from a mass of semi-legendary material on principles which are at best uncritical, at worst merely propagandist. Nor is there much internal evidence of any scientific interest in the recording of historical facts for their own sake. It is at least evident that no direct reference to the Jutish settlement of southern Hampshire and the Isle of Wight has been allowed to find a place in the story of Alfred's ancestors in this region, and that the dates assigned to the stages in their conquests can only be reconciled with Gildas's contemporary evidence for the forty years of peace in the first half of the sixth century, by depriving the recorded events of all the importance which the chronicler clearly intended us to attach to them. If the chronology of the story is even approximately correct it can hardly be the record of a national migration; at best it can describe little more than the movements of a single family and its retainers whose activities were not felt, in the circles from which Gildas derived his information, to be of sufficient importance to ruffle the precarious calm achieved by Mons Badonicus.

It remains to consider the other possible lines of inquiry into the settlement of the chalk downland between the upper Thames valley and the English Channel, to ask what light the archaeology and the place-names of this region can throw upon the date and character of its earliest Teutonic occupation. Does the outcome of our investigation of the literary story find support in the quality and distribution of the cemeteries and the local names?

The scarcity of pagan Saxon burial-grounds in Hampshire and Wiltshire and the comparative poverty in grave-goods of those whose existence is known has been a standing puzzle to scholars ever since the archaeological evidence for this period began to receive serious consideration.[1] It was this fact which first drove Mr. Leeds to add his archaeological doubts to the array of objections which had already been raised on other grounds against the credibility of the West Saxon annals, and led him to seek a route other than the traditional advance from the south for the passage of the early West Saxon communities to their homes in the upper Thames region. And it is worth noting that such archaeological material as does exist in the

[1] The Saxon remains of Wiltshire are conveniently listed by Mrs. Cunnington in *Wilts. Arch. Mag.* xlvi (1933), 147–75.

chalk uplands of the later Wessex has given little or no suggestion that it belongs to the earliest phase of the settlement.[1] The few sites which are known in southern Hampshire seem like those of the Isle of Wight to indicate Kentish rather than Saxon connexions, and the earliest material from the only considerable cemetery in Wiltshire south of the Kennet, that of Harnham Hill near Salisbury, seems also to be distinctly Jutish in character.[2] And since we have seen good reason to believe that these Jutish settlements themselves did not begin before the traditional dating for the West Saxon arrival on the Hampshire coast at the turn of the fifth and sixth centuries, it would seem that here at any rate the Saxon influence, which is certainly present, was superimposed on a Jutish phase and must therefore itself belong to a somewhat later period.[3] Elsewhere in this region this sequence of cultures is less clear, but the remains in general seem to preclude the idea of any widespread settlement at an early date. For they are composed either of groups of inhumation-burials, accompanied only by the scantiest of furniture— cemeteries, in fact, whose general quality is similar to those which seem characteristic of the seventh century in the Cambridge region and elsewhere—or else of isolated burials, nearly always of men, which have been found scattered up and down the chalk uplands, either as intrusions into prehistoric barrows or as primary interments in mounds built specially for the purpose. Such burials are notoriously difficult to date. It may, however, be remarked that the secondary interment of isolated male bodies in pre-existing barrows points far more strongly to the disposal of casualties incurred in raiding than to the habits of a settled population, and that the whole number of such interments known in Wiltshire amounts in any case in terms of immigrant population to no more than the contents of a single small cemetery.[4] So far as primary barrow-burial is concerned, there would seem to be reason for believing that it was at least

---

[1] See E. T. Leeds in *Antiquaries Journal*, xiii (1933), 249-51. The Roundway Down jewellery, to which an early date is assigned by Kendrick (*Trans. South-Eastern Union of Scientific Socs.* (1934), 15), belongs in Mr. Leeds's opinion to the seventh century.

[2] See Baldwin Brown, *Arts in Early England*, iv (1915), 619-20 and Fig. 21.

[3] See above, p. 366. The traditional date of 552 for the West Saxon victory at Searoburh may well be approximately correct for the first appearance of Saxon elements at the Harnham Hill settlement. It does not, of course, imply a thorough Saxon occupation of all the surrounding country.

[4] Some twenty-five are known at present.

as popular among Saxon chieftains in the later as in the earlier part of the conquest period,[1] and its frequent occurrence in Wiltshire is not to be taken as a sign of early occupation. On the contrary, the numerous barrow-burials in this region, suggesting as they do the unusual strength and persistence of habits acquired under the necessities of a campaigning life, point to the probable continuance here of raiding and unstable nomadic conditions at a time when in Kent, Sussex, or the upper Thames valley that phase had long since given way to the establishment of settled village communities.

It has recently been suggested that the scantiness of pagan Saxon remains in the districts portrayed by the *Anglo-Saxon Chronicle* as the nucleus of the West Saxon kingdom can be sufficiently explained by assuming that 'Cerdic and his chiefs were clever and adaptable men who saw that the depositing of weapons and jewellery with the corpses was an unnecessary extravagance'.[2] It would be easier to accept this assumption, and to agree that archaeology here is rather a hindrance than a help in our task, if there was any independent support from the place-name evidence to reinforce the admitted weakness of the literary tradition. If the valleys of Hampshire and Wiltshire contained even half as many of those archaic names in *-ingas* which, as has been shown, replace the archaeological evidence in Essex and permit us there to accept a Saxon settlement widely if not thickly spread in the pagan period, then it would be possible to ignore the paucity and poverty of the cemeteries and legitimate to explain away their evidence in any manner that might carry conviction. But in Wessex the early place-names are even more conspicuous by their absence than are the pagan cemeteries,[3] and it is hardly to be supposed that the skill and foresight which on this assumption enabled Cerdic and his

[1] The Taplow and Asthall barrows are both, on the ordinary dating, late: so are several of the barrow-burials of Derbyshire. An instance of a barrow being built in the seventh century over the body of a criminal in Thanet is in the *Passio SS. Ethelberti et Ethelredi*, § 8 (*Symeon of Durham* (Rolls Series), i. 9).

[2] R. H. Hodgkin, *History of the Anglo-Saxons* (1935), i. 131.

[3] See *Eng. Place-name Soc. Sussex* (1929), i, xv, xvi. The few early names in Hants are either in the Jutish area on the south coast, or in the north-west, and clearly related to those of the Thames and Wey valleys. In Wilts. the only group of early names is in the north, suggesting penetration from the Thames and the Kennet. The unusual frequency of Celtic names in central Hants and Wilts. (Micheldever, Candover, Andover, Fovant, &c.) completes the general coherence of the testimony from archaeology and place-names in favour of the thesis here put forward.

followers to leave so few traces for the archaeologist would extend to the suppression of any tell-tale place-names. It is indeed difficult to believe that, in a land so little disturbed by later invasion as were the chalk uplands of Wessex, so few early names would have survived had the main mass of the West Saxon people followed the traditional founders of their dynasty at the traditional date into their homes in Hampshire and Wiltshire.

Nor is there, when all the evidence is analysed, much reason to believe that they did so. The only piece of contemporary literary evidence, as we have already seen, rules out any widespread advance of the Saxon invaders in southern England during the first half of the sixth century, and this testimony of Gildas is by itself sufficient to show that the events recorded in the West Saxon annals in the *Chronicle* were, if correctly dated, of very minor importance. The internal evidence of those annals themselves suggests, as we have observed, that they owe their origin to a rationalization at once prejudiced and uncritical of a group of family traditions preserved by the medium of heroic poetry.[1] The events described, reduced to their true scale as a selection of picturesque but not necessarily important incidents in the marauding careers of some professional bandits, fit well enough into the background of prolonged raiding and unsettlement indicated by the archaeological evidence; and the scarcity of early place-names is there to suggest that the permanent occupation of the chalk downland by Saxon communities had made little progress before the end of the sixth century.

How that occupation eventually took place, and from what point of the compass the settlers came, is unfortunately a topic on which direct evidence is lacking, but there is at least one notable and material proof that the population of Wiltshire and Dorset in this period anticipated invasion and conquest rather from the north than from the south. The Wansdyke, the most impressive and mysterious of all the monuments of this age, runs from the Kennet valley south of Hungerford to the neighbourhood of the Bristol Channel facing a danger from the

---

[1] 'The chronicler is not composing a history: he is only setting down in a very rough—perhaps a quite mistaken—chronological framework, headlines or mottoes, as it were, of famous stories handed down from father to son.' G. M. Young, *Origin of the West Saxon Kingdom* (1934), 15. Many matters of detail pointing to a dual origin of Wessex in a fusion of northern (Saxon) and southern (Jutish) elements may be found in this suggestive pamphlet.

north. It was built at some time in the fifth or sixth century,[1] and can only represent a political situation before the beginnings of the historic Wessex, a time when a well-organized power was proposing to hold the chalk uplands of the south against a foe already in possession of the upper Thames and Kennet valleys. It is intelligible in the light of just such an early and thorough settlement of the Oxford district and north Berkshire as is suggested by the general pattern of cemeteries and place-names; but any reconstruction of the story which brings the main mass of the later Saxon population into Wessex from the south has first to explain away this substantial and enigmatic frontier.

But when all is said and done there remains this stubborn tradition of a southern origin for the royal family of Wessex, and this tradition there seems no adequate reason for rejecting. Indeed it may be that behind the word Gewissae, which Bede uses as an alternative name for the West Saxons, there lies a further hint of the distinction between the bulk of the people and their southern masters. For it seems clear, not only from the appearance of Gewis himself in the royal pedigree, but from the long-continued use of the phrase *rex Gewissorum* as a formal style, that the word was primarily applicable to the kingly family and its immediate dependants.[2] And while, as we have seen, the first employment of the term West Saxons is likely to have arisen for the folk on the upper Thames, it is significant that in the few passages in which any geographical position seems to be attached to the Gewissae it is in connexion with the people of Hampshire:[3] Bede's usage, it is true, is not altogether con-

---

[1] The Wansdyke was proved to be late Roman or post-Roman by Pitt-Rivers. Its apparently deliberate exclusion of Bath might naturally suggest that it was built to demarcate the Saxon-British frontier after the Battle of Deorham in 577. An earlier date for at least its eastern part would be more acceptable on other grounds. I cannot agree with Sir Charles Oman's contention (*Arch. Journal*, lxxxvii (1930), 60) that this tremendous work may represent a frontier between two of the petty British states described by Gildas.

[2] The usual explanation of Gewissae as meaning 'confederates' would be applicable enough to the mixed traditions of the West Saxon folk here envisaged. Its acceptance, however, involves the rejection of Gewis himself as a fictitious personage interpolated into the West Saxon pedigree. No adequate ground has ever been given for such an interpolation, and the increasing tendency of scholars to treat the genealogies as archaic and primitive documents makes it safer to believe that the Gewissae owe their name to an historic Gewis than that he owes his existence merely to their name.

[3] The more significant passages are *Hist. Eccles.* iii. 7, Birinus arriving in Britain, presumably in Hampshire, 'first entered the land of the Gewissae'; iv. 16, the Isle

sistent,[1] and he seems generally to have thought of the term merely as an obsolescent synonym for the more familiar West Saxons, but this is in no way surprising when it is realized that the kings of the house of Cerdic admittedly dominated the Thames valley Saxons as early as the reign of Ceawlin, and that the geographical distinction between the two words was thus losing its meaning a century and a half before Bede's day. It is, in view of this, all the more interesting to find him on one occasion defining the Gewissae as 'those of the West Saxons who were in Winchester', for it is evident that the Winchester district in early times was peculiarly associated with the royal family. While St. Birinus had naturally made Dorchester the centre of his evangelization of the West Saxons, Winchester sprang at once into ecclesiastical importance as soon as the king of the Gewissae and his court had been converted; and it is easy to guess that behind the personal quarrels to which Bede attributes the supplanting of Dorchester by Winchester as the centre of West Saxon Christianity in the middle of the seventh century[2] lay a deeper political rivalry between the West Saxons of the upper Thames and the land of the Gewissae, which was becoming under royal patronage more and more the focus of the kingdom as the years went by. In these circumstances, and with the final loss of the original West Saxon district to the rising power of Mercia, it is hardly surprising that an element of confusion entered into the folk-memory of Wessex,[3] and that the part played by the Thames valley in its early history became overlaid by the southern traditions of a royal house, which, however weak and disunited

of Wight is 'set opposite the middle of the South Saxons and the Gewissae'; iv. 15, the Gewissae are 'those of the West Saxons who were in Winchester'.

[1] See, e.g., *Hist. Eccles.* iv. 13: on the other hand Augustine's Oak is placed rightly, if the view here suggested is sound, 'on the bounds of the Hwiccii and the West Saxons' (not the Gewissae) in ii. 2.

[2] Ibid. iii. 7.

[3] It has sometimes been argued that this confusion extended to the adoption into the Gewissan family and pedigree, of kings—Ceawlin in particular—whose real homeland was in the West Saxon area on the upper Thames: see G. M. Young, op. cit., 33 ff. It is certain that Ceawlin's empire was based on the upper Thames: indeed his final disaster at Wodnesbeorh (in the vale of Pewsey) may be read, if we will, as implying an unsuccessful effort to force his way southward into Gewissan territory. But the uniform alliteration in C of all the early West Saxon rulers—Cerdic, Cynric, Ceawlin, Ceolwulf, Cuthwulf, &c.—is strong evidence that we are dealing with one family. To assume that both the Thames valley Saxons and the Gewissae had kings who practised C-alliteration is not impossible, but it involves recourse to one of those coincidences which, however attractive, are best avoided in this period.

it might often show itself, remained none the less both exceptionally prolific and remarkably tenacious of the popular affec-
tion.

It has been necessary to discuss the early history of Wessex
at such length, and to trespass in this way on ground outside
the chronological limits of the present volume, in order to make
clear what appear to have been the historical connexions between the settlement of the upper Thames region and that of
the country between it and the Hampshire coast. The result
of the discussion has been to suggest that so far from the West
Saxon communities of the upper Thames being derived from
the south, they were themselves in all probability the source
from which late in the sixth and early in the seventh century
much of this region obtained its Saxon population, and that
they accepted in return little but the political dominance of a
southern royal family. If there is any truth in this view, it will
thus be necessary to turn, in the search for the origin of the
upper Thames valley Saxons, to one or other of the remaining
alternatives, the route by the Icknield Way from Middle Anglia,
or the Thames valley itself.

The archaeological and topographical evidence in favour of
a Middle Anglian origin has already been briefly summarized:
it remains to inquire what the Thames valley has to show in
answer to this claim. The employment of the river route by
prehistoric man, as a main artery of penetration into England
at all periods, is amply demonstrated by the remarkable and
varied assortment of objects which have been recovered from
time to time from all parts of its bed during dredging operations.
The evidence of archaeology and place-names in the valley
itself lends weight to the argument that in this period also it was
in use.

That Saxon settlers made use of the lower Thames valley at
an early date has already been demonstrated in discussing the
archaeological evidence from Kent, Surrey, and Middlesex, and
while the discoveries in the middle reaches of the river between
Shepperton and the Goring gap are less impressive than those
which mark its course both east and west of this region, they
are quite sufficient to show that the valley was open for settlement throughout its length. In particular the burnt burials at
Lower Shiplake and Reading can be pointed out as links in a
chain which may have united the cremating folk of Northfleet,

Croydon, and Shepperton with those of Long Wittenham, Frilford, and Abingdon. And there is a regular procession of early
folk-names such as Sonning, Reading, and Goring to reinforce
the archaeological evidence, and some of these names are of unusual interest, for they seem to have preserved an outline of the
primitive social geography of this region into far later times.[1] It
is clear, however, from the distribution both of the cemeteries
and the place-names that the earliest settlement hereabouts was
based rather rigidly on the line of the river. On the north bank
'the deserts of Chiltern', as they are described by Eddius early
in the eighth century, long remained, with their precipitous
lateral valleys and densely tangled undergrowth, a haunt of
outlaws and brigands, and may have retained elements of unabsorbed Romano-British folk to an unusually late period. On
the south the barren heathland of east Berkshire and Surrey
was almost equally unattractive to a farming population.[2] Only
beyond the Goring gap did the country open out into that
natural paradise of the primitive agriculturalist which, as we
have seen, the West Saxon communities soon made their own.

However easy such a line of approach may appear, it must
none the less be admitted that the archaeological parallels between the upper and the lower Thames are hardly as close as
one might expect if the one region had been the sole cultural
parent of the other. Few, if any, of the specific fashions in
pottery which distinguished the Saxons of Kent and Surrey
reappear on the upper reaches of the river, and some of those
which are common to the Oxford district and Middle Anglia,
while they occur as far down the Thames as Reading, seem

---

[1] The *provincia* 'quae appellatur Sunninges', in the Chertsey charter (Birch, *Cart.
Sax.* 34), whose claims to historical significance have been demonstrated by Prof.
Stenton in *Eng. Hist. Rev.* xxxiii (1918), 435, n. 11, was still in part preserved in
the middle ages as the great manor of Sonning; east of it the wording of the charter
implies that the 'land of three hundred *manentes*' which formed the subject of the
Chertsey grant was originally another such *provincia*, possibly that of the Fullingas,
for their eastern boundary was the *Fullingadic*: west of the Sunningas another similar
unit has left its name at Reading, which was still in 1086 a manor covering 'an area
at least seven miles wide . . . quite large enough for an early *folc*' (Stenton in
Introd. to Survey of Eng. Place-names (1924), 50): beyond that lie other early names
at Goring and Pangbourne (Pægeingaburna): and on the other side of the river
the *villa regalis* of the Benesingas once dominated the whole country between
Dorchester and Henley later comprised by the vast manor of Bensington.

[2] For an excellent account of this barrier of unattractive lands which encircle
the lower Thames basin, and of its importance in the understanding of early Saxon
history, see S. W. Wooldridge and D. L. Linton in *Geography*, xx (1935), 161–75,
especially Fig. 2.

curiously alien to the traditions of Northfleet or Croydon. It would be foolish to press these differences too strongly, however, for the range of ceramic material available for study from the Thames valley cemeteries as a whole is very much narrower than that which is preserved in Middle Anglia, and conclusions based on the absence of parallel forms are correspondingly less reliable.

On the whole, however, it would appear that something more than a general probability can be established for the Thames route, but the evidence for its use is certainly not strong enough to rule out the alternative origin in Middle Anglia which has been championed by Mr. E. T. Leeds. Here, as we have seen, the positive archaeological parallels are undoubted, and the geographical facts and prehistoric analogies are there to support and explain the obvious cultural connexions. Yet it is worth noting that here too the archaeology, when closely examined, hardly provides quite the continuous chain of certainly early material that we should like to see. It will take, as we have seen, fifth-century Teutonic immigrants as far south from the Fens as Luton and Kempston, but between these communities and the equally early folk at Frilford, Long Wittenham, or Sutton Courtenay on the upper Thames there remains a gap in east Oxfordshire and Buckinghamshire in which, though cemeteries are not uncommon, the signs of really early date are at present lacking.[1] Here too, however, it would be very unwise to insist on such negative evidence, and the point would hardly be worth making were there not some other reasons for believing that the Saxon occupation of the country between east Bucks and the Thames came late rather than early in the pagan period. The place-name evidence for this region in which a paucity of early Saxon types is accompanied by a rather high proportion of Celtic elements is one significant fact pointing in this direction,[2] and there would appear some reason for postulating also a considerable survival of the pre-Saxon population.[3] Nor can we forget the entry in the *Anglo-Saxon Chronicle* for 571, which

---

[1] It may not be accidental that the earliest objects known in this area, the Bishopstone plates (G. Baldwin Brown, *Arts in Early England*, iv (1915), Pl. CLV. 1) are in the classical rather than the Saxon tradition.

[2] *Eng. Place-name Soc. Bucks.* (1925), Introduction.

[3] J. Beddoe's views on this district are borne out by more recent if not necessarily more reliable methods than his. See W. Bradbrooke and F. G. Parsons in *Journ. Royal Anthr. Inst.* lii (1920), 113.

appears to record at this surprisingly late date a decisive Saxon
victory over the Britons at a site which may or may not be Bedford,[1] followed by the occupation of Aylesbury and Limbury,
in the region under discussion, as well as by that of Bensington
and Eynsham on the Oxfordshire side of the upper Thames.
Many difficulties in the past have been felt in accepting this
annal at its face value. Mr. Leeds would like to think that the
battle was fought nearly a century before 571 and that it helped
to clear the passage for his early Saxon settlers working south
along the Icknield Way:[2] Sir Charles Oman finds it difficult to
believe in the persistence of British communities here so late as
571 and would prefer to turn the Saxons' opponents into Angles.[3]
But in the light of the archaeological and place-name evidence
both the alleged date and the British identity of the losing side
in this fight are in no way improbable, and the battle of Bedcanford may fortify our tentative conclusion that something of a
British enclave did still remain between the southern limit of
the early settlements deriving from the Fens and the Saxons of
the upper Thames. At the same time it would hardly appear
that this conclusion need jeopardize Mr. Leeds's argument, for
we are not bound to believe that such a British enclave would
necessarily, in the confusion of those times, have blocked the
through passage of Saxon bands along the Icknield Way. To
grant such bands a free passage may even have been the easiest
method of preserving the British enclave itself from molestation;
and that something did prevent much Saxon settlement in central and north Buckinghamshire before the formation of Ceawlin's empire in the third quarter of the sixth century would seem
to be a natural conclusion from the present state of the evidence.

If a discreet refusal to rule out either the Thames valley or
the Icknield Way as the route by which the earliest West Saxons
reached their homes may lend an air of indecision to this part
of our analysis, there can at least be no doubt about one further
addition to the lands conquered by the invaders in the midlands
early in the settlement period. There is conclusive archaeological evidence for their presence at a number of sites in the valley
of the Warwickshire Avon at quite an early date. Amongst these

---

[1] The editors of the English Place-name Society do not accept the identification:
Hodgkin (*History of the Anglo-Saxons*, i. 375), following W. H. Stevenson and
probably Æthelweard, is prepared to do so.

[2] *History*, x (1925), 105.   [3] *England before the Norman Conquest* (1910), 230.

may be noticed the partly-cremation cemeteries at Bidford-on-Avon and Baginton near Coventry, further cremations at Marton, the early burials on the line of the Watling Street at Cestersover near Rugby, and the recent important discoveries at Stratford. The provenance of these settlers, who exhibit a culture in which Anglian and Saxon elements are blended, is no doubt to be sought both in the Fenland settlement-area and in the Oxford district.[1] This dual origin is indeed suggested as well by the place-names as by the archaeological evidence. There is little doubt, for example, that one group of these settlers were the founders of the later kingdom or province of the Hwicce whose ecclesiastical centre was soon to be established at Worcester, and it would seem that Wychwood Forest in north-west Oxfordshire preserves along with their name a memory of the route by which they reached their later homes, as well, perhaps, as a hint of a social organization similar to that of the primitive *provinciae* of Kent. Midway between Worcester and Stratford, on the other hand, a small stream, still known as the Whitsun Brook, recalls a settlement here of the Wixna, one of those mysterious folk of the Tribal Hidage, who soon lost their identity in the formation of larger political units. In that document the Wixna appear already divided into an eastern and a western group, and while their position in the list suggests that their original homes were in close proximity to the Gyrwe and Spalda of the north-western Fens, it is by no means impossible that one branch had migrated at an early date up the Welland and so across the easy watershed and down the valley of the Warwickshire Avon. It may even be that this division is itself recognized in the distinction of the East and West Wixna of that catalogue; and their appearance in Worcestershire is in any case an excellent illustration of the Anglian element already evidenced in the archaeology of the Avon valley.[2]

The main interest of this early penetration lies in the fact that it took place in an area much of which consists of dense natural

[1] It is sometimes assumed that 'the original English settlers of Worcestershire were West Saxons' and that the Anglian influence is a subsequent intrusion consequent on the rise of Mercia: see *Eng. Place-name Soc. Worcs.* (1927), xvi–xvii. It is, however, clear from the archaeological evidence that both elements were present in the Avon valley from the earliest times.

[2] Ibid. xviii–xix. A further illustration is also there given in the village-name Phepson, whose earliest inhabitants, the Fepsaetan, must have been an offshoot of the Feppingas, whom both Bede and the Tribal Hidage locate in Middle Anglia.

forest. The evidence of the place-names in Worcestershire, which include a notable group with heathen elements in the triangle north of the confluence of the Severn and Avon, shows even better than the known archaeological distribution the extent to which this exploitation had gone in pagan times. If we may take as typical the graphic description of a property hemmed in by surrounding forest which is given in an eighth-century charter referring to the region somewhat farther north between the Severn and the Stour, this exploitation had proceeded in a spasmodic and piecemeal fashion, and long remained in a pioneering stage;[1] but the evidence of the heathen names, and the existence of other primitive groups like the Stoppingas, whose *regio* lay on the Alne north-west of Stratford,[2] shows beyond question that the steady process of forest-clearing, which makes the Anglo-Saxon conquest so vitally different from any earlier invasion of Britain, had already made some progress in the western midlands before the middle of the seventh century. And here, in the lands of the Hwicce, we are not far from the central districts of Mercia, and the rise of Mercia to predominance among the other kingdoms at this time was unquestionably due in part to early and successful forest-clearance.[3] To appreciate this fact in its proper context, however, it will be necessary to turn to the third great radiating-point of the Anglo-Saxon immigration, the river-system of the Humber.

[1] Birch, *Cart. Sax.* 154: 'The said property lies on both sides of the river (the Stour) being bounded on the north by the woodland which they call Cynibre and on the west by another forest called Moerheb of which the greatest part belongs to the said property.'   [2] Ibid. 157.

[3] The striking occurrence of Penda's name in two place-names in Worcestershire and one in Gloucestershire, coupled with that of his father Pybba in three or four others in the former county, may even suggest that the Mercian royal family had early connexions with the Hwicce: *Eng. Place-name Soc. Worcs.* (1927), xxii.

XXIII

THE HUMBRENSES

THE view of this third main area of Anglo-Saxon settlement which must now be considered involves a rearrangement of the current ideas of its political geography, ideas which are derived from the outlook of Bede and later writers. For in Bede's day, and perhaps from as early as the middle of the seventh century, the estuary of the Humber was regarded as a barrier or dividing line between the northern and the southern English, a frontier which held apart the peoples whom Bede himself seems to have been among the first to call Northumbrians, from those Southumbrian tribes who were falling in his lifetime under the domination of Mercia. Bede himself repeatedly speaks of the Humber in this sense: the sway of the early Bretwaldas, he tells us, extended over those provinces 'which are separated from the Northerners by the river Humber and boundaries adjacent to it',[1] and the Mercian supremacy at the end of his life is described as covering all southern England 'as far as the limit of the river Humber'.[2]

But there are many reasons for believing that this was not the function of the Humber in the earliest times. Elsewhere, as we have seen, the river-systems of eastern England became the centres rather than the boundaries of the first Teutonic settlements. On the lower Thames the name of Surrey still bears witness to a primitive political unit which included settlers on both banks of the river, and in the Fenland streams we have seen the natural lines of penetration which carried peoples of a common cultural equipment ever farther into the southern midlands. To appreciate the similar attraction which the Humber exercised, and to understand the part which it played as a focus of settlement, is our next concern: we must force our way behind the political conditions of Bede's day to the more primitive circumstances of the age of settlement.

To do so is not, in fact, so difficult as might at first sight appear. For there is clear evidence from our literary sources that as late as the end of the seventh century it was still customary, if not universal, to refer to those whom, following the usage adopted by Bede in the *Ecclesiastical History*, we have since called

[1] *Hist. Eccles*. ii. 5.   [2] Ibid. v. 23.

Northumbrians, as Humbrenses or Hymbronenses, the men of
the Humber itself. And when we remember that the name
Humber, now restricted in its use to the lower part of the estuary
between Trent Falls and the sea, had once a far wider geographical extension, and could be applied, for example, to the
Ouse as far north as York, to the Don, and to at least the lower
course of the Trent, it becomes easy to visualize the Humbrenses
as eventually settling the whole region drained by the tributaries of that river-system. On the north, indeed, as the position
and name of the present-day Northumberland suggest, it may
be justifiable to carry the settlement of folk based on the Humbrensian system far beyond the limits of the Humber basin to
the lands watered by other rivers of the north-east coast, of
which the most important are the Tees, Tyne, and Tweed. We
shall thus find ourselves discussing in this part of our survey the
beginnings of Bernicia as well of Deira, Lindsey, and Mercia.[1]

It will be as well to begin the discussion with some general
considerations. Of direct literary evidence for the settlement
period in the Humber basin there is practically none. A tradition in the *Historia Brittonum* that the first Teutonic leaders in
Northumbria were a son and nephew of Hengist would be
hardly worth mentioning were it not for the striking archaeological parallels between the Deiran cemeteries and those of
Frisia. The probable Frisian connexions both of Hengist himself and of some elements in the archaeology of Kent have already been mentioned, and certain direct similarities of a kind
whose significance should not be over-emphasized may be held
to link the more Saxon elements of the ceramic material from
Kent with that of Yorkshire. That the bulk of the latter points
to Frisia as the immediate provenance of its owners is, however,
certain, but this need not, for reasons mentioned earlier, be any
bar to our acceptance of Bede's general designation of the
northern English as Angles. Apart from this tradition the only
direct literary evidence concerns the later part of our period,
when the struggles of Ida and his descendants in Bernicia in the
second half of the sixth century have left a few echoes in British

---

[1] For detailed discussion of the evidence on which the argument of this and the
preceding paragraph is based see J. N. L. Myres in *History*, xx (1935), 250–62.
The possibility of a connexion between the Humbrenses and the Ambrones whose
name survives in that of the Frisian island Amrum—a connexion apparently taken
for granted by the author of the *Historia Brittonum*, §§ 57 and 63—is also there
discussed.

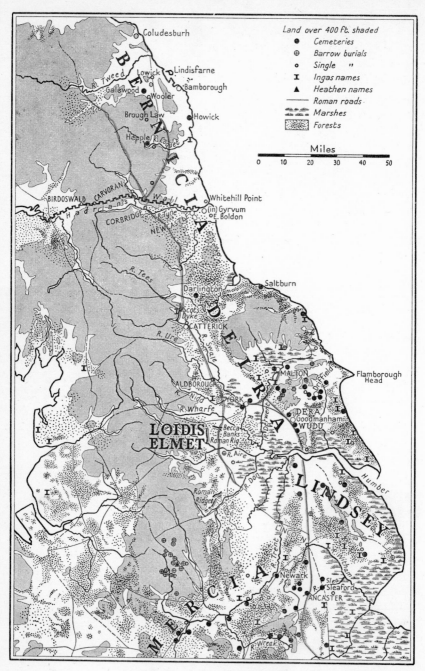

MAP IX. THE HUMBRENSES

legends reported by Nennius.[1] Bede, though himself a Northumbrian, has little or nothing to say of his people's earliest history: their conversion to Christianity came later than in the south, and this no doubt in part accounts for his silence. It is none the less possible to obtain many interesting sidelights on the economic and social conditions of Northumbria in pagan times from Bede's account of later events; and especially, perhaps, on the relations between invader and invaded in a land whose earlier history bore but little similarity to that of the more southern and more civilized districts which have hitherto concerned us.

For it must be remembered that in the Humbrensian area we are on the borderland between the civil and military parts of Roman Britain. In Lindsey, it is true, civil conditions are still predominant, as the *colonia* of Lincoln and the known sites of some ten or twelve villas may suggest; but while the lands bordering on the Trent were but scantily populated in Roman times, in east and central Yorkshire the military and civilian elements balance one another, and in the western dales and beyond the most northerly of the Roman cantonal capitals at Aldborough (Isurium Brigantum) Roman provincial culture had made but little impression on a scanty native population whose main contacts with southern civilization lay through the blockhouses of an increasingly barbarized army. No account of the wide differences between the north and south of the Humbrensian area, differences which, for example, rendered impossible a genuine fusion of interest and sentiment between Bernicia and Deira, can be complete which does not bring home the profound contrast of cultural background between the last outposts of the lowland zone in Yorkshire and the Celtic uplands beyond. In no other part of the Roman province can the combined influences of geography and native culture on the character of the Saxon settlement be more profitably studied than in the divergent and discordant histories of the Bernician and Deiran peoples.

Geographical conditions, indeed, played a more obviously dominant part in determining the whole pattern of settlement in the Humbrensian area than in the lands opening on the Fens. South of the estuary the confines of the kingdom of Lindsey were as clearly marked out by swamps and heaths as if it had been actually an island, and it has been truly remarked that 'among

[1] *Hist. Britt.*, §§ 62-3.

all the earliest English kingdoms only Sussex is surrounded by more definite and formidable barriers than those which encircle Lindsey'.[1] There is evidence here to suggest that, while the shallow and waterlogged coast-line from Grimsby to the Wash was extensively protected against direct settlement by dangerous and obstructive sandbanks, the natural lines of entry to the habitable regions of the Wolds and Lincoln Edge lay up the tributary valleys from the Humber estuary on the north. For it has been plausibly argued that the pattern of the existing parish boundaries in north Lincolnshire indicates a progressive extension of riverside settlement up these tributary streams, giving way southwards, as the rivers ceased to be conveniently navigable, to the series of villages whose lands are carefully alined upon both sides of the Roman road from the Humber to Lincoln.[2]

The position of Lincoln itself in the period of Teutonic settlement is one of peculiar interest. Lying as it did at the important intersection of the easy highway down Lincoln Edge by the Witham valley which formed the natural route westwards from the Wolds to the Trent, it dominated the whole area available for settlement, and its impressive tactical position might have been expected to attract the early occupation of Anglian bands. It is therefore a matter for some surprise to find that with the exception of a single cremation-urn believed to have come from near the Eastgate, and one recorded cemetery six miles away to the south, no remains of the pagan Saxon period are known within ten miles of the city in any direction.[3] The blank area round Lincoln at this time contrasts so strikingly with its focal position in the distribution-maps of the remains of the Roman centuries, and indeed of earlier prehistoric ages, as to raise the possibility that the Humbrensian penetration of Lindsey from the north may either have spent its force before reaching the Roman colony or else may have been prevented for a while from occupying the lands adjacent to it. Such a possibility brings to mind other facts which may perhaps be thought to

[1] F. M. Stenton in *Essays in History presented to R. Lane Poole* (1927), 148.
[2] W. Page in *Antiquity*, i (1927), 454–61.
[3] See the maps published by C. W. Phillips in *Archaeological Journal*, xc (1933) and xci (1934). The Bronze Age distributions here as in Cambridge are strikingly parallel to that of pagan Saxon times, with the one exception of the Lincoln neighbourhood itself. I owe the knowledge of the Eastgate urn to Mr. Phillips, who tells me that it has only recently been returned to Lincoln, by the enlightened authorities of the Dorchester Museum, after a long and unexplained exile. See p. 456.

point in the same direction. Lincoln retained through the dark
ages not only its Roman name with a minimum of perversion,
but also its Roman fortifications, in what seems to have been an
unusual state of preservation: the so-called Newport arch still
exists as a unique survival in Britain of a town gate of the Roman
period.[1] More interesting, perhaps, is the fact that in the second
quarter of the seventh century, before the coming of Christianity, which seems to have been necessary as a stimulant to the
reawakening of town life on many Roman sites, there was
already an Anglian *praefectus Lindocolinae civitatis* whose presence
in the city implies some degree of population within the old
walls.[2] There is, further, at least one figure in the line of Lindsey's kings whose Celtic name, Caedbaed, may be indicative of
an unusual degree of contact in the sixth century between native
and Saxon princes.[3] These facts may lead archaeologists to
devote closer scrutiny than might otherwise be thought necessary to such claims as have been made recently for the survival
of some traces of the *territorium* of the Roman colony in the
rectangular lay-out of parish boundaries which is so marked a
feature of the countryside both north and south of Lincoln, over
an area which to a large extent equates with that which we have
already noticed as devoid of early Saxon remains. It cannot
indeed be denied that the notion of an unusual degree of native
survival in and around the Roman colony, culminating perhaps
in a peaceful absorption of the whole enclave with far less disturbance than occurred on most other Roman sites, possesses an
attractive plausibility.

It would, however, be unwise to state the case more strongly.
The antiquities of Lincolnshire have not in the past received
that careful attention which makes it possible to argue with any
confidence from the apparent lack of finds to a denial of early
settlement, and, while the discovery of further cemeteries in
neighbouring villages is in no way improbable, the single urn
from Lincoln itself may well be the sole survivor of a pagan
graveyard comparable in extent and significance to those which
encircle York. The Roman age of the parish boundaries is not
a matter to be lightly assumed, and is scarcely susceptible of

[1] When the Norman castle was built its earthen ramparts completely buried,
and so preserved, another gate which was still standing and thus remained almost
intact until it was uncovered and destroyed in quite recent times.

[2] Bede, *Hist. Eccles.* ii. 16.

[3] F. M. Stenton in *Essays in History presented to R. Lane Poole* (1927), 139.

proof; and the survival of the Roman name of Lincoln itself may have no significance at all. If the *praefectus civitatis*, whom Paulinus converted, presided over a community that possessed any recognizable continuity with Roman times, it would seem that that continuity was soon lost, for the church which the saint built was roofless and all but deserted in Bede's day, and the city, in spite of its traditions, had to wait many centuries before it became once more the centre of a Christian bishopric.[1]

Westward from Lindsey the flooded country covering the lower reaches of the Trent and the Idle was no bar to the progress upstream of those Humbrensian bands who, finding at last drier riverside lands in south Nottinghamshire and Leicestershire, seem to have laid there the foundations of the Mercian people. From Newark, at any rate, a line of cremation-cemeteries, mostly on the right bank of the Trent stretching away to Burton and beyond, indicates an early and substantial incursion which penetrated also up such southern tributaries of the main river as the Soar, and there met and mingled with settlers from the Fenland region coming down these valleys from Northamptonshire and Rutland. It is not possible to estimate at present the relative strength of the contributions made by these two groups to the earliest Mercian federation. There is, however, good reason to believe that political cohesion was here late in achievement: apart from the mysterious Cearl who was the father-in-law of Edwin of Deira, but does not appear in the pedigree of the later Mercian dynasty, there is no record of a king of Mercia before the accession of Penda in 626,[2] and indeed the close, if hostile, relations between Edwin and Cuichelm of Wessex make it difficult to believe that a people of any political consequence existed in the country between them much before this date.[3] It is true that the dynasty of Penda is known to have claimed descent from the royal family of the continental Angles, and the fact that the stock was known later on as Iclingas may lend colour to the notion that the Icel who appears in the pedi-

---

[1] *Hist. Eccles.* ii. 16. There is no reason to believe that the kings of Lindsey, who maintained an obscure existence until the eighth century, made use of Lincoln as an *urbs regia*. It is probable, however, that Blaecca, the converted *praefectus*, was connected with the dynasty, for his name alliterates suggestively with the Beda, Bubba, and Biscop who were successive kings about this time.

[2] Or 633, if Bede's authority (Ibid. ii. 20) be preferred to that of the *Anglo-Saxon Chronicle*.

[3] As was pointed out by J. Beddoe (*Races of Britain* (1885), 50).

gree five generations earlier than Penda was the first of the line
to hold sway in Britain. There is, however, no means of knowing whether it was under the leadership of Icel that the earliest
Mercians poured into the middle Trent valley from the estuary
of the Humber, or whether it was the later arrival of this illus-
trious family bringing a strong reinforcement to the pre-existent
settlers perhaps from the Fenland region[1] that led to the territorial expansion and political achievements of the Mercians in
the seventh century. It is, however, clearly of some importance
to find Penda described as the king who first separated the
Mercians from the *Regnum Nordorum*.[2] Until his day, it would
appear, Mercia had remained politically dependent on the
Humbrenses, the Men of the North.

There is furthermore a suggestion of duality in the settlement
of Mercia which may perhaps be held to give support to this
view. It has already been noticed that the earliest Mercian
people are represented archaeologically by the cremation-cemeteries on the right bank of the middle Trent and on its southern
tributaries. In Bede's day the Trent itself separated the five
thousand families of these southern Mercians from the seven thousand families of the northern Mercians beyond the river,[3] and
it is interesting to observe the marked archaeological contrast
between the two areas. North of the river cremation, so
common to the south, is conspicuous by its absence, while poorly
furnished inhumation-cemeteries, and barrow-burials similar to
those of Wiltshire, suggest as in that area that an unusually prolonged period of raiding preceded and delayed the final occupation.[4] It may even be guessed that the term Mercians—the men
of the frontier or march—may have first come into use in this
early period when the Trent itself marked the boundary between the settled lands to the south and the insecurely held
country stretching northwards to the foot-hills of the Peak.[5]

---

[1] Or from the land of the Hwicce; see p. 410, n. 3.

[2] *Hist. Britt.*, § 65.   [3] *Hist. Eccles.* iii. 24.

[4] See Baldwin Brown, *Arts in Early England* (1915), iv. 773, for the late date of
the barrow-burials in this region.

[5] It is interesting to observe that another Mercia, represented now by the place-
names Markington and Markenfield near Ripon, seems nearly to have developed
in the West Riding of Yorkshire between Deira and Elmet. (*Eng. Place-name Soc.
Yorks. North Riding* (1928), xiv.) That the districts south of the Trent were the
earliest focus of Mercia is suggested further by the fact that both its religious centres
(Repton and Lichfield) and the most important *villa regalis* of its kings (Tamworth)
were all in this part of the kingdom.

However that may be, the absorption of these and other areas and the rapid rise of Mercia to political dominance in the seventh and eighth centuries is of the greatest interest from an economic point of view. For much of the Trent basin and of the northern midlands as a whole was covered with dense natural forest, and had carried only the scantiest population in the Roman period. The Mercians were the first of the Anglo-Saxon peoples to demonstrate in a practical way that revolution in political and economic geography which the systematic exploitation of the heavy forested soils was to entail in the development of England.

Northwards beyond the Humber the line of the Lincolnshire wolds is picked up and emphasized by those of Yorkshire, which, sweeping on towards the Malton gap and then eastwards along the south side of the vale of Pickering, finally plunge into the sea at Flamborough Head. These chalk hills, with their steep escarpments to west and north and their gentler slopes and fertile valleys south-eastwards towards the low-lying and forested Holderness, constitute another natural and clearly demarcated region, even more obviously attractive than Lindsey to the earliest Anglo-Saxon settlers. Here, there can be no doubt, lay the core of the kingdom of Deira, and from this, as from another Sussex, pioneers spread out, as the years passed, on three sides: eastwards into Holderness, where the place-name In Dera Uuda, associated by Bede with the later monastery of Beverley, seems to preserve a memory of the common forest pastures of the earliest Deirans; northwards into the lagoons and morasses of the vale of Pickering; and westwards down the valley of the Derwent, and by the Roman road from Malton into the plain of York. On the Wolds themselves especially round Driffield and along their western fringes the archaeological signs of an occupation beginning as early as the fifth century are thickly spread: we know from Bede that the religious centre of the Deirans in pre-Christian times was at Goodmanham,[1] and that there was an administrative centre, a *villa regalis*, in Edwin's day, somewhere on the Derwent,[2] in all likelihood at or near Malton, where the ruins of the Roman fortress which had perhaps controlled the last attempts at coastal defence in the previous period still emphasized the strategic importance of the site.

---

[1] *Hist. Eccles.* ii. 13.   [2] Ibid. ii. 9.

Inland much of the plain of York, along the lower courses of the Ouse, the Aire, and the Wharfe, was as waterlogged as were the lower reaches of the Don and the Trent, and behind this wide natural barrier of flooded country the British kingdom of Elmet, defended perhaps also by lines of earthworks of which traces may still remain in the Roman Rig and the Becca Banks, maintained its woodland independence until the second quarter of the seventh century, when it was conquered by Edwin of Deira. Farther north a cluster of early cremation-cemeteries at York, some of them deliberately set in ground already full of Roman burials, may suggest a history different from that of the colony at Lincoln; it points further to a realization among the new-comers of the nodal position of the site at the crossing of the Ouse by the most important natural highway east and west across the forested plain. Whether these early settlements in and round the legionary fortress originated from the Wolds by way of this ancient route along the terminal moraines of a long-forgotten glacier, or whether they were the outcome of independent expeditions following the course of the Ouse, is uncertain. The similarities between the cremation-pottery of the York cemeteries and those of the Wolds show at least that the two groups possessed close cultural affinities; and by the second quarter of the seventh century in any case the York settlers owed political allegiance to Edwin of Deira, who allowed Paulinus to make the city the centre of his evangelizing activities.[1] Further sporadic finds at Aldborough, Catterick, and Darlington would suggest a northward movement from York up the Roman roads, and confirm the suspicion that the neighbourhood of what had once been the important Roman centres of this district remained in the sixth century the more obvious points from which the agricultural development of a naturally forested region could most easily radiate. And it is possible that, behind the Gododdin poems attributed to the sixth-century poet Aneirin, with their memories of a British disaster at Catraeth (Catterick), there may survive traditions of this northward advance of the Deirans, an advance which seems to have been held up eventually rather by the broken and difficult country in Durham beyond the valley of the Tees than by any successful British resistance.

In the Tees valley, at any rate, we are reaching the limits

[1] Bede, *Hist. Eccles.* ii. 15.

beyond which Roman civilian culture had scarcely penetrated, and in Bernicia the impact of the Anglo-Saxon invaders fell upon a land of Celtic traditions whose scanty pastoral population still lived largely in the moorland and mountain fastnesses from which the Roman armies had but temporarily and partially dislodged them. Such a country-side, poor by nature and poorer still after the destructive raids of Picts and Scots had repeatedly passed over it on their way to the richer lowlands beyond, was not one to attract the earliest Saxon settlement, and the traditional date 547 for the beginning of the reign of Ida, 'from whom the royal stock of the Northumbrians claims descent',[1] may well mark the winning of the earliest effective Anglian foothold in Bernicia.

There are several reasons for believing that the direct assault of Ida and his followers on their future homes was from the sea rather than the land. The coastal distribution of such pagan archaeological remains as have yet been found in Bernicia points irresistibly to this conclusion. It suggests a concentration in two main areas:[2] one was the estuary of the Tyne from which raiding-parties, if not settlers, passed easily westward along the river valley and the line of the Roman Wall and left signs of their presence in the Roman centres of Corbridge and Birdoswald as well as an early *villa regalis Ad Murum* whose site is not certainly identified. The other lay farther north between the Tweed and the Coquet with a focus in the country behind Lindisfarne and Bamborough, and was by far the more important. The promontory fortress of Bamborough, a natural stronghold for sea-faring invaders, became the political centre, the *urbs regia*, of the Bernician kings; Lindisfarne was the first centre of Bernician Christianity; and inland at Yeavering in Glendale was a *villa regalis* on a site which has retained its Celtic name and is significantly marked by a large hill-fort and other striking evidences of British as well as of Anglian occupation.

That the obviously coastal distribution of the earliest Bernician remains is good evidence that the invaders came by sea is suggested further by the complete absence of similar remains to the south between the Tyne and the most northerly Deiran

---

[1] Bede, *Hist. Eccles.* v. 24.

[2] I owe this grouping of the Bernician remains to my pupil, Mr. G. S. Keeney, who has kindly allowed me to use his unpublished thesis on the occupation of Northumberland, Durham, &c., from the fourth to the eighth centuries.

settlements at Darlington in the Tees valley or at Saltburn on the north Yorkshire coast. There is indeed good reason to accept the later tradition that the county of Durham was at this period almost entirely uninhabited owing to its forested and broken character,[1] for the native hill-forts so frequent in Northumberland are here very much more thinly scattered, and we have seen previous instances of Teutonic avoidance in early times of areas which had not been occupied by their predecessors, for these were in general the least attractive to the new-comers.

But if the settlement of Bernicia took place by sea there are reasons for believing that the settlers came from the south rather than direct from the Continent. The late date of the movement makes this at least probable, and there is some positive evidence to reinforce it. According to the local traditions at any rate Ida himself first landed in Britain at Flamborough Head in the homeland of Deira and subsequently moved northwards,[2] and the evidence, slight but significant, that the Bernician kings as late as the end of the seventh century still called themselves kings of the Humbrensians is hardly explicable on any other assumption than that their people sprang from the southern stock of the Deirans.[3] It is indeed possible to see in such seaboard cemeteries as those of Robin Hood's Bay and Saltburn the first phase of this northward movement of the Humbrenses up the forbidding Yorkshire coast-line from Flamborough Head to Tees mouth, once dominated by late Roman signal-stations, and to imagine the later and more adventurous expedition of Ida passing by the cliff-villages of these earlier pioneers on the precipitous edges of Cleveland, and making with a sure instinct

---

[1] In the twelfth-century Life of St. Oswald, the early boundary between Bernicia and Deira is said to have been uncertain because the whole country between Tees and Tyne had been 'a deserted waste and was thus nothing but a hiding-place and home for wild and woodland beasts' (*Symeon of Durham* (Rolls Series), i. 339).

[2] Ibid. i. 338.

[3] Ecgfrid, for example, seems to have used it as an official style. For the philological connexion between Lindisfarne and Lindsey, which would strongly corroborate this idea of a southern origin for the Bernicians already suggested, for example, by the parallelism of the Gyrwe of the Fens with Bede's *In Gyrvum* (Jarrow), see E. Ekwall, *Oxford Dict. of Eng. Place-names* (1936), s.v. The word Bernicia itself, if rightly derived from the Brigantes, also implies a southern origin, for it is clear, both from the distribution of their inscribed coinage and from the location of their tribal capital in Roman times at Aldborough (Yorks.), that the focus of the British Brigantes was not in the later Bernicia but in Yorkshire. The word is thus likely to have been taken north by an expedition some of whose members came from Deira.

for the impregnable fortresses of Bamborough or St. Abb's Head
(Coludesburh)[1] on which to base a military domination of what
to this day we still call Northumberland.

It is clear that for twenty or thirty years from the appearance
of Ida in 547 this movement was strenuously fought by the un-
tamed British kings whose names and exploits are preserved in
the *Historia Brittonum* and became the basis for native sagas and
elegies, some of which are still preserved. At one time we read
of four kings—Urien, Ridderch, Guallanc, and Morcant—who
fought against Hussa, at another of his successor Theodoric
besieged by Urien for three days and nights in Lindisfarne;[2]
and it would seem that it was hardly before the days of Æthelfrid in the last quarter of the sixth century that the Bernician
warriors were able to turn a struggle for bare existence on the
Northumberland coast into a political supremacy which could
make its power felt alike by the Picts of Scotland, the Britons
of Lancashire and north Wales, and the parent stock of the
Angles in Deira. Æthelfrid at any rate was still remembered
in Bede's day as the king who above all others 'had laid waste
the nation of the Britons . . . for no one before him had rendered
more of their lands either habitable for the English by the
extermination of the natives, or tributary by their conquest'.[3]
Bede's terse phrase throws a flood of light not merely on the
methods of Æthelfrid, but on the whole question of British
survival in Northumbria and the mutual relations of invaders
and invaded in the centuries of conquest. And the striking persistence of Celtic institutions, Celtic language, and Celtic place-
names coupled with the peculiarities of the later agricultural
system may lead us to believe that in Bernicia a far greater
proportion of the native lands were at first left for tributary
British subjects of the new military aristocracy than was the
case in those parts of Britain where the invaders were rather
seeking habitable lands for themselves than to live on the rents
of a dependent native population.[4]

The beginning of the career of Æthelfrid marks the limit of
our period in Northumbria and forms an excellent illustration

---

[1] *Antiquity*, viii (1934), 202–4.
[2] *Hist. Britt.*, § 63.   [3] *Hist. Eccles.* i. 34.
[4] On the Celtic elements in Northumbrian institutions see J. E. A. Jolliffe in
Eng. Hist. Rev. xli (1926), 40–2. On Northumbrian agriculture see H. L. Gray,
English Field Systems (1915), 225–7.

of the new phase into which the history of the conquest is turning in the century from A.D. 550 to 650. That phase sees the
creation in their later forms of the traditional kingdoms of the
Heptarchy out of the confusion of the previous century. We
have attempted to analyse that confusion by examining in turn
the three main centres from which the Teutonic conquerors
radiated to the settlement of eastern and midland Britain. In
each case, in spite of substantial local differences, the process
has seemed to be similar, for in each we have watched the break-
down of those common interests which naturally bound together
at first the groups who found their way through the same door-
way into the promised land. The military necessities which first
demanded joint action gave way under the disintegrating influences of geographical divergence and the development of local
patriotisms. In this way we have seen in the south-east how the
postulate of big military movements growing out of the successful activities of the earliest Teutonic leaders as *foederati* is
necessary to explain both the British story in Gildas, with its culmination at Mount Badon, and also the Saxon attribution of a
Bretwaldaship to Ælle of Sussex; we have seen, too, how these
mobile hordes broke up in the second or third generation into
the territorial kingdoms of Essex, Sussex, and Kent and the
Jutish *provinciae* in Hampshire and the Isle of Wight. So too the
Fenland settlers lost their original cohesion in circumstances of
which no memory is preserved and split apart into the maze of
provinciae and *regiones* which present themselves in the Tribal
Hidage; while in the north there are traces in local nomenclature and tradition which suggest the common Humbrensian
origin of the men of Lindsey, Deira, Bernicia, and the valley of
the Trent.

But the pattern of the historic kingdoms was not yet complete. A further consolidation and rearrangement of the smaller
units was necessary to produce the familiar outlines of Wessex,
Mercia, and Northumbria. And this last process was the natural
outcome of the rising population, of the growth of territorial
monarchies, and of the consequent development of political
ambition. With its later expressions the next volume will have
to deal, and the unification of the lands north of the Humber
begun by Æthelfrid and continued by Edwin, Oswald, and
Oswy need not concern us; nor need the creation of a greater
Mercia by Penda and his successors with the absorption first of

Middle Anglia and Lindsey and eventually 'of all those provinces which are known by the general name of the South
Angles'.[1]

But the earliest and most striking example of the process falls
within our period and concerns the formation of the historic
Wessex. Here, if we are not mistaken, it was Ceawlin who
contrived, by imposing the dominance of his southern dynasty
upon the prosperous West Saxon settlements of the upper
Thames valley, to make that fertile and well-populated region
the temporary centre of a military despotism which pressed
Kent heavily on the east,[2] broke up such British enclaves as still
remained in the Chilterns and north Bucks.,[3] forced back the
Welsh from the Cotswolds and the lower Severn,[4] and absorbed
the old-established British and Anglo-Saxon communities in the
valley of the Warwickshire Avon.[5] This mushroom empire
collapsed, it is true, in the face of internal dissension even before
600, and the growing power of Mercia in the seventh century
drove Ceawlin's successors to abandon the homeland of the
West Saxon communities on the upper Thames. But his work
had not been in vain. There still remained to the new Wessex
a nucleus of rich and varied agricultural land, an imperialistic
tradition, and a powerful dynasty whose members devoted their
energies as the years passed with ever-increasing success to an
irresistible if largely unrecorded expansion over the downland
and the fertile valleys of the south-west, and to the peaceful
absorption of their still numerous British population. And in
this methodical agricultural exploitation and the steady increase of numbers and wealth of which it was both the cause
and the effect, no less than in the capacity for compromise and
understanding shown in the quiet amalgamation of subject
peoples, lay the seeds of something greater than the conquests of
Ceawlin, the beginnings of the kingdom of England.

[1] Birch, *Cart. Sax.* 154.
[2] '568: Ceawlin and Cutha fought with Æthelberht and drove him into Kent.'
[3] '571: Cuthwulf fought with Britons at Bedcanford and took four towns, Aylesbury, Limbury, Bensington, and Eynsham.'
[4] '577: Cuthwine and Ceawlin fought with Britons . . . at the place called Deorham; and they took three *castra*, Gloucester, Cirencester, and Bath.'
[5] '584: Ceawlin and Cutha fought with Britons at the place called Fethanleag . . .
Ceawlin took many *tunas* and countless booty and returned in anger to his own.'
Fethanleag has not been certainly identified: the most plausible suggestion is the
Fachanleage near Stratford-on-Avon mentioned in the bounds of two tenth-
century charters. (E. T. Leeds, *Archaeology of the Anglo-Saxon Settlements* (1913), 63.)

XXIV

THE CHARACTER OF THE CONQUEST

THE time has not yet come when definitive answers can be given to the questions which present themselves for solution in this part of our inquiry. It is, indeed, far less possible than it was twenty or fifty years ago to speak with confidence of the character of the Anglo-Saxon conquest, to estimate the extent to which the old population survived, and the degree of continuity, if any, which may have linked the cities and villas of the Roman province with the *burhs* and manors of late Saxon England. Universal agreement on such topics there has, of course, never been, but questions which in the Victorian age could be answered with a clear-cut Yes on one side, and a determined No on the other, are now too often regarded as themselves anachronistic or irrelevant,[1] and at best receive replies so hedged with qualifications and reserves as to suggest rather the evasions of diplomacy than the precision of science. In this matter, indeed, there is some excuse for the belief that an increase of knowledge has led only to a growth of ignorance.

In these circumstances the most useful form which a discussion of these questions can take will be one in which on the negative side the weakness of some earlier lines of inquiry is suggested, and on the positive side such facts are mentioned as appear likely to repay more detailed study than they have yet received. If finally a general survey of the state of England in the middle of the sixth century is attempted it will be in the full consciousness that the development of research along these and other lines may render it at any time, in whole or part, obsolete.

One example may be given to illustrate the growth of ignorance. It is obvious that the only direct evidence which can be used to answer the question 'What proportion of the pre-Saxon population survived?' is the evidence of physical anthropology. What is essentially an anthropological problem can only be tackled directly by anthropological methods. But whereas in

---

[1] The problem of villa-survival as it was left after nineteenth-century research may be studied, for example, in the careful summary of E. Lipson, *Economic History of England*, i (1915), ch. i; but the problem as he discussed it has become in the light of recent study little more than an academic exercise: it bears little relation to the facts at present regarded as significant.

the past distinctions between human stocks were often held to be easily recognizable in differences of physical structure—especially, for example, in skull-form or in the colour of hair and eyes—it is now generally recognized, firstly that the laws governing the inheritance of such physical characteristics are so complicated as to make distinctions based upon them most unreliable in the present state of knowledge,[1] and secondly, that even if they were reliable, neither the Romano-Britons nor the Anglo-Saxons can be regarded, in view of their previous history, as a sufficiently homogeneous group to enable such distinctions as have hitherto been considered, to be used with confidence in their differentiation.[2] To mention but one instance to illustrate this point, it may be noted that recent work on the Belgic peoples and on the character and extent of their invasions of south-eastern Britain in the immediately pre-Roman period has demonstrated more clearly than ever before their origin in a fusion of German and Celtic strains.[3] Any future attempt to evaluate anthropologically the relation of native and Saxon in the Belgic area of Britain will thus have first to determine the extent to which the population was already Germanized even before the Claudian conquest. Meanwhile we can be confident only that the easy distinctions of earlier days, the far-reaching conclusions derived from a study of cephalic indices or tables of nigrescence, however important they may be as landmarks in the history of anthropological method, however useful as a collection of statistics, can no longer be employed by themselves as direct evidence on our present problem: and until the anthropologists are agreed on a more reliable approach[4] it would seem mere waste of time for others to continue the discussion.

Of the indirect lines of inquiry into the two problems of the survival of pre-Saxon institutions and of pre-Saxon population

[1] See the letter of G. R. de Beer quoted in R. H. Hodgkin, *History of the Anglo-Saxons* (1935), i. 382 d.

[2] On the Romano-Britons see L. H. D. Buxton in *J.R.S.* xxv (1935), 35–50, particularly his statement that they are anthropologically 'extremely closely related, if identity of measurement be a criterion of relationship, to . . . the Anglo-Saxons'.

[3] C. F. C. Hawkes and G. C. Dunning in *Archaeological Journal*, lxxxvii (1930), 150 ff.

[4] The most suggestive recent study is that of the Saxons of the Oxford district by L. H. D. Buxton in *Custom is King* (1936). He concludes that the bulk of the Saxons from the Oxford district were craniologically indistinguishable from the Romano-Britons, though the Abingdon skulls are of a more distinct and normal type. Dr. Buxton kindly allowed me the use of his paper before publication.

the study of place-names which has made such important recent advances is more likely in the long run to throw light on the first than on the second. For the detailed county surveys now in course of publication have shown that not merely in the south and east of Britain, but also in such areas as Devon or Worcestershire, which were far less affected by Anglo-Saxon penetration in our period, Teutonic place-names almost everywhere supplanted Celtic except for such natural features of the countryside as rivers, forests, or conspicuous hills. On any showing the survival of pre-Saxon folk in Worcestershire must have been proportionately much greater than in Surrey or Sussex, and the fact that such differences are barely reflected in the place-names is a clear enough indication of their fallibility as a guide to the degree of human survival in different parts.[1]

Even in the matter of institutional survival the place-name evidence can be very easily misused. It is, for example, ludicrous to suppose that those Roman towns whose names were preserved more or less recognizably in later times, say Gloucester (Glevum), or Cirencester (Corinium), are for that reason alone more likely to have survived the storms of the dark centuries than those whose names were lost or distorted out of all recognition, such as Chichester (Noviomagus) or Leicester (Ratae).[2] For Roman towns, whether inhabited or not, must have been conspicuous objects in the Anglo-Saxon landscape, and the survival or loss of their names was in general determined by the same principle, or lack of it, as that which led to the survival or loss of the names of other prominent features of that landscape, such as rivers or hills. Where, as in Kent, there is other evidence for

---

[1] It is, of course, highly probable, though the probability has received little attention, that many place-names now to all appearances thoroughly Teutonic are in reality basically Celtic, and owe their present form to popular substitution of a Germanic for a similarly sounding Celtic word. Thus if we did not know that the Celtic Eboracum lay behind such early forms of York as Eoforwic, the name would almost certainly have been derived by students of place-names from the Saxon word for a boar, and its Celtic origin would have been very naturally denied. Where pre-Saxon forms are not preserved it is in the nature of the case impossible to determine the extent to which this factor of sound-assimilation may have operated, and any arguments based on the small extent of Celtic survival behind our place-names are thus necessarily devoid of value. The exceptional agility displayed by the British Army in the Great War in thus perverting the names of French villages to English equivalents makes it easier to visualize a similar attitude of their Anglo-Saxon ancestors to the Celtic place-names of Britain.

[2] As is argued by R. E. Zachrisson, *Romans, Celts and Saxons in Ancient Britain* (1927), 60–3.

an uncommon degree of native survival, it is certainly tempting and perhaps legitimate to regard the almost unaltered persistence of the names of several Roman walled sites such as Reculver (Regulbium), Dover (Dubris), and Lympne (Lemanis) as evidence for an unusually close contact between invader and invaded. But far more significant than such persistence for the problem of urban continuity in this area is, as it happens, the loss by Canterbury of its name Durovernum. For here the substitution of the British tribe-name of the Cantiaci, in the Teutonic dress of the Cantware, recalls with some force the parallel history of many tribal capitals in northern Gaul, such as Paris (Lutetia Parisiorum), Reims (Durocortorum Remorum), or Amiens (Samarobriva Ambianorum), of whose continuous occupation in some form or other there need be little doubt. Canterbury, however, is the sole example of this phenomenon in Britain, and its occurrence in the one urban centre for which in other ways a good case for an unbroken life can be made, may serve as an additional warning against basing theories of the survival of urban conditions elsewhere on the mere persistence of a non-tribal Roman name.

The problem of urban survival is in any case one which can only be solved after the consideration of many other factors besides the place-names, and these factors will include the topographical evidence as well as such information as can be supplied from the literary sources. But first of all it is necessary to consider what we mean by urban survival. Do we mean merely that for no appreciable time during these centuries was the site of a town wholly devoid of human habitation, or do we mean that in some attenuated but recognizable form there was also a continuity of civic consciousness? It is clear that without a survival of population there can be no survival of institutions, but it would also be quite possible for a site to be in some sense continuously occupied and yet to lose every trace of its former organization, every characteristic which distinguishes urban life either from the life of another sort of organic unit—say a village community—or from that of a chance concourse of refugees or squatters. It is hardly justifiable to claim urban survival except where there is a reasonable certainty not merely that the town was continuously occupied but that the occupiers were conscious of the links which bound them to the past and endeavoured, however feebly, to conform to civic custom.

A good deal of confusion has been caused in the past by attempts to utilize the topographical evidence in the absence of any complete collection of the relevant material. At present very few even of the more important Roman towns have received adequate topographical study from this point of view, and it is clear that no conclusions can be reached and no generalizations justified until a far more extensive survey has been made. From the evidence at present available it is already clear that the problem of urban survival is more complicated than has sometimes been supposed.

Not only, however, is the topographical evidence incompletely assembled but it is also subject to unusual difficulties of interpretation. One of the more obvious questions which must be considered in any estimate of probable urban survival is the relation which each site bears to the pattern of early Teutonic settlement in its neighbourhood. There are sites such as York (Eburacum) or Caistor-by-Norwich (Venta Icenorum) where the closest relationship seems to exist between a Roman centre and the early Saxon cemeteries. There are others such as London or Verulam of which the reverse is true. Yet it would be equally plausible and equally fallacious to argue either that York and Caistor are instances of continuity because the sites attracted the earliest Teutonic settlement, or that London and Verulam survived because they were strong enough to hold the new-comers at arm's length. Indeed in the case of two of these examples, Caistor and Verulam, the close presence of barbarian settlers to the one, and their marked absence from the other, are equally consistent with the probability that both lost in these centuries not merely their urban institutions but also their population, for neither emerged from the dark ages as more than a negligible hamlet. Meanwhile neither the Anglian settlements at York nor the lack of pagan cemeteries near London can be used by themselves as evidence for institutional continuity, though both are clearly significant factors in estimating the extent to which each of these sites enclosed a human population of some sort throughout our period.

Another difficulty of the same kind may also be mentioned. It has sometimes been argued that the surest evidence for continuity of occupation from Roman to medieval times would lie in the survival of the street-plan of the Roman town.[1] Where

[1] See, for example, W. Page, *London, its Origin and Early Development* (1923), 31.

the main lines of communication within a town remained unchanged, there and there only would it be justifiable to claim
continuity of occupation and perhaps of urban life. Where, on
the other hand, there appears little or no similarity between the
position of Roman streets and that of their medieval successors,
there, it is argued, the claim to continuity must fail, for any
radical alteration of street-plan, involving as it must not only
a change in the lines of communication but also a wholesale
shifting of property boundaries, is unthinkable on a continuously inhabited site, and must imply a period of desolation
sufficient for the obliteration of old landmarks and the elimination of old claims. It has, however, been recently contended
that this argument is valueless, that a contrast between the
Roman and medieval street-plan can be best explained as the
result of continuous occupation in conditions of 'indifferent
civic discipline', and that a period of desolation would in fact
be more likely to lead to a survival than a disappearance of the
Roman plan, for it would be possible, when the time came for
reoccupation, to clear and reopen the old lines, unhampered
by the distortions and obstructions brought about in a period
of decadent but unbroken existence.[1]

It is impossible here to discuss the relative merits of these two
lines of thought. They are mentioned only to emphasize the
lack of agreement in the interpretation of the evidence, and it is
clear that both are over-simplified as explanations of the actual
situation. Before either is made the basis of a dogmatic generalization it will be necessary to examine the topography of each
site in order to determine if possible whether the facts suggest
such a radical alteration of street-plan as would naturally result
from reoccupation after a period of abandonment, or such a
progressive distortion of the original lay-out as might be consistent with continuous occupation in conditions of indifferent
civic discipline. None of the crucial instances have yet been
considered adequately from this point of view, and it will be
impossible to use their evidence until such detailed studies are
available. Meanwhile it may merely be noted that the more
marked is the contrast between the Roman and medieval street-
plan, the weaker is the case for any continuity of civic consciousness, for it is admittedly only where such consciousness is dead
or moribund that the practice of living in what had once been

[1] R. E. M. Wheeler, *London and the Saxons* (1935), 80–2.

a street or using as a street what had once been private property is readily understandable. Such practices may be consistent with a bare continuity of human occupation, but hardly with that persistence of institutional order or municipal life which we have seen to be properly inherent in the notion of urban survival. On the other hand the existence of a rectangular street-plan in the middle ages on a Roman site is in itself no proof of urban survival: it is not even a proof of Roman origin. For it must be remembered that towns planned with a gridiron arrangement of the principal streets were frequently laid down afresh in the burghal centres of late Saxon times, and these were as often on virgin as on Roman sites.[1] A rectangular planning of streets may thus be no older than the tenth century and as such irrelevant to the present purpose. To prove its relevance it must be shown that the medieval streets overlie Roman predecessors on the same alinement.

It would thus appear that from the topographical evidence little direct information is at present to be drawn, and that much detailed study will have to be devoted to individual sites before arguments based on them can be properly used in an historical connexion. If we turn to the literary evidence it may be possible to obtain a somewhat clearer picture. It has already been suggested that even in the later part of the Roman period many of the towns were in an advanced state of decay and that all had suffered severely from that creeping paralysis of economic activity which characterized urban life all over the western empire after the third century. In conditions of increasing political insecurity, however, the possession of easily defensible walls made them the natural centres of escape from the raids of Picts, Scots, and Saxons; and it would not be an improbable guess that the influx of refugees from the country-side and the concentration of the more romanized classes in the towns in the late fourth and early fifth centuries may have arrested, if not temporarily reversed, the tendency they had long been showing to a decreasing population. However that may be, it seems plain that the check was short-lived and that civic enterprise, in spite of the responsibility laid upon it by Honorius, played little part in such organized opposition as was put up to Saxon settlement. If there is any justifiable inference to be drawn for our purposes from the story of St. Germanus's visits, it is that of

[1] e.g. Oxford, Wallingford, or Wareham.

the helpless incompetence of such urban organization as remained in southern Britain. The leading men of Verulamium may have been vigorous enough in theological disputation, as Celtic society indeed has always shown itself both in an urban and non-urban environment, but no steps whatever had apparently been taken to protect the country-side of southern Britain, which though 'Romanized to an extent unparalleled elsewhere'[1] remained at the mercy of every passing raid. It is similarly of some significance to notice the non-urban background of Gildas's account of the earliest Teutonic settlement. Political authority on the British side, so far from being in the control of municipal officials, or even, as was coming to be the case increasingly in contemporary Gaul, in that of the urban episcopate,[2] has already passed to 'a proud tyrant' in whose counsels no recorded part is played by the spokesmen of urban interests—a man who is able, according to the later versions of the story, to dispose of considerable territorial areas without any mention of resistance or concurrence on the part of the towns which they contained.[3]

Gildas indeed is unusually precise on this matter of urban survival. He attributes a general destruction of the towns of Britain to the period of disastrous raids following the rupture of relations between 'the proud tyrant' and the first federate settlers.[4] This period preceded the British revival begun by Ambrosius Aurelianus which culminated at Mount Badon; and it has been suggested earlier on[5] that it reached its climax with the reign of Ælle of Sussex in the last quarter of the fifth century. Gildas adds to this assertion the interesting comment that even in his own day the cities of Britain still lay uninhabited and destroyed,[6] as the direct consequence of these events, which, as we have seen, he places no earlier than the generation before his own birth. It is important to gauge the significance of Gildas's testimony on this point, for if it were possible to accept it at its face value it would be unnecessary to continue this discussion further. Such a definite statement from an almost contempo-

---

[1] R. E. M. Wheeler, *London and the Saxons* (1935), 58.

[2] The spirited resistance of Clermont under Bishop Sidonius Apollinaris to Visigothic aggression occurred within a generation of the 'Adventus Saxonum' to Britain.

[3] The only protest, significantly enough, came, according to the *Hist. Britt.*, § 37, from Guoyrancgon, a local king in Kent.

[4] Ch. 24. [5] See pp. 379–82. [6] Ch. 26.

rary source would be sufficient to settle the problem of urban survival once and for all with a negative answer.

Two main lines of argument can be used to discredit the evidence of Gildas. It can be said that his avowed purpose was not to write history for its own sake, but to lead his countrymen to a more moral life by attributing their political misfortunes to divine vengeance on their sins, and that his rhetorical method permitted, if it did not compel, him to exaggerate those misfortunes for the strengthening of his moral argument. It may also be urged that he had difficulty on his own confession in securing accurate information about the condition of Britain as a whole, that in fact his knowledge even of contemporary events was strictly limited to the west, and that in consequence a generalization on the fate of the towns all over Britain made by one in his position can have little or no value to us. Now the validity of the second argument may be admitted at once: we cannot use Gildas's statement as evidence that all the towns of eastern Britain had been destroyed before the end of the fifth century, and since the problem is one which has its focus in eastern Britain, where native society had been most thoroughly urbanized, this is more than enough to deprive his evidence of finality. But within his limited western horizon it is hard to reject it altogether, if only because he does use this destruction of towns as one of the planks in his moral argument. A preacher is not likely to win so great a reputation for sagacity as Gildas achieved among his countrymen if his sermons are illustrated with demonstrably untrue statements of easily verifiable contemporary facts. It was indeed precisely because he thought that he had an explanation of facts which were as familiar to his audience as to himself that he ever wrote his book at all. We are thus compelled to agree that in south-western Britain such urban centres as retained any vitality in the last quarter of the fifth century received at that time a blow from which, in the middle of the sixth, they had not yet recovered.

Beyond this point, however, the direct literary evidence will not take us very far. One entry in the *Anglo-Saxon Chronicle* has sometimes been thought to imply a degree of urban survival in the generation after Gildas. After the battle of Deorham in 577 we are told that Ceawlin and the West Saxons took Gloucester, Cirencester, and Bath.[1] But it would be highly precarious to

[1] The reputed grant by Æthelred of Mercia to Osric prince of the Hwicce of

conclude from such a statement that these places remained in any significant sense urban centres, or that, if their walls still proved serviceable in times of need, the defenders had any direct connexion with the Roman past. Indeed, in these western parts it would be legitimate to quote the direct statement of Gildas as precluding any such continuity, and it is at least arguable that the compiler of the *Chronicle* made use of the three names as no more than convenient geographical expressions to indicate the extent of country which fell, after the battle, under Saxon domination.

Such entries, in fact, serve merely to emphasize the non-urban atmosphere which is as striking a feature of the *Anglo-Saxon Chronicle* and the other Saxon sources as it is of the native tradition preserved by Gildas or Nennius. And this is true not only of those parts of Britain where town life had scarcely taken firm root even in the securest days of the Roman occupation, but also of the more highly urbanized south-east. Even in Kent, as we have seen, Canterbury and Rochester play no part in the traditions of the settlement; London is not mentioned between 457 and 604; Colchester appears in no Saxon source before the tenth century; no incident connected with Winchester or Silchester found a place in the West Saxon legends, and though Chichester may have been renamed after a son of Ælle, the slaughter of Anderida in 491 is significantly located, not in a town, but in a Saxon Shore fort. Most remarkable, however, is the case of Verulamium, for here the continuous memory of St. Alban's martyrdom on the neighbouring hill-side[1] serves only to throw into the strongest relief the complete collapse of municipal life after the middle of the fifth century; for, if any analogies from Roman Gaul were applicable in Britain, this juxtaposition of saint and city should have been sufficient to secure the transference of the urban tradition from the municipal authorities to the safe keeping of the Church.

It is, indeed, the contrast in the ecclesiastical situation

---

300 *tributarii* at Gloucester (? 681) (Birch, *Cart. Sax.* 60) would, if it could be relied upon as genuine, be valuable evidence of the survival at that date of something very like the *territorium* of the Roman colony, for the grant is subsequently referred to in the same document as *civitatem cum suo agro*. Unfortunately, though it preserves archaic features, the text in its present form can hardly be original.

[1] Bede's words (*Hist. Eccles.* i. 7) that on the site of St. Alban's martyrdom 'miracles of healing do not cease to be performed right up to the present day' are most naturally read as implying continuity of cult from Roman times.

between Britain and Gaul which illuminates most strongly the
fate of the British towns in the sixth century. For in Gaul, even
when the break-down of the imperial system had deprived the
towns of their official significance, they retained an administrative importance as the seats of the bishops and the centres of
ecclesiastical life. There can be little doubt that it was the
Church and the urban episcopate which more than any other
factor kept alive the civic traditions of Gaul until the beginning
of the middle ages. But in Britain there is no hint of such a
process, and its absence is perhaps the strongest argument
against the survival of town life through this period. In the
east Christianity itself all but entirely disappeared before the
onslaught of heathen invaders,[1] and in the west the church of
Gildas and David lost utterly the traditions of its urban origin.
For it is important to remember that Christianity in the western
provinces of the Roman empire had been essentially an urban
faith: a fact illustrated aptly enough in the history of the word
pagan, which from its original meaning of countryman acquired
the religious sense of non-Christian, and in Britain the paganism
of the country-side was apparently more profound even than in
Gaul. Thus, while in the second quarter of the fifth century
St. Germanus could dispute subtle points of Christian theology
with the townspeople of Verulamium, he found it advisable to
open the campaign which culminated with the Alleluia victory
by a wholesale baptism of his apparently pagan peasant army.
His action is of great interest as symbolizing that movement of
Christianity from town to country which led eventually to the
peculiar structure of Celtic Christianity, but it is clear that
before this process had made much headway in the lowland
zone of Britain both country-side and towns alike were engulfed
by Saxon conquest. Thus, while the substitution by the British
church of a tribal structure and a monastic organization for the
urban episcopate of Roman times affords striking confirmation
of Gildas's testimony to the desolation of the western towns, the
elimination of Christianity itself in the east is hardly consistent
with their survival in a region in which they had been pre-

---

[1] Some peculiar features of the Saffron Walden cemetery (H. Ecroyd-Smith,
An Ancient Cemetery at Saffron Walden) in north-west Essex are most easily explained
on the assumption that it represents a community of *Wealas* (Romano-Britons:
hence probably the name Walden, *Eng. Place-name Soc. Essex* (1935), 537) who
remained more or less undisturbed and probably Christian throughout this period.
(C. Fox, *Archaeology of the Cambridge Region* (1923), 265–6.)

eminently the centres of the church's life. When Bede ascribes
the failure of St. Augustine's attempt to establish a bishopric in
London to the obstinate heathenism of the inhabitants, his words
are clear enough proof that the Londoners of the early seventh
century were no survivors of Roman Londinium, but a body of
pagan Saxons squatting within the shelter of its walls.[1]

The presence of such a community, if it is scarcely relevant
to the problem of urban continuity, illustrates the form in which
some Roman towns, especially those which, like London, occupied positions of exceptional strategic importance, may have
been displaying, even before the coming of Christianity, a trickle
of human if not of urban life. Yet it would be unwise to deduce
from such phenomena that the Anglo-Saxon invaders had themselves any contribution to make at this time to the maintenance
or restoration of civic conditions. Ammianus Marcellinus speaks
from his own knowledge of the reluctance of the German tribes
to settle within the walls of the captured cities of the Rhineland
in the fourth century,[2] and if this was true of folk whose contact
with Roman society had been comparatively close, it was, we
may be sure, far truer of the more destructive and barbaric
peoples of the north. The Anglo-Saxons were, in fact, pagans in
both senses of the word, men whose vision of life in peace-time
was limited to the bare satisfaction of physical needs by the
cultivation of the land, and whose primitive notions of social
and domestic comfort left no room for the economic and architectural complexities of town life.[3]

It is only in Kent that there is any reason to qualify this
general statement. There we have already seen how the structure of the new provinces or lathes grew up round some of the
main centres of Romano-British population, and how the Cantware, in taking over the name of the British Cantiaci, came to
regard the former tribal capital as their own *burh*. Before the
end of the sixth century Canterbury was not only the residence
of the kings of Kent but also, in Bede's phrase, the *metropolis*
of their *imperium*, and this royal adoption of urban habits was
probably unparalleled at this time in any other part of Saxon
England. It was, moreover, only in Kent that the Augustinian

---

[1] *Hist. Eccles.* ii. 6.   [2] xvi. 2.
[3] The village sites of the pagan period as excavated, for example, at Sutton
Courtenay (Berks.) (E. T. Leeds in *Archaeologia*, lxxiii (1923), 147, and lxxvi
(1927), 59) show the extraordinary squalor of the invaders' life and the primitive
poverty of their cultural equipment.

mission was able to establish its new episcopate upon the traditional urban basis, and the success of this experiment at so small a place as Rochester emphasizes more vividly than the settlement of St. Augustine himself at Canterbury the contrast with other parts of England. Even so near as London, not to mention Paulinus' later plans for York and probably Lincoln, the attempts to follow the Kentish example were for a time unsuccessful, and the seventh-century episcopate eventually evolved on principles more suited to the rural atmosphere of the heptarchic kingdoms. And in Kent itself the disappearance of organized British Christianity and the ruinous churches which St. Augustine found to repair in Canterbury may serve to remind us that even here, under the most favourable circumstances, the continuity of urban conditions was by the end of the sixth century probably more a matter of moribund tradition than of vital fact.

Reference has been made to the light which may be thrown on the situation in London by the failure of the Augustinian bishopric. This is, however, only one among many reasons which justify a sceptical attitude towards the many attempts which have been made to prove the continuity of London's life through the dark centuries.[1] It is impossible to discuss these attempts in detail here.[2] The elements of Roman law in the city's medieval custom can be more plausibly explained than as institutional survivals from imperial times:[3] the medieval traditions ascribing a Roman origin to St. Peter's-on-Cornhill are very late and quite worthless as historical evidence; and while it is true that Saxon London grew up round a centre different from that which had been the focus of Roman Londinium, this interesting fact is more significant as an illustration of Saxon aversion to life in a built-up area than as an argument for the

---

[1] See p. 372, n. 2, for another.

[2] The most recent and most thorough statement of the case for survival is in R. E. M. Wheeler, *London and the Saxons* (1935): for a criticism of some of his arguments see *J.R.S.* xxvi (1936), 87–92, and *Antiquity*, viii (1934), 437–42.

[3] As rightly emphasized by Wheeler, op. cit., 77–80. In Bede, *Hist. Eccles.* v. 12, there is a striking and little noticed example of the adoption by an Anglian 'paterfamilias' in the seventh century of the Roman law of inheritance as later known in London—a third to the wife, a third to the children, and a third to be freely disposed of: it is, however, clear that the man in the story was acting under strong ecclesiastical influence, and the incident provides a remarkable illustration of the extent to which such influence could modify, even quite unconsciously, the institutional customs of the invaders.

survival of the Romano-British population. It has been urged that certain linear earthworks in the Chilterns, in Middlesex, and in Kent can be regarded as 'tangible evidence for the effective survival of London through the Dark Ages',[1] but at present there is no direct proof from excavation that any one of these earthworks is of dark-age date, and even when such evidence is forthcoming there will be other more probable if less dramatic ways of explaining them than by the postulate of a London 'still vital and watchful of her territorial interests'.[2] It is at least clear both from the archaeological evidence for early Saxon settlement and from the continuous line of very primitive place-names along the Thames valley that civic authority did not, in fact, control in any significant sense the Saxon settlement of the London basin;[3] and if a handful of Britons still haunted the ruins of the Roman city, they are more likely to have supported themselves by their wits than by the straightforward commerce which alone could supply the life-blood of London's urban vitality. For London, after all, has always depended for her existence on close commercial contact with the Continent, on the continuance of sea-borne trade, and on the maintenance of that peace and order in the interior of Britain which alone makes it possible for the goods which she handles to find their way over the country-side. At no time in her long history have these indispensable conditions of London's existence been less in evidence than in the fifth and sixth centuries. It was not long after this, perhaps, that the increasing consolidation of the heptarchic kingdoms restored the possibility of London's recovery and made her again, in Bede's words, 'the mart of many nations'. But if London retained a civic consciousness throughout our period, it was indeed an astonishing triumph over economic fact.

In review, the evidence for urban survival in these years has led us provisionally to a negative verdict. It has suggested that

---

[1] Wheeler, op. cit., 83.

[2] Wheeler in *Antiquaries Journal*, xiv (1934), 262. We know, for example, that in the seventh century 'the deserts of Chiltern' were the haunt of Saxon outlaws, and even of political exiles of some consequence, such as Caedwalla of Wessex (Eddius, *Vita S. Wilfridi*, ch. 42): the dykes in question may well be visible protests against the depredations of such people; or again they may be relevant in part to the situation created by the battle of Bedcanford in 571 as argued by W. M. Hughes in *Antiquity*, v (1931), 291 ff.

[3] See above, p. 406, n. 1.

while many towns prolonged a precarious existence far into the fifth century it was rather as passive receptacles for the congregation of refugees than as the centres of active municipal life. And as the last quarter of the fourth century saw a blow dealt to the rural life of Roman Britain from which it never recovered, so a century later, it would seem, the chaotic years which preceded the British revival under Ambrosius Aurelianus extinguished in many places what still remained of civic tradition. And when at last that revival had established a temporary equilibrium in southern Britain, there was little hope of immediate urban recovery, for a new society was already taking shape on both sides of the shifting frontier in which for the time at least town life was to play no part.

In Celtic Britain some five territorial kingdoms were in existence in Gildas's day between Cornwall and north Wales.[1] Their rulers were mainly distinguished, in the eyes of that section of their subjects which still clung tenaciously to the fading memories of Roman culture, by a lack both of moral principle and of coherent policy. In a society revolving inconsequently round the melodramatic activities of this *ménagerie de bêtes féroces*[2] there was little hope for the continuance or the recovery of urban life, and the church, the one surviving symbol of that life, soon learnt by a revolution in its organization to acclimatize itself to the new conditions. In the east, as we have seen, the prospects before the civic tradition were equally, if less permanently, unfavourable. It had no meaning to a stolid agricultural peasantry who thought of towns only as 'tombs surrounded by nets'.[3] If towns contained no loot they could be ignored, and those that were least roughly handled owed their comparative immunity to their weakness rather than their strength. Here and there local circumstances may have delayed the process of progressive decadence, and before the point of extinction had been reached may have handed over a Roman city to a Saxon ruler who could appreciate the nature of his acquisition. In this way, perhaps, Canterbury passed to the kings of Kent; and farther north the *praefectus civitatis* whom Paulinus converted at Lincoln

---

[1] Those of Constantine in Dumnonia; Aurelius Caninus somewhere in the western midlands; Vorteporius in Demetia (SW. Wales); Cuneglasus presumably in central Wales; and Maglocunus, who was the most powerful of the group, in north Wales and Anglesey.

[2] F. Lot, *Bretons et Anglais aux Ve et VIe siècles* (1931), p. 12.

[3] Ammianus Marcellinus, xvi. 2. 12.

and that other *civitatis praepositus* at Carlisle who was proudly displaying to St. Cuthbert 'the wall of the city and the fountain once marvellously built there by the Romans' on the day when King Ecgfrid fell before the Pictish onslaught at Nechtansmere[1] may have been symbols of a similar history. But such exceptions, if they were exceptions, only serve to emphasize the weakness of the link which binds the towns of Roman Britain to those of Anglo-Saxon England.

If, however, the partial survival of the names of Roman towns provides a very insecure argument for urban survival, the complete disappearance of the estate-names of the Romano-British villas is a far more interesting and important matter. For if the villa system had remained as a fact of any significance in the agricultural organization of Anglo-Saxon times, even if the Teutonic settlement had in the first instance taken place, as it did in many parts of Gaul, within the existing framework of the Romano-British estates, one might surely expect that here and there at least the names of some of these estates would have perpetuated themselves as the names of Saxon villages. The contrast between Britain and Gaul is here most illuminating, for, however the phenomenon may be explained, it is generally recognized that names based on those of Gallo-Roman estates remain to this day one of the commonest basic elements among the village-names of France. The absence of such names in this country may serve not only to remind us of the reasons already given for the earlier and more drastic elimination of the cultured land-owning classes in Britain than in Gaul,[2] but also to emphasize the more complete collapse of the old social order which the disappearance of estate-boundaries and estate-names implies. And that this is apparently as true of Kent as of the rest of the conquered territory will help us to remember the great gulf fixed between the character of Teutonic settlement in Gaul and that of even those parts of Britain in which in other ways the closest parallels to it are to be observed.

The archaeological evidence for the break-down of the villa system has already been considered:[3] it fully bears out the evidence of the place-names for the disuse of the old agricultural estates. There is hardly a case in England in which a Saxon

---

[1] Anon., *Vita S. Cuthberti*, § 37.
[2] See pp. 303–5.
[3] See pp. 317–18.

object of early date has been found in a Roman villa,[1] nor are there even any known examples of that use of a ruined villa as a Teutonic burial-ground, of which the occasional instances in Gaul seem to indicate a sort of inverted continuity of occupation, a suggestion at least that a Frankish village was somewhere very close at hand.[2]

It is easy to make this undoubted break-down of the villa system in England the starting-point for an argument whose conclusion will be a denial of any continuity between the agricultural institutions and methods of Roman Britain and those of Saxon England. Such an argument for a great part of the south and midlands it would indeed be hard to combat. In certain areas, notably on the chalk hills of Wessex and Sussex, the new weapon of air photography has been employed to demonstrate the contrast between the upland Romano-British villages with their system of small arable plots, spreading downwards towards the valleys, and the river-side townships of the Saxons, whose great open fields cultivated in bundles of acre and half-acre strips left the ploughlands of the earlier population on the chalk plateaux to return to pasture and waste.[3] In such regions as these the conclusion can hardly be avoided that the conquest involved a complete break with the agricultural past; and the new distribution of the villages, as well as the new pattern of the fields, can be rightly used to illustrate the possession by the new-comers of an agricultural equipment of tools and implements capable of exploiting for the first time the heavier soils which primitive man had always shunned.

It is clear from the general trend of Saxon history that this would be in the main a just conclusion, yet it is easy to be misled by the visual impression of the Wessex air photographs into over-estimating the general extent of local discontinuity between Saxon and British villages. It was by no means everywhere that the character of the terrain or the social antipathy of invaders and invaded justified or demanded the immediate

---

[1] An unpublished pot of Saxon character from the Hartlip villa (Kent), now in the Maidstone museum, is the only certain instance known to me: it may not be merely accidental that this one example should be in Kent, where, as we have seen, the relations of invader and invaded seem to have been unusually close.

[2] Instances of this are at Gondrexange (Moselle); Le Bois Flahaut (Seine Inf.); Furfooz (Belgium). I owe two of these references to Mr. C. E. Stevens. The burials found in the Scampton villa (C. Illingworth, *Topographical Account of . . . Scampton* (1808), 7–8, 13) are probably to be connected with a medieval chapel on the site. [3] O. G. S. Crawford, *Air Survey and Archaeology* (ed. 2, 1928).

occupation of new land. We have seen the gravel terraces of the Thames and other midland valleys spread as thickly with native as with early Saxon villages, and if we are right in thinking that the settlement of the Wessex downland marks, on the whole, a late stage in the conquest of southern Britain, then it may be that the abrupt contrast between the two distributions there was a product not only of cultural difference but also of the passage of time.[1] And where this contrast is less strongly marked, and the Saxon penetration apparently earlier in date, it is less easy to be certain that the older methods of cultivation had no influence whatever on the new.

One further consideration may also give us pause before we postulate everywhere a complete break in agricultural method. It is no longer possible to make a clear-cut distinction between the systems of cultivation employed in this country before and after the Teutonic conquest. In Wessex, indeed, it is generally supposed that the change-over from the small 'Celtic' fields of the pre-Saxon villages to open-field agriculture indicates the first appearance here of the heavy plough which alone made cultivation of the new lands practicable; but there is a growing accumulation of evidence to suggest that already in the Roman period, and perhaps even earlier, a heavy plough was in use in other parts of southern and midland Britain, and there is some reason to believe that its natural accompaniment of open-field agriculture was already here and there in vogue.[2] Whether this heavy plough was related to the Teutonic *pflug*, was the equivalent of the Gaulish *caruca*, or was an improved version of the lighter *aratrum*; whether its introduction was due to the Belgic immigration, to the improvements effected by progressive villa-owners during the Roman period, or to local invention, are questions on which there is no general agreement. We may guess that a heavy plough of some sort was as familiar on the villa estates as was the light *aratrum* in the village areas,[3] but we cannot estimate the survival-value of the improved system in the confusion which brought ruin to the villas and uprooted all classes of the population from their agricultural routine. None the less the possibility of some survival makes it

[1] See also p. 223 for the possibility of extensive depopulation in the village areas of Wessex in late Roman times.

[2] J. B. P. Karslake in *Antiquaries Journal*, xiii (1933), 455 ff. See also ch. xiii.

[3] See above, pp. 210-13. I owe much in this discussion to the ideas of Mr. C. E. Stevens.

unwise to argue without misgivings that the open-field villages of Saxon England have inherited no legacy whatever from Roman Britain.

The difficulties inherent in this problem of agricultural continuity may be illustrated once more from the peculiar circumstances of Kent. Here the nucleated villages with their open fields and communal agriculture, characteristic of midland England, never took root at all, and the widespread occurrence of a system based on single, compact farms held in severalty under the custom of gavelkind and similar in many of its tenurial and social features to the normal arrangements in the Celtic lands or in half-Celtic Northumbria has led many scholars to the belief that here direct continuity can be demonstrated with a pre-Saxon agricultural order.[1] Such a conclusion would not be inconsistent with the historical evidence which, as has been seen, can be interpreted as implying that the Teutonic settlement of Kent took place in the first instance within the structure of the old society. But it is equally possible to maintain, as has recently been done,[2] that the peculiarities of Kentish tenure owe nothing whatever to survival from British times, but were brought in by Teutonic invaders who came from the middle Rhine, a region characterized not merely by pre-feudal institutions parallel in many ways to those of Kent, but also by the closest archaeological similarities in the actual period of the migrations.

Between these two opposite interpretations it would appear at present that there is no sure means of deciding. No criterion is yet available which will enable us to distinguish with certainty between the indigenous institutions of the Cantiaci, which no doubt reflected the amalgamation of earlier Celtic folk with the half-Teutonized Belgae who poured into Britain in the first century before Christ, and those of the middle Rhineland, which were likewise the offspring of Teutonic pressure on a basic Celtic society. And perhaps the search for such a criterion may be merely a waste of time, for it is not impossible that both interpretations are simultaneously true, and that the exceptional tenacity of Kentish institutions may have sprung not only from the vigour and prosperity of unusually civilized invaders, but also from the similarities which linked their social habits with

---

[1] H. L. Gray, *English Field Systems* (1915), ch. vii.
[2] By J. E. A. Jolliffe, *Pre-Feudal England: The Jutes* (1933).

those which were already native to the soil. Such a view would provide an easy explanation both of the early predominance of Kent among the Teutonic kingdoms, and of some unusual features in its social hierarchy. The contrast between the agricultural situation here and in Wessex is in any case a notable illustration of the strange variety which the confusion of these centuries produced in the institutional background of the English people.

It would thus appear that of the characteristic institutions of Roman Britain neither the towns nor the villas survived in any significant sense. Our survey has brought us to the point of saying that the Saxon conquest caused a real break in the continuity of urban life, that, even if the possibility of some influence of the old agriculture on the new be allowed, yet the whole structure of rural society was shattered and reformed, and that the towns and manors of late Saxon England can claim no demonstrable connexion with the Roman past. What light do these facts throw upon the other half of our problem, the extent to which the British population survived to influence the anthropological make-up of the modern Englishman? Even if the time has not come when physical anthropology can supply a direct answer to this question it may be that its general lines can be determined by other considerations.

While there have been few advocates at any time of the idea that the native population was completely annihilated, there have been many scholars who displayed the tendency to reduce its survival to the lowest terms and to speak of it as an altogether negligible factor.[1] Such an attitude is very easy to understand. The obvious contrasts in language and place-names between England and France, the admitted disappearance of the villas and of urban life, and the almost complete absence of archaeological remains other than those of the invaders in this period, seemed only explicable on the assumption that the older population was almost wholly replaced by the new. And yet such an explanation is not the only one possible. We have already noticed that the elimination of the older place-names in Devon and Worcestershire, regions but little affected by Saxon settle-

---

[1] e.g. Freeman's point of view, quoted by T. Hodgkin, *Political History of England*, i (1906), 110: 'though the literal extirpation of a nation is an impossibility, there is every reason to believe that the Celtic inhabitants of those parts of Britain which had become English at the end of the sixth century had been as nearly extirpated as a nation can be.'

ment until after the invaders had abandoned any efforts which they may earlier have made at wholesale extermination, is nearly as complete as in the east of England; and if on the borders of Wales the germanization of place-names is consistent with a considerable degree of native survival may not the same be true of Kent or Essex? So, too, the absence of British archaeological remains is almost as marked in the unconquered west of England as it is in the east and the midlands: it is thus no evidence for the absence of a native population, which in fact is known to have existed in the west, but only for the poverty of its material culture. And the elimination of the villas and of urban life, while it is certainly symptomatic of the break-down of Roman civilization, is no proof of the extermination of the British people, who had survived for centuries before the Roman conquest without any of these things: it may thus merely mean that the standard of civilized life had reverted in these respects to the level of pre-Roman days. Only so long as the question of native survival is thought of as bound up with the survival of Roman institutions and material culture need these factors be regarded as relevant to the question under discussion: once the independence of the two is appreciated, then the elimination of the one may actually be of assistance in explaining the survival of the other. For it will be apparent from the contrast with Gaul that in Britain those classes of the population alone can have survived in any numbers whose material culture when the invasions began was already almost devoid of survival-value. How large those classes might have been on the eve of the conquest will be apparent from Chapter XIX.

So far, however, we have only admitted the possibility of the survival of such native elements as were in the main culturally negative, and have reminded ourselves that by the middle of the fifth century such elements constituted a rapidly increasing proportion of an undoubtedly dwindling population. Are there any means of determining the extent to which such elements did in fact survive? While the inability of the physical anthropologists to provide a direct answer to this question at present has already been observed, it is none the less true that the best anthropological opinion would appear to envisage a very considerable degree of British survival. 'There can be little doubt', runs a typical judgement, 'that the physical inheritance of a great proportion of the present population of the country is derived from its pre-Roman inhabitants who were already of many breeds established side by side.'[1] And it would also seem that even where the Teutonic settlers were most numerous at first, the characteristics of some of these pre-Roman breeds reasserted their influence as time went on. While such judgements as these can only be accepted as provisional, they do constitute an *a priori* case for a greater degree of survival than has often been envisaged by historians, and it would appear most unlikely that the anthropological evidence will ever point towards the extermination of the British people.

Of direct evidence on the extent of such survival in different parts there can, in the nature of the case, be very little trace. A population so reduced in material culture as to be almost unrecognizable to the archaeologist is hardly likely to have left many signs of its presence for the philologist or the student of social custom. We have already noticed in other connexions those areas in the more completely germanized regions in which the occurrence of Celtic place-names or other evidence can be most plausibly interpreted as implying an unusual extent of native survival. Among these, apart from Kent, are parts of west Suffolk, Essex, the Chilterns and north Bucks., areas in the main of fen, heath, or forest, which for one reason or another did not attract at first the attentions of the invaders, and so became natural refuges for the natives. Beyond the limits of the earliest conquered districts the survival was doubtless much greater, and it is perhaps significant that Celtic personal names seem to occur among the invaders more commonly in the Humbrensian area and in Wessex than in the other kingdoms. The number of such names in the royal family of Wessex is indeed remarkable; and while their occurrence cannot, of course, be properly used to discredit the story of the invasion in the *Anglo-Saxon Chronicle*, it does strongly suggest that the house of Cerdic had intermarried on more than one occasion with persons of British stock. And it is reasonable to suppose that in this as in other ways the fashion set by royalty was followed in humbler West Saxon circles.

In Wessex it happens that clearer evidence is preserved of native persistence than in any other part of England. For not only are there many survivals of Celtic place-names in Hampshire and Wiltshire, but in the Laws of Ine and of Alfred there are several important references to the position of Welsh classes

<hr />

[1] H. J. Fleure, *Races of England and Wales* (1923), 19.

in the West Saxon social system. It would indeed be improper to use legislation of Alfred's time to illustrate the conditions of the sixth century, and even by Ine's day (688–725) West Saxon penetration had made notable strides into the Celtic west since the collapse of Ceawlin's empire. But it is interesting to find at that time mention not merely of Welsh slaves but of Welshmen holding as much as five hides of land, with wergelds of 600 shillings,[1] of at least three other classes of Welsh freemen,[2] and yet others whose protection is increased because they are in the personal service of the king. Although the wergelds of the Welsh are apparently reckoned on half the scale of the corresponding Saxon classes—a practice which seems also to have prevailed in later Northumbria,[3] it was still possible for principles characteristic of Celtic custom to find a place in their calculation.[4] Social contact with the native population may perhaps also be inferred from the mention of Welsh ale at this time among the food rents of West Saxon estates.[5]

Elsewhere, no doubt, the survivors of the native population were mostly to be found in the slave-class, which appears to have been very large in early times.[6] It is tempting to see in the Kentish *laets*, whose three grades are allotted wergelds in Æthelberht's code which place them in a position markedly inferior to that of the substantial *ceorls* of Kent, a reference to a surviving British population which we have seen reason to believe was here larger than elsewhere.[7] But the clear equivalence between these *laets* and the *lazzi*, *liti*, or *lati* who appear in a similar social position in the codes of many Teutonic peoples on the Continent, shows that the *laets* were not peculiar to Kent, although no similar class is to be found in Wessex, nor, so far as the scanty evidence goes, in any other English kingdom. The most that can be said, therefore, is that whereas in Wessex the Welsh

---

[1] Laws of Ine, c. 74. Wergeld is the compensation payable by a murderer or his representative to the kindred of a murdered man. It varied with the social status of the deceased. [2] Ibid., c. 32.

[3] H. M. Chadwick, *Studies in Anglo-Saxon Institutions* (1905), 91–3.

[4] F. L. Attenborough, *Laws of the English Kings* (1922), 186.

[5] Laws of Ine, c. 70.

[6] There were 250 slaves on Wilfrid's Selsey estate of 87 hides (Bede, *Hist. Eccles.* iv. 13). If this was at all a normal number, Chadwick has calculated from the figures in the Tribal Hidage that there may have been as many as half a million slaves in seventh-century England. (*Studies in Anglo-Saxon Institutions* (1905), 373: this figure cannot, of course, be used with any confidence.)

[7] Laws of Æthelberht, c. 26.

classes were retained as separate entities within the West Saxon community, in Kent the surviving Britons may have found a place along with Teutonic freedmen and other dependents in the class of *laets* which already existed in the society of the Cantware; and it would be possible to take this as pointing once again to the more complete and successful fusion of the two peoples of which in Kent other signs have been noticed. If this is so, however, it must be admitted that the Britons had been here uniformly reduced to a more subordinate social position than seems to have prevailed in the Wessex of Ine's day, some three-quarters of a century later. By that time, however, the westward advance of the West Saxons must have brought them into contact with lands in Dorset or Somerset where Celtic society may well have survived in a far less confused state than is likely to have been the case in sixth-century Kent.

Another line of inquiry, whose relevance to the present problem has only recently been emphasized, is that which concerns the burial-customs of the Teutonic settlers. It is a familiar fact that to the Teutonic inhabitants of north Germany, from whom the bulk of our invaders sprang, the ancestral tradition was to cremate the dead and to bury the ashes afterwards in urns, while in the western provinces of the Roman empire the universal rite in the fourth and fifth centuries was inhumation. Along the fringes of the empire the Germans everywhere showed great readiness to abandon cremation under the influence of cultural contact with their romanized neighbours, but at the time of the invasions of Britain this tendency had hardly begun to infect the Anglo-Saxon homeland, and such instances of inhumation as have there been noticed serve only to emphasize the general rule of cremation.[1] It would thus be natural to expect that after the migration to Britain the peoples of this region would have continued with some consistency to cremate their dead, but in fact this was not the case. From the beginning both rites are practised with a tendency much stronger in some districts than others towards a general abandonment of cremation, which none the less persisted here and there down to the eve of the conversion to Christianity. Long before this, however, inhumation had everywhere become the normal practice, and

---

[1] See the discoveries at Nesse and at the Galgenberg near Cuxhaven discussed by F. Roeder, *Neue Funde auf kontinental-sächsischen Friedhöfen der Völkerwanderungszeit* (1933).

in some parts, especially in the south-east, it had been all but universal from the beginning. It is clear that the difference between the two rites is not merely one of time.

But if the practice of cremation among the new-comers is not simply a test of date, it must surely be a test of something else: the pattern made by plotting the cremation, inhumation, and mixed cemeteries on the map can hardly be the result of chance. The natural conclusion is that the areas in which cremation is commonest are those in which cultural contact with the native population was slightest, and that in the primarily inhuming regions we must allow for a survival of the Britons on a scale sufficient to influence promptly and effectively the burial-customs of their conquerors. The clue thus provided to the possible extent of British survival in different parts of the country has not yet received the detailed study which it would repay, but there is nothing improbable about the general conclusions which it suggests. Thus the Humbrensian area, where romanization had always been thinnest, and East Anglia, where the native population was scanty and backward, are the chief homes of persistent cremation. The rite also occurs commonly in those *foci* of early settlement, the Cambridge region, the Oxford district, and the whole course of the Thames valley, suggesting that here the mere weight of numbers was sufficient to prevent an immediate adoption of more civilized habits. In Sussex and Kent, on the other hand, it is not very common, and in upland Wessex, and Essex, quite unknown. In Kent, of course, it is probable that if the Britons preached the advantages of inhumation to their conquerors, they were preaching in great part to the converted, for if the latter came mainly from the lower or middle Rhine or from Holland they had mostly discarded cremation before their arrival in Britain. Thus in the matter of burial-customs, as perhaps also in the wider spheres of agriculture and social organization, the similarities between the Cantiaci and the Cantware may have been so close that the part each played in the formation of the Kentish tradition is now barely distinguishable. Elsewhere, however, it would seem that the varying prevalence of inhumation among the earliest settlers may provide a welcome test of the areas in which a culturally negative British population was sufficiently numerous to record its otherwise invisible persistence.

It would be a mistake, however, to overdo our insistence upon the culturally negative character of these survivals. For it has recently been more fully recognized that at least one element of the artistic production of these years in lowland Britain can be claimed as evidence for the continuance of native craftsmanship. The art-forms of this period in Britain can be broadly divided into three main groups. There are firstly the classical *motifs*, taken more or less directly from the standard repertoire of late Roman artists; there are secondly the elements of the Teutonic tradition, and notably the various developments of animal ornament; and thirdly there is the remarkable revival of the so-called 'Celtic' curvilinear style, which, in the seventh and eighth centuries and in combination with *motifs* drawn from the other two traditions, was to become the dominant partner in the Hiberno-Saxon art of the manuscripts and the crosses. With the Teutonic art, represented in every pagan cemetery, we are not at present concerned; nor can we linger over the classical tradition, for while there are some examples of it which many archaeologists would claim as the products of British craftsmen, and many others which some would thus claim, yet the established tendency of the barbarians to adopt and imitate every expression of classical culture renders the assignment of the racial parentage to these romanizing objects an unusually precarious business.[1]

This is, however, not the case with the renaissance of Celtic design in this period. For while it may be legitimate to explain away the occurrence of romanizing objects by the alternative pleas of loot and deliberate imitation, it is hardly possible to account in either way for the revival of a purely British tradition which, after an original florescence of astonishing beauty in the first centuries before and after Christ, had been largely driven off the market by the mass-produced goods of Roman capitalist enterprise. It is hardly possible to doubt that both the Celtic designs and the enamel technique in which they were frequently carried out on metal objects in this period were alike the products of a reviving native craftsmanship; and it has been possible, by plotting the distribution of the so-called hanging bowls, the

---

[1] It is none the less a striking fact that the bulk of these romanizing objects have been found in the south-eastern counties, the great majority being from Kent and Sussex. Mr. Leeds tells me that he believes them all to be the products of sub-Roman craftsmen working for the most part in the early fifth century before the period of Saxon settlement began: in this case they are, of course, irrelevant to the survival-problem.

most conspicuous group of objects which exemplify this Celtic revival, to demonstrate the surprising fact that its focus lay, not in the unconquered west, nor even, as was once believed, in Ireland, but in the heart of lowland Britain, probably in Kent and in the home counties.[1] Whether the revival was a spontaneous result of the disappearance of standardized Romano-British goods, or was strangely stimulated by the otherwise disastrous incursions of the savage Picts, who had paradoxically remained the artistic guardians of the older Celtic tradition;[2] whether the craftsmen worked in the first instance for surviving Romano-British notables or for Anglo-Saxon chieftains in whose graves so many examples of their work found lasting homes, may remain matters for discussion. The moral for our present argument is clear enough. Not only, it would seem, have we to reckon anthropologically with the flotsam and jetsam left by the ebb-tide of Roman imperialism, with frightened and bewildered bands of underfed and under-equipped provincials eking out, as Gildas describes them, a precarious and pathetic existence in forests, swamps, and caves: we have also to find room in the picture for small groups of native craftsmen, men whose minds were steeped in the delicate subtleties of Celtic design, who were unsurpassed in their day in the difficult techniques of bronze-working and enamelling, who had the leisure and the security to produce artistic masterpieces, and the patrons, whether Saxon or British, to purchase and appreciate their wares. It is not easy to understand the position of these men in the chaotic conditions of the age of conquest, but somehow or another they were there.

It is by following such clues as these that we may hope some day to reach a surer knowledge of the extent to which, in different parts of the country, the shattered remnants of the native population merged themselves slowly and painfully in the growing Anglo-Saxon states. And if, bearing these clues in mind, we were to attempt a provisional survey, with the eye of faith, of the state of England soon after the middle of the sixth century, when that process of mergence was in its earlier stages, the first impression such a survey would create would be one of kaleidoscopic variety.

In Kent we should see the prosperous and luxurious aristo-

---

[1] See T. D. Kendrick in *Antiquity*, vi (1932), 161–84.
[2] As argued by A. W. Clapham in *Antiquity*, viii (1934), 43–57.

cracy of the Cantware already firmly established on a sure basis
of trade and agriculture. They were in a position to admire and
develop the skill with gold and garnets of their own and Frankish
jewellers and could afford to encourage the native craftsmanship
of the hanging bowls. Their dependents were laying out the
limits of their self-contained arable farms, here and there making use of pre-existing territorial divisions between the lands of
long-deserted Roman villas. They could often command the
services of a numerous native peasantry, whose methods of cultivation, social habits, and customary law were perhaps assimilated the more readily from the close likeness of their general
character to those of their Teutonic masters. Rents were paid
and justice administered in the *villa regalis* of the lathe or *provincia*, often in the decayed ruins of a Romano-British town,
whose name was sometimes half-retained; and at Canterbury
the king's hall and the houses of his immediate followers, standing self-consciously among the tumbled wreckage of Roman
shops, tenements, and churches, bore witness at once to the new
Teutonic order and to a precarious continuity with the urban
past.

But beyond the limits of Kent that continuity had already all
but disappeared. In the waste of broken buildings that had
once been Roman London an unusually acute eye might detect
a handful of squatters or refugees, men of dubious ancestry and
uncertain occupation; in Essex an occasional clearing in the
woodland, accessible by Roman road or navigable stream,
marked the site of a new Saxon village, or the head-quarters of
a predatory band of Britons, and between the two it must often
have been difficult to distinguish. Westward, in Hertfordshire
and the Chilterns, the settled Saxon communities became rarer
and the surviving natives proportionately more numerous; the
walls of Roman Verulam enclosed in all probability a city of the
dead, though, on the hill-side a mile away, the half-forgotten
sanctuary of St. Alban may never have quite lost the service of
its devotees. In the Thames valley to the south the riparian
lands were thickly settled by immigrant Saxon folk; and
a continuous line of *provinciae* or *regiones* may already have extended all the way from the Geddinges of Middlesex to the West
Saxons of Dorchester and Bensington. Already, perhaps, enterprising pioneers, defying or defeating British opposition, were
spreading into the backlands, like the Hycga who has left the

memory of his extensive Chiltern estate in the Buckinghamshire place-names of Hitcham, Hedgerley, and Hughenden.[1]

Along the English Channel the coastal settlements of the Haestingas, the South Saxons, and the Hampshire Jutes had ignored, eliminated, or enslaved the Celtic agriculturalists of the chalk hills, whose lyncheted fields had already in part reverted to the downland turf from which some of them had been won far back in the Bronze Age; but while the Wealden forest was as yet scarcely touched by Celt or Saxon, the main chalk uplands of Hampshire and Wiltshire were still full of wary British villagers, men of scanty possessions and mobile habits, whom the transient passage of a Cerdic or Ceawlin had temporarily terrorized but neither exterminated nor subdued. Northwards the Wansdyke may have marked a living frontier between a region they still largely controlled and the populous Saxon communities now pressing south and west from the upper Thames into the Berkshire downs and the Severn valley.

Up the east coast various bodies of cremating Angles had found their way into the valleys of Norfolk and Suffolk, and were perhaps already coalescing under the rule of the Wuffingas. Such British survivals as remained in this backward region had probably taken refuge on the heaths and brecklands or plunged westward into the Fens; and we need not wonder that the Angles who cremated their dead in such numbers within a stone's throw of the Roman walls of *Venta Icenorum* were uninfluenced by the more civilized habits of its last British citizens, for these had been massacred in their houses perhaps a hundred years before.

Ignorance and neglect had combined with geological changes to turn the once prosperous farmlands of the Fens into a waste of swamp and reed-bed, and such human population as they supported at this time consisted mainly of British refugees and political exiles of all sorts. Round their margins, on the other hand, and in the valleys that radiated from them, the countryside was already thickly spread with Saxon and Middle Anglian immigrants; it was only in the upland forest towards Essex, on the wooded ridges between the rivers, and south-westwards in Buckinghamshire that any considerable enclaves of British population remained. North of the Fens it is possible that the advancing settlers round Sleaford and on the site of Roman Causennae (Ancaster) were still separated from the

---

[1] *Eng. Place-name Soc. Bucks.* (1925), Introd.

Humbrenses by an unabsorbed Lincoln whose central position and dominating site gave its native occupants the natural advantages of a hill-top stronghold combined with the solid protection of Roman walls and gates. But in Lindsey and East Anglia as a whole, as in the new settlements in the Trent valley, it would seem, from the prevalence of cremation, that contact with natives who retained any noticeable Roman culture was much less frequent than in the south: such British elements as here survived were not of a kind to modify at first in any significant fashion the habits or outlook of the invaders.

This, too, was the case with the Humbrenses of Deira, who from their stronghold in the Yorkshire wolds could look eastwards over their tribal woodlands into Holderness, and westwards across a land still largely unoccupied to York, where the walls of the Roman fortress, long deserted by the legionaries, looked down upon the clustering huts and cremation-cemeteries of other Humbrensian bands. Northwards from the wolds the wind-swept moors of Hambleton and Cleveland remained, as they had done throughout prehistoric time, a refuge of broken peoples, a home of lost cultural causes, in which, as Bede was to put it so aptly later on, *vel bestiae commorari vel homines bestialiter vivere consuerant.*[1]

Beyond the Tees the Celtic north had as yet barely felt the first inroads of Ida and his followers as something more disturbing than the normal routine of passing raids; in the Derbyshire valleys Mercian incursions were giving place to permanent occupation; and across the forested midlands from Staffordshire to Bath a host of Anglo-Saxon river-side settlers were alternately hampered and assisted in their struggle with natural obstacles by the presence of hostile or renegade Britons in every stage of social and cultural collapse. No single generalization can cover the varieties of their piecemeal progress, but the evidence of later agricultural methods throws perhaps the clearest light on its diversity. In Staffordshire, for example, the regular open-field system which became normal in the Trent valley indicates early and complete dominance by the new-comers, but the irregularity of arrangements elsewhere in the county is evidence of slow progress in the long struggle with forest conditions. Farther west, in Shropshire and Herefordshire, while the Saxons

---

[1] Bede, *Hist. Eccles.* iii. 23; and see F. Elgee, *Early Man in North-east Yorkshire* (1930), 219–20.

were eventually strong enough to impose three-field agriculture and many place-names of their own making, yet they could only do so within a society still largely organized on a Celtic basis of hamlets and isolated farms, and nucleated villages of normal Teutonic type are here uncommon.[1] In our period, of course, Shropshire and Herefordshire were still beyond the reach of Anglo-Saxon penetration, but what was true of them in later times was true, we may be sure, of much of the midlands in the sixth and seventh centuries, and may be safely taken to illustrate a stage in the ultimate domination of this area by Teutonic social custom.

It is interesting to contrast this evidence for the slow and piecemeal advance of a Saxon peasantry, gradually permeating with its own methods a pre-existing social system, with the state of affairs in Bernicia, where the fusion of the two peoples took a different form. While Northumberland, for example, is 'a county of villages rather than one of hamlets',[2] many features of its agricultural system are alien to Teutonic tradition, and it retains elements both of language and of local custom which go back to Celtic times. It is impossible to resist the conclusion that here, in place of a slow penetration of humble Saxon cultivators, we are viewing the effects of a military conquest, and that while nucleated villages of Teutonic type grew up round the residences of the new Anglian aristocracy and their followers, a far greater share in the daily routine of cultivation had been left in the hands of the conquered natives. The contrast, not only with the regular Teutonic arrangements of the Deirans and of midland England, but with other half-Celtic areas like the Welsh marches, as well as with the self-contained gavelkind tenements of Kent, well illustrates the enduring influence left by the variegated circumstances of the age of conquest on the ultimate mosaic pattern of the English people.

And there we must leave the fascinating and vital problems of the darkest centuries in English history. If at the end they may seem as dark as they were at the beginning, that is in part the fault not of ourselves but of the inadequacy of the evidence before us. But in part too—and from this we may take comfort —it arises directly from the character of the times. For they were times whose quality cannot be portrayed without serious

---

[1] H. L. Gray, *English Field Systems* (1915), 153 and 189.
[2] Ibid., p. 226.

distortion in those broad and rational sequences of cause and effect so beloved by the historian. The conflicts are too complex, the issues too obscure, the cross-currents too numerous, and the decisions too local, to make possible the application of any single formula to their solution; and it is at least reassuring sometimes to remember that, if we found such a formula, we should unquestionably be wrong. *Uno itinere non potest perveniri ad tam grande secretum.* And if we leave the subject with little more than a blurred impression in our minds we can none the less maintain that that blurred impression represents more faithfully than any clear-cut picture the spirit of the age that we have been trying to understand.

NOTE

p. 414. In addition to the cremation urn recently deposited in the Lincoln Museum by the Dorchester Museum there has long been another urn from Lincoln in the Museum there, and it is this specimen, not that from Dorchester (whose exact findspot is unknown), which was found near the Eastgate. Mr. C. W. Phillips's statement in *Archaeological Journal*, xci (1934), 149, that 'nothing of the pagan period is known from Lincoln city' thus requires modification; and since the presence of more than one urn considerably increases the probability of early Anglian settlement at Lincoln, the argument for British survival there which I derived from the apparent absence of Teutonic finds in its neighbourhood loses most of its force.   J. N. L. M.

IN these two maps an attempt has been made to illustrate the expansion of the earliest English settlements during the period covered by Book V of this volume. The first shows those cemeteries which have produced Teutonic antiquities of whose manufacture, whether in England or on the Continent, before the year A.D. 500 we can be reasonably certain. Many other sites have produced objects which can with considerable probability be ascribed to this early period—this is especially true of the pottery—but it has been thought best to exclude rather than include all doubtful cases. It must thus be realized that while the map may give a fairly satisfactory picture of the *extent* of Anglo-Saxon settlement in its earliest phase—and even so there are areas such as the Trent and Warwickshire Avon valleys where more signs of early occupation should probably be shown—it should not be used in any part as evidence for the *density* of that settlement. We are looking at the skeleton rather than at the fully clothed body of the earliest Anglo-Saxon occupation.

The point can be further appreciated by comparing the entries on this map with those on the second. Here it has been possible to use the evidence not only of archaeology but of the earliest types of place-names, and it is at once obvious that the distribution of the latter supplements in a remarkable way that of the archaeological remains. Several explanations have been offered to account for this phenomenon,[1] but the point here to notice is that many of these names may have been current as early as the fifth century and so really deserve inclusion on the first map. It is, however, impossible to say which these should be, and the first map in consequence is in this matter also not strictly comparable with the second.

For convenience of reference the sites chosen for inclusion on the first map are here listed under the three main areas discussed in Book V.

I. *The South-east*: Sarre, Faversham, Howletts, Milton-next-Sittingbourne (brooches and metalwork); Sturry, Northfleet, Alfriston, High Down (pottery); Mitcham, Croydon (pottery and metalwork).

II. *Middle Anglia, East Anglia, and the upper Thames*: Croxton, Mildenhall, West Stow, Ixworth, Trumpington, Little Wilbraham, Soham, Malton, Brixworth, Castle Acre, Cestersover, Glen Parva, Sleaford, Carlton Scroop, Baston, Luton, Frilford, East Shefford, Dorchester, Long Wittenham, Sutton Courtenay (brooches and metalwork); Ickwell, Sandy, Somersham, Kettering, Great Addington, Stamford, North Luffenham, Souldern, Osney, Shropham, Fakenham, Culford, Eye (pottery); Girton, St. John's (Cambridge), Haslingfield, Kempston, Abingdon, Caistor-by-Norwich (pottery and metalwork).

III. *The Humbrenses*: Searby, Driffield, Rudston, Kilham (brooches); Newark, Sancton, Heworth, Saltburn (pottery).

The second map is based mainly on the two small maps issued with the *Map of Dark Age Britain* (Ordnance Survey). Certain classes of names have, however, been omitted from those there shown, since their date is less securely established, and a few cemeteries have been added which were there left out. Single burials are not shown on this map.

[1] See, for example, S. W. Woolridge in *An Historical Geography of England before 1800* (1936), 88–126 ; and J. N. L. Myres in *Antiquity*, ix (1935), 455–64.

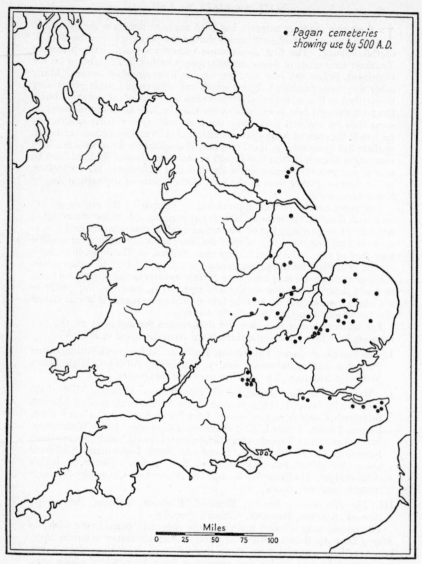

MAP X*a*. THE GROWTH OF THE ENGLISH SETTLEMENTS

Pagan cemeteries
showing use by 500 A.D.

Miles

0   25   50   75   100

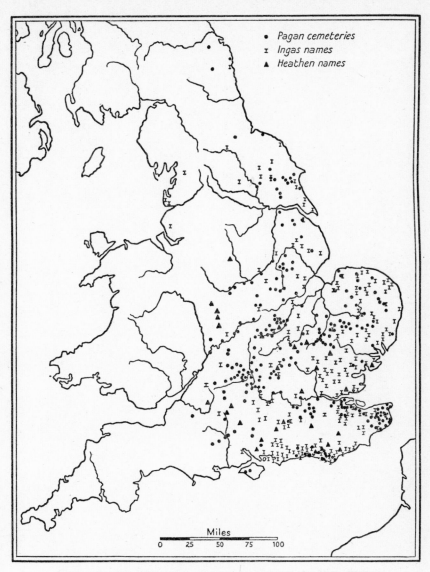

Miles

0   25   50   75   100

MAP X*b*. THE GROWTH OF THE ENGLISH SETTLEMENTS

APPENDIX I

(See pp. 327, 358, 365, 367, 380)

(a) The Conquest of Kent, as recorded in the 'Anglo-Saxon Chronicle' [A].

449 Mauricius [for Marcianus, as corrected by MS. E] and Valentines [for Valentinianus] obtained the kingdom; and reigned seven winters. In their days Hengist and Horsa, invited by Wyrtgeorn, king of the Britons, sought Britain at a place called Ypwines fleot, at first to help the Britons but later they fought against them.

455 Hengist and Horsa fought King Wyrtgeorn in the place called Agæles threp, and Horsa his brother was killed. After that Hengist took the kingdom and Æsc his son.

457 Hengist and Æsc fought the Britons at a place called Crecganford and slew there four thousand men, and the Britons left Kent and fled to London in great terror.

465 Hengist and Æsc fought the Welsh near Wippedes fleot, and there slew twelve leaders of the Welsh, and one of their own thanes was slain whose name was Wipped.

473 Hengist and Æsc fought the Welsh and took countless spoil; and the Welsh fled from the English like fire.

488 Æsc succeeded to the kingdom and was king of the Cantware for twenty-four winters.

There are no further Kentish entries until 565 [E].

For the name Æsc, mistakenly substituted by the *Chronicle* for the correct form Oisc, see note on p. 380.

(b) The Conquest of Sussex, as recorded in the 'Anglo-Saxon Chronicle'.

477 Ælle came to Britain and his three sons Cymen, Wlencing, and Cissa with three ships at the place called Cymenes ora and there they slew many Welsh and drove some to flight in the wood that is called Andredes leag.

485 Ælle fought the Welsh near Mearc rædesburna.

491 Ælle and Cissa beset Andredes cester, and slew all who dwelt in it, nor was there one Briton left.

There are no further South Saxon entries in this period.

APPENDIX II

(*See pp. 327, 365, 396–9*).

The West Saxon Annals from the 'Anglo-Saxon Chronicle'

495 Two chieftains came to Britain, Cerdic and Cynric his son, with five ships at the place called Cerdices ora and the same day they fought the Welsh.

501 Port came to Britain and his two sons Bieda and Mægla with two ships at the place called Portes mutha and slew a young Briton, a very noble man.

508 Cerdic and Cynric slew a British king whose name was Natanleod and five thousand men with him. Afterwards the land was called Natan leag as far as Cerdices ford.

514 [E] The West Saxons came to Britain with three ships at the place called Cerdices ora. And Stuf and Wihtgar fought the Britons and put them to flight.[1]

519 Cerdic and Cynric took the kingdom, and the same year they fought with Britons where it is now called Cerdices ford.

527 Cerdic and Cynric fought with Britons at the place called Cerdices leaga.

530 Cerdic and Cynric took the Isle of Wight and slew a few men at Wihtgaræsbyrg.

534 Cerdic died: and his son Cynric reigned on for twenty-six winters, and they gave the Isle of Wight to their kinsfolk Stuf and Wihtgar.

544 Wihtgar died and was buried at Wihtgara byrg.

552 Cynric fought with Britons at the place called Searo byrg and put the Brit-Welsh to flight.

556 Cynric and Ceawlin fought with Britons at Beran byrg.

560 Ceawlin began to reign in Wessex.

568 Ceawlin and Cutha fought with Æthelberht and drove him into Kent, and they slew two chieftains Oslaf and Cnebba at Wibbandun.

571 Cuthwulf fought with Brit-Welsh at Bedcanford and took four townships, Lygeanburg and Ægelesburg, Benesington and Egonesham, and the same year he died.

577 Cuthwine and Ceawlin fought with Britons and slew three kings, Coinmail and Condidan and Farinmail at the place called Deorham, and they took three 'chesters', Gleawanceaster and Cirenceaster and Bathanceaster.

---

[1] In MS. A this entry reads: 'The West Saxons . . . place called Cerdices ora, Stuf and Wihtgar: and they fought the Britons . . .', &c. See note on p. 366.

584 Ceawlin and Cutha fought with Britons at the place called Fethanleag and Cutha was killed, and Ceawlin took many townships and countless spoil and returned in anger to his own.

592 There was a great slaughter at Wodnesbeorg and Ceawlin was driven out.

593 Ceawlin and Cwichelm and Crida perished.

(*See pp. 320, 333, and 379*)

The date of the Obsessio Montis Badonici

IT may be worth while briefly setting out the evidence which enables one to date this important event between 490 and 516, and at the same time makes it impossible to tie it down much more closely. The relevant facts are as follows.

Gildas (ch. 26) says of it: *quique quadragesimus quartus ut novi orditur annus mense iam uno emenso qui et meae nativitatis est.* The wording is obscure, but it will perhaps just translate intelligibly as it stands, in some such way as this: 'and this begins the forty-fourth year as I know with one month elapsed and it is also that of my birth'. Gildas is thus apparently trying to say that Mons Badonicus occurred nearly forty-four years ago, and he knows that this is so because it was in the same year as his birth, and he is now nearly forty-four. Mommsen proposed to read *est ab eo qui* for *ut novi*, an emendation which would greatly simplify the construction of the sentence but is too remote from the text to carry immediate conviction. A simpler change would be to read *quia* for *qui*, and some support for this may be derived from a manuscript reading *qui iam*: Gildas would then definitely be explaining that his knowledge that Mons Badonicus was nearly forty-four years ago is derived from the fact that he is himself now nearly forty-four. This is, on the whole, the best and most usually accepted interpretation of the passage, though it is not, as will be shown later, the only one.

But even this interpretation does not give us a close date for Mons Badonicus, for we do not know in what year Gildas wrote his book. It is, however, often assumed that he must have written it before 547, for Maglocunus, the king of North Wales who is amongst the British princes whom he attacks by name, is credibly reported by the tenth-century *Annales Cambriae* to have died of the great pestilence in that year. This should give us a date some time before 503 for Mons Badonicus. Unfortunately, however, the *Annales Cambriae* also have a direct date, 516, for Mons Badonicus itself, and we are thus faced with a contradiction, insoluble on the sources we possess, between the chronology of Gildas as interpreted above and the two dates in the *Annales Cambriae*, one of which, if we have correctly interpreted Gildas, must be wrong. It may also be noted that if the death of Gildas is rightly dated by the *Annales* to 570, and if he was born in the year of Mons Badonicus, we can be fairly certain that that event did not take place more than ten or fifteen years before 503 at the earliest.

There is, however, a further difficulty in the interpretation of

Gildas's text. Bede, who used the passage in *Hist. Eccles.* i. 16, either had a text before him which read *adventus eorum in Brittaniam* in place of the whole or some part of the phrase *ut novi orditur annus mense iam uno emenso*, or else he interpreted the text as we have it as meaning that the forty-four years were to be reckoned not backwards from the time of writing but forwards from the *Adventus Saxonum*.[1] Bede may, of course, be simply misreading an admittedly obscure text, but since the manuscript of Gildas which he used must have been at least three hundred years nearer to Gildas's *ipsissima verba* than any we now possess, we cannot help taking his view into serious consideration, for it is possible that he has preserved what is really the correct phrasing of the original.

Now Bede, as we have seen above (p. 354), never gives an exact year for the *Adventus Saxonum*. It lies for him between the extremes of 446 and 455, and Mons Badonicus would therefore have taken place some time between 490 and 499. This in itself is in no way improbable, for both dates fall within the limits set by the earlier line of inquiry: but it does not bring us much nearer to a definite year or even a definite decade in which we can be quite certain that the siege of Mons Badonicus occurred. All that we can say is that it did occur; and that a date either earlier than 490 or later than 516 seems to be excluded by the available evidence.[2]

---

[1] I cannot agree with Plummer's view (see his note on *Hist. Eccles.* i. 16) that Bede's authority for the forty-four years may be entirely distinct from Gildas. If we reject the *Annales* it is indeed quite possible, as he points out, that Mons Badonicus may have lain both forty-four years after the *Adventus* and forty-four years before the date of Gildas's book, which would thus have been written between 534 and 543. But Bede is following Gildas much too closely in this passage for it to be the least probable that he has suddenly switched over to another authority, and to one which by an extraordinary coincidence was using the same number of years to date the same event from a totally different angle.

[2] A number of other interpretations of the passage in Gildas could be mentioned, but most of them do not materially advance our knowledge and have little but ingenuity to recommend them. E. W. B. Nicholson, for example, thought that the forty-four years were to be reckoned from the appearance of Ambrosius: unfortunately we are even less able to date this event closely than any of the other suggested *termini*. G. H. Wheeler (*Eng. Hist. Rev.* xli (1926), 497) for *ut novi orditur* reads *ut novi ordinant*, 'as recent writers reckon', providing us once more with an unknown era from which to count the forty-four years, nor are his attempts to fix it very convincing. F. Seebohm (*Tribal System in Wales*, 189, n. 3) thought that Gildas meant that he was himself forty-three at the time of Mons Badonicus; this sense can, it is true, be squeezed out of Gildas's Latin, but if, as Seebohm thinks, Mons Badonicus was in 516, and Gildas died in 570, he must in that case have lived to be nearly ninety-eight. It is, of course, quite possible that the *qui et meae nativitatis est* may refer, not to the year of Mount Badon at all, but to the extra month mentioned in the immediately preceding phrase. This is just the sort of irrelevant piece of information which a man of Gildas's mentality might have thought worth giving, but few historians have had the audacity to adopt this view, and to lose in so doing the last hope of dating Mons Badonicus.

BIBLIOGRAPHY

ROMAN BRITAIN

In conformity with the general practice of these volumes, this bibliography is a review of the sources in general, not a collection of references for individual statements in the text. I have indicated the books and periodicals where the most important evidence is to be found, not as a rule mentioning again publications already mentioned in footnotes, and hardly ever referring to individual papers in the periodicals which have been my chief source throughout. I have, however, called special attention to works in which copious references of this kind are to be found, and have marked the most useful of these with an asterisk*. As a rule, no work is here mentioned twice, and the more general contain material (often very important) bearing on more special subjects.

In one way, however, this bibliography is not comparable with those of other volumes in this series. In the later periods of English history our knowledge is mainly based on the study of written or printed documents, so that a bibliography can refer readers directly to the sources themselves. Our knowledge of Roman Britain is based only to a very small extent on texts: most of it depends on archaeological material, and a bibliography can only refer a reader to descriptions and discussions of this material, not to the material itself. Even inscriptions, as historical sources, depend for their value not merely on what they say, but on their style as examples of stone-cutting and lettering: cf. footnote to p. 120.

ANCIENT WRITERS

The texts of ancient writers dealing with Britain have been collected in *Monumenta Historica Britannica*, vol. i (all published), folio 1848, edited by Petrie and Sharpe; where they are in Greek, an English translation is added. From the point of view of textual criticism and scholarship, this work is, of course, out of date, and should not be used without being checked. Standard editions of the chief ancient writers are as follows:

Diodorus Siculus, ed. Fischer (Teubner, 1905).
Strabo, ed. Meineke (Teubner, 1866).
Ptolemy, *Geographia* (cf. H. Bradley, 'Ptolemy's Geography of

the British Isles', *Archaeologia*, xlviii. 379, reprinted in *Collected Papers*, 1928).

Itinerarium Antonini Augusti (latest ed. is *Itineraria Romana*, ed. Otto Cuntz, vol. i, Teubner, 1929. K. Muller's folio ed., *Itineraria Romana*, is not satisfactory. The English section has been often edited separately, with commentaries: William Burton, 1658; Thomas and Roger Gale, 1709; Reynolds, 1799).

Notitia Dignitatum, ed. Seeck (Berlin, 1876).

Ravennatis Anonymi Cosmographia, ed. Pinder and Parthey (Berlin, 1860).

Caesar, *de Bello Gallico*. Text with notes, T. Rice Holmes (1914). The best commentary is T. Rice Holmes's *Ancient Britain and the Invasions of Julius Caesar* (1907).

Tacitus, *de vita Agricolae*, *ed. Furneaux, revised by J. G. C. Anderson with contributions by F. Haverfield (a valuable edition with historical and archaeological commentary) (1922).

Tacitus, *Annals*, ed. Furneaux and others, vol. ii (1907).

Suetonius, *de vita Caesarum*, ed. Ihm (Teubner, 1908). Separate lives with commentaries: *Divus Iulius*, H. E. Butler and M. Cary (1927); *Divus Vespasianus*, Braithwaite (1927).

Cassius Dio, *Historia Romana*, ed. Boissevain (1895–1931).

Herodian, *Ab excessu divi Marci*, ed. Mendelssohn (1883).

Historia Augusta: (cf. N. H. Baynes, *The Historia Augusta, its date and Purpose*, 1926).

Panegyrici Latini, ed. Baehrens (Teubner, 1874).

Aurelius Victor, *De Viris Illustribus* and *Epitome*, ed. Schraeter (1831).

Eutropius, *Breviarium Historiae Romanae*, ed. Ruehl (Teubner, 1887).

Ammianus Marcellinus, *Historiae*, ed. Gardthausen (Teubner, 1874–5).

Zosimus, *Historia Nova*, ed. Mendelssohn (1887).

Orosius, *Historiae*, ed. Zangemeister (Teubner, 1889).

Gildas, *De Excidio et Conquestu Britanniae*, and *Historia Brittonum cum additamentis Nennii*, ed. Mommsen: *Mon. Hist. Germ., chronica minora*, vol. iii (1896).

BOOKS OF REFERENCE

Standard works of every kind on the Roman Empire are, of

course, necessary, but there is no space to enumerate them in this bibliography. The same is true of standard works on the neighbouring provinces, Gaul and Germany. The numerous articles on matters relating to Britain in such works of reference as Pauly-Wissowa's *Realenzyklopädie* must not be overlooked. Continental periodicals seldom contain useful articles on Romano-British subjects; an exception is *Germania*, where contributions from English scholars or Germans acquainted with British work are not infrequent.

INSCRIPTIONS

For every part of the Roman Empire, Britain not excepted, inscriptions constitute a source of high importance. In Britain, however, their distribution is curious and gives rise to some difficulties. Throughout the lowland zone they are relatively rare; in the highland zone they are extremely common. The result is that for every aspect of the life of the frontier armies (until the late third century, when inscriptions of every kind except milestones and a few tombstones disappear) they give us voluminous evidence; for the more civilized parts of the country they give us very little indeed, and this is one of the reasons why archaeology is so overwhelmingly important as a source of information on the general life of the people.

The standard collection is *Corpus Inscriptionum Latinarum*, vol. vii (1873), ed. E. Hübner. This volume contains a somewhat unduly large number of omissions and errors. Supplements to it by Hübner himself appeared in the now defunct periodical *Ephemeris Epigraphica*, two in vol. iii and a third in vol. iv. Larger and much more scholarly supplements were added later by F. Haverfield: a fourth in vol. vii and a fifth in vol. ix, bringing the material down to 1913. Since 1921 annual notes on new and re-deciphered inscriptions have been published in the *Journal of Roman Studies*. A complete new *corpus* of Romano-British inscriptions is in preparation.

GENERAL WORKS ON ROMAN BRITAIN

At the head of these must be placed the masterly essay of Mommsen in vol. v of his *Römische Geschichte* (Berlin, 1886; English translation, *The Provinces of the Roman Empire*, 1909, with additions by Haverfield). Chapters on the subject occur in T. Hodgkin's *History of England from the Earliest Times to the*

Norman Conquest (1906) and Sir C. Oman's *England before the Norman Conquest* (1910), both valuable though now out of date; and by Haverfield in *Cambridge Medieval History*, vol. i (1911; ch. xiii (*a*)). Mention may be made, too, of the present writer's brief sections in the later volumes of the *Cambridge Ancient History*.

Modern books wholly dealing with Roman Britain are not very numerous. H. M. Scarth's volume in the S.P.C.K. series (*Roman Britain* [1883]) was the work of a scholar. When it became out of date it might profitably have been revised; but instead it was superseded by a new book with the same subject and of the same size, by E. Conybeare (1903) which was by no means satisfactory. A large book in French was written by F. Sagot (*La Bretagne romaine*, 1911). It was an attempt to trace the history of Roman Britain on the strength of literary and epigraphic evidence, with little attention to archaeological data. This was the method brilliantly used by Camille Jullian in his *Histoire de la Gaule*; Sagot's book demonstrated its inadequacy in the case of Britain. Haverfield never wrote the comprehensive book for which his contemporaries hoped. His *Romanization of Roman Britain* (ed. 4, by G. Macdonald, 1923) is a classic, and the standard work on the subject is his *Roman Occupation of Britain*, a course of lectures given in 1907 and worked up into a book by Sir G. Macdonald (1924). Sir B. Windle's *The Romans in Britain* (1923) is untrustworthy. A. R. Burn's *The Romans in Britain, an anthology of inscriptions* (1932), is good, but not invariably accurate. The present writer has published a short sketch (*Roman Britain*) whose latest edition is 1934.

The specially economic aspects of the subject (for which cf. especially M. Rostovtzeff, *Social and Economic History of the Roman Empire*, 1926) are dealt with by the present writer in a contribution on *Britain to Tenney Frank's *Economic Survey of Rome* (forthcoming), with bibliographical matter. L. C. West's *Roman Britain: the Objects of Trade* (1931) is a painstaking compilation which suffers from lack of first-hand knowledge of the material and is not sufficiently exhaustive.

ARCHAEOLOGY AND TOPOGRAPHY

The reconstruction of Romano-British history from archaeological sources involves the collection of material from sites all over the country, and the extraction of historical conclusions from this material, in relation to the place and context of its discovery, by classifying it according to character and date and comparing it with similar material from elsewhere. Collection and interpretation are not entirely separable processes, but to some extent collection must precede interpretation. The process of collecting such material, first by inspecting and recording remains visible on or above the ground and those accidentally brought to light, and then by searching for it, by means of increasingly scientific excavation, has been continuously going forward ever since the sixteenth century. The systematic interpretation of this material has already made some progress, but in this respect a great deal remains to be done.

The beginnings of systematic topographical study may be placed in the reign of Henry VIII, with the work of J. Leland, whose *Itinerary* ('*The Laboryouse Iourney and Serche of Johan Leylande, for Englandes antiquitees*'), the record of a complete perambulation of England, was begun about 1538 (ed. 1, 1549; edited by T. Hearne, 1710). The same antiquary's *Collectanea* were also edited by Hearne (1715). Some time later William Lambarde compiled a *Topographical and Historical Dictionary of England* (about 1577; printed 1730). The greatest work of this kind was William Camden's *Britannia* (first ed. 1586; 6th, and first folio, 1607; translated into English by Philemon Holland, 1610; edited with many additions by Edmund Gibson (ed. 1, 1695) and Robert Gough (1789)). With Camden's work may be compared the *Itinerarium Curiosum* of Stukeley (early eighteenth century; published 1776); his diaries and letters (Surtees Society, 3 vols., 1880–5) also contain much valuable material. A student of the same type, but peculiar in being a specialist on Roman remains, was John Horsley, whose *Britannia Romana* (1732) includes a corpus of inscriptions illustrated with engraved facsimiles, and admirable accounts of Roman sites, together with studies of the literary evidence, and may be regarded as the first and in many ways still the best book on Roman Britain as a whole.

These writers established the precedent of dividing their topographical material according to counties; and their example (especially the enormous and deserved prestige of Camden) encouraged the idea that this was the best way of arranging it. As knowledge increased it was natural that individual writers should specialize on separate counties, and thus grew up the 'county history' literature which will be considered in the next section. In recent times the necessity of taking a wider view and recognizing that county boundaries have nothing to do with Roman history has resulted in various attempts to review this material as a single whole, and has produced works of which the following are examples.

Two pioneer volumes were published in 1911 by John Ward (*The Roman Era in Britain* and *Romano-British buildings and earthworks*). Both are valuable works, but suffer through being in the main compiled from other writings rather than based on personal acquaintance with the material, and neither is uniformly accurate in detail. The present writer has published a book on *The Archaeology of Roman Britain* (1930) containing much bibliographical matter, which may here be referred to once for all. A. H. Lyell's *Bibliographical List descriptive of Romano-British Architectural Remains* (1912) is not sufficiently critical to be of great value. Reviews of recent discoveries were published by F. Haverfield in two pamphlets (*Roman Britain in 1912, Roman Britain in 1913*); since 1921 similar annual summaries have appeared in the *Journal of Roman Studies*. Research over a space of years has been admirably summarized by Sir G. Macdonald (*Roman Britain 1914–1928*) and by T. D. Kendrick and C. F. C. Hawkes (*Archaeology in England and Wales 1914–1931* (1932)). For the relation of archaeology and history to physical geography, Sir C. Fox, *The Personality of Britain* (ed. 2, 1933) is fundamental: also the Ordnance Survey Map of *Roman Britain* (1/1,000,000: ed. 2, 1928). In this connexion the companion map of *Britain in the Dark Ages* (1935) should be mentioned.

Topographical works of importance, not mentioned in any of the following sections, include such things as the following. Alexander Gordon, *Itinerarium Septentrionale* (mostly on the two walls: 1726); Pennant, *Tour in Wales* (1784); Stuart, *Caledonia Romana* (1852); A. C. Smith, *British and Roman Antiquities of North Wiltshire* (1884); S. Lysons, *Reliquiae Romano-Britannicae* (1813, 1817; a magnificent publication, splendidly illustrated, of villas and other sites); General W. Roy, *Military Antiquities of the Romans in Britain* (1793; mainly consisting of a splendid series of plans); C. Roach Smith, *Collectanea Antiqua* (7 vols., 1848–80, an invaluable collection of illustrated notes on sites and finds); the same writer's *Antiquities of Richborough, Reculver and Lymne* (1850); T. Wright and Fairholt, *The Archaeological Album*

(1845; contains articles on Burgh Castle, Roman London, Silchester, &c.); Bowman, *Reliquiae antiquae Eboracenses* (finds in York and district, 1855); W. T. Watkin, *Roman Lancashire* (1883) and *Roman Cheshire* (1886) (admirable studies of Roman remains in single counties); General Pitt-Rivers, *Excavations in Cranborne Chase* (1887–1905; a classical example of archaeological method, especially important for Romano-British villages); T. Codrington, *Roman Roads in Britain* (1903); and modern works, abreast of present-day standards, like Sir C. Fox's *Archaeology of the Cambridge Region* (1923), R. E. M. Wheeler's *Prehistoric and Roman Wales* (1924), I. A. Richmond's *Huddersfield in Roman Times* (1925), and F. Elgee's *Early Man in North-East Yorkshire* (1930).

Much archaeological information is contained in museum catalogues and handbooks, notably those of the British Museum (*Guide to Antiquities of Roman Britain*, 1922), Guildhall Museum, London Museum (*London in Roman Times* (1930), a monograph in itself) Devizes, Chester, Durham (Cathedral Library), Glasgow (Hunterian Collection), &c. Good guide-books to individual Roman sites can often be had, e.g., those published by H.M. Office of Works for sites in their charge.

COUNTY HISTORIES AND KINDRED WORKS

So-called county histories, which in fact are not so much histories as collections of materials for history (documents, pedigrees, descriptions of ancient remains, &c.), have been continuously published ever since the sixteenth century; but their great age was the later eighteenth and early nineteenth centuries, when the total quantity of material had outgrown even the enlarged editions of Camden. The authors of these works were as a rule not professional scholars. Sometimes they were hack-writers who wrote the history of any county which seemed to require it; but the best of them were residents (landowners, clergy, &c.), educated men whose interests were centred in their own counties and whose appetite for information connected with their home-district was omnivorous. Hence the local knowledge contained in these works is almost always of an extremely high order: it is accurate, critical, and intelligent. But the general equipment of historical and archaeological learning in the light of which the local facts are interpreted is often defective, so that the authors observe their facts correctly but are apt to misunderstand their significance. In the case of Roman remains, these writers suffer from an 'idol of the tribe', deluding them into conceiving everything Roman in military terms: a town becomes a fortress and its inhabitants legionaries; a villa becomes the residence of an officer, and so forth. But it is easy for a modern reader to correct this illusion, and as storehouses of topographical information these county histories are invaluable.

A few examples may be given. Lambarde's *Perambulation of Kent* (1576) stands at the head of the series. R. Carew's *Survey of Cornwall* (1602) is a fine work, worthy of a contemporary and friend of Camden. Another seventeenth-century example is Thoroton's *Antiquities of Nottinghamshire* (1677). The eighteenth century, after a few in its earlier years, such as Thoresby's *Ducatus Leodiensis* (1715), produced a flood of them: e.g., Borlase's *Antiquities of Cornwall* (1754), Morant's *History and Antiquities of the County of Essex* (1768), Wallis's *Natural History and Antiquities of Northumberland* (1769), Whittaker's *History of Manchester* (1771), Nicolson and Burn's *History of Westmorland and Cumberland* (1777), Brand's *History and Antiquities of the Town and County of Newcastle-upon-Tyne* (1789), and Hutchinson's *History and Antiquities of the County Palatine of Durham* (1785–94) and *History of Cumberland* (1794). Similar works, but on the whole rising in quality, continued to appear during the first half of the nineteenth century. Colt Hoare's *Ancient Wiltshire* was published 1812–19, Ormerod's *History of Cheshire* in 1819. Whittaker published a *History of Craven* in 1805 and a *History of Richmondshire* in 1823. Phelps's *History and Antiquities of Somersetshire* was published in 1836. Surtees's *History and Antiquities of the County Palatine of Durham* appeared from 1816 to 1840. During the same period the volumes of Hodgson's *History of Northumberland*, the best of all these works, were coming out (1820–40). A few similar works appeared at later dates: e.g. Warne's *Ancient Dorset* in 1872.

A few attempts were made to gather up this mass of literature, or the cream of it, into single comprehensive works. The most important was the *Magna Britannia* of S. and D. Lysons, planned as a series of volumes dealing with counties alphabetically, the first published in 1806, but only six volumes (ten counties) appeared. The quality of the Lysons' work was excellent, and their accounts of Roman remains in particular very good; but the task they set themselves was an impossible one. A less scholarly collection of a similar kind was Britton and Brayley's *Beauties of England and Wales*, begun in 1801.

By the middle of the nineteenth century, even these works were becoming incapable of containing the quantities of topographical knowledge and the constant revisions to which old knowledge was subject. A new form of publication, at once larger and more elastic, was needed. To meet this need local societies began to be formed all over the country, whose chief function was to publish periodicals in which topics of local history and archaeology were discussed in separate papers. These will be considered in the next section. The writing of large 'county histories' did not die out, but late in the century a new type of county history began to appear: no longer encyclopaedic collections of undigested material, but shorter works, expressing the conclusions based on interpreting this material in the light of specialized knowledge and scientific archaeological methods. Thus, apart from the vast periodical literature to be discussed below, the following classes of publications have grown up in the last fifty years to take the place of the county histories described above.

1. Compact studies of the history and archaeology of single counties or districts, often produced by publishers in the form of volumes in series. One of these was Elliot Stock's *Popular County Histories*, of which a few volumes were published about 1890–1900. The latest is Messrs. Methuen's series of *County Archaeologies* which provide useful summaries and discussions of the archaeological material of single counties.

2. The *Victoria County Histories*, a vast series of which the first volume was published in 1900; after a long interval, publication has now recommenced under the auspices of the Institute of Historical Research. The volume or group of volumes dealing with each county contains a *chapter on its Roman remains. For a long time these chapters were written by Haverfield, who spared no pains to collect and publish exhaustive lists of discoveries, with a thoroughly scientific commentary. Among the most important of the monographs which he thus produced are his chapters on Hampshire, Somerset, and Shropshire. These and similar chapters are the best sources for any account of the state of Britain during the Roman period, and have been constantly used in the present volume. Similar

chapters published since Haverfield's death have been either based on materials collected by him or at least planned on the model of his own work, and continue to maintain a high standard of accuracy and completeness.

At the same time, as Haverfield pointed out in every one of his contributions to this ponderous work, the materials for a topographical survey of Roman Britain are seriously damaged by being forced into the Procrustean bed of the English county system. This division of facts by counties is harmless so long as the material is merely described, with no attempt at comparison and interpretation; but in an age of scientific archaeological research when comparison and interpretation are indispensable, it is a positive detriment to historical study. In order to use Haverfield's magnificent chapters, the student must first rearrange the material they contain in a less unnatural order.

3. Northumberland stands in a class by itself. John Hodgson's vast and scholarly *History of Northumberland*, left unfinished at his death in 1845, became the nucleus of a further work undertaken by the antiquaries of that county, and thus arose the great *History of Northumberland* whose first volume was published in 1858 and of which down to the present thirteen volumes have appeared. In view of this, Northumberland was omitted from the scheme of the *Victoria County Histories*. The volumes deal with separate districts in the county, and contain very valuable accounts of the Roman remains in these districts, notably Haverfield's chapter on Corbridge in vol. x, and descriptions of various parts of Hadrian's Wall in later volumes (Rudchester Burn to Matfen Piers, vol. xii; Wallsend to Rudchester Burn, vol. xiii; the outpost forts north of the Wall will be dealt with in vol. xiv). While preparing a volume on one district, the editorial committee promotes excavation on important sites in that district, so that the *History* is an organ of original archaeological research as well as a repository of information already in existence.

4. There are Royal Commissions on Historical Monuments for England, Wales, and Scotland, which publish inventories of ancient monuments, with descriptions, plans, and illustrations, county by county. The primary aim of these is to facilitate not the advancement of historical knowledge but the preservation of historical relics; and they are of less interest to the historian

than the foregoing publications because they describe only structures and not the small finds (pottery, coins, inscriptions, &c.) which form so valuable a part of the material discussed in the Victoria and other county histories. An exception must be made for the volume on *Roman London* (1928), which contains chapters on inscriptions, &c., and offers an historical interpretation of the evidence as a whole.

PERIODICALS, ETC.

The bulk of the archaeological material for Roman Britain (especially that which has accumulated in the last half-century since the advent of scientific methods in archaeology, and therefore the most valuable part) is contained in periodicals, general or local. Access to a large number of these periodicals is therefore indispensable for any student of the subject; and anything like a bibliographical list of the articles contained in them is impossible in the compass of a volume like this. The following are some of the most important, with the year of first issue. General periodicals: *Archaeologia* (1804); *Proceedings of the Society of Antiquaries of London* (1843–1920), replaced by the *Antiquaries Journal* (1921); *Archaeological Journal* (1844); *Journal of the British Archaeological Association* (1862); *Classical Review* (1887); *Numismatic Chronicle* (1861); *Journal of Roman Studies* (1911); *Antiquity* (1927); also the defunct *Philosophical Transactions* (1665), *Gentleman's Magazine* (1731) (there are three volumes of excerpts, *The Gentleman's Magazine Library: Archaeology*, parts I, II, ed. S. L. Gomme (1886), *Romano-British Remains*, same editor (1887)); *The Antiquary* (1880), *The Academy* (1869), *The Athenaeum* (1828).

Of local journals, Wales is covered by *Archaeologia Cambrensis* (1846) and the *Transactions of the Honourable Society of Cymmrodorion*, alternatively entitled *Y Cymmrodor* (1877); Scotland by the *Proceedings of the Society of Antiquaries of Scotland* (1852); few county or city journals are of any importance. For England, most counties have their own journals. The following are the chief: for Northumberland and Durham, *Archaeologia Aeliana* (1822) and *Proceedings of the Society of Antiquaries of Newcastle-upon-Tyne* (1855); *Transactions of the Cumberland and Westmorland Antiquarian and Archaeological Society* (1866); *Yorkshire Archaeological Journal* (1870); *Transactions of the Lancashire and Cheshire Antiquarian Society* (1884); *Liverpool Annals of Archaeology and Anthro-*

pology (1908); *Journal of the Chester and North Wales Architectural, Archaeological, and Historical Society* (1850); *Journal of the Derbyshire Archaeological and Natural History Society* (1879); *Transactions of the Thoroton Society* (1898, for Nottinghamshire); various publications of the Cambridge Antiquarian Society (1851); *Transactions of the Essex Archaeological Society* (1858); *Transactions of the East Hertfordshire Archaeological Society* (1899); *Records of Buckinghamshire* (1854); *Berks., Bucks., and Oxon. Archaeological Journal* (1895; since 1931 the *Berkshire Archaeological Journal*); *Proceedings of the Woolhope Club* (1852, for Herefordshire); *Transactions of the Bristol and Gloucestershire Archaeological Society* (1876); *Proceedings of the Somersetshire Archaeological and Natural History Society* (1850); and of its Bath and district branch (1904); *Proceedings of the Bath Field Club* (1869); *Wiltshire Archaeological Magazine* (1854); *Proceedings of the Hampshire Field Club* (1887); *Hampshire Notes and Queries* (1883); *Surrey Archaeological Collections* (1858); *Sussex Archaeological Collections* (1848); *Sussex Notes and Queries* (1926); *Archaeologia Cantiana* (1858, for Kent); *Proceedings of the Dorset Natural History and Archaeological Society* (1877); *Proceedings of the Devon Exploration Society* (1929).

Together with periodicals it is convenient to mention certain series of publications not strictly in periodical form. Among these the most important are the Reports of the Research Committee of the Society of Antiquaries of London (I: on Wroxeter, 1912, by J. P. Bushe-Fox (1913); II: ditto 1913, by the same (1914); III: on Hengistbury, by the same (1915); IV: on Wroxeter, 1914, by the same (1916); V: on Swarling urnfield, by the same (1925); VI, VII, X, on Richborough, by the same (1926, 1928, 1932); VIII: on Ospringe cemetery, by Whiting, Hawley, and May (1931); IX: on Lydney, by R. E. M. and T. V. Wheeler (1932); XI: on Verulamium, by the same (1936); excavation reports on Scottish sites published by the Glasgow Archaeological Society (on Balmuildy, by S. N. Miller (1922); on Old Kilpatrick, by the same (1928); on Cadder, by John Clarke (1933)); and Reports of the Roman Antiquities Committee of the Yorkshire Archaeological Society (I: Roman Pottery at Crambeck, by P. Corder (1928); II: Defences of the Roman Fort at Malton, by the same (1930); III: Roman pottery at Throlam, Holme-on-Spalding-Moor, by the same (1930); IV: Roman Villa at Langton, by the same and J. L. Kirk (1932); V: Gazeteer of Roman remains in E. Yorks, by M. Kitson Clark.

MONOGRAPHS ON SEPARATE SITES

Most of these are contained in the periodicals and other serial publications mentioned in the preceding section, or from separate articles or chapters in more comprehensive works. Here will be enumerated only some especially important separate publications.

Frontier-works.—Antonine Wall: Sir G. Macdonald, *The Roman Wall in Scotland*, ed. 2 (Oxford, 1934), is definitive and gives references to earlier literature.

Hadrian's Wall: there is no definitive work to be compared with the above. The fullest account is still J. Collingwood Bruce, *The Roman Wall*, ed. 3 (1867); the best survey, that of H. MacLauchlan (atlas, 1857, and accompanying volume of text). Bruce's *Handbook of the Roman Wall* was brought up to date in 1933 (9th ed.) by the present writer, but subsequent discoveries have already superseded the views there put forward. Recent research is described in the local periodicals and the *Journal of Roman Studies*.

Towns.—In addition to descriptions in the *Victoria County Histories* and similar works, articles in periodicals on individual sites and on excavations, and excavation reports already mentioned in this bibliography, there are numerous monographs of which the following is a selection. Royal Commission on Historical Monuments, *Roman London* (1928). Among older monographs may be mentioned F. Drake, *Eburacum* (1736); E. T. Artis, *Durobrivae* (1828); H. Eckroyd Smith, *Reliquiae Isurianae* (1852); Buckman and Newmarch, *Remains of Roman Art at Cirencester* (1850); H. M. Scarth, *Aquae Solis* (1864); T. Wright, *Uriconium* (1872).

Military sites.—With the same qualification as above, the following may be mentioned. Rauthmell, *Antiquitates Bremetonacenses* (1746); Lee, *Isca Silurum* (1862); Hooppell, *Vinovia* (1891); J. Ward, *The Roman fort at Gellygaer* (1903); R. S. Conway, *Melandra Castle* (1906); F. A. Bruton, *Roman Fort at Manchester* (1909); F. A. Bruton, *Castleshaw* (1911). A new era in the study of such sites opened with J. Curle's *Roman Frontier Post* (on Newstead, 1911), both in methods of excavation and in the full and scholarly publication of finds; this book still remains the fullest monograph on any Roman fort in Britain. The influence of the same new movement in archaeology is seen in subsequent works like T. May's *Roman Forts at Templebrough* (1922); J. P. Hall's *Caer Llugwy* (1923); R. E. M. Wheeler's *Roman Fort near Brecon* (Cymmrodorion Soc., 1926); F. Oswald's *Margidunum* (Nottingham Art Gallery, 1927); and D. Atkinson's edition (3rd) of J. H. Hopkinson's *Roman Fort at Ribchester* (1928).

Villas.—Again the material is mostly contained in periodicals. But, apart from works already mentioned, there are separate monographs such as S. Lysons, *Roman Antiquities at Woodchester* (1817), R. Colt Hoare, *The Pitney Pavement* (1832), J. E. Price and F. G. Hilton Price, *Roman Buildings near Brading, I.O.W.* (1881), and a pleasant popular account of an excavation, S. E. Winbolt, *Roman Folkestone* (1925).

Miscellaneous Sites.—The following separate publications may be mentioned: W. H. Bathurst and C. W. King, *Roman Antiquities at Lydney Park* (1879); T. May, *Warrington's Roman Remains* (1904); D. Atkinson, *The Romano-British Site on Lowbury Hill in Berkshire* (1916); Fieldhouse, May, and Wellstood, *A Romano-British industrial settlement near Tiddington, Stratford-on-Avon* (1931).

SPECIAL SUBJECTS

1. *Early Britain.*—T. Rice Holmes's *Ancient Britain and the Invasions of Julius Caesar* deals with the subjects discussed in chapter ii. It is a monument of industry and learning, but the author has tried to cover too much ground (his survey goes back to the beginnings of human life in Britain) and his personal experience of archaeological work was inadequate to prepare him for dealing with the material of prehistoric archaeology. Apart from the chapters on Caesar's invasion, therefore, it has never been an entirely satisfactory work and has been superseded by the advance of knowledge in the last thirty years. With regard to physical anthropology, J. Beddoe, *Races of Britain* (1885) is still valuable, but the numerous papers by Sir Arthur Keith and other writers (see footnotes) have placed this study on a new footing. Sir J. Rhŷs, *Celtic Britain* (1884), is also out of date in many respects: his theory about Goidels and Brythons (though still accepted by some archaeologists, e.g. H. J. Peake, *The Bronze Age and the Celtic World*, 1922), is abandoned by philologists. With regard to early British civilization, the material is mostly archaeological and is contained in the books and periodicals already mentioned, together with some others such as J. R. Mortimer, *Forty Years' Researches in*

the Burial Mounds of East Yorkshire (1905), A. Bulleid and H. St.G. Gray, *The Glastonbury Lake Village* (1911), B. H. Cunnington, *All Cannings Cross* (1923). Although as a rule articles in periodicals are not separately quoted here, exception must be made for Sir Arthur Evans's classical paper on 'The Late-Celtic Cemetery at Aylesford' (*Archaeologia*, lii. 1890, p. 315), and C. Hawkes and G. C. Dunning's important article on 'The Belgae of Gaul and Britain' (*Arch. Journal*, lxxxvii, 1930, p. 150). On coinage, Sir John Evans, *The Coins of the Ancient Britons* (1864), must be corrected by reference to recent work, e.g. G. C. Brooke's paper quoted on p. 59. The importance of the name Pretani was recognized by Rice Holmes (op. cit. 459–61); see further, E. MacNeill, 'The Pretanic Background' (*Journal of the Royal Soc. of Ant. of Ireland*, lxiii, p. 1); T. F. O'Rahilly, 'The Goidels and their Predecessors' (*Proc. Brit. Acad.*, vol. xxi).

Julius Caesar's notes on Britain (*de Bell. Gall.* v. 12–14) are by some scholars regarded as spurious. In a literary sense they are rough and unfinished; but from the point of view of a British historian their substantial genuineness is beyond question. They include a certain amount of information that can apply only to the middle of the last century B.C., and a certain number of truths and errors which could only have arisen from the writer's personal knowledge being confined to Kent and the lower Thames basin.

The Roman Evacuation.—All previous discussions were put out of date by J. B. Bury, 'The *Notitia Dignitatum*, in *J.R.S.* x (1920). But this was primarily a paper (of first-rate importance) on that document, and only dealt with the British problem in a secondary manner. Bury showed ignorance of British archaeological results; he took up an untenable position as to the impossibility of out-of-date material in an official document; but he also made the vital point about the *Comes Britanniarum*. The present writer, 'The Roman Evacuation of Britain', *J.R.S.* xii (1922), replied, criticizing him effectively on the first point, showing his inconsistency on the second, and overlooking the importance of the third; adding by way of counter-attack an argument to show that coin-evidence was decisive for the traditional dating. In some quarters this argument has been accepted as valid, but subsequent work, especially on the Richborough coins, by F. S. Salisbury and others (Soc. of

Antiqs. *Richborough* report, ii); Salisbury in *Antiqs. Jour.* vii (1927), p. 268), and search in French museums by C. E. Stevens (who undertook it for this express purpose and has put his notes generously at the writer's disposal) has shown the weakness of the assumptions on which it was based. Bury's point about the *Comes* has been admirably worked out by E. Stein in *xviii Bericht der röm.-germ. Kommission* (1928), p. 92. H. S. Schultz, 'The Roman evacuation of Britain', *J.R.S.* xxiii (1933), p. 36, is of value only for the comments by Stein on Danubian coin-finds which it contains. The treatment of the fifth century by E. Foord (*The Last Age of Roman Britain*, 1925) is unscientific. G. Sheldon, *The Transition from Roman Britain to Christian England* (1932) is attractive and stimulating, but not based on a thorough acquaintance with the evidence.

Britain in the Fifth Century.—Apart from general works and the special studies mentioned in the preceding paragraph, mention should be made of Hugh Williams, *Christianity in Early Britain* (1912); Windisch, *Das keltische Britannien bis zu Kaiser Arthur* (1912); Zimmer, *Nennius Vindicatus* (1893; with comments by Mommsen in his ed. of the *Historia Brittonum*), Bury, *Life of St. Patrick* (1905). Most of the extensive Arthurian literature is connected not with the historical Arthur but with the literary history of the medieval legends. Rhŷs, *Studies in the Arthurian Legend* (1891), is a farrago of unscientific 'comparative mythology' and arbitrary etymology, much too leniently treated by most subsequent writers. Sir E. K. Chambers, *Arthur of Britain* (1927), approaches the problem of the historical Arthur from a sane point of view but without sufficient knowledge of the late Roman Empire. Kemp Malone, 'The Historicity of Arthur' (*Journal of English and Germanic Philology*, 1924, p. 463) is quite vague and subjective in his opinions, and approaches the subject as a mythologist, not as an historian. The most careful and scholarly discussion which I have come across is that of Faral, *La légende arthurienne* (vols. 255–7 (1929) of the Bibliothèque de l'école des hautes études). He regards the Arthuriana as probably part of the original *Historia Brittonum* (i. 133), although he is not satisfied that Mommsen is right in thinking that Bede used that work, and will not commit himself to a closer dating for it than between 687 and 801 (ibid. 73). He thinks (rashly, in my opinion) that one of Arthur's battles can be located (Guinnion =

Vinovia = Binchester) and infers that the historical Arthur was
a British chief in the north, though the silence of Bede (himself
a north-countryman) shows that he was not very famous by
Bede's time (pp. 146–53). Even so able an historian as F. Lot
is infected by the wild philology which vitiates so much Arthurian literature: he tolerates the traditional location of Camlann on the Cornish river Camel, and stoops to supporting
this by quoting the fact that there is on that river a place
called 'Slaughter Bridge' (*Romania*, xxx. 16); cf. art. 'Camel' in
Ekwall's *English River-names*, 1928.

THE ENGLISH SETTLEMENTS

To compile a bibliography for the period covered by Book V
of the present volume presents unusual difficulty. The student
of this period must be prepared to find significant material in
a very great variety of different and often unexpected places,
and to become familiar with the techniques of several different
sciences; but many of the works which will help him to achieve
that familiarity contain in themselves little or nothing that is
directly relevant to our present subject. It is a subject touched
marginally by many others, and much of the light by which it
is illuminated is derived from the friction of these marginal
contacts.

Much, too, of the evidence can be more appropriately surveyed
in the bibliographies for the periods before and after. Some of
the original sources coincide with those for Roman and sub-
Roman Britain and have been dealt with above: others belong
to the later Saxon centuries. Nearly all the topographical and
most of the periodical literature surveyed in the bibliography
for Roman Britain is as relevant to this period as to that; and
on the other hand there is little point in partially anticipating
here the fuller survey of the literature for Saxon social, legal,
and cultural history, which will appropriately accompany
volume ii of this series, for there are very few works dealing
with these topics in our period which do not do so as a mere
preface or introduction to their fuller treatment in later Saxon
times. Thus some subjects will be discussed below much more
thoroughly than others, not because they are in themselves of
greater importance but because this is the most appropriate
place for their full discussion. Works mentioned in the bibliography for Roman Britain are only mentioned again here when

there are special reasons for emphasizing their importance for the early Saxon period.

ANCIENT TEXTS, INSCRIPTIONS, AND DOCUMENTS

Mommsen's edition of Gildas and Nennius (see above) provides the standard text for these authors: but mention should be made of F. Lot's new edition of the latter, *Nennius et l'Historia Brittonum* (1934), a characteristically original and lively work, of which the usefulness is somewhat marred by the editor's habit of dismissing statements of his text whose meaning is not self-evident as mere instances of Nennian imbecility. Collections of the dark-age inscribed tombstones of Wales and Cornwall are in E. Hübner, *Inscriptiones Brittanniae Christianae* (1876) and J. O. Westwood, *Lapidarium Walliae* (1876–9); both are obsolete, and a scholarly *corpus* of these inscriptions with proper commentary is one of the main *desiderata* of the dark-age historian.

The standard edition of Bede's *Ecclesiastical History* is that of C. Plummer, *Baedae Opera Historica* (1896), an excellent and scholarly work not yet seriously out of date; C. Plummer and J. Earle, *Two of the Saxon Chronicles Parallel* (1892–9), remains the best edition of the *Anglo-Saxon Chronicle*. Other standard collections of texts belonging in themselves to later times but indirectly relevant to this period may be found in F. Liebermann, *Die Gesetze der Angelsachsen* (1898–1916), A. W. Haddan and W. Stubbs, *Councils*, &c. (1869–78), J. M. Kemble, *Codex Diplomaticus Aevi Saxonici* (1839–48), W. de G. Birch, *Cartularium Saxonicum* (1885–93), C. W. M. Grein and R. P. Wülker, *Bibliothek der angelsachsischen Poesie* (1883–98), and in the publications of the Early English Text Society (1864–   ), especially H. Sweet's edition of the Oldest English Texts (No. LXXXIII, 1885). The editions by R. W. Chambers of *Beowulf* (1929) and *Widsith* (1912) are both very valuable: as is his *England before the Norman Conquest* (1928), which contains a selection from the more important historical sources with a well balanced and constructive commentary.

BIBLIOGRAPHIES, BOOKS OF REFERENCE, AND PERIODICALS

Surveys of the earlier literature for the period can be found in many of the standard works on English history, and in the *Cambridge Mediaeval History*, i (1911), ch. xiii (*b*): these are, however, now becoming obsolete, and even the sections in

C. Gross, *Sources and Literature of English History* (ed. 1915), though valuable and comprehensive, do not adequately cover the field of the auxiliary sciences. J. F. Kenney's useful *Sources for the Early History of Ireland*, i (1929), includes a good deal of bibliographical material bearing on the sources, especially on Germanus, Patrick, Gildas, and Nennius: perhaps the best way to compile the nucleus of an up-to-date general bibliography would be to run through the footnotes and abbreviations in R. H. Hodgkin, *History of the Anglo-Saxons* (1935) (see below). *The Dictionary of National Biography* must be used with cautious discrimination for the early Saxon heroes and the Celtic saints. There are a number of articles bearing on early Saxon history and cognate subjects in such continental reference books as M. Ebert, *Reallexikon der Vorgeschichte* (1924–32), Pauly-Wissowa, *Realenzyclopädie* (1904–), and J. Hoops, *Reallexikon der germanischen Altertumskunde* (1911–19).

Much of the best work on every aspect of the period is to be found in periodicals, but in accordance with general practice no attempt to list individual articles is here made: many of the more important are referred to in footnotes to the text. All the general and most of the local periodicals listed in the bibliography for Roman Britain contain material for the early Saxon period, and students should be warned that many of the earlier discoveries of Saxon remains were described on publication either as Roman or as British. In addition to these archaeological journals the following are among the English and foreign periodicals which contain matter more or less relevant to this period (the dates are those in which each was first published): *English Historical Review* (1886); *Transactions of the Royal Historical Society* (1871); *History* (1916); *Geography* (1915); *Journal of the Royal Anthropological Institute* (1871); *Man* (1901); *Biometrika* (1901); *Proceedings of the British Academy* (1904); *Modern Language Review* (1905); *Essays and Studies by members of the English Association* (1910); *English Studies* (1919); *Englische Studien* (1877); *Anglia* (1877); *Zeitschrift für Celtische Philologie* (1896); *Revue Celtique* (1870); *Revue Historique* (1876); *Acta Archaeologica* (1930); *Prähistorische Zeitschrift* (1909); *Mannus* (1909); and access to a large number of Danish, German, Dutch, and Belgian local publications would be necessary for an adequate study of the continental background to the English settlements. These cannot be listed here, but mention may perhaps be made of the important excavation reports issued by the Dutch *Vereeniging voor Terpenonderzoek.*

GENERAL WORKS ON EARLY SAXON ENGLAND

Nearly all historians of medieval England have included one or more chapters on the pagan Saxon period, and it is only possible to mention those whose scale of treatment or special interest enabled them to make contributions of more or less permanent value to this part of their subject. The first two volumes of J. M. Lappenberg's *Geschichte von England* (1834) were translated by B. Thorpe as *History of England under the Anglo-Saxon Kings* (1845), and had much influence on historical thought before W. Stubbs, *Constitutional History of England,* vol. i (1874), diverted attention from the effort to base political history on the literary sources to the institutional problems at which those sources also hinted. In this part of his subject, however, Stubbs had been already to some extent anticipated by J. M. Kemble, who in his *Saxons in England* (1849, best edition 1876) had applied extraordinarily modern methods of inquiry to the elucidation of the Saxon settlement. Kemble was a pioneer whose work, containing as it did many over-statements and some perversities, was easy to criticize, but his penetrating appreciation of all the essential lines of inquiry deserves more recognition than it has obtained. He was the first to see the institutional importance of the land charters, a *corpus* of which he published in the *Codex Diplomaticus* (see above); he pointed out the significance of the early place names; he was a pre-eminent student of Teutonic philology and mythology and edited *Beowulf*; he wrote as fluently in German as in English, and besides demonstrating for the first time the similarities between the dark-age antiquities of north Germany and those of England in an epoch-making paper in *Archaeologia*, xxxvi (1856), reprinted in *Horae Ferales* (1863), he even conducted excavations in Hanover with the express purpose of throwing light on the conquest of Britain. But when he died in 1857 at the age of fifty he had no successors in this versatility, and the criticism which some aspects of his historical work incurred —particularly his 'mark' theory of the settlements which arose from over-emphasis on the early place-names—led later profes-sional historians to undervalue the importance and originality of his outlook. Such compilations as C. Elton's *Origins of English*

History (1882) pointed the way back to reliance on the literary sources, which was followed by E. A. Freeman in the relevant parts of *Four Oxford Lectures* (1888) and by Sir J. M. Ramsay in *Foundations of England* (1898). Meanwhile E. Guest had won a temporary popularity with his fantastically uncritical *Origines Celticæ* (1883), whose reputation was not finally punctured until W. H. Stevenson's destructive article in *Eng. Hist. Rev.* xvii (1902), 625 ff., and J. R. Green in his *Making of England* (1881, best edition 1897), and other works, had carried the dramatic reconstruction of the political history to such lengths as to be accused of writing 'as if he had been present at the landing of the Saxons and had watched every step of their subsequent progress'.[1] A somewhat more critical attitude was taken up by T. Hodgkin in the first volume of the *Political History of England* (1906), and C. W. C. Oman in *England before the Norman Conquest* (1910) wrote the fullest and most reliable general account available until a few years ago, although it was still based mainly on a wide and critical appreciation of the literary sources and showed little attempt to make use of the auxiliary sciences. Meanwhile, H. M. Chadwick's *Origin of the English Nation* (1907) had not merely thrown fresh critical light on the Saxon sources, but had again demonstrated the importance of Teutonic legend and mythology for the historian: his book, though superseded in parts, is of great permanent value; some lines of its thought were developed by M. G. Clarke in *Sidelights on Teutonic History during the Migration Period* (1911), especially useful for its analysis of the historical allusions in *Beowulf* and *Widsith*.

All earlier general works are now superseded by R. H. Hodgkin, *History of the Anglo-Saxons* (1935), a beautifully produced and sensibly written work of wide knowledge in which a conscientious and on the whole successful attempt has been made to use the evidence of the auxiliary sciences in a single coherent exposition of the settlement period.

There are few books dealing specifically with social, institutional, or economic history in the pagan period, but among those which have most relevance are the two classical works of F. Seebohm, *Tribal Custom in Anglo-Saxon Law* (1902) and *The English Village Community* (1883). Seebohm's arguments for institutional and agrarian continuity with Roman times are

---

[1] Plummer's note on Bede, *Hist. Eccles.* i. 15.

many of them fallacious, as was pointed out by Round, Maitland, and Vinogradoff, but his books are valuable both for their method and as landmarks in the history of the subject. J. H. Round's paper on 'The Settlement of the South and East Saxons' in *The Commune of London* (1899) and P. Vinogradoff, *Growth of the Manor* (1905) should be read to correct the balance. On the agrarian side, H. L. Gray, *English Field Systems* (1915), contains a mass of well-digested and important material, though his conclusions, particularly in the case of Kent, are over-confident. J. E. A. Jolliffe, *Pre-Feudal England: the Jutes* (1933), is an important attempt to elucidate the earliest agrarian and administrative organization of south-eastern England: the facts revealed in his analysis are fundamental; his attempt to link the system with the invading Jutes and both with the middle Rhineland is less convincing. His article on 'The Era of the Folk' in *Oxford Essays ... presented to H. E. Salter* (1934) in so far as it suggests that many features of this early organization were not limited to the south-east may be used to modify his previous arguments: but there is much controversial matter in it. In another sphere O. G. S. Crawford has demonstrated by means of air-photographs the breach in agricultural method and in the distribution of population which occurred in Wessex in our period: see the Introduction to *Air Survey and Archaeology* (ed. 2, 1928). Air photography in general has, however, thrown more light on prehistoric than on dark-age studies at present.

A list of the earlier books bearing on the religious aspects of pagan society can be found in the bibliography of the *Cambridge Mediaeval History*, ii (1913), chs. xv and xvi. A useful recent addition is A. E. Philippson, *Germanisches Heidentum bei den Angelsachsen* (1929), which also contains a bibliography.

ARCHAEOLOGY AND TOPOGRAPHY

For the general principles underlying these studies, and for the history of their development in England, see the Bibliography for Roman Britain. While the Anglo-Saxon antiquities received archaeological recognition much later than did the Romano-British, the earlier topographers, travellers, and county historians whose works are there listed have preserved a good deal of relevant material, often unrecognized by them as Anglo-Saxon, but classed either as Roman or British remains: they cannot therefore be ignored by students of this period.

Perhaps the earliest work dealing directly, if unconsciously, with Anglo-Saxon antiquities is the charming *Hydriotaphia, or Urne buriall* of Sir Thomas Browne (1658), to the composition of which he was moved by the discovery of 'sad sepulchral pitchers' in what was clearly an Anglian cremation cemetery at Walsingham, Norfolk.[1] He, however, thought that they were Roman, and the same view was still held a century later by the Rev. B. Faussett of the objects unearthed by him during careful excavations in various Kentish cemeteries between 1757 and 1773; these were afterwards published with Faussett's notes by C. Roach Smith in the *Inventorium Sepulchrale* (1856). Meanwhile, however, the Rev. James Douglas had also carried out systematic excavations in Kent, especially on Chatham Lines, from 1779 and had published his discoveries, correctly attributed to the Saxons, in the stately folio *Nenia Britannica or a Sepulchral History of Great Britain* (1793). During the nineteenth century the subject was farther advanced, first by the publication of individual sites in periodicals and in such works as W. M. Wylie, *Fairford Graves* (1852), and R. C. Neville, *Saxon Obsequies* (1852), a sumptuous book on the Little Wilbraham cemetery with excellent and copious illustrations; secondly by their notice in such regional studies as Sir R. Colt Hoare, *Ancient Wiltshire* (1812–19), G. Hillier, *History and Antiquities of the Isle of Wight* (1855), for the Chessel Down cemetery, T. Bateman, *Ten Years' Diggings* (1861), and J. R. Mortimer, *Forty Years' Researches in the Burial Mounds of East Yorkshire* (1905), or in general antiquarian collections like C. Roach Smith, *Collectanea Antiqua* (7 vols., 1848–80), which contains a quantity of important Anglo-Saxon material; and thirdly by attempts, some of them premature, to survey the material as a whole, like J. Y. Akerman, *Archaeological Index* (1847), his important *Remains of Pagan Saxondom* (1855), a valuable work with beautiful plates, and J. de Baye, *Industrie Saxonne* (trans. T. B. Harbottle, *The Industrial Arts of the Anglo-Saxons* (1893)), or to relate it to that of other periods and countries as in T. Wright, *The Celt, the Roman and the Saxon* (1852), and J. M. Kemble's posthumously published *Horae Ferales* (1863).

[1] As Leeds has observed (*Archaeology of the Anglo-Saxon Settlements* (1913), 38), one of these Walsingham urns may have survived in the specimen once in 'Tradescants' Ark', which formed the nucleus of the Ashmolean Collections, and is still preserved at Oxford. This urn is in any case likely to have come from Norfolk, for it shows several features especially characteristic of the cemeteries in that county.

Except for the publication of freshly discovered material in periodicals and the appearance of de Baye's book, Anglo-Saxon archaeology made little progress between Kemble's death and 1900, but in the first decade of the twentieth century came R. A. Smith's masterly surveys of the material county by county in the *Victoria County History* as follows: *Hampshire and the Isle of Wight* (1900); *Norfolk* and *Worcester* (1901); *Hertford, Northampton*, and *Surrey* (1902); *Essex* (1903); *Bedford* and *Warwickshire* (1904); *Buckingham* and *Sussex* (1905); *Berkshire, Nottingham*, and *Somerset* (1906); *Leicester* (1907); *Kent, Rutland*, and *Stafford* (1908); *London* (1909); *Suffolk* (1911); *Yorkshire* (1912); *Huntingdon* (1926). Though subject to the disadvantage of an irrational sub-division along the lines of the county system, these surveys reached a high standard of completeness, and made far easier the study of particular groups of objects, of which the pioneer work on the saucer-brooches by E. T. Leeds in *Archaeologia*, lxiii (1912), 159–202, deserves special mention. In 1913 appeared the same author's *Archaeology of the Anglo-Saxon Settlements*, a slim volume of permanent value containing the first real attempt to assess the contribution of archaeology to the history of the times and to force it upon the reluctant attention of historians. G. Baldwin Brown in *The Arts in Early England*, iii and iv (1915), gave an extremely thorough and well-illustrated analysis of every class of Anglo-Saxon antiquities, which remains the standard work on the subject, though both his and Leeds's acceptance of the chronology of Teutonic ornament laid down by such works as Salin's *Die altgermanische Thierornamentik* has lately been subjected to criticism which may necessitate revision of the dating; see Kendrick and Hawkes, *Archaeology in England and Wales* (1932), and papers by Kendrick in *Antiquity* and elsewhere mentioned in footnotes to pp. 362, 400, based on the work of S. Lindqvist, *Vendelkulturens Ålder och Ursprung* (1926). The older chronology, however, has not lacked recent supporters: see for example the British Museum *Guide to Anglo-Saxon Antiquities* (1923), the careful and useful survey of the brooches and other metal work by N. Åberg, *Anglo-Saxons in England* (1926), and E. T. Leeds, *Early Anglo-Saxon Art and Archaeology* (1936).

Besides these general works a number of regional studies, based wholly or mainly on the archaeological and topographical evidence, deserve mention. Such are the illuminating Anglo-

Saxon chapters in C. Fox, *Archaeology of the Cambridge Region* (1923), and those in the County Archaeologies which include in each case a useful gazetteer and bibliography of the local finds, viz.: *Middlesex and London*, by C. E. Vulliamy (1930); *Kent*, by R. F. Jessup (1930); *Berkshire*, by H. J. E. Peake (1931); *Somerset*, by D. P. Dobson (1931); *Surrey*, by D. C. Whimster (1931); *Yorkshire*, by F. Elgee (1933); see also F. Elgee, *Early Man in North-east Yorkshire* (1930), M. E. Cunnington, *Introduction to the Archaeology of Wiltshire* (1933, enlarged ed. 1934), and R. E. M. Wheeler, *London and the Saxons* (1935), important not only for its local interest and controversial introduction (see p. 437) but also for the useful classification of some types of Anglo-Saxon weapons. A. Gray, *Dual Origin of the Town of Cambridge* (1908), uses institutional rather than archaeological evidence to supplement an essentially topographical study: and this is perhaps the best place to notice F. M. Stenton's valuable account of Lindsey in *Essays . . . presented to R. Lane Poole* (1929).

Most excavation reports are, of course, published in the general and local periodicals listed above, but the following among recent exceptions to this practice should be noticed: E. J. Hollingworth and M. M. O'Reilly, *Anglo-Saxon Cemetery at Girton College, Cambridge* (1925), T. C. Lethbridge, *Recent Excavations in Anglo-Saxon Cemeteries in Cambridgeshire and Suffolk* (1931), and E. T. Leeds and D. B. Harden, *Anglo-Saxon Cemetery at Abingdon, Berks.* (1936). *The Proceedings of the First International Congress of Prehistoric and Protohistoric Sciences, London*, 1932 (pub. 1934), contain résumés of some important papers on Anglo-Saxon subjects: and the Anglo-Saxon chapter in the *Handbook of the Prehistoric Archaeology of Britain* (1932), issued in connexion with the same Congress, should also be studied.

The Map of Dark Age Britain (1935) published by the Ordnance Survey is an indispensable aid to topographical study in this period, though a few cemeteries, single burials, and early names not at present shown could be added with advantage to the next edition: it is likely to stimulate further that co-operation between archaeologist and topographer, of which S. W. Woolridge's instructive chapter on the Anglo-Saxon settlement in *An Historical Geography of England before 1800* (1936), ed. H. C. Darby, should be mentioned as the most important recent example.

PLACE-NAMES

No subject has attracted the attention of more misguided enthusiasts and ignorant amateurs than the study of English place-names; and the student seeking enlightenment on their historical significance must pick his way with especial caution among the pitfalls which beset his path. The safest rule that can be laid down is to pay no attention to any suggested etymology that is not securely based upon the collation of all the available early forms. This is the method now adopted by the English Place-name Society, whose county surveys will eventually provide a sure and comprehensive guide both to the major and the minor names of the countryside: the volumes at present available are *Buckinghamshire* (1925); *Bedfordshire* and *Huntingdonshire* (1926); *Worcestershire* (1927); *Yorkshire, North Riding* (1928); *Sussex* (1929–30); *Devon* (1931–2); *Northamptonshire* (1933); *Surrey* (1934); *Essex* (1935); *Warwickshire* (1936). Their Introductions contain in every case important historical discussions.

For other parts of the country recourse may be had to E. Ekwall's recent monumental *Concise Oxford Dictionary of English Place-names* (1936); and to the more secure of the unofficial county studies, among which may be noted, E. Ekwall, *Place-names of Lancashire* (1922); F. M. Stenton, *Place-names of Berkshire* (1911); A. Mawer, *Place-names of Northumberland and Durham* (1920); E. Ekblom, *Place-names of Wiltshire* (1917); W. W. Skeat, *Place-names of Cambridgeshire* (1911) and *Place-names of Suffolk* (1913), in the octavo publications of the Cambridge Antiquarian Society; J. E. B. Gover, *Place-names of Middlesex* (1922); and J. K. Wallenberg, *Kentish Place-names* (1931) and *Place-names of Kent* (1934), who deliberately reacts against what he regards as the excessive tendency in the Place-name Society's editors to explain doubtful elements by the supposition of unrecorded personal names. All these and many other local studies too unreliable to be listed here must be used with varying degrees of caution. W. J. Watson, *History of the Celtic Place-names of Scotland* (1926), contains interesting material bearing on the early history of Bernicia. Special classes of names may be studied in E. Ekwall, *English River-names* (1928), the same author's extremely important *English Place-names in -ing* (1923), and S. Karlström, *Old English compound Place-names in -ing* (1927). There is a useful list of the *Weala-* names (Walton, Walcot, &c.), and a discussion of their significance in R. E. Zachrisson, *Romans, Kelts and Saxons in Ancient Britain* (1927), constituting the most valuable part of this otherwise rather unsatisfactory pamphlet. The general principles of place-name study in its historical setting and some of the results obtained by its means are discussed in the first volume issued by the English Place-name Society, *Introduction to the Survey of English Place-names* (1924), and by A. Mawer in *Problems of Place-name Study* (1929).

THE CONTINENTAL BACKGROUND

It would be beyond the scope of this volume to enter into a discussion of the copious literature bearing on Germany in the migration period. Of up-to-date general works for early Germanic history L. Schmidt, *Geschichte der deutschen Stämme* (1911), is perhaps the most useful, and may be supplemented by the more recent production of G. Schütte, conveniently accessible for English readers as *Our Forefathers the Gothonic Nations* (1929–33). The student of agrarian history must still start with A. Meitzen, *Siedelung und Agrarwesen der Westgermanen und Ostgermanen* (1895), and may pass on to such special studies as G. des Marez, *Le Problème de la Colonisation Franque* (1926), M. Bloch, *Les caractères originaux de l'histoire rurale française* (1931), and K. Rhamm, *Grosshufen der Nordgermanen* (1905). Various problems directly concerning the English settlements are discussed by A. Erdmann, *Über die Heimat und den Namen der Angeln* (1892), who brings the Angles from Schleswig; E. Wadstein, *On the Origin of the English* (1927), who unconvincingly denies the connexion with Angeln, but puts forward good reasons for associating the Jutes with the Frisians; K. Schreiner, *Die Saga von Hengest und Horsa* (1921), who gives a useful analysis in her opening chapter of the evidence for the legend before Geoffrey of Monmouth; J. Hoops, *Waldbäume und Kulturpflanzen im germanischen Altertum* (1905), who considers, amongst other topics, the evidence for the continental homes of the invaders provided by the names used for wild and cultivated plants; and D. J. H. Nyessen, *The Passing of the Frisians* (1927), an anthropological study, to which is conveniently prefixed a good discussion of the purpose, distribution, and chronology of the Frisian mound-settlements or *terpen*.

Of more strictly archaeological literature, the standard works of Salin and Lindqvist have already been mentioned. The only reasonably full recent survey of the immediate cultural background to the Saxon invasions is that of A. Plettke, *Ursprung und Ausbreitung der Angeln und Sachsen* (1921); but his treatment is not definitive, for he does not deal adequately with the material from Schleswig, his chronology is probably for most of the critical period about fifty years too high, and he was not acquainted with the English evidence at first hand. H. Schetelig, *The Cruciform Brooches of Norway* (1906), and B. Hougen, *The Migration Style in Norway* (1936), are important for the typology of the copious comparative material in England. General archaeological surveys of different parts of the continental homelands are P. C. J. A. Boeles, *Friesland tot de elfde eeuw* (1927); J. H. Holwerda, *Nederlands vroegste geschiedenis* (1925); P. Zylmann, *Ostfriesische Urgeschichte* (1933), and K. H. Jacob-Friesen, *Einführung in Niedersachsens Urgeschichte* (1934). F. Roeder has been responsible for several important studies of types of objects found both in Germany and in England and has thus materially helped to clarify the chronology of the settlements: see his *Die sächsische Schalenfibel der Völkerwanderungszeit* (1927) for saucer brooches; 'Die sächsische Fenstergefässe in *Röm.-germ. Kommission*, xviii (1928), 149, for window-urns; 'Die Henkelgussurnen' in *Mannus*, Ergänzungsband VI (1928), 190 ff., for spout-handled urns; *Typologisch-chronologische Studien zu Metallsachen der Völkerwanderungszeit* (1930); and finally his *Neue Funde auf kontinental-sächsischen Friedhöfe der Völkerwanderungszeit* (1933).

INDEX

Aaron, Christian martyr, 270.
Aberdeen, 17, 159.
Åberg, N., 349 n., 361 n., 362 n., 386 n.
Abergavenny (Gobannium), map I.
Aberystwyth, 112.
Abingdon, Anglo-Saxon cemetery at, map VIII, 396.
Abone (Sea Mills), map I.
Abus, see Humber.
-acum, place-names in, 220.
Addedomarus, 59.
Adelphius, bishop, 271.
Adrianople, battle of, 287, 322, 342, 359.
Adur, river, 56.
adventus Saxonum, 315; date of, 352-6, 461.
Aediles, 166.
Ægelesburg (Aylesbury), 408, 458.
Aelius, see Hadrian, Antoninus.
Ælle of Sussex, 366-9, 380-2, 423, 432, 434, 457.
Æsc (Oisc), 356, 380-1, 457.
Aesica (Great Chesters), map I, 257, 260.
Æthelbald of Mercia, 372.
Æthelberht, 362, 389, 458; Laws of, 447.
Æthelfrid, 422-3.
Aetius, 293, 301, 307, 313, 315, 321, 354-5.
Agæles threp, 457.
ager attributus (attributio), 165, 168, 171.
Agitius (= Aetius), 293.
Agricola, see Calpurnius, Julius.
Agriculture, early British, 9, 10, 20, 27, 56, 68; of Belgae, 27; Romano-British, 208 seqq.; Anglo-Saxon, 441-4, 454-5.
Ahenobarbus, Cn. Domitius, 61 n.
Aire gap, 110.
Aire, river, map IX, 419.
Airedale, 14.
Air-photography, 210.
Aisne valley, 27.
ala, auxiliary, 138.
Alaisiagae, 268.
Alamanni settled in Britain, 183, 287.
Alaric, 291-2, 328.
Alban, St., 270-1, 434, 452.
Albinus, see Clodius.
Aldborough (Isurium), map I, 149, 168, 171, 193, 196, 413, 419.
Alde, river, map VII, 390.
Alemanni, 344.
Alesia, 53, 55, 187, 267.
Alfenus Senecio, L., 158.
Alfred of Wessex, 383, 391; and the Anglo-Saxon Chronicle, 327, 366, 397-9; Laws of, 446-7.

Alfriston, Anglo-Saxon cemetery at, map VI, 370.
All Cannings Cross, 22.
Allectus (usurper), 277.
Alleluia, 306, 435.
Almondbury, 67 n.
Alne, river, map VII, 410.
Alone (Watercrook), map I.
Alpine race, 16, 184.
Alston Moor, 230.
Amber, 70.
Ambleside (Galava), map I.
Ambleteuse, 36-8.
Ambrose, St., 310.
Ambrosius Aurelianus, 314, 319, 333, 379, 381-2, 432, 439.
Amiens (Samarobriva Ambianorum), 428.
Ammianus Marcellinus, 183 n., 243 n., 286 n., 294, 302, 324, 436.
Amminius, 75-6.
Amphitheatres, 192, 201-2.
Amphorae, pre-Claudian, 71.
Anavio (Brough, Derbyshire), map I, 149.
Ancasta, 264, 268.
Ancaster (Causennae), map I; Anglo-Saxon cemetery at, 386, 453.
Anderida, see Pevensey.
Andescocis, 264, 268.
Andoco . . ., 57.
Andover, map VIII, 272, 401 n.
Andredescester, see Pevensey.
Andredesweald, 368, 453, 457.
Aneirin, 419.
Angel, 346; called Oghgul, 346.
Angeln, 337, 347, 349.
Angles: on the Continent, map V, 336-8, 342-6, 348, 350; in England, 336; and see separate kingdoms, &c.; English dynasties descended from, 347, 416; and see Anglo-Saxon, Jutes, &c.
Anglesey (Mona), map I, 13-14, 98-9, 114, 228, 231, 289.
Anglia, East, see East Anglia.
Anglia, Middle, see Middle Anglia.
Anglo-Saxon: agriculture, 441-4, 454-5; art, 258, 450-1; brooches and jewellery, 333, 348-9, 361-3, 369, 386, 395; burial customs, 349, 351, 361-3, 368-71, 373, 377, 381, 393, 400-1, 405-6, 414, 416-17, 419, 448-9, 453-4; ceramics, 349, 362-3, 387, 396, 406-7, 412, 419; charters, 335; invasions, 15, 306 sqq.; laws, 446-8; physical type, 184; and see Angles, Saxons, Jutes, &c., and Table of Contents.